Blackwell Handbook of Social Psychology: Intergroup Processes

Blackwell Handbook of Social Psychology

Series editors: Miles Hewstone and Marilynn Brewer

The four volumes of this authoritative handbook each draw together 25–30 newly commissioned chapters to provide a comprehensive overview of specific topics in the field of social psychology. Designed to have considerable depth as well as breadth, the volumes encompass theory and research at the intraindividual, interpersonal, intergroup, and group levels. Editors have been chosen for their expertise and knowledge of the subject, making the *Blackwell Handbook of Social Psychology* an invaluable companion for any serious social psychology scholar.

Intraindividual Processes, edited by Abraham Tesser and Norbert Schwartz

Interpersonal Processes, edited by Garth J. O. Fletcher and Margaret S. Clark

Intergroup Processes, edited by Rupert Brown and Samuel L. Gaertner

Group Processes, edited by Michael A. Hogg and Scott Tindale

Blackwell Handbook of Social Psychology: Intergroup Processes

Edited by

Rupert Brown and Samuel L. Gaertner

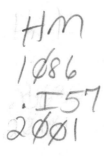

First published 2001

2 4 6 8 10 9 7 5 3 1

Blackwell Publishers Inc.
350 Main Street
Malden, Massachusetts 02148
USA

Blackwell Publishers Ltd
108 Cowley Road
Oxford OX4 1JF
UK

Library of Congress Cataloging-in-Publication data has been applied for.

British Library Cataloguing in Publication Data

A CIP catalogue record for this book is available from the British Library.

ISBN 0 631 21062 8 (hbk)

Typeset in 10.5 on 12.5 pt Adobe Garamond
By Best-set Typesetter Ltd., Hong Kong
Printed in Great Britain by T.J. International, Padstow, Cornwall

This book is printed on acid-free paper.

Contents

Series Editors' Preface

The idea for a new, international handbook series for social psychology was conceived in July 1996 during the triannual meeting of the European Association of Experimental Social Psychology (EAESP) in the idyllic setting of Gmunden, Austria. Over a glass of wine and pleasant breezes from the Traunsee, Alison Mudditt (then Psychology Editor for Blackwell Publishers) engaged the two of us in a "hypothetical" discussion of what a multi-volume handbook of social psychology at the start of the 21st century might look like. By the second glass of wine we were hooked, and the project that has culminated in the publication of this four-volume *Blackwell Handbook of Social Psychology* was commissioned.

The EAESP meeting provided a fitting setting for the origin of a project that was intended to be an international collaborative effort. The idea was to produce a set of volumes that would provide a rich picture of social psychology at the start of the new millennium – a cross-section of the field that would be both comprehensive and forward-looking. In conceiving an organizational framework for such a venture, we sought to go beyond a simple topical structure for the content of the volumes in order to reflect more closely the complex pattern of cross-cutting theoretical perspectives and research agendas that comprise social psychology as a dynamic enterprise. Rather than lengthy review papers covering a large domain of social psychological research, we felt that a larger number of shorter and more focused chapters would better reflect the diversity and the synergies representative of the field at this point in time.

The idea we developed was to represent the discipline in a kind of matrix structure, crossing levels of analysis with topics, processes, and functions that recur at all of these levels in social psychological theory and research. Taking inspiration from Willem Doise's 1986 book (*Levels of Explanation in Social Psychology*) four levels of analysis – intrapersonal, interpersonal, intragroup, and intergroup – provided the basis for organizing the Handbook series into four volumes. The content of each volume would be selected on the basis of cross-cutting themes represented by basic processes of social cognition, attribution, social motivation, affect and emotion, social influence, social comparison, self and identity, as they operate at each level. In addition, each volume would include methodological issues and areas of applied or policy-relevant research related to social psychological research at that level of analysis.

Armed with this rough organizational framework as our vision for the series, our role was to commission editors for the individual volumes who would take on the challenging task of turning this vision into reality. The plan was to recruit two experts for each volume who would bring different but complementary perspectives and experience to the subject matter to work together to plan, commission, and edit 25–30 papers that would be representative of current and exciting work within their broad domain. Once selected, co-editors were encouraged to use the matrix framework as a heuristic device to plan the coverage of their volume but were free to select from and embellish upon that structure to fit their own vision of the field and its current directions.

We have been extremely fortunate in having persuaded eight exceptionally qualified and dedicated scholars of social psychology to join us in this enterprise and take on the real work of making this Handbook series happen. Once they came on board, our role became an easy one: just relax and observe as the project was brought to fruition in capable hands. We are deeply indebted and grateful to Abraham Tesser and Norbert Schwarz, Margaret Clark and Garth Fletcher, Michael Hogg and Scott Tindale, Rupert Brown and Samuel Gaertner for their creative leadership in producing the four volumes of this series. Through their efforts, a rough outline has become a richly textured portrait of social psychology at the threshold of the 21st century.

In addition to the efforts of our volume editors and contributors, we are grateful to the editorial staff at Blackwell who have seen this project through from its inception. The project owes a great deal to Alison Mudditt who first inspired it. When Alison went on to new ventures in the publishing world, Martin Davies took over as our capable and dedicated Commissioning Editor who provided guidance and oversight throughout the operational phases. Our thanks to everyone who has been a part of this exciting collaborative venture.

Miles Hewstone
Marilynn Brewer

Preface

Finding an adequate way to introduce a volume such as this, comprising as it does nearly a quarter of a million words penned by most of the world's leading authorities on intergroup relations, proved to be rather a daunting task. It seemed to us to be not very informative – and also rather tedious for the reader – simply to provide a series of brief summaries of what each had written. For the most part, such snapshots are readily available from the authors' own introductions. Instead, what seemed more worthwhile was to identify what struck us as being the three salient features of the volume as a whole.

The first noteworthy characteristic is the diversity of different perspectives employed by our contributors. Readers of this book will surely gain an impression of theoretical pluralism rather than hegemony. Thus, several authors drew heavily and eclectically on current models in social cognition (e.g., Fiedler & Schmid; Operario & Fiske; Rothbart; and Wilder & Simon); others relied more exclusively on social identity and self-categorization theories (e.g., Ellemers & Bareto; Oakes; Simon, Aufderheide, & Kampmeier; and Turner & Reynolds); others used or developed accounts in which competing conceptions of social justice or normative appropriateness play a central explanatory role (e.g., Mummendey & Otten; Tyler; Wright); and still others were concerned with the interplay of social psychological and cultural variables (e.g., Aboud & Amato; Liebkind; and Triandis & Trafimow). It seems to us that this variety rather accurately reflects the current state of the field of intergroup relations and that an important task for the future will be to achieve some integration of these different approaches, as Mackie and Smith (1998) have also argued quite recently.

Despite this heterogeneity, it is possible to detect at least three common themes running through the volume. The first is undoubtedly the importance of social categorization. As the pioneers of our field had the foresight to realize, it is impossible to understand – or hope to change – intergroup relationships without appreciating the social psychological significance of this most basic of cognitive processes (Allport, 1954; Campbell, 1956; Tajfel, 1969). Categorization takes center stage in several chapters (e.g., Aboud & Amato; Bourhis & Gagnon; Brewer & Gaertner; Dovidio, Kawakami, & Beach; Fiedler

& Schmid; Mackie & Wright; and Oakes) and is implicit in most of the others. Thanks to social identity theory (SIT; Tajfel & Turner, 1986), categorization has come to be seen as almost indissolubly linked to the second communality in the volume, the concept of identity. As has been noted elsewhere (Brown & Capozza, 2000), over the past 20 years SIT has come to assume a pre-eminent position among theories of intergroup relations and it is thus unsurprising to find social identity figuring so prominently in the chapters of this book. Whether this takes the form of a reprise of some of the central ideas of SIT (Turner & Reynolds), examinations of the social psychological consequences of belonging to minority or underprivileged groups (Crocker & Quinn; Ellemers & Bareto; Simon, Aufderheide, & Kampmeier; and Wright), the role of justice in the maintenance of group identity (Tyler), or the impact of culture on identity construction and expression (Triandis & Trafimow), social identity makes frequent appearances in our contributors' analyses. Thirdly, the concept of ambivalence emerges as another linking idea. Operario and Fiske draw attention to the fact that intergroup stereotypes are seldom wholly positive or wholly negative but contain elements of both. The same point is made in different contexts by Swim and Campbell in their analyses of modern forms of sexism, and by Dovidio, Kawakami, and Beach commenting on the frequent disjunctures between intergroup behavior, attitudes, and covert beliefs: What we do may not be the same as what we say, and that may also differ from what we think. The coexistence of apparently contradictory beliefs or behavioral tactics is also noted by Bourhis and Gagnon in the context of allocation strategies in the minimal group paradigm (MGP), by Kramer and Carnevale in discussing negotiation tactics, and by Devine, Plant, and Blair in their examination of discrepancies between personal and normative beliefs about the treatment of outgroups.

As the field of intergroup relations has developed, so has the range of methods employed by its practitioners, and this is the second significant feature of this handbook. We were enjoined by the series editors to focus at least some of the chapters explicitly on methodological issues. This is most apparent in the analysis of the MGP by Bourhis and Gagnon, and in the account by Dovidio, Kawakami, and Beach of contemporary efforts to measure the variegated forms which modern prejudice can take. But just as intergroup relations tends to be theoretically eclectic, so too are its methods far from being confined to laboratory techniques. The chapters by Aboud and Amato; Brewer and Gaertner; and Schofield and Eurich-Fulcer vividly illustrate how systematic research in field and applied settings can yield important insights into intergroup relations problems. But what is perhaps most noteworthy of all about the plethora of paradigms discussed or drawn upon by our authors is that they are all underpinned by a common assumption of the value of objective and quantitative research methodology. Apparently, however fashionable post-modern or discourse-analytic approaches may be in some quarters in psychology, they have made little impact on the four dozen contributors to this volume.

The third interesting characteristic to emerge from the chapters of this handbook is how many of them were, directly or indirectly, concerned with current social issues. Perhaps it is inevitable that the topic of this volume should be more politically embedded than in the other volumes in the series, but still we were struck by how many of our contributors attempted to link their analyses to the resolution of social problems. This was most obviously true of the authors of the three chapters in the final section (Crosby,

Ferdman, & Wingate; Pettigrew; and Schofield & Eurich-Fulcer), all of whom were specifically invited because of their expertise in applied domains. But the messages of several other chapters have obvious practical implications too: In different ways, Brewer and Gaertner; Devine, Plant, and Blair; and Kramer and Carnevale are all concerned with finding workable strategies for the reduction of intergroup conflict and prejudice; while Crocker and Quinn; Liebkind; and Simon, Aufderheide, and Kampmeier all focus on problems experienced by minority groups, especially those who have suffered discrimination at the hands of dominant groups. It was particularly refreshing for us as editors to see such clear evidence of social psychology's historical concern with social injustice reflected in the thoughtful practical recommendations made by so many of our contributors.

These, then, are the three themes that stood out most noticeably for us and they find their expression throughout the eight sections of the volume. As the series editors note in their preface, most of these section headings came from them, reflecting the structure which links the four volumes of the series. Roughly speaking, the eight sections represent a continuum from a focus on individual processes to a more societal level of application, and they have been ordered with that in mind. Some of the chapters could have sat just as happily in other sections and some of the sections could easily have had different headings. Nevertheless, it is our hope that, one way or another, the 25 chapters of this volume form a coherent and useful resource for those readers interested in learning most of what there is to know about the field of intergroup relations as we enter the 21st century.

References

Allport, G. W. (1954). *The nature of prejudice*. Reading, MA: Addison-Wesley.

Brown, R., & Capozza, D. (2000). Social identity theory in prospect and retrospect. In D. Capozza & R. Brown (Eds.), *Social identity processes: Trends in theory and research*. London: Sage.

Campbell, D. T. (1956). Enhancement of contrast as a composite habit. *Journal of Abnormal and Social Psychology, 53*, 350–355.

Mackie, D. M., & Smith, E. R. (1998). Intergroup relations: insights from a theoretically integrative approach. *Psychological Review, 105*, 499–529.

Tajfel, H. (1969). Cognitive aspects of prejudice. *Journal of Social Issues, 25*, 79–97.

Tajfel, H., & Turner, J. C. (1986). An integrative theory of social conflict. In S. Worchel & W. Austin (Eds.), *Psychology of intergroup relations*. Chicago, IL: Nelson Hall.

Acknowledgments

We would like to acknowledge the part played by our 48 contributors in the successful completion of this volume. Their *punctuality* in meeting our unreasonable deadlines, their *patience* in responding to our draconian requests for page cuts, and, above all, their consummate *professionalism* in writing such insightful and informative chapters have made our task of editing this volume more pleasurable than we anticipated when we accepted the series editors' invitation four years ago. We are grateful to Miles Hewstone and Marilynn Brewer for that invitation and also to Martin Davies and Alison Dunnett at Blackwell Publishers for their helpfulness in bringing this volume to fruition. Further, we thank our wives, Lyn and Shelley, for their loving support and patience with us during this book's long gestation and production. Finally, we are indebted to the three scholars whose seminal works have shaped the field of intergroup relations in the 20th century and who thereby influenced each of the chapters herein. We dedicate this volume to them: Gordon Allport, Muzafer Sherif, and Henri Tajfel.

PART I

Sociocognitive Processes

CHAPTER ONE

The Root of all Evil in Intergroup Relations? Unearthing the Categorization Process

Penelope Oakes

1 Introduction

The social psychology of intergroup processes has a long and venerable history. As evidenced by this volume, our understanding of intergroup phenomena is rich, complex, and ripe with possibility in both scientific and social terms. At the heart of all this lies one pivotal process without which the modern social psychology of intergroup relations is almost impossible to imagine – categorization.

We can define categorization as "the process of understanding what some thing is by knowing what other things it is equivalent to and what other things it is different from" (McGarty, 1999, p. 1). It is through categorization that we identify things, *know what they are*. Henri Tajfel, viewed by many as laying the foundations of the categorization analysis of intergroup relations, always emphasized this elaborative, meaning-giving function of the process. He argued that social categorization works to "structure the causal understanding of the social environment" as a guide to action. Importantly, it also provides a system of orientation for *self-reference*, creating and defining the individual's place in society. Our "self-definition in a social context" (1978, p. 61) always depends upon social categorization. Where the relevant categorization produces a subjective division into social groups – we are Australians, you are New Zealanders; we are police, you are protesters – *action within that context will take on the distinct meaning and significance of intergroup relations*.

Developing the legacy of theorists such as Asch (1952) and Sherif (1967), Tajfel urged recognition of a qualitative discontinuity between interpersonal and intergroup behavior.

Grateful thanks to Alex Haslam, Kate Reynolds, and the editors for comments on an earlier draft, and to Kate Reynolds and Peter Reid for their invaluable support and encouragement during the writing of this chapter.

At the same time, the subdiscipline of social cognition was developing apace. With it came discussions of the categorization process, which had more to say about distortion and bias than they did about self-definition and behavior. Indeed, it has been as a source of *bias* rather than contextually variable knowledge and understanding that categorization has featured so centrally in the social psychology of intergroup processes. For example, in 1986 David Wilder published an influential paper entitled, "Social categorization: Implications for creation and reduction of intergroup bias", in which he comments that "categorization, per se, propels the individual down the road to bias" (p. 292). And this view has prevailed. Retaining the road metaphor, Bodenhausen and Macrae recently commented that "the road to . . . discrimination begins with the simple act of categorization" (1998, p. 7). Essentially, categorization stands accused of leading us to perceive something other than reality, of generating efficient but inaccurate interpretations of social life.

Is this what happens when perceivers categorize? Does categorization place us out of touch with reality, almost helplessly propelled down roads to bias and discrimination? Can it therefore be held accountable, at least in part, for the real evils of social mistreatment and bigotry which, though sometimes in mutated forms, continue to pervade society?

This chapter addresses these questions by *unearthing* social categorization, in the sense of laying bare, making explicit, its role within both the social psychology of group processes and the social reality of intergroup relations. The "road to bias" is thought to pass through three vital staging posts: activation, construal, and discrimination (see Bodenhausen, Macrae, & Garst, 1998). We visit each of these in turn, asking questions about what categorization is actually *doing* at each stage. Importantly, are categories activated automatically, without due regard for the realities of context? Do the known manifestations of category-based construal – accentuation and assimilation to category meaning – constitute bias? And is categorization responsible for intergroup discrimination?

2   Activation

In a highly influential paper published in 1978, Taylor, Fiske, Etcoff, and Ruderman presented seven hypotheses concerning "the perceptual and cognitive underpinnings" of intergroup discrimination. Building on the groundbreaking work of Tajfel (1969; Tajfel, Billig, Bundy, & Flament, 1971; Tajfel & Wilkes, 1963), Taylor and colleagues contributed to the development of a categorization approach to intergroup behaviour and stereotyping. In particular, they raised the issue of the "contextual bases" of group phenomena, suggesting that stereotyping would only happen when categorization happened. Thus, understanding the factors responsible for activating social categories became a priority.

Taylor et al. (1978, p. 779) hypothesized that perceivers would use "physical and social discriminators such as race and sex" to categorize people, and that this was especially likely when the relevant cues were highly distinctive, novel, within the current social context.

Moreover, activation of the category would lead to an accentuation of within-group similarity and between-group difference (following Tajfel & Wilkes, 1963) and stereotypical interpretation of targets' behavior (see section 3 below). While the specific hypothesis about the prepotence of distinctive cues has attracted some controversy (Biernat & Vescio, 1993, 1994; Oakes, 1994), the basic idea that certain stimulus cues can almost automatically (at least, with conditional automaticity; Bargh, 1989) activate social categories has remained highly influential – "theories of stereotyping generally hold that stereotype activation is an automatic process that operates when the appropriate situational cue is present" (Blair & Banaji, 1996, p. 1143).

In recent work the unconscious automaticity of social category activation has been emphasized. For example, Blair and Banaji (1996) measured how long it took for participants to identify first names as either male or female. Presentation of the names was preceded by a 150-millisecond prime which was male stereotypical (e.g., strong, mechanic), female stereotypical (e.g., gentle, ballet) or gender-neutral. As predicted, reaction times were significantly reduced when primes were stereotypic (e.g., gentle – Jane) rather than counterstereotypic (e.g., gentle – John), providing evidence of the "automatic activation of gender stereotypes" (p. 1148) by the preconscious gender-relevant primes.

Work initiated by Devine (1989) has argued that the automatic activation of categories is so powerful it can produce "prejudice-related discrepancies" (Monteith, 1993, p. 469) in which category content that the perceiver does not actually endorse or believe in is activated by highly salient cues (such as skin color). Thus, perceivers become the victims of "spontaneous, unintentional stereotype use" (ibid.), applying beliefs which are not their own but are foisted upon them by cultural currency. Similarly, Bodenhausen and Macrae suggest that the effects of automatic categorization are "typically not consciously intended by perceivers; rather, they arise spontaneously because of basic properties of the information processing system" (1998, p. 20). Thus, we have a view of categorization as the root cause of "unwanted thoughts" which might lead individuals to act in ways counter to their real beliefs (e.g., to appear prejudiced when they believe they are not; but see Haslam & Wilson, 2000). Other recent work has, however, questioned aspects of this evidence of automaticity (e.g., Lepore & Brown, 1997), and the true significance of these "semantic priming" type effects is unclear, once real social contexts and pressing perceiver goals enter the analytic picture.

The effects of perceiver goals on category activation receive serious consideration in the continuum model of impression formation developed and tested by Fiske and her colleagues (Fiske, Lin, & Neuberg, 1998; Fiske & Neuberg, 1990). Briefly, the model distinguishes between individuated impressions formed through piecemeal integration of attributes and stereotyping based on categorization, placing these at opposite ends of an impression formation continuum. Movement along the continuum is dependent upon attention: the more attention perceivers invest in the impression formation process the more they will analyze current attribute information rather than rely on predigested category-based information, increasing the likelihood of individuation over stereotyping. Conversely, lack of attentional investment increases reliance on available cues to categorization and produces stereotyping.

One factor thought to increase attentional investment in impression formation, and therefore reduce the likelihood of categorization, is interdependence. Neuberg and Fiske

(1987) suggest that interdependence motivates perceivers to discover the other's "true attributes" (e.g., see Ruscher, Fiske, Miki, & Van Manen, 1991; cf. Reynolds & Oakes, 2000). This argument has been extended (Fiske, 1993) to provide an account of the way in which power differentials affect categorization. Fiske suggests that, because of their dependence on the powerful, the powerless direct their attention up the hierarchy and don't categorize those with power. The powerful, on the other hand, are too busy, too unconcerned with accuracy, and possibly too dominance-oriented to invest any attention in their appraisals of the powerless. They tend, therefore, to categorize and to form highly stereotypical impressions of those over whom they can exert power (Fiske & Dépret, 1996).

Fiske views social perceivers as "versatile, flexible . . . remarkably skilled and often quite attuned in their use of situation-appropriate strategies" (Fiske & Neuberg, 1990, p. 62), and her work on the way in which categorization is responsive to perceiver goals and motives (through, she believes, their effects on attention) is consistent with this emphasis. None the less, Fiske and her colleagues remain convinced of categorization's tendency to *over*simplify and thus distort, bias, and otherwise degrade impressions.

Thus far, the exemplar-category relationship, the ability of given cues to trigger given categories, has been presented as relatively unproblematic. Straightforward associations are assumed between the isolated attributes of isolated stimuli (e.g., an Irish accent) and a category ("Irish") with fairly fixed meaning. It is not difficult to see how this contributes to ideas about the biasing effects of categorization – many of these cues and the categories they relate to may be *irrelevant* in the present context, but it seems that the cues spark the categories regardless. Indeed, some argue that the attribute-category trigger is so automatic, some cued categories have to be actively inhibited in order for one single category to emerge as a clear basis for impression formation (Bodenhausen & Macrae, 1998).

We turn now to ideas generated mainly within the study of stereotype change, ideas about the conditions under which the presence of "consistent" or "confirming" cues is more or less likely to trigger the relevant categorization. This work is important because it moves us towards consideration of the *relationships between* attributes and between categorizable stimuli as potentially important influences on the categorization process.

In their cognitive analysis of intergroup contact Rothbart and John (1985) comment on "the often autonomous relationship between category attributes and the attributes of individual category members" (p. 101). They are referring to a syndrome we all know about – the homophobe who declares that some of his best friends are gay, the White member of an explicitly racist political organization who gets along perfectly well with her Asian workmates. The presumably positive attributes of some individual category members appear unrelated to the presumably negative defining attributes of the category. Rothbart and John's analysis of this shaky exemplar-category relationship, and more specifically of the conditions under which exemplar atypicality might succeed in challenging category meaning, has been elaborated by Hewstone and colleagues into a cognitive model of stereotype change (see Hewstone, 1996). The model is founded on a prototype approach to categorization in which "goodness of fit" to the category prototype, rather than the simple presence of relevant cues, determines whether or not a stimulus is perceived in terms of a given category. This is important for stereotype change because by definition potential change agents are somewhat aprototypical and thus likely to be seen as individual exceptions, or categorized as members of some group other than the one targeted for change. Change requires that exemplars with some degree of aprototypicality gain acceptance as category members. When does this happen?

Hewstone's research manipulates the way in which constant amounts of category confirming and disconfirming information are distributed across a number of category members (e.g., Johnston & Hewstone, 1992). This work has consistently demonstrated that the dispersal of disconfirming information across several members, such that each remains *relatively* prototypical, produces significantly more change than does concentrated disconfirmation which defines some highly typical but also some highly atypical category members. The lack of change under concentrated conditions is attributed to a process of subtyping, in which atypical members are corralled into a subdivision within the overall category, leaving the latter intact (Hantzi, 1995).

This work clearly demonstrates that categorization is not a matter of isolated cues triggering given categories (cf. Blair & Banaji, 1996, p. 1143, cited above). Individuals can carry crucial cues (e.g., appropriate uniform) to the categorization of interest ("police officer") but under certain conditions may be categorized in ways that the presence of the cue, in itself, could not predict (e.g., as more of a "welfare worker" than an agent of law enforcement; see Hewstone, Hopkins, & Routh, 1992). Findings of the kind reported by Hewstone suggest that relations between stimulus aspects contribute to categorization in two ways. First, the role of each "cue" in the categorization process is clearly conditioned by its relationship to other cues characterizing the target (cf. Kunda & Thagard, 1996). A police uniform does not mean the same when it is on a person talking about road safety in a classroom as it does when it is on someone exercising their move-on powers on a Saturday night (Hewstone et al., 1992), and "Black skin" is not the same thing when it appears in conjunction with "highly educated, famous biochemist" (Rothbart & John, 1985, p. 88) as when it characterizes a cool and groovy blues singer (Asch, 1946; Reynolds, 1996).

Second, the characteristics of *other people* within the salient context affect the categorization of any given target. In other words, being a police officer in comparison with welfare workers is not the same thing as being a police officer in comparison with prison guards, and this obviously affects the "cues" relevant for category "activation" (cf. Haslam, Turner, Oakes, McGarty, & Hayes, 1992). We have recently explored this issue in experiments which have introduced explicit comparison outgroups into Hewstone's dispersed/concentrated disconfirmation paradigm (Oakes, Haslam, & Reynolds, 1999). In one study students at the Australian National University (ANU) read about six students at a Catholic university who were generally believed to be conservative and conventional. The information presented included both confirming and disconfirming traits, the latter portraying the Catholic students as progressive, frivolous, and rebellious. This information was either concentrated in three of the stimulus students or dispersed across all six (cf. Johnston & Hewstone, 1992). Half of the participants also expected to read about members of the Call to Australia Party, an extremely conservative, fundamentalist right-wing religious group.

As we had predicted, under these "extended context" conditions the usual dispersed/concentrated effect was reversed, i.e., presentation of concentrated disconfirmation produced *more* stereotype change than did dispersed disconfirmation. Our interpretation of these findings focused on the variable definition of social categories across different comparative contexts. Indeed, it was evident from the data provided by control subjects, who received no information about individual category members, that the "typical attributes" of Catholic students were different – more progressive – under comparison with Call to Australia than when only the ANU participants and the Catholic targets defined the comparative context. Under these conditions the rebellious, frivolous concentrated disconfirmers had more impact on definition of the Catholic student category than did the (now rather atypical) largely conservative, tradition-loving dispersed disconfirmers.

This brings us to the self-categorization theory (SCT) analysis of category activation, or "salience", in which features of the current comparative context play a crucial role (Oakes, 1987). In fact, there are two important ways in which the category activation question as asked by SCT researchers is different from that posed by the approaches discussed so far. First, the question for SCT is not "when do we categorize, when don't we?" The theory regards all person perception as the outcome of a process of categorization, but a process which operates at varying *levels of abstraction*. The difference between individuated and stereotypical impression formation is that the latter is more abstract, more inclusive, than the former, defining differences between and similarities within *groups* of people. Categorization at the individual level, on the other hand, defines interpersonal differences and intra-individual consistency, and there can be social categorization both more and less abstract than these two intergroup and interpersonal levels.

Second, SCT places a strong emphasis on categorization as context-specific *process* rather than activation of cognitive structure (Turner, Oakes, Haslam, & McGarty, 1994). Together with Medin and colleagues, it considers the attribute-matching approach to categorization untenable in both its classical and prototype forms, because relevant "attributes" cannot be defined without reference to perceivers' purposes and prior understandings (see Medin, Goldstone, & Gentner, 1993). Relevant evidence comes from Medin and Wattenmaker (1987) who presented participants with a set of children's drawings divided into two categories and asked them to explain the basis of the categorization. In addition, participants were given a "theory" to guide this rule induction process; some were told that the pictures had been drawn by farm versus city children, others that they came from mentally healthy versus disturbed children, and so forth. It was found that the theories altered the meaning of "attributes", such that they had to be seen as emergent products of, rather than fixed inputs to, the categorization process. For example, uniformly smiling faces in one group of drawings was often used to explain their attribution to mentally healthy (versus disturbed) children in the appropriate condition. In another condition, exactly the same attribute was used as evidence that the drawings were done by noncreative (versus creative) children: "the faces show little variability in expression". Medin concludes that judgments of similarity are emergent and variable rather than based on a hit-or-miss attribute matching process: "similarity is always dynamic . . . and discovers and aligns features rather than just adding them up . . . the constituents are determined in the context of the comparison, not prior to it" (Medin et al., 1993, p. 275).

SCT views "relevant attributes" (see Medin et al., 1993) and salient categories as mutually emergent outcomes of an inherently *comparative* process working towards the resolution of the stimulus field that is most meaningful to the perceiver. To this end, categorization operates to maximize perceived similarity within and difference between categories in terms of contextually and normatively relevant dimensions. Formally, the hypothesis is that categorization is determined by an interaction between category-stimulus *fit* (both comparative and normative; i.e., in terms of both the pattern and the substantive content of perceived similarity and difference) and *perceiver readiness*. These factors define a dynamic interplay between stimulus information and the perceiver's perspective, values and motives which produces highly variable outcomes. *It is this complete dependence on variable features of both perceivers and contexts that enables categorization to fulfil its meaning-giving, identity-conferring function in perception.* We know that meaning varies with context – tears at a wedding are not the same as tears at a funeral. Accordingly, if categorization is to serve the knowledge function with which it is credited it too has to vary with context. The fixed cue-category relationships implied in cognitive structure/attribute-matching approaches do not easily accommodate the fact that meaning, identity, always varies with context. No wonder that categorization thus understood has been considered a hindrance to valid perception rather than a help.

In terms of the important differentiation between individuated and intergroup categorization, the prediction is that where perceived similarities and differences covary with a potential division into social groups in a way that makes sense in terms of the perceiver's motives and his or her background theories about the contextual significance or purpose of those groups, an ingroup-outgroup categorization will become salient and attitudes and actions will become inter*group* rather than interpersonal (or interspecies, or whatever). On the other hand, where individuals are perceived to vary within more than between groups categorization will be interpersonal and impression formation individuated (for relevant evidence see Oakes, Turner, & Haslam, 1991; Van Knippenberg, Van Twuyver, & Pepels, 1994; Yzerbyt, Rogier, & Fiske, 1998).

Two important assumptions underlying the SCT analysis of category salience deserve emphasis here. First, the crucial role of *self*-categorization (cf. Tajfel, 1978, discussed above). The self always features in the categorization work of the perceiver, is always an element of the to-be-categorized domain – "categorization works to *align the person with the realities of the social context*, to produce dynamic, context-specific definitions of self and others which both reflect and make possible the almost infinitely variable pattern of human social relations" (Oakes et al., 1999, p. 58, emphasis in original).

Second, distinctive amongst the approaches we have discussed in this section (with the exception of Hewstone's work) SCT follows Tajfel in emphasizing a qualitative discontinuity between interpersonal and intergroup contexts. The difference between categorization at the interpersonal and intergroup levels, as a cognitive process, is inalienably related to an assumed difference between interpersonal and intergroup *social reality* (see Oakes, 1996; Oakes, Reynolds, Haslam, & Turner, in press). Life – social life, work, political processes, cultural activity, and so forth – proceeds through the coordinated actions of groups as well as the private or idiosyncratic acts of individuals, and in order to be *accurate*, our social perceptions must register this distinctive group reality. This point was perhaps best expressed by Solomon Asch:

> Group-properties are the forms that interrelated activities of individuals take, not simply the actions of separate individuals. A flying wedge of policemen has a quality of power or threat that is a direct consequence of its organization. A picket line in front of a plant has a quality of unity that is a product of its organization. In each of these instances the group property cannot be rediscovered in the individuals taken singly (1952, p. 225).

Note that Asch locates distinctive group properties in the "*interrelated* activities of individuals", in other words it is the contextual relations between people which must be apprehended in order to access these group properties. SCT argues that, through comparative and normative fit, it is precisely these context-specific relationships which categorization represents.

To summarize the work discussed in this section, many argue that category activation is essentially a matter of an appropriate cue triggering a category and its contents, and impression formation proceeding accordingly. Motives and context are considered in some variants of this approach, but all endorse the idea of a cognitive category activated by given attributes. In an explicitly alternative view, SCT argues that cue-category relations are not enough, and indeed do not exist independent of context. Further, the theory insists that social categorization is not just about cognitive events; it is also always about social reality. To apply a category to an individual (e.g., "police officer") is not to *stereotype* them unless relevant aspects of the current context lead the category to be applied at an ingroup-outgroup level of inclusiveness, indicating interchangeability with other "police officers" and contrast from an appropriate outgroup.

3   Construal

> Does the mere act of categorizing actors into a group lead to a different set of inferences than if they are perceived to be unrelated to one another? (Wilder, 1986, p. 296)

The answer, of course, is yes. That categorization into groups transforms inference is not in doubt, and we shall discuss two basic manifestations of this – accentuation and assimilation to category meaning. These effects demonstrate that both the perceived structure and the substantive meaning of input are significantly affected by categorization, and because they have been understood as instances of bias and distortion in social perception it is these effects (together with ingroup favouritism, discussed in the next section) that have earned social categorization such a bad name.

In one of the most famous categorization experiments in social psychology, Tajfel and Wilkes (1963) found that division into categories can produce "a tendency to exaggerate the difference . . . between items which fall into distinct classes, and to minimize these differences within each of the classes" (Tajfel, 1969, p. 83). Numerous studies explored the potential for extrapolation of Tajfel and Wilkes' findings to the social domain (see McGarty, 1999, for review and a critical discussion of the robustness of this effect). For example, Allen and Wilder (1979; following Tajfel et al., 1971, see below) divided participants into two groups, in fact randomly but allegedly on the basis of preferences for paintings, then assessed their beliefs on a range of topics including art, politics, and college life. Participants also completed the beliefs measure as if they were either another ingroup member or an outgroup member. Responses revealed an assumed within-group similarity and between-group difference of opinion on both relevant (art) and entirely irrelevant (e.g., politics) dimensions. Put simply, accentuation effects reveal that when we believe (on whatever basis) that individuals share a salient group membership we expect them to be similar, more so than when such a shared identity is not salient (see McGarty & Turner, 1992). We also expect people divided by categorization to be different from each other, more so than when they are not distinguished from each other in this way.

One development of this basic accentuation finding has been exploration of the *outgroup homogeneity effect*. This refers to the apparent tendency for within-group accentuation of similarity to apply to outgroups rather more than it does to ingroups – "*they* all look alike to me" (e.g., Park & Rothbart, 1982; for review see Haslam, Oakes, Turner, & McGarty, 1996). Symptomatic of the assumed robustness of this pattern of asymmetrical perceived homogeneity, Park and Rothbart refer to it as "the *principle* of outgroup homogeneity" (1982, p. 1051, emphasis added) which, together with the "principle" of ingroup favoritism (see below) they see as a major cause of negative outgroup stereotypes and intergroup conflict. Attempts to explain the asymmetry have focused on identifying fundamental differences in the way in which ingroup and outgroup categories are represented.

Tajfel understood the accentuation effects of categorization as a distortion of perception – stimuli are being perceived as more similar and different *than they really are*, than they would appear to be if the perceiver made more effort or took "a closer look" (Tajfel, 1972). However, in recent work, Haslam and Turner (e.g., 1992) have turned our understanding of accentuation effects on its head, and argued that an *absence* of what we have come to know as "accentuation" would indicate distortion, would reflect perception which was insufficiently sensitive to context. At the heart of their argument is a point we have already emphasized – that, through categorization, *all perception is relative to context.* If this is the case, how can we establish a "standard" in comparison to which other impressions are "distorted" or "accentuated"? Theoretically, we could just as well define participants' awareness of interindividual differences in interpersonal contexts as an accentuated distortion of the "real" similarities perceived when group memberships are salient. The fact that stereotyping and individuation have not been construed in this way simply indicates that researchers have, without explicit justification, defined interpersonal differences as the objectively accurate "standard".

Haslam and Turner argue that it is inappropriate to refer to the judgment effects of ingroup-outgroup categorization as "accentuation", because this suggests that to be non-accentuated (i.e., accurate) impression formation should always proceed as if it were operating in an interpersonal context, with reference to individual differences (see Fiske & Neuberg, 1990; cf. Oakes & Reynolds, 1997). However, once we accept the real distinctiveness of group-level behavior, we can understand that it would make no sense to see people as individuals when they were behaving as group members, or as group members when they were behaving idiosyncratically. At the same time, Haslam and Turner emphasize that their re-analysis of accentuation is not restricted to conditions where group influences do in fact transform the character of individual "stimuli", such as where conformity processes produce relatively homogeneous behavior within groups. This is, of course, part of a clear dynamic within which stereotyping processes operate, but even where the stimulus is incapable of effecting change itself (as in most studies of social judgment), veridical perception will still involve accentuation (at some level of categorization), because accentuation simply reflects cognizance of the *relational* properties of stimuli within the current context.

Returning briefly to the outgroup homogeneity (OGH) effect mentioned above, recall that the apparently asymmetrical pattern of accentuation observed was held partially responsible for unwarranted derogation of outgroups and social conflict. Work by Simon and colleagues (e.g., Simon, 1992) and by self-categorization researchers (e.g., Haslam et al., 1996) has now produced extensive evidence inconsistent with a generalized OGH "effect" and consequently inconsistent with its proposed basis in entrenched differences between ingroup and outgroup representations. This work demonstrates that perceived group homogeneity – both ingroup and outgroup – is a predictable outcome of the categorization process as driven by the comparative, normative, and motivational principles specified in SCT and social identity theory. Again, the view of accentuation effects as distortions of a sovereign individuated, interpersonal social reality can be challenged – homogenization of both ingroups and outgroups occurs in a predictable manner which indicates that social perception is sensitive to the comparative and normative realities of the social context, and individuals' goals within that context.

In addition to findings of categorical accentuation effects, there is much accumulated evidence that the encoding, retrieval and interpretation of stimulus information is affected by category content (see Kunda & Thagard, 1996 for review). Wilder (1986, p. 294) refers to this as evidence of "categorical blinders" which restrict perceivers' perspectives on new information producing confirmation of pre-existing category-based expectations, sometimes even when disconfirming, inconsistent evidence is available and particularly when the available evidence is ambiguous (e.g., Kunda & Sherman-Williams, 1993).

The classic example comes from Duncan (1976) who manipulated the race (Black/White) of both the perpetrator and the victim of an "ambiguous shove". White participants tended to see the shove as fooling around when perpetrated by a White actor, but as violent behavior when perpetrated by a Black actor, particularly when the victim was White. Interpretation of the Black actor's behavior was guided by category content that defined Blacks as "impulsive and given to crimes and violence" (Duncan, 1976, p. 591).

Also widely cited under this heading is the work of Snyder and his colleagues (e.g., Snyder & Swann, 1978) which demonstrates that category-based expectations can affect the way in which perceivers structure their intake of information from the environment and the way in which they behave towards others, such that those expectations tend to be confirmed rather than disconfirmed (for discussion of limitations on this effect see Neuberg, 1994). Further, patterns of recall indicate information processing that favours category confirmation (e.g., Snyder & Uranowitz, 1978). Given the longstanding assumption that social category content is an inaccurate misrepresentation of the characteristics of group members (e.g., Judd & Park, 1993), it is not surprising that this sort of construal through categorization has been defined as a distortion of the "true attributes" of individuals. Again, it is assumed that these true attributes would be apparent to a motivated perceiver prepared to take "a closer look."

But is this a defensible assumption? As with accentuation, it appears to require some un-construed form of social perception as an accurate standard against which the outcomes of categorization can be defined as "biased". Indeed, this idea is quite explicit in Fiske and Neuberg's (1990) continuum model, which proposes that fully individuated impression formation involves a piecemeal, bottom-up appreciation of "true attributes", "uncontaminated" by categorization. It is in comparison with this effortful accuracy that the quick-fix categorical alternative is defined as "unfortunate", oversimplified and distorted.

In contrast, as we outlined above, SCT explicitly rejects the idea of uncategorized social perception. It argues that all impression formation involves categorization, that categorization varies with context, and therefore that the validity (accuracy) of *all* impression formation is relative to context (Oakes & Reynolds, 1997). It is, moreover, relative to the currently salient *self*-categorization of the perceiver, a perceiver who approaches every perceptual act armed with the theories, motives, values, and so forth that are relevant to that salient identity (Turner & Oakes, 1997).

Who is to establish the "correct" interpretation of Duncan's explicitly *ambiguous* shove? Apparently, it is the experimenter and the social-scientific community, people who are not placed in a salient relationship with the stimulus individuals, and who reject the stereotype of Blacks as violent. The White participants in the study, on the other hand, were asked to engage with, and make sense of, the scenario. Their potentially differing relationships to the White and to the Black protagonists – respectively, intragroup and intergroup (especially when the victim was White) – evidently did affect their own salient identity and therefore the motives, values, background theories that they brought to bear in interpreting events. At least some of the White participants experienced the encounter as one involving "a Black person and a White person" (rather than two individuals, or two students, or whatever) and the meaning that those categories had for them included an expectation of conflict and hostility. The Black actor's "ambiguous shove" was given meaning within that theoretical context, while the same action from a White actor was interpreted with reference to different expectations and theories. Note that *both* judgments require categorization – the conclusion that the White actor was "fooling around" was a product of his categorization as "ingroup", just as the judgment of "violence" followed from categorization of the Black actor as "outgroup".

What are we really doing when we interpret Duncan's findings as evidence that categorization produces bias and distortion? In fact, we are making value judgments about the *end products* of categorization. We want to say that race shouldn't matter, and that Blacks certainly shouldn't be stereotyped as violent. We are making a *political* statement, as is our right, but we cannot condemn categorization as a source of *psychological* inadequacy simply because we don't like some of its outcomes.

We have discussed these issues at length in the context of the question of stereotype accuracy (Oakes et al., 1994; Oakes & Reynolds, 1997) and of the general validity of social perception (Turner & Oakes, 1997). Our aim is not to defend political or social relativ*ism* (the fatal stumbling block for social-constructionist analyses with which we disagree in some fundamental ways) but to emphasize the inherent, inescapable *relativity* of human social perception. The categorization process is heavily implicated in this, as it produces the variable, context-dependent identities from which perceptual relativity flows. However, it cannot, in our view, be indicted as producing *bias* through this process. If it does, then all human perception, all human life, is bias because we are not computers or omniscient, all-seeing beings and there is no neutral, disinterested thought – "perception and thought . . . are actively involved in representing and understanding the world *from the point of view of the participating perceiver*" (Turner & Oakes, 1997, p. 367, emphasis added). As active participants in the political processes of social life, we may well wish to reject and protest "the point of view of the participating perceiver" in Duncan's study, but that is a matter of politics rather than psychology.

Finally, recent work also indicates that the influence of category content is more a matter of context-dependent, emergent interpretation than the imposition of fixed, over-simplified preconceptions on a complex reality. First, early indications of the context-dependence of stereotype content (e.g., Diab, 1963) have been confirmed (e.g., Haslam et al., 1992; Verkuyten, 1997). Consistent with both SCT and the analysis offered by Medin, discussed above, the attribute-category relationship appears to be far more fluid than had been presumed, with categories and attributes mutually emergent products of an "interaction of intelligent systems with aspects of their perceptual world" (Medin & Wattenmaker, 1987, p. 50). Second, it has been argued (often with direct reference to Medin's work) that categorization does not represent the efficient but relatively brutal wielding of the blunt instrument so frequently selected from the toolbox of the cognitive miser (Macrae, Milne, & Bodenhausen, 1994). On the contrary, this categorical deployment of knowledge is actually a highly complex interpretive, explanatory process with fairly hefty resource requirements (e.g., Nolan, Haslam, Spears, & Oakes, 1999; Spears & Haslam, 1997; Wittenbrink, Park, & Judd, 1998; Yzerbyt et al., 1998). Typical of the tone of this work, Wittenbrink and colleagues treat stereotypes as "a kind of shorthand for a *more elaborate theory* of what a group is like" (1998, p. 192, emphasis added).

In summary, we have discussed two major aspects of categorical influence in the construal of social stimuli – accentuation and assimilation to category content. In both instances, we have argued that the "bias" perspective can be usefully, and without great difficulty, jettisoned in favour of a more dynamic view in which the categorization process, in all its forms, is simply doing its job of producing *meaning* by defining stimuli in context-dependent, relational and self-relative terms.

4   Discrimination

In what must stand as one of the most influential and provocative experiments in the study of intergroup processes, Tajfel and colleagues (1971) divided schoolboys into minimal groups and asked them to distribute rewards between two anonymous others, an ingroup member and an outgroup member (see Bourhis & Gagnon, this volume, chapter 5). The results are well known. This apparently meaningless division into groups was sufficient to provoke ingroup-favoring responses in the allocation of rewards, even at the expense of absolute ingroup gain.

It was the fact that the "the mere act of categorizing" (Wilder, 1986, p. 296) apparently produced these ingroup-favoring responses that drew researchers' attention.

Conclusions about the irrationality and meaninglessness of intergroup conflict and discrimination were drawn by some, but not by Tajfel, who insisted that it was the very need to create meaning in an "otherwise empty situation", particularly meaning for the *self* – identity – that led participants to act in terms of the minimal categories (see 1972, pp. 39–40). In fact, one can turn the triviality argument on its head and argue that the power of minimal categorizations to produce group-based behavior reflects the customary significance and usefulness of categorical perception which participants import to the laboratory – when a context is defined in social-categorical terms *participants expect the categories to mean something*. McGarty and colleagues have used this argument in interpretation of the illusory correlation effect, presenting evidence that what had been seen as an automatic bias in social perception actually reflects "normal sense-making processes involving differentiation between groups which can be seen as both sensible and logical in the unusual context in which subjects are asked to make judgments" (McGarty & De la Haye, 1997, p. 169).

The crucial link Tajfel had drawn between social categorization and the self helped to make sense of minimal intergroup discrimination; insofar as participants' identities became engaged with the minimal groups ingroup favouritism could be seen as positive *self*-evaluation. This interpretation catalyzed the development of social identity theory, Tajfel and Turner's (1979) more general analysis of intergroup relations, and it is the subtle complexity of this analysis that stands as the true legacy of the minimal categorization experiments.

The social identity analysis of intergroup relations has been outstandingly fruitful. Perhaps most importantly it has challenged researchers, provoking disagreement and debate from which new clarity has emerged. We shall not discuss this work here because it is reviewed in detail elsewhere in the present volume (see Turner & Reynolds, chapter 7). For present purposes we shall simply note that the intergroup literature abounds with attempts to psychologize intergroup conflict by misusing aspects of the social identity analysis (see Turner, in press). Most relevant for the present discussion, many conclude from both minimal categorization findings and social identity theory that categorization, minimal or otherwise, automatically and inevitably produces intergroup discrimination (e.g., Stangor & Jost, 1997; Stephan, 1985). In fact, it was always clear that this was not the case. The first essential step is psychological identification, the engagement of the self such that a category is transformed into an *ingroup* (in contrast to a relevant outgroup) and this does not always occur within the minimal group paradigm (Turner, 1975) or elsewhere. What one then does about, with and in relation to that ingroup, discrimination or otherwise, emerges in interaction with both perceived social-structure (as discussed in social identity theory; e.g., see Ellemers, 1993) and other contextual and social-psychological factors (e.g., Ellemers, Spears, & Doosje, 1999). Again, as we noted in section 2, the workings of social categorization are always about social reality as much as they are about cognition.

Thus, the social identity analysis describes a road from categorization to discrimination that is rather more circuitous, offering many more possibilities for alternative destinations, than some commentaries on this literature have suggested. We cannot hold categorization, *per se*, responsible for intergroup discrimination. Indeed, we know that *exactly the same process of categorical self-definition* can, under appropriate conditions, *reduce* hostility (e.g., Gaertner, Mann, Murrell, & Dovidio, 1989; Hewstone & Brown, 1986) and produce cooperation (Morrison, 1997), a sense of justice and fairness (Tyler & Dawes, 1993), and the potential for extreme heroism and individual self-sacrifice. Recognition of the all-round validity of this process might prove more fruitful than persisting with the good cop/bad cop routine.

5   Conclusions: Categorization and Intergroup Conflict

This chapter has discussed the pivotal role of categorization in the social psychology of intergroup processes. We have followed the sequence of category activation, category-based construal, and (as one possible outcome of such construal) intergroup discrimination. Our mission has been to dispute the widely endorsed view that what categorization does, at every stage of this process, is to impose both informational and motivational "blinders" through cognitive laziness and self-interest which produce distorted perception and social hostility.

The explanation of conflict has always been at the top of the agenda for social theorists. Harmony and peaceful coexistence are desired and straightforwardly acceptable, but conflict is usually seen as a problem that needs to be dealt with. It falls to our discipline to specify the psychological underpinnings of social hostility, and our main response has been to identify various scapegoats (dysfunctions of the personality, shortcomings of cognition) which serve to disconnect human social conflict from human rationality – we don't *mean* to fight, we just can't help it. Categorization has been the most successful scapegoat thus far, a universally essential process, often automatic and mindless, but with negative side effects.

We can see that the starting point of this analysis is the definition of conflict as pathology, as problematic. We reject conflict and then portray its psychological underpinnings as themselves pathological and irrational. In effect, social psychology has defined some of the most significant events of history and some of the most engaging and forceful of human motivations as, in psychological terms, unintended byproducts, irrational, pathological, meaningless. There is, however, an alternative view in which intergroup conflict is taken seriously as a normal and perfectly healthy aspect of the political process that is social life. Consistent with this meta-theoretical perspective, social identity and self-categorization theories have presented categorization as the process through which individuals achieve "self-definition in a social context" (Tajfel, 1978, p. 61), context-specific identities which are emergent outcomes of human cognition engaging in the active interpretation of social reality. There is nothing irrational, distorting, oversimplifying, or biased about this process. It works to align the individual with the current social context and the outcome is that perception and thought operate from the specific vantage point, the singular perspective, of the self currently salient. Inevitably, then, there are differences of opinion, varying interpretations of reality.

It seems ironic that subjectivity, "the notion . . . that we actively construe reality instead of passively registering our environment" (Wittenbrink, Gist, & Hilton, 1997, p. 526), has been one of the defining principles of social psychology, and yet we have condemned what is probably its major basis, categorization, as a source of *bias*. We seem to pay lip service to subjectivity when we should be taking it seriously as a basic element of the human condition. Perhaps this is because social categorization can produce, within a single social context, not one, consensual subjectivity but a plethora of conflicting, contradictory statements of "fact" (e.g., see Bar-Tal, 1990). How can this be? Many have cried "bias"; others have argued that the reality of social disagreement cannot be defused in this way, and that we must "fac[e] the specific political, historical, and ideological facts of society" (Turner, 1999, p. 34) – conflict, contempt, disagreement, and denigration included. In this chapter I have advocated an analysis of categorization which, in my view, allows social psychology to do this. Our discipline may, in the process, become a far more powerful force in opposition to the real social injustices with which intergroup theorists have been rightly preoccupied.

References

Allen, V. L., & Wilder, D. A. (1979). Group categorization and attribution of belief similarity. *Small Group Behaviour, 10*, 73–80.

Asch, S. E. (1946). Forming impressions of personality. *Journal of Personality and Social Psychology, 41*, 258–290.

Asch, S. E. (1952). *Social Psychology*. New York: Prentice-Hall.

Bar-Tal, D. (1990). *Group beliefs*. New York: Springer-Verlag.

Bargh, J. (1989). Conditional automaticity: Varieties of automatic influence on social perception and cognition. In J. S. Uleman & J. A. Bargh (Eds.), *Unintended thought* (pp. 3–51). New York: Guilford Press.

Biernat, M., & Vescio, T. K. (1993). Categorization and stereotyping: Effects of group context on memory and social judgement. *Journal of Experimental Social Psychology, 29*, 166–202.

Biernat, M., & Vescio, T. K. (1994). Still another look at the effects of fit and novelty on the salience of social categories. *Journal of Experimental Social Psychology, 30*, 399–406.

Blair, I. V., & Banaji, M. (1996). Automatic and controlled processes in stereotype priming. *Journal of Personality and Social Psychology, 70*, 1142–1163.

Bodenhausen, G., & Macrae, C. N. (1998). Stereotype activation and inhibition. In R. S. Wyer (Ed.), *Stereotype activation and inhibition* (Advances in social cognition Vol. XI) (pp. 1–52). Mahwah, NJ: Erlbaum.

Bodenhausen, G., Macrae, C. N., & Garst, J. (1998). Stereotypes in thought and deed: Social-cognitive origins of intergroup discrimination. In C. Sedikides, J. Schopler, & C. A. Insko (Eds.), *Intergroup cognition and intergroup behaviour* (pp. 311–336). Mahwah, NJ: Erlbaum.

Devine, P. G. (1989). Stereotypes and prejudice: Their automatic and controlled components. *Journal of Personality and Social Psychology, 56*, 5–18.

Diab, L. N. (1963). Factors determining group stereotypes. *Journal of Social Psychology, 61*, 3–10.

Duncan, B. L. (1976). Differential social perception and attribution of intergroup violence: Testing the lower limits of stereotyping of Blacks. *Journal of Personality and Social Psychology, 34*, 590–598.

Ellemers, N. (1993). The influence of socio-structural variables on identity enhancement strategies. *European Review of Social Psychology, 4*, 27–57.

Ellemers, N., Spears, R., & Doosje, B. (Eds.), (1999). *Social identity: Context, commitment, content*. Oxford, UK: Blackwell.

Fiske, S. T. (1993). Controlling other people: The impact of power on stereotyping. *American Psychologist, 48*, 621–628.

Fiske, S. T., & Dépret, E. (1996). Control, interdependence and power: Understanding social cognition in its social context. In W. Stroebe & M. Hewstone (Eds.), *European review of social psychology* (Vol. 7, pp. 31–61). Chichester, UK: Wiley.

Fiske, S. T., Lin, M., & Neuberg, S. L. (1998). The continuum model: Ten years later. In S. Chaiken & Y. Trope (Eds.), *Dual process theories in social psychology*. New York: Guilford Press.

Fiske, S. T., & Neuberg, S. L. (1990). A continuum of impression formation, from category-based to individuating processes: Influences of information and motivation on attention and interpretation. In M. P. Zanna (Ed.), *Advances in experimental social psychology* (Vol. 23, pp. 1–73). New York: Random House.

Gaertner, S. L., Mann, J., Murrell, A., & Dovidio, J. F. (1989). Reducing intergroup bias: The benefits of recategorization. *Journal of Personality and Social Psychology, 57*, 239–249.

Hantzi, A. (1995). Change in stereotypic perceptions of familiar and unfamiliar groups: The pervasiveness of the subtyping model. *British Journal of Social Psychology, 34*(4), 463–477.

Haslam, S. A., Oakes, P. J., Turner, J. C., & McGarty, C. (1996). Social identity, self-categorization and the perceived homogeneity of ingroups and outgroups: The interaction between social motivation and cognition. In R. M. Sorrentino & E. T. Higgins (Eds.), *Handbook of Motivation and Cognition* (Vol. 3). New York: Guilford Press.

Haslam, S. A., & Turner, J. C. (1992). Context-dependent variation in social stereotyping 2: The relationship between frame of reference, self-categorization, and accentuation. *European Journal of Social Psychology, 22*, 251–278.

Haslam, S. A., Turner, J. C., Oakes, P. J., McGarty, C. A., & Hayes, B. K. (1992). Context-dependent variation in social stereotyping 1: The effects of intergroup relations as mediated by social change and frame of reference. *European Journal of Social Psychology, 22*, 3–20.

Haslam, S. A., & Wilson, A. (2000). In what sense are prejudiced beliefs *personal?* The importance of an ingroup's shared stereotypes. *British Journal of Social Psychology, 39*, 45–63.

Hewstone, M. (1996). Contact and categorization: Social psychological interventions to change intergroup relations. In C. N. Macrae, C. Stangor, & M. Hewstone (Eds.), *Foundations of stereotypes and stereotyping* (pp. 323–368). New York: Guilford. Press.

Hewstone, M., Hopkins, N., & Routh, D. A. (1992). Cognitive models of stereotype change: (1) Generalization and subtyping in young people's views of the police. *European Journal of Social Psychology, 22*, 219–234.

Johnston, L., & Hewstone, M. (1992). Cognitive models of stereotype change: (3) Subtyping and the perceived typicality of disconfirming group members. *Journal of Experimental Social Psychology, 28*, 360–386.

Judd, C., & Park, B. (1993). Definition and asssessment of accuracy in social stereotypes. *Psychological Review, 100*, 109–128.

Kunda, Z., & Sherman-Williams, B. (1993). Stereotypes and the construal of individuating information. *Persoanlity and Social Psychology Bulletin, 19*, 90–99.

Kunda, Z., & Thagard, P. (1996). Forming impressions from stereotypes, traits and behaviors: A parallel-constraint-satisfaction theory. *Psychological Review, 103*, 284–308.

Lepore, L., & Brown, R. (1997). Category and stereotype activation: Is prejudice inevitable? *Journal of Personality and Social Psychology, 72*, 275–287.

Macrae, C. N., Milne A. B., & Bodenhausen, G. V. (1994). Stereotypes as energy-saving devices: A peek inside the cognitive toolbox. *Journal of Personality and Social Psychology, 66*, 37–47.

McGarty, C. (1999). *The categorization proces in social psychology*. London: Sage.

McGarty, C., & de la Haye, A.-M. (1997). Stereotype formation: Beyond illusory correlation. In R. Spears, P. Oakes, N. Ellemers, & S. A. Haslam (Eds.), *The social psychology of stereotyping and group life* (pp. 144–170). Oxford, UK: Blackwell.

McGarty, C., & Turner, J. C. (1992). The effects of categorization on social judgement. *British Journal of Social Psychology, 31,* 147–157.

Medin, D. L., Goldstone R. L., & Gentner, D. (1993). Respects for similarity. *Psychological Review, 100,* 254–278.

Medin, D. L., & Wattenmaker, W. D. (1987). Category cohesiveness, theories, and cognitive archeology. In U. Neisser (Ed.), *Concepts and conceptual development: Ecological and intellectual factors in categorization.* Cambridge, UK: Cambridge University Press.

Monteith, M. J. (1993). Self-regulation of prejudiced responses: Implications for progress in prejudice-reduction efforts. *Journal of Personality and Social Psychology, 65,* 469–485.

Morrison, B. E. (1997). *Social cooperation: Re-defining the self in self-interest.* Unpublished Ph.D. thesis, The Australian National University.

Neuberg, S. L. (1994). Stereotypes, prejudice, and expectancy confirmation. In M. P. Zanna & J. M. Olson (Eds.), *Psychology of prejudice: The seventh Ontario symposium on personality and social psychology.* Hillsdale, NJ: Erlbaum.

Neuberg, S. L., & Fiske, S. T. (1987). Motivational influences on impression formation: Outcome dependency, accuracy-driven attention, and individuating processes. *Journal of Personality and Social Psychology, 53,* 431–444.

Nolan, M. A., Haslam, S. A., Spears, R., & Oakes, P. J. (1999). An examination of resource-based and fit-based theories of stereotyping under cognitive load and fit. *European Journal of Social Psychology, 29,* 641–664.

Oakes, P. J. (1987). The salience of social categories. In J. C. Turner et al., *Rediscovering the social group: A self-categorization theory.* Oxford, UK: Basil Blackwell and Madrid: Ediciones Morata (1990).

Oakes, P. J. (1994). The effects of fit versus novelty on the salience of social categories: A response to Biernat & Vescio (1993). *Journal of Experimental Social Psychology, 30,* 390–398.

Oakes, P. J. (1996). The categorization process: Cognition and the group in the social psychology of stereotyping. In P. Robinson (Ed.), *Social groups and identity: Developing the legacy of Henri Tajfel.* Oxford, UK: Butterworth-Heinemann.

Oakes, P. J., Haslam, S. A., & Reynolds, K. J. (1999). Social categorization and social context: Is stereotype change a matter of information or of meaning? In D. Abrams & M. A. Hogg (Eds.), *Social identity and social cognition* (pp. 55–79). Oxford, UK: Blackwell.

Oakes, P. J., & Reynolds, K. J. (1997). Asking the accuracy question: Is measurement the answer? In R. Spears, P. Oakes, N. Ellemers, & S. A. Haslam (Eds.), *The social psychology of stereotyping and group life.* Oxford, UK: Blackwell.

Oakes, P. J., Reynolds, K. J., Haslam, S. A., & Turner, J. C. (in press). Part of life's rich tapestry: Stereotyping and the politics of intergroup relations. In E. Lawler & S. Thye (Eds.), *Advances in group processes* (Vol. 16) Greenwich, CT: JAI Press.

Oakes, P. J., Turner, J. C., & Haslam, S. A. (1991). Perceiving people as group members: The role of fit in the salience of social categorizations. *British Journal of Social Psychology, 30,* 125–144.

Park, B., & Rothbart, M. (1982). Perception of outgroup homogeneity and levels of social categorization: Memory for the subordinate attributes of ingroup and outgroup members. *Journal of Personality and Social Psychology, 42,* 1051–1068.

Reynolds, K. J. (1996). Beyond the information given: Capacity, context, and the categorization process in impression formation. Unpublished Ph.D. thesis, The Australian National University.

Reynolds, K. J., & Oakes, P. J. (2000). Variability in impression formation: Investigating the role of motivation, capacity, and the categorization process. *Personality and Social Psychology Bulletin, 26,* 355–373.

Rothbart, M., & John, O. P. (1985). Social categorization and behavioral episodes: A cognitive analysis of the effects of intergroup contact. *Journal of Social Issues, 41,* 81–104.

Ruscher, J. B., Fiske, S. T., Miki, H., & Van Manen, S. (1991). Individuating processes in competition: Interpersonal versus intergroup. *Personality and Social Psychology Bulletin, 17,* 595–605.

Sherif, M. (1967). *Group conflict and co-operation: Their social psychology.* London: Routledge and Kegan Paul.

Simon, B. (1992). The perception of ingroup and outgroup homogeneity: Re-introducing the social context. In W. Stroebe & M. Hewstone (Eds.), *European review of social psychology,* (Vol. 3). Chichester, UK: Wiley.

Snyder, M., & Swann, W. B. (1978). Hypothesis-testing processes in social interaction. *Journal of Personality and Social Psychology, 36,* 1202–1212.

Snyder, M., & Uranowitz, S. W. (1978). Reconstructing the past: Some cognitive consequences of person perception. *Journal of Personality and Social Psychology, 36,* 941–950.

Spears, R., & Haslam, S. A. (1997). Stereotyping and the burden of cognitive load. In R. Spears, P. Oakes, N. Ellemers, & S. A. Haslam (Eds.), *The social psychology of stereotyping and group life* (pp. 171–207). Oxford, UK: Blackwell.

Stangor, C., & Jost, J. T. (1997). Commentary: Individual, group, and system level of analysis and their relevance for stereotyping and intergroup relations. In R. Spears, P. Oakes, N. Ellemers, & S. A. Haslam (Eds.), *The social psychology of stereotyping and group life* (pp. 336–358). Oxford, UK: Blackwell.

Stephan, W. G. (1985). Intergroup relations. In G. Lindzey & E. Aronson (Eds.), *Handbook of social psychology* (Vol. 2). New York: Random House.

Tajfel, H. (1969). Cognitive aspects of prejudice. *Journal of Social Issues, 25,* 79–97.

Tajfel, H. (1972). Social categorization. In S. Moscovici (Ed.), *Introduction à la psychologie sociale* (Vol. 1). Paris: Larousse.

Tajfel. H. (Ed.), (1978). *Differentiation between social groups: Studies in the social psychology of intergroup relations.* London: Academic Press.

Tajfel, H., Billig, M. G., Bundy, R. F., & Flament, C. (1971). Social categorization and intergroup behaviour. *European Journal of Social Psychology, 1,* 149–177.

Tajfel, H., & Turner, J. C. (1979). An integrative theory of intergroup conflict. In W. G. Austin & S. Worschel (Eds.), *The social psychology of intergroup relations.* Monterey, CA: Brooks/Cole.

Tajfel, H., & Wilkes, A. L. (1963). Classification and quantitative judgement. *British Journal of Psychology, 54,* 101–114.

Taylor, S. E., Fiske, S. T., Etcoff, N. L., & Ruderman, A. J. (1978). Categorical and contextual bases of person memory and stereotyping. *Journal of Personality and Social Psychology, 36,* 778–793.

Turner, J. C. (1975). Social comparison and social identity: Some prospects for intergroup behaviour. *European Journal of Social Psychology, 5,* 149–178.

Turner, J. C. (1999). Some current issues in reserach on social identity and self-categorization theories. In N. Ellemers, R. Spears, & B. Doosje (Eds.), *Social identity: Context, commitment, content* (pp. 6–34). Oxford, UK: Blackwell.

Turner, J. C., & Oakes, P. J. (1997). The socially structured mind. In C. McGarty & S. A. Haslam (Eds.), *The message of social psychology.* Oxford, UK: Blackwell.

Turner, J. C., Oakes, P. J., Haslam, S. A., & McGarty, C. M. (1994). Self and collective: Cognition and social context. *Personality and Social Psychology Bulletin, 20,* 454–463.

Tyler, T. R., & Dawes, R. M. (1993). Fairness in groups: Comparing the self-interest and social identity perspectives. In B. A. Mellers & J. Baron (Eds.), *Psychological perspectives on justice: Theory and applications.* Cambridge, UK: Cambridge University Press.

Van Knippenberg, A., Van Twuyver, M., & Pepels, J. (1994). Factors affecting social categorization processes in memory. *British Journal of Social Psychology, 33,* 419–432.

Verkuyten, M. (1997). Discourses of ethnic minority identity. *British Journal of Social Psychology, 36,* 565–586.

Wilder, D. A. (1986). Social categorization: Implications for creation and reduction of intergroup bias. In L. Berkowitz (Ed.), *Advances in experimental social psychology* (Vol. 19). New York: Academic Press.

Wittenbrink, B., Gist, P. L., & Hilton, J. L. (1997). Structural properties of stereotypic knowledge and their influences on the construal of social situations. *Journal of Personality and Social Psychology, 72*, 526–543.

Wittenbrink, B., Park, B., & Judd, C. (1998). The role of stereotypic knowledge in the construal of person models. In C. Sedikides, J. Schopler, & C. A. Insko (Eds.), *Intergroup cognition and intergroup behaviour* (pp. 177–202). Mahwah, NJ: Erlbaum.

Yzerbyt, V. Y., Rogier, A., & Fiske, S. T. (1998). Group entitativity and social attribution: On translating situational constraints into stereotypes. *Personality and Social Psychology Bulletin, 24*, 1089–1103.

CHAPTER TWO

Stereotypes: Content, Structures, Processes, and Context

Don Operario and Susan T. Fiske

> For the real environment is altogether too big, too complex, and too fleeting for direct acquaintance. We are not equipped to deal with so much subtlety, so much variety, so many permutations and combinations. And although we have to act in that environment, we have to reconstruct it on a simpler model before we can manage it.
>
> Lippmann (1922, p. 16)

Walter Lippmann introduced the word "stereotypes" to the social sciences in his ground-breaking text *Public Opinion* (1922), referring to them as "pictures in our heads" that simplify how people think about human groups. Lippmann argued that people rely on simplistic pictures and images when forming and expressing opinions about others. Accordingly, thus derives the basis for social misunderstanding, tension, and conflict: People's stereotypes of human groups cloud reality, distorting actual experience with biased preconceptions. Lippmann argued, "For the most part we do not first see, and then define, we define first and then see" (1922, p. 81).

Almost 80 years later, the concept of stereotypes has spread throughout popular discourse. Discussion of stereotypes abounds: Newspaper and magazine articles describe how stereotypes impede social progress; college orientation programs inform new students about stereotypes permeating the culture; and business organizations provide workshops urging employees to suppress their stereotypes. Although most popular discussions of stereotypes recognize their destructive potential, few explicitly address what they communicate, why they exist, how they operate, and where they originate.

Does social psychology research enlighten this ubiquitous discussion of stereotypes? Indeed, following the publication of Lippmann's classic work, social psychologists have investigated almost every facet of stereotypes and stereotyping, from the cultural contexts that shape their meaning to the mental structures that shape their use. Literally thousands of studies published in psychological journals have addressed the bases for stereotypes and stereotyping, and dozens of review articles summarize the conclusions derived along the way. This wealth of knowledge is intellectually inspiring, yet intimidating in scope. A thorough review of this work leaves even the most expert reader wondering, "What core messages can be extracted from this corpus of knowledge?"

This chapter advances two core principles derived from a review of this literature. First, stereotypes are more ambivalent than people commonly recognize; stereotypes contain both positive and negative attributes about social groups, and, thus, their potency is largely determined by the social context within which they arise. Second, stereotypes are an inherent byproduct of the human cognitive system, yet controllable with personal motivation and effort. The novelty of this framework lies in explicit disentanglement of stereotypes as *a constellation of beliefs* about members of social groups, versus stereotyping as *a manner of thinking* about people and the groups to which they belong. Although both principles are intimately interconnected – each embedded in Lippmann's (1922) original treatise – most work focuses on one theme (thinking) exclusively, treating the other (beliefs) as an assumption. We argue that social scientists and lay people alike must consider both dimensions to appreciate the problem of stereotypes and seek solutions for their effects.

This chapter proceeds with four sections addressing, respectively, the what, why, how, and where of stereotypes: The content of stereotypes, the cognitive structures of stereotypes, the processes of stereotyping, and the context of stereotypes. The first and fourth sections, on content and context, argue that stereotyping involves negative or ambivalent belief systems that vary in potency according to the situation. The second and third sections, on structures and processes, argue that stereotyping is inherent to the cognitive system. Organized thus, each section supports either or both of our two core principles.

Several limitations (mostly space and feasibility) preclude an exhaustive discussion of relevant literature. Interested readers can seek recent work published elsewhere, for example, Fiske's (1998) chapter on stereotyping, prejudice, and discrimination (a companion piece to the present article, with a thorough examination of specific findings); as well as outstanding reviews, including Bodenhausen and Macrae (1998), Hilton and von Hippel (1996), and Stangor and Lange (1994).

Stereotype Content

Most lay discussions of stereotypes focus on content. In American culture, stereotypic content describes the "characteristics" of people who are ethnic minorities, women, elderly, overweight, and homosexual, among other categories. Stereotypes overgeneralize, misattribute, prescribe, and often condemn the behavior and personal characteristics associated with these categories. As this section discusses, such is the nature of stereotype content.

In contrast to popular discussion, social psychology has devoted considerably less research to content, focusing more on structures and processes (discussed in subsequent sections). However, studies of stereotype content matter just as much, for they illuminate *what*, rather than how and why, people think about others. Insight into stereotype content can elucidate intergroup relations, political attitudes, social tension, and other societal phenomena, whereas knowledge of process and structure may be less helpful in these domains.

One of the first studies to address the content of stereotypes was Katz and Braly's (1933) classic examination of ethnic stereotypes, which concluded that ethnic stereotypes were uniformly negative and consensually shared. However, follow-up studies observed over time diminishing negative attitudes toward minorities, concluding that these stereotypes were fading (Gilbert, 1951; Karlins, Coffman, & Walters, 1969). Prior research was claimed ungeneralizable (cf. Gergen, 1973); stereotype content allegedly provided historically sensitive descriptions of social attitudes, but fell outside the purview of general psychological principles.

The thesis in this section, however, is that stereotype content indeed follows general psychological principles. A review of research reveals basic principles that underlie stereotype content. These principles are that (a) stereotypes contain ambivalent beliefs reflecting relationships between groups, (b) stereotypes augment perceptions of negative and extreme behavior, and (c) stereotypes maintain division between ingroups ("us") and outgroups ("them"). This section briefly addresses the issue of stereotype accuracy and the debates about whether a "kernel of truth" underlies the content of stereotypes.

Ambivalent belief systems: Competence versus niceness

The content of stereotypes described in Allport's (1954) groundbreaking text *The Nature of Prejudice* reflects antipathy toward members of derogated groups. However, emerging perspectives in social psychology indicate that stereotype-based antipathy is rare. Instead, stereotypes more likely contain ambivalent beliefs, with a mixture of mostly negative but some positive attributes. The blend of these traits indeed reflects overall disparagement, but not utter repugnance.

For example, the Black stereotypes endorsed in Katz and Braly's (1933) study included *superstitious, lazy, happy-go-lucky, ignorant, musical, ostentatious*, and *religious*. Thus, even when explicit endorsement of negative Black stereotypes was somewhat acceptable, Katz and Braly's respondents in 1933 reported more ambivalent disapproval than outright antipathy. However, some stereotypes, even today, remain resolutely negative, including beliefs about terrorists and criminals. But again, ambivalence is more common than antipathy in stereotypes of outgroups.

The ambivalence of most social stereotypes reflects the structural relationship between groups, determined by (a) groups' relative status and (b) the nature of interdependence between groups. Relative status predicts whether the target group is perceived as competent or incompetent, and interdependence (cooperation versus competition) predicts whether the target group is perceived as nice or not (Fiske, Xu, Cuddy, & Glick, in press). In this view, competence and niceness represent core dimensions of ambivalent belief systems.

Stereotypes ensue from groups' structural relationships, such that non-majority groups tend to be viewed as high on one domain but low on the other: either highly competent but not nice, or extremely incompetent but nice. Stereotype content adheres to this pattern. Recent data (Fiske et al., in press) indicate that people believe the following groups are nice but incompetent: retarded people, housewives, elderly people, disabled people, and blind people. In contrast, people believe the following groups are not nice but competent: feminists, business women, Black professionals, Asians, and Jews. The beliefs associated with these two clusters reflect their relationship with the dominant majority (White, male, middle-class, able-bodied). The first group presents no threat to the majority, whereas the second group presents significant threat.

The payoff between perceived niceness and competence corroborates many common cultural stereotypes about categories and their subtypes (Rosenberg, Nelson, & Vivkananthan, 1968). Business women are stereotypically industrious and aggressive (high competence–low niceness), whereas "pink-collar" workers are stereotypically nice but not very smart. Middle-class or wealthy African Americans are often viewed as ambitious but defensive about racism (high competence–low niceness). According to this analysis, only members of the dominant majority profit from being both competent and nice.

The dimensions of competence and niceness, which derive from groups' status and interdependence, reflect a trans-historical principle of stereotyping. Most common stereotypes contain ambivalent, rather than purely negative, beliefs about outgroup categories, which can influence perceivers' attitudes and behaviors in subtle yet powerful ways (e.g., Gaertner & Dovidio, 1986). Situational context can determine the overall valence and potency of ambivalent stereotypes (Oakes, Haslam, & Reynolds, 1999). An example of stereotypes about Asians demonstrates this point. Recent findings (Lin & Fiske, 1999) showed that some Anglo-Americans believe Asians are intelligent, shy, upwardly mobile, hardworking, and socially awkward – truly a heterogeneous combination of traits. Social context can trigger how perceivers use this stereotype: In a social situation, Asians are irrelevant and non-threatening, but in a competitive situation, Asians are dominating and menacing.

Negative and extreme behavior

A second principle of stereotype content is that stereotypes augment negative and extreme behavior. This simple principle has permeated social cognition research for decades (see Fiske, 1980), and impacts how people think about outgroup members.

Negative and extreme information captures people's attention (Skowronski & Carlston, 1989; Taylor, 1991). For example, research on salience (Taylor & Fiske, 1978) indicates that attention flows to negative and extreme stimuli – such as inappropriate behavior (crimes) or unanticipated accidents (car accidents). This occurs because people generally expect other people and events to be slightly positive or benign (Matlin & Stang, 1978), and in contrast, negative and extreme stimuli stand out. Consequently, perceivers assume that negative and extreme stimuli are diagnostic of a person or situation, and thus become central to subsequent formed impressions (Skowronski & Carlston, 1989).

Perceptions of outgroups are particularly vulnerable to the cognitive effects of negative and extreme behavior. Perceivers associate minority groups with negative or extreme behavior – known as the illusory correlation (Hamilton & Sherman, 1989) – because both are rare occurrences that represent exceptions to the rules (i.e., the majority group and positive events). When encountering both an unusual group and a rare event, perceivers assume the two are directly associated. For example, people tend to view AIDS as a homosexual disease because both are novel stimuli – homosexuals are a minority group and AIDS is a negative occurrence – when they happen to co-occur. Although the incidence of AIDS is higher among other groups (e.g., heterosexual women), the illusory correlation between AIDS and homosexuality persists. Other examples include the illusory correlation between African Americans and welfare recipients (most recipients are White) and between Mexicans and illegal immigration to the United States (just as many, if not more, illegal immigrants come from Canada, Europe, and Asia).

Stereotypes capitalize on the distinctiveness of negative and extreme concepts stored in people's mental representations. Minority group members tend to be novel or unique to majority group members, so are vulnerable to the cognitive processes that pair their distinctiveness with socially undesirable traits and behavior.

Us and them

The third principle of stereotype content is the advantage given to the ingroup and relative disadvantage given to the outgroup. This principle is the cornerstone of social identity theory (Tajfel & Turner, 1986), and an elementary concept in social psychology (see also Brewer & Brown, 1998).

People allocate more rewards to ingroup members than outgroup members (Brewer, 1979), have more positive reactions to ingroup versus outgroup stimuli presented unconsciously (Perdue, Dovidio, Gurtman, & Tyler, 1990), and engage in more cooperative rather than competitive behavior with ingroup members (Schopler & Insko, 1992). Stereotypic beliefs of the outgroup are implicated in all of these findings (Fiske, 1998). Although most laboratory evidence reveals ingroup favoritism rather than outgroup derogation *per se*, the realities of social life and resource scarcity suggest that the two are at least partially correlated (Brewer & Brown, 1998). Moreover, mere presence of an outgroup might suggest that one's own personal goals are at risk (Fiske & Ruscher, 1993), thereby prompting motivated stereotyping.

Stereotype accuracy?

Recent years have witnessed increased studies addressing the relative accuracy of stereotypes. Do they reflect a "kernel of truth" about outgroups? This perspective was highlighted in a volume by Lee, Jussim, and McCauley (1995), which countered the dominant view of stereotypes as incorrect, biased, and socially harmful. Lee, Jussim, and their colleagues argue that stereotype content has some factual basis. They cite evidence indicating that societies consensually agree about groups' traits and attributes; that minority group members themselves endorse stereotypes about their group; and that objective criteria, such as grades, standardized test scores, and job evaluations, corroborate the validity of stereotypes (see Ottati & Lee, 1995, for a summary of this evidence).

The perspective gleaned from our review of the literature, however, is less accommodating of the stereotype accuracy movement. Several lines of research indicate the sheer difficulty in establishing accuracy criteria. Judd, Park, and their colleagues have shown wide variability in people's judgments of what constitutes accuracy (Judd & Park, 1993; Ryan, Park, & Judd, 1996). For example, how could one measure whether African Americans conform to stereotypes that they are athletic, loud, superstitious, and academically unmotivated? Would accuracy be determined by group differences on these traits, by the amount of within-group variability on these traits, or by the trans-situational endurance of these traits among different subgroups? Judgments of accuracy are indeed complex, and the "kernel of truth" criteria will likely remain elusive.

Rather than focus on the a priori veracity of stereotype content, more compelling evidence supports behavioral confirmation of stereotype content. Research on self-fulfilling prophecies (Snyder, 1992) reveals that people who hold stereotypes about others can elicit confirmatory behavior, making their biases appear grounded in reality. For example, a biased individual who believes "Black people are hostile" might act cold, distant, and suspicious when interacting with an African American (Chen & Bargh, 1997). The African-American person might respond reciprocally, displaying resentment and hostility toward the biased perceiver. The stereotype thus becomes confirmed in the perceiver's eyes.

Another line of research by Steele and Aronson (1995) shows that members of stereotyped groups can be vulnerable simply to the awareness of their group's stereotype, and act in ways that support the stereotype (see Crocker & Quinn, this volume, chapter 12). For example, African Americans who are reminded of their group membership (and therefore made aware of alleged academic deficiencies) and women who are reminded about women's alleged math deficiencies, perform significantly worse on standardized tests compared to other group members who are not reminded of the stereotype (see also Steele, 1997). In this instance, stereotype-confirming behavior is not elicited by a biased perceiver; simply knowing that the stereotype exists can lead a target group member to confirm it.

Understanding *what* people do with the content of their stereotypes, rather than whether the content of those stereotypes is true or not, supports a social psychological account of influence processes, rather than degenerating into measurement debates.

Stereotype Structures

A second way of understanding stereotypes examines cognitive structures from which they arise. The preceding discussion of stereotype content assumed existence of internal structures that store stereotypic beliefs and information. This section explores the nature of these cognitive structures to understand how stereotypes draw support from basic mental architecture.

Earlier discussion focused on content rules of category-based beliefs. By categorizing people into groups – such as women, Blacks, Asians, college professors – people ascribe qualities associated with the group to the individual target. One might wonder, What exactly is a cognitive category? Is it a theoretical abstraction, or an actual mental construct? This section addresses these questions by surveying four major social cognitive approaches that clarify how people store information in their minds – that is, how they mentally represent the world as it exists "out there" – and how that organization of information influences subsequent perception and judgment. These four approaches are prototype, exemplar, associative network, and connectionist models of mental representation (see also Fiske & Taylor, 1991; Smith, 1998, for more discussion).

Prototype models

A prototype refers to the average or most typical member of a category. According to prototype models, people organize category information around the category's statistical average. However, the prototype of a category need not represent a veridical instance or member of the category; in most cases, the prototype does not actually exist (Posner & Keele, 1968; Reed, 1972). One would be hard-pressed to identify the embodiment of the average professor, African American, or lawyer, although one can describe the average attributes associated with these categories.

Prototype models posit that people represent categorical information in "fuzzy sets." That is, attributes about the category have no definite boundaries or systematic organizing criteria, except for mere association with the prototype. Category attributes cluster around the prototype according to family resemblance, wherein attributes share similar features, but their direct association makes sense only in the context of the prototype (Fiske & Taylor, 1991). For example, the attributes *intelligent, disorganized, distinguished,* and *awkward* make little sense as a coherent personality description, but organized professor prototype can describe many familiar individuals.

Prototypes have important implications for forming impressions and making judgments about group members. When forming impressions of people, perceivers compare the target individual with a category prototype; if the target overlaps sufficiently with the prototypical representation, perceivers assimilate the target into the category (Fiske & Neuberg, 1990). Stereotypes take hold when perceivers assume that fuzzy-set attributes associated with the general category describe the target individual. Following this logic, prototypes can influence all stages of social cognition, from initial impressions people form of others, to the way they interpret subsequent information, to the way they recall targets' attributes (Fiske, Lin, & Neuberg, 1999).

Prototype-based stereotyping is strongest when perceivers have little direct experience with the category yet possess strong group expectancies (Smith & Zàrate, 1990), for example, when people learn about an outgroup through cultural socialization rather than actual interaction. Such might be the case for racial stereotypes, wherein perceivers hold strong beliefs transmitted by culture, yet have little intergroup interaction due to racial segregation (cf. Pettigrew, 1997). According to prototype models, changing perceivers' beliefs about typical members of a given category (e.g., the "average" African American or woman) can dilute the stereotype (Hantzi, 1995).

Exemplar models

Exemplar models emphasize the role of concrete examples in mental representation (Medin & Schaffer, 1978), and are based on actual experience with category members (Carlston & Smith, 1996). Accordingly, perceivers compare target individuals with mental representations of actual category members when forming impressions and judgments (e.g., "He reminds me of my graduate school advisor"), rather than relying on prototypical abstractions (e.g., "He reminds me of the typical professor").

Exemplar models suggest that mental representations involve variability – that is, several discrete instances of the category – rather than typicality and homogeneity, as in the case for prototype models (Linville, Fischer, & Salovey, 1989). Exemplar models resonate with the notion of subgroups of general categories, which acknowledge within-group heterogeneity and allude to the potential for stereotype change via the accumulation of sufficient group variability (Maurer, Park, & Rothbart, 1995; Rothbart, 1996).

According to exemplar models, stereotyping ensues from the match between individual target and category exemplar (Smith & Zàrate, 1990, 1992). When targets resemble the exemplar, perceivers impute characteristics of the exemplar to the target. Although similar to prototype-based processes, exemplar-based stereotypes involve the application of concrete attributes associated with the exemplar, rather than abstract attributes associated with a prototype (Smith, 1998). Research suggests that exemplar-based stereotyping is strongest when perceivers have undeveloped beliefs about the general category (Sherman, 1996), and when discrete exemplars are highly accessible in the perceiver's memory (see Higgins, 1996 for review). However, stereotyping diminishes when perceivers use an exemplar as a frame of reference for forming impressions, and when targets contrast with the exemplar (Stapel & Koomen, 1998).

Associative networks

Associative network models can clarify basic assumptions of prototype and exemplar models, meanwhile offering unique predictions about stereotyping. According to associative network models (e.g., Anderson, 1983), information is stored in discrete mental structures called nodes. Each node corresponds to one and only one concept, whether it be a name, place, object, visual concept, personality trait, affective response, evaluation, or any other form of raw data (Carlston, 1994). Nodes are systematically interconnected by links, which map out meaningful associations between the concepts contained in each node. Inter-nodal linkages structure people's mental representations. Some links are particularly strong, denoting significant association between concepts, whereas others are relatively weak. The nature of nodal linkages fluctuates according to perceivers' experiences: Links increase or decrease in strength depending on the perceived correlation between concepts, and new nodal links can develop according to new associations between previously unpaired concepts.

Network models suggest that all knowledge and experiences are cognitively represented and organized by interlinked nodes. But most nodes lie dormant – that is, stored in long-term memory – and only a small portion are currently active, thus influencing conscious or unconscious cognition (Carlston & Smith, 1996). Impressions, judgments, and memories depend on which nodes are active at any given time, and the activation of one particular node implies the activation of closely related concepts (see also Smith, 1998, for more discussion).

Associative network models can explain how stereotypes ensue from mere categorization. According to prototype and exemplar models, perceivers infer targets' attributes associated with either a typical member (prototype) or a discrete instance (exemplar) of the general category. Network models extend this analysis, suggesting that stereotypes occur from spread of activation (Collins & Loftus, 1975), whereby the excitation of one node (e.g., the social category "professor") flows across links to stimulate other nodes (e.g., attributes such as intelligent and forgetful, visual concepts such as eyeglasses and disorganized desks, affective responses such as feeling intimidated). According to network models, excitation travels rapidly across strong links, triggering automatic associations between linked concepts.

This analysis resonates with findings in the stereotyping literature, particularly priming studies that measure response latency and strength of judgment (e.g., rapidly identifying the word "good") following the presentation of a single concept (e.g., seeing the word "white"). Some of the best-known studies in the stereotyping literature (e.g., Devine, 1989; Higgins, Bargh, & Lombardi, 1985; Perdue et al., 1990) employ this technique, suggesting that stereotypes represent the strength between two or more conceptual nodes stored in people's mental representations. Because of the emphasis on micro-level cognitive structures, network models suggest that stereotyping via associated nodes occurs largely outside of the perceiver's awareness (see also Banaji & Hardin, 1996, for discussion).

Parallel-distributed processing (PDP) models

Emerging from cognitive and neuroscience laboratories over the past decade (e.g., McClelland, Rumelhart, & Hinton, 1986), PDP, or connectionist, models of mental representation have infused social psychological research with new theoretical perspectives on the structures guiding thought (see Smith, 1996, for review). Like associative network models, PDP models posit that knowledge is represented in nodes, which are interconnected by associative links. But whereas network models focus on the information contained in activated nodes, PDP models suggest that a given node has no inherent meaning by itself, and nodes are not category specific. Rather, meaning comes from the patterns of activation across nodes, and nodes are general mental structures non-specific to any particular category. The focus, then, moves away from the discrete properties of each particular node, and is instead on the blend of impulses that arise from activation across a pattern of nodes.

With the focus now on the patterns across nodes, research emphasizes the properties of pattern activation, which has implications for research on stereotypes (see Smith, 1996, 1998, for more general discussion). Activation patterns – for example, from node a to nodes b, c, and d – function from the excitation level of initial node a and the weight of a–b, a–c, a–d nodal connections (as well as b–c, b–d, and c–d connections). Activation between nodes can be positive or negative; positive activations facilitate the connection between nodes, and negative connections inhibit connection. Given repeated stimulus exposure and experience, the activation of a few nodes within a pattern can lead to the completion of prior learned patterns; triggering nodes *a* and *b* alone can complete the pattern by stimulating *c* and *d*. Pattern activation is constrained by the initial information input, and by prior weights (positive or negative) between nodes. Multiple simultaneous patterns of activation occur at the same time, reflecting people's capacity for concurrent on-line cognitions.

Applications of PDP models to social psychology have been few thus far, largely because theoretical models are still developing. However, a few programs of research apply PDP models to stereotyping phenomena. One particular new trend in the stereotyping literature is the focus on both facilitatory and inhibitory mechanisms that underlie stereotypic thought (see Bodenhausen & Macrae, 1998, for review). Extending the emphasis on both positive and negative nodal connections, recent research has examined the variables that undermine or dampen stereotypes (e.g., Macrae, Bodenhausen, & Milne, 1998; Macrae, Bodenhausen, Milne, & Ford, 1997; Monteith, 1993), rather than focusing solely on variables that set them in motion. Another new trend in stereotyping research, derived from PDP models, is the explicit focus on constraint satisfaction processes (Kunda & Thagard, 1996; Miller & Read, 1991), in which activated nodes (e.g., individuating traits or personal motives) can counter the overwhelming effects of other nodes (e.g., categorical beliefs) when forming impressions and making judgments.

Social and cognitive psychology offer several models of mental representation, each model overlapping significantly with others, yet providing unique explanations and predictions. Prototype, exemplar, associative network, and PDP models have contributed valuable insight into the cognitive structures that sustain stereotypes. They indicate that stereotypes emerge from basic cognitive units that store prior beliefs and expectations, and are thus embedded within our mental architecture.

Stereotyping Processes

Another way of understanding stereotypes looks at the mental processes involved when people think about members of other groups. The thesis here: That the process of stereotyping – independent of the specific content of stereotypes – is a fundamental human mechanism for perceiving and making sense of the world. This idea traces back to the earliest theorizing on stereotyping (e.g., Lippmann, 1922; Allport, 1954), and counters the notion that stereotyping is entirely destructive, for the perceiver, at least.

This section reviews research on the functional properties of stereotyping processes, focusing on the automatic nature of categorization and stereotype activation, the cognitive and motivational processes that guide subsequent perception, and the mechanisms of stereotype maintenance and change. Viewed as such, stereotyping can be a pragmatic human process, controllable by motivation and attention to additional information, and not entirely faulty. Stereotypes are most detrimental for their targets, but can also disserve perceivers when accuracy or interdependence matters.

The utility of social categories

As Lippmann (1922) remarked in the chapter's opening quotation, humans cannot handle the complexity of their environment, and therefore "reconstruct it on a simpler model" (p. 16) to function within such complexity. Gordon Allport's (1954) *The Nature of Prejudice* elaborated on Lippmann's theme of simplifying the world, introducing a cognitive perspective to the stereotyping literature. So remarkable were his insights on the mental processes guiding stereotypes that even the most recent empirical findings can trace their theoretical origins to his text, and his insights are taken for granted.

Allport (1954) argued, in a now familiar analysis, that categorization of objects is adaptive and necessary to function effectively: "A new experience must be redacted into old categories. We cannot handle each event freshly in its own right" (p. 19). People categorize furniture such as tables and chairs; kitchen devices such as cookware and eating utensils; places such as restaurants and office buildings; and people such as professors, lawyers, and housewives. Categorization allows people to extract meaning from environmental objects by attending to a few diagnostic cues, rather than perceiving every attribute of every object – a time-consuming and labor-intensive task. In Allport's words, "All categories engender meaning upon the world. Like paths in a forest, they give order to our life-space" (1954, p. 171).

According to Allport's analysis, the processes guiding categorization are the same for all objects. Upon encountering objects in the environment – whether furniture, utensils, locations, or people – individuals first *select* certain characteristics that define the object, then *accentuate* those characteristics in their formed impressions (overlooking other characteristics), and finally *interpret* the object by generalizing from those particular characteristics (see Allport, 1954, chapter 10 for more discussion). Although subsequent research refined this outline of stages (e.g., Brewer, 1988; Fiske & Neuberg, 1990, reviewed shortly), Allport's initial work suggested that stereotyping follows basic rules associated with mere categorization, from which no perceivers or objects are exempt.

Although by now most current stereotyping research hinges on the role of categorization, Allport noted a fundamental distinction between categories and stereotypes. Categories refer to associated concepts, properties, or objects that overlap in meaning or purpose. Stereotypes refer to exaggerated beliefs associated with a category of people that function to rationalize behavior toward that category (see Allport, 1954, chapter 12). Stereotypes are specific consequences of the more general categorization process. The importance of this distinction lies in the difference between basic mental processes ensuing from categorization, versus interpersonal and social processes ensuing from generalized beliefs about group members.

Models of category-based stereotyping

Social cognition researchers developed models to track the progression of people's perceptions about others, from initial categories that promote stereotypes to piecemeal impressions that incorporate detailed information. The two most commonly cited models are Brewer's (1988) dual process model of impression formation and Fiske and Neuberg's (1990) continuum model of impression formation. Superficially, both share similar features, particularly their emphasis on categorization and its effects on subsequent information processing, but vary in specific theoretical postulates (Fiske, 1988). This subsection extracts the core themes from the vast empirical research supporting one or both of these models: (a) Perceivers automatically categorize other people; and (b) whenever possible, perceivers interpret information about others according to their initial categorization, which can result in stereotypes. However, when motivated, perceivers can (c) make use of category-inconsistent information to revise their categorical beliefs; as well as (d) view others as individuated beings, rather than as stereotyped category members. Note the temporal nature of these themes – as proposed in the original theoretical models, each theme represents a discrete stage in the impression formation process.

Automatic categorization. Perceivers categorize other people immediately upon meeting them. Repeated findings, using computer-aided timing techniques, reveal that initial categorization can occur within milliseconds after first encounter (Banaji & Hardin, 1996; Devine, 1989; Dovidio, Evans, & Tyler, 1986; Zàrate & Smith, 1990). Perceivers typically categorize others using obvious, visually salient cues, usually based on race, gender, and age (McCann, Ostrom, Tyner, & Mitchell, 1985; Perdue & Gurtman, 1990; Stangor, Lynch, Duan, & Glass, 1992); but other initial categories are also common, such as body size (Crandall, 1994; Ryckman, Robbins, Kaczor, & Gold, 1989), physiognomy (Kleck & Strenta, 1980; Zebrowitz, 1997), and social roles (Macrae, Bodenhausen, & Milne, 1998). Initial categorization often occurs outside of perceivers' awareness, and the effects of categories on perception can go unnoticed (Macrae, Milne, & Bodenhausen, 1994).

Once a target is placed within a category, numerous cognitive effects that facilitate stereotyping can take immediate hold (see Fiske & Taylor, 1991). For example, perceivers minimize differences between the target and other category members (Taylor, 1981), and ascribe stereotypic attributes to the person (Devine, 1989; Dovidio et al., 1986). Hence, upon categorizing a new acquaintance as a lawyer, perceivers might infer that he or she possesses stereotypical characteristics, such as ambition, intelligence, dishonesty, and greed.

The effects of initial categorization can have undeniably negative consequences for targets, who are perceived as interchangeable category members rather than as unique individuals, but this process confers advantages to the perceivers. By using automatic categories to assist their perceptual processes, people can make quick judgments and conserve cognitive energy for other tasks (Macrae et al., 1994). Thus, initial categorization organizes perceivers' complex environments, directing attentional flow along an orderly trajectory.

Information interpretation. After automatic initial categorization, perceivers sometimes engage in more thoughtful processing. This depends on motivation to exert cognitive effort beyond the categorization stage, as well as available information for forming impressions (Fiske & Neuberg, 1990). With modest amounts of motivation, perceivers make use of additional information (Erber & Fiske, 1984; Neuberg & Fiske, 1987; Ruscher & Fiske, 1990), but are biased by their initial categories.

Following categorization, perceivers' attention flows primarily to category-consistent information (Hamilton, Sherman, & Ruvolo, 1990). So after categorizing someone as "Black" or "female," perceivers tend to pay close attention to attributes consistent with those categories. Category-based information processing increases when perceivers have limited attentional resources – that is, when they have little time or energy to think accurately (Macrae, Milne, & Bodenhausen, 1994).

Although perceivers bias information processing toward category-consistent information, other types of information exert influence on impression formation. Perceivers can encounter three types of information when forming impressions of others: information that matches the category, information irrelevant to the category, and information that disconfirms the category. When information matches the category, expectations are confirmed and categories strengthened (Hamilton et al., 1990; Oakes, Turner, & Haslam, 1991); stereotypes proceed from the alleged fit between target information and prior beliefs (cf. Snyder, 1984). When information is irrelevant to the category, perceivers either overlook it (Belmore, 1987; Fiske, Neuberg, Beattie, & Milberg, 1987) or interpret it according to category-based expectations (Hilton & Von Hippel, 1990; Nelson, Biernat, & Manis, 1990); stereotypes thus capitalize on informational ambiguity. When information disconfirms the category, perceivers tend to perceive that information as non-representative of the general category (Krueger & Rothbart, 1990; Kunda & Oleson, 1995); stereotypes can thus "explain away" deviant information (e.g., Weber & Crocker, 1983). According to meta-analyses, perceivers tend to recall expectancy-inconsistent information only under very specific conditions (Stangor & McMillan, 1992), for example, when expectancies are weak, when incongruencies are strong, and when perceivers have explicit impression formation goals.

People assimilate information into their pre-existing beliefs about the category. This work resonates with Fiske and Neuberg's (1990) idea of confirmatory categorization, whereby perceivers preserve their categories and prior beliefs via selected information searches. Stereotypes appear resilient to irrelevant and incongruent information, as perceivers find creative ways of reinterpreting discrepant information. But as we will see, stereotyping is not inevitable. Provided sufficiently disconfirming information and sufficient motivation to pay attention, perceivers can alter their categorical beliefs and view others as individuals, not only as category members.

Revising categorical beliefs. When highly motivated to attend and when provided adequate information, perceivers can modify both their a priori expectations and the very nature of their categories. Thus, stereotype change can occur by revising categorical beliefs through motivated attention to information (Hilton & Von Hippel, 1996).

Several models postulate the processes by which categories can change. An early model of change contrasted two processes (Rothbart, 1981). According to the bookkeeping process, people change their stereotypes gradually over time, by attending to category-discrepant targets and incorporating new information into that category. Categorical expectations change incrementally by averaging new information with prior beliefs. According to the conversion process, people change their stereotypes more rapidly, as a result of encountering highly discrepant category members. Accordingly, one prominent category member can individually alter the nature of the category (see Weber & Crocker, 1983, for empirical tests of this distinction).

Therefore, stereotypes can change when people attend to and incorporate new information into prior categories. Perceivers can form more specific categories subsumed within the broader stereotype, known as subtyping. Conversely, they can develop elaborated beliefs about the category, referred to as subgrouping (see Rothbart, this volume, chapter 3), which can ultimately dilute the stereotype. The latter process, wherein category variability diminishes stereotypic beliefs, presents the more promising avenue for stereotype change.

Forming individuated impressions. Models of impression formation posit that perceiving individuals according to their unique personal traits, rather than category-consistent attributes, represents the most individuated form of person perception (Brewer, 1988; Fiske & Neuberg, 1990). However, these models suggest that individuation occurs under rare instances; even subtyping and subgrouping processes prioritize categories over individual traits. Category-based perception is more common because full individuation takes enormous effort from the perceiver.

Under rare conditions, perceivers are motivated to form piecemeal impressions that integrate all the target's attributes. This motivation can come from outcome dependency (Erber & Fiske, 1984; Neuberg & Fiske, 1987), accountability (Tetlock, 1992), accuracy goals (Chen, Schechter, & Chaiken, 1996; Neuberg, 1989), and personal values of fairness (Monteith, 1993), in addition to other social motives (see Fiske, 1998, for review).

To arrive at an individuated impression, perceivers must proceed through all stages of perception just described – from categorization to information search and interpretation to recategorization. When no single category can explain the target person, perceivers treat the category as just another attribute. Perceivers appraise the individual's unique attributes, incorporating them into a piecemeal impression (cf. Anderson, 1981). Categories, thus, reduce to just another piece of information, and carry equal weight with other idiosyncratic information in the impression formation process (Fiske & Neuberg, 1990; see also Kunda & Thagard, 1996).

Stereotype Context

A discussion of stereotypes would be incomplete without reference to the social context of stereotype agents and targets. The first section of this paper focused on the interpersonal level, suggesting that stereotype content adheres to basic psychological principles of interpersonal and intergroup relations. The next two sections focused on the cognitive level, indicating that stereotypes arise from basic mental structures and processes that allow people to simplify the world and think efficiently. This final section argues that the larger context of stereotypes, reflected in social hierarchy and history, defines their truly insidious nature.

Two facets of social context determine the potency of stereotypes: (a) power dynamics and group hierarchy, plus (b) status quo justification. Macro-level contextual variables can have profound psychological effects that influence all levels of stereotyping – from formation of mental representations to endorsement and legitimization of their descriptive content.

Power and hierarchy

The nature of societal power dynamics and group hierarchy render stereotypes particularly oppressive for certain individuals and groups (Operario, Goodwin, & Fiske, 1998). In particular, individuals whose outcomes are controlled by others, and groups low in the social hierarchy, are vulnerable to the demeaning content of their stereotypes. Conversely, individuals who control others' outcomes, and groups near the top of the social hierarchy, are more likely to employ stereotypes about others, and even benefit from their own stereotypes (Fiske, 1993).

Individuals who have power over others are likely to engage in more stereotyping processes (Dépret & Fiske, 1993), because powerful people simply pay less individuating attention to their subordinates (Goodwin, Gubin, Fiske, & Yzerbyt, in press). Rather than examine subordinates' unique traits and attributes, powerful perceivers often rely on categorical assumptions to guide their inferences and judgments. Three mechanistic explanations account for this effect. First, powerful perceivers might lack motivation to form accurate impressions of their subordinates, and instead remain satisfied with categorical sketches of subordinates' personalities. Second, powerful perceivers might lack cognitive capacity, allocated elsewhere, to attend to their subordinates. And third, powerful perceivers who prefer to dominate others might simply desire to stereotype their subordinates (see Goodwin et al., in press; Lee-Chai, Bargh, & Chen, 1998; Operario & Fiske, 1999, for support of these postulates). In addition, people who identify with powerful groups tend to assume the cognitive and attitudinal tendencies associated with that group (Turner, Hogg, Oakes, Reicher, & Wetherell, 1987), and thus are prone to stereotyping their subordinates (see also Sachdev & Bourhis, 1985, 1991). Some findings suggest that stereotyping increases under threat or resource scarcity, wherein powerholders must protect their privileged status (Ellemers, Doosje, van Knippenberg, & Wilke, 1992). However, when people with power have communal orientations with their subordinates, they stereotype less (Lee-Chai et al., 1998).

Subordinate individuals or groups are less likely to stereotype the powerful (Fiske & Dépret, 1996). Subordinates pay more scrutinizing attention to powerholders' individuating attributes compared to their categorical attributes, and they sometimes form unrealistically positive impressions of powerholders (Stevens & Fiske, in press), ostensibly in an effort to increase their sense of prediction and control about future outcomes (see also Erber & Fiske, 1984; Neuberg & Fiske, 1987).

Thus, although all perceivers are prone to stereotyping, power increases the tendency to form category-based judgments, and likewise decreases the need to form individuated impressions. Aggregated across individuals and over time, the psychological effects of power on stereotyping can have profound societal effects (Martell, Lane, & Emrich,

1996). Not only does power perpetuate beliefs associated with social subordinates and minority groups, it also enables people to act upon stereotypic beliefs through legislation, economic policies, and institutional practices (Banks & Eberhardt, 1998; Goodwin, Operario, & Fiske, 1998; Sidanius, Levin, & Pratto, 1998).

Status quo justification

As noted, powerful people's stereotypes of social subordinates can have long-term ramifications for the status quo. Powerholders who consensually agree that disadvantaged groups possess negative or undesirable traits tend to act in ways that maintain power differentials (Pratto, Sidanius, Stallworth, & Malle, 1994; Sidanius, 1993). But given our understanding of the stereotyping content, structures, and processes, the tendency for powerholders to stereotype makes some intuitive sense: People strive to protect themselves and their ingroup, and consequently must derogate or impair the outgroup, at least relatively, if not absolutely.

A counterintuitive finding is the tendency for powerless or disadvantaged people to express outgroup favoritism and show biases that justify and maintain their group's low status (Jost, in press; Mlicki & Ellemers, 1996). Some explanations for the phenomenon suggest that members of disadvantaged groups accept the status quo when they perceive that their societal or institutional context follows appropriate social justice standards (Major, 1994; Martin, 1986). Social injustice can endure within cultures or contexts that outwardly endorse egalitarianism and equity. People in those contexts may believe hierarchy-maintaining stereotypes reflect the truth about social groups, rather than see stereotypes as myths that perpetuate power differentials (Sidanius, 1993).

Although people all along the social hierarchy might accept the status quo, members of low-status groups do not necessarily internalize negative stereotypes (see Crocker, Major, & Steele, 1998, for review). Members of low-power groups tend to acknowledge their groups' disadvantaged status, but minimize perceptions of personal vulnerability to discrimination (e.g., Taylor, Wright, Moghaddam, & Lalonde, 1990). In doing so, members of disadvantaged groups can maintain levels of self-esteem and personal control (Ruggiero & Taylor, 1997), and avoid feeling personally victimized. Future research on how members of disadvantaged groups react to prejudice can clarify the apparent tension between acknowledging societal bias and preserving perceptions of self-efficacy.

Stereotypes can be powerful tools for maintaining social hierarchies, rationalizing societal inequalities, and advocating intergroup hostility. Social context can "get inside the head" by influencing the very nature of people's cognitions about group members all along the social hierarchy.

Conclusion

This chapter has argued that stereotypes must be understood at multiple levels of analysis to appreciate their complexity and understand their universality. At the cognitive level, stereotypes are functional mechanisms for thinking about the world. At the interpersonal level, stereotypes reflect the structural relationships between groups – particularly groups' relative status and interdependence. At the societal level, stereotypes reflect the larger context of group life. This analysis of stereotype content, structures, processes, and context indicates that stereotypes are both (a) basic human tendencies, inherent within our mental architecture; and (b) potentially damaging belief systems, depending on the power of the situation. Both principles of stereotypes must be acknowledged in theory, research, or intervention.

Social psychology's understanding of stereotypes and stereotyping has evolved considerably from Lippmann's (1922) introduction of the word. Aided by advances in theory and technology, more complex and multifaceted models guide our insight into stereotyping and group phenomena. Future research will undoubtedly capitalize on the recent body of work, spanning levels of analysis to understand and ameliorate the dilemmas rooted in stereotypes. But while social psychologists continue to seek sophisticated resolutions for stereotype-based problems, we are reminded of Lippmann's (1922) earlier wisdom:

> What matters is the character of the stereotypes, and the gullibility with which we employ them. . . . If our philosophy tells us that each man is only a small part of the world, that his intelligence catches at best only phases and aspects in a coarse net of ideas, then, when we use our stereotypes, we tend to know that they are only stereotypes, to hold them lightly, to modify them gladly. (p. 90)

Social psychologists and lay people alike, we hope, will uncover ways to achieve Lippmann's ideal.

References

Allport, G. W. (1954). *The nature of prejudice.* Reading, MA: Addison-Wesley.

Anderson, J. R. (1983). *The architecture of cognition.* Cambridge, MA: Harvard University Press.

Anderson, N. H. (1981). *Foundations of information integration theory.* New York: Academic Press.

Banaji, M. R., & Hardin, C. (1996). Automatic stereotyping. *Psychological Science, 7,* 136–141.

Banks, R. R., & Eberhardt, J. L. (1998). Social psychological processes and the legal bases of racial categorization. In J. L. Eberhardt & S. T. Fiske (Eds.), *Confronting racism: The problem and the response* (pp. 54–75). Thousand Oaks, CA: Sage.

Belmore, S. M. (1987). Determinants of attention during impression formation. *Journal of Experimental Psychology: Learning, Memory, and Cognition, 13,* 480–489.

Bodenhausen, G. V., & Macrae, C. N. (1998). Stereotype activation and inhibition. In R. S. Wyer (Ed.), *Advances in social cognition* (Vol. 11, pp. 1–52). Mahwah, NJ: Erlbaum.

Brewer, M. B. (1979). Ingroup bias in the minimal intergroup situation: A cognitive motivational analysis. *Psychological Bulletin, 86,* 307–324.

Brewer, M. B. (1988). A dual process model of impression formation. In R. Wyer & T. Srull (Eds.), *Advances in social cognition* (Vol. 1, pp. 1–36). Hillsdale, NJ: Erlbaum.

Brewer, M. B., & Brown, R. J. (1998). Intergroup relations. In D. T. Gilbert, S. T. Fiske, & G. Lindzey (Eds.), *Handbook of social psychology* (4th ed., Vol. 2, pp. 554–594). New York: McGraw-Hill.

Carlston, D. E. (1994). Associated systems theory: A systematic approach to cognitive representations of persons. In T. K. Srull & R. S. Wyer (Eds.), *Advances in social cognition* (Vol. 7, pp. 1–78). Mahwah, NJ: Erlbaum.

Carlston, D. E., & Smith, E. R. (1996). Principles of mental representation. In E. T. Higgins & A. W. Kruglanski (Eds.), *Social psychology: Handbook of basic principles* (pp. 184–210). New York: Guilford Press.

Chen, M., & Bargh, J. A. (1997). Nonconscious behavioral confirmation processes: The self-fulfilling consequences of automatic stereotype activation. *Journal of Experimental Social Psychology, 33*, 541–560.

Chen, S., Schechter, D., & Chaiken, S. (1996). Getting the truth or getting along: Accuracy- vs. impression-motivated heuristic and systematic processing. *Journal of Personality and Social Psychology, 71*, 262–275.

Collins, A. M., & Loftus, E. F. (1975). A spreading-activation theory of semantic processing. *Psychological Review, 82*, 407–428.

Crandall, C. S. (1994). Prejudice against fat people: Ideology and self-interest. *Journal of Personality and Social Psychology, 66*, 882–894.

Crocker, J., Major, B., & Steele, C. (1998). Social stigma. In D. T. Gilbert, S. T. Fiske, & G. Lindzey (Eds.), *The handbook of social psychology* (4th ed., pp. 504–553). New York: McGraw-Hill.

Dépret, E. F., & Fiske, S. T. (1993). Social cognition and power: Some cognitive consequences of social structure as a source of control deprivation. In G. Weary, F. Gleicher, & K. Marsh (Eds.), *Control motivation and social cognition.* New York: Springer-Verlag.

Devine, P. G. (1989). Stereotypes and prejudice: Their automatic and controlled components. *Journal of Personality and Social Psychology, 56*, 5–18.

Dovidio, J. F., Evans, N., & Tyler, R. B. (1986). Racial stereotypes: The contents of their cognitive representations. *Journal of Experimental Social Psychology, 22*, 22–37.

Ellemers, N., Doosje, B. J., Knippenberg, A. V., & Wilke, J. (1992). Status protection in high status minority groups. *European Journal of Social Psychology, 22*, 123–140.

Erber, R., & Fiske, S. T. (1984). Outcome dependency and attention to inconsistent information. *Journal of Personality and Social Psychology, 47*, 709–726.

Fiske, S. T. (1980). Attention and weight in person perception: The impact of negative and extreme behavior. *Journal of Personality and Social Psychology, 38*, 889–906.

Fiske, S. T. (1993). Controlling other people: The impact of power on stereotyping. *American Psychologist, 48*, 621–628.

Fiske, S. T. (1998). Stereotyping, prejudice, and discrimination. In D. T. Gilbert, S. T. Fiske, & G. Lindzey (Eds.), *The handbook of social psychology* (4th ed., Vol. 2, pp. 357–411). New York: McGraw-Hill.

Fiske, S. T., & Dépret, E. (1996). Control, interdependence, and power: Understanding social cognition in its social context. *European Review of Social Psychology, 7*, 31–61.

Fiske, S. T., Lin, M., & Neuberg, S. L. (1999). The continuum model: Ten years later. In S. Chaiken (Ed.), *Dual-process theories in social psychology* (pp. 231–254). New York: Guilford Press.

Fiske, S. T., & Neuberg, S. L. (1990). A continuum model of impression formation: From category-based to individuating processes as a function of information, motivation, and attention. In M. P. Zanna (Ed.), *Advances in experimental social psychology* (Vol. 23, pp. 1–74). New York: Academic Press.

Fiske, S. T., Neuberg, S. L., Beattie, A. E., & Milberg, S. J. (1987). Category-based and attribute-based reactions to others: Some informational conditions of stereotyping and individuating processes. *Journal of Experimental Social Psychology, 23*, 399–427.

Fiske, S. T., & Ruscher, J. B. (1993). Negative interdependence and prejudice: Whence the affect? In D. M. Mackie, & D. L. Hamilton (Eds.), *Affect cognition, and stereotyping: Interactive processes in group perception* (pp. 239–268). New York: Academic Press.

Fiske, S. T., & Taylor, S. E. (1991). *Social cognition* (2nd ed.). New York: McGraw-Hill.

Fiske, S. T., Xu, J., Cuddy, A. J. C., & Glick, P. (in press). Respect versus liking: Status and interdependence underlie ambivalent stereotypes. *Journal of Social Issues.*

Gaertner, S. L., & Dovidio, J. F. (1986). The aversive form of racism. In J. F. Dovidio & S. L. Gaertner (Eds.), *Prejudice, discrimination, and racism* (pp. 61–89). Orlando, FL: Academic Press.

Gergen, K. (1973). Social psychology as history. *Journal of Personality and Social Psychology, 26,* 309–320.

Gilbert, G. M. (1951). Stereotype persistence and change among college students. *Journal of Abnormal and Social Psychology, 46,* 245–254.

Goodwin, S. A., Gubin, A., Fiske, S. T., & Yzerbyt, V. (in press). Power can bias impression formation: Stereotyping subordinates by default and by design. *Group Processes and Intergroup Relations.*

Goodwin, S. A., Operario, D., & Fiske, S. T. (1998). Situational power and interpersonal dominance: Factors that perpetuate bias and inequality. *Journal of Social Issues, 54,* 677–698.

Hamilton, D. L., & Sherman, S. J. (1989). Illusory correlations: Implications for stereotype theory and research. In D. Bar-Tal, C. F. Graumann, A. W. Kruglanski, & W. Stroebe (Eds.), *Stereotypes and prejudice: Changing conceptions* (pp. 59–82). New York: Springer-Verlag.

Hamilton, D. L., Sherman, S. J., & Ruvolo, C. M. (1990). Stereotype-based expectancies: Effects on information processing and social behavior. *Journal of Social Issues, 46,* 35–60.

Hantzi, A. (1995). Change in stereotypic perceptions of familiar and unfamiliar groups: The pervasiveness of the subtyping model. *British Journal of Social Psychology, 34,* 463–477.

Higgins, E. T. (1996). Knowledge activation: Accessibility, applicability, and salience. In E. T. Higgins, & A. W. Kruglanski (Eds.), *Social psychology: Handbook of basic principles* (pp. 133–168). New York: Guilford Press.

Higgins, E. T., Bargh, J. A., & Lombardi, W. (1985). The nature of priming effects of categorization. *Journal of Experimental Psychology: Learning, Memory, and Cognition, 11,* 59–69.

Hilton, J. L., & von Hippel, W. (1990). The role of consistency in the judgment of stereotype-relevant behaviors. *Personality and Social Psychology Bulletin, 16,* 430–448.

Hilton, J. L., & von Hippel, W. (1996). Stereotypes. In J. T. Spence, J. M. Darley, & D. J. Foss (Eds.), *Annual review of psychology* (Vol. 47, pp. 237–271). Palo Alto, CA: Annual Reviews.

Jost, J. T. (in press). Outgroup favoritism and the theory of system justification. In G. Moskowitz (Ed.), *Future directions in social cognition.* Hillsdale, NJ: Erlbaum.

Judd, C. M., & Park, B. (1993). Definition and assessment of accuracy in social stereotypes. *Psychological Review, 100,* 109–128.

Karlins, M., Coffman, T. L., & Walters, G. (1969). On the fading of social stereotypes: Studies in three generations of college students. *Journal of Personality and Social Psychology, 13,* 1–16.

Katz, D., & Braly, K. (1933). Racial stereotypes in one hundred college students. *Journal of Abnormal and Social Psychology, 28,* 280–290.

Kleck, R. E., & Strenta, A. (1980). Perceptions of the impact of negatively valued physical characteristics on social interactions. *Journal of Personality and Social Psychology, 39,* 861–873.

Krueger, J., & Rothbart, M. (1990). Contrast and accentuation effects in category learning. *Journal of Personality and Social Psychology, 59,* 651–663.

Kunda, Z., & Oleson, K. C. (1995). Maintaining stereotypes in the face of disconfirmation: Constructing grounds for subtyping deviants. *Journal of Personality and Social Psychology, 68,* 565–579.

Kunda, Z., & Thagard, P. (1996). Forming impressions from stereotypes, traits, and behaviors: A parallel-constraint-satisfaction theory. *Psychological Review, 103*, 284–308.

Lee, Y., Jussim, I., & McCauley, C. R. (Eds.). (1995). *Stereotype accuracy.* Washington, DC: American Psychological Association.

Lee-Chai, A. Y., Bargh, J. A., & Chen, S. (1998, August). *Questioning the metamorphosis effect: A longitudinal study of social power.* Paper presented at the meeting of the Society for the Psychological Study of Social Issues, Ann Arbor, Michigan.

Lin, M. H., & Fiske, S. T. (1999). *Attitudes toward Asian Americans: Developing a prejudice scale.* Unpublished manuscript, University of Massachusetts at Amherst.

Linville, P. W., Fischer, G. W., & Salovey, P. (1989). Perceived distributions of the characteristics of in-group and out-group members: Empirical evidence and a computer simulation. *Journal of Personality and Social Psychology, 57*, 165–188.

Lippmann, W. (1922). *Public opinion.* New York: Harcourt Brace.

Macrae, C. N., Bodenhausen, G. V., & Milne, A. B. (1998). Saying no to unwanted thoughts: Self-focus and the regulation of mental life. *Journal of Personality and Social Psychology, 74*, 578–589.

Macrae, C. N., Bodenhausen, G. V., Milne, A. B., & Ford, R. (1997). On the regulation of recollection: The intentional forgetting of stereotypical memories. *Journal of Personality and Social Psychology, 72*, 709–719.

Macrae, C. N., Milne, A. B., & Bodenhausen, G. V. (1994). Stereotypes as energy-saving devices: A peek inside the cognitive toolbox. *Journal of Personality and Social Psychology, 66*, 37–47.

Major, B. (1994). From social inequality to personal entitlement: The role of social comparisons, legitimacy appraisals, and group membership. *Advances in Experimental Social Psychology, 26*, 293–355.

Martell, R. F., Lane, D. M., & Emrich, C. (1996). Male-female differences: A computer simulation. *American Psychologist, 51*, 157–158.

Martin, J. (1986). The tolerance of injustice. In J. M. Oleson, C. P. Herman, & M. P. Zanna (Eds.), *Relative deprivation and social comparison: The Ontario symposium* (Vol. 4, pp. 217–242). Hillsdale, NJ: Erlbaum.

Matlin, S., & Stang, D. (1978). *The Pollyanna principle.* Cambridge, MA: Schenkman.

Maurer, K. L., Park, B., & Rothbart, M. (1995). Subtyping versus subgrouping processes in stereotype representation. *Journal of Personality and Social Psychology, 69*, 812–824.

McCann, C. D., Ostrom, T. M., Tyner, L. K., & Mitchell, M. L. (1985). Person perception in heterogeneous groups. *Journal of Personality and Social Psychology, 49*, 1449–1459.

McClelland, J. L., Rumelhart, D. E., & Hinton, G. E. (1986). The appeal of parallel distributed processing. In D. E. Rumelhart, J. L. McClelland, & the PDP Research Group (Eds.), *Parallel distributed processing: Explorations in the microstructure of cognition* (Vol. 1, pp. 3–44). Cambridge, MA: MIT Press.

Medin, D. L., & Schaffer, M. M. (1978). Context theory of classification learning. *Psychological Review, 85*, 207–238.

Miller, L. C., & Read, S. J. (1991). On the coherence of mental models of persons and relationships: A knowledge structure approach. In G. J. O. Fletcher & F. Fincham (Eds.), *Cognition in close relationships* (pp. 69–99). Hillsdale, NJ: Erlbaum.

Mlicki, P. P., & Ellemers, N. (1996). Being different or being better? National stereotypes and identifications of Polish and Dutch students. *European Journal of Social Psychology, 26*, 97–114.

Monteith, M. J. (1993). Self-regulation of prejudiced responses: Implications for progress in prejudice-reduction efforts. *Journal of Personality and Social Psychology, 64*, 198–210.

Nelson, T. E., Biernat, M. R., & Manis, M. (1990). Everyday base rates (sex stereotypes): Potent and resilient. *Journal of Personality and Social Psychology, 59*, 664–675.

Neuberg, S. L. (1989). The goal of forming accurate impressions during social interactions: Attenuating the impact of negative expectancies. *Journal of Personality and Social Psychology, 56,* 374–386.

Neuberg, S. L., & Fiske, S. T. (1987). Motivational influences on impression formation: Outcome dependency, accuracy-driven attention, and individuating processes. *Journal of Personality and Social Psychology, 53,* 431–444.

Oakes, P. J., Haslam, S. A., & Reynolds, K. J. (1999). Social categorization and social context: Is stereotype change a matter of information or of meaning? In D. Abrams (Ed.), *Social identity and social categorization* (pp. 55–79). Malden, MA: Blackwell.

Oakes, P. J., Turner, J. C., & Haslam, S. A. (1991). Perceiving people as group members: The role of fit in the salience of social categorizations. *British Journal of Social Psychology, 30,* 125–144.

Operario, D., & Fiske, S. T. (1999). *Effects of trait dominance on powerholders' judgments of subordinates.* Unpublished manuscript, University of California, San Francisco.

Operario, D., Goodwin, S. A., & Fiske, S. T. (1998). Power is everywhere: Social control and personal control both operate as stereotype activation, interpretation, and response. In R. S. Wyer (Ed.), *Advances in social cognition* (Vol. 11, pp. 163–176). Hillsdale, NJ: Erlbaum.

Ottati, V., & Lee, Y. (1995). Accuracy: A neglected component of stereotype research. In Y. Lee, L. J. Jussim, & C. R. McCauley (Eds.), *Stereotype accuracy: Toward appreciating group differences* (pp. 29–59). Washington, DC: American Psychological Association.

Perdue, C. W., Dovidio, J. F., Gurtman, M. B., & Tyler, R. B. (1990). Us and them: Social categorization and the process of intergroup bias. *Journal of Personality and Social Psychology, 59,* 475–486.

Perdue, C. W., & Gurtman, M. B. (1990). Evidence for the automaticity of ageism. *Journal of Experimental Social Psychology, 26,* 199–216.

Pettigrew, T. F. (1997). Generalized intergroup contact effects on prejudice. *Personality and Social Psychology Bulletin, 5,* 461–476.

Posner, M. I., & Keele, S. W. (1968). On the genesis of abstract ideas. *Journal of Experimental Psychology, 77,* 353–363.

Pratto, F., Sidanius, J., Stallworth, L. M., & Malle, B. F. (1994). Social dominance orientation: A personality variable predicting social and political attitudes. *Journal of Personality and Social Psychology, 67,* 741–763.

Reed, S. K. (1972). Pattern recognition and categorization. *Cognitive Psychology, 3,* 382–407.

Rosenberg, S., Nelson, C., & Vivkananthan, P. S. (1968). A multidimensional approach to the study of personality impressions. *Journal of Personality and Social Psychology, 9,* 283–294.

Rothbart, M. (1981). Memory processes and social beliefs. In D. L. Hamilton (Ed.), *Cognitive processes in stereotyping and intergroup behavior* (pp. 145–181). Hillsdale, NJ: Erlbaum.

Rothbart, M. (1996). Category-exemplar dynamics and stereotype change. *International Journal of Intercultural Relations, 20,* 305–321.

Ruggiero, K. M., & Taylor, D. M. (1997). Why minority group members perceive or do not perceive the discrimination that confronts them: The role of self-esteem and perceived control. *Journal of Personality and Social Psychology, 72,* 373–389.

Ruscher, J. B., & Fiske, S. T. (1990). Interpersonal competition can cause individuating impression formation. *Journal of Personality and Social Psychology, 68,* 826–838.

Ryan, C. S., Park, B., & Judd, C. M. (1996). Assessing stereotype accuracy: Implications for understanding the stereotyping process. In C. N. Macrae, C. Stangor, & M. Hewstone (Eds.), *Stereotypes and stereotyping* (pp. 121–157). New York: Guilford Press.

Ryckman, R. M., Robbins, M. A., Kaczor, L. M., & Gold, J. A. (1989). Male and female raters' stereotyping of male and female physiques. *Personality and Social Psychology Bulletin, 15,* 244–251.

Sachdev, I., & Bourhis, R. Y. (1985). Social categorization and power differentials in group relations. *European Journal of Social Psychology, 15*, 415–434.

Sachdev, I., & Bourhis, R. Y. (1991). Power and status differentials in minority and majority group relations. *European Journal of Social Psychology, 21*, 1–24.

Schopler, J., & Insko, C. A. (1992). The discontinuity effect in interpersonal and intergroup situations: Generality and mediation. In W. Stroebe & M. Hewstone (Eds.), *European review of social psychology* (Vol. 3, pp. 121–151). Chichester, UK: Wiley.

Sherman, J. W. (1996). Development and mental representation of stereotypes. *Journal of Personality and Social Psychology, 70*, 1126–1141.

Sidanius, J. (1993). The psychology of group conflict and the dynamics of oppression: A social dominance perspective. In S. Iyengar & W. J. McGuire (Eds.), *Explorations in political psychology* (pp. 183–219). Durham, NC: Duke University Press.

Sidanius, J., Levin, S., & Pratto, F. (1998). Hierarchical group relations, institutional terror, and the dynamics of the criminal justice system. In J. L. Eberhardt & S. T. Fiske (Eds.), *Confronting racism: The problem and the response* (pp. 136–165). Thousand Oaks, CA: Sage.

Skowronski, J. J., & Carlston, D. E. (1989). Negativity and extremity biases in impression formation: A review of explanations. *Psychological Bulletin, 105*, 131–142.

Smith, E. R. (1996). What do connectionism and social psychology offer each other? *Journal of Personality and Social Psychology, 70*, 893–912.

Smith, E. R. (1998). Mental representation and memory. In D. T. Gilbert, S. T. Fiske, & G. Lindzey (Eds.), *Handbook of social psychology* (4th ed., Vol. 1, pp. 391–445). New York: McGraw-Hill.

Smith, E. R., & Zàrate, M. A. (1990). Exemplar and prototype use in social categorization. *Social Cognition, 8*, 243–262.

Smith, E. R., & Zàrate, M. A. (1992). Exemplar-based model of social judgment. *Psychological Review, 99*, 3–21.

Snyder, M. (1984). When beliefs create reality. In L. Berkowitz (Ed.), *Advances in experimental social psychology* (Vol. 18, pp. 248–306). New York: Academic Press.

Snyder, M. (1992). Motivational foundations of behavioral confirmation. In M. P. Zanna (Ed.), *Advances in experimental social psychology* (Vol. 25, pp. 67–114). San Diego, CA: Academic Press.

Stangor, C., & Lange, J. E. (1994). Mental representations of social groups: Advances in understanding stereotypes and stereotyping. In M. P. Zanna (Ed.), *Advances in experimental social psychology* (Vol. 26, pp. 357–416). San Diego, CA: Academic Press.

Stangor, C., Lynch, L., Duan, C., & Glass, B. (1992). Categorization of individuals on the basis of multiple social features. *Journal of Personality and Social Psychology, 62*, 207–218.

Stangor, C., & McMillan, D. (1992). Memory for expectancy-congruent and expectancy-incongruent information: A review of the social and social developmental literatures. *Psychological Bulletin, 1*, 42–61.

Stapel, D. A., & Koomen, W. (1998). When stereotype activation results in (counter)stereotypic judgments: Priming stereotype-relevant traits and exemplars. *Journal of Personality and Social Psychology, 34*, 136–163.

Steele, C. M. (1997). A threat in the air: How stereotypes shape intellectual identity and performance. *American Psychologist, 52*, 613–629.

Steele, C. M., & Aronson, J. (1995). Stereotype vulnerability and the intellectual test performance of African-Americans. *Journal of Personality and Social Psychology, 69*, 797–811.

Stevens, L. E., & Fiske, S. T. (in press). Forming motivated impressions of a powerholder: Accuracy under task dependency and misperception under evaluative dependency. *Personality and Social Psychology Bulletin.*

Tajfel, H., & Turner, J. C. (1986). The social identity theory of intergroup behaviour. In S. Worchel & W. G. Austin (Eds.), *Psychology of intergroup relations* (pp. 7–24). Chicago, IL: Nelson.

Taylor, D. M., Wright, S. C., Moghaddam, F. M., & Lalonde, R. N. (1990). The personal/group discrimination discrepancy: Perceiving my group, but not myself, to be a target for discrimination. *Personality and Social Psychology Bulletin, 16,* 254–262.

Taylor, S. E. (1981). A categorization approach to stereotyping. In D. L. Hamilton (Ed.), *Cognitive processes in stereotyping and intergroup behavior* (pp. 88–114). Hillsdale, NJ: Erlbaum.

Taylor, S. E. (1991). Asymmetrical effects of positive and negative events: The mobilization/minimization hypothesis. *Psychological Bulletin, 110,* 67–85.

Taylor, S. E., & Fiske, S. T. (1978). Salience, attention, and attribution: Top of the head phenomena. In L. Berkowitz (Ed.), *Advances in experimental social psychology* (Vol. 11, pp. 249–288). New York: Academic Press.

Tetlock, P. E. (1992). The impact of accountability on judgment and choice: Toward a social contingency model. In M. P. Zanna (Ed.), *Advances in experimental social psychology* (Vol. 23, pp. 331–376). San Diego, CA: Academic Press.

Turner, J. C., Hogg, M. A., Oakes, P. J., Reicher, S. D., & Wetherell, M. S. (1987). *Rediscovering the social group: A self-categorization theory.* Oxford, UK: Blackwell.

Weber, R., & Crocker, J. (1983). Cognitive processes in the revision of stereotypic beliefs. *Journal of Personality and Social Psychology, 45,* 961–977.

Zàrate, M. A., & Smith, E. R. (1990). Person categorization and stereotyping. *Social Cognition, 8,* 161–185.

Zebrowtiz, L. A. (1997). *Reading faces: Windows to the soul?* Boulder, CO: Westview.

CHAPTER THREE

Category Dynamics and the Modification of Outgroup Stereotypes

Myron Rothbart

The tendency to disparage groups different from our own represents a social problem of enormous proportion, and one whose solution needs little justification. The last hundred years of this millennium may come to be described as a century of genocide, in which mass murder of outgroup members, thought to be a monopoly of impoverished third world countries, reached peak efficiency when practiced by the most advanced and civilized nation on earth. Few nations of the world, whether first or third world, remain untarnished by the dehumanization or mistreatment of outgroups. The goal of this chapter is to explore the nature and modifiability of outgroup stereotypes, with particular emphasis on the role of categorization processes in stereotype change. Given the strength – and often the fury – of outgroup hostility, is it possible to do justice to this by focusing on those causal mechanisms most removed from human emotion and from the conflictual nature of intergroup relations? No single approach is adequate to explain the complex, multi-faceted nature of intergroup hostility. Stereotypes play an important role in intergroup relations, and categorization processes play an important role in stereotyping. The approach taken in this chapter regards categorization as playing a very important – although by no means exclusive – role in the process of stereotype change.

The focus of this chapter is on the modification of outgroup rather than ingroup stereotypes. It is not assumed that the processes governing ingroup and outgroup stereotypes are fundamentally different, but that the more negative and more homogeneous image of the outgroup is in greater need of change.

This chapter explores three basic, related questions about the nature of outgroup stereotypes: (1) To what degree do image and reality correspond in our perception of outgroups? (2) When does our contact and/or experience with individual outgroup members

This research was supported by National Institute of Mental Health Grant MH40662. I wish to thank Ellen Peters and Mary Rothbart for their astute comments on an earlier draft of this manuscript.

alter our perceptions of the outgroup? (3) Are there some general strategies for making our perceptions of the outgroup more like our perceptions of the ingroup? The first two questions are closely linked, since there is evidence that our perceptions of the outgroup are unrealistically extreme, and that these extreme images are often not moderated by our experiences with outgroup members who do not fit the stereotype. It will be argued that categorization processes play an important role in insulating the stereotype from disconfirming information. The third question examines whether categorization processes can be recruited for the purpose of changing outgroup stereotypes to make them more like our images of the ingroup – that is, more favorable and more complex.

Image and Reality

Assessing the accuracy of stereotypic perception is a daunting task (Judd & Park, 1993; Judd, Ryan, & Park, 1991; Lee, Jussim, & McCauley, 1995), and it is not surprising that there is significant disagreement about the definition and assessment of stereotype accuracy. Judges may show accuracy in their ordering of social objects or in terms of absolute discrepancy of their estimates from "known" characteristics. This approach immediately raises the problem of deciding what benchmark of "reality" is to be used in assessing accuracy. Consider two important studies in this area. During the Vietnam War, samples of self-described Doves and Hawks on the War were obtained, based on advertisements placed in the campus newspaper (Dawes, Singer, & Lemons, 1972). Each subject was asked to write attitude statements that would accurately describe both Doves' and Hawks' views on the war. Since each subject was either a Dove or a Hawk, they were writing one set of statements to describe their ingroup and one to describe the outgroup. The statements were then given to outgroup members or other ingroup members to be rated for accuracy. Judges could rate the statements along a continuum from "too mild" to "too extreme" in describing their own attitudes, with the midpoint of the scale reflecting an accurate assessment.

The clearest prediction, based on the Gestalt principle of contrast from an anchoring stimulus (Sherif & Hovland, 1966) – where one's own position serves as the anchor – was that each group of subjects would write statements that "overshot" the actual attitudes of the outgroup, and this prediction was strongly confirmed. Statements describing the attitudes of Doves were more likely to be judged as too extreme when they were written by Hawks than by Doves, and statements describing the attitudes of Hawks were more likely to be judged as too extreme when written by Doves than Hawks. Although the perceptions of the outgroup were exaggerated in this work, there was evidence that ingroup members also overestimated the extremity of their own group – although not as much as for the outgroup. That is, both ingroup and outgroup members were viewed as more extreme than they really were, but this "distortion" was clearly stronger for outgroup than ingroup.

The problem of the criterion for accuracy is evident in this study. Judges are inaccurate only if the sample of Doves and of Hawks in this study is truly representative of their respective populations. That is, perhaps this particular sample of Doves and Hawks is "in reality" less extreme than Doves and Hawks in general, in which case the judges would have been accurate had the stimulus groups been the general population of Doves and Hawks. Judd et al. (1991) corrected this problem in an analogous study, in which business and engineering majors were *randomly* sampled from their respective populations and used as judges (and stimulus groups) in their study. Using measures of both central tendency and dispersion, and using each subject's own judgments about the self as the criterion, Judd et al. obtained the same basic findings as Dawes et al. (1972). That is, both business and engineering majors were estimated as more extreme than they really were by both ingroup and outgroup judges, but the effect was clearly stronger for the latter. Since these groups were selected to be representative of their parent populations, a stronger inference of inaccuracy can be made. Moreover, Judd et al. found that the two effects – a general tendency to exaggerate the position of the target group, and a greater tendency to exaggerate the outgroup than the ingroup – were found for measures of both central tendency and dispersion. That is, the outgroup in particular was viewed as both more extreme and more homogeneous than it really was (with the criterion for reality being the aggregated self-judgments).

It should be emphasized that the Judd et al. research strongly corroborates and extends the Dawes et al. findings with different measures and different groups. Dawes et al. used two groups that were strongly opposed to each other's views, while Judd et al. used two relatively mundane college majors who, although not in conflict, had somewhat contrasting characteristics. The tendency to view a group in a way that is both more extreme and more homogeneous than warranted by reality can be thought of as a form of "idealization," and this idealization is clearly stronger for outgroup than for ingroup. Note that the difference between the perception of ingroup and outgroup resides not only in the degree of idealization but in the direction of the differences as well. That is, when the overwhelming tendency to judge the ingroup more favorably than the outgroup (Brewer, 1979) is combined with the tendency to extremitize the outgroup as well, the outgroup is idealized in an unfavorable direction while the ingroup tends to be idealized in a favorable direction.

There is reason to think that this idealization works for many different stimulus groups. First, there is a great deal of evidence indicating that a group is viewed as more homogeneous and monolithic by outgroup than ingroup members (Judd & Park, 1988; Park & Judd, 1990; Park & Rothbart, 1982). Second, Mauro (1981) noted the same inaccuracy and simplification in an important social context. To explain jurors' strong support for the death penalty in the abstract, and their strong reluctance to impose the death penalty in a specific case, Mauro argued that jurors' abstract image of "murderers" is extreme, corresponding to such serial killers as Charles Manson, for whom they would impose the death penalty. Garden-variety defendants accused of murder, however, typically have killed only their spouse, are not serial killers, have children and a job, and generally do not fit the extreme image that jurors associate with the category "murderers." Given what we know about crime statistics, the typical murderer is far less extreme than is the public image of murderers. More generally, the tendency to idealize outgroups is strong, we suspect, not only for such emotionally charged categories as murderers, rapists, schizophrenics, and Republicans, but for mundane categories as well, such as business majors, engineering majors, librarians, cab drivers, and professors.

Lakoff (1987) argued that social categories can be represented by a number of differ-ent structures, where the "characteristic" exemplar is not necessarily the most frequent or typical instance, and may well be the paragon, or most extreme, exemplar of the category (e.g., "Mother Teresa," when used as a category name, defines the extreme example of the altruistic, nurturing individual). Although category structure based strictly on paragons may be uncommon, it seems probable that the "characteristic" category member is dis-placed toward extreme instances, and away from the statistically frequent exemplars, for the same reason that people estimate death by fire to be more probable than death by a bee sting (Lichtenstein, Slovic, Fischhoff, Layman, & Combs, 1978). The media is far more likely to describe deaths caused by spectacular fires than by bee stings, and serial killers receive more coverage than do the more frequent, but less dramatic, spouse mur-derers. The availability of dramatic instances may be only one of several possible reasons for the displacement of "characteristic" members toward the extreme (cf. Lakoff, 1987).

Data from the Dawes, et al. (1972) and the Judd et al. (1991) research indicate that the discrepancy between image and reality – the idealization of group impressions – is present for both ingroup and outgroup judges, but is considerably stronger for the latter. One way to approach the question of changing outgroup stereotypes, then, is to ask how we can make our perceptions of outgroup members less discrepant from reality and more like our perceptions of ingroup members. As the research above indicates, stereotypes are not absent in our perceptions of the ingroup, but they are less extreme and more complex (i.e., more heterogeneous) than are our perceptions of the outgroup. The question of how we can reduce the discrepancy between the image and the reality of the outgroup will be addressed after examining the question of how experiences with outgroup members influ-ence perceptions of the outgroup as a whole.

When does contact with individual outgroup members modify the stereotype of the outgroup?

Newcomb (1947) used the concept of "autistic hostility" to describe the self-amplifying nature of interpersonal and intergroup conflict. He proposed that mutually antagonistic parties avoid contact and the isolation between the parties then allows each to generate unrealistically negative attributions about the other – since isolation does not allow the attributions to be tempered by reality. The cycle of hostility, isolation, and unrealistically negative attributions constitutes a positive feedback loop which putatively can be reversed by re-established contact. Through contact, the disparity between image and reality is reduced, with a corresponding reduction in hostility. In the case of intergroup hostility, the individual members of the category are recognized as being less negative than the cat-egory as a whole, and it is assumed that the latter is adjusted in the direction of the former.

Whereas Newcomb assumed that unrealistically negative group images would natu-rally be ameliorated by contact, Allport, in his *Nature of Prejudice*, made a more complex argument (Allport, 1954; Pettigrew, 1986, 1998). Allport argued that contact does not always lead to favorable attitude change, and posited four necessary conditions for favor-able, contact-induced change: equal status, common goals, intergroup cooperation, and support from legal authorities and/or custom (Pettigrew, 1998).

The problem of contact-induced stereotype change may be even more difficult than commonly assumed given the nature of category-exemplar relations (Rothbart, 1996; Rothbart & John, 1985; Rothbart, John, & Duncan, in prep.; Rothbart & Lewis, 1988; Rothbart, Sriram, & Davis-Stitt, 1996). The reader is referred to Rothbart (1996) for a general statement of the argument; a brief summary follows.

Responding to a call by Amir (1976) and by Cook (1970) for a theoretical analysis of the psychological factors involved in contact-induced stereotype change, Rothbart and John (1985) proposed a multi-step model for stereotype change. First, it was deemed necessary that category members engage in behaviors perceived as counter to the stereotype. This is a simple point, but its importance is frequently ignored. Some stereotypic attributions are more susceptible to behavioral disconfirmation than others (Rothbart & Park, 1986) and behavior itself is frequently ambiguous and thus easily assimilable to the group stereotype (Kunda & Sherman-Williams, 1993). Stereotypes are unlikely to be changed by contact if the contact is perceived as consistent with the stereotype. This may be one of the severest shortcomings of Newcomb's assumption: As inaccurate as our images may be, ambiguous behaviors are easily assimilable to the stereotype. Allport recognized that contact may support rather than negate the stereotype, and indeed the first three of his four facilitating factors (equal status, common goals, and intergroup cooperation) can be viewed as conditions most likely to bring out behaviors counter to the stereotype. That is, for low-status outgroups, equal status violates the stereotype; and for outgroups with whom we have a competitive relation, common goals and cooperative interactions also conflict with expectation.

Assuming, then, that the first step is satisfied in which behaviors engaged in by outgroup members are perceived as violating the stereotype, the second step becomes of cardinal importance: When do the stereotype-disconfirming attributes of the category member generalize to the category as a whole? Rothbart and John argued that the positions taken by Newcomb and Allport assume an Aristotelean view of category structure. That is, since all category members have the same status and are all "equally good" exemplars, generalization is as likely to occur for members with stereotype-disconfirming attributes as it is for members with stereotype-confirming attributes. The contact hypothesis is specifically concerned, of course, with the impact of category members whose attributes are inconsistent with the category, and assumes strong generalizability from poor-fitting examples of the category.

An alternative view of categorization, based on a graded view of category structure – in which members differ in their goodness of fit to the category – is more consistent with the psychological literature (Rosch, 1973, 1978), but has serious implications for the problem of generalization associated with the contact hypothesis. At the level of mechanism, as the goodness of fit between category and exemplar decreases, there would be less inference from category to exemplar, and from exemplar to category (cf. Rips, 1975; Rothbart & Lewis, 1988). At the level of phenomenology, a logical member of the category thus may not be perceived as a member of the category. The question of what is meant by "perceived" deserves elaboration. A fraternity member, Doug, who is shy, quiet, writes poetry, and plays the oboe may be a card-carrying member of his fraternity, but is not thought of as a member, given the poor fit between his attributes and the public image of fraternity members. Doug does not spontaneously activate the category "fraternity men" in others' thoughts, nor is the category "fraternity men" likely to activate Doug as an exemplar.

Rothbart and John argued that poor-fitting exemplars often become "functionally isolated," or compartmentalized, from the category, and thus the stereotype-disconfirming attributes do not generalize to the category as a whole. In essence, stereotype-disconfirming attributes are thought to have two contradictory effects. First, they increase the disparity between image and reality (category and exemplar), exerting force on the stereotype to moderate and to move into line with the exemplar (à la Newcomb). Second, the decreasing goodness of fit between exemplar and category psychologically removes the exemplar from the category-making generalization less likely. There is now a great deal of experimental evidence indicating that as an exemplar's stereotype-disconfirming attributes increase, the likelihood of those attributes being incorporated into the stereotype decrease (Brown, Vivian, & Hewstone, 1999; Desforges, Lord, & Pugh, 1997; Hewstone, 1994; Johnston & Hewstone, 1992; Kunda & Oleson, 1995; Lord, Desforges, Ramsey, Trezza, & Lepper, 1991; Weber & Crocker, 1983).

To summarize to this point, Rothbart and John (1985) argued simply that not all category members are "equally good," and that inference between exemplar and category is directly related to the goodness of fit between the two; in short, generalization will be proportional to an exemplar's typicality. The importance of typicality as an important determinant of contact-induced stereotype change was presaged by Lewin half a century ago (Lewin & Grabbe, 1945). Referring to research combating prejudice based on age and race, they argued:

> . . . [these studies] indicate that favorable experiences with members of another group, even if they are frequent, do not necessarily diminish prejudices toward that group . . . Only if a psychological linkage is made between the image of specific individuals and the stereotype of a certain group, only when the individuals can be perceived as "typical representatives" of the group, is the experience with individuals likely to affect the stereotype. (Lewin & Grabbe, 1945, p. 58)

The problem, of course, is that the same member characteristics that disconfirm the stereotype also serve to reduce the typicality of that group member. The challenge is to pair stereotype-disconfirming information with an otherwise "typical representative of the group" despite the inverse relation between disconfirming attributes and typicality – a difficult but not impossible task that will be discussed later (for an excellent, recent review of this issue, see Hewstone & Lord, 1998).

Because Rothbart and John expect generalization to be more likely for good- than for poor-fitting category members, they predict a bias in information processing that favors stereotype stability over stereotype change. Whether the model is too pessimistic about the possibilities for contact-induced stereotype change will depend largely upon the findings of field research, preferably using a longitudinal design. Hovland's (1959) early analysis of attitude change research showed considerable change within the laboratory, but little change in the field – an analysis that may be as applicable today in the domain of stereotype change as in the earlier analysis of attitude change.

To assess the degree of stability and change in stereotypic beliefs, Rothbart and John conducted a four-year, four-panel, longitudinal study of the stereotypic beliefs of University of Oregon college students from their freshman to senior year (Rothbart & John, 1993; Rothbart, John, & Duncan, in prep.). Subjects judged 14 target groups on a number of stereotype measures, and provided us with detailed self-reports of the nature and extent of contact with each target group, as well as providing demographic and attitudinal data. For each target group, subjects rated approximately 40–50 trait descriptive terms at each of the four testing sessions. One measure of stereotype change is agreement over time in the ordering of the trait terms, corresponding to the test-retest reliability of the traits. Using aggregated means (computed across subjects, but within target groups), we found the average test-retest for the 14 different target groups over a four-year period – from the beginning of their freshman year to the end of their senior year – to be .92. A base-rate against which this can be judged is a comparable, non-longitudinal sample over a seven-day period, which produced a correlation of .96. The drop from .96 to .92 can be thought of as one measure of change over a four-year period – clearly very strong evidence for stability. This correlation is not the only measure of stability, however, and there was evidence of change for some of the target groups. Interestingly, the one group for which there was a great deal of change – in an unfavorable direction – was also the group for which there was a great deal of contact. Indeed, across all subjects, changes in the degree of self-reported direct contact (an index of amount and closeness of contact) correlated – .01 with changes in the favorability of the stereotype. There is considerable complexity to this data set, but thus far no strong evidence has emerged indicating that the *amount*, as opposed to judged quality of contact, is related to favorable stereotype change. Judged favorability of the contact did correlate significantly with changes in favorability toward the group, but the measure of favorability was based on retrospective self-report and may overlap conceptually with other indices of group favorability. In summary, at least one measure of stereotype change – consistency in the ordering of stereotypic attributes – showed enormous stability over an important four-year period in subjects' lives, providing evidence generally consistent with predictions from Rothbart and John (1985).

In the author's view, the Rothbart and John model is not an argument against contact in the amelioration of intergroup relations. Providence has given us rather few weapons in the fight against outgroup hostility, and contact is one of the few that has been effective, although not universally so. The arguments made by Rothbart and John attempt to define those conditions that might increase the likelihood of generalization for atypical exemplars. The first of these is that because the association of the category with the exemplar is a necessary condition for generalization to occur, it is especially important for atypical exemplars to be presented as clear – if not typical – members of the category. Second, if possible, disconfirming information should be associated with otherwise typical, rather than atypical members of the category. Finally, it may be useful to differentiate between group attributes that are more central or essential to group membership from those that are more peripheral. Greater generalization may be possible when highly typical peripheral attributes are presented to remind us of category membership, and atypical but central attributes are presented to challenge the more central aspects of the stereotype. To use an example (based more on fantasy than reality), assume that the image of a typical campus fraternity member is of a male who (1) wears a baseball cap backwards, (2) is clean shaven, (3) is politically conservative, and (4) conforms to the group. Assume the first two features are peripheral and the latter two are more central to group membership. If we were to try to change either of the more essential features, by presenting a liberal and/or non-conforming fraternity member, it would be useful to have the member typical on the peripheral features. Having group membership salient, even when presented with atypical members, is particularly helpful in weakening the stereotype (e.g., Maurer, Park, & Rothbart, 1995).

Individuation and Decategorization

What happens when we acquire individuating information about a category member? A number of thoughtful models have been proposed to account for the complex relation between individuating and categorical information (Brewer, 1988; Fiske & Neuberg, 1990; Locksley, Hepburn, & Ortiz, 1982; Nisbett, Zukier, & Lemley, 1981; Rothbart & John, 1985). This relation is important because one putative effect of sustained contact with a category member is the acquisition of information that is either irrelevant to or incongruent with the category. This newly acquired information about a category member should result, through generalization, in stereotype change. Indeed, at least two models hold individuation/decategorization to be an important component of stereotype change (Brewer & Miller, 1984; Pettigrew, 1998).

According to Rothbart and John, individuation and generalization may work against each other to produce stereotype change. The same counter-stereotypic behavior that disconfirms the stereotype also reduces the goodness of fit between category and category member, making generalization less likely. Qualms about the efficacy of personalization and decategorization in producing stereotype change are shared by Brown and Turner (1981), Hewstone and Brown (1986), and Brown et al. (1999), albeit for somewhat different theoretical reasons. Change at the interpersonal level is not necessarily mirrored by change at the intergroup level, and indeed there is reason to think that decategorizing an outgroup member may inhibit stereotype change.

Two recent sets of studies examine the effect of individuating information on categorical judgments. The first re-examines the interesting work by Nisbett, et al. (1981) on the dilution effect. Nisbett et al. argued that information nondiagnostic of a target behavior could none the less dilute the predictive power of diagnostic information. For example, consider a target behavior "child abuse," which is predicted by "having a drinking problem," but not by "managing a hardware store." The category "having a drinking problem" is diagnostic of child abuse, but the behavior "managing a hardware store" is not. Nisbett et al. found that the addition of nondiagnostic information systematically decreased (diluted) the predictive strength of diagnostic information. Tversky's (1977) features of similarity model, which assumes similarity to be a function of common minus distinctive features, was invoked to account for dilution. The addition of nondiagnostic information increases the number of distinctive features, and thus reduces perceived similarity.

Peters and Rothbart (2000) argued that the dilution effect may be intimately related to category-exemplar dynamics, rather than to Tversky's features of similarity. Specifically, they argued that the nondiagnostic information may have influenced the perceived strength of the diagnostic information, which in turn influenced prediction. Thus, a person who "has a drinking problem *and* who manages a hardware store" may be viewed as less of an alcoholic than a person who is simply described as "having a drinking problem." Peters and Rothbart argued that the specific nondiagnostic behaviors used may have inadvertently reduced the strength of the diagnostic category by making the exemplar less typical of the category. If so, then it ought to be possible to create nondiagnostic behaviors that increase, decrease, or do not change the typicality of the stimulus person vis-à-vis the diagnostic category. Peters and Rothbart provided subjects with either 1, 3, or 5 pieces of nondiagnostic, individuating information that were either typical, atypical, or unrelated to the diagnostic category. Consistent with the Nisbett et al. research, as the amount of atypical information increased, the impact of the diagnostic information decreased, entirely consistent with the dilution effect. However, contrary to the dilution effect, as typical nondiagnostic information increased, enhanced categorical prediction – the opposite of dilution – was obtained. With irrelevant nondiagnostic information, there was no change in prediction as the amount of that information increased. Thus the critical variable – the typicality of the categorical information – seemed to be an essential ingredient in determining whether dilution would or would not occur.

In general, however, it was easier to dilute than to enhance the diagnostic category. Although there were a number of possible reasons for this finding, one explanation is based on the nature of categorical representation, as discussed earlier (Lakoff, 1987). A pure category alone may already contain a large number of typical elements, making it difficult, for example, to make an "alcoholic" even more alcoholic, although it is relatively easy to reduce the degree of alcoholism by including incongruent elements. This means that dilution may be the most frequently observed effect – as originally argued by Nisbett et al. – but for reasons related to the dynamics of stereotyping rather than to Tversky's model of similarity.

Are mothers women?

Given the idealized nature of category labels, in which features consistent with the category predominate, it is probable that the addition of individuating information is more likely to weaken than strengthen the link between category and exemplar. Although at first blush the ease of "decategorizing" a category member may seem desirable, since it "releases" the individual from the tyranny of the category, it may be undesirable from the point of view of generalization.

There is a story told by an eminent developmentalist studying the gender role expectations of young girls whose mothers were employed in highly atypical occupations. In one case, where the mother's job was driving a tractor-trailer cross country for a large trucking company, the daughter provided a list of the usual occupations appropriate for women: Secretaries, nurses, librarians, etc. When asked whether women could be truck drivers, the daughter said no. When the interviewer called attention to her mother's own occupation, the daughter commented that "that is my mother, that is not women." This anecdote illustrates the inverse relation between the amount of individuating information and the amount of generalization. Those category members about whom we have the greatest amount of individuating information, and who could potentially exert the greatest force for humanizing our abstract impressions of social categories, may well be those individuals whose attributes are least likely to generalize to the category as a whole.

An interesting experiment that examines this question directly was conducted by Scarberry, Ratcliff, Lord, Lanicek, and Desforges (1997). They created an experience with a category member (a male homosexual) under conditions that were most likely to show generalization to the category as a whole. The factors identified by Allport to facilitate contact-induced stereotype change were included in the present experiment. Subjects interacted cooperatively with a confederate under equal-status conditions to work interdependently on a task to achieve a mutually desired goal, and under conditions in which the confederate was viewed in a highly favorable way. On the cooperative task, the homosexual confederate provided help to the subject through the use of analogies, but the nature of the analogies was varied experimentally. For some subjects the analogies were given in the abstract, such as "like when someone squeezes every bit of toothpaste out of the tube"; in the other condition the analogies were given as self-examples, such as "like when I squeeze every bit of toothpaste out of the tube." Subjects' attitudes toward homosexuals and toward three other stigmatized groups were assessed both pre- and post-contact, and attitudes toward the homosexual confederate were also assessed. Confederates who used abstract or self-based analogies were both highly liked and, most importantly, equally well liked. However, favorable attitudes toward homosexuals in general were greater in the condition where the confederate used abstract, rather than personal, analogies. A nice feature of this experiment is the careful control of the nature of the information presented to subjects. The informativeness of the analogies was virtually the same across conditions, and only the referent (abstract vs. self) varied. When the analogies referred to the personal behavior of the homosexual confederate, there was less generalization than when the analogies were abstract and unrelated to the confederate. It appears that the individuating information, seemingly quite unrelated to the stereotype of homosexuals, succeeded in isolating the individual from the category.

There may be at least two ways to interpret the findings of Scarberry et al. One possibility is that some of the analogies used (e.g., woodworking) may actually be slightly disconfirming of the stereotype of homosexuals, and those analogies when personally associated with the confederate made him less typical of the category. This interpretation would be consistent with Peters and Rothbart's interpretation of Nisbett et al.'s dilution findings. It is also possible, however, that even mundane, truly stereotype-irrelevant information can reduce the goodness of fit between category and exemplar, particularly for "strong" categories, that is, categories which carry strong implication or have high "inductive potential" (Rothbart & Taylor, 1992). Strong categories, such as homosexual, often connote a highly limited, and evaluatively potent set of behaviors, and it is possible that even common, mundane, nondiagnostic behaviors may function to reduce the goodness of fit between category and exemplars for such strong categories.

When Allport (1954) wrote that some labels are ". . . exceedingly salient and powerful. They tend to prevent alternative classification, or even cross-classification. . . . 'labels of primary potency' . . . act like shrieking sirens, deafening us to all finer discriminations that we might otherwise perceive," he was referring to such strong categories, and his intuition is compelling: Once these categories are applied to individuals they may inhibit the application of other, even independent or neutral categories. Saltz and Medow (1971) found that young children have difficulty in applying more than one social category to an individual, and the same may be true for adults when the categories are strong (that is, have high inductive potential). For very strong categories, any individuating information that is not directly implied by the category label may serve to decategorize the individual by making the exemplar a less good fit to the category. If so, the fact that almost any information can liberate the individual from the stigma of category membership may be received as good news, but again the downside is that the unrealistically extreme image of such categories may remain unperturbed by the reality of the members who make up that category.

To summarize the argument thus far, there are powerful categorization processes that work against contact-induced stereotype change. The same processes that individuate the category member – that is, that distance the member from the category – work against generalization from the individual to the category. The limitations of contact-induced stereotype change are not in the author's view a moral imperative, but a theoretically derived prediction with considerable empirical support. Indeed, the arguments made can be used to inform research on contact to increase the likelihood of stereotype change, as shown by Hewstone and Lord (1998). Most generally, any techniques that remind an observer that atypical group members are none the less category members should increase the likelihood of generalization. The problem of intimately known outgroup members is particularly vexing, however, since high levels of individuating information about outgroup members may lead them to be only weakly associated with the category label. Emphasizing their category membership, and particularly their category attributes that are typical, may be of value, but the power to compartmentalize poor-fitting group members should not be underemphasized (cf. Kelman's (1992) work on small-group interactions between Jews and Arabs in Israel).

Our discussion thus far has been focused on the complex relation between a category and its members, and we now wish to turn to the basic question of how we define, explicitly or implicitly, the nature of category membership through the placement of category boundaries.

The nature of group boundaries

Any discussion of ingroup–outgroup relations accepts as a basic premise the importance of a boundary dividing one's own group from others. There is little need to remind social psychologists raised in the tradition of Asch (1948) and Lewin and Grabbe (1945) that the importance of such boundary markers lies, not necessarily in the reality of the external world, but in the phenomenal representation of that world. Two studies dealing with issues of boundary markers, one explicitly and the other implicitly, will be summarized and used to speculate on the relation of such boundary markers to the modification of outgroup stereotypes.

A study by Rothbart, Davis-Stitt, and Hill (1997) examined the impact of category labels and visual boundary markers on similarity judgments. In one experiment, they presented subjects with pairs of names of male actors located along a continuous, percentile scale of political liberalism (e.g., Alan Alda was located at point that makes him more liberal than 85% of the population). Each subject judged the similarity between a number of pairs, some placed 10 units apart and others placed 15 units apart. The presence of boundary markers at the quartiles of the scale was systematically varied across subjects. Boundary markers were either verbal labels (e.g., "moderately conservative," "moderately liberal") or visual markers (solid vertical "tick" marks). One group received a continuum with no markers of any kind (a baseline control), another received a continuum with *both* verbal and visual boundary markers, and in the two other conditions there was the presence of one type of boundary marker but not the other. The results were clear: A given pair of actors was judged most similar to each other when no boundaries existed between them, and perceived similarity decreased as a function of the number of interposed boundary markers. The effects of the verbal and visual boundary markers were each significant and additive. Thus, even though the verbal and visual markers added nothing to the underlying reality of the scale, both types of markers – when interposed between stimulus persons – decreased the perceived similarity between them. A comparison between the baseline control condition and the condition with two boundary markers present indicates that there were two effects of category boundaries: 1) To increase the perceived similarity within categories, and 2) to decrease the perceived similarity between categories. These two effects constitute the phenomenon Turner, Hogg, Oakes, Reicher, and Wetherell (1987) have called "metacontrast" (cf. also Tajfel & Wilkes, 1963).

The design of the experiment also allowed a comparison between "reality" and categorization. Consider two different types of pairs: Those separated by 10 units and those separated by 15 units. The unit distance between the pairs represents the "reality" of the scale, and the judgments in the control baseline condition, where no boundaries are present, appropriately show greater similarity for the 10 unit than for the 15 unit pairs. Now consider the case in which the actors separated by 10 units are in different categories, and those separated by 15 units are present in the same category: Now the 15 unit pairs are judged more similar than are the 10 unit pairs. At least for this range of scale values, categorization is able to override the effects of reality. Category boundaries appear to be treated as informative even when they add little or no information to what is already known about the objects subsumed by the categories. If the opening example from that article is paraphrased, it is as if a farmer living at the boundary of Poland and Russia, after learning that his house is just inside the Polish border, exclaims with relief, "Thank God, no more Russian winters!" Similar findings have been obtained by Allison and Messick (1985) and Mackie and Allison (1987) in the context of group attributions, where the criterion for electoral success is varied.

Rothbart et al. explicitly manipulated the presence of boundary markers and examined the effects on perceived similarity. A study by Maurer, Park, and Rothbart (1995), although not explicitly designed to examine the effects of category boundaries, may usefully be interpreted in this way. Maurer et al. tested some important ideas put forth earlier by Park, Ryan, and Judd (1992) about subgrouping and perceived intragroup variability, and considered how subtyping may differ from subgrouping. Earlier work by Park et al. showed that subjects who first thought about the characteristics of the subordinate groups that make up the larger superordinate group then rated the superordinate group as *less* homogeneous. This phenomenon, referred to as subgrouping, has important implications for modifying the perceived complexity/heterogeneity of outgroups. How, then, does subgrouping differ from subtyping, where poor-fitting members of a category are also relegated to a subordinate category resulting in a *more* homogeneous view of the super-ordinate group (e.g., Johnston & Hewstone, 1992; Weber & Crocker, 1983)? The goal of the Maurer et al. research was to determine whether the creation of subgroups and subtypes – both of which involve the establishment of subordinate categories – leads to different effects on the perceived strength of the stereotype.

Subjects were given information about a group of 16 stimulus persons involved in a Big Brother program, where the group members varied in typicality. One group was given this information without any instructions (the control condition), and then were asked to make typicality judgments as well as judgments about the group as a whole (including judgments of intragroup variability). A second group was given "subtyping" instructions to sort the group members into those who fit and those who do not fit the image of the group before making the same judgments as did the control condition. A third group was given "subgrouping" instructions to sort the members into as many piles as they wished, trying to minimize differences within subgroups while maximizing differences between subgroups before making their judgments. Compared to the control condition, the subtyping condition had a more stereotyped and homogeneous image of the target group, while the subgrouping condition had a less stereotyped and more heterogeneous image. We believe the reason for this was that the subjects were implicitly drawing the group boundaries differently for the different conditions. In the subtyping condition, atypical members were functionally excluded from group membership, a conclusion which was supported by a mediational analysis based on typicality ratings; in the subgrouping condition, the boundaries enclosed all of the subgroups, and the heterogeneity of the included groups was apparent. Stated differently, the same atypical stimulus persons were functionally excluded from the group representation in the subtyping condition, while they were included in the subgrouping condition.

There are two potentially important implications of this research. One is that the perception of typicality is influenced not only by the "computation" of matching features between category and exemplar, but also by the processing goals of the subjects. Context can determine whether subjects do or do not include the atypical members in their implicit calculations of group impressions, and this is an important phenomenon that needs to be better understood. In this research, the subtyping and subgrouping instructions had very different effects on how subjects thought about the relation of group members to the group as a whole. The relatively simple dichotomous judgments (good fit vs. poor fit) required by the subtyping instructions may have led subjects to view group members in a unidimensional way, promoting an exaggerated difference between the attributes of good- and poor-fitting members (in comparison to the control condition). In contrast, the more complex subgrouping instructions, which encouraged subjects to examine similarities and differences between and among individual stimulus persons and between and among subgroups, may have had at least two important consequences. First, subjects may have been led to realize that each stimulus person was a complex set of attributes some of which fit and some of which did not fit the stereotype. In contrast to the subtyping instructions, the multiattribute nature of the stimulus persons was emphasized, leading to more moderate judgments of atypicality (cf. Judd & Lusk, 1984). Second, whereas the judgments under subtyping instructions may have led subjects to think of atypical members as outside the group, or as nonmembers of the group, the subgrouping instructions may have encouraged subjects to make discriminations *within* the context of an activated superordinate category. To state this somewhat differently, there is a difference between sorting a list of occupations into those that fit or do not fit our stereotype of women (the subtyping instructions) versus a task in which we classify a list of occupations, *all engaged in by women*, into subcategories (the subgrouping instructions). In the former case, the atypical exemplars may be *dissociated* from the superordinate category, and in the latter case may be actively *associated* with that category.

The second general implication of this work is the importance of implicit group boundaries. One way to think about the Maurer et al. (1995) results is that subjects in the subtyping condition are implicitly drawing the group's boundaries in a way that is different from subjects in the subgrouping condition. For the former, the boundaries appear to exclude atypical group members, whereas for the latter, the boundaries appear to be drawn in a more inclusive manner. Although the concept of "implicit group boundaries" remains vague, it has precedence in Allport's concept of "refencing" (referring to the isolation of poor-fitting group members outside the category) and in Lewin's treatment of psychological barriers. In both cases, it is argued that one function of psychological boundaries is to seal off or isolate one region of the "life-space" from another. The isolated regions may be individual group members from the group as a whole, one social category from another, the ingroup from the outgroup, or any concept or idea that remains isolated or inaccessible from another (cf. Nissen, Ross, Willingham, Mackenzie, & Schacter, 1988).

Group Boundaries and Stereotype Change

In this last section, a number of general boundary-related strategies are considered that might be useful in modifying perceptions of the outgroup, guided by the question: "How can we make our images of the outgroup more like those of the ingroup?" Park and Rothbart (1982) have provided one approach to answering this question. When asked to describe female dance and female physics majors, female college students based their ratings primarily on college major, whereas male college students based their ratings primarily on gender. For male dance and male physics majors, now male judges used college major, while female judges used gender. In other words, each group of judges used the more differentiating dimension (college major) when rating its own gender and the less differentiating dimension (gender) when rating the other gender. How can we get judges to think about outgroup members in terms of their most differentiating rather than their least differentiating attributes?

Subgrouping

One strategy for making the outgroup more like the ingroup is to increase the perceived variability of the outgroup, particularly with respect to increasing subordinate bases for classification – that is, by making it clear that a number of subgroup category labels comprise the superordinate group. This is exactly the program of research being carried out by Park and her colleagues (e.g., Park, Judd, & Ryan, 1992). There may be a number of ways of enhancing the perceived variability of a group, and consistent with the reasoning offered earlier, presenting the subgroupings in the context of the superordinate grouping may be particularly effective.

Augmentation of underrepresented subgroups. One source of bias in the perception of outgroups is the overrepresentation of particular subgroups for reasons of extremeness, memorability, threat, etc. (Rothbart, Fulero, Jensen, Howard, & Birrell, 1978), and the underrepresentation of others. For example, Whites' images of Blacks may be disproportionately influenced by the image of "young Black males." Even though violent behavior occurs in a minority of "young Black males," this subgroup itself represents only a minority of Blacks, a category which also includes Black females, elderly Blacks, middle-class Blacks, etc. Perhaps due to media attention directed at violent crime among young Black males, other subgroups are inadequately represented in our impressions of the group as a whole. This is an instance where increased public awareness of other Black subgroups may lead both to a more heterogeneous, and less negative, image of the group as a whole.

Aggregation of categories. Often an outgroup category retains its homogeneous, negative characteristics by remaining isolated or compartmentalized from both relevant category members and from other, affectively inconsistent, labels. In a classic study on the effects of consensual information, Asch (1948) had judges rank the favorability of a set of occupations, one of which was "politicians." In one condition, judges were informed that other subjects had rated politicians highly favorably, and in another condition, unfavorably. Judges were strongly influenced by these consensual ratings, but when Asch probed their thinking, it was clear that in the first condition, judges interpreted the category to mean "statesmen" and in the second condition to mean "political hacks" (cf. Sia, Lord, Blessum, Ratcliff, & Lepper, 1997, Lord & Lepper, 1999). Indeed, the exemplars activated in both conditions were politicians, by any reasonable definition of the term, and the categories "statesman" and "politician," although separated by an implicit boundary, could easily be aggregated to yield a single, more heterogeneous category.

Although there is little enthusiasm to change the public perception of politicians, there are many important social categories, such as "disabled" and "mentally ill," in which the categories retain their extreme character by virtue of excluding many other relevant classes of exemplars. The category "disabled" includes not only paraplegics or quadriplegics, but also individuals with less obvious impairments to hearing or vision. The mentally ill are not just dangerous psychotics, but include individuals with other disabling mental states (anxiety, fear, depression, etc.). Part of the problem with these categories is the ambiguity associated with category membership: How do we define a disability and how do we define mental illness? Although these two cases may constitute extreme examples of ambiguity, most social categories have fuzzy boundaries, and the consequence of such ambiguity is the exclusion or underrepresentation of more moderate exemplars. The process of aggregation joins together previously separated categories into a superordinate, but more heterogeneous grouping (cf. Abelson's (1959) concept of "transcendence").

Redefining category boundaries. Probably one of the clearest examples of altering category boundaries for the purpose of modifying outgroup stereotypes is the imposition of a superordinate category inclusive of ingroup and outgroup members, in effect removing the implicit boundary marker between the two groups. The classic research by M. Sherif, Harvey, White, Hood, & C. Sherif (1988) on the use of superordinate goals to reverse the destruction effects of intergroup competition can be thought of as an instance of removing category boundaries. Although Sherif preferred to explain the beneficial effects of cooperation on the "functional relations" between groups, it is also possible to interpret the results as due either to common fate (e.g., Rabbie & Horwitz, 1969) or to the redefinition of category boundaries to yield a single ingroup (Gaertner, Mann, Murrell, & Dovidio, 1989; Dovidio, Gaertner, Validzic, Matoka, Johnson, & Frazier, 1997; Gaertner, Mann, Dovidio, Murrell, & Pomare, 1990). These ideas are discussed extensively in the chapter by Brewer and Gaertner, this volume, chapter 22, and will not be pursued here.

In summary, two possible routes to modifying the stereotypes of outgroup members have been considered in this paper. One route, through contact with individual exemplars, can be problematic due to the dynamics of category-exemplar relations. Specifically, those exemplars most disconfirming of the stereotype are least likely to be associated with the category and least likely to produce generalization to the category as a whole. None the less, category-exemplar dynamics can also be exploited to increase the probability of generalization by making sure that atypical exemplars – through a variety of techniques – become strongly associated with the category. A second route attempts a modification of the relations among the categories themselves, by augmenting, combining, and redefining category boundaries in a way that yields a less extreme and more heterogeneous view of the outgroup. In the author's view, there is as yet no magic bullet that vanquishes the unfavorable, simplified images of the outgroup. Our categorical structures, which represent the mind's attempt to simplify the complexities of the social world, play a significant role in such stereotypes. The difficulty of modifying these categorical structures, to make them more complex and more reflective of the actual variety of the social world, should not be underestimated. The importance of achieving this goal also should not be underestimated.

References

Abelson, R. P. (1959). Modes of resolution of belief dilemmas. *Journal of Conflict Resolution, 3,* 343–352.

Allison, S. T., & Messick, D. M. (1985). The group attribution error. *Journal of Experimental Social Psychology, 21,* 563–579.

Allport, G. W. (1954). *The nature of prejudice.* Cambridge, MA: Addison-Wesley.

Amir, Y. (1976). The role of intergroup contact in change of prejudice and ethnic relations. In P. A. Katz (Ed.), *Towards the elimination of racism* (pp. 245–308). New York: Pergamon Press.

Asch, S. E. (1948). The doctrine of suggestion, prestige, and imitation in social psychology. *Psychological Review, 55,* 250–276.

Brewer, M. B. (1979). Ingroup bias in the minimal intergroup situation: A cognitive-motivational analysis. *Psychological Bulletin, 86,* 307–324.

Brewer, M. B. (1988). A dual process model of impression formation. In T. K. Srull & J. Wyer (Eds.), *Advances in social cognition* (pp. 1–36). Hillsdale, NJ: Erlbaum.

Brewer, M. B., & Miller, N. (1984). Beyond the contact hypothesis: Theoretical perspectives on desegregation. In N. Miller & M. B. Brewer (Eds.), *Groups in contact: The psychology of desegregation.* New York: Academic Press.

Brown, R. J., & Turner, J. C. (1981). Interpersonal and intergroup behavior. In J. C. Turner & H. Giles (Eds.), *Intergroup behavior* (pp. 33–65). Chicago IL: University of Chicago Press.

Brown, R., Vivian, J., & Hewstone, M. (1999). Changing attitudes through intergroup contact: The effects of group membership salience. *European Journal of Social Psychology, 29*(5–6), 741–764.

Cook, S. W. (1970). Motives in a conceptual analysis of attitude-related behavior. In W. J. Arnold & D. Levine (Eds.), *Nebraska symposium on motivation, 1969* (pp. 179–235). Lincoln, NE: University of Nebraska Press.

Dawes, R. M., Singer, D., & Lemons, F. (1972). An experimental analysis of the contrast effect and its implications for intergroup communication and the indirect assessment of attitude. *Journal of Personality and Social Psychology, 21*(3), 281–295.

Desforges, D. M., Lord, C. G., & Pugh, M. A. (1997). Role of group representativeness in the generalization part of the contact hypothesis. *Basic and Applied Social Psychology, 19,* 183–204.

Dovidio, J. F., Gaertner, S. L., Validzic, A., Matoka, K., Johnson, B., & Frazier, S. (1997). Extending the benefits of recategorization: Evaluations, self-disclosure, and helping. *Journal of Experimental Social Psychology, 33,* 401–420.

Fiske, S. T., & Neuberg, S. L. (1990). A continuum of impression formation from category-based to individuating processes: Influences of information and motivation on attention and interpretation, *Advances in experimental social psychology* (Vol. 23). New York: Academic Press.

Gaertner, S. L., Mann, J., Murrell, A., & Dovidio, J. F. (1989). Reducing intergroup bias: The benefits of recategorization. *Journal of Personality and Social Psychology, 57,* 239–249.

Gaertner, S. L., Mann, J. A., Dovidio, J. F., Murrell, A. J., & Pomare, M. (1990). How does cooperation reduce intergroup bias? *Journal of Personality and Social Psychology, 59,* 692–704.

Hewstone, M. (1994). Revision and change of stereotypic beliefs: In search of the elusive subtyping model. In W. Stroebe & M. Hewstone (Eds.), *European review of social psychology* (Vol. 5, pp. 69–109). New York: Wiley.

Hewstone, M., & Brown, R. (1986). Contact is not enough: An intergroup perspective on the "Contact Hypothesis". In M. Hewstone & R. Brown (Eds.), *Contact and conflict in intergroup encounters* (pp. 1–44). Oxford, UK: Blackwell.

Hewstone, M., & Lord, C. G. (1998). Changing intergroup cognitions and intergroup behavior: The role of typicality. In C. Sedikides, J. Schopler, & C. A. Insko (Eds.), *Intergroup cognition and intergroup behavior.* Mahwah, NJ: Erlbaum.

Hovland, C. I. (1959). Reconciling conflicting results derived from experimental and survey studies of attitude change. *American Psychologist, 14,* 8–17.

Johnston, L., & Hewstone, M. (1992). Cognitive models of stereotype change. 3. Subtyping and the perceived typicality of disconfirming group members. *Journal of Experimental Social Psychology, 28,* 360–386.

Judd, C. M., & Lusk, C. M. (1984). Knowledge structures and evaluative judgments: Effects of structural variables on judgmental extremity. *Journal of Personality and Social Psychology, 46*(6), 1193–1207.

Judd, C. M., & Park, B. (1988). Out-group homogeneity: Judgments of variability at the individual and group levels. *Journal of Personality and Social Psychology, 54,* 778–788.

Judd, C. M., & Park, B. (1993). Definition and assessment of accuracy in social stereotypes. *Psychological Review, 100,* 109–128.

Judd, C. M., Ryan, C. S., & Park, B. (1991). Accuracy in the judgment of in-group and out-group variability. *Journal of Personality and Social Psychology, 61*, 366–379.

Kelman, H. C. (1992). Coalitions across conflict lines: The interplay of conflicts within and between the Israeli and Palestinian communities. In S. Worchel & J. A. Simpson (Eds.), *Conflict between people and groups* (pp. 236–258, 293–294). Chicago, IL: Nelson-Hall.

Kunda, Z., & Oleson, K. C. (1995). Maintaining stereotypes in the face of disconfirmation: Constructing grounds for subtyping deviants. *Journal of Personality and Social Psychology, 68*, 565–579.

Kunda, Z., & Sherman-Williams, B. (1993). Stereotypes and the construal of individuating information. *Personality and Social Psychology Bulletin, 19*, 90–99.

Lakoff, G. (1987). Cognitive models and prototype theory. In U. Neisser (Ed.), *Concepts and conceptual development: ecological and intellectual factors in categorization* (pp. 63–100). New York: Cambridge University Press.

Lee, Y.-T., Jussim, J., & McCauley, C. R. (1995). *Stereotype accuracy: Toward appreciating group differences.* (1st ed.). Washington, DC: American Psychological Association.

Lewin, K., & Grabbe, P. (1945). Conduct, knowledge, and acceptance of new values. *Journal of Social Issues, 2*, 53–64.

Lichtenstein, S., Slovic, P., Fischhoff, B., Layman, M., & Combs, B. (1978). Judged frequency of lethal events. *Journal of Experimental Psychology: Human Learning and Memory, 4*, 551–578.

Locksley, A., Hepburn, C., & Ortiz, V. (1982). Social stereotypes and judgments of individuals: An instance of the base-rate fallacy. *Journal of Experimental Social Psychology, 18*, 23–42.

Lord, C. G., Desforges, D. M., Ramsey, S. L., Trezza, G. R., & Lepper, M. R. (1991). Typicality effects in attitude-behavior consistency: Effects of category discrimination and category knowledge. *Journal of Experimental Social Psychology, 27*, 550–575.

Lord, C. G., & Lepper, M. R. (1999). Attitude representation theory. In M. P. Zanna (Ed.), *Advances in Experimental Social Psychology* (Vol. 31). San Diego, CA: Academic Press.

Mackie, D. M., & Allison, S. T. (1987). Group attribution errors and the illusion of group attitude change. *Journal of Experimental Social Psychology, 23*, 460–480.

Maurer, K. L., Park, B., & Rothbart, M. (1995). Subtyping versus subgrouping processes in stereotype representation. *Journal of Personality and Social Psychology, 69*, 812–824.

Mauro, R. (1981). *Effects of the complexity and extremity of social prototypes on perceptions of individual category members.* Unpublished Masters, Yale University, New Haven, CT.

Newcomb, T. M. (1947). Autistic hostility and social reality. *Human Relations, 1*, 69–86.

Nisbett, R. E., Zukier, H., & Lemley, R. E. (1981). The dilution effect: Nondiagnostic information weakens the implications of diagnostic information. *Cognitive Psychology, 13*, 248–277.

Nissen, M. J., Ross, J. L., Willingham, D. B., Mackenzie, T. B., Schacter, D. L. (1988). Memory and awareness in a patient with multiple personality disorder. *Brain and Cognition, 8*, 117–134.

Park, B., & Judd, C. M. (1990). Measures and models of perceived group variability. *Journal of Personality and Social Psychology, 59*, 173–191.

Park, B., & Rothbart, M. (1982). Perception of out-group homogeneity and levels of social categorization: Memory for the subordinate attributes of in-group and out-group members. *Journal of Personality and Social Psychology, 42*(6), 1051–1068.

Park, B., Ryan, C. S., & Judd, C. M. (1992). Role of meaningful subgroups in explaining differences in perceived variability for in-groups and out-groups. *Journal of Personality and Social Psychology, 63*, 553–567.

Peters, E., & Rothbart, M. (2000). Typicality can create, eliminate, and reverse the dilution effect. *Personality and Social Psychology Bulletin, 26*, 177–187.

Pettigrew, T. F. (1986). The intergroup contact hypothesis reconsidered. In M. Hewstone & R. Brown (Eds.), *Contact and conflict in intergroup encounters* (pp. 169–195). Oxford, UK: Blackwell.

Pettigrew, T. F. (1998). Intergroup contact theory. *Annual Review of Psychology, 49,* 65–85.

Rabbie, J. M., & Horwitz, M. (1969). Arousal of ingroup-outgroup bias by a chance win or loss. *Journal of Personality and Social Psychology, 13,* 269–277.

Rips, L. J. (1975). Inductive judgments about natural categories. *Journal of Verbal Learning and Verbal Behavior, 14,* 665–681.

Rosch, E. H. (1978). Principles of categorization. In E. Rosch & B. Lloyd (Eds.), *Cognition and categorization* (pp. 27–48). Hillsdale, NJ: Erlbaum.

Rosch, E. H. (1973). On the internal structure of perceptual and semantic categories. In T. E. Moore (Ed.), *Cognitive development and the acquisition of language* (pp. 111–144). New York: Academic Press.

Rothbart, M. (1996). Category-exemplar dynamics and stereotype change. *International Journal of Intercultural Relations, 20,* 305–321.

Rothbart, M., Davis-Stitt, C., & Hill, J. (1997). Effects of arbitrarily placed category boundaries on similarity judgments. *Journal of Experimental Social Psychology, 33*(2), 122–145.

Rothbart, M., Fulero, S., Jensen, C., Howard, J., & Birrell, P. (1978). From individual to group impressions: Availability heuristics in stereotype formation. *Journal of Experimental Social Psychology, 14,* 237–255.

Rothbart, M., & John, O. P. (1985). Social categorization and behavioral episodes: A cognitive analysis of the effects of intergroup contact. *Journal of Social Issues, 41,* 81–104.

Rothbart, M., & John, O. P. (1993). Intergroup relations and stereotype change: A social-cognitive analysis and some longitudinal findings. In P. M. Sniderman, P. E. Tetlock, & E. G. Carmines (Eds.), *Prejudice, politics, and the American dream* (pp. 32–59, 307–332). Stanford, CA: Stanford University Press.

Rothbart, M., John, O., & Duncan, T. (in preparation). A longitudinal analysis of stereotype change.

Rothbart, M., & Lewis, S. (1988). Inferring category attributes from exemplar attributes: Geometric shapes and social categories. *Journal of Personality and Social Psychology, 55,* 861–872.

Rothbart, M., & Park, B. (1986). On the confirmability and disconfirmability of trait concepts. *Journal of Personality and Social Psychology, 50,* 131–142.

Rothbart, M., Sriram, N., & Davis-Stitt, C. (1996). The retrieval of typical and atypical category members. *Journal of Experimental Social Psychology, 32,* 309–336.

Rothbart, M., & Taylor, M. (1992). Category labels and social reality: Do we view social categories as natural kinds? In G. R. Semin & K. Fiedler (Eds.), *Language, interaction and social cognition* (pp. 11–36). London: Sage.

Saltz, E., & Medow, M. L. (1971). Concept conservation in children: The dependence of belief systems on semantic representation. *Child Development, 42,* 1533–1542.

Scarberry, N. C., Ratcliff, C. D., Lord, C. G., Lanicek, D. L., & Desforges, D. M. (1997). Effects of individuating information on the generalization part of Allport's contact hypothesis. *Society for Personality and Social Psychology, Inc., 23,* 1291–1299.

Sia, T., Lord, C., Blessum, K., Ratcliff, C., & Lepper, M. (1997). Is a rose always a rose? The role of social category exemplar change in attitude stability and attitude-behavior consistency. *Journal of Personality and Social Psychology, 72,* 501–514.

Sherif, M., Harvey, O. J., White, B. J., Hood, W. R., & Sherif, C. W. (1988/1961). *The Robbers Cave experiment: Intergroup conflict and cooperation.* Middletown, CT: Wesleyan University Press.

Sherif, M., & Hovland, C. I. (1966). *Social judgment: Assimilation and contrast effects in communication and attitude change.* New Haven, CT: Yale University Press.

Tajfel, H., & Wilkes, A. L. (1963). Classification and quantitative judgment. *British Journal of Social Psychology, 54,* 101–114.

Turner, J. C., Hogg, M. A., Oakes, P. J., Reicher, S. D., & Wetherell, M. S. (1987). *Rediscovering the social group: A self-categorization theory.* Oxford, UK: Blackwell.

Tversky, A. (1977). Features of similarity. *Psychological Review, 84,* 327–352.

Weber, R., & Crocker, J. (1983). Cognitive processes in the revision of stereotypic beliefs. *Journal of Personality and Social Psychology, 45,* 961–977.

CHAPTER FOUR

Developmental and Socialization Influences on Intergroup Bias

Frances E. Aboud and Maria Amato

Over the past 25 years, our understanding of how children come to perceive and prefer certain ethnic groups has expanded greatly. Since 1974, when Brand, Ruiz, and Padilla published their *Psychological Bulletin* article reviewing children's ethnic identification and preference, a number of reviews have presented quite a different perspective (Aboud, 1988; Brown, 1995; Hirschfeld, 1996; Katz, 1976; Schofield, 1982). In particular, two traditionally held views have undergone major revision. One view, that children become gradually more prejudiced with age, is no longer tenable. Empirical research now typically shows an inverted-U relation between age and prejudice. The second view, that children learn stereotypes and prejudice solely from parents and peers, has also not been supported. Rather, children are now seen to play a more active role in the biases they develop. Perhaps the revisions are due in part to a decline in normative forms of prejudice and thus greater variability in attitudes of parents and children. We now have a diversity of developmental trends and causal variables to be studied. Research from different cultures and historical periods has contributed to the observed diversity. Finally, theories of cognitive development, social cognition, interpersonal relations, and social change have been added to traditional learning theory to help explain age- and culture-specific phenomena.

For readers who are familiar with adult social psychology research on stereotyping, prejudice, and discrimination, the developmental field provides a closer look at the origins of prejudice and the different routes children take as they become prejudiced or tolerant adults. From our perspective, stereotyping, prejudice, and discrimination are not inevitable, normal, pragmatic, and adaptive. Individual differences and age changes belie such a conclusion. While social psychologists have focused primarily on normative cognitive processes driven by contextual cues to form and use ethnic categories (Fiske, 1998), developmental psychologists examine when these cognitive processes develop in relation to emotional processes, and how they impact on prejudice. Context is relevant to the acquisition and reduction of prejudice, but stable social influences rather than temporary environmental cues have greater explanatory value. To understand why certain social influences are greater than others, developmentalists consider children's motivation to make sense of their social world and their place in it – a cognitively driven motivation – in addition to their desire for approval and other short-term goals. Consequently, the two explanatory frameworks currently used in developmental research, namely social influences in the environment and cognitive/emotional developments in the child, take a longer term perspective but are not incompatible with the prevailing social psychology view.

Our chapter focuses on ethnic/racial intergroup bias. Although biases based on gender, disability, and other criteria also exist in children, their development does not always follow the same trajectory (Fishbein, 1996; Powlishta, Serbin, Doyle, & White, 1994). Ethnic bias has been particularly harmful in imposing constraints on the social and academic opportunities afforded minority children, and on the social relationships of majority children. Gender stereotypes impose the same harmful constraints on development; however, we know that boys and girls will eventually be dating and mating. The ethnic divide only becomes larger with age, not necessarily because of personal bias, but because of societal structures such as marriage and religion that keep us apart.

We review several aspects of the development of intergroup bias: attitudes, categorical perceptions and cognitions about ethnicity, and cross-ethnic peer relations. These different ways of understanding ethnicity and relating to members of ethnic groups may not show consistent levels of bias. Moreover, they may not necessarily reflect bias. For example, awareness of different ethnic groups and the formation of social categories are not in themselves harmful. However, the over-use of categories when making judgments about individuals often leads to inaccuracy because of an exaggeration of between-group differences and within-group homogeneity. This can interfere with recognition and respect for an individual's qualities. Although schema-driven judgments are arguably more normative (i.e., prevalent) than data-driven judgments, they are not necessarily inevitable or normal. Our theories of development will eventually have to explain not only the universal tendency to categorize (the focus of social cognitive and evolutionary frameworks) but also the age, individual and cultural differences that are so apparent in heterogeneous societies.

To organize the recent developmental research on intergroup bias, we will discuss measurement issues and then review findings with respect to age and majority-minority status of children. The final section will deal with explanatory frameworks, such as the influence of significant others, cultural-historical variables, and cognitive development.

1   Conceptual and Measurement Issues

Although a number of definitions of prejudice have been proposed, Brown's (1995, p. 8) captures the essence: "the holding of derogatory social attitudes or cognitive beliefs, the expression of negative affect, or the display of hostile or discriminatory behavior towards members of a group on account of their membership of that group." The existence of such attitudes, beliefs, affect, or behavior in an individual demonstrates intergroup bias to the extent that they are based on only one item of information about a person, namely his or her group membership. What they hold in common is a predisposed negativity toward a group of people.

A discussion of measurement techniques leads to the question of how children's prejudice differs from adults' prejudice. This question often arises because teachers and parents express disbelief at the early high levels of prejudice reported by researchers. They claim to be unaware of prejudice in all but a few young children. Most people identify spontaneous slurs and stereotypic remarks as indications of prejudice. Children, however, differ from adults in verbal and emotional sophistication. Consequently, they do not frequently express their prejudice in racial slurs. Furthermore, the emotional underpinnings of children's prejudice is less likely to be anger and hostility and more likely to be suspicion, fear, sadness, and expectations or projections of rejection, harm, and avoidance. Early childhood prejudice may reflect a developmental phenomenon more than a stable personality characteristic in some children whose levels change dramatically between 6 and 9 years (Doyle & Aboud, 1995).

In addition, prejudice, stereotyping, and discrimination do not develop simultaneously in children, so there is little consistency among the different components of bias. At 4 and 5 years, they often express prejudice without any accurate recognition of the groups they dislike (Bar-Tal, 1996). Similarly, youngsters hold prejudiced attitudes without knowing any of the attributes included in adults' stereotypes. They may not use their attitudes or beliefs to guide their behavior or choice of playmates (Hirschfeld, 1996). One behavior often considered as an index of discrimination is ethnic conflict, accompanied by name-calling, hassling, fighting, and intimidation; however, higher levels of conflict are directed to ingroup than outgroup peers and seem to be associated with certain aggressive individuals (Aboud, 1992; Patchen, 1982; Schofield, 1982). More closely associated with prejudice are avoidance and exclusion in peer relations, yet even the possession of outgroup friends does not strongly correlate with attitudes. The components of intergroup bias may converge, if at all, only in middle childhood when the child has some control over these mental and behavioral processes and can bring them to bear on each other. This understanding has guided our selection of age-appropriate constructs measured in the pre-adolescent years.

Measurement of prejudiced attitudes in children focuses on negative evaluation of group members. The Doll Test, developed by Clark (1955) was most commonly used before 1975. Children were asked to point to one doll in response to questions such as: Which is the nice color? Typically the sample's responses to each separate item were analyzed by comparing the frequencies with chance (usually 50%). This meant that the degree of consensus in the sample was addressed, rather than the prevalence of prejudice or the identification of prejudiced children. Despite the limitations of this methodology, the findings fairly accurately reflected the common tendency of White children to show negative attitudes toward brown-skinned figures.

Since the development of the Preschool Racial Attitude Measure (PRAM) by Williams, Best, and Boswell (1975), it has become possible to measure the level of prejudice in individual children. By including multiple items, researchers can derive a more reliable prejudice score by aggregating many responses, assessing convergent or predictive validity, and correlating scores with age, parental attitudes, and other potentially causal variables. More recent measures of this variety include Katz' (Katz & Zalk, 1978) Projective Prejudice Test, Davey's (1983) post box technique, and Doyle and Aboud's Multi-response Racial Attitude (MRA) measure (1995). A distinct advantage is obtained with measures such as the MRA, where the respondent is allowed to assign the same positive and negative evaluations (e.g., plays fair, bossy) to more than one group. They allow for the assessment of attitudes that run counter to ingroup bias, namely positive evaluations of outgroups and negative evaluations of the ingroup. These counter-bias attitudes may be more or less accessible than biased attitudes, depending on the age, individual, situation, and training. The rise of counter-bias attitudes, rather than the decline of bias, appears to change most during middle childhood.

One common criticism of conventional measures is that children may mask their true attitudes in order to appear socially desirable. This criticism is based on the notion that older children in particular know that prejudice is undesirable and so make unprejudiced evaluations to obtain approval from the experimenter. Several studies have attempted to rule out this explanation (Aboud & Doyle, 1996a; Aboud & Fenwick, 1999). The studies have found that responses to the Children's Social Desirability Scale do not correlate with prejudice. They have also found that while social desirability concerns should minimize negative evaluations of minorities, it is not these evaluations that change with age; rather negative evaluations of Whites and positive evaluations of minorities increase. In addition, children verbalize evaluations in line with their prejudice test scores when talking with peers. Finally, when children are asked to report on their friends' prejudice, a method that should reduce social desirability concerns, low-prejudice children do not demonstrate a self–friend discrepancy. High-prejudice children do show a slight discrepancy, reporting higher prejudice for their friend than for themselves, though they report high prejudice for both.

Another criticism is that children are forced to evaluate categories of stimulus persons (Carrington & Short, 1993), in that they are given the evaluative descriptors and only one "representative" of the category. In answer to this criticism, researchers have used spontaneous open-ended formats, with unresolved problems. One is to simply ask children how they feel about familiar or unfamiliar pictured children from different groups (Holmes, 1995; Lerner & Schroeder, 1975; Ramsey, 1991). Questions include: What do you think this person is like? Is it good or bad to be a person like this? Why? Who would you like/not like to have as a friend (and why)? Would you like to be this person (and why)? The more unstructured questions fail to elicit many comments from young children, those elicited are generally neutral in tone, and reasons are not explicitly racial. The same children who spontaneously described mostly neutral descriptors also assigned over 70% of positive attributes to Whites and negative attributes to Blacks (Lerner & Schroeder, 1975). Does this imply that structured evaluative questions make children appear prejudiced when in fact they are not? A more likely explanation is that spontaneous descriptions reflect a lack of verbal sophistication and cognitive access to the racial basis of judgments.

In summary, this outline of the measures points to their various strengths and limitations in the hope that researchers will converge on a common set of measures for the construct of prejudice. Consensus on measures has the advantage of producing data that can be compared directly – data that are valid in addressing the theoretical questions of how and why children develop intergroup bias.

2 Documenting the Development of Prejudice, Ethnic Categorization, and Intergroup Peer Relations

In this section, we document the evidence for the development of intergroup bias by answering the following three questions:

1. At what age do children acquire prejudice and how does this change with age in majority White children and minority children?
2. At what age do children begin to form ethnic categories and use them to organize information about people, and how does this change with age?
3. What is the nature of intergroup peer relations?

Ethnic attitudes of majority and minority children

Because the development of attitudes differs greatly according to the ethnic status of the child, each group will be described separately.

Majority children. Regardless of the measure used, White children as young as 3 years show a bias in favor of Whites and prejudice toward minorities. This bias at first increases with age, reaching very high levels between 5 and 6 years (Bigler & Liben, 1993; Clark, Hocevar, & Dembo, 1980; Fox & Jordan, 1973; Johnson, 1992; Katz & Kofkin, 1997; Yee & Brown, 1992). However, numerous studies have shown that by age 7, over half of White children begin to show a significant decrease in prejudice (Bigler & Liben, 1993; Black-Gutman & Hickson, 1996; Clark et al., 1980; Doyle & Aboud, 1995). In many children, this decrease continues until age 12 and beyond (Kalin, 1979). This literature has been reviewed extensively elsewhere (Aboud, 1988; Brown, 1995).

Minority children. Children from Black, Hispanic, Native Indian, and Asian groups also begin to develop ethnic attitudes as young as 3 years of age. An earlier review of studies (Aboud, 1988) found a great deal of variability in the ethnic evaluations of Black children between 5 and 7 years: 6 samples were in the pro-Black range, 10 in the pro-White range, and 16 had means in the unbiased range for both Black and White stimuli (where perhaps some children were pro-Black, some pro-White, and others unbiased). One longitudinal study, following children from 6 months to 5 years, found that although Black children were pro-Black or unbiased at 3 years, 37% were pro-White by age 5; that is, 20% of the children had shifted from the pro-Black to the pro-White position during this period (Katz & Kofkin, 1997). Others have found that children are more pro-Black when asked for their personal preferences, yet more pro-White when assigning rewards for accomplishments (Banks & Rompff, 1973). Family background may also account for some of this variability. Bagley and Young (1998) found that while most 5- to 6-year-old Black children of Caribbean descent had a pro-White (and anti-Black) bias, most Black children of recent African descent had no bias. However, parental attitudes did not always explain these differences (Branch & Newcombe, 1986), and neither did attending an integrated or segregated school (Fox & Jordan, 1973; Stephan, 1999). Research on Mexican-American and Asian children showed similar heterogeneity at this young age (e.g., Bernal, Knight, Ocampo, Garza, & Cota, 1993; Fox & Jordan, 1973; Milner, 1973; Morland & Hwang, 1981), though Native Indian children were largely pro-White (e.g., Corenblum & Annis, 1993).

By the time minority children are between 7 and 10 years old, any pro-White bias seems to have disappeared, and they either no longer exhibit any clear bias or express pro-ingroup bias (Aboud & Doyle, 1995; Averhart & Bigler, 1997; Bernal et al., 1993; Corenblum & Annis, 1993; Davey, 1983; Katz, Sohn, & Zalk, 1975; Kelly & Duckitt, 1995; Semaj, 1980; Williams & Morland, 1976). In general, most studies did not reveal any gender difference in ethnic attitudes (see Aboud, 1988). However, there was evidence that some minority girls felt more pro-White than did minority boys (Fox & Jordan, 1973; Marsh, 1970).

What are we to make of this early variability in minority children's attitudes? Some have interpreted White preference as self-hatred. However, group- and self-esteem are not correlated – Black children with a negative evaluation of their ethnic group simultaneously show high self-esteem (Rosenberg & Simmons, 1972; Verkuyten, 1994).

Others have suggested that minority children are confused about their group identity. This is not supported by the evidence. Two measures of ethnic identification have been used: selecting a label to describe oneself (label matching), and selecting the doll or person one most looks like (perceptual matching). Minority children express ethnic self-identification at an earlier age when the question is direct, as with the use of an ethnic label or a specific question about skin color, than when it is based on an ambiguous question about global appearance (e.g., Bernal et al., 1993; Greenwald & Oppenheim, 1968; Katz & Kofkin, 1997; Ramsey & Myers, 1990; Vaughan, 1987). Children who know their ingroup label may still say they are most similar to an outgroup stimulus. Clearly they may look most like an outgroup member in all respects but ethnicity. However, minority children are less likely spontaneously to use ethnic labels to describe themselves than White children, and perhaps do not feel clearly identified as simply and solely members of one ethnic group. Their position in a largely White society is bicultural in that they are members of both their ethnic community and the White society (Cross, 1987; Phinney & Devich-Navarro, 1997).

The greater variability in minority children's attitudes points to the need for a multivariate explanation of the acquisition and development of ethnic attitudes. While majority children receive consistent information from their environment to help them form ethnic categories, preferences, and identification, minority children receive variable information. Not surprisingly, their preferences and identifications reflect this variability. An analogy to language acquisition may be instructive here. Children exposed to two languages may use words from both languages in the same sentence until they sort out the distinctions between the two language systems.

Ethnic categorization

Although forming ethnic categories of people and identifying with a category does not in and of itself imply prejudice, these can be the first steps that pave the way to differential evaluation of ingroups and outgroups (see a review of the adult research by Brewer & Brown, 1998). Moreover, categories foster perceived outgroup homogeneity, which is more directly linked with prejudice. In contrast, the actual content of ethnic categories, known as stereotypes, is very fragmentary in childhood (Bar-Tal, 1996; Ramsey, 1991). In this section we ask: At what age do children become aware of ethnic groups and treat them as undifferentiated categories distinct from one another?

Measures of matching, sorting, identifying and comparing allow the child to use perceptual, cognitive, or verbal labels to categorize. The use of perceptual/cognitive criteria appears at an earlier age (Katz & Kofkin, 1997; Ramsey & Myers, 1990; Vaughan, 1987; Williams & Morland, 1976) than verbal labels (Bar-Tal, 1996; Bernal et al., 1993; Corenblum & Annis, 1993; Greenwald & Oppenheim, 1968; Gregor & McPherson, 1966), though it is not always clear what criteria are being used when children sort or match by appearance. While verbally labeled categories develop somewhat later than perceptually based ones, children reach ceiling levels of accuracy in their labels relatively early. Minority and majority children progress through this sequence at roughly the same ages.

While young children's dichotomous sorting and verbal labeling indicate the early development of ethnic awareness, a more serious aspect of categorization is the over-use of ethnic categories to mask individual features. This is demonstrated with measures that highlight a fixation on ethnic classification over multiple classification. For example, children have been asked to sort pictures of people into as many groups as they like, based on whatever criteria are salient to them ("Make groups of children who go together or who are similar"). In some studies, race was a particularly salient cue for sorting, more salient than gender or age (e.g., Davey, 1983; Ramsey, 1991), whereas in others race was less salient (Bennett, Dewberry, & Yeeles, 1991; Bigler & Liben, 1993; Hirschfeld, 1996; Verkuyten, Masson, & Elffers, 1995). When children were asked to reclassify pictures they had already sorted based on one dimension, for example, race, they found this difficult at 4 and 5 years, but generally were able to resort at 6 or 7 years (Bigler & Liben, 1993). More difficult was the simultaneous multiple classification task which requires that the child use two criteria such as race and gender to classify people.

Rise of the homogeneity effect – the mistaken perception that all Black people are the same and all White people are the same – has been demonstrated directly by asking children to rate the similarity of pairs of stimuli or verbally describe what is similar and different. Children aged 4 and 5 often rate same-race stimuli as different, thus indicating attention to individual differences as much as ethnic differences. At 5 and 6 years, their perception of individual differences declines in favor of ethnic differences, an indication of the homogeneity effect. Between 5 and 12 years, there are great differences between children in the degree to which they perceive outgroup homogeneity, which in turn is associated with prejudice (Davey, 1983; Doyle & Aboud, 1995; Katz et al., 1975).

In summary, children become aware of ethnicity at a young age and begin to use it to form categories of people at 4 or 5 years. Once formed, these categories, which may initially be based on perceptual or verbal cues, eventually become elaborated in content through the acquisition of knowledge about an ethnic group (e.g., Bernal et al., 1993). Although at first this knowledge may be organized in a simplistic structure, accentuating homogeneity within ethnic groups, later in middle childhood it can become more elaborated in structure, thus allowing children to differentiate within ethnic groups (e.g., Bar-Tal, 1996; Schofield, 1982) and to use multiple cross-cutting categories (Verkuyten et al., 1995). Homogeneity and the inability to use multiple categories are associated with higher prejudice.

Intergroup peer relations

Voluntary contact with peers and the development of stable relationships is the most important index of intergroup behavior among children. This is obviously best studied in schools or neighborhoods where children from different ethnic groups are available as potential friends or acquaintances. Typically, voluntary contact has been equally high in a classroom setting with same- and cross-race peers, but outside the classroom, relationships with same-race peers were more common (e.g., Finkelstein & Haskins, 1983; Schofield, 1982). Age was also an important variable in that White children in particular had fewer cross-race friends with age (DuBois & Hirsch, 1990; Hallinan & Teixeira, 1987; Shrum, Cheek, & Hunter, 1988). Most studies do not report the number of children who have close cross-race friends, but when they do, the percentages appear to be less than 50% during pre- and early adolescence (Aboud & Mendelson, 1999; DuBois & Hirsch, 1990; Graham & Cohen, 1997). Although studies generally report gender effects, there has been no consistent finding that girls or boys have more cross-race friends.

Black, Hispanic, and Asian students have generally, but not always, reported more cross-race friends than White students (Clark & Ayers, 1988; Davey, 1983; Denscombe, Szulc, Patrick, & Wood, 1986; Hallinan & Teixeira, 1987; Howes & Wu, 1990). Overall, Blacks nominated more classmates as friends and therefore made more unreciprocated nominations; they also tended to spend more time in and out of school with their friends. Living in the same neighborhood as one's cross-race school friends made an important difference to Black children by increasing contact and closeness; those in integrated neighborhoods also reported having many cross-race friends outside school (DuBois & Hirsch, 1990). Responses of Black adults to a national U.S. survey revealed that 57% had had at least one White friend in their youth, and those who had such a friend were more likely to have trusting attitudes toward Whites and social/work relations with Whites (Ellison & Powers, 1994).

How are we to account for the decline in cross-race friendships during pre- and early adolescence when there is no evidence for increasing prejudice at this age? There is also little evidence that cross-race friendships lack an important quality of same-race friendships (Aboud & Mendelson, 1999). Hallinan and Kubitschek (1990) have examined the possibility that cross-race triads of friends are fragile and may dissolve if the three do not feel equally positive toward each other. A second explanation focuses on the way preadolescents prepare to date (Schofield, 1982). Social factors related to peer approval need to be examined more closely to determine how they contribute to self-segregation in group settings, and extend to dyadic friend relations. Because of the obvious benefits to social and work relations, research is currently focusing on conditions that improve the number, stability, and quality of cross-race friendships, with a view to reducing the self-segregation that takes place in group and dyadic settings.

3　Explanatory Frameworks: How the Theories Stack Up

Several theories have been formulated over the years to explain the development of prejudice. The most commonly held theory of prejudice is that it is learned from parents (Allport, 1954). Most lay people, educators, and psychologists explain the ethnic conflicts and name-calling of young children in this manner. "If children are not born prejudiced, then they must have learned it from their parents" is the logic employed. The alternative cognitive-developmental theory proposes that cognitive maturation leads children at a young age to construct and evaluate categories from available information, and that subsequent maturation leads children to differentiation within these categories (Aboud, 1988; Katz, 1976; Piaget & Weil, 1951). Individual differences in the way children use these categories (Levy & Dweck, in press) may explain why some children maintain prejudice into adolescence. We now describe the theories and the evidence pertaining to them.

Social influences

Based on Allport's (1954) theory, research has examined whether influences from parents, peers, cultural background, media, and school programs have an impact on the attitudes children develop. Although naturally occurring social events do not seem to show a strong, direct impact, specifically designed interventions have a more profound effect.

Parent socialization. Direct and indirect teaching by parents is the mechanism used to explain how children are socialized to adopt prejudiced attitudes. Allport (1954) described several forms of learning that might take place beyond the age of 4 to change children from being "normally interested, curious, and appreciative of differences in racial groups" (p. 289) to being prejudiced. According to Allport, the labels and associated emotions expressed by parents are imitated by children, initially independent of the referent, in order to gain parental approval. Later with exposure to outgroup members, the labels and emotions become attached to the referent. In adolescence, these emotions become integrated with the person's personality.

　Before examining the evidence for how children learn ethnic attitudes, we might question whether imitation is a feasible mechanism and whether the desire to gain parental approval is a likely motive. Evidence from Kuczynski, Zahn-Waxler, and Radke-Yarrow (1987) for spontaneous imitations in family settings supports the claim that young children imitate emotional expressions and specific behaviors, and that parents are imitated more than peers or television characters. However, in this study, emotions were more commonly imitated in the second year of life and their frequency declined with age. Furthermore, with age these imitated emotions took on a more contrived quality, dissociated from the child's internal state. By 3 years of age, the emotions of peers, and the task-oriented behaviors of parents were more likely to be imitated. Because children do not imitate most of the words, emotions, and behaviors they observe in their parents, we are forced to ask, why ethnic attitudes? The need for parental approval may underlie children's eagerness to learn task behaviors, but not their acquisition of language, gender preferences, or social categorization (Lytton & Romney, 1991). Ethnic categories may be constructed by children in the preschool years, because they are motivated to organize their social world and so use whatever information allows them to create simple rules. Children in the middle childhood years, who are capable of forming more complex categories, would be expected to seek and use information to elaborate and differentiate their categories.

The simplest way to demonstrate parental influence on the acquisition of prejudice is to correlate the attitudes of parents and children. Some studies have found a small correlation (Carlson & Iovini, 1985; Mosher & Scodel, 1960). Others found no significant relationship between White parents and their children (Aboud & Doyle, 1996b; Davey, 1983) or Black parents and their children (Branch & Newcombe, 1986). Children of 10 years could not accurately predict the attitudes of their parents or best friends, but their own attitudes correlated significantly with what they thought were others' attitudes (Aboud & Doyle, 1996b; Epstein & Komorita, 1966). Children generally seem to perceive in others levels of prejudice comparable to their own, either because they egocentrically distort others' attitudes or because they have little real evidence on which to base judgments to the contrary.

Most children receive very little information about race or ethnicity from their parents. Kofkin, Katz, and Downey (1995) reported that only 26% of White parents of 3-year-old children had ever commented on race, usually for the purpose of teaching their children about equality and appreciating differences, or merely to answer their children's questions. The correlation between parent and child attitudes was .33 in families where race had been discussed, and nonsignificant in families where race had not been discussed. This suggests that children are influenced by their parents' attitudes only when parents explicitly talk about their views. Typically it is in regions where ethnic conflict is high that parents explicitly and emotionally express their attitudes (e.g., Bar-Tal, 1996; Duckitt, 1988), leading to the one-sided conclusion that high prejudice in children comes from parents. However, parents are just as likely to be responsible for lowering the levels of prejudice in their children.

Socio-cultural influences. Minority group children may be more exposed to parental talk and teaching about their own cultural background and social discrimination. A number of recent studies have examined how Black and Mexican-American parents influence their children. For example, in the Kofkin et al. (1995) study, Black parents were much more likely than White parents to discuss race with their 3-year-olds (54%), reportedly to protect their children from, or prepare them for, experiences of discrimination. However, there was no relation between Black parents' talk of race and their child's attitudes (see also Branch & Newcombe, 1986). This changes with age, because as children mature their parents may discuss race in terms of civil rights (Spencer & Markstrom-Adams, 1990), conveying pride and assertiveness rather than protection. Exposure to sophisticated talk about race may explain differences in ingroup preferences among Black and Mexican-American children older than 7 years who identify with their group (Knight, Bernal, Garza, Cota, & Ocampo, 1993). In contrast with gender socialization, which appears to decline with age during childhood, minority ethnic socialization may increase as parents detect their children's receptivity to the more complex aspects of ethnic group membership. Likewise, it is thought that minority children derive important ideas about minority group identity from watching television programs, which to date have not provided the kinds of models that parents find desirable (Graves, 1993).

Finally, there is ample evidence that historical and cultural differences exist in prejudice, not only in the targets of prejudice but in the prevalence of prejudice. These can only be explained in terms of society- or culture-wide influences on children. In the past, it was common for children to overhear racial slurs and racial jokes in adult company. This would provide them with labels and attributes, made memorable by the emotions expressed in the context, and it would also signal that such opinions gained approval from others. Currently, immigration patterns (e.g., Black-Gutman & Hickson, 1996), violent conflicts (Rouhana & Bar-Tal, 1998), and affirmative action programs (Pratkanis & Turner, 1996) may be discussed fearfully and angrily by parents, allowing children to learn labels and their associated emotions. With greater understanding of the threatening aspects of ethnic conflict, adolescents in some cultures show a return to high levels of prejudice (Black-Gutman & Hickson, 1996) while others follow a linear decline (Bar-Tal, 1996).

In some cultures and for some children, the labels and perceptual cues are complex and subtle. Australian children, for example, do not easily create consistent categories and evaluations for people from Southeast Asia (e.g., Robinson, 1998). Likewise, minority children in heterogeneous societies may be exposed to variable and inconsistent information about race because they have models and peers from different races. They may identify with different people regardless of race and so create categories that are not dichotomous or race-based.

Experimental intervention studies. The lack of a consistent relation between the attitudes of children and their parents or peers may result from the lack of direct expression of attitudes. Conditions could be created to study social influence by asking parent and child, or two children, to discuss their attitudes. Aboud and Doyle (1996a) paired high-prejudice children with a low-prejudice friend to talk about their racial evaluations. Both made comments in line with their initial levels of prejudice; but when tested afterwards, only high-prejudice children were influenced to adopt more tolerant attitudes, in direct relation to the comments made by their friend. Unbiased children, in contrast, did not adopt their friend's prejudiced attitudes. The inference is that when talk about race is directed to the specific concerns and justifications of the high-prejudice child, it will have a beneficial influence. The results of this and other studies on coordinated discussions between children suggest that social influence takes place not solely because of imitation, dominance, conformity, need for approval, or compromise on some middle ground. Rather the process is one of gradually constructing a perspective of reality by repeating each other's phrases and evaluating them. It appears that children must be somewhat active in the process, because when they passively listen to vignettes that are inconsistent with their race or gender stereotypes and evaluations, the information is disregarded or distorted (e.g., Bigler & Liben, 1993). Respect for the person who provides an opposing view and personal engagement, rather than simply counter-stereotype information, may be necessary to change children's attitudes (Madge, 1976; Moe, Nacoste, & Insko, 1981).

Research has also examined how children learn social categories from contextual cues and whether they automatically translate category differences into evaluations. In a classroom experiment of category formation, Bigler, Jones, and Lobliner (1999, in press) had children wear yellow or blue T-shirts. Only when teachers imposed extra meaning on the T-shirts, by using their colors to organize children and their activities, did children use the categories to make evaluations. Specifically, they applied positive evaluations to more students of their color group and negative evaluations to fewer of their group than did control children whose teachers did not make use of color groupings. The conclusion here is that simple exposure to groupings and belonging to one of them does not promote categorical evaluation unless an adult makes use of the categories. This conclusion appears inconsistent with results from the minimal group paradigm used by Tajfel and colleagues (1978; Turner, 1982), where simply assigning a person to a category resulted in their allocating rewards to maximize the superiority of the ingroup. There are at least two reasons why minimal group findings are not always consistent with real-group findings. One is that allocating rewards, especially between only two groups, arouses a competitive spirit and a desire to demonstrate that "we" are the best (Harstone & Augoustinos, 1995). A second is that because the social categories existed in a vacuum, norms about fairness and information about individuals were absent. Results tend to be more extreme in analogue studies, where complex information is unavailable, than in natural settings (Aboud, 1992; Jetten, 1997; Kawakami & Dion, 1993, 1995).

Integrated schooling and cooperative learning groups are types of intervention, though less controlled than the previously described ones (see Schofield & Eurich-Fulcer, this volume, chapter 23). Though increased contact of this nature has not significantly altered students' attitudes toward ethnic outgroups as a whole (e.g., Weigel, Wiser, & Cook, 1975), work and social relations appear to benefit from such school programs.

In summary, while children do learn through imitation and approval to acquire the categories and evaluations of significant others, the process depends on many conditions. It takes place more frequently when children are young, and when parents or teachers explicitly express their emotions and values. Older children have access to a variety of inputs from their school and peers and are better able to integrate information into a differentiated stereotype of others. They are also cognitively equipped to evaluate both tolerant and biased perspectives and may be more influenced by tolerant attitudes or by attitudes that are consistent with their self-identity. Changes taking place within the child, due to cognitive development, determine which social inputs will be influential.

Cognitive developmental theory

Piaget's theory proposed that children develop preferences for groups with which they identify (Piaget & Weil, 1951). According to Piaget, preoperational children are egocentric and unaware of national or ethnic groups, basing their preferences on individual characteristics of stimulus persons. When children enter the concrete operational stage at 7 years, they begin to categorize people into ethnic groups and to exaggerate differences; they then map contrasting evaluations onto these categories in line with personal and family preferences. At first glance, these age changes seem to fit the data on minority children's attitudes, while majority children use race-based categories earlier. Finally, Piaget expected children over 11 years to justify prejudice with the concept of reciprocity, translated as "outgroups dislike us as much as we dislike them." However, many of his Swiss interviewees expressed a more mature form of reciprocity known as reconciliation. Reconciliation is expressed as "their ingroup preference is as valid as my ingroup preference," a view more likely to be associated with tolerance and respect.

Katz (1976) elaborated on this framework by suggesting eight stages in the development of prejudice. Initially, from 3 to 5 years of age, children observe differences, learn labels and evaluations from others, and begin to add instances of members who fit the label and the evaluations. After 5 years, children elaborate on their categories, in terms of seeing racial cues as a constant feature of people, accumulating more perceptual and cognitive cues to accentuate differences between groups and homogeneity within the racial categories. Finally, prejudice becomes crystallized, bringing together the perceptual, cognitive, and attitudinal components. Aboud (1988) further distinguished between prejudice in the early preschool years when affective reactions dominate a child's response, and in the later years when cognitive processes such as self-identity serve as guides for ingroup preference, and reconciliation along with flexibility promote more balanced evaluations.

Cognitive correlational studies. Certain propositions from these theories, concerning age changes and perceptual-cognitive correlates of prejudice, have been confirmed or modified by subsequent research. Evidence is strong that prejudice is present in many White children at 5 years, reaches a peak between 5 and 7, and then declines in some but not all children (see references given previously). This has two implications for research on the cognitive-developmental bases of prejudice. One is that we ought to be looking for preoperational processes involved in the acquisition of prejudice, and concrete operational processes involved in its decline. The second is that simple correlations among prejudice, age, and cognitive processes will be masked to the extent that the sample includes children on both sides of the peak.

The origins of prejudice appear to lie in the early formation of ethnic categories, their use for self-identification, and the way they are used to exaggerate distinctions between groups and homogeneity within (Bigler & Liben, 1993; Katz & Kofkin, 1997). In addition to categorical thinking, there are a number of other perceptual and cognitive processes in preoperational children that could potentially be instrumental in the acquisition of prejudice, including egocentrism and the assumption that race is an immutable biological category (Hirschfeld, 1996). However, more research is necessary to identify which processes directly initiate prejudice.

That prejudice appears to increase during the preoperational years of 5 to 7, rather than after 7 years as proposed by Piaget, is not surprising. As in the acquisition of language, children are cognitively motivated to make sense of their social world by deriving simple rules. The phenomenal success they show in discovering patterns of language attests to both their ability and their motivation. Where regularities exist in a social milieu with respect to defining and distinguishing ethnic groups, children will create categories and sometimes over-use them. Where regularities do not exist, as in the ethnically mixed world of minority children or the Switzerland of Piaget, they may not form or use ethnically based categories, but instead rely on other regularities such as gender or occupation. The latter may acquire bipolar ethnic attitudes after 7 years, following the Piagetian framework, with stronger input from concrete operational skills such as reciprocity.

Finally attitudes do seem to become more consistent with self-identification and behavior in the middle childhood years, though they do not necessarily become crystallized and unchangeable. Several concrete operational capabilities, namely conservation, reconciliation, multiple classifications, perceived similarity of groups, and attention to individual differences within groups, are influential in breaking down the over-use of exaggerated, homogeneous categories and reducing prejudice (Bigler & Liben, 1993; Black-Gutman & Hickson, 1996; Clark et al., 1980; Doyle & Aboud, 1995; Katz & Zalk, 1978). Because many children who have these concrete operational skills persist in holding biased attitudes, other approaches are needed to explain individual differences. Levy and Dweck (1999) have characterized these children as lay entity theorists who assume that others' traits and abilities are unchangeable. Children who hold such views about human nature tend to perceive groups as more homogeneous than children who assume that human nature is more changeable. Thus, general schemata about the stability of personality may be related to the persistence of bias.

Cognitive developmental theory lacks a clear explanation of why, in the process of acquiring attitudes, children attach positive evaluations to one group and negative to others. The socialization explanation, namely that evaluations are learned from the family, is not supported by low parent–child correlations. Alternative sources of evaluation may arise from the child's own emotional development, in areas such as self-esteem and attachment to others. Thus, one cognitive developmental explanation focuses on a connection between self-esteem and ethnic self-identification; once children form ethnic categories, they identify with one, and generalize their own self-worth – which is unrealistically high in the preoperational years – to that group. Another source of evaluation is the child's own emotional attachments to family, teachers and friends. These attachments may generalize to unfamiliar but similar people whether or not they are consistent with the child's ethnic identity. So even though minority children know their ethnic group, their attachments to majority teachers and peers might form the basis of their ethnic evaluations. A different explanation, based on egocentrism or sociocentrism, is needed to explain the devaluation of outgroups. As children distinguish between ethnic categories, outgroup members are perceived as different, inferred to have different preferences and different ways of life, and so judged as wrong (Aboud, 1981).

Social identity theory (Tajfel, 1978; Turner, 1982) proposes another explanation for the positive evaluations given by some minority children to Whites rather than to their ingroup. As we saw, this may happen around age 5. They suggest that once ethnic categories are formed, children begin to identify themselves with one and try to gain positive self-worth through group belonging. If through social comparison one's group is perceived to be devalued, one will identify with the outgroup to gain worth. Many of these assumptions do not hold for 5-year-olds. First, although present, ethnic self-identity is not a salient component of self at this age, and therefore unlikely to be used as a basis for self-worth. Secondly, children rarely seek evaluative information for between-group comparisons (Aboud, 1976), and do not translate comparisons into self-evaluations until the age of 8 or 9 (Ruble & Goodnow, 1998). Thus, although the target group's status may influence evaluations, it is not clear that self-enhancement rather than self-consistency is the motive underlying attitudes, or that the theory explains ethnic attitudes of children as young as 5 years. It seems more parsimonious to suggest, as we did in the previous paragraph, that young children generalize their self-esteem or their personal attachments to whomever they perceive as similar.

There may be two ways of viewing age and group status differences in intergroup attitudes. If children's attitudes reflect the societal status hierarchy, then we need to ask: Why do preoperational children, regardless of their group, prefer the high status group? and why is concrete operational thought necessary (but not sufficient) for children, regardless of their group, to see the value of minority or lower status groups? If children's attitudes are tied to ethnic self-identification, then we would ask: Why is preoperational thought sufficient for majority children to derive ingroup identification and preference? and why is concrete operational thought necessary for minority children to understand the importance of race-based categories for self-identification and preference?

Intervention experimental studies. Because category formation and outgroup homogeneity appear at a young age, researchers have not attempted to train these skills in order to observe their role in the formation of prejudice. However, a number of cognitive approaches have been used in schools to reduce prejudice. The common one is to provide knowledge about the cultural ways of minority groups. This is unrelated to cognitive developmental theory in that it makes no reference to age-related cognitive structures, but rather to the idea that prejudice is based on ignorance. Typically these studies find no consistent effect of information on reducing prejudice (Pate, 1988; Furuto & Furuto, 1983). In fact, the presentation of information about typical cultural patterns, simplified for young schoolchildren, runs the risk of contributing to group stereotypes. Even if the goal is to instill a positive stereotype, say about the eating habits of Chinese people, it is quite inappropriate to teach children that Chinese Americans use chopsticks, when many of them do not.

More successful are role-playing programs, where students re-examine their attitudes after experiencing powerlessness or discrimination in a simulation game (McGregor, 1993). Another cognitive approach, called antiracist teaching, seeks to reduce prejudice by discussing the social/historical inequalities that underlie racism and discrimination. Role-playing and antiracist teaching, however, are limited in scope and application. First, they are rarely used with elementary schoolchildren because they require a certain amount of social and emotional sophistication. Secondly, they may unintentionally portray minority members as helpless victims, rather than as potentially respectable friends. Thirdly, they are directed to a White audience only, and the material is often inappropriate for non-White ethnic group members. Fourthly, they may raise feelings of guilt that young children cope with in unproductive ways, for example, by blaming the victim or denying wrongdoing. Although these programs were developed to fill the need for antibias programs in all-White schools, they are potentially harmful and inappropriate for young and/or non-White students.

Based on the empirical finding that those who perceive less homogeneity within groups are less prejudiced, Katz and Zalk (1978) trained children in one session to learn the individual names of outgroup children. Compared to a control group of children who learned the names of ingroup children, the experimental group showed reduced prejudice. This intervention was also more effective than a mere contact or conditioning intervention. To extend these findings, Aboud and Fenwick (1999) evaluated an 11-week curriculum program which attempted to strengthen the appreciation and use of internal qualities that make for individuality, rather than racial cues. Specific classroom activities required students to continually process, store, and recall individual information. Although racism was not discussed directly, the student book included thirty photographs of students from several ethnic groups, and there was some discussion of the invalid all-or-none assumption underlying ethnic stereotypes. In comparison to control students, those who received the program increased their use of internal descriptors, and initially high-prejudice students became significantly less prejudiced when assessed later. These studies demonstrate the potential for reducing prejudice of programs that address, in a social context, the cognitive processes indirectly associated with prejudice.

Conclusion

In summary, there may be several routes to the acquisition and reduction of prejudice. Children appear to have a predisposition to create ethnic categories around age 4 or 5, and then to use these to infer group distinctions and homogeneity of members within categories. If evaluations from parents are explicit, preoperational children may adopt these evaluations. However, a more likely scenario is that prejudice is acquired when children identify with one ethnic category and generalize their self-esteem to their group, or without a salient identification they generalize from social attachments to similar others. As a function of age and familiarity, children become more flexible in their thinking and more reciprocal in their social relations; this results in fewer distinctions between ethnic groups, more differentiation within groups, better reconciliation of differences, and use of multiple cross-cutting categories. These social-cognitive abilities, developing in the concrete operational stage, appear to contribute to a post-7 year reduction in prejudice. Minority group children differ from White children only in their greater attitude variability pre-7 years. They may not all follow the ingroup preference route to the extent that ingroup identification is not salient or personal attachments are multiethnic. Why some but not all children develop balanced attitudes in middle childhood is not clear, though there may be individual differences in cognitive assumptions about people or the presence of other controlled, as opposed to automatic, processes such as belief in fairness. Research published over the next decade will address questions about social and cognitive inputs to prejudice by designing experimental interventions to prevent early high levels of prejudice and to reduce prejudice and discrimination in school children (see Aboud & Levy, 2000).

References

Aboud, F. E. (1976). Self-evaluation: Information-seeking strategies for interethnic social comparisons. *Journal of Cross-Cultural Psychology, 7*, 289–300.

Aboud, F. E. (1981). Egocentrism, conformity, and agreeing to disagree. *Developmental Psychology, 17*, 791–799.

Aboud, F. E. (1988). *Children and prejudice.* Cambridge, MA: Blackwell.

Aboud, F. E. (1992). Conflict and group relations. In C. U. Shantz & W. W. Hartup (Eds.), *Conflict in child and adolescent development* (pp. 356–379). New York: Cambridge University Press.

Aboud, F. E., & Doyle, A. B. (1995). The development of in-group pride in Black Canadians. *Journal of Cross-Cultural Psychology, 26*, 243–254.

Aboud, F. E., & Doyle, A. B. (1996a). Does talk of race foster prejudice or tolerance in children? *Canadian Journal of Behavioural Science, 28*, 161–170.

Aboud, F. E., & Doyle, A. B. (1996b). Parental and peer influences on children's racial attitudes. *International Journal of Intercultural Relations, 20*, 371–383.

Aboud, F. E., & Fenwick, V. (1999). Exploring and evaluating school-based interventions to reduce prejudice in preadolescents. *Journal of Social Issues, 55*, 767–785.

Aboud, F. E., & Levy, S. R. (2000). Interventions to reduce prejudice and discrimination in children and adolescents. In S. Oskamp (Ed.), *Reducing prejudice and discrimination.* Mahwah, NJ: Erlbaum.

Aboud, F. E., & Mendelson, M. J. (1999). *Do cross-race friendships decline with age in quantity and quality?* Presented at Society for Research in Child Development meetings, 1999.

Allport, G. W. (1954). *The nature of prejudice.* Cambridge, MA: Addison-Wesley.

Averhart, C. J., & Bigler, R. S. (1997). Shades of meaning: Skin tone, racial attitudes, and constructive memory in African-American children. *Journal of Experimental Child Psychology, 67*, 363–388.

Bagley, C., & Young, L. (1998). Evaluation of color and ethnicity in young children in Jamaica, Ghana, England, and Canada. *International Journal of Intercultural Relations, 12*, 45–60.

Banks, W. C., & Rompff, W. J. (1973). Evaluative bias and preference in Black and White children. *Child Development, 44*, 776–783.

Bar-Tal, D. (1996). Development of social categories and stereotyping in early childhood: The case of "the Arab" concept of formation, stereotype, and attitudes by Jewish children in Israel. *International Journal of Intercultural Relations, 20*, 341–370.

Bennett, M., Dewberry, C., & Yeeles, C. (1991). A reassessment of the role of ethnicity in children's social perception. *Journal of Child Psychology & Psychiatry, 32*, 969–982.

Bernal, M. E., Knight, G. P., Ocampo, K. A., Garza, C. A., & Cota, M. K. (1993). Development of Mexican-American identity. In M. E. Bernal & G. P. Knight (Eds.), *Ethnic identity: Formation and transmission among Hispanics and other minorities.* (pp. 31–46). Albany, NY: State University of New York Press.

Bigler, R. S. (in press). When groups are not created equal: Effects of group status on the formation of intergroup attitudes in children. *Child Development.*

Bigler, R. S., Jones, L. C., & Lobliner, D. B. (1997). Social categorization and the formation of intergroup attitudes in children. *Child Development, 68*, 530–543.

Bigler, R. S., & Liben, L. S. (1993). A cognitive-developmental approach to racial stereotyping and reconstructive memory in Euro-American children. *Child Development, 64*, 1507–1518.

Black-Gutman, D., & Hickson, F. (1996). The relationship between racial attitudes and social-cognitive development in children: An Australian study. *Developmental Psychology, 32*, 448–456.

Branch, C. W., & Newcombe, N. (1986). Racial attitude development among young Black children as a function of parental attitudes: A longitudinal and cross-sectional study. *Child Development, 57*, 712–721.

Brand, E. S., Ruiz, R. A., & Padilla, A. M. (1974). Ethnic identification and preference: A review. *Psychological Bulletin, 81*, 860–890.

Brewer, M. B., & Brown, R. J. (1988). Intergroup relations. In D. T. Gilbert, S. T. Fiske, & G. Lindzey (Eds.), *The handbook of social psychology* (Vol. 2, pp. 554–594). New York: McGraw-Hill.

Brown, R. (1995). *Prejudice: its social psychology.* Cambridge, MA: Blackwell.

Carlson, J. M., & Iovini, J. (1985). The transmission of racial attitudes from fathers to sons: A study of Blacks and Whites. *Adolescence, 20*, 233–237.

Carrington, B., & Short, G. (1993). Probing children's prejudice: A consideration of the ethical and methodological issues raised by research and curriculum development. *Educational Studies, 19*, 163–179.

Clark, A., Hocevar, D., & Dembo, M. H. (1980). The role of cognitive development in children's explanations and preferences for skin color. *Developmental Psychology, 16*, 332–339.

Clark, K. B. (1955). *Prejudice and your child.* Boston, MA: Beacon Press.

Clark, M. L., & Ayers, M. (1988). The role of reciprocity and proximity in junior high school friendships. *Journal of Youth and Adolescence, 17*, 403–407.

Corenblum, B., & Annis, R. C. (1993). Development of racial identity in minority and majority children: An affect discrepancy model. *Canadian Journal of Behavioural Science, 25*, 499–521.

Cross, W. E. (1987). Two-factor theory of Black identity: Implications for the study of identity development in minority children. In J. S. Phinney & M. J. Rotheram (Eds.), *Children's ethnic socialization: Pluralism and development* (pp. 117–133). Newbury Park, CA: Sage.

Davey, A. G. (1983). *Learning to be prejudiced: Growing up in multi-ethnic Britain.* London: Edward Arnold.

Denscombe, M., Szulc, H., Patrick, C., & Wood, A. (1986). Ethnicity and friendship: The contrast between sociometric research and fieldwork observation in primary school classrooms. *British Educational Research Journal, 12*, 221–236.

Doyle, A. B., & Aboud, F. E. (1995). A longitudinal study of White children's racial prejudice as a social-cognitive development. *Merrill-Palmer Quarterly, 41*, 209–228.

DuBois, D. L., & Hirsch, B. J. (1990). School and neighborhood friendship patterns of Blacks and Whites in early adolescence. *Child Development, 61*, 524–536.

Duckitt, J. (1988). Normative conformity and racial prejudice in South Africa. *Genetic, Social and General Psychology Monographs, 114*, 413–437.

Ellison, C. G., & Powers, D. A. (1994). The contact hypothesis and racial attitudes among Black Americans. *Social Science Quarterly, 75*, 385–400.

Epstein, R., & Komorita, S. S. (1966). Childhood prejudice as a function of parental ethnocentrism, punitiveness and outgroup characteristics. *Journal of Personality and Social Psychology, 3*, 259–264.

Finkelstein, N. W., & Haskins, R. (1983). Kindergarten children prefer same-color peers. *Child Development, 54*, 502–508.

Fishbein, H. D. (1996). *Peer prejudice and discrimination: Evolutionary, cultural, and developmental dynamics.* Boulder, CO: Westview Press.

Fiske, S. T. (1998). Stereotyping, prejudice, and discrimination. In D. T. Gilbert, S. T. Fiske, & G. Lindzey (Eds.), *The handbook of social psychology*, (Vol. 2, pp. 357–411). New York: McGraw-Hill.

Fox, D. J., & Jordan, V. B. (1973). Racial preference and identification of Black, American Chinese, and White children. *Genetic Psychology Monographs, 88*, 229–286.

Furuto, S. B., & Furuto, D. M. (1983). The effects of affective and cognitive treatment on attitude change toward ethnic minority groups. *International Journal of Intercultural Relations, 7,* 149–165.

Graves, S. B. (1993). Television, the portrayal of African Americans on the development of children's attitudes. In G. L. Berry & J. K. Asamen (Eds.), *Children and television: images in a changing socio-cultural world* (pp. 179–190). Thousand Oaks, CA: Sage.

Greenwald, H. J., & Oppenheim, D. B. (1968). Reported magnitude of self-misidentification among Negro children: Artifact? *Journal of Personality & Social Psychology, 8,* 49–52.

Gregor, A. J., & McPherson, D. A. (1966). Racial preferences and ego-identity among White and Bantu children in the Republic of South Africa. *Genetic Psychology Monographs, 73,* 217–253.

Hallinan, M. T., & Kubitschek, W. N. (1990). Sex and race effects of the response to intransitive sentiment relations. *Social Psychology Quarterly, 53,* 252–263.

Hallinan, M. T., & Teixeira, R. A. (1987). Students' interracial friendships: Individual characteristics, structural effects, and racial differences. *American Journal of Education, 95,* 563–583.

Hartstone, M., & Augoustinos, M. (1995). The minimal group paradigm: Categorization into two versus three groups. *European Journal of Social Psychology, 25,* 179–193.

Hirschfeld, L. A. (1996). *Race in the making: Cognition, culture, and the child's construction of human kinds.* Cambridge, MA: MIT Press.

Holmes, R. M. (1995). *How young children perceive race.* Thousand Oaks, CA: Sage.

Howes, C., & Wu, F. (1990). Peer interactions and friendships in an ethnically diverse school setting. Special Issue: Minority children. *Child Development, 61,* 537–541.

Graham, J. A., & Cohen, R. (1997). Race and sex as factors in children's sociometric ratings and friendship choices. *Social Development, 6,* 355–372.

Jetten, J. (1997). *Dimensions of distinctiveness: Intergroup discrimination and social identity.* Amsterdam: Universiteit van Amsterdam.

Johnson, D. J. (1992). Racial preference and biculturality in biracial preschoolers. *Merrill-Palmer Quarterly, 38,* 233–244.

Kalin, R. (1979). Ethnic and multicultural attitudes among children in a Canadian city. *Canadian Ethnic Studies, 11,* 69–81.

Katz, P. A. (1976). The acquisition of racial attitudes in children. In P. A. Katz (Ed.), *Toward the elimination of racism* (pp. 125–154). New York: Pergamon Press.

Katz, P. A., & Kofkin, J. A. (1997). Race, gender, and young children. In S. S. Luthar, J. A. Burack, D. Cicchetti, & J. Weisz (Eds.), *Developmental psychopathology: Perspectives on adjustment, risk, and disorder* (pp. 51–74) New York, NY: Cambridge University Press.

Katz, P. A., Sohn, M., & Zalk, S. R. (1975). Perceptual concomitants of racial attitudes in urban grade-school children. *Developmental Psychology, 11,* 135–144.

Katz, P. A., & Zalk, S. R. (1978). Modification of children's racial attitudes. *Developmental Psychology, 14,* 447–461.

Kawakami, K., & Dion, K. L. (1993). The impact of salient self-identities on relative deprivation and action intentions. *European Journal of Social Psychology, 23,* 525–540.

Kawakami, K., & Dion, K. L. (1995). Social identity and affect as determinants of collective action: Toward an integration of relative deprivation and social identity theories. *Theory and Psychology, 5,* 551–577.

Kelly, M., & Duckitt, J. (1995). Racial preference and self-esteem in Black South African children. *South African Journal of Psychology, 25,* 217–223.

Knight, G. P., Bernal, M. E., Garza, C. A., Cota, M. K., & Ocampo, K. A. (1993). Family socialization and the ethnic identity of Mexican-American children. *Journal of Cross-Cultural Psychology, 24,* 99–114.

Kofkin, J. A., Katz, P. A., & Downey, E. P. (1995). *Family discourse about race and the development of children's racial attitudes.* Presented at SRCD Indianapolis.

Kuczynski, L., Zahn-Waxler, C., & Radke-Yarrow, M. (1987). Development and content of imitation in the second and third years of life: A socialization perspective. *Developmental Psychology, 23,* 276–282.

Lerner, R. M., & Schroeder, C. (1975). Racial attitudes in young White children: A methodological analysis. *Journal of Genetic Psychology, 127,* 3–12.

Levy, S. R., & Dweck, C. S. (1999). The impact of children's static vs. dynamic conceptions of people on stereotype formation. *Child Development.*

Lytton, H., & Romney, D. M. (1991). Parents' differential socialization of boys and girls: A meta-analysis. *Psychological Bulletin, 109,* 267–296.

Madge, N. J. (1976). Context and the expressed ethnic preferences of infant school children. *Journal of Child Psychology & Psychiatry & Allied Disciplines, 17,* 337–344.

Marsh, A. (1970). Awareness of racial differences in West African and British children. *Race, 11,* 289–302.

McGregor, J. (1993). Effectiveness of role-playing and antiracist teaching in reducing student prejudice. *Journal of Educational Research, 86,* 215–226.

Milner, D. (1973). Racial identification and preference in Black British children. *European Journal of Social Psychology, 3,* 281–295.

Moe, J. L., Nacoste, R. W., & Insko, C. A. (1981). Belief versus race as determinants of discrimination: A study of southern adolescents in 1966 and 1979. *Journal of Personality & Social Psychology, 41,* 1031–1050.

Morland, J. K., & Hwang, C. H. (1981). Racial/ethnic identity of preschool children: Comparing Taiwan, Hong Kong and the United States. *Journal of Cross-Cultural Psychology, 12,* 409–424.

Mosher, D. L., & Scodel, A. (1960). Relationships between ethnocentrism in children and the ethnocentrism and authoritarian rearing practice of their mothers. *Child Development, 31,* 369–376.

Patchen, M. (1982). *Black-White contact in schools: Its social and academic effects.* West Lafayette, IN: Purdue University Press.

Pate, G. S. (1988). Research on reducing prejudice. *Social Education, 52,* 287–289.

Phinney, J. S., & Devich-Navarro, M. (1997). Variations in bicultural identification among African-American and Mexican-American adolescents. *Journal of Research on Adolescence, 7,* 3–32.

Piaget, J., & Weil, A. M. (1951). The development in children of the idea of the homeland and of relations to other countries. *International Social Science Journal, 3,* 561–578.

Powlishta, K. K., Serbin, L. A., Doyle, A. B., & White, D. R. (1994). Gender, ethnic and body type biases: The generality of prejudice in childhood. *Developmental Psychology, 30,* 526–536.

Pratkanis, A. R., & Turner, M. E. (1996). The proactive removal of discriminatory barriers: Affirmative action as effective help. *Journal of Social Issues, 52,* 111–132.

Ramsey, P. G. (1991). The salience of race in young children growing up in an all-White community. *Journal of Educational Psychology, 83,* 28–34.

Ramsey, P. G., & Myers, L. C. (1990). Salience of race in young children's cognitive, affective, and behavioral responses to social environments. *Journal of Applied Developmental Psychology, 11,* 49–67.

Robinson, J. A. (1998). The impact of race and ethnicity on children's peer relations. In K. Rigby & P. Slee (Eds.), *Children's peer relations.* London: Routledge.

Rosenberg, M., and Simmons, R. G. (1972). *Black and White self-esteem; the urban school child.* Washington: American Sociological Association.

Rouhana, N. N., and Bar-Tal, D. (1998). Psychological dynamics of intractable ethnonational conflicts: The Israeli–Palestinian case. *American Psychologist, 53,* 761–770.

Ruble, D. N., & Goodnow, J. J. (1998). Social development in childhood and adulthood. In D. T. Gilbert, S. T. Fiske, & G. Lindzey (Eds.), *The handbook of social psychology*, (Vol. I, pp. 741–787). New York: McGraw-Hill.

Schofield, J. W. (1982). *Black and White in school: trust, tension or tolerance?* New York: Praeger.

Semaj, L. (1980). The development of racial evaluation and preference: A cognitive approach. *Journal of Black Psychology, 6*, 59–79.

Shrum, W., Cheek, N. H., & Hunter, S. M. (1988). Friendship in school: Gender and racial homophily. *Sociology of Education, 61*, 227–239.

Spencer, M. B., & Markstrom-Adams, C. (1990). Identity processes among racial and ethnic minority children in America. *Child Development, 61*, 290–310.

Stephan, W. G. (1999). *Improving intergroup relations in the schools.* New York: Columbia Teachers College.

Tajfel, H. (1978). Social categorization, social identity, and social comparison. In H. Tajfel (Ed.), *Differentiation between social groups* (pp. 61–98). New York: Academic Press.

Turner, J. C. (1982). Towards a cognitive redefinition of the social group. In H. Tajfel (Ed.), *Social identity and intergroup relations* (pp. 15–40). Cambridge, MA: Cambridge University Press.

Vaughan, G. M. (1987). A social psychological model of ethnic identity development. In J. S. Phinney & M. J. Rotheram (Eds.), *Children's ethnic socialization: pluralism and development* (pp. 73–91). Beverly Hills, CA: Sage.

Verkuyten, M. (1994). Self-esteem among ethnic minority youth in Western countries. *Social Indicators Research, 32*, 21–47.

Verkuyten, M., Masson, K., & Elffers, H. (1995). Racial categorization and preferences among older children in the Netherlands. *European Journal of Social Psychology, 25*, 637–656.

Weigel, R. H., Wiser, P. L., & Cook, S. W. (1975). The impact of cooperative learning experiences on cross-ethnic relations and attitudes. *Journal of Social Issues, 31*, 219–244.

Williams, J. E., Best, D. L., & Boswell, D. A. (1975). The measurement of children's racial attitudes in the early school years. *Child Development, 46*, 494–500.

Williams, J. E., & Morland, J. K. (1976). *Race, color, and the young child.* Chapel Hill, NC: University of North Carolina Press.

Yee, M. D., & Brown, R. (1992). Self-evaluations and intergroup attitudes in children aged three to nine. *Child Development, 63*, 619–629.

PART II

Motivation

CHAPTER FIVE

Social Orientations in the Minimal Group Paradigm

Richard Y. Bourhis and André Gagnon

> Whereas prejudice is an attitude, discrimination is a selectively unjustified negative behaviour towards members of target groups.
>
> (Dovidio & Gaertner, 1986, p. 3)

Discriminatory behavior can range from the avoidance of outgroup members, antilocution, differential allocation of resources, physical attack (hate crimes), ethnic cleansing, and genocide (Allport, 1954). Many of the early social psychological explanations of discrimination focused on intrapersonal processes such as authoritarianism and frustration-aggression as key individual factors accounting for such dissociative behaviors (Adorno, Frenkel-Brunswick, Levinson, & Sanford, 1950; Billig, 1976; Taylor & Moghaddam, 1994). However, it was the situational approach of Sherif, Harvey, White, Hood, and Sherif (1961) stressing the functional nature of intergroup relations that provided a more societal framework for the study of prejudice and discrimination. Sherif et al. (1961) showed how competition over scarce resources could lead to discrimination while cooperative interdependence was related to more favorable attitudes and behaviors toward outgroups.

Though Sherif's realistic conflict theory (RCT) received much empirical support in the literature, results from Tajfel's minimal group paradigm (MGP) experiments showed that conflicting group interests was not a necessary condition for intergroup discrimination. In the now classic minimal group studies, Tajfel and colleagues sought to uncover

This chapter was made possible thanks to a grant awarded to the first author by the Social Sciences and Research Council (SSHRC) of Canada. Comments or suggestions concerning this chapter would be much appreciated and should be addressed to Richard Y. Bourhis, Départment de psychologie, Université du Québec à Montréal, C. P. 8888, Succ. Centre Ville, Montréal, Québec, Canada, H3C 3P8.

the necessary and sufficient conditions fostering intergroup discrimination (Tajfel, Flament, Billig, & Bundy, 1971). In the minimal group paradigm (MGP), participants were randomly categorized as members of either one of two arbitrary groups (e.g., group K, group W) specifically created for the purpose of the experiment (Rabbie & Horwitz, 1969). Factors known to contribute to discriminatory behavior were systematically eliminated from the MGP, namely objective conflict of interest, intergroup contact, intragroup friendships and loyalties, self-interest, a history of intergroup rivalry, and any ideological context legitimizing the disparagement of outgroup members relative to ingroup members. Despite these minimal intergroup circumstances, results showed that the mere categorization of subjects as "us and them" was sufficient to trigger intergroup discrimination (Tajfel et al., 1971). During the last three decades a large number of studies have corroborated the link between social categorization, ingroup identification, and intergroup discrimination (see reviews by Brewer, 1979; Brewer & Brown, 1998; Deaux, 1996; Diehl, 1990; Ellemers, Spears, & Doosje, 1999; Hogg & Abrams, 1988; Messick & Mackie, 1989; Rubin & Hewstone, 1998; Tajfel, 1978; Turner & Bourhis, 1996).

Social identity theory (SIT) proposes that this minimal group discrimination effect reflects competition for a positive social identity (Tajfel & Turner, 1979, 1986). The arbitrarily imposed "us–them" categorization provides subjects with the cognitive structure on which to base their social identities. Individuals' desire for a positive social identity is achieved by seeking favorable comparisons between the ingroup and the outgroup on the only available dimension of comparison in the MGP experiment, namely the distribution of more resources to members of the ingroup than the outgroup (e.g., money, symbolic points). Discrimination on such measures allows individuals to establish the "differentiation" they need to establish a positive social identity relative to the outgroup.

A number of laboratory studies have supported this SIT account of discrimination (Lemyre & Smith, 1985). Though early studies showed a weak correlation between degree of ingroup identification and discriminatory behavior (Hinkle & Brown, 1990), more recent laboratory and field studies have documented the link between ingroup identification, discrimination, and evaluative bias in favor of the ingroup (Jetten, Spears, & Manstead, 1999; Rubin & Hewstone, 1998; Wann & Branscombe, 1995). For instance, in their MGP study, Gagnon and Bourhis (1996) showed that individuals who identified strongly with their ad hoc ingroup discriminated while those who weakly identified did not discriminate at all but instead only used parity in their allocations of resources to ingroup and outgroup others. In other MGP studies, Perreault and Bourhis (1998, 1999) showed that the more participants identified with their own group *prior* to engaging in the resource distribution task (money), the more they discriminated. Also, compared to ingroup identification measured *prior* to discrimination, participants identified more *after* they had discriminated, suggesting that the act of discrimination can also contribute to stronger identification with the ingroup, which in turn may lead to even more discrimination. Results also showed that group members felt more happy, satisfied, confident, and liked being members of their own group more *after* they had discriminated than *before*. In line with SIT, these before–after "quality of social identity" measures provide causal evidence that people can discriminate in order to achieve a more positive social identity (Rubin & Hewstone, 1998; Tajfel & Turner, 1979).

The focus of this chapter is both methodological and conceptual. The first section of the chapter provides a brief methodological account of how and why the Tajfel matrices were first developed as a dependent variable used to monitor resource allocations within the minimal group paradigm (MGP). The second part of the chapter discusses what we consider fundamental allocation strategies adopted by group members to distribute resources between ingroup and outgroup members within laboratory and field situations. Using social identity theory (SIT) as a conceptual backdrop, the third part of the chapter provides a critical analysis of social psychological and sociostructural processes recently proposed to account for intergroup behaviors such as parity and discrimination.

1 The Minimal Group Paradigm and the Tajfel Matrices

Within minimal group paradigm (MGP) studies, group members make decisions about the distribution of valued resources such as money or points to anonymous ingroup and outgroup individuals. The distribution of such resources is usually made using allocation options known as the "Tajfel Matrices" (Tajfel et al., 1971). These matrices are used to assess how much group members are "tempted" by contrasting orientations such as parity (P), ingroup favoritism (FAV), maximum differentiation (MD), and maximum joint profit (MJP).

The first matrices used by Tajfel et al. (1971) opposed the strategy of ingroup favoritism (FAV = MIP + MD) against the more economically rational strategy of maximum joint profit (MJP; pull of FAV on MJP; pull of MJP on FAV). Note that ingroup favoritism (FAV) is a combination of two strategies: maximum ingroup profit (MIP) and maximum differentiation (MD). Another matrix is designed to pit maximum differentiation (MD) against a combination of maximum ingroup profit (MIP) and maximum joint profit (MJP; pull of MD on MIP + MJP; pull of MIP + MJP on MD). In this case, respondents choosing the MD option do so at the cost of sacrificing absolute ingroup gain (MIP and MJP) for the sake of achieving a maximum differentiation between the ingroup and outgroup outcome, this difference being in favor of the ingroup. In another matrix, Billig and Tajfel (1973) pitted the parity (P) option (equal number of points to each group) against ingroup favoritism (pull of P on FAV; pull of FAV on P).

By comparing each allocation response on these classic matrices, distinct "pull scores" were derived which represented the relative strengths of the different distribution strategies adopted by group members. Note that within each matrix, the option to choose the parity (P) response was ALWAYS available. The advantage of using the Tajfel matrices lies in the fact that one can measure the strength of different types of discrimination strategies (MD, FAV on P, FAV on MJP) independently of more socially desirable strategies such as parity (P) and maximum joint profit (MJP). Methodological, statistical, and scaling issues related to the use of the Tajfel matrices were discussed by Brown, Tajfel, and Turner (1980) while Bourhis, Sachdev, and Gagnon (1994) provided a step-by-step guide to construct and calculate "pull scores" from the Tajfel matrices.

Both theory and data suggest that social orientations measured using "pull scores" based on the Tajfel matrices do provide a "convenient and representative description of the actual distribution strategies" employed by group members in laboratory and field intergroup situations (Brown et al., 1980, p. 409). Post-experimental questionnaires have been used in various MGP studies to verify the congruence between participants' self-reported and actual use of the distribution strategies measured by the Tajfel matrices. For instance, we conducted correlations between actual use of distribution strategies on the Tajfel matrices and self-reports obtained in post-session questionnaire items for the following MGP studies: Gagnon and Bourhis (1996) $n = 116$; Gagnon and Bourhis (1997) $n = 470$; Rabbie, Schot, and Visser (1989) $n = 131$; and Sachdev and Bourhis (1985) $n = 200$. For computation purposes correlations were weighted as a function of the number of respondents in each study. Combining the above studies, results showed positive and significant correlations between actual use of distribution strategies and the allocation motives expressed by subjects in the questionnaires for parity: P on FAV: $r = .44$; and for the three discrimination strategies: FAV on MJP: $r = .51$; FAV on P: $r = .46$; MD on MIP + MJP: $r = .46$. However, correlations between actual allocations and reported use were not significant for maximum joint profit: MJP on FAV: $r = .08$ and the MIP + MJP on MD strategy: $r = .07$. Thus group members correctly report their use of key strategies such as parity and discrimination while they tend to systematically overestimate their use of the maximum joint profit (MJP) relative to the virtual absence of this strategy in actual use.

The Tajfel matrices have been adapted successfully for use in various laboratory and field settings. The Tajfel matrices have been modified to measure: performance evaluations (Sachdev & Bourhis, 1987); real-life salary increases and salary cuts (Bourhis & Hill, 1982); teachers' allocation of financial resources to rival labor federations (Bourhis, Gagnon, & Cole, 1997); the distribution of punishments such as obnoxious noise and unpleasant tasks (Otten, Mummendey, & Blanz, 1996); the allocation of additional course credits for participation in experiments (Bourhis, 1994a) and the allocation of sweets by children using three-column matrices presented as dominoes (Vaughan, Tajfel, & Williams, 1981). The diversity of these measures shows that the Tajfel matrices can be adapted to suit the valued resources of contrasting group members in different types of intergroup laboratory and field settings.

The classic minimal group discrimination effect is a robust phenomenon which can be monitored using evaluative and resource allocation measures other than the Tajfel matrices. As Brown et al. (1980) stated ". . . the minimal group paradigm is defined solely in terms of the independent variable, social categorization per se. It is not defined by dependent variables or response techniques and strategies" (p. 400). Resource allocation measures other than the Tajfel matrices have included the distribution of a fixed sum of money (or points) between ingroup and outgroup members using a "zero-sum" allocation rule (Ng, 1981; Perreault & Bourhis, 1999) and the "free-choice" distribution of up to 100 points to ingroup members and of up to another 100 points to outgroup members (Locksley, Oritz, & Hepburn, 1980). Binary choice matrices have been used by Brewer and Silver (1978) while multiple alternative matrices (MAM) were proposed by Bornstein, Crum, Wittenbraker, Harring, Insko, & Thibaut (1983a,b). Researchers using the Tajfel matrices also proposed that discrimination could be measured more simply by using a "difference score" between points given to ingroup members over those assigned to outgroup members (rather than the more complicated "pull scores"; Diehl, 1990; Platow, Harley, Hunter, Hanning, Shave, & O'Connel, 1997).

The above measurement alternatives tend to provide parity and discrimination options which are not as diversified and subtle as the strategies monitored using "pull scores" based on the Tajfel matrices. For instance, measures of ingroup favoritism using "difference scores" calculated from ingroup/outgroup allocations (free choice, zero sum, Tajfel matrices) cannot distinguish orientations such as maximum ingroup profit (MIP) and maximum differentiation (MD). Furthermore, such "difference scores" do not reveal whether ingroup favoritism was achieved at the cost of maximum ingroup profit (MIP) or maximum joint profit (MJP). Moreover, "difference scores" cannot distinguish when an equal distribution of resources between ingroup and outgroup members (ingroup − outgroup = zero) actually reveals a systematic strategy of parity (P) or the use of maximum joint profit (MJP) or minimum joint benefit (MJB).

Perhaps because of the initial lack of clear information on how to construct and score the Tajfel matrices, the measures were the focus of a methodological and conceptual debate in the 1980s. For instance, one debate centered on whether group members used mainly "pure" allocation strategies (Bornstein et al., 1983a,b) or were instead tempted by a combinations of both single strategies and compromises between alternative allocation strategies (Turner, 1983a,b). For Bornstein et al. (1983a), "the basic assumption of the multiple alternative matrices (MAM) is an outcome maximization assumption . . . that the preferred orientation will have a relatively high frequency of choice, and the remaining alternatives will have low or approximately equal frequencies of choice" (pp. 370–371). Using the MAM, group members were instructed to choose a single allocation option out of those presented in each matrix. The allocation orientations offered as choices on each matrix always included the following options: Parity (P), ingroup favoritism (MIP, MD), maximum joint profit (MJPi, MJPo), and outgroup favoritism (OF). Matrices offering these same options were presented numerous times to the respondents, each matrix differing simply by the actual numbers portraying each orientation. For instance, the same parity option could be presented across five different matrices as: 34/34, 35/35, 36/36, 37/37, and 38/38. Repeated presentation of the matrices allowed respondents to consistently choose the same allocation orientation on each matrix or to choose different allocation options from one matrix to the other. Results obtained with MAM measures showed that only 22% to 49% of respondents limited their allocations choice to a unique distribution orientation (Bornstein et al., 1983a, table 8, p. 338). These results showed that the majority of respondents either had difficulty opting for only one strategy at a time, or preferred to compromise between pure orientations, a mode of resource distribution more in line with the premises of the Tajfel matrices. The latter assume that the measurement of resource allocations is similar to the measurement of attitudes representing continuous variables which on each Tajfel matrix can include combinations of ingroup favoritism, parity, outgroup favoritism, and maximum joint profit (Turner, 1983a). Results obtained with the Tajfel matrices demonstrate that group members do prefer to compromise between such orientations while they rarely opt for unique orientations across sets of matrices.

Though not all issues of the debate have been settled, it remains that much empirical evidence suggests that the Tajfel matrices do monitor subjects' social orientations in a valid, reliable, and sensitive manner (Brewer, 1979; Diehl, 1990; Messick & Mackie, 1989; Rabbie et al., 1989; Turner, 1980, 1983a,b). Consequently, and as noted by

Messick and Mackie (1989), it remains fruitful to devote attention to the conceptual and economic underpinnings of the Tajfel matrices, a theme which is the focus of the second part of this chapter.

2   Fundamental Orientations in Resource Allocations

A total of 13 "pure" allocation orientations can be measured using the Tajfel matrices. It is by considering the pattern of results obtained across the six "pull scores" that one can identify which of the 13 distinctive orientations are adopted by group members in their allocation of resources to ingroup and outgroup members (Bourhis et al., 1994). As mentioned earlier, actual results obtained with the Tajfel matrices usually show that group members choose resource allocations which represent compromises between these "pure" strategies depending on the type of intergroup situation they happen to be in. For instance, group members may have a general tendency to discriminate against a disparaged outgroup but on occasion will show some parity towards this same outgroup depending on the immediate intergroup situation, the importance of the comparison dimension, ingroup identification, and personal mood state (Forgas & Fiedler, 1996).

As can be seen in Figure 5.1, the 13 allocation orientations measured using the Tajfel matrices can be situated on a two-dimensional space with point allocations to ingroup members situated on the X axis and point allocations made to outgroup members situated on the Y axis. This two-dimensional view of ingroup/outgroup allocation is based on earlier two-dimensional depictions of how *individuals* distribute resources to themselves versus others (Liebrand & Dehue, 1996).

For the purpose of our discussion and based on the classic Tajfel matrices used in the literature (Bourhis et al., 1994; Bourhis, Gagnon, & Sachder, 1997), the number of points that can be awarded to either ingroup or outgroup members ranges from a minimum of 36 to a maximum of 132 "points". The range of allocation orientations that can be situated within this two-dimensional space is extensive and Figure 5.1 can be used to compare ingroup/outgroup allocations made on a broad range of measures other than the Tajfel matrices including binary-choice matrices, free-choice, zero-sum, and multiple-alternative matrices (MAM). The basic allocation strategies are situated within the four quadrants of Figure 5.1 with parity being situated at the center of the figure. Clockwise, the four quadrants reflect the basic allocation orientations of: ingroup favoritism; maximum joint profit; outgroup favoritism; and minimum joint benefit. The 13 "pure" allocation strategies situated within each of these quadrants can now be discussed.

Fairness or more precisely parity (P) consists of a choice which awards EQUAL numbers of points to ingroup and outgroup members on each of the six classic Tajfel matrices usually offered to respondents. As can be seen in Figure 5.1 the parity strategy is situated at the intersection of the X and Y axis and corresponds to an allocation of 84 points to both ingroup and outgroup members. Note that the term "parity" is more precise than the term "fairness" because parity clearly refers to the numerically equal distribution of points to ingroup and outgroup members. The term fairness is less adequate because group members may distribute points unequally between ingroup and outgroup

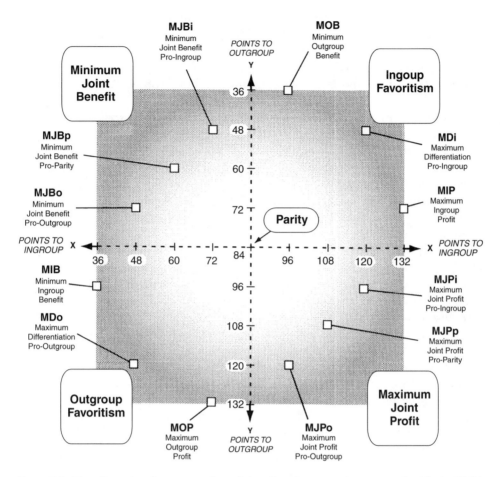

Figure 5.1. Two-dimensional representation of the allocation strategies measured with the Tajfel matrices.

members while rationalizing that this distribution is only "fair" given the "superiority" of one group over the other. Psychologically, parity is a fundamental allocation orientation in the distribution of resources to ingroup and outgroup members and is expressed most clearly at the center of Figure 5.1. Parity was shown to be a strong orientation in most laboratory and field studies using the Tajfel matrices in the last three decades.

As can be seen in Figure 5.1, the *ingroup favoritism* quadrant includes three types of discrimination orientations: minimal outgroup benefit (MOB); maximum differentiation (MD); and maximum ingroup profit (MIP). *Maximum ingroup profit* (MIP) is a strategy which awards the highest ABSOLUTE number of points to ingroup members (132/132; 100%) regardless of awards made to outgroup members (72/132; 55%). Cognitively, MIP is the simplest and most common discrimination strategy, measured not only with the

Tajfel matrices but also with other types of allocation measures such as zero-sum distributions and multiple-allocation matrices (MAM). Affectively, maximum ingroup profit (MIP) represents a type of discrimination which arises from "the positive consequences of ingroup formation: enhanced favoritism toward ingroup members without any change in affect toward those who do not share the group identity" (Brewer & Brown, 1998, p. 559).

Maximum differentiation (MD) is a discrimination strategy "par excellence" and refers to a choice that maximizes the DIFFERENCE in points awarded to ingroup and outgroup recipients, the difference being in favor of the ingroup member but at the cost of sacrificing maximum ingroup profit (MIP). The maximum differentiation (MD) strategy is not economically rational though it offers the greatest possible "differentiation" outcome between ingroup and outgroup fate. As seen in Figure 5.1, the MD strategy does maximize the difference between ingroup and outgroup fate ($120 - 48 = 72$) but at the cost of gaining less ingroup profit (91% of the potential) and less total joint profit from the experimenter (78% of the potential). In contrast, the maximum ingroup profit (MIP) strategy saturates ingroup profit ($132 = 100\%$) while providing less differentiation between ingroup and outgroup fate ($132 - 72 = 60$). Maximum differentiation is a discrimination strategy which is "the product of intergroup social competition: the attainment of a relative advantage by the ingroup over the outgroup" (Brewer & Brown, 1998, p. 559). The MD strategy has been well documented in MGP studies using the Tajfel matrices and is usually associated with ingroup identification and differentiation processes as proposed within SIT (Perreault & Bourhis, 1998, 1999).

Is the MD strategy only obtained in studies using the Tajfel matrices or can the orientation also be found in real-life settings? Maximum differentiation at the cost of optimal ingroup profit can be documented in the long-standing language conflict between the English and French communities in Canada. In the 1988–89 period, over 70 medium to small English municipalities in Ontario adopted English-only laws denying French minority citizens the possibility of obtaining selected municipal services in the French language. The English majority town councilors who adopted these anti-French laws did so at the cost of sacrificing full funding by the Ontario provincial government for the provision of French language services including the payment of bilingual civil servant salaries and costs associated with the publication of bilingual municipal documents and flyers. At the cost of improving the range of services offered to its citizens with provincially paid civil servants and gaining national prominence as bigoted anti-French towns, these English majority municipalities asserted their distinctiveness as unilingual English towns in a province where only 5% of the population are French mother tongue and do not constitute a threat to the dominant majority status of English.

Minimal outgroup benefit (MOB) is a discrimination strategy which focuses on allocating as few resources as possible to the outgroup (36/132; 27% of the potential) without being too concerned by the amount of resources awarded to ingroup members (96/132; 73% of the potential). MOB is a vindictive discrimination strategy as it seeks to deny outgroup members as many valued resources as possible within the intergroup situation. MOB is a strategy which "reflects the negative consequences of outgroup differentiation: enhanced derogation, hostility, and distrust of groups that are different from oneself" (Brewer & Brown, 1998, p. 559). As such the MOB strategy is perhaps a behavioral outcome of "hot prejudices" which are usually based on negative and hostile attitudes toward disparaged outgroups (Fiske, 1998). Historical examples of dominant groups adopting measures akin to the MOB strategy come to mind in the case of institutional discrimination such as the Nuremberg laws of Nazi Germany (1933–45) and the apartheid laws of South Africa up to the early 1990s. These cases of institutional discrimination share in common denying disparaged minorities access to positively valued resources such as employment and promotion, access to state services, and denial of democratic rights such as voting and equal representation in government and private institutions.

The MOB strategy is the most dissociative allocation strategy measured with the Tajfel matrices. This is so not only when positive resources are allocated (e.g., money, promotions) but also in cases when negative outcome allocations are distributed such as unpleasant tasks, burdens, and punishments. The Tajfel matrices have been successfully adapted to monitor the full range of allocation strategies with negative outcome allocations (Otten et al., 1996). For instance the MOB strategy with negative outcomes would consist of distributing the maximum burdens and physical punishments possible to outgroup members.

Field situations characterized by long-standing and intense intergroup conflict (e.g., civil war, ethnic strife) are most likely to be associated with the use of MOB strategies. Individual differences related to authoritarianism, social dominance, and ethnocentrism have also been invoked to account for group members who adopt MOB strategies toward scapegoat and pariah minorities in settings involving both institutional and social discrimination (Allport, 1954; Altemeyer, 1998; Sidanius & Pratto, 1999). So far not enough attention has been devoted to the social psychology of group members who adopt the MOB strategy within laboratory and field settings.

The *maximum joint profit (MJP)* quadrant represents choices that maximize the total COMBINED number of points to BOTH ingroup and outgroup recipients. The Tajfel matrices distinguish between three types of MJP strategies, namely one that slightly favors the ingroup *(MJPi)*, one that focuses on parity oriented allocations *(MJPp)*, and another that slightly favors outgroup members *(MJPo)*. As shown in Bourhis et al. (1994), these three MJP orientations maximize the total number of points possible for ingroup and outgroup members *combined* and as such they are economically more rational than the classic parity (P) strategy which results in a joint profit of only 78% of the possible maximum joint outcome (84 + 84 = 168/264). The three MJP orientations shown in Figure 5.1 represent economically rational strategies to the ultimate disadvantage of implicitly third party others such as the experimenter in laboratory studies, the government or the employer, some third-party outgroup in multiple group situations. Most MGP studies using the Tajfel matrices have shown that the MJP strategies are seldom used by group members while self-reports of the use of MJP strategies usually overestimate the use of this orientation. More studies should explore the intergroup circumstances likely to increase the use of the MJP strategies in both laboratory and field settings (Bourhis & Hill, 1982; Bourhis et al., 1997).

The Tajfel matrices also allow the measurement of what is known as *outgroup favoritism (OF)* strategies which consist of allocating more points to outgroup members than to ingroup members. As can be seen in Figure 5.1, the outgroup favoritism quadrant consists of three variations of the OF strategy, these are namely maximum outgroup profit (MOP), maximum differentiation in favor of the outgroup (MDo), and minimum benefit for the ingroup (MIB). The *maximum outgroup profit (MOP)* strategy focuses on allocating the maximum possible resources to outgroup members (132 = 100%) regardless of the number of points allocated to ingroup members (72/132 = 55%). Outgroup favoritism can also be reflected in a strategy for maximizing differentials between ingroup and outgroup allocations, but this time in favor of the outgroup *(MDo)*. The *minimum ingroup benefit (MIB)* is an outgroup favoritism strategy focusing on allocating as few valued resources to the ingroup as possible (36/132 = 27%) regardless of how many points are allocated to outgroup members (96/132 = 73%). As can be seen in Figure 5.1, the outgroup favoritism (OF) orientations are least economically rational from the point of view of ingroup members relative to the maximum joint profit, the ingroup favoritism, and the parity orientations.

Group members who have internalized the low status ascription imposed on them by dominant high status outgroups are likely to adopt outgroup favoritism allocations especially on dimensions of comparison related to their status inferiority (Sachdev & Bourhis, 1987). More research is needed to understand under what circumstances group members are likely to use maximum differentiation in favor of the outgroup rather than maximum outgroup profit or minimum ingroup benefit.

As seen in Figure 5.1, the *minimum joint benefit (MJB)* quadrant represents choices that minimize the total combined number of valued resources to both ingroup and outgroup recipients. The Tajfel matrices can distinguish between three types of minimum joint benefit (MJB) strategies, namely MJB that slightly favors the ingroup (MJBi), MJB that focuses on parity oriented allocations (MJBp) and MJB that slightly favors outgroup members (MJBo). The MJB orientations are economically irrational strategies because they minimize the number of resources obtained for both ingroup and outgroup members to the benefit of an implicitly third party in the intergroup situation, the experimenter in laboratory studies, or some third-party group in multigroup relation situations.

The descriptions of the above strategies demonstrate the internal validity of the Tajfel matrices which can be used as a subtle tool for monitoring a broad range of resource distribution strategies adopted by group members in different intergroup situations (Bourhis et al., 1994). In the final section of the chapter we will review some of the social psychological and sociostructural factors which have been found to affect how group members use the resource allocation strategies depicted in Figure 5.1. This third section will close with a discussion of current alternative explanations of the minimal group discrimination effect.

3.1   Psychological and Sociostructural Correlates of Allocation Strategies

One important goal of the intergroup relation research has been to uncover the social psychological mechanisms most likely to foster harmonious and egalitarian relations between social groups. What structural and social psychological conditions are most likely to encourage group members to choose resource allocation strategies that are parity oriented rather than discriminatory? Figures 5.2A–E provide three-dimensional depictions of the five major allocation orientations already described in Figure 5.1. In the name of justice and equity, the implicit goal of most efforts to reduce discrimination is the eventual adoption by group members of the parity strategy in the distribution of valued resources to ingroup and outgroup members. This desired outcome is depicted in the "resource allocation landscape" in which parity is the only strongly endorsed strategy (largest volume) in Figure 5.2A. Note that the absence of the other four types of strategies is depicted by the flat surfaces in the quadrants surrounding the parity strategy.

The strong parity response presented in Figure 5.2A is also the allocation outcome that Henri Tajfel and colleagues expected in their classic minimal group paradigm study (MGP) (Tajfel et al., 1971). By excluding from the intergroup situation known factors contributing to discrimination other than the "us–them" categorization, the MGP was designed to foster the parity response depicted in Figure 5.2A. With parity established as the baseline condition of the MGP, the next step of the research program was to add "one-by-one" intergroup bias producing factors such as objective conflict of interest, intragroup loyalties, historical rivalries between the groups, threat to ingroup identity and group distinctiveness, self-interest, and ideologies legitimizing the glorification of the ingroup and the disparagement of outgroups (Turner, 1996). In their distinctive ways, each of these "aggravating factors" was expected to shift the allocation strategies from mainly parity responses to the various permutations of ingroup favoritism responses presented in Figure 5.1 (MIP; MD, MOB).

Of course, what in fact happened in the classic MGP was that the "us–them" categorization was sufficient to trigger intergroup discrimination of the kind depicted in Figure 5.2B. To the degree that individuals do identify with their assigned group within MGP studies, resource allocations using the Tajfel matrices show that group members both discriminate and are parity oriented toward outgroup members. MGP studies show that parity is usually somewhat stronger than ingroup favoritism strategies such as MIP and MD. This trend is depicted in Figure 5.2B by the greater volume obtained for the parity orientation than for the ingroup favoritism strategies. Thus, within laboratory studies using the classic MGP, group members deciding on how to distribute positive resources between contrasting groups are concerned with reaching a *compromise* between systematically favoring members of their own group (MIP, MD) and sharing resources equally between ingroup and outgroup members (parity). The fact that maximum differentiation (MD) is obtained in most classic MGP studies supports the SIT explanation that the desire to positively differentiate from the outgroup (social competition) is involved in the minimal group discrimination effect. However, the most extreme form of social competition against outgroups depicted in Figure 5.1, namely minimum outgroup benefit (MOB) has not been observed or explored in studies using the MGP.

As in some real-life intergroup situations, outright discrimination without the moderating effect of parity (see Figure 5.2C) was obtained in a MGP study exploring the impact of sociostructural variables on the resource distribution strategies of undergraduates in Ontario (Sachdev & Bourhis, 1991). Using the MGP, students were randomly

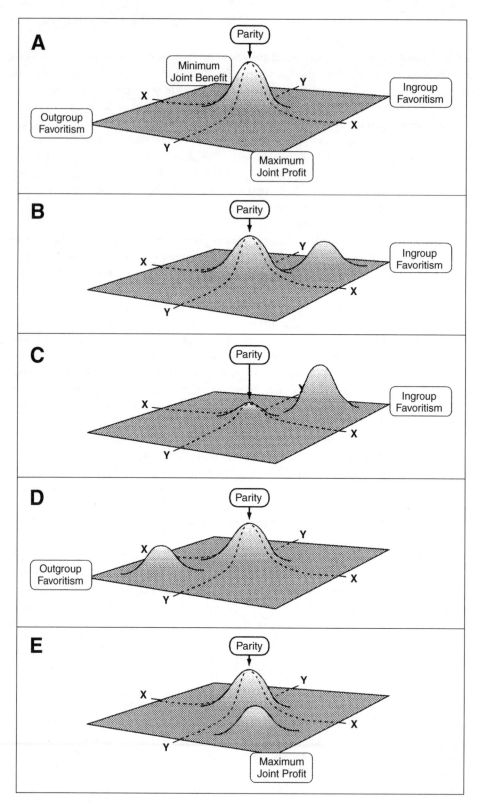

Figure 5.2. Three-dimensional representations of social orientations in the intergroup distribution of resources.

assigned to groups which varied in power, status, and group numbers and were asked to make decisions concerning the distribution of valued resources to anonymous ingroup and outgroup others. Results showed that dominant group members were much more discriminatory (MIP, MD) and less parity (P) oriented toward outgroup members than were subordinate group members. High status group members were more discriminatory (MIP, MD) and less parity oriented than members of low status groups. More importantly for our current concern, results showed that dominant high status minority group members were exceptional in engaging in discriminatory behavior (MIP, MD) without moderating this strategy with any parity whatsoever. It is as though this dominant elite could not afford the "noblesse oblige" of granting any parity toward the subordinate low status outgroup whose strength in numbers as a majority nevertheless had the potential of threatening the hegemony of the dominant elite. In line with SIT (Tajfel, 1978), one could expect that high status dominant groups could be even more likely to discriminate without the moderating effect of parity in circumstances where the power and status differential between the groups was challenged as being illegitimate and unstable by subordinate majorities thus making dominant groups less secure in their social identity. Classic factors such as realistic conflict of interest with the outgroup (Sherif et al., 1961), perceived threat from the outgroup (Stephan, Ybarra, Martinez, Schwarzwald, & Tur-Kaspa, 1998), prejudicial and disparaging attitudes against the outgroup (Dovidio, Brigham, Johnson, & Gaertner, 1996), social dominance orientation (SDO, Sidanius & Pratto, 1999), and "submissive" right-wing authoritarianism (Altemeyer, 1998) are likely, singly or in combination, to foster the type of clear-cut discrimination depicted in Figure 5.2C.

The clearest case of the combined parity and outgroup favoritism strategies depicted in Figure 5.2D was also obtained by Sachdev and Bourhis (1991). In this MGP study it was undergraduates assigned to the subordinate, low status minority group position who not only were quite parity oriented (P) but also gave more resources to members of the outgroup than to members of their own group (−MD and −MIP; outgroup favoritism). Though moderated by parity, why did subordinated low status minorities deny resources to members of their own group and instead favor members of the dominant high status minority? Implicitly, this outgroup favoritism acknowledged the superior status of the minority elite on the pertinent and legitimated dimension of comparison established by the experimenter acting as an authority figure.

Outgroup favoritism responses in both evaluative and resource allocations have been observed in the field among subordinated low status minorities who have internalized their inferiority on specific comparison dimensions within stable stratified societies. For instance in the Canadian setting, the classic "matched guise" studies conducted in Montreal during the 1960s showed that Quebec francophones not only evaluated French speakers of their own group less favorably than English stimulus speakers but also provided ratings of their own group which were even more negative than those provided by English Quebecers who themselves had also rated French speakers less favorably than English speakers of their own group (Bourhis, 1994b).

Though *maximum joint profit (MJP)* is a more economically rational allocation strategy than parity, results of classic MGP studies rarely obtain the combination of parity (P) and maximum joint profit (MJP) responses depicted in Figure 5.2E. One exception stands out and this is a study in which three types of intergroup power relations were established between ad hoc groups: an absolute power group (100% power) faced with a powerless outgroup (0% power); a high power group (70% power) faced with a low power group (30% power); and two equal power groups (50%–50%) as in classic MGP studies (Sachdev & Bourhis, 1985). Results showed that participants in dominant group position (100% and 70% power) used their power advantage to discriminate against subordinated outgroups (FAV on P, FAV on MJP, MD) while also being parity oriented. Participants in the equal power position engaged in both parity and discrimination in their allocations, thus replicating the classic MGP effect. Even group members who were subordinate but had some power (30%) did use the little power they had to discriminate (MD, FAV on P) against the dominant outgroup while also adopting parity. No-power group members (0%) did not discriminate at all, eliminating the classic MGP effect and confirming that usable power is a necessary condition for effective discrimination (Ng, 1981). However, these no-power group members were exceptional in adopting the most rational combination of strategies in the study: maximum joint profit (MJP) and parity (Figure 5.2E). For powerless group members, MJP and P were the optimal strategies for claiming valued resources within an intergroup situation totally controlled by the dominant outgroup.

The laboratory and field research of the last decades could be portrayed as exploring ways of shifting group members from using mainly the discriminatory strategies depicted in Figures 5.2B and 5.2C to using the parity and joint profit strategies depicted in Figures 5.2A and 5.2E (Brewer & Brown, 1998). Extrapolating from prejudice and ingroup favoritism research, one can identify numerous factors likely to shift resource allocations from the discrimination to the parity and joint profit orientations. Measures likely to reduce ingroup bias are the following: intergroup cooperation to reach superordinate goals or avoid superordinate threats (Sherif et al., 1961); the establishment of social norms favoring fairness rather than ingroup favoritism (Jetten, Spears, & Manstead, 1996); stressing individual merit and equity concerns for intergroup allocations (Ng, 1984; Platow et al., 1997); the fostering of equal status contact between groups (Pettigrew, 1997); the decategorization of group members as individuals rather than as ingroup versus outgroup members (Brewer & Miller, 1984); the recategorization of ingroup and outgroup members into a single superordinate common identity representation (Gaertner, Dovidio, Anastasio, Bachman, & Rust, 1993); cross-cutting categorization and multiple category membership as factors reducing intergroup bias (Vanbeselaere, 1991).

As is well known in the literature, most of these ingroup bias-reducing mechanisms more or less suffer from the problem of generalizability. Their positive impact in reducing prejudice tends to degrade with time especially as group members return to their respective status and power positions within stratified societies. While much is known about how the above motivational and cognitive processes can reduce prejudice, less is known about their impact on reducing actual discriminatory behaviors as measured in resource allocation tasks such as the Tajfel matrices. Our point therefore is that the Tajfel matrices offer a sensitive measure of a wide range of resource allocation strategies which can be especially suitable for assessing the impact of motivationally and cognitively inspired methods of reducing discrimination and promoting intergroup harmony.

3.2   Alternative Explanations of the MGP Discrimination Effect

Alternative explanations

While SIT has become the prevalent intergroup theory used to explain the minimal group discrimination effect, Rabbie and colleagues argued against SIT's explanation of the minimal group effect. According to the behavioral interaction model (BIM) (Rabbie et al., 1989) the minimal group discrimination effect results from mutual interdependence for the achievement of some rewarding outcome related to the satisfaction of individual self-interest. Perceiving that one shares the same fate as other ingroup members within the MGP gives rise to reciprocity expectations from ingroup members. Reciprocity expectations motivate participants to favor the ingroup rather than the outgroup in their resource distributions. Giving more resources to one's ingroup is the best way for individuals to maximize their personal gain because they expect that other ingroup members will do the same for them.

In one experiment specifically designed to test the BIM account of the minimal group discrimination effect, Rabbie et al. (1989) showed that discriminatory behavior did vary as a function of the interdependence structure established between groups within their MGP experiment. Group members who were exclusively dependent on ingroup others discriminated by favoring ingroup recipients over outgroup ones on the Tajfel matrices of MIP and MD. Group members who were totally dependent on outgroup others discriminated in favor of the outgroup, thus reversing the classic minimal group effect. Participants in the control condition whose fate depended *equally* on ingroup and outgroup others (as in the usual MGP), not only used parity and maximum joint profit as expected from the BIM reciprocity hypothesis but also were also quite discriminatory in their use of the FAV and the economically irrational MD strategy. Though these latter results also supported the SIT account of the MGP effect, Rabbie et al. (1989) concluded that self-interest and interdependence of fate rather than social identity processes were at the root of the minimal group discrimination effect.

Conceptual accounts of the rival BIM and SIT explanations of the MGP discrimination effect were provided by Turner and Bourhis (1996) and Bourhis, Turner, and Gagnon (1997). Gagnon and Bourhis (1996) provided an empirical test of the relative merit of the BIM and SIT explanations of the minimal group discrimination effect. The control condition consisted of the usual MGP interdependence situation in which respondents' individual fates depended equally on ingroup and outgroup resource distributions. However, in the positively autonomous condition, participants were secretly told that in their individual case they would receive the maximum number of points possible in the experiment. The aim of this manipulation was to break the link between participants' personal self-interest and the distribution of resources to ingroup and outgroup members. According to the BIM, positively autonomous participants should not discriminate because interdependence on other ingroup members was eliminated by satiating the personal self-gains of individuals who received all the possible points. In contrast, according to SIT, autonomous participants should discriminate as much as interdependent individuals given that group members in both conditions still need to achieve a positive social identity within the intergroup setting. Results failed to support the BIM: autonomous individuals discriminated as much as interdependent participants on matrices such as FAV and MD. When the discriminatory behaviors of strong and weak identifiers were analyzed, results showed that strong identifiers discriminated whereas weak identifiers did not. Results also showed that discrimination contributed to positive social identity only to the degree that participants identified strongly with their own group. Without ingroup identification, discrimination did not contribute to a more positive social identity. In an extension of the above study, Perreault and Bourhis (1998) showed that negatively autonomous participants, that is participants who were secretly told that they would personally receive no money at all in the study, discriminated just as much as both interdependent and positively autonomous participants. In line with Dawes, van de Kragt, and Orbell (1990) these results suggest that ingroup identification can override concerns for personal self-interest. Taken together, these results show that ingroup identification (SIT) is a better explanation of discrimination in the MGP than self-interest and interdependence as postulated within the BIM.

Although the above studies do not support the BIM they do not contradict Sherif et al.'s (1961) realistic conflict theory (RCT) conceptualization of interdependence and its complementarity with SIT (Turner & Bourhis, 1996). To the degree that individuals do identify with their own group, it is clear from Sherif's field studies that cooperative versus competitive group interdependence does have an impact on intergroup discrimination. In the Gagnon and Bourhis (1996) study, interdependence was manipulated at an *individual* level and not at the *collective* level. A manipulation of negative autonomy at the collective level in which group members are denied valued resources by virtue of their group membership could be seen as illegitimate and unjust, thus triggering retaliatory behaviors such as discrimination against an outgroup seen as the cause of this inequity.

Uncertainty reduction

Using self-categorization theory as a conceptual backdrop, Hogg and Mullin (1999) proposed that the need for "uncertainty reduction" may be more fundamental than motivation for a positive social identity (SIT) as an explanation of discrimination in the MGP. The role of subjective "uncertainty reduction" in social identity processes is based on the premise that people have a basic need to feel certain about their social environment and their place within it. While subjective certainty contributes positively to the self by making existence meaningful and guiding behavior, uncertainty is aversive as it reduces mastery over one's environment. It is proposed that individuals are more strongly motivated to reduce uncertainty in situations which are ambiguous than in those which are clear-cut, stable, and predictable.

According to Grieve and Hogg (1999), the classic minimal group paradigm (MGP) situation is high in subjective uncertainty due to the novelty of the ad hoc categorization (group X/Y), the undefined nature of relations between participants, and the "strangeness" of the Tajfel matrices as a resource allocation task. They propose that participants within classic MGP conditions categorize themselves as members of their ad hoc ingroup mainly to reduce "subjective uncertainty" which in turn guides discriminatory behavior and fosters ingroup identification. To better test their uncertainty reduction hypothesis, Hogg and Mullin (1999) manipulated the ambivalence of the MGP by creating experimental conditions which were less uncertain than the classic MGP situation. In three studies a "low uncertainty" condition was manipulated by giving participants a chance to practice with the Tajfel matrices for allocating points to uncategorized, individually numbered recipients. Across the three studies results showed that categorized subjects in the usual "high uncertainty" MGP conditions did discriminate (composite score of FAV on P; FAV on MJP; MD), thus replicating the classic minimal group effect. However, the MGP effect was eliminated in the "low uncertainty" condition as subjects did not discriminate at all and tended to identify less with their own group than those in the classic "high uncertainty" condition. With the MGP situation clarified in the "low uncertainty" condition, individuals did not need to discriminate or to identify strongly with their ad hoc group as a way of reducing their subjective uncertainty. However, support for the uncertainty hypothesis was undermined by results showing that self-categorization and discrimination did not systematically reduce the pre-post uncertainty felt by participants in the experiments.

Though Hogg and Mullin (1999) did use pre-post measures of uncertainty reduction they only assessed ingroup identification *after* subjects completed the resource allocation task. Given that discrimination can increase both ingroup identification and positive social identity (Perreault & Bourhis, 1998), differential ingroup identification scores used as evidence of uncertainty reduction in the Hogg and Mullin (1999) studies may be the result of both uncertainty effects and the role of discrimination in increasing ingroup identification. Furthermore, the 10-item identification scale used in the three studies combined identification items with quality of social identity items thus confounding the distinctive effects of discrimination on self-categorization (SCT) and on positive–negative social identity (SIT). As Rubin and Hewstone (1998) concluded, confounds within ingroup identification scales have contributed to the complexity of results exploring the link between collective self-esteem (quality of social identity) and discrimination. It is frustration with this very complexity that motivated some researchers to redirect explanations of discrimination from social identity needs (SIT) to uncertainty reduction needs.

It is clear that ongoing research must explore the distinctive and complementary roles of social identity and uncertainty reduction as key motives accounting for discrimination within the MGP. Moreover, within the usual "high uncertainty" condition of the classic MGP, Perreault and Bourhis (1999) did find that ethnocentric individuals were more likely to identify with their ad hoc ingroup (pre-post measures) than less ethnocentric persons (E and F scale measured a week before the MGP study proper). These results suggest that some individuals enter the MGP with a greater concern than others for identifying with their ingroup and/or reducing uncertainty. Path analysis in the Perreault and Bourhis (1999) study also showed that unconfounded ingroup identification measured *prior* to resource allocations acted as a mediator variable predicting discrimination, while high–low ingroup identification manipulated as an independent variable also predicted discrimination. Thus, in line with SIT, identification with the ingroup category is a necessary antecedent condition for intergroup discrimination while unconfounded degree and quality of ingroup identity were each shown to increase following discrimination.

The positive–negative asymmetry effect

It is one thing to favor the ingroup through the distribution of positive allocations such as money, but quite another to discriminate by imposing negative outcomes such as burdens and punishments on outgroup members. In a series of MGP studies, Mummendey and Otten (1998) showed that categorization per se was not sufficient to trigger discriminatory behavior in the distribution of negative outcomes such as tedious tasks or unpleasant sounds. The failure to obtain the "minimal group discrimination effect" on negative outcome allocations poses a challenge to the generality of social identity theory (SIT) as an "explanation" of discrimination in the MGP.

Numerous studies conducted by Mummendey and colleagues have corroborated the "positive–negative asymmetry effect" (PNAE) with both evaluative ratings (on positive versus negative traits) and on resource distributions (e.g., Tajfel matrices) using positive (money) versus negative allocations (unpleasant noise). Why is it that group members do not discriminate on negative outcome allocations in the MGP? Mummendey and Otten (1998) propose two classes of explanations to account for the PNAE within the MGP: the *normative* and the *cognitive*. The normative perspective suggests that within the MGP, discrimination on negative outcome allocations is seen as even less socially acceptable than discrimination on positive outcome allocations. However, Mummendey and Otten (1998) concur with Billig and Tajfel (1973) in recognizing the circularity of post hoc normative accounts for predicting parity and discriminatory behaviors.

The cognitive account draws from findings showing that negative outcome allocations elicit more careful information processing than positive ones. Mummendey and Otten (1998) propose that more accurate and deeper information processing for negative outcome allocations may make respondents more aware that there are no obvious grounds for treating ingroup and outgroup members differently within the MGP. From a self-categorization theory perspective (SCT) (Turner, Hogg, Oakes, Reicher, & Wetherell, 1987), this awareness may shift self-categorizations from the group level categorization (us vs. them) to a supra-ordinate level: "all of us undergraduates" involved in the unpleasant task of distributing punishments to "fellow" undergraduates. From the recategorization framework proposed by Gaertner et al. (1993), the task of distributing negative outcome allocations may raise the salience of this supra-ordinate category (all of us undergraduates) thus reducing the pertinence of discrimination based on the experimenter-imposed "us–them" categories.

Otten et al. (1996) showed that low status and minority group members did discriminate on negative outcome allocations while subjects in identical "aggravating" conditions discriminated even more on positive outcome allocations. Invoking SIT, Otten et al. (1996) suggested that being in a low status or minority group position can threaten group members' positive social identity. It is under such "aggravating" circumstances that discrimination on negative outcome allocations can be used to achieve a more secure and positive social identity. Unfortunately, Otten et al. (1996) did not measure feelings of group insecurity, perception of group threat, and pre-post quality of group identity to support their account of discrimination on negative outcomes in their studies. Recently, Blanz, Mummendey, and Otten (1998) found that degree of ingroup identification was not related to valence asymmetry in their discrimination measures, a result leading to their rejection of social identity theory (SIT) as a heuristic explanation of the PNAE. Unfortunately in this study, degree of ingroup identification was measured only *after* outcome allocations rather than both *before* and *after*, suggesting that exclusion of SIT as a contributing explanation of the PNAE may be premature. Furthermore, from an SIT perspective, group members may consider that giving more "punishments" to the out-group than to the ingroup does not contribute to positive social identity. Unlike positive resources, negative outcome allocations may not constitute a valued or favorable comparison dimension on which group members can "positively differentiate" from outgroup members.

Though current research is being conducted to replicate the positive–negative asymmetry effect in laboratories other than that of Mummendey and colleagues in Germany, a fundamental point remains: One can document numerous historical and current cases in which dominant group members systematically inflict extreme punishments on outgroup others for an ideologically "good ingroup cause" while being self-aware of the socially unacceptable nature of their destructive actions (e.g., apartheid, ethnic cleansing, genocide).

Concluding Note

Recently, a number of social psychologists have argued in favor of a long overdue "rapprochement" between the individualistic and intergroup traditions of research on stereotyping, prejudice, and discrimination (Brewer, 1994; Leyens & Bourhis, 1994). The individualistic tradition focuses mostly on the social cognition of stereotyping while the intergroup tradition deals mainly with prejudice, discrimination, and intergroup conflict. While noting the lack of cross-referencing between these two traditions of research, one can also observe that it is the social cognition of stereotyping that generated the greatest amount of research activity within mainstream social psychology in the last decade. This state of affairs has led Fiske (1998) to warn that: "Documenting discriminatory behavior has not been social psychology's strong suit. Like the attitude–behaviour debacle that almost destroyed the foundation of persuasion research, a debacle threatens stereotyping research if it does not soon address behavior" (p. 374). The pendulum of research interest has perhaps already shifted to a more balanced approach as was evident in the 4th edition of the *Handbook of Social Psychology* (1998) which included two chapters rather than the usual combined one devoted to group phenomena. The first chapter, while focusing on the social cognition of stereotyping, also addressed conceptual and empirical links between stereotyping, prejudice, and discrimination (Fiske, 1998; see also Dovidio et al., 1996). The second chapter on intergroup relations focused on the nature of prejudice and discrimination and ways to reduce intergroup animosities (Brewer & Brown, 1998). What we hope this chapter has shown is that the minimal group paradigm (MGP) along with the Tajfel matrices remain key methodological and conceptual tools for researchers interested not only in discrimination but also for those investigating the social psychology of prejudice, stereotyping, and the promotion of intergroup harmony.

References

Allport, G. W. (1954). *The nature of prejudice.* Reading, MA: Addison-Wesley.

Adorno, T. W., Frenkel-Brunswick, E., Levinson, D. J., & Sanford, R. N. (1950). *The authoritarian personality.* New York: Harper.

Altemeyer, B. (1998). The other "Authoritarian Personality". In M. Zanna (Ed.), *Advances in Experimental Social Psychology, 30,* 47–92.

Billig, M. (1976). *Social psychology and intergroup relations.* London & New York: Academic Press.

Billig, M., & Tajfel, H. (1973). Social categorization and similarity in intergroup behaviour. *European Journal of Social Psychology, 3,* 27–52.

Blanz, M., Mummendey, A., & Otten, S. (1998). Ingroup identification as an explanatory concept for the positive–negative asymmetry in social discrimination? *Revue Internationale de Psychologie Sociale.*

Bornstein, G., Crum, L., Wittenbraker, J., Harring, K., Insko, C. A., & Thibaut, J. (1983a). On the measurement of social orientations in the minimal group paradigm. *European Journal of Social Psychology, 13,* 321–350.

Bornstein, G., Crum, L., Wittenbraker, J., Harring, K., Insko, C. A., & Thibaut, J. (1983b). Reply to Turner's comments. *European Journal of Social Psychology, 13,* 369–381.

Bourhis, R. Y. (1994a). Power, gender and intergroup discrimination: Some minimal group experiments. In M. P. Zanna & J. M. Olson (Eds.), *The psychology of prejudice: The Ontario symposium* (Vol. 7, pp. 209–232). Hillsdale, NJ: Erlbaum.

Bourhis, R. Y. (1994b). Ethnic and language attitudes in Quebec. In J. Berry & J. Laponce (Eds.), *Ethnicity and culture in Canada: The research landscape* (pp. 322–360). Toronto: Toronto University Press.

Bourhis, R. Y., Gagnon, A., & Cole, R. (1997). Sexe et pouvoir: Une recherche de terrain sur un cas de ségrégation sexuelle de deux syndicats au Canada. *Revue Internationale de Psychologie Sociale, 10,* 109–134.

Bourhis, R. Y., Gagnon, A., & Sachdev, I. (1997). Les matrices de Tajfel: Un guide méthodologique pour la recherche intergroupes. *Les Cahiers Internationaux de Psychologie Sociale, 34,* 11–28.

Bourhis, R. Y., & Hill, P. (1982). Intergroup perceptions in British higher education: A field study. In H. Tajfel (Ed.), *Social identity and intergroup relations.* Cambridge, UK & Paris: Cambridge University Press and Edition de la Maison des Sciences de l'Homme.

Bourhis, R. Y., Sachdev, I., & Gagnon, A. (1994). Intergroup research with the Tajfel Matrices; Methodological notes. In M. P. Zanna & J. M. Olson (Eds.), *The psychology of prejudice: The Ontario symposium* (Vol. 7, pp. 209–232). Hillsdale, NJ: Erlbaum.

Bourhis, R. Y., Turner, J. C., & Gagnon, A. (1997). Interdependence, social identity, and discrimination. In R. Spears, P. J. Oakes, N. Ellemers, & A. Haslam (Eds.), *The social psychology of stereotyping and group life* (pp. 273–295). Oxford, UK: Blackwell.

Brewer, M. B. (1979). Ingroup bias in the minimal group situation: A cognitive-motivational analysis. *Psychological Bulletin, 86,* 307–324.

Brewer, M. B. (1994). The social psychology of prejudice: Getting it all together. In M. P. Zanna & J. M. Olson (Eds.), *The psychology of prejudice: The Ontario symposium* (Vol. 7, pp. 315–329). Hillsdale, NJ: Erlbaum.

Brewer, M. B., & Brown, R. J. (1998). Intergroup relations. In D. Gilbert, S. Fiske, & G. Lindzey (Eds.), *The handbook of social psychology* (pp. 554–594). Boston, MA: McGraw-Hill.

Brewer, M., & Miller, N. (1984). Beyond the contact hypothesis: Theoretical perspectives on desegregation. In N. Miller & M. B. Brewer (Eds.), *Groups in contact: The psychology of desegregation* (pp. 281–302). New York: Academic Press.

Brewer, M. B., & Silver, M. (1978). Ingroup bias as a function of task characteristics. *European Journal of Social Psychology, 8*, 393–400.

Brown, R. J., Tajfel, H., & Turner, J. C. (1980). Minimal group situations and intergroup discriminations: Comments on the paper by Aschenbrenner and Schaefer. *European Journal of Social Psychology, 10*, 399–414.

Dawes, R. M., van de Kragt, A., & Orbell, J. (1990). Cooperation for the benefit of us-not me, or my conscience. In J. J. Mansbridge (Ed.), *Beyond self-interest* (pp. 97–110). Chicago, IL: University of Chicago Press.

Deaux, K. (1996). Social identification. In T. E. Higgins & A. Kruglanski (Eds.), *Social psychology: Handbook of basic principles* (pp. 777–798). New York: Guilford Press.

Diehl, M. (1990). The minimal group paradigm: Theoretical explanations and empirical findings. In W. Stroebe & M. Hewstone (Eds.), *European review of social psychology* (Vol. 1, pp. 263–292). Chichester, UK: Wiley.

Dovidio, J., & Gaertner, S. L. (1986). Prejudice, discrimination, and racism: Historical trends and contemporary approaches. In J. Dovidio & S. L. Gaertner (Eds.), *Prejudice, discrimination, and racism*. Orlando, FL: Acadamic Press.

Dovidio, J., Brigham, J., Johnson, B., & Gaertner, S. (1996). Stereotyping, prejudice, and discrimination: Another look. In C. N. Macrae, C. Stangor, & M. Hewstone (Eds.), *Stereotypes and stereotyping* (pp. 276–319). New York: Guilford Press.

Ellemers, N., Spears, R., & Doosje, B. (Eds.), (1999). *Social identity*. Oxford, UK: Blackwell.

Fiske, S. T. (1998) Stereotyping, prejudice and discrimination. In D. Gilbert, S. Fiske, & G. Lindzey (Eds.), *The handbook of social psychology* (pp. 357–411). Boston, MA: McGraw-Hill.

Forgas, J., & Fiedler, K. (1996). Us and them: Mood effects on intergroup discrimination. *Journal of Personality and Social Psychology, 70*, 28–40.

Gaertner, S. L., Dovidio, J. F., Anastasio, P. A., Bachman, B. A., & Rust, M. C. (1993). The common ingroup identity model: Recategorization and the reduction of intergroup bias. In W. Stroebe & M. Hewstone (Eds.), *European review of social psychology* (Vol. 4, pp. 1–26). Chichester, UK: Wiley.

Gagnon, A., & Bourhis, R. Y. (1996). Discrimination in the minimal group paradigm: Social identity or self-interest? *Personality and Social Psychology Bulletin, 22*, 1289–1301.

Gagnon, A., & Bourhis, R. Y. (1997). *The polarization of discriminatory behaviour between dominant and subordinate group members*. Paper presented at the Conference of the Society for Experimental Social Psychology (SESP). University of Toronto, Ontario.

Grieve, P., & Hogg, M. (1999). Subjective uncertainty and intergroup discrimination in the minimal group situation. *Personality and Social Psychology Bulletin, 25*, 8, 926–940.

Hinkle, S., & Brown, R. (1990). Intergroup comparisons and social identity: Some links and lacunae. In D. Abrams & M. Hogg (Eds.), *Social identity theory: Constructive and critical advances* (pp. 48–70). New York: Harvester-Wheatsheaf.

Hogg, M. A., & Abrams, D. (1988). *Social identifications: A social psychology of intergroup relations and group processes*. London: Routledge.

Hogg, M. A., & Mullin, B. (1999). Joining groups to reduce uncertainty: subjective uncertainty reduction and group identification. In D. Abrams & M. Hogg (Eds.), *Social identity and social cognition* (pp. 249–279). Oxford, UK: Blackwell.

Jetten, J., Spears, R., & Manstead, A. (1996). Intergroup norms and intergroup discrimination: Distinctive self-categorization and social identity effects. *Journal of Personality and Social Psychology, 71*, 1222–1233.

Jetten, J., Spears, R., & Manstead, A. (1999). Group distinctiveness and intergroup discrimination. In N. Ellemers, R. Spears, & B. Doosje (Eds.), *Social identity* (pp. 107–126). Oxford, UK: Blackwell.

Lemyre, L., & Smith, P. (1985). Intergroup discrimination and self-esteem in the minimal group paradigm. *Journal of Personality and Social Psychology, 49*, 660–670.

Leyens, J. P., & Bourhis, R. Y. (1994). Epilogue: Perceptions et relations intergroupes. In R. Y. Bourhis & J. P. Leyens (Eds.), *Stéréotypes, discrimination et relations intergroupes* (pp. 347–360). Liege, Belgium: Mardaga.

Liebrand, W. B., & Dehue, F. M. (1996). Social values. In A. S. R. Manstead & M. Hewstone (Eds.), *The Blackwell Encyclopedia of Social Psychology* (pp. 609–614). Oxford, UK: Blackwell.

Locksley, A., Oritz, V., & Hepburn, C. (1980). Social categorization and intergroup behavior: Extinguishing the minimal group discrimination effect. *Journal of Personality and Social Psychology, 39*, 773–783.

Messick, D. M., & Mackie, D. M. (1989). Intergroup relations. *Annual Review of Psychology, 40*, 45–81.

Mummendey, A., & Otten, S. (1998). Positive-negative asymmetry in social discrimination. In W. Stroebe & M. Hewstone (Eds.), *European review of social psychology.* Chichester, UK: Wiley.

Ng, S. H. (1981). Equity theory and the allocations of rewards between groups. *European Journal of Social Psychology, 11*, 439–443.

Ng, S. H. (1984). Equity and social categorization effects on intergroup allocation of rewards. *British Journal of Social Psychology. 23*, 165–172.

Otten, S., Mummendey, A., & Blanz, M. (1996). Intergroup discrimination in positive and negative outcome allocations: Impact of stimulus valence, relative group status, and relative group size. *Personality and Social Psychology Bulletin, 22*, 568–581.

Perreault, S., & Bourhis, R. Y. (1998). Social identification, interdependence, and discrimination. *Group Processes & Intergroup Relations, 1*, 49–66.

Perreault, S., & Bourhis, R. Y. (1999). Ethnocentrism, social identification, and discrimination. *Personality and Social Psychology Bulletin, 25*, 92–103.

Pettigrew, T. (1997). Generalized intergroup contact effects on prejudice. *Personality and Social Psychology Bulletin, 23*, 173–185.

Platow, M., Harley, K., Hunter, J., Hanning, P., Shave, R., & O'Connel, A. (1997). Interpreting in-group-favouring allocations in the minimal group paradigm. *British Journal of Social Psychology, 36*, 107–117.

Rabbie, J., & Horwitz, M. (1969). Arousal of ingroup–outgroup bias by a chance win or loss. *Journal of Personality and Social Psychology, 13*, 269–277.

Rabbie, J. N., Schot, J. C., & Visser, L. (1989). Social identity theory: A conceptual and empirical critique from the perspective of a behavioural interaction model. *European Journal of Social Psychology, 19*, 171–202.

Rubin, M., & Hewstone, M. (1998). Social identity's self-esteem hypothesis: A review and some suggestions for clarification. *Personality and Social Psychology Review, 2*, 40–62.

Sachdev, I., & Bourhis, R. Y. (1985). Social categorization and power differentials in group relations. *European Journal of Social Psychology, 15*, 415–434.

Sachdev, I., & Bourhis, R. Y. (1987). Status differentials and intergroup behaviours. *European Journal of Social Psychology, 17*, 277–293.

Sachdev, I., & Bourhis, R. Y. (1991). Power and status differentials in minority and majority group relations. *European Journal of Social Psychology, 21*, 1–24.

Sherif, M., Harvey, O. J., White, B. J., Hood, W. R., & Sherif, C. (1961). *Intergroup conflict and co-operation: The Robbers Cave experiment.* Norman, OK: University of Oklahoma.

Sidanius, J., & Pratto, F. (1999). *Social dominance: An intergroup theory of social hierarchy and oppression.* Cambridge, UK: Cambridge University Press.

Stephan, W., Ybarra, O., Martinez, C. M., Schwarzwald, J., & Tur-Kaspa, M. (1998). Prejudice toward immigrants to Spain and Israel: An integrated threat theory analysis. *Journal of Cross-Cultural Psychology, 29*, 559–576.

Tajfel, H. (1978). The psychological structure of intergroup relations. In H. Tajfel (Ed.), *Differentiation between social groups* (pp. 27–98). London: Academic Press.

Tajfel, H., Flament, C., Billig, M., & Bundy, R. (1971). Social categorization and intergroup behaviour. *European Journal of Social Psychology, 11*, 149–178.

Tajfel, H., & Turner, J. C. (1979). An integrative theory of intergroup conflict. In W. G. Austin & S. Worchel (Eds.), *The social psychology of intergroup relations* (pp. 33-47). Monterey, CA: Brooks/Cole.

Tajfel, H., & Turner, J. C. (1986). The social identity theory of intergroup behavior. In S. Worchel & W. G. Austin (Eds.), *Psychology of intergroup relations* (2nd ed.). Chicago, IL: Nelson-Hall.

Taylor, D. M., & Moghaddam, F. (1994). *Theories of intergroup relations* (2nd ed.). Westport, CT: Praeger.

Turner, J. C. (1980). Fairness or discrimination in intergroup behaviour? A reply to Branthwaite, Doyle, and Lightbown. *European Journal of Social Psychology, 10*, 131–147.

Turner, J. C. (1983a). Some comments on . . . "the measurement of social orientations in the minimal group paradigm." *European Journal of Social Psychology, 13*, 351–367.

Turner, J. C. (1983b). A second reply to Bornstein, Crum, Wittenbraker, Harring, Insko, and Thibaut on the measurement of social orientations. *European Journal of Social Psychology, 13*, 383–387.

Turner, J. C. (1996). Henri Tajfel: An introduction. In W. P. Robinson (Ed.), *Social groups and identities: Developing the legacy of Henri Tajfel* (pp. 1–23). Oxford, UK: Butterworth-Heinemann.

Turner, J. C., & Bourhis, R. Y. (1996). Social identity, interdependence, and the social group: A reply to Rabbie et al. In W. P. Robinson (Ed.), *Social groups and identities: Developing the legacy of Henri Tajfel* (pp. 25–63). Oxford, UK: Butterworth-Heinemann.

Turner, J. C., Hogg, M. A., Oakes, P., Reicher, S., & Wetherell, M. (1987). *Rediscovering the social group: A self-categorization theory*. Oxford, UK: Blackwell.

Vanbeselaere, N. (1991). The different effects of simple and crossed categorizations: A result of the category differentiation process or differential category salience. In W. Stroebe & M. Hewstone (Eds.), *European review of social psychology, 2* (pp. 247–278). Chichester, UK: Wiley.

Vaughan, G. M., Tajfel, H., & Williams, J. (1981). Intergroup and interindividual discrimination in British children. *Social Psychology Quarterly, 44*, 37–42.

Wann, D., & Branscombe, N. (1995). Influence of level of identification with a group and physiological arousal on perceived intergroup complexity. *British Journal of Social Psychology, 34*, 223–235.

CHAPTER SIX

Aversive Discrimination

Amélie Mummendey and Sabine Otten

Introduction

"I don't want my grave blasted in the air – like Heinz Galinski's grave. Regrettably, the danger that the dignity of the dead is violated is still serious in this country." Ignaz Bubis, the president of the Central Council of Jews in Germany uttered this sentence in July 1999, in an interview where he came up with the resigned conclusion that more than half a century after the defeat of Nazi Germany, Jews, although German citizens, remain foreigners in Germany, and Jewish graveyards are still targets of destruction. Of course, in today's Germany, these attacks are prosecuted as criminal acts and there is a high sensitivity with regards to the explicit expression of negative attitudes toward Jewish people. However, in Germany as in other societies, there are plenty of other groups whose differentiation and exclusion are much more deliberate or even accepted: Ethnicity, religion, gender, sexual orientation, age, disabilities, and regional or national origin are all well-known criteria for social differentiation. Besides, social psychological research provides ample evidence that even arbitrary categorizations can elicit ingroup–outgroup differentiation effects (e.g., Brewer, 1979; Brown, 1999; Messick & Mackie, 1989).

The questions we want to deal with in this chapter are twofold: (1) Why do particular categorizations become relevant for differentiation between ingroup and outgroup, and when does social differentiation lead to discrimination? (2) What are the determinants of derogation, hostility, and antagonism against outgroups? Dealing with these issues, we will not emphasize instances of mild ingroup favoritism, but will focus on negative treatments, that is, on derogation, hostility, and dehumanization based on social category membership. However, first, we will analyze the psychological definition of social discrimination and its crucial constituents: Social categorization, normative context, position-specific perspectives, and the quality of behavior manifesting intergroup discrimination.

Discrimination as Social Interaction

Most of the theoretical and empirical work on social discrimination refers to Gordon Allport (1954), who defines discrimination as behavior that ". . . comes about only when we deny to individuals or groups of people equality of treatment which they may wish" (p. 51). This definition comprises two crucial aspects: First, social discrimination necessitates social categorization; and second, it involves not only an actor, that is, somebody deciding about and realizing an intergroup treatment, but also a recipient, who *disagrees* with this treatment.

A more recent definition by Dovidio and collaborators describes social discrimination as "inappropriate treatment to individuals due to their group membership" (Dovidio, Brigham, Johnson, & Gaertner, 1996, p. 279). By reference to the issue of inappropriateness, this statement illustrates a further decisive aspect: Processes of judgment and interpretation, not just clear-cut, "objective" characteristics of the intergroup treatment determine what we conceive of as social discrimination (Otten & Mummendey, 1999a). Correspondingly, Graumann and Wintermantel (1989) state that "the concept of social discrimination is inextricably connected to notions of justice and equ(al)ity . . ." (p. 183).

Instances of discrimination are not only restricted to category-based transgressions of the equality-norm, but can also imply transgressions of the equity-norm. Neither do equal distributions of resources guarantee that there is *no* discrimination, nor is unequal intergroup allocation a reliable criterion to identify instances of bias, favoritism, and derogation. A key criterion is some *dissent* between allocating group (member) and targeted group (member) about the appropriateness of their relative treatment. Accordingly, the subsequent analysis will focus upon the different facets that might determine such dissent.

Differentiation versus discrimination

Social differentiation does not necessarily imply social discrimination, but forms the basis for both consensual and conflictual forms of unequal intergroup treatment. Thus, it is a necessary, but not a sufficient condition for social discrimination. As such, it can take different forms: First, it can refer to a *quantitative* dimension – for example, those who work longer get more salary. Second, category-based treatment can follow a *qualitative* differentiation – for instance, more money for those with better qualifications. Third, social differentiation can determine the access to opportunities and rights by reference to *descriptive*, inherited characteristics – for example, giving the right to vote only to citizens of 18 years and above. In all of these cases the parties involved can be demarcated into those who get more and those who get less, into those who have access to a certain resource and those who do not. None the less, for the examples given, we can also assume a shared consensus about the adequacy of the criteria applied or the dimension underlying differentiation. However, if there is dissent about the categorization that has been applied, or about the consequences derived from the categorical distinction, then social differentiation will turn into social discrimination.

Historical and cultural differences. Depending on the social context, the identical differentiation might be perceived as adequate and functional or as illegitimate and aversive. Such contextual differences can be due to historical change. For example, the changed ideas on gender equality demonstrate the *inter-time perspective* on the (in)appropriateness of social differentiation: Until the 20th century women were typically conceived of as predisposed to raise children, keep the house, feed their family, while men were obliged to provide for their families materially. Gender-specific roles were assumed to fit gender-specific abilities (see Eagly, 1987). Even in democratic systems, it took a long time until the claim "Women and men are equal!" was heard and translated into social reality. For example, not until the 1960s were women accepted as students at prestigious American universities such as Princeton. Today, however, the same universities would be sued if they rejected a student based on gender. In addition to such variations over time, there are also examples of diverging *inter-cultural perspectives* on certain categorical distinctions (see Triandis & Trafimow, this volume, chapter 18, for a discussion of cultural differences).

Discrimination and social categorization

Social discrimination can involve individual group members or groups as a whole. What makes it a *social* phenomenon is not the number of persons involved but the fact that it presupposes social identities and is based upon categorical distinctions among groups of individuals. As outlined in the previous sections, the distinction of individuals in terms of social categories is not problematic per se, but its application as a basis of resource allocations might cause conflict and dissent. Accordingly, a crucial question for the social psychological analysis of social discrimination is: Why does a certain categorization of persons into members of ingroup and outgroup become the adequate basis for their differential treatment? Mere category salience does not necessarily imply a differential treatment according to the lines of this categorization. For example, article 3, 3 of the German constitution explicitly says: Nobody should be (dis)advantaged because of gender, descent, race, language, origin, faith, religious or political beliefs. Although these are highly accessible, frequently applied social categories, their members have to be treated equally before the law, and are guaranteed equal opportunities.

Mere categorization effects. Although salient social categories *must* not imply unequal treatment based on this distinction, a huge body of research on so-called minimal groups (Rabbie & Horwitz, 1969; Tajfel, Billig, Bundy, & Flament, 1971) documents that simply by introducing a categorization into "we" and "they," even when based on fully arbitrary criteria and without directly serving realistic self-interest, ingroup bias and intergroup discrimination occur (e.g., Brewer, 1979; Brown, 1999). "Social identity theory" (Tajfel & Turner, 1986) offered an account for this "mere categorization effect" by emphasizing the motivational functions of social categorization. People's desire to see themselves positively can partly be derived from their membership of social groups (Tajfel, 1981); by perceiving and treating own groups in a way that distinguishes them positively from other groups, individuals can enhance or ensure their positive social identity. Thus, even positive differentiation of a minimal ingroup can serve an overall positive self-concept.

Social categorization and identification. According to Tajfel and Turner (1986), identification with the ingroup is necessary for the assumed sequence from categorization via social comparison to positive ingroup distinctiveness. Research showed, however, that when measuring ingroup identification and intergroup bias, especially under minimal conditions, correlations are often only weak (see Hinkle & Brown, 1990). More recently, ingroup identification has been manipulated as an independent variable (Perreault & Bourhis, 1999). Here, the relation between identification and favoritism turned out to be straightforward: Under conditions increasing ingroup-identification (chosen group membership) discriminatory behavior was significantly stronger than under conditions with lower identification (assigned minimal group membership). Other studies manipulating or measuring ingroup identification independently of the intergroup treatment similarly reveal that ingroup-identification can be understood as a key variable of discriminatory behavior (e.g., Branscombe & Wann, 1994; Ellemers, Van Rijswijk, Roefs, & Simons, 1997).

Police officers and police dogs: Defining adequate levels of categorization. It is beyond the scope of this chapter to deal with empirical and theoretical work criticizing and extending the theoretical explanation of the "mere categorization effect" as provided by social identity theory (e.g., Diehl, 1989; Mummendey, 1995). In the present chapter we can state that understanding social discrimination as a result of positive distinctiveness striving cannot suffice to explain why certain category distinctions are taken as rationales for (unequal) distributions of resources while others are not. Here, self-categorization theory (Turner, Hogg, Oakes, Reicher, & Wetherell, 1987) allows more precise predictions: An individual will apply a certain social categorization, if it subjectively gives meaning to the given situation. Such meaning and, thus, category salience is determined by three aspects: accessibility, structural fit, and normative fit (Oakes, 1987). Accessibility refers to the perceiver's readiness to apply a certain categorization, which is due to prior experiences or to situational goals. Structural fit is defined by the meta-contrast ratio, the proportion of perceived intra-category differences and inter-category differences; the more the latter outscore the former, the higher is the structural fit (Turner et al., 1987). Finally, normative fit refers to the match between category and the content properties of its stimuli (cf. Oakes, 1996), that is, it indicates whether in a given situation a categorization in fact allows appropriate behavioral predictions (e.g., in a decision about building of a new atomic reactor, the members of the Christian Democrats might predominantly stress economic interests while members of the Green Party will mainly focus on environmental risks).

The notion of fit, however, presupposes a general comparability of the two categories. In order to guide intergroup treatment a social categorization must be linked to a superordinate, inclusive category defining a frame for the comparison. Consider a member of the police wondering whether his salary is fair. He might compare salaries of members of the secret service with those from the mounted police, but not consider relevant what the State spends for its human police members compared to its police dogs. A dissent about the intergroup treatment necessitates that there is an inclusive category (e.g., human police members) within which ingroup (e.g., secret service) and outgroup (e.g., mounted police) can compete for their entitlements in a certain allocation decision.

Categorization and justice. We have argued that discrimination is inextricably linked to both justice and social categorization (see also Tyler, this volume, chapter 17). Both aspects are taken into account in an approach by Wenzel (1997; 2000) who combined self-categorization theory (Turner et al., 1987) with theories of distributive justice. According to self-categorization theory, ingroup favoritism implies that the own group is seen as more prototypically representing dimensions that are defined as crucial for the superordinate category including both ingroup and outgroup (Turner et al., 1987; Mummendey & Wenzel, 2000). For example, a male employer could argue: Jobs in business necessitate advanced skills in math. Males are better at math than females; thus, male applicants should be preferred. Wenzel (1997; in press) argues and provides evidence that perceptions of social justice follow the same logic: Perceived entitlements are bound to the positive or negative evaluation of the own subcategory compared to the corresponding other subcategory in terms of relevant dimensions of the *primary category*, which includes all potential recipients in the given allocation situation.

Crucial is the social categorization of the target entity: As one possibility, the target may be categorized as a member of the category that includes the potential recipients in a certain allocation situation. In this case, the target is perceived to be equal to the other members of the primary category and, consequently, entitled to the same treatment. If, however, the primary category is further divided into subcategories (e.g., gender), then the subgroups' prototypicality in terms of comparison dimensions relevant for the primary category (e.g., math skills) will determine perceived entitlement. Thus, we can conclude that salience and abstraction level of a certain categorization crucially determine whether social inequality will be perceived, accepted, neglected, questioned, or protested against (see also Major, 1994).

Discrimination as perspective-specific

As mentioned above, Allport's (1954) definition of the term "social discrimination" involves the issue of perspective. None the less, until recently, the overwhelming body of social-psychological theorizing and research on social discrimination has focused on the agents of social discrimination. Such one-sided focus on an *interactional* phenomenon is not a deficiency unique to the domain of intergroup research, but has also been criticized in traditional aggression research (e.g., Mummendey, Linneweber, & Löschper, 1984; Mummendey & Otten, 1993; Tedeschi, 1984). While recently there has been a growing interest in the consequences of social inequality and social discrimination on the targets' side (see Crocker & Quinn and Ellemers & Barreto, this volume, chapters 12 and 16, respectively), the *relation* between target and actor still lacks a thorough theoretical empirical investigation.

Specific to the perspectives of either allocating/privileged group (member) or receiving/disadvantaged group (member) the single groups' entitlement to the resources in question will be estimated. As outlined in the previous section, social categorization provides a basis for judging this entitlement: Those who are categorized as equal or prototypical within the primary category of recipients deserve equal treatment, while those who are categorized as unequal may legitimately be treated unequally (Wenzel, 1997). Accordingly, a perspective-specific dissent can involve three aspects: (1) Is the division of the primary category into subcategories appropriate (e.g., should job candidates be distinguished in terms of gender)? (2) Is the value differentiation linked to the categorization appropriate (e.g., is it true that women are worse in math than men)? (3) Are the decisions about intergroup treatment derived from categorization and value differentiation appropriate (e.g., does the job require high proficiency in math)? In other words, social discrimination as an interactional phenomenon is characterized by a lack of consensus about the fit (Oakes, 1987) of the given social categorization in the respective social context.

As outlined above, an unequal or negative treatment of a group per se does not yet define an instance of social discrimination, but it might be accepted as finally functional, or as legitimized by different needs or different inputs on behalf of the differentiated groups. Groups might be willing to take serious burdens without complaint. Relative deprivation theories (see Taylor & Moghaddam, 1994) state that it is not hardship and negative living conditions per se, which make people feel unjustly treated: The key point is the experience that there are others who are better off, although they are perceived as equal in terms of entitlement or deservingness (see Mikula, 1994 for a respective analysis in interpersonal relations).

However, acknowledging perspectivity in social discrimination and defining a judgmental dissent as its manifesting characteristic might provoke a serious misunderstanding. Our position does not imply that we do not have to care about the exploitation of groups so long as they do not complain about their fate. First, the dissent may not only be located between target and allocating party, but also between an outside observer and the allocating party. Second, such conclusion would imply a confound between the analysis of social discrimination from a political point of view with our attempt to clarify the *psychological processes* that are at stake for the individuals involved in specific instances of implementing or receiving socially discriminating intergroup treatment. Only by analyzing how *both* allocators and recipients differ in their understanding of the appropriateness of certain categorizations, value differentiations and, finally, intergroup allocations, can social discrimination as an interactional phenomenon be fully understood and convincingly dealt with.

Valence, behavioral mode, and discriminating behavior

The reflection on the distinction between differentiation and discrimination already implied that the quality of the "treatment" which might be perceived as discrimination needs a careful analysis. It is not sufficient to take into account whether a certain evaluation or allocation violates norms of equality or equity; in addition its specific characteristics and the dimension to which it refers have to be considered.

A taxonomy of social discrimination. Mummendey and Simon (1991) have offered a taxonomy of social discrimination, which distinguishes two aspects: (a) the valence of resources (positive or negative) that are distributed between groups; and (b) the type of behavioral mode (direct/inflicting or indirect/withdrawing) by which this distribution is established. In each of the resulting four cells, ingroup favoritism or outgroup antagonism can be realized: One might opt for the own professional group getting a higher salary than another professional group, but expect the latter to pay more money when taxes are increased (direct and indirect discrimination in the positive domain); one might vote for another rather than the own home town as a place for an additional large garbage dump, but claim that the own community should be first in line when the township starts the re-naturation of areas that have been destroyed by the coal-mining industry (direct and indirect discrimination in the negative domain).

This variety of possibilities for differentiation and discrimination between groups is not reflected in the empirical work in this domain: Although everyday life provides many examples of a category-based infliction of burdens or costs in ways that the outgroup suffers relatively more than the ingroup, research has overwhelmingly dealt with differential positive treatments.

Positive–negative asymmetry in social discrimination. Findings by Mummendey and collaborators about the so-called positive–negative asymmetry in social discrimination (for a survey, see Mummendey & Otten, 1998; Otten & Mummendey, 2000) indicate that – at least for direct forms of discrimination – results obtained in the domain of positive resources should not be simply extrapolated to the negative area. The experiments mostly followed a typical minimal categorization procedure, but varied the valence of resources that were distributed between groups: On matrices like the ones in the original study by Tajfel and collaborators (1971) participants either allocated points that were allegedly to be transferred either into money, or into the duration of unpleasant noise or the number of unpleasant tasks (see Mummendey et al., 1992; Otten, Mummendey & Blanz, 1996). In other studies, the manipulation of valence was realized by asking participants to evaluate the novel ingroup and outgroup on either positive or negative trait dimensions (Blanz, Mummendey, & Otten, 1995). These and a number of subsequent experiments consistently showed that for both intergroup allocations and evaluations there were no favoritism effects if negative resources or evaluation dimensions were involved. In the positive domain, however, the typical "mere categorization effect" was replicated: The (minimal) ingroup was significantly and positively differentiated from the respective outgroup.

Integrating the empirical evidence from their studies, Mummendey and Otten (1998) propose the following explanation: Social categories that are minimal do not offer a legitimate rationale for unequal intergroup treatment. Accordingly, in the negative domain a more elaborate cognitive processing (Otten, Mummendey, & Buhl, 1998) and a stronger concern about normative inhibitions (Blanz, Mummendey, & Otten, 1997; Otten & Mummendey, 1999b) will raise the probability that the minimal categorization will be considered irrelevant. Thus, group members will re-categorize as a common ingroup (Gaertner, Dovidio, Anastasio, Bachman, & Rust, 1993) and refrain from differential intergroup treatment (Mummendey, Otten, Berger, & Kessler, in press). These findings were further corroborated in a recent study by Gardham and Brown (in press), demonstrating that subgroup and superordinate group identification were crucial for the effects of stimulus valence on intergroup treatment. Besides, this study is noteworthy as it manipulated not only valence but also behavioral mode (allocation, withdrawal). In fact, only for instances of beneficiary decisions (i.e., allocating positive stimuli and withdrawing negative stimuli) was there significant ingroup favoritism. Finally, the importance of category salience in understanding the differential effects of stimulus valence on category salience was underlined in recent studies by Reynolds, Turner, and Haslam (2000), who argue that the positive–negative asymmetry might rely on valence-specific differences in the normative fit of the social categorization and the intergroup comparison dimension.

However, when testing the explanations for the potential explanations of the positive–negative asymmetry effect, Mummendey and collaborators also documented that there are conditions, where ingroup favoritism and outgroup derogation were shown irrespective of valence. Introducing so-called "aggravating conditions" (Blanz, Mummendey, & Otten, 1995; Otten, Mummendey, & Blanz, 1996), such as inferior status and/or minority status, which increased the salience of the intergroup distinction and – possibly – elicited a threat towards positive social identity, resulted in significant favoritism effects in both valence conditions.

We can conclude from the above that negative forms of social discrimination can be demonstrated in the laboratory and in fairly reduced forms of intergroup settings. However, when we turn from allocating minutes of unpleasant noise or samples of boring experimental tasks to much more dramatic negative treatments, then these effects necessitate a salient, subjectively meaningful social categorization that provides even greater legitimization for a category-based intergroup treatment. In the following, we will analyze what such legitimizing rationales might look like, and how an allocating party might come up with the decision that it is appropriate or even inevitable to treat another group negatively.

Determinants of Social Discrimination

Collective beliefs and social norms

Ordinary people typically perceive and describe themselves as friendly, and will claim that their normal everyday activities are primarily motivated to gradually improve their and their families' living conditions, to live in good relations with friends, to be fair to other people, and to achieve further positive goals. Hardly anybody would perceive him- or herself as primarily and explicitly aiming at excluding, insulting, injuring, or even killing somebody else. Nevertheless, aversive discrimination is undoubtedly a social reality. Social norms as part of the belief systems prevailing in a society can – at least partly – account for this apparent paradox.

Norms tell people which kind of differentiation is normal or even necessary, and which differentiation is unacceptable or even sanctioned by authorities. They may dictate against which groups (e.g., Jews, African Americans) public expressions of prejudice are unacceptable, and against which groups (e.g., overweight, asylum seekers) such prejudice may be tolerated or even positively sanctioned. Beyond a simple dichotomous differentiation between own and other groups, norms may prescribe a further differentiation between different outgroups. Pettigrew (1998) differentiates seven different types of minorities in Western Europe according to their status, ranging from the most favored national migrants (e.g., "Aussiedler" "returning home" from Romania after eight centuries) to rejected illegal immigrants. Depending on their respective status assigned by authorities and legislation, members of these groups are treated more or less negatively. Often, illegal immigrants are officially expelled by the host country's police, who will apply severe physical coercion "if necessary." These events are not kept secret from ordinary citizens, but are occasionally shown in TV programs or reported in the newspapers. Little protest is heard on these occasions: Coercion and violence against such groups maybe seem regrettable, but can be normatively justified. With minority groups holding a higher status, negative treatment is not accepted officially, but since these groups are not viewed as belonging to the host nationalities, differentiation in terms of employment, public accommodation, housing, insurance, banks, etc. is still widespread.

Moral exclusion and delegitimization. A remote observer would notice an inconsistency between a country's constitution and its fundamental paragraphs against any discrimination and the apparently accepted and legitimate differential treatment of people in terms of their group membership. Members of the society itself won't necessarily recognize it because of the consensual acceptance of the normative beliefs. Opotow (1990, 1995) has coined the term "scope of justice" as a fundamental psycho-social orientation toward others. It refers to the fact that people have psychological boundaries of fairness or form a defined and limited moral community. For members of social categories inside this community and within the scope of justice, rules of justice and morality apply. For members of categories outside this scope, the same rules don't apply or seem irrelevant. Thus, members of other social categories might be excluded from the moral community, ". . . permitting justifications – even jubilation – for harm that befall outsiders" (Opotow, 1995, p. 348). In a similar way, Bar-Tal (1989) sees "delegitimization" as categorization of groups into extreme negative social categories which are excluded from human groups that are considered as acting within limits of acceptable norms and/or values (p. 170). Ways to delegitimize outgroups are to dehumanize them, to attribute negative personality traits generalized to the group, to use political labels and associations with consensually despised groups. Delegitimization functions as justification for extreme negative behavior against the dehumanized outgroup.

Social norms, the scope of justice, and moral exclusion lead to differential awareness of legitimate differentiation, on the one hand, or discrimination as illegitimate differentiation, on the other hand. Societal beliefs and norms provide not only the frame for consensual differentiation, but also for dissent and conflicts about the appropriateness of a category to serve as a differentiation basis.

Violence against minorities. Analyses of anti-minority violence in various European countries committed since the beginning of the 1990s showed that the perpetrators were not predominantly from the far right. Moreover, a mixed group of people, adolescents, young adults, and large crowds of ordinary people actively committed, applauded, or refrained from interfering against violence and brutality against foreigners and other minorities. These incidents were often paralleled by the political elite legitimizing the view of foreigners as unbearable burdens or, as the political scientist Thränhardt (1995) puts it, by "playing the race card." Supported by a social climate of intergroup tension, in which outgroups are declared as cause of unsatisfying life conditions, some people might feel legitimized actively to attack outgroups in order to solve social problems (see Pettigrew, 1998, for further discussion of this point). Group members might mutually reinforce each other in their view that they are all behaving appropriately (Mummendey & Otten, 1993; Otten, Mummendey, & Wenzel, 1995; Postmes & Spears, 1998).

The most extreme case of moral exclusion and violence against outgroups is *genocide*. Again, the smaller group of active perpetrators as well as the large majority of bystanders act with support and justification of the dominant ideology. Following Staub (1989), in situations where societies are unstable and provide difficult living conditions, where citizens are unable to improve by individual effort, simple ideological solutions become attractive: "The Jews are our evil." Here, from the perspective of perpetrators, "ethnic cleansing" fulfils social functions; the expulsion of the minority is assumed to solve social problems. The severity of atrocities develops gradually. The society and its authorities provide norms and laws which successively justify more and more extreme actions against the minority. By this stepwise adaptation to severe derogation and harm as normality, perpetrators, bystanders but also victims gradually undergo changes. Increasing levels of harm can be inflicted together with an increasingly firm sense of "justification." Repression, expulsion, and finally extermination are done to protect the own group. This protection is needed not against threat from attacks by enemies from outside, as in wartime; rather, attacks are perceived from within, threatening "essence purity" of the own group, be that essence defined in terms of biology such as race, or in terms of political or religious beliefs.

Intragroup deviance and group threat. In the incidents outlined above, the majority agrees that certain minorities are threatening the ingroup's identity. There are other cases where there is dissent within the majority itself about which of two conflicting views or beliefs would contradict the essence of group identity. Following these lines, Sani and Reicher (1998, 1999) provide an explanatory approach toward the process of group-schism. Schism of a group stands for collective agreement about the essence of group identity being ruptured: Two opposing fractions mutually claim that the other fraction is negating the group's identity. The perspective-specific divergence about who is supporting and who is negating group identity becomes crucial. Some group members put forward beliefs or values which are viewed by other group members as "destroying" their identity. Sani and Reicher propose that in such situation, intergroup differences become non-negotiable, dissent will be exacerbated, and schism as the state of conflict and incompatibility arises. Convincing evidence for their model is presented by their analysis of two political incidents, namely the split in the Italian Communist Party into two new fractional parties (Sani & Reicher, 1998) and the split in the Church of England following the decision to ordain women to priesthood (Sani & Reicher, 1999).

The actor's perspective

Looking from the actor's perspective, we can see basically three types of differentiation between ingroup and outgroup, differing in terms of the intentionality of outgroup derogation and rejection, and, correspondingly, differing in terms of the (in)consistency between evaluative attitude and behavior toward own and other group.

Mindless ingroup favoritism. An ingroup might be evaluated positively simply due to its automatic association with the typically positive self, without explicit social comparison between ingroup and outgroup. In line with this assumption, Perdue, Dovidio, Gurtman, and Tyler (1990) documented that ingroup or outgroup designators (like "us" and "them") can produce affective congruency effects when combined with previously neutral verbal material, or when presented subliminally in masked affective priming tasks. Recently, such intergroup bias on the implicit level could be shown in three studies even with minimal groups (Otten & Moskowitz, 2000; Otten & Wentura, 1999). Thus, positive ingroup evaluation might result from mindless intergroup differentiation. However, as soon as the individual reflects on the rationale for this differentiation more consciously or is asked to account for it, the differentiation is likely to be given up (Dobbs & Crano, in prep.; Otten et al., 1998).

Ambivalent discrimination. Second, and in line with the "aversive racism" approach (Dovidio, Mann, & Gaertner, 1989; Gaertner & Dovidio, 1986), many actors endorse principles of egalitarianism and fairness, and want to avoid discrimination. Simultaneously, they possess negative beliefs and affect about outgroups, just because they grew up in a society in which stereotypes and prejudice against certain groups still prevail. Differentiation in favor of the own group might be shown only if it can be rationalized by reasons independent of prejudice and without deliberate intention to disadvantage the outgroup. Aversive racists avoid overt displays of intergroup distinctions when the normative structure of a situation is clear, but when the situation is normatively ambiguous, intergroup distinction may occur.

Intentional discrimination. Finally, actors might differentiate deliberately and be able to account for it. They may apply criteria for distinction which they consider justified and based on social norms. In this case, actors perceive outgroups as being distinct and as deserving less positive or even negative treatment. Consistently, they will behave negatively toward these groups or will support others in doing so. Realistic conflict between groups (Sherif, 1966), delegitimization (Bar-Tal, 1989), and moral exclusion (Opotow, 1995) or non-negotiable differences about ingroup identity essence (Sani & Reicher, 1999) provide rationales for deliberately downgrading a particular outgroup.

Accounting for social discrimination. It is the intentional, fully reflected decision to treat ingroup and outgroup differently that is of particular interest when looking for antecedents of explicit derogation, rejection, and aversive treatment of outgroups. If actors can refer to social justifications for their behavior toward outgroups, the question is how these justifications are provided or developed.

Traditional beliefs. First, justifications might be a feature of traditional beliefs and thus a facet of normality in a stable society. In Germany, for example, until 1994, the constitutional right for equal opportunities did not encompass disabled people. It was taken for granted and adequate to keep them separated from non-disabled people in schools, housing facilities, and at the workplace, where they still get only minimum salary for their work. In the German courts, tourists successfully sued travel agents for damage, because they felt disturbed while on their holidays by a group of disabled people in their hotel and restaurants. People maintaining this situation won't have recognized that they were blocking an outgroup from resources it was entitled to.

Threat. Second, in situations of instability and major social change, people might experience threat to their group status, economically and with respect to their values and belief systems. Macro-social studies show a clear coincidence of high percentages of immigrant minorities and low gross national product, on the one hand, and pronounced xenophobic attitudes, on the other hand (Quillian, 1995). Besides, laboratory experiments provide evidence for the crucial function of perceived threat to positive ingroup identity. In line with social identity theory, Branscombe and Wann (1994) showed that for individuals identifying highly with their threatened ingroup, derogating the threatening outgroup apparently serves motivational functions. Only if an outgroup is threatening the status of the own group, and if positive identity is based upon membership in that group, then positive collective self-esteem is negatively affected, and is re-established by actively derogating the outgroup.

Individual differences. Beyond situation-specific experiences, people differ individually with respect to a generalized experience of negative interdependence and threat from outgroups leading to a disposition to react against these outgroups in a hostile manner. Several personality constructs have been proposed to explain interindividual variance of outgroup hostility and rejection. In response to the authoritarian-personality-approach (Adorno, Frenkel-Brunswik, Lewinson, & Sanford, 1950), Rokeach (1960) created the politically "neutral" concept of *dogmatism* which stresses the importance of value-differences: dogmatic people with a "closed mind" will conceive value-differences as incompatibility and therefore feel threat to their own values and beliefs by those held by outgroups. *Right-wing authoritarianism* (Altemeyer, 1988, 1994) implies submission to established authorities, aggression directed at targets sanctioned by established authorities, and adherence to traditional social conventions. Like nationalistic orientations (Eckhardt, 1991) it is related to both evaluative bias in favor of ingroup and to the perception of outgroups as inferior to the own group. A related concept to authoritarianism is the concept of *social dominance orientation* as the basic desire to have one's own primary ingroup considered to be superior to and dominant over relevant outgroups (Sidanius, 1993).

Batson and Burris (1994) provide evidence for a close relationship between *prejudice and religion*. Based upon their three-dimensional model of personal religion, they see especially their "religion as quest" dimension associated with outgroup rejection. Individuals whose religious beliefs face the complexity of the human condition, who accept doubts and open questions, show much less inclination toward prejudice than those whose religious beliefs predominantly comprise clear-cut answers and simplistic views of the world as either good or bad.

From a survey of seven representative samples drawn from four European countries, Wagner and Zick (1995) report strong evidence for a positive correlation between level of formal education and outgroup rejection, a correlation which, however, is mediated by social psychological variables such as perceived fraternal relative deprivation (Runciman, 1966; Vanneman & Pettigrew, 1972), or political conservatism and conventional values (Crandall & Cohen, 1994).

In their distinction between blatant and subtle prejudice as two types of intergroup prejudice, Pettigrew and Meertens (1995) take into account the possible effect of societal norms and social desirability striving on individuals' expressing negative attitudes toward outgroups. Subtle prejudice stands for defense of traditional values, exaggeration of cultural differences, and denial of positive emotions; as such, it is in line with today's socially accepted forms of rejecting minorities. Blatant prejudice stands for direct rejection of minorities on the basis of perceived threat from outgroups. Blatant prejudice sees inferior positions of outgroups as biologically or naturally given; hence, differential treatment is justified. From the perspective of a blatant racist, discrimination against ethnic minorities does not exist.

Social emotion and discrimination. Experience of category-based threat, either induced by a particular intergroup conflict situation, or by a generalized expectation of an outgroup's intentions and actions, refers to an aversive event, which evokes emotions associated with motivations to fight or flight. Emotions such as hostility, but also anger and contempt, are connected to behavioral tendencies to attack, to aggress, or to retaliate against the source of aversion. Fear or disgust accompany avoidance tendencies. Ample evidence in aggression research shows that anger arousal and feelings of provocation on the actor's side are instigated when the opponent's behavior is perceived as illegitimate and norm-violating (Averill, 1982; Tedeschi & Felson, 1994). The actor's subsequent reaction will aim at a subjectively justified payback to the aggressor. Feelings of hostility and anger against outgroups, therefore, can be expected by those people holding a prejudice which explicitly represents such an "offense-retaliation" scheme. In this vein, Smith (1993) stresses the important function of emotion for explaining discrimination. He defines prejudice as "a social emotion experienced with respect to one's social identity as a group member, with an outgroup as a target" (p. 304). Discrimination is seen as the behavior consistent with and driven by emotional action tendencies. Evidence from relative deprivation research supports Smith's predictions: Beyond social categorization in ingroup and outgroups, effects of fraternal relative deprivation on outgroup discrimination require an affective reaction (Pettigrew, 1998).

The target's perspective

As outlined in previous sections of this chapter, we think that an appropriate approach to social discrimination as social interaction necessitates reference to both the actor's and the target's perspective. In addition to the aspects dealt with below, we would like to refer to two other contributions in this volume: Crocker and Quinn (this volume, chapter 12), for the issue of social stigmatization and stereotype threat, and Ellemers and Barreto (this volume, chapter 16), for more details on strategies to cope with negative social identity.

The experience of relative deprivation. Similar to actors differing in terms of the intentionality of social differentiation, targets either may not realize unequal treatment, or accept it as normatively adequate, or, on the contrary, feel discriminated against. Relative deprivation theory (Crosby, 1982; Folger, 1986) offers concepts about how these diverging views between targets evaluating group-based social inequality may be explained. There is little relationship between objective standard of living and personal dissatisfaction with own income. In order to know whether their own situation is adequate and satisfying, people need an acceptable standard of reference. In addition, the perception of personal entitlement within a context of social inequality is determined by legitimizing beliefs and attributions of the causes for the status quo (see Major, 1994, for an extended discussion of this issue). For example, the more people believe in a just world, the more they feel that they are in personal control of their own outcomes, and the more they believe that their outcomes are deserved (Crocker & Major, 1994).

If people perceive a gap between their expectations and their outcomes, then feelings of relative deprivation such as hostility, grievance, moral outrage, or resentment will arise. The concept of relative deprivation encompasses a cognitive component, the perceived is-ought discrepancy, and an affective component, the feeling of resentment. Egoistical deprivation refers to a person's position within his or her ingroup, while fraternal deprivation refers to an ingroup's status compared to other groups in society (Runciman, 1966). Fraternal rather than egoistic deprivation is expected to affect intergroup behavior (Dion, 1986): Feelings of group-level dissatisfaction have been found to be correlated with negative attitudes toward ethnic outgroups (Applegryen & Nieuwoudt, 1988), with support for nationalist movements (Guimond & Dubé-Simard, 1983), and with a desire for social change and militancy (Koomen & Fränkel, 1992).

The personal/group discrepancy of social discrimination. Often, when describing their present status quo, members of underprivileged minorities clearly perceive their group as a target of discrimination, but claim they personally would experience little if any discrimination. This meanwhile often-replicated "personal/group discrimination discrepancy" (Taylor, Wright, Moghaddam, & Lalonde, 1990), originally regarded as a phenomenon restricted to minorities and negative evaluations, was recently generalized to majorities and positive evaluations (Moghaddam, Stolkin, & Hutcheson, 1997).

There have been several attempts to explain this seemingly irrational effect. One category of explanations refers to motivational processes. First, denying personal discrimination might protect the self from negative emotional consequences and threat (Crosby, 1984). Second, exaggerating the amount of group discrimination might be functional, as it raises feelings of fraternal relative deprivation and increases the probability of actions to improve the group's status (Taylor, Wright, & Porter, 1994). In contrast to motivated reasoning assumptions, Moghaddam et al. (1997) conceive of the effect as result of the differential availability of incidents of discrimination on the personal and the group level. In a recent longitudinal study, Kessler, Mummendey, and Leiße (in press) showed that the person/group discrepancy might stem from the integration of separate non-overlapping sets of comparative information which are derived from different levels of self-categorization. Depending on the salient level of self-categorization different comparison referents, either persons or groups are selected and provide different comparison outcomes.

Strategies to cope with group-based inequality. According to social identity theory, a positive social identity is to a large extent based on favorable comparisons of the ingroup with some relevant outgroup on salient comparison dimensions (Turner, 1975). Belonging to a less privileged group results in an unsatisfactory or negative social identity (Tajfel & Turner, 1986). Individuals therefore are expected to engage in "identity management strategies" (Van Knippenberg, 1989). Tajfel and Turner (1986) distinguish three classes of strategies, namely individual mobility, social creativity, and social competition. These strategies can be categorized further as individualistic versus collectivistic and as behavioral versus cognitive. Beliefs about the socio-structural characteristics of the intergroup relations are expected to influence the choice of coping strategies. Principally important is the question whether individuals can conceive of an alternative intergroup situation to the status quo. This manifests itself in the perceived stability and legitimacy of status differences, as well as in the perceived permeability of intergroup boundaries. Besides socio-structural variables, the extent to which individuals identify with their ingroup constitutes an important determinant of whether individual or collective strategies are chosen (see Ellemers & Barreto, this volume, chapter 16).

Typically, experimental studies in this field referred to an intergroup situation where the continuous existence of the two groups was beyond doubt. This is different in a merger situation, where two groups are expected to exchange their previous identity against a broader, common ingroup identity (Gaertner et al., 1993). Such a situation was examined in a field study on the relation between East and West Germans after the unification and hence after the merger into the inclusive group of Germans. Here the typically reported effect of perceived stability of status differences was reversed: The pessimistic alternative to the promised change and to the extinction of obvious (material) status differences between East and West was the stability and endurance of the status quo. Consequently, perception of stability rather than instability strengthened East Germans' identification as well as their preferences for collective strategies (Mummendey, Klink, Mielke, Wenzel, & Blanz, 1999).

The prediction of preferences for identity management strategies can be significantly improved by combining assumptions of social identity theory and relative deprivation theory into an integrative model: Individual strategies such as actual or cognitive individual mobility are directly and negatively related to ingroup identification. Collective strategies such as social competition or readiness to participate in social protest are directly connected to negative feelings of resentment and deprivation (Mummendey, Kessler, Klink, & Mielke, 1999).

Conclusions

Differentiation between people because of their group membership is a *necessity* because it is needed by individuals as a basis for orientations and decisions in their everyday life. *Discrimination* between people is a *problem* because it is an inappropriate and unjustified differentiation between people because of their group membership. It is judgment and interpretation and not clear-cut "objective" characteristics of the intergroup treatment itself which define instances of social discrimination. Differentiation changes into discrimination when two parties disagree about the appropriateness and justifiability of a respective distribution and of the underlying categorization. Dissent results from perspective-specific evaluations of a group's entitlement to certain shares of resources derived from the categorization which provided the basis of judging this entitlement. The dissent may be located between actors and targets, or it may exist between actors and targets on the one hand and external observers on the other. With this conception of social discrimination as social interaction we obviously do not intend to "define away" the social problem but to clarify the psychological processes breeding it.

As evidence on the positive–negative asymmetry in social discrimination exemplifies, in the negative more than in the positive domain, differential treatment of own group and outgroup in the negative domain requires elaborate and substantial justifications on behalf of the actor. The abundance of incidents of derogation, rejection, and hostility against outgroups across time and societies demonstrates that ample justifications must be available. Strong ingroup identification and beliefs which interpret unstable or insecure situations as threat from outgroups seem to be key candidates to provide these types of justification. Some approaches see the roots of these social and political beliefs in personality variables such as right-wing authoritarianism, social dominance orientation, or dogmatism. Personality differences, however, cannot account for the homogeneity of people belonging to dominant groups which is necessary for a broad consensus either actively or, in most cases, passively, to support disadvantageous treatment of minorities. As Staub (1989) convincingly demonstrates, even "the roots of evil" could not generate such extreme cases as dehumanization or genocide in a society, if a vast majority would not yield more or less direct support to the whole elimination machinery.

Moreover, it is the interplay between ethnocentric and other discrimination-legitimizing ideologies, created and defended by political and religious elites, gradually coagulated in collective beliefs and social norms and, finally, the sometimes blind, often utilitarian conformity with these norms, which account for the obvious homogeneity in dominant group members' aversive behavior toward minorities. It would be naive to think that a tolerant society would ever be constituted of solely tolerant, non-authoritarian, individual citizens. Rather, a society is tolerant because people conform to norms prescribing tolerance (Kinder, 1998; Pettigrew, 1991). Unfortunately, after a major political change, these people would not have much difficulty in gradually conforming to very different norms. This is exactly the sad lesson that the Kosovo conflict recently taught us: Victims can easily turn into perpetrators as soon as political power changes, and their retaliatory violence is in no way less dehumanizing and cruel than what they have suffered before.

References

Adorno, T. W., Frenkel-Brunswik, E., Lewinson, D., & Sanford, R. N. (1950). *The authoritarian personality*. New York: Harper.

Allport, G. W. (1954). *The nature of prejudice*. Reading, MA: Addison-Wesley.

Altemeyer, B. (1988). *Enemies of freedom: Understanding right-wing authoritarianism*. San Francisco, CA: Jossey-Bass.

Altemeyer, B. (1994). Reducing prejudice in right-wing authoritarians. In M. P. Zanna & J. M. Olson (Eds.), *The psychology of prejudice: The Ontario symposium* (Vol. 7, pp. 131–148). Hillsdale, NJ: Erlbaum.

Appelgryen, A. E., & Nieuwoudt, J. M. (1988). Relative deprivation and the ethnic attitudes of Blacks and Afrikaans-speaking Whites in South Africa. *Journal of Social Psychology, 128,* 311–323.

Averill, J. R. (1982). *Anger and aggression. An essay on emotion.* New York: Springer.

Bar-Tal, D. (1989). Delegitimization: The extreme case of stereotyping and prejudice. In D. Bar-Tal, C. F. Graumann, A. W. Kruglanski, & W. Stroebe (Eds.), *Stereotyping and prejudice* (pp. 169–182). Berlin: Springer.

Batson, C. D., & Burris, C. T. (1994). Personal religion: Depressant or stimulant of prejudice and discrimination? In M. P. Zanna & J. M. Olson (Eds.), *The psychology of prejudice: The Ontario symposium* (Vol. 7, pp. 149–170). Hillsdale, NJ: Erlbaum.

Blanz, M., Mummendey, A., & Otten, S. (1995). Positive-negative asymmetry in social discrimination: The impact of stimulus-valence, size- and status-differentials in intergroup evaluations. *British Journal of Social Psychology, 34*(4), 409–419.

Blanz, M., Mummendey, A., & Otten, S. (1997). Normative evaluations and frequency expectations regarding positive versus negative outcome allocations between groups. *European Journal of Social Psychology, 27,* 165–176.

Branscombe, N. R., & Wann, D. L. (1994). Collective self-esteem consequences of outgroup derogation when a valued social identity is on trial. *European Journal of Social Psychology, 24,* 641–657.

Brewer, M. B. (1979). In-group bias in the minimal intergroup situation: A cognitive-motivational analysis. *Psychological Bulletin, 86*(2), 307–324.

Brown, R. J. (1999). *Group processes: Dynamics within and between groups.* Oxford, UK: Blackwell.

Crandall, C. S., & Cohen, C. (1994). The personality of the stigmatizer: Cultural world view, conventionalism, and self-esteem. *Journal of Research in Personality, 28,* 461–480.

Crocker, J., & Major, B. (1994). Reactions to stigma: The moderating role of jusifications. In M. P. Zanna & J. M. Olson (Eds.), *The psychology of prejudice: The Ontario symposium* (Vol. 7, pp. 289–314). Hillsdale, NJ: Erlbaum.

Crosby, F. (1982). *Relative deprivation and working women.* New York: Oxford University Press.

Crosby, F. (1984). The denial of personal discrimination. *American Behavioral Scientist, 27,* 371–386.

Diehl, M. (1989). Justice and discrimination between minimal groups: The limits of equity. *British Journal of Social Psychology, 28,* 227–238.

Dion, K. L. (1986). Responses to perceived discrimination and relative deprivation. In J. M. Olson, C. P. Herman, & M. P. Zanna (Eds.), *Relative deprivation and social comparison: The Ontario symposium* (Vol. 5, pp. 159–179). Hillsdale, NJ: Erlbaum.

Dobbs, M., & Crano, W. D. (in prep.). *Accountability in the Minimal Group Paradigm: Implications for aversive discrimination and social identity theory.*

Dovidio, J. F., Brigham, J. C., Johnson, B, T., & Gaertner, S. L. (1996). Stereotyping, prejudice, and discrimination: Another look. In C. N. Macrae, C. Stangor, & M. Hewstone (Eds.), *Stereotypes and stereotyping* (pp. 276–319). New York: Guilford Press.

Dovidio, J. F., Mann J., & Gaertner, S. L. (1989). Resistance to affirmative action: The implications of aversive racism. In F. A. Blanchard & F. J. Crosby (Eds.), *Affirmative action in perspective* (pp. 85–102). New York: Springer.

Eagly, A. H. (1987). *Sex differences in social behavior: A social-role interpretation.* Hillsdale, NJ: Erlbaum.

Eckhardt, W. (1991). Authoritarianism. *Political Psychology, 12,* 97–124.

Ellemers, N., Van Rijswijk, W., Roefs, M., & Simons, C. (1997). Bias in intergroup perceptions: Balancing group identity with social reality. *Personality and Social Psychology Bulletin, 23,* 186–198.

Folger, R. (1986). A referent cognition theory of relative deprivation. In J. M. Olson, C. P. Herman, & M. P. Zanna (Eds.), *Relative deprivation and social comparison: The Ontario symposium* (Vol. 4, pp. 33–55). Hillsdale, NJ: Erlbaum.

Gaertner, S. L., & Dovidio, J. F. (1986). The aversive form of racism. In J. F. Dovidio & S. L. Gaertner (Eds.), *Prejudice, discrimination, and racism* (pp. 61–90). San Diego, CA: Academic Press.

Gaertner, S. L., Dovidio, J. F., Anastasio, P. A., Bachman, B. A., & Rust, M. C. (1993). The common ingroup identity model: Recategorization and the reduction of intergroup bias. In W. Stroebe & M. Hewstone (Eds.), *European review of social psychology* (Vol. 4, pp. 1–26). Chichester, UK: Wiley.

Gardham, K., & Brown, R. J. (in press). Two forms of intergroup discrimination with positive and negative outcomes: Explaining the positive-negative asymmetry effect. *British Journal of Social Psychology*.

Graumann C. F., & Wintermantel, M. (1989). Discriminatory speech acts. A functional approach. In D. Bar-Tal, C. F. Graumann, A. W. Kruglanski, & W. Stroebe (Eds.), *Stereotyping and prejudice* (pp. 183–204). New York: Springer.

Guimond, S., & Dubé-Simard, L. (1983). Relative deprivation theory and the Québec nationalist movement: The cognition-emotion distinction and the personal-group deprivation issue. *Journal of Personality and Social Psychology, 44,* 526–535.

Kessler, T., Mummendey, A., & Leiße, U. K. (in press). The personal/group discrepancy: Is there a common information basis?

Hinkle, S., & Brown, R. J. (1990). Intergroup comparisons and social identity: Some links and lacunae. In D. Abrams & M. Hogg (Eds.), *Social identity theory: Constructive and critical advances.* Hemel Hempstead, UK: Wheatsheaf.

Kinder, D. R. (1998). Opinion and action in the realm of politics. In D. T. Gilbert, S. T. Fiske, & G. Lindzey (Eds.), *The handbook of social psychology* (Vol. 2, pp. 778–867). Boston, MA: McGraw-Hill.

Koomen, W., & Fränkel, E. G. (1992). Effects of experienced discrimination and different forms of relative deprivation among Surinamese, a Dutch ethnic minority group. *Journal of Community and Applied Social Psychology, 2,* 63–71.

Major, B. (1994). From social inequality to personal entitlement: The role of social comparisons, legitimacy appraisals, and group membership. In M. P. Zanna (Ed.), *Advances in experimental social psychology* (Vol. 26, pp. 293–355). San Diego, CA: Academic Press.

Messick, D. M., & Mackie, D. M. (1989). Intergroup relations. *Annual Review of Psychology, 40,* 45–81.

Mikula, G. (1994). Perspective-related differences in interpretations of injustice by victims and victimizers: A test with close relationships. In M. J. Lerner & G. Mikula (Eds.), *Injustice in close relationships: Entitlement and the affectional bond* (pp. 175–203). New York: Plenum.

Moghaddam, F. M., Stolkin, H. J., & Hutcheson, L. S. (1997). A generalized personal/group discrepancy: Testing the domain specificity of a perceived higher effect of events on one's group than on one's self. *Personality and Social Psychology Bulletin, 23,* 724–750.

Mummendey, A. (1995). Positive distinctiveness and intergroup discrimination: An old couple living in divorce. *European Journal of Social Psychology, 25,* 657–670.

Mummendey, A., Kessler, T., Klink, A., & Mielke, R. (1999). Strategies to cope with negative social identity: Predictions by Social Identity Theory and Relative Deprivation Theory. *Journal of Personality and Social Psychology, 76,* 229–245.

Mummendey, A., Klink, A., Mielke, R., Wenzel, M., & Blanz, M. (1999). Socio-structural relations and identity management strategies: Results from a field study in East Germany. *European Journal of Social Psychology, 29,* 259–285.

Mummendey, A., Linneweber, V., & Löschper, G. (1984). Aggression: From act to interaction. In A. Mummendey (Ed.), *Social psychology of aggression: From individual behavior to social interaction* (pp. 69–106). New York: Springer.

Mummendey, A., & Otten, S. (1993). Aggression: Interaction between individuals and social groups. In R. B. Felson & J. T. Tedeschi (Eds.), *Aggression and violence. Social interactionist perspectives* (pp. 145–167). Washington, DC: American Psychological Association.

Mummendey, A., & Otten, S. (1998). Positive-negative asymmetry in social discrimination. In W. Stroebe & M. Hewstone (Eds.), *European review of social psychology* (Vol. 9, pp. 107–143). New York: John Wiley & Sons Ltd.

Mummendey, A., Otten, S., Berger, U., & Kessler, T. (in press). Positive-negative asymmetry in social discrimination: Valence of evaluation and salience of categorization. *Personality and Social Psychology Bulletin.*

Mummendey, A., & Simon, B. (1991). Diskriminierung von Fremdgruppen: Zur Asymmetrie im Umgang mit positiven und negativen Bewertungen und Ressourcen. In D. Frey (Ed.), *Berichte über den 37. Kongreß der Deutschen Gesellschaft für Psychologie in Kiel 1990* (Vol. 2, pp. 359–365). Göttingen, Germany: Hogrefe.

Mummendey, A., Simon, B., Dietze, C., Grünert, M., Haeger, G., Kessler, S., Lettgen, S., & Schäferhoff, S. (1992). Categorization is not enough: Intergroup discrimination in negative outcome allocations. *Journal of Experimental Social Psychology, 28*, 125–144.

Mummendey, A., & Wenzel, M. (1999). Social discrimination and tolerance: Reactions to intergroup difference. *Personality and Social Psychology Review, 3*, 158–174.

Oakes, P. J. (1987). The salience of social categories. In J. C. Turner, M. A. Hogg, P. J. Oakes, S. Reicher, & M. Wetherell (Eds.), *Rediscovering the social group: A self-categorization theory* (pp. 117–141). Oxford, UK: Blackwell.

Oakes, P. J. (1996). The categorization process: Cognition and the group in the social psychology of stereotyping. In W. P. Robinson (Ed.), *Social groups and identities* (pp. 95–119). Oxford, UK: Butterworth.

Opotow, S. (1990). Moral exclusion and injustice: An introduction. *Journal of Social Issues, 46*, 1–20.

Opotow, S. (1995). Drawing the line. Social categorization, moral exclusion, and the scope of justice. In B. B. Bunker & J. Z. Rubin (Eds.), *Conflict, cooperation, and justice: Essays inspired by the work of Morton Deutsch* (pp. 347–369). San Francisco, CA: Jossey-Bass.

Otten, S., & Moskowitz, G. B. (2000). Evidence for implicit evaluative ingroup bias: Affect-biased spontaneous trait inference in a minimal group paradigm. *Journal of Experimental Social Psychology, 36*, 77–89.

Otten, S., & Mummendey, A. (1999a). Aggressive Interaktionen und soziale Diskriminierung: Zur Rolle perspektiven – und kontextspezifischer Legitimationsprozesse. *Zeitschrift für Sozialpsychologie, 30*, 126–138.

Otten, S., & Mummendey, A. (1999b). To our benefit or at your expense? Justice considerations in intergroup allocations of positive and negative resources. *Social Justice Research, 12*, 19–38.

Otten, S., & Mummendey, A. (2000). Valence-dependent probability of ingroup-favoritism between minimal groups: An integrative view on the positive-negative asymmetry in social discrimination. In D. Capozza & R. Brown (Eds.), *Social identity processes* (pp. 33–48). London: Sage.

Otten, S., Mummendey, A., & Blanz, M. (1996). Intergroup discrimination in positive and negative outcome allocations: The impact of stimulus valence, relative group status, and relative group size. *Personality and Social Psychology Bulletin, 22*, 568–581.

Otten, S., Mummendey, A., & Buhl, T. (1998). Accuracy in information processing and the positive-negative asymmetry in social discrimination. *Revue Internationale de Psychologie Sociale, 11*, 69–96.

Otten, S., Mummendey, A., & Wenzel, M. (1995). Evaluation of aggressive interactions in interpersonal and intergroup contexts. *Aggressive Behavior, 21*, 205–224.

Otten, S., & Wentura, D. (1999). About the impact of automaticity in the Minimal Group Paradigm: Evidence from affective priming tasks. *European Journal of Social Psychology, 29*, 1049–1071.

Perdue, C. W., Dovidio, J. F., Gurtman M. B., & Tyler, R. B. (1990). Us and them: Social categorization and the process of intergroup bias. *Journal of Personality and Social Psychology, 59*, 475–486.

Perreault, S., & Bourhis, R. Y. (1999). Ethnocentrism, social identification, and discrimination. *Personality and Social Psychology Bulletin, 25*, 92–103.

Pettigrew, T. F. (1991). Normative theory in intergroup relations: Explaining both harmony and conflict. *Psychology and developing societies, 3*, 3–16.

Pettigrew, T. F. (1998). Reactions toward the new minorities of Western Europe. *Annual Review of Sociology, 24*, 77–103.

Pettigrew, T. F., & Meertens, R. W. (1995). Subtle and blatant prejudice in Western Europe. *European Journal of Social Psychology, 25*, 57–75.

Postmes, T., & Spears, R. (1998). Deindividuation and anti-normative behavior: A meta-analysis. *Psychological Bulletin, 123*, 1–21.

Quillian, L. (1995). Prejudice as a response to perceived group threat: Population composition and anti-immigrant and racial prejudice in Europe. *American Sociology Review, 60*, 586–611.

Rabbie, J. M., & Horwitz, M. (1969). Arousal of ingroup–outgroup bias by a chance win or loss. *Journal of Personality and Social Psychology, 13*, 269–277.

Reynolds, K., Turner, J. C., & Haslam, A. (2000). When are we better than them and they worse than us? A closer look at social discrimination in positive and negative domains. *Journal of Personality and Social Psychology, 78*, 64–80.

Rokeach, M. (Ed.). (1960). *The open and closed mind.* New York: Basic Books.

Runciman, W. G. (1966). *Relative deprivation and social justice.* London: Routledge & Kegan Paul.

Sani, F., & Reicher, S. (1998). When consensus fails: An analysis of the schism within the Italian Communist Party (1991). *European Journal of Social Psychology, 28*, 623–645.

Sani, F., & Reicher, S. (1999). Identity, argument, and schism: Two longitudinal studies of the split in the Church of England over the ordination of women to the priesthood. *Group Processes and Intergroup Relations, 2*, 279–300.

Sidanius, J. (1993). The psychology of group conflict and the dynamics of oppression: A social dominance perspective. In S. Iyngar & W. McGuire (Eds.), *Current approaches to political psychology* (pp. 173–211). Durham, NC: Duke University Press.

Sherif, M. (1966). *Group conflict and cooperation.* London: Routledge & Kegan Paul.

Smith, E. R. (1993). Social identity and social emotions: Toward new conceptualizations of prejudice. In D. M. Mackie & D. L. Hamilton (Eds.), *Affect, cognition, and stereotyping* (pp. 297–315). San Diego, CA: Academic Press.

Staub, E. (1989). *The roots of evil. The origins of genocide and other group violence.* Cambridge, UK: Cambridge University Press.

Tajfel, H. (1981). *Human groups and social categories: Studies in social psychology.* Cambridge, UK: Cambridge University Press.

Tajfel, H., Billig, M. G., Bundy, R. P., & Flament, C. (1971). Social categorization and intergroup behaviour. *European Journal of Social Psychology, 1*, 149–178.

Tajfel, H., & Turner, J. C. (1986). The social identity theory of intergroup behavior. In S. Worchel & W. G. Austin (Eds.), *Psychology of intergroup relations* (pp. 7–24). Chicago, IL: Nelson-Hall Publishers.

Taylor, D., & Moghaddam, F. M. (1994). *Theories of intergroup relations.* New York: Praeger.

Taylor, D. M., Wright, S. C., Moghaddam, F. M., & Lalonde, R. N. (1990). The personal/group discrimination discrepancy: Perceiving my group, but not myself, to be a target for discrimination. *Personality and Social Psychology Bulletin, 16,* 254–262.

Taylor, D. M., Wright, S. C., & Porter, L. E. (1994). Dimensions of perceived discrimination: The personal/group discrimination discrepancy. In M. P. Zanna & J. M. Olson (Eds.), *The psychology of prejudice: The Ontario symposium* (Vol. 7, pp. 233–255). Hillsdale, NJ: Erlbaum.

Tedeschi, J. T. (1984). A social psychological interpretation of human aggression. In A. Mummendey (Ed.), *Social psychology of aggression: From individual behavior to social interaction* (pp. 5–20). Berlin: Springer.

Tedeschi, J. T., & Felson, R. B. (1994). *Aggression and coercive actions: A social interactionist perspective.* Washington, DC: American Psychological Association.

Thränhardt, D. (1995). The political uses of xenophobia in England, France, and Germany. *Party Politics, 1,* 323–345.

Triandis, H. C., & Trafimow, D. (this volume).

Turner, J. C. (1975). Social comparison and social identity: Some prospects for intergroup behaviour. *European Journal of Social Psychology, 5,* 5–35.

Turner, J. C., Hogg, M. A., Oakes, P. J., Reicher, S. D., & Wetherell, M. S. (1987). *Rediscovering the social group. A self-categorization theory.* Oxford, UK: Blackwell.

Tyler, T. R. (this volume).

Van Knippenberg, A. (1989). Strategies of identity management. In J. P. Oudenhoven & T. M. Willemsen (Eds.), *Ethnic minorities: Social-psychological perspectives* (pp. 59–76). Amsterdam: Swets & Zeitlinger.

Vanneman, R. D., & Pettigrew, T. F. (1972). Race and relative deprivation in the urban United States. *Race, 13*(4), 461–486.

Wagner, U., & Zick, A. (1995). Formal education and ethnic prejudice. *European Journal of Social Psychology, 25,* 41–56.

Wenzel, M. (1997). *Soziale Kategorisierungen im Bereich distributiver Gerechtigkeit.* Münster, Germany: Waxmann.

Wenzel, M. (2000). Justice and identity: The significance of inclusion for perceptions of entitlement and the justice motive. *Personality and Social Psychology Bulletin, 26,* 157–176.

CHAPTER SEVEN

The Social Identity Perspective in Intergroup Relations: Theories, Themes, and Controversies

John C. Turner and Katherine J. Reynolds

Introduction

There has been a steady growth of research on intergroup relations in the last 30 years and the social identity perspective, comprising social identity theory (SIT; Tajfel & Turner, 1979) and self-categorization theory (SCT; Turner, Hogg, Oakes, Reicher, & Wetherell, 1987), has played a leading role in this development. In fact, research in this tradition is being pursued more vigorously now than ever before (e.g., Abrams & Hogg, 1999; Ellemers, Spears, & Doosje, 1999; Haslam, in press; Mummendey & Wenzel, 1999; Oakes, Haslam, & Turner, 1994; Spears, Oakes, Ellemers, & Haslam, 1997; Tyler, Kramer, & John, 1999; Worchel, Morales, Paez, & Deschamps, 1998). Its basic ideas about the role of social categorization and social identities in group processes are now widely accepted throughout the field (e.g., Brewer & Brown, 1998; Fiske, 1998). These ideas are moreover finding their way into new areas (Abrams & Hogg, 1999; Haslam, in press; Turner & Haslam, in press; Turner & Onorato, 1999).

This chapter will provide an overview of the social identity perspective by discussing key ideas and addressing important misunderstandings. The latter are worth discussing to identify themes in current research and directions for the future. It will be argued that there has been a failure to take seriously the metatheory behind the perspective. The tendency has been to divorce psychological processes from the social forces that structure their functioning. SIT and SCT emphasize that intergroup relations cannot be reduced

Note: This research was supported by a Large Australian Research Council grant to John Turner, Kate Reynolds, and Alex Haslam.

to individual psychology but emerge from an interaction between psychology and society (Tajfel, 1972a, 1979; Turner, 1996).

The first section summarizes the basic ideas of SIT and SCT while highlighting the similarities and differences between them. In the second section a series of questions, which raise key themes and controversies within social identity research, are addressed. The final section attempts to identify and examine the necessary features of a comprehensive social psychological analysis of social conflict between groups. It is concluded that the social identity perspective, although not intended as a "sovereign" approach to intergroup conflict, has made a significant contribution toward understanding intergroup relations, and that future progress depends on the metatheoretical ideas within which SIT and SCT developed being fully understood and embraced.

The Theories: Similarities and Differences

Many researchers tend to confuse SIT and SCT. Some use the term "social identity theory" to refer to ideas from both theories indiscriminately. Others, in distinguishing the theories, misattribute ideas from one to the other. For these reasons it is useful to highlight the main points of similarity and difference between SIT and SCT. Space is not available for detailed summaries of the theories but these are widely available (e.g., Turner, 1999).

SIT attempts to make sense of intergroup relations in real societal contexts (Tajfel, 1978; Tajfel & Turner, 1979). It provides a comprehensive theory of intergroup relations and social change in socially stratified societies (the term social identity theory was first employed by Turner & Brown, 1978, to describe this complex analysis of intergroup relations) and addressed ingroup bias, social conflict, intergroup relations: "Why do people in groups discriminate against each other?", "Why are they ethnocentric?". Its response to these questions was the idea that people have a need for positive social identity which requires them to establish a positively valued distinctiveness for their own group compared to other groups.

The theory has *three* indispensable elements (or "legs of a conceptual tripod," as Tajfel, 1979, put it). As well as (1) an analysis of aspects of collective psychology (i.e., the need for a positive social identity), the theory delineated how this motivation interacted with (2) specific intergroup status differences in society and (3) the tendency to deal with one's identity problems as either an "individual" or as a "group" (defined as movement along a continuum from interpersonal to intergroup behavior).

SIT was used to explore the psychological consequences for members of the relative status position of their group (high or low status) and the perceived nature of intergroup status differences (secure vs. insecure, i.e., legitimate or stable vs. illegitimate or unstable), and to elaborate the different ways in which group members could and would react to the challenges posed to their social identities by their different locations in the social structure and their shared beliefs about the nature of the social structure (the main strategies identified being "individual mobility," "social creativity," and "social competition").

Tajfel developed the idea of the "interpersonal–intergroup continuum" (the extent to which one acted as an individual in terms of interpersonal relationships or as a group member in terms of intergroup relationships) to explain when social identity processes were likely to come into operation and how social interaction differed qualitatively between these extremes (Tajfel, 1974, 1978). He argued that as behavior became more intergroup, attitudes to the outgroup within the ingroup tended to become more consensual and that outgroup members tended to be seen as homogeneous and undifferentiated members of their social category.

Shift along the continuum was a function of an interaction between psychological and social factors. He emphasized the degree to which group members shared an ideology of "individual mobility" or "social change" and saw the social system as characterized by rigid and intense social stratification. He suggested that the perceived impermeability of group boundaries tended to be associated with an ideology of "social change," characterized by a belief that people cannot resolve their identity problems through individual action and mobility but are only able to change their social situation by acting collectively in terms of their shared group membership.

Contrary to many reviews the basic psychological idea of SIT was not the distinction between personal and social identity. As Tajfel stated on numerous occasions, it was the notion that social comparisons between groups were focused on the establishment of positive ingroup distinctiveness. Social identity was distinguished from the rest of the self-concept but not from personal identity. The interpersonal–intergroup continuum in SIT was not related to personal versus social identity but to "acting in terms of self" versus "acting in terms of group" (Tajfel, 1974).

The distinction between personal and social identity was the beginning of SCT and was not made until the end of the 1970s. SCT began with the insight that Tajfel's distinction between interpersonal and intergroup behavior could be explained by a parallel and underlying distinction between *personal* and *social identity* (Turner, 1978, 1982). SCT was not concerned with ethnocentrism or discrimination but with psychological group membership: "What is a psychological group?", "How are people able to act psychologically in a collective way as group members?". It tried to explain how people became a group and the psychological basis of group processes.

The basic idea was that self-perception or self-conception varies between personal and social identity and that as one moves from defining self as an individual person to defining self in terms of a social identity, group behavior becomes possible and emerges. In other words, when a shared social identity is psychologically operative or salient there is a depersonalization of self-perception such that people's perceptions of their mutual and collective similarities are enhanced. Subsequently the distinction between personal and social identity was related to the more general hypothesis that there are different levels of self-categorization, but this was a reconceptualization of the founding notion, that personal and social identity can be distinguished and that group behavior is simply people acting more in terms of social than personal identity.

A fundamental point of SCT which has been central to the analysis of stereotyping and other group phenomena is that when we perceive ourselves as "we" and "us" as opposed to "I" and "me," this is ordinary and normal self-experience in which the self is defined in terms of others who exist outside of the individual perceiver and is therefore not purely personal. It is a shared cognitive representation of a collective entity which exists reflexively in the minds of individual group members and is structured by the realities of group life in a particular social system. Social identity is a collective self, not a "looking-glass" self – it is not an "I" as perceived by the group, but a "we" who are the group and who define ourselves for ourselves (Turner, Oakes, Haslam, & McGarty, 1994; Turner & Onorato, 1999).

Just as SIT provides a new way of approaching intergroup relations, so SCT provides a new way of thinking about social groups. It has provided new analyses of group formation and cohesion, social cooperation, social influence (conformity, polarization, minority influence, and leadership), crowd behavior, "de-individuation," the contact hypothesis, social stereotyping, the self-concept, and personality. Current work on the theory has in fact gone far beyond traditional group issues (Turner, 1999).

Attributing the distinction between personal and social identity (and the hypothesis that the shift from personal to social identity transforms individual into group behavior) to SIT acts therefore to strip SCT of its core idea. The result is that the theory loses its force as an explanation of group psychology. It tends to be reduced to a purely cognitive analysis of categorization processes, an application of Tajfel's (1969) accentuation theory to self-perception but with a more developed analysis of the contextual factors determining the "salience" of social categorizations. SCT is then described as "social-cognitive" (Abrams & Hogg, 1999), as a turn away from the more "social" and "motivational" SIT to less social and more individual-cognitive ideas. It is assumed to ignore or reject the role of self-esteem in social identity processes, and to have been developed to replace SIT (Operario & Fiske, 1999). SIT in turn is reduced to a "self-esteem" theory, one which explains intergroup relations in terms of the need for positive self-esteem and has little interest in cognitive analysis. The failure of its supposed self-esteem predictions then leads it to be dismissed as a "macro-social" metatheory (Operario & Fiske, 1999), a polite way of saying that it has been empirically falsified.

In fact, both SIT and SCT are "cognitive" in the classic social psychological sense that they assume that to explain and predict behavior we need to understand how people perceive, define, and make sense of the world and themselves. Both are in the Gestalt (as opposed to behaviorist) tradition which derives from Sherif, Asch, Lewin, Heider, Festinger, and others. Both are also part of the cognitive tradition which goes back to Bruner's "New Look" in perception through Tajfel's (1957) analysis of categorization and values (other "cognitive" influences on SCT include Rosch, Medin, and Barsalou and colleagues). Neither is an individual-level cognitive theory of the form that dominated social cognition research in the 1980s. Further, despite assertions to the contrary, SCT assumes explicitly that "self-categories tend to be evaluated positively and that there are motivational pressures to maintain this state of affairs" (Turner et al., 1987, p. 57). SCT provides a specific analysis of self-esteem, seeing it as an expression of the degree to which self at any level is perceived as relatively prototypical of a higher-order, valued self-category. SCT does not discuss self-esteem in the same terms as SIT for the simple reason that SIT had already done the job and SCT was not seen as a replacement for SIT but as complementary to it (see Turner & Oakes, 1989, for a summary of how SCT emerged from social identity work).

Themes and Controversies

Are social groups the same as categories?

Rabbie, Schot, and Visser (1989) contrast social groups, which they define as "dynamic wholes," social systems characterized by perceived interdependence among members, with social categories, which they define as collections of individuals who share at least one attribute in common. They suggest that the social identity perspective assumes that groups are the same as categories.

Social groups are, of course, not the same as cognitive categories and the social identity perspective does not suggest that they are. In answering this charge, Tajfel (1982) criticized Rabbie and Horwitz for confusing two types of categories. The term "category" can mean an objective collection of people as defined by an outsider in terms of some common characteristic – a sociological category, for example, such as single-parent families. Such a group exists objectively, but it is a "membership" group (Turner, 1991). It need have no psychological or subjective significance for its members. It is not a "reference" group in classic terms.

The social identity perspective is explicitly and specifically addressed to reference groups. It uses the term "category," not in the sense of sociological categories, but in the sense of self-categories. Such "categories" are psychological representations in the mind; they are cognitive structures which people use *to define themselves* and to change their behavior. The point of SCT is to explain how a sociological group becomes a psychological group, how a membership group becomes a reference group. The idea is that people create cognitive categories to represent themselves as a higher-order entity and that, insofar as they represent themselves in terms of such categories, in terms of psychological concepts which become part of their mental functioning, they are able to transform their relationships to each other. As one moves from the "I" to the "we," we transform our behavioral and psychological relationships to each other so that we can now act in terms of a higher-order, emergent entity called a psychological group.

Rabbie and others confuse sociological categories (objective collections) with self-categories (psychological concepts). A social group, on the other hand, is a body of real people that acts in the world; it is a social system. The members interact, behave, and have relationships with each other. They share an identity, have goals, are interdependent, and they have social structures. A group has a social as well as a psychological reality. Such groups cannot be confused with either type of category above, but nevertheless their existence requires explanation. As psychologists, we assume that part of the explanation has to do with the psychology of their members. And part of their psychology is the way in which they create higher-order social categorical representations of themselves to transform their relations to each other and themselves. This does not mean that a group is only psychological, or that it is explained solely by social psychology. But self-categorization theorists are entitled to point to the psychological processes involved in group formation as a contribution to their explanation.

Rabbie et al. also suggest that the social identity perspective rejects the role of goal interdependence in group formation and that the "minimal group" studies which inspired the development of SIT and SCT were misinterpreted by Tajfel and Turner. They claim that minimal intergroup behavior is motivated by personal self-interest and hence does not provide evidence that self-categorization is alone sufficient for psychological group formation. Their points have been answered in detail by Turner and Bourhis (1996) but it is important to note that relevant studies demonstrate that ingroup bias is influenced by participants' degree of identification with minimal ingroups rather than by the degree to which they stand to gain financially from ingroup favoritism (e.g., Bourhis, Turner, & Gagnon, 1997).

Does SIT predict a positive correlation between ingroup identification and ingroup bias?

Hinkle and Brown (1990) propose that one of the basic propositions of SIT is that there should be a direct causal link between ingroup identification and ingroup bias. This translates into the hypothesis that positive correlations should be obtained between individual differences in identification with some ingroup and individual differences in the degree to which that group is favored over the outgroups in the setting. In fact, such correlations are not uniformly positive but often tend to be weak and quite variable (Brown, Hinkle, Ely, Fox-Cardamone, Maras, & Taylor, 1992; Hinkle & Brown, 1990). These findings are then cited as evidence against the theory and are used to justify attempts at major revision (Brown et al., 1992). The lack of simple positive relationships between ingroup identification and bias is probably the single most frequently cited empirical "disconfirmation" of SIT. We suggest that such an inference is unjustified (see also Turner, 1999).

The proposition is a version of SIT's basic idea that positive social identity requires positive ingroup distinctiveness, but SIT did not equate this idea with a direct causal connection between ingroup identification and ingroup bias. On the contrary, the causal relationship was always assumed to be mediated by a number of complicating factors and "ingroup bias" ("social competition") is only one of several individual and group strategies which can be pursued to achieve positive distinctiveness (others being "individual mobility" and "social creativity").

SIT assumed that whether or not ingroup bias was observed was a function, inter alia, of the specific intergroup comparison being made and the interaction between the relative status position of the ingroup, the perceived impermeability of group boundaries, and the nature of the perceived status differences on the relevant dimension. Turner and Brown (1978), for example, showed early on just how complex the relationship between ingroup bias and different intergroup status differences could be. Low status groups tended to be discriminatory when their position was unstable and illegitimate but not when it was secure; high status groups tended to be particularly discriminatory when their position was legitimate but unstable but not when it was both illegitimate and unstable. In this light the variable relationship between measures of ingroup identification and ingroup bias is in line with the theory and only to be expected. Nothing in the summary of the theory above implies simple positive correlations.

Another issue is that identification in the relevant studies is often not experimentally manipulated but is an individual difference variable. The use of individual difference methodology is inconsistent with the SCT hypothesis that there is a psychological discontinuity between people acting as individuals and people acting as group members (e.g., Turner & Onorato, 1999). The role of social identity salience is fundamental to this point. If one obtains intergroup attitudes from subjects responding in terms of their personal differences from others, in terms of their personal identities, then the attitudes obtained are not likely to remain unchanged when the subjects' social identities become salient. SCT predicts directly that depersonalizing participants enhances intragroup homogeneity and thus will modify correlations between the intergroup responses and a prior individual difference score (Haslam & Wilson, 2000; Reynolds, Turner, Haslam, & Ryan, 1999; Verkuyten & Hagendoorn, 1998).

These and related issues are elaborated elsewhere (Turner, 1999). An important point to be made here is that differences in ingroup identification, conceptualized appropriately, are of central interest to the social identity perspective (see Ellemers et al., 1999). What we need to avoid is the idea that identification expresses some kind of fixed and stable self-structure or personality trait which is chronically salient across situations and directly expressed in just one collective strategy independently of the social meaning of the intergroup relationship. From a self-categorization viewpoint, measures of identification may be a way of getting at the individual's readiness to self-categorize in terms of some identity, reflecting the psychological resources a person will tend to bring to the task of understanding self and constructing self-categories in some setting. They will reflect the centrality of some group membership in a person's understanding of their place in the social order and their relationships to others and also their commitment to that identity as a consequence of that understanding and their social values.

Does SIT actually contain the so-called "self-esteem hypothesis"?

The "self-esteem hypothesis" in this context refers to two supposed corollaries of SIT advanced by Hogg and Abrams (1990): that (1) successful intergroup discrimination elevates self-esteem and (2) depressed or threatened self-esteem promotes intergroup discrimination. The predictions which tend to be made and which receive mixed support are that ingroup bias should enhance or be correlated with (individual) self-esteem and that low (individual) self-esteem or ingroup status should enhance or be correlated with ingroup bias. The lack of support for these predictions is another widely cited "disconfirmation" of SIT.

Some of the problems with these corollaries have been discussed by Farsides (1995), Long and Spears (1997), Rubin and Hewstone (1998), and Turner (1999). The first point to note is that they are not actually contained in SIT. In fact, the theory can be seen as inconsistent with them. The theory assumes that there is a need for positive self-evaluation, but it does not equate this need with an individual-level motive. On the contrary, it is concerned with positively valued social identity, not individual-level self-esteem, and it does not even predict main effects of low group status or depressed social identity on ingroup bias, let alone such effects as a function of low personal self-esteem. Under conditions where social identity is salient, it is *insecure* (unstable and/or illegitimate) *social identity* in *interaction with low or high* status that prompts the need for positive distinctiveness and the search for positive distinctiveness *can take a variety of forms*. Social identity processes are only expected to come into play where social identity is salient and under such conditions people act in terms of their shared social identity, not in terms of their individual-level self-esteem.

For example, a low status group whose inferiority is stable and legitimate on the status dimension and which sees group boundaries as impermeable may seek positive distinctiveness on alternative dimensions (social creativity) but it is not likely to discriminate on the status dimension. A high status group with positive social identity which perceives its superiority as legitimate but unstable and under threat may be highly discriminatory. The personal self-esteem of group members is of no relevance to these predictions, and not even does positive or negative social identity in isolation lead to any consistent outcome. What matters is status position in interaction with the perceived nature of status differences and group boundaries.

Where discrimination takes place and successfully achieves positive distinctiveness, this might be reflected in a relevant status-related measure of collective self-esteem (but perhaps not for a high status group protecting what it has), but there is no reason why it should necessarily be reflected in a measure of personal self-esteem. If positive distinctiveness is achieved through some strategy other than social competition on the status dimension, then collective self-esteem could increase or be maintained without any basis in intergroup discrimination. To determine whether ingroup bias or some other intergroup strategy enhances positive social identity, one has to measure the self-evaluative aspects of the specific social not personal identity in relation to the specific situational dimension of comparison, what Rubin and Hewstone (1998) refer to as "social," "specific," and "state" self-esteem, not "personal," "global," and "trait" self-esteem. Why would a more positive social identity affect personal, global, and trait self-esteem? Perhaps where there is no other outlet, the participants may sometimes employ whatever measure is available to express the situationally relevant intergroup comparison, but this cannot be taken for granted.

The social identity perspective provides a different way of thinking about self-esteem from the traditional view that it is an individual psychological property which drives and motivates behavior independently of the social context. It makes a core assumption of a psychological discontinuity between individual and group behavior, personal and social identity and therefore personal and social categorical self-esteem (Branscombe & Ellemers, 1998; Brewer & Weber, 1994; Crocker & Luhtanen, 1990; Turner, 1982; Turner et al., 1987, pp. 57–65). The need for a positive social identity is not driven by some fixed "inner" motive but arises from the interaction of social identities, social comparison, and social values in specific intergroup relationships (Tajfel, 1972b; Turner, 1975). There are different levels of self-esteem just as there are different levels of self-categorization (e.g., Brewer & Weber, 1994) and self-esteem at any level is a function of judgments of self in relation to higher-level identity-based norms and values through relevant self-other comparisons on specific dimensions.

Are ingroup bias and therefore prejudice universal and inevitable features of relations between human social groups?

Two widespread misconceptions are that the social identity perspective sees ethnocentrism as a universal feature of relations between human social groups and that ingroup bias can be directly equated with social conflict and prejudice between groups. For example, using minimal groups, Mummendey and colleagues (e.g., Mummendey & Otten, 1998) have systematically demonstrated positive–negative asymmetry in social discrimination. Although the ingroup is favored on positively evaluated dimensions, there is a tendency toward fairness or outgroup favoritism on negative dimensions. It is only when the positive distinctiveness of the ingroup is threatened (e.g., through minority or insecure low status) that ingroup favoritism in the negative domain arises. Because ingroup bias in the minimal group paradigm is assumed by many to be the same as prejudice and because it is not found on negative dimensions (which is equated with overt hostility or aggression), the claim is then made that SIT has proved itself unable to deal with aggression and hostility in the full-blown sense, because it can only deal with bias on positive dimensions. The same kind of idea is found in more general assertions that SIT is an argument for the universality of prejudice.

In fact, SIT never equated ingroup bias with social hostility. It conceptualized it as a strategy for comparative, positively valued ingroup distinctiveness. Ingroup bias expressed evaluative (social) competition, evaluative differentiations between groups. It was never identified directly with aggression or hostility. It was of interest because of the processes to which it pointed in intergroup relations, processes which had hitherto been largely ignored. The value of SIT was that it identified these processes explicitly and used them to create an analysis of socially structured intergroup relations. On the basis of this novel theoretical analysis one could then derive hypotheses about the generation of social conflict and aggression.

There are several ways that one can get from SIT to a prediction of aggression, but they are all theoretical rather than merely an empirical assertion that ethnocentrism and social conflict are the same thing. Social conflict cannot be equated with the outcome of just one psychological process but must be understood in terms of the interplay of many as they are shaped by the historical, social, economic, and political structure of society. In Tajfel and Turner (1979), for example, it is hypothesized that one of the ways in which intergroup conflict develops is where insecure identities and a socially competitive need for positively valued distinctiveness are correlated with a salient division into groups and a realistic conflict of interests. SIT linked realistic conflict and insecure identity processes to explain the specific conditions under which aggression might develop.

In relation to ethnocentrism, there are suggestions that the theory is refuted by evidence that groups sometimes show outgroup favoritism. But the theory never claimed that ingroup favoritism was a universal feature of intergroup relations. For example, if members of low status groups define their inferiority as legitimate and stable, then they will see their group as consensually inferior on that dimension. There are many consensual status systems in which groups agree with each other about their respective inferiorities and superiorities. SIT did not assert that groups never see themselves as inferior, it argued that such self-perceived inferiority will have psychological consequences and motivate a range of responses.

Part of the issue is that the term "ingroup bias" has come to be used as a synonym for ingroup favoritism, implying that the latter always reflects an irrational, indiscriminate, reality-distorting psychological bias. It is assumed that ingroup favoritism (being a "bias") always accompanies ingroup–outgroup categorization, regardless of the specific nature of the intergroup relationship. But for a researcher to define ingroup favoritism as a bias is to make a value judgment from the perspective of an outside observer. Such a judgment often reflects no more than the fact that the relevant groups disagree with each other (both asserting that they are superior to each other). Groups may disagree with each other without irrationality being involved (Mummendey & Wenzel, 1999; Reynolds, Turner, & Haslam, 2000; Turner & Oakes, 1997). Diversity in opinion between individuals does not necessarily indicate bias or irrationality and the same is true for group-based disagreement. Group differences of opinion arise from the natural relativity of perception in which meaningful and veridical representations of reality are constructed from each group's singular perspective and from attempts to (in)validate certain views over others (Turner & Oakes, 1997).

Where there is consensual inferiority and superiority between groups in a particular social system then there is agreement about the nature of social reality. Groups share a similar interpretation of their respective strengths and weaknesses and if members are asked to evaluate their own and other groups on dimensions characteristic of each group, their responses will reflect both ingroup and outgroup favoritism. Conversely, with some (insecure) group relations there is less agreement regarding the extent to which attributes characterize one group compared to another. Expressions of ingroup favoritism are most likely when the same valued dimension is claimed as characteristic of both groups and are part of the process of social competition and potential group conflict. In these terms ingroup favoritism is not indiscriminate ethnocentrism or a psychological bias but rather depends on self-categorization as an ingroup member and the extent to which the relationship to the outgroup is secure or insecure and the comparative dimension important and relevant to the group comparing itself. In SIT so-called ingroup biases are expressions of the fact that the social reality of intergroup relations is being contested rather than that it is being perceptually distorted.

These considerations have implications for the explanation of positive–negative asymmetry in minimal groups (Reynolds et al., 2000). SIT and SCT maintain that in order to behave in terms of a particular group membership, self-definition in terms of the social category *must be psychologically salient.* SCT argues that the extent to which perceivers can meaningfully categorize themselves in terms of more (or less) inclusive categories depends on the interaction between context-specific judgments of similarity and difference (comparative and normative fit) and the perceivers' expectations, motives, and goals (perceiver readiness). Perceivers seek meaningful self-definition in terms of the comparative and normative features of the stimulus information available. It is possible that, where groups are minimal, it is less meaningful for perceivers to categorize and define themselves on the basis of negative than positive dimensions. It may be difficult for ingroup members to discriminate on negative dimensions because they provide a less appropriate, less fitting basis for self-definition.

To display ingroup favoritism in the negative domain ingroup members have to indicate that they are "less bad than the outgroup" on particular dimensions. This means that in order to discriminate, ingroup members have to accept, or at least countenance, a negative self-definition. Because participants may not believe that they are defined by particular negative dimensions they may be unwilling to define themselves and act in these terms. Negative dimensions may not fit participants' normative beliefs about themselves as well as positive dimensions and consequently, identification and intergroup discrimination will be minimized.

An implication is that it should be possible to find ingroup favoritism on both positive and negative dimensions when both provide a meaningful and relevant basis for self-definition in ingroup–outgroup terms. Recent empirical work supports this analysis (Reynolds et al., 2000). In one study, ingroup members evaluated the ingroup and the outgroup on positive and negative dimensions that were typical of the ingroup, typical of the outgroup, typical of both groups, and typical of neither group. There was no evidence of positive–negative asymmetry and ingroup favoritism was found on certain negative traits. Responses were ingroup-favouring on (a) positive traits that were typical of the ingroup and (b) negative traits that were typical of the outgroup, and outgroup-favouring on (a) positive traits that were typical of the outgroup and (b) negative traits that were typical of the ingroup.

A different pattern of results characterized responses on traits typical of both groups. In line with such evaluations being less consensual (the traits are fitting for both groups) ingroup favoritism was evident on both positive and negative traits. With traits typical of neither group, the pattern of discrimination was either fairness or outgroup favoritism. Such non-fitting dimensions (as with evaluations of minimal groups on negative dimensions) are not relevant to self and are therefore of little consequence for group-based status concerns.

This analysis and evidence indicate that ingroup favoritism is not the result of a generic drive or bias for ethnocentrism triggered automatically by being in a group. Nor is it the equivalent of outgroup hostility and aggression. These judgments (and the degree to which social hostility is involved) are constrained by social realities, varying with the degree to which the relevant social identity provides a meaningful fit between the perceiver and the situation and the degree to which the social structure of intergroup status differences is secure and consensual or insecure, contestable, and open to dispute (e.g., Ellemers, 1993; Ellemers, van Rijswijk, Roef, & Simons, 1997; Tajfel & Turner, 1979; Turner, 1996).

Social Identity: Implications and Future Directions

SIT and SCT are grounded in the metatheory of social psychological interactionism (Tajfel, 1972a, 1979; Turner & Oakes, 1997), which holds that social psychological processes emerge from a functional interaction between mind and society. The theories deal with psychological processes which are socially structured and which are qualitatively transformed by their interaction with social life and social processes. The interactionist perspective leads to a very different analysis of prejudice and intergroup relations from that currently dominant.

An alternative to the "prejudice" model of intergroup relations and human social conflict

As implied above, researchers sometimes appear to believe that SIT holds that ethnocentrism and prejudice are inevitable and irrational. The analysis goes as follows: People form groups; inherent in group formation is the need for superiority, which in turn is motivated by the drive for positive self-esteem; hence once one is in a group, one displays ethnocentrism, and ethnocentrism is the same as prejudice. The need for positive social identity is thus used to argue for the hypothesis that ethnocentrism is inevitable, an automatic and therefore irrational product of group formation. Intergroup attitudes are seen as products of irrational psychological biases, implying that unjustifiable prejudice is inherent in group life.

The social identity perspective is actually an argument against this view. It not only provides a specific theory of intergroup relations, it also resurrects the intergroup approach to social conflict pioneered in social psychology by Sherif (e.g., 1967) and his colleagues. Although Sherif was a realistic group conflict theorist, pointing to the role of conflicts of interests between groups in social antagonism, he stressed as fundamental the idea that intergroup relations rather than individual and interpersonal processes determined intergroup attitudes. SIT and SCT are intergroup theories in exactly the same sense. They argue that intergroup attitudes are always the product of an interaction between people's collective psychology as group members and the perceived social structure of intergroup relationships. The interaction between collective psychology and social reality is assumed to be mediated by group members' socially shared and socially mediated understanding of their intergroup relations (i.e., their collective beliefs, theories, and ideologies about the nature of the social system and the nature of the status differences between groups).

In this respect, as has been argued elsewhere (Turner, 1996), the social identity perspective provides a way of going beyond the "prejudice" model of social conflict which has dominated the field since the 1920s. The implicit orthodoxy in intergroup relations research is that social antagonism in its various forms is a product of prejudice, that is, of defect, irrationality, and pathology at the level of individual psychology. Negative outgroup attitudes are assumed to be inherently pathological, irrational, invalid, and unjustifiable.

This notion is summarized by three main ideas that pervade much research: That specific dysfunctional individual-difference or personality factors more or less directly predispose people to more or less hostility against outgroups; that there are individual-level cognitive and/or motivational processes which directly produce negative outgroup attitudes and which are socially irrational since they are purely psychologically caused; and that intergroup attitudes are inherently mindless, meaningless, and devoid of rational content. Personality, cognitive limitations, and ignorance become possible explanations of intergroup relations precisely because they ignore issues of social structure, but, in our view, this oversight also renders these explanations limited and incoherent.

The social identity perspective rejects each of these ideas. It emphasizes that we need to understand social conflict as psychologically meaningful, as an expression of how people define themselves socially, and of their understanding of the reality of their intergroup relationships. Social conflict can be a rational reaction to people's historically evolved understanding of themselves in interaction with their theories of the social world and the reality of social structure. We do not need to posit defective personality types, individual-level psychological processes which directly cause outgroup hostility as a result of some single variable, factor, or state (social categorization, ingroup identification, frustration, low self-esteem, low social status, positive or negative mood, etc.), or inherent defects in human cognition, motivation, or emotions (e.g., the supposed over-simplification and over-generalization of stereotyping) to explain social antagonism. It is a result of ordinary, adaptive, and functional psychological processes in interplay with the realities of social life. This is an important and radically different approach to social conflict from the traditional emphasis on "prejudice."

One example of the difference in approach is provided by research on stereotyping. Much SCT work has been done over the last decade to argue for its rationality and validity (Oakes et al., 1994). An aspect of the "prejudice" model is the social cognition view that stereotyping is due to limited attentional resources and shortcuts in information processing. Such impressions are interpreted as less valid and accurate than individuated judgments which reflect a person's true personal characteristics (Fiske, 1998). This view is not surprising if the influence of group realities and social structure is denied in theory and research. If groups do not exist and there are only individuals, then any judgment of people as a group must be invalid, must be erroneous. If there is not an analysis of collective psychology and social structure that can be used to explain stereotypes and stereotyping then the explanation must be sought in individual psychology. The end point is a view that stereotypes and intergroup perceptions are a function of individual psychology (and pathology).

The alternative view is that stereotypes and intergroup attitudes are expressions of collective cognition, of people's attempt to make sense of the world, to create a meaningful but collectively shaped representation of group realities. Stereotypes are not just held by individuals perceiving individuals, they describe people's group attributes and are shared within groups; they are products of group interaction and anchored in group memberships. They serve group purposes and are products of social influence and communication as much as they are products of an individual cognitive process. They also have an ideological content related to people's theories, beliefs, ideologies about the nature of the intergroup relationship.

This view does not see stereotyping as psychologically defective, invalid, or unjustifiable, but rather as an outcome of an adaptive, rational, and reality-oriented psychological process. This does not mean that every specific stereotype is valid but that the same reasonable psychological process is behind everybody's stereotypes (both those with which we agree and those with which we disagree). Validity is not purely a psychological question. It is also a social and a political question and we are entitled to argue about stereotypes, to accept some and reject some, to try, as a society, to put right those we think are wrong. The fact that we engage in social and political debate over differing stereotypes is not proof that they are psychologically defective. Rather it speaks to the functional aspects of human collective psychology, to the fact that we seek to produce higher-order collective truths from the relativities of lower-level group judgments (see Oakes et al., 1994, chapter 8; Turner & Oakes, 1997).

It is paradoxical in light of these points that the social identity perspective is sometimes reduced to a "prejudice" theory. Arguments that SIT predicts that social categorization automatically and inevitably leads to ingroup bias, that intergroup relations should be characterized by universal ethnocentrism, that ingroup bias is inherent in group formation, that low status groups should always be more biased than high status groups, that intergroup discrimination is driven by an individual need for self-esteem and should directly enhance individual self-esteem, and so on, interpret it in this way. They imply that the theory is simply the assertion of a universal, irrational drive for ethnocentrism, unconstrained by social realities or the social meaning of intergroup attitudes and that some simple, single factor which triggers or relates to this drive should be positively correlated with intergroup discrimination virtually independent of social context or the perceived nature of intergroup relations. As we have seen, this is a misconception.

What do we need to explain human social conflict?

Is the social identity perspective a "sovereign" theory of intergroup conflict? Were social identity processes ever meant to provide exclusive or comprehensive explanations of human social conflict? The point is sometimes made that the social identity perspective does not provide a complete account of intergroup relations, as if it had ever been claimed that it did. Suffice it to say, Tajfel and Turner both stated that social identity processes were not the only factor in intergroup relations, that realistic group interests, for example, were important. The social identity perspective never rejected the insights of Sherif's realistic conflict analysis. It did reconceptualize the relationship between realistic group interests, psychological group formation, and intergroup relations (Turner & Bourhis, 1996), but it never denied the empirical importance of conflicting group interests in intergroup conflict. Indeed Tajfel and Turner were also clear that one cannot explain human social conflict through social psychology alone. Social psychology *in toto* is only a part of the story, let alone any particular theory of intergroup processes.

What does one need to explain human intergroup conflict and how does the social identity analysis fit into the picture? There are, of course, different views on this matter, but the elements of an "intergroup" view consistent with the spirit of the social identity perspective can be found in Sherif's work, in Tajfel's writings, in the self-categorization analysis of stereotyping, and in the preceding discussion of the relative role of "prejudice" or "intergroup relations" in intergroup attitudes.

SIT and SCT assume that intergroup attitudes are always an outcome of an interaction between people's collective psychology as group members and the social structure of intergroup relationships. They further assume that this interaction is mediated by people's collective beliefs, theories, and ideologies about intergroup relationships and the wider social system, by socially structured cognition. Thus human social conflict is not a matter of psychological irrationality, pathology, or error. It must be seen as an outcome of the social, psychological, and historical processes which have shaped people's collective understandings of themselves, their ingroups and outgroups, and their relationships with other groups. It is an outcome of the collective theories and ideologies which they have developed to make sense of, explain, and justify intergroup relationships, of the ways in which people are influenced by these ideas, and of the particular kinds of social psychological processes that are relevant to predicting how their shared understandings of intergroup relationships will translate into attitudes and actions.

From this perspective, restricting ourselves to social psychology, there are four general requirements for an account of intergroup conflict:

1. An analysis of the *psychological group*; one must know when and why people form groups and what groups are psychologically and be able to answer the question of when people will behave individually or collectively.
2. An idea of the *processes* that come into play in *intergroup relations*; one must know what processes shape how people behave toward ingroups and outgroups as a function of intergroup relationships.
3. A *theory of social influence*; one must know how group identities, goals, and beliefs become consensual, shared, and normative, how they are validated, spread, changed, and anchored in group interaction and how collective beliefs about intergroup relationships, how stereotypes about one's own and other groups, are disseminated and/or changed. It is also necessary to confront the facts of political and other forms of leadership and the role of moderates and extremists in shaping group ideology.
4. An ability to analyze the *content of group beliefs* relevant to intergroup relations and the wider society; one must know how groups understand themselves, their relationships with other groups and who they see as outgroups. What are the collective theories and ideologies which they have developed to make sense of, explain, justify, and rationalize their intergroup relationships and how are we to describe and explain the development of these collective social theories?

In terms of these components social psychology has made good progress in understanding social conflict. We have much work relevant to the main elements of the picture and the social identity perspective is central to it. SCT is a theory of the psychological group. In terms of intergroup processes, we have realistic conflict theory, which looks at the role of group goals and collective group interests, SIT, which looks at the interaction between identity, social values, and intergroup comparisons, and we have (fraternal) relative deprivation theory, which is relevant to social comparisons between groups and the collective emotions of anger, resentment, and frustration. SCT also provides a detailed and systematic analysis of social influence that has been applied to conformity, crowd behavior, group polarization, leadership, minority influence, and even political rhetoric (Haslam, in press; Reicher & Hopkins, 1996; Turner, 1991, 1999; Turner & Haslam, in press). We also know to some degree (or can speculate) on the basis of existing theory how these processes interact with each other. For example, SCT shows how identity processes and self-categorization are relevant to perceived interdependence, cooperation, and competition between groups. We know how conflicts of interests are relevant to the salience of social categorizations. We know that shared ideologies are relevant to the identities and stereotypes one forms (Brown, P. & Turner, in press) and play a role in mutual influence (Reicher, 1987). We know that social identities are social comparative and provide a basis for the experience of collective emotions (E. Smith, 1993).

What is it that we do not have? There are two definite weaknesses. Despite the theoretical insights into how psychological group membership, intergroup processes, social influence, and collective beliefs are likely to affect each other, relatively little systematic research into these interrelationships has been conducted (although there are honorable exceptions). We have, for example, not much tried to integrate what we know from SCT and social identity processes with what we know about realistic conflict and relative deprivation, although it is evident that relative deprivation is intimately linked to realistic conflict and social identity processes. In addition, we still know very little about how groups create the content of their collective beliefs. How and why do groups develop specific ideologies? How do certain ideologies win out over others? How are they spread? Researchers have noted this neglect for years but little real progress seems to have been made in terms of testable social psychological theory.

The social identity perspective contributes to our general understanding in several ways, in relation to the group, intergroup processes, and social influence, and is relevant to the role of ideology. It helps also to clarify where future research needs to be directed for integrative progress, at the synthesis of all the main elements of the picture, at the links between the intergroup processes, and at the development of a social psychological approach to the content of group beliefs.

Conclusion

The social identity perspective emphasizes that we need to understand intergroup relations as psychologically meaningful, as an expression of how people define their social identities, and an interaction between their collective psychology as group members and the perceived social structure of intergroup relations. Social antagonism can be a (psychologically) rational reaction to people's collective understanding of themselves in interaction with their theories of the social world and social structural realities. We do not need to posit sick or defective personality types, individual-level psychological processes operating in a social vacuum, or intergroup perceptions as inherently distorting of social reality to explain stereotypes, "prejudice," and social conflict.

Part of the reason for the prevalence of traditional views has to do with metatheory. Social psychology is still dominated by "the individualistic thesis" (Asch, 1952). The social identity perspective also tends willy-nilly to be assimilated to this thesis (and reduced to a prejudice analysis). It tends to be divorced from the interactionist metatheory within which it developed. In reality, SIT and SCT take for granted that it is not possible to develop adequate social psychological theories, which do not distort the phenomena under consideration, unless one accepts that the relevant psychology is socially structured, emergent, and always functions in a social context. Social psychology is not biology, nor sociology, nor general (i.e., individual) psychology; its focus is on the socially systematic regularities of psychological functioning and human conduct. Its processes must take such an interaction between the psychological and the collective for granted and be explanatory of and consistent with its effects.

To fail to appreciate that SIT and SCT were intended to unravel aspects of the mind–society interaction and to divorce the psychological processes they posit from the social processes with which they were assumed to interact, is to individualize them and misconstrue their psychological ideas. Misinterpretations of SIT and SCT are not an accident and neither are they wilful; they represent the intellectual influence of individualism, an influence which is felt whenever social identity ideas are divorced from their proper metatheoretical home. Understanding the metatheory of social identity is not a luxury; it is a crucial part of its legacy and a prerequisite for the full development of social psychology's analysis of intergroup relations and human social conflict.

References

Abrams, D., & Hogg, M. A. (1999). *Social identity and social cognition.* Oxford, UK: Blackwell.

Asch, S. E. (1952). *Social psychology.* Englewood Cliffs, NJ: Prentice-Hall.

Bourhis, R. Y., Turner, J. C., & Gagnon, A. (1997). Interdependence, social identity, and discrimination: Some empirical considerations. In R. Spears, P. J. Oakes, N. Ellemers, & S. A. Haslam (Eds.), *The social psychology of stereotyping and group life.* Oxford, UK: Blackwell.

Branscombe, N. R., & Ellemers, N. (1998). Coping with group-based discrimination: Individualistic versus group-level strategies. In J. K. Swim & C. Stangor (Eds.), *Prejudice: The target's perspective* (pp. 243–266). New York: Academic Press.

Brewer, M. B., & Brown, R. J. (1998). Intergroup relations. In D. T. Gilbert, S. T. Fiske, & L. Gardner (Eds.), *The handbook of social psychology* (4th ed., Vol. 2. pp. 554–594). Boston, MA: McGraw-Hill.

Brewer, M. B., & Weber, J. G. (1994). Self-evaluation effects of interpersonal versus intergroup social comparison. *Journal of Personality and Social Psychology, 66,* 268–275.

Brown, P. M., & Turner, J. C. (in press). The role of theories in the formation of stereotype content. In C. McGarty, V. Y. Yzerbyt, & R. Spears (Eds.), *Stereotypes as explanations: The formation of meaningful beliefs about social groups.* Cambridge, UK: Cambridge University Press.

Brown, R. J., Hinkle, S., Ely, P. G., Fox-Cardamone, L., Maras, P., & Taylor, L. A. (1992). Recognizing group diversity: Individualist-collectivist and autonomous-relational social orientations and their implications for intergroup processes. *British Journal of Social Psychology, 31,* 327–342.

Crocker, J., & Luhtanen, R. (1990). Collective self-esteem and ingroup bias. *Journal of Personality and Social Psychology, 58,* 60–67.

Ellemers, N. (1993). The influence of socio-structural variables on identity-enhancement strategies. *European Review of Social Psychology, 4,* 27–57.

Ellemers, N., Spears, R., & Doosje, B. (1999). *Social identity: Context, commitment, content.* Oxford, UK: Blackwell.

Ellemers, N., van Rijswijk, W., Roefs, M., & Simons, C. (1997). Bias in intergroup perceptions: Balancing group identity with social reality. *Personality and Social Psychology Bulletin, 23,* 186–198.

Farsides, T. (1995). *Why social identity theory's self-esteem hypothesis has never been tested – and how to test it.* Paper presented to BPS Social Psychology Section Conference, York, UK, September.

Fiske, S.-T. (1998). Stereotyping, prejudice, and discrimination. In D. T. Gilbert, S. T. Fiske, & L. Gardner (Eds.), *The handbook of social psychology* (4th ed., Vol. 2, pp. 357–411). Boston, MA: McGraw-Hill.

Haslam, S. A. (in press). *The psychology of organizations: A social identity approach.* London: Sage.

Haslam, S. A., & Wilson, A. (2000). In what sense are prejudicial beliefs *personal?* The importance of an ingroup's shared stereotypes. *British Journal of Social Psychology, 39,* 45–63.

Hinkle, S., & Brown, R. J. (1990). Intergroup comparisons and social identity: Some links and lacunae. In D. Abrams & M. A. Hogg (Eds.), *Social identity theory. Constructive and critical advances* (pp. 48–70). London: Harvester Wheatsheaf.

Hogg, M. A., & Abrams, D. (1990). Social motivation, self-esteem, and social identity. In D. Abrams & M. A. Hogg (Eds.), *Social identity theory. Constructive and critical advances* (pp. 28–47). London: Harvester Wheatsheaf.

Long, K., & Spears, R. (1997). The self-esteem hypothesis revisited: Differentiation and the disaffected. In R. Spears, P. J. Oakes, N. Ellemers, & S. A. Haslam (Eds.), *The social psychology of stereotyping and group life* (pp. 296–317). Oxford, UK: Blackwell.

Mummendey, A., & Otten, S. (1998). Positive–negative asymmetry in social discrimination. In W. Stroebe, & M. Hewstone (Eds.), *European review of social psychology* (Vol. 9, pp. 107–143). Chichester, UK: Wiley.

Mummendey, A., & Wenzel, M. (1999). Social discrimination and tolerance in intergroup relations: Reactions to intergroup difference. *Personality and Social Psychology Review, 3,* 158–174.

Oakes, P. J., Haslam, S. A., & Turner, J. C. (1994). *Stereotyping and social reality.* Oxford, UK: Blackwell.

Operario, D., & Fiske, S. (1999) Integrating social identity and social cognition: A framework for bridging diverse perspectives. In D. Abrams & M. A. Hogg (Eds.), *Social identity and social cognition* (pp. 26–54). Oxford, UK: Blackwell.

Rabbie, J. M., Schot, J. C., & Visser, L. (1989). Social identity theory: A conceptual and empirical critique from the perspective of a Behavioural Interaction Model. *European Journal of Social Psychology, 19,* 171–202.

Reicher, S. (1987). Crowd behaviour as social action. In J. C. Turner, M. A. Hogg, P. J. Oakes, S. D. Reicher, & M. S. Wetherell, *Rediscovering the social group: A self-categorization theory* (pp. 171–202). Oxford, UK: Blackwell.

Reicher, S., & Hopkins, N. (1996). Self-category constructions in political rhetoric: An analysis of Thatcher's and Kinnock's speeches concerning the British Miners' Strike (1984–5). *European Journal of Social Psychology, 26,* 353–372.

Reynolds, K. J., Turner, J. C., Haslam, S. A., & Ryan, M. K. (1999). *The role of personality and group factors in explaining prejudice.* Manuscript submitted for publication.

Reynolds, K. J., Turner, J. C., & Haslam, S. A. (2000). When are we better than them and they worse than us? A closer look at social discrimination in positive and negative domains. *Journal of Personality & Social Psychology, 78,* 64–80.

Rubin, M., & Hewstone, M. (1998). Social identity theory's self-esteem hypothesis: A review and some suggestions for clarification. *Personality and Social Psychology Review, 2,* 40–62.

Sherif, M. (1967). *Group conflict and co-operation: Their social psychology.* London: Routledge and Kegan Paul.

Smith, E. R. (1993). Social identity and social emotions: Toward new conceptualizations of prejudice. In D. M. Mackie & D. L. Hamilton (Eds.), *Affect, cognition, and stereotyping: Individualistic processes in group perception* (pp. 297–315). San Diego, CA: Academic Press.

Spears, R., Oakes, P. J., Ellemers, N., & Haslam, S. A. (Eds.), (1997). *The social psychology of stereotyping and group life.* Oxford, UK: Blackwell.

Tajfel, H. (1957). Value and the perceptual judgment of magnitude. *Psychological Review, 64,* 192–204.

Tajfel, H. (1969). Cognitive aspects of prejudice. *Journal of Social Issues, 25,* 79–97.

Tajfel, H. (1972a). Experiments in a vacuum. In J. Israel & H. Tajfel (Eds.), *The context of social psychology.* London: Academic Press.

Tajfel, H. (1972b). La catégorisation sociale (Social categorization). In S. Moscovici (Ed.), *Introduction à la psychologie sociale* (pp. 272–302). Paris: Larousse.

Tajfel, H. (1974). Social identity and intergroup behaviour. *Social Science Information, 13,* 65–93.

Tajfel, H. (1978). (Ed.). *Differentiation between social groups: Studies in the social psychology of intergroup relations.* London: Academic Press.

Tajfel, H. (1979). Individuals and groups in social psychology. *British Journal of Social and Clinical Psychology, 18,* 183–190.

Tajfel, H. (1982). (Ed.). *Social identity and intergroup relations.* Cambridge, UK: Cambridge University Press.

Tajfel, H., & Turner, J. C. (1979). An integrative theory of intergroup conflict. In W. G. Austin & S. Worchel (Eds.), *The social psychology of intergroup relations* (pp. 33–47). Monterey, CA: Brooks/Cole.

Turner, J. C. (1975). Social comparison and social identity: Some prospects for intergroup behaviour. *European Journal of Social Psychology, 5,* 5–34.

Turner, J. C. (1978). *Towards a cognitive redefinition of the social group.* Paper presented to the Research Conference on Social Identity, European Laboratory of Social Psychology (L.E.P.S.), Université de Haute Bretagne (Rennes II), Rennes, France.

Turner, J. C. (1982).,Towards a cognitive redefinition of the social group. In H. Tajfel (Ed.), *Social identity and intergroup relations* (pp. 15–40). Cambridge, UK: Cambridge University Press and Paris: Editions de la Maison des Sciences de l'Homme.

Turner, J. C. (1991). *Social influence.* Milton Keynes, UK: Open University Press.

Turner, J. C. (1996). *Social identity theory and the concept of prejudice.* Invited Keynote Lecture, 40th Kongress der Deutschen Gesellschaft für Psychologie (40th Congress of the German Psychological Society), Ludwig-Maximilians-Universität, Munich, Germany, September 22–26.

Turner, J. C. (1999). Some current issues in research on social identity and self-categorization theories. In N. Ellemers, R. Spears, & B. Doosje (Eds.), *Social identity: Context, commitment, content* (pp. 6–34). Oxford, UK: Blackwell.

Turner, J. C., & Brown, R. J. (1978). Social status, cognitive alternatives, and intergroup relations. In H. Tajfel (Ed.), *Differentiation between social groups* (pp. 201–234). London: Academic Press.

Turner, J. C., & Bourhis, R. Y. (1996). Social identity, interdependence, and the social group: A reply to Rabbie et al. In W. P. Robinson (Ed.), *Social groups and identities: Developing the legacy of Henri Tajfel* (pp. 25–63). Oxford, UK: Butterworth-Heinemann.

Turner, J. C., & Haslam, S. A. (in press). Social identity, organizations, and leadership. To appear in M. E. Turner (Ed.), *Groups at work. Advances in theory and research.* Hillsdale, NJ: Erlbaum.

Turner, J. C., Hogg, M. A., Oakes, P. J., Reicher, S. D., & Wetherell, M. S. (1987). *Rediscovering the social group: A self-categorization theory.* Oxford, UK: Basil Blackwell.

Turner, J. C., & Oakes, P. J. (1989) Self-categorization theory and social influence. In P. B. Paulus (Ed.), *The psychology of group influence* (2nd ed., pp. 233–275). Hillsdale, NJ: Erlbaum.

Turner, J. C., & Oakes, P. J. (1997). The socially structured mind. In C. McGarty & S. A. Haslam (Eds.), *The message of social psychology* (pp. 355–373). Oxford, UK: Blackwell.

Turner, J. C., Oakes, P. J., Haslam, S. A., & McGarty, C. (1994). Self and collective: Cognition and social context. *Personality and Social Psychology Bulletin, 20,* 454–463.

Turner, J. C., & Onorato, R. (1999). Social identity, personality, and the self-concept: A self-categorization perspective. In T. R. Tyler, R. Kramer, & O. John (Eds.), *The psychology of the social self* (pp. 11–46). Hillsdale, NJ: Erlbaum.

Tyler, T. R., Kramer, R., & John, O. (Eds.), (1999). *The psychology of the social self.* Hillsdale, NJ: Erlbaum.

Verkuyten, M., & Hagendoorn, L. (1998). Prejudice and self-categorization: The variable role of authoritarianism and ingroup stereotypes. *Personality and Social Psychology Bulletin, 24*, 99–110.

Worchel, S., Morales, J. F., Paez, D., & Deschamps, J.-C. (Eds.), (1998). *Social identity: International perspectives.* London, UK & Newbury Park, CA: Sage.

CHAPTER EIGHT

Affect as a Cause of Intergroup Bias

David Wilder and Andrew F. Simon

In this chapter we will consider the role of affect in intergroup bias. Does a person's affective state influence the likelihood of engaging in bias against outgroups? Venerable common sense suggests a relationship. Whether at a rally before a football game or a political demonstration, agitation and emotional fervor appear to exacerbate hatred of rivals and enemies. Certainly the social psychological literature on the antecedents of aggression supports this premise. Research has consistently demonstrated that aversive stimuli generate anger which, in turn, frequently accentuates social aggression (e.g., Berkowitz, 1990, 1993). When our feelings are unpleasant, should we not be more distrustful of and hostile toward others? When our feelings are pleasant, should we not be more beneficent in our thoughts and behaviors?

Indeed, the proposition that affect affects intergroup bias surely seems redundant. Prejudice is an attitude toward members of a social group or category and therefore, as an attitude, has an affective component. More broadly, intergroup bias has traditionally been viewed as having three components: prejudice, stereotypes, and discrimination. Although conceptually distinct, these components of bias are related. In a recent literature review, Dovidio, Brigham, Johnson, and Gaertner (1996) reported a significant correlation of .32 between prejudice and discrimination among Whites. The classic treatise on prejudice by Gordon Allport (*The Nature of Prejudice*, 1954) is chock full of examples in which affect is both a cause and an effect of bias between groups.

Several theories of prejudice and intergroup bias have considered affect to be either a direct antecedent or a contributing factor to intergroup bias. In the theory of the authoritarian personality, Adorno and colleagues (Adorno, Frenkel-Brunswick, Levinson, & Sanford, 1950) argued that prejudice is the result of conflict and anxiety generated by children's relationships with their parents. Reflecting the influence of behaviorism and psychoanalytic theory, Dollard and associates (Dollard, Doob, Miller, Mowrer, & Sears, 1939) proposed that intergroup bias is the product of displaced hostility triggered by frustration. As a vast literature of aggression research would later demonstrate, frustration generates anger that, in turn, fosters harmful behaviors including aggression and discrimination (Berkowitz, 1990, 1993). The realistic conflict theory of prejudice (e.g., Levine & Campbell, 1972; Sherif, 1966) offered a similar argument: Conflict between groups over limited resources or incompatible goals gives rise to enmity between the groups which, in turn, is manifested in biased attitudes and behaviors. Social identity theorists (Tajfel, 1982; Turner, 1987) have hypothesized that one function of intergroup bias is to maintain and even enhance the self-esteem of group members. Consequently, threats to one's self-esteem should generate negative affect and foster bias against outgroups as a means of maintaining a favorable sense of self (Hunter, Platow, & Howard, 1996; Hunter, Platow, Bell, & Kypri, 1997; Lemyre & Smith, 1985; Messick & Mackie, 1989; Meindl & Lerner, 1984; Oakes & Turner, 1980).

Just as negative affect appears to foster bias, there is also evidence that persons respond to bias with intense negative reactions (Allport, 1954; Brewer, 1981; Campbell, 1975; Kramer & Messick, 1998; Stephan & Stephan, 1985; Trivers, 1971). Quite often this negative reaction takes the form of anger accompanied by a desire for retribution and revenge against the offending outgroup (Bies, 1987; Bies, Tripp, & Kramer, 1996). Although most likely to yield negative affect, victims of bias can at times take solace in making downward social comparisons to others who are even worse off than themselves (e.g., Wills, 1981).

Certainly those who perpetrate bias may derive both material and psychological benefit from their actions. Such benefit can include enhanced self-esteem (e.g., Hunter et al., 1996, 1997; Messick & Mackie, 1989). Nevertheless, engaging in bias does not inevitably yield positive affect. Inflicting bias can be a source of disquiet if retaliation is likely. In addition, bias may generate guilt if it violates personal standards or internalized norms of equity. Of course, rationalization and justification of bias may be attempted to assuage any discomfort. Furthermore, one need not engage in bias to reap its rewards nor suffer from bias to feel its pains. These effects can be experienced vicariously through shared membership in groups or empathy toward groups in which others mete out or receive bias.

Domain and Definitions

In this chapter we will review the theory and research that have examined how affective states influence the display of intergroup bias. Before plunging into this pool of research, we need to define "affect" and "bias." Affect refers to either a mood state or an emotion. An emotion, in turn, is a specific feeling that has an identifiable source and target (Isen, 1984, 1987). Emotions (e.g., anger, disgust, joy) often impel a person to act and are, therefore, considered "hot." A mood generally refers to a more diffuse feeling (e.g., unpleasantness) that is often less intense and less focused than an emotion. Distinctions between emotions and moods are not consistently made in this literature. Consequently, mood and emotion will be lumped together under the broader term, "affect." Thus, affect includes emotions such as fear and anger that are frequently provoked by specific threats as well as more diffuse moods such as happiness and sadness (Forgas, 1995).

Bias encompasses discrimination, prejudice, or stereotypes. Discrimination is differential treatment of groups because of their group labels; in particular, favoritism of one's own group (ingroup) relative to another group (outgroup) in the absence of a legitimate basis for that favoritism. Prejudice is dislike of an outgroup or greater liking of an ingroup relative to an outgroup. Stereotypes refer to beliefs about attributes or characteristics generally held by members of a group; especially beliefs that are unflattering or unfavorable.

Simply put, will the presence of affect increase or decrease bias between groups? Although it is a simple question, research does not answer with a simple yes or no. Part of this may be due to differences in procedures across studies and especially to differences in the manipulation of affective states. In the typical experiment, affect is induced and then subjects read about or interact with a member (or members) of an outgroup. Finally, subjects evaluate those outgroup members or the outgroup as a whole. For purpose of experimental control, the affect manipulation is usually independent of the outgroup and is induced in a number of ways such as giving subjects a reward (e.g., Dovidio, Gaertner, Isen, & Lawrence, 1995), threatening subjects with embarrassment or pain (e.g., Wilder & Shapiro, 1989a), asking subjects to recall a pleasant or unpleasant past event (e.g., Forgas, 1989), or having subjects read or view unpleasant information (e.g., Mackie, Queller, & Stroessner, 1994). Thus, manipulation of affect is usually independent of the outgroup (incidental affect) rather than caused by the outgroup (integral affect; Bodenhausen, 1993). Use of incidental affect avoids the confounding present in natural groups that have a specific affect associated with them.

The Impact of Affect on Bias: Explanations and Literature Review

Five reasonable hypotheses have been proposed by researchers to account for the relationships they have observed between affect and intergroup bias. These explanations are not mutually exclusive or necessarily independent of one another. Three of these (affect consistency, affect as information, affect infusion) are related in that they posit some degree of consistency between affective valence and intergroup judgments. The other two (mood and general knowledge, distraction) do not presume consistency between affect and judgments. Rather, the mood and general knowledge hypothesis predicts an asymmetry such that positive affect promotes superficial processing and the use of stereotypes whereas negative affect encourages more careful consideration of information. Finally, the distraction hypothesis argues that strong affect, regardless of valence, distracts the perceiver from careful attention to the outgroup and, consequently, leads to increased reliance on existing stereotypes and prejudice.

Affect consistency

Affect primes consistent cognitions and, therefore, disposes consistent behaviors. Positive affect should trigger positive cognitions and actions, and negative affect should foster negative thoughts and behaviors. This hypothesis fits with spreading-activation models of cognitive organization (e.g., Bower, 1981), cognitive consistency theories (e.g., Abelson et al., 1968), and learning theory based on temporal association (e.g., Byrne & Clore, 1970; Clore & Byrne, 1974; Staats & Staats, 1958; see also Zillman, 1983, for a conceptually similar argument that links arousal to aggression via excitation transfer). Extrapolating from these various, but convergent, approaches yields the simple prediction that the induction of positive affect should lessen negative affect, beliefs, and behavior directed toward an outgroup. If we are feeling good, then we should be less likely to respond unkindly to those around us. Conversely, negative affect should activate unpleasant thoughts and, therefore, encourage bias between groups.

In an experiment showing support for the affect consistency hypothesis, Forgas and Moylan (1991) showed subjects films that provoked either a positive, negative, or neutral mood. As part of an unrelated experiment, subjects viewed drawings of heterosexual dyads in which both persons were members of the same race or one person was Asian and one was Caucasian. Overall, subjects in a pleasant mood rated the stimulus persons more positively than subjects in an unpleasant mood did. In addition, there was a significant interaction between mood and the racial pairing: Subjects in a good mood rated the same-race and mixed-race pairs similarly; however, subjects in an unpleasant mood rated the mixed-race pairs as less competent and likable than the matched-race pairs. According to Forgas and Moylan, the mixed-race pairs presented a more complex, unusual stimulus for subjects and, therefore, demanded greater processing when evaluations were made. Consequently, a subject's mood was likely to influence judgments in a manner consistent with the literature on affect-cognition consistency (e.g., Bower, 1981; Isen, 1984). A negative mood made salient more negative conditions than a positive mood did.

Dovidio et al. (1995) also reported findings showing consistency between affect and judgments. When subjects were made happy, they responded more positively to members of an outgroup. Consistent with their theory of the benefits of a superordinate categorization, they found that subjects' perception of being in a common group with the target outgroup members mediated the relationship between affect and evaluation. Positive affect was significantly related to feelings of a common ingroup identity with members of the outgroup and that, in turn, was significantly predictive of a positive response to the outgroup.

Affect as information

Awareness of affect should instigate an attempt to explain it (Schachter & Singer, 1962). If the source of the affect is not apparent, the affect will be used as information to interpret the situation (Schwarz, 1990; Schwarz & Bless, 1991; Schwarz & Clore, 1988). The affect as information hypothesis can be viewed as a restricted relative of the affect consistency premise. The latter stipulates a generalization of affect to stimuli present when the affect is present. The former maintains that spreading occurs only when the affect has not been explained away; in other words, when the affect has not been compartmentalized and separated from ongoing thought. Therefore, if there is unexplained affect, predictions of the affect as information hypothesis should be similar to the affect consistency hypothesis. In an intergroup setting unexplained positive affect may be attributed to the outgroup and reduce bias whereas unexplained negative affect should exacerbate bias.

Affect infusion

Recently Forgas (1995) proposed the affect infusion model (AIM) to explain the influence of affect on social judgments. Forgas argued that the processing strategies a person adopts determine the extent to which affect infuses or influences judgments. He identified four judgmental strategies that perceivers use: direct access, motivated, heuristic, and substantive processing. Direct access (direct retrieval of stored information) and motivated processing (directed processing in response to motivational pressures; e.g., motivation to be accurate) result in little affect infusion. These strategies involve relatively narrow and closed search processes which, in turn, allow little opportunity for affect to influence cognition.

On the other hand, heuristic and substantive strategies are more constructive and take longer to complete. As a result, heuristic and substantive strategies afford more opportunity for affective states to influence information processing. Heuristic processing occurs when perceivers lack prior information and a strong motivational goal yet desire to minimize their effort. They, therefore, rely on shortcuts or heuristics (e.g., Brewer, 1988; Paulhus & Lim, 1994). Using heuristics opens judgments to the infusion of prevailing affect. Heuristic processing according to Forgas appears to be comparable to what others refer to as category-based processing (Brewer, 1988; Fiske & Neuberg, 1990) or peripheral processing (Petty & Cacioppo, 1986a, 1986b). Finally, substantive processing involves the selection and integration of novel information. This is the most complex type of judgment and requires the most cognitive effort. The process of learning and integrating new information opens perceivers to the influence of their current affective state. Substantive processing is similar, if not identical, to what others refer to as individual-based processing in which careful consideration is given to individuating or personal information about the targets (Brewer, 1988; Fiske & Neuberg, 1990). It is also reminiscent of the concept of central processing in the attitude change literature (Petty & Cacioppo, 1986a, 1986b).

Which strategy a perceiver adopts is determined by task requirements. In general, perceivers are thought to be cognitive misers and will adopt the processing strategy that requires the least effort yet is sufficient to be responsive to task and social demands. If affect does influence or infuse judgments, then it does so in a manner consistent with the mood state. Like the affect consistency hypothesis, the AIM model predicts greater intergroup bias when perceivers are experiencing negative affect. However, the AIM model forecasts mood effects only when perceivers use heuristic or substantive processing strategies.

In support of the affect infusion hypothesis, Forgas (1989, 1995) reported that atypical targets elicited longer and more elaborate processing by subjects. Longer processing resulted in greater mood infusion; that is, the effects of the subjects' mood state had more impact on judgments of targets when processing time increased. As a result, subjects in a positive mood made more favorable judgments of atypical targets. But those subjects who experienced a negative mood made more unfavorable judgments of atypical targets. The effect of mood state on outgroup judgments was mediated by the amount of time processing information about the outgroup targets which, in turn, was determined by the typicalness of the target. Thus, based on Forgas' findings, one would expect that judgments of atypical or unusual outgroup members will be more influenced by a perceiver's mood state than judgments of more representative outgroup members. Moreover, the direction of influence will be consistent with the valence of the mood state.

Mood and general knowledge

Mood may affect judgments by influencing a person's motivation to do detailed processing. Specifically, a positive mood may signal that the present situation is safe and, therefore, vigilance is unnecessary (Bless, 1994, cited in Bless, Schwarz, & Kemmelmeier, in press; Bless & Fiedler, 1995; Schwarz, 1990; Schwarz & Bless, 1991). On the other hand, a negative mood signals an aversive, and perhaps threatening, environment in which vigilance is important. Consequently, greater attention should be paid to the external environment under conditions of unpleasant than pleasant mood. This, in turn, should encourage more substantive examination of stimuli by persons in a negative mood state relative to those who are happy. The bottom line is that the use of stereotypes should be greater among happy than among sad or angry persons.

Evidence from the persuasion literature is consistent with this train of thought. Sad persons are more influenced by strong than by weak arguments which suggests that sadness fosters more substantive or central processing. On the other hand, happy persons are equally influenced by strong and weak arguments, indicative of heuristic or peripheral processing (Bless, Mackie, & Schwarz, 1992; Clore, Schwarz, & Conway, 1994; Fiedler, 1991; Mackie & Worth, 1989; Schwarz, Bless, & Bohner, 1991; Sinclair, Mark, and Clore, 1994).

Turning to research on affect and bias, Mackie and her colleagues have conducted a program of research examining the role of positive mood on bias (Mackie, Queller, Stroessner, & Hamilton, 1996; Stroessner & Mackie, 1993). Overall, they have found that positive affect is associated with greater stereotyping. Their findings are most easily explained by the mood as general knowledge and distraction hypotheses (to follow).

In one of their earlier investigations (Mackie, Hamilton, Schroth, Carlisle, Gersho, Meneses, Nedler, & Reichel, 1989), they had subjects read a series of trait statements about target persons following a mood induction. As the first of two experiments, subjects watched a videotape designed to create a happy, sad, or neutral mood. Then they read statements containing two attributes (either positive or negative) about fictitious persons who were either described as construction workers, lawyers, or policemen. Subjects estimated the frequency with which each trait had described the members of each job category. Results revealed an illusory correlation effect (Hamilton & Rose, 1980) in which subjects overestimated the association between stereotypic traits and occupations. Of interest was that the illusory correlation was strongest for happy subjects.

Stroessner and Mackie (1992) induced either a positive or a neutral mood using the manipulation cited in the last paragraph. Then all subjects read descriptions of members of an unnamed group. Descriptions gave trait information relevant to intelligence, sociability, stupidity, and friendliness. The variability of the information was manipulated so that subjects had information indicating either high or low variability of these traits among the unnamed target group. Subjects in the neutral mood condition accurately reported greater variability in the group when they had seen more variable information. However, subjects experiencing a positive mood reported relatively low variability (or greater homogeneity) even when they had seen highly variable information.

Mackie, Queller, and Stroessner (1994) examined the impact of a pleasant mood on perceptions of outgroup homogeneity by varying the dispersion of information inconsistent with stereotypes of a group. For some subjects stereotype inconsistent behavior was concentrated in a few group members; for other subjects the stereotype inconsistent information was dispersed across many group members. In the neutral mood condition, subjects accurately estimated less consistency and greater atypicality among group members when counterstereotypic information was dispersed. However, when subjects had experienced a positive mood, they reported that the information they had seen was typical and consistent with stereotypes in both the dispersed and concentrated conditions. Hence, a positive mood appeared to enhance perceptions of outgroup homogeneity which might well contribute to the development of stereotypes.

Using a similar procedure in which subjects were exposed to both stereotypic and non-stereotypic information about an outgroup, Stroessner and Mackie (1992) asked subjects to rate the extent to which two stereotypic and two nonstereotypic traits were represented in the group. Subjects in the neutral condition rated the group equally across the traits (which, as the authors argued, most likely reflected the mix of information given them). Happy subjects, however, rated the stereotypic traits as more characteristic of the group and the nonstereotypic traits as less characteristic of the group.

Bodenhausen, Kramer, & Susser (1994) also examined the relationship between positive mood and judgments of an outgroup. Consistent with research reported by Mackie and her colleagues, they found that positive mood led to greater stereotypic judgments of an outgroup target. In a series of experiments they found no evidence that this relationship was due to cognitive deficits such as distraction. (To do so, they used mood manipulations that were unlikely to diminish cognitive capacity such as smells and having subjects contort their faces to display the desired affect.) Apparently, subjects did not stereotype more because they were distracted by their pleasant mood and paid less attention to information about the outgroup target. However, this effect for happy mood was eliminated when subjects were made accountable for their judgments. The accountability manipulation presumably caused subjects to focus more carefully on the individuating information presented to them, so their judgments of the targets were less affected by group stereotypes.

In a series of experiments, Bless, Schwarz, and Kemmelmeier (in press) varied both the mood of subjects (happy, neutral, sad) and the consistency of a target person vis-à-vis subjects' expectations about the target person's group. Target characteristics were either positive or negative, and stereotypes of the target group were either positive or negative. When subjects were feeling sad, evaluations of the target person were influenced only by the valence of the individuating information. Sad subjects rated the target with positive characteristics more favorably than the target with negative characteristics. Stereotypes based on the target's group membership had no influence on judgments. On the other hand, subjects experiencing a happy mood rated the target most favorably when the target had positive characteristics and the target's group was also thought to be positive. Thus, subjects made more stereotypic judgments of the target outgroup member when his behavior matched the expectations of the outgroup. This finding is consistent with the general pattern that happy subjects stereotype more than sad subjects. However, when the target's characteristics were negative, happy subjects showed a contrast effect and rated the target most unfavorably when the target's group was positive.

Overall, these studies by Mackie, Bodenhausen, Bless and their co-authors have found that positive affect usually causes superficial processing and greater stereotyping. Among the five hypotheses presented at the outset of this section, their findings are most consistent with the mood as general knowledge hypothesis and the distraction hypothesis (discussed next) and less supportive of the consistency-based explanations (affect consistency, affect as information, affect infusion).

Distraction

Affect may sap attention from other ongoing activities. Attending to and coping with affect can distract a person from other stimuli and, consequently, may disrupt processing of other activities (Wilder & Simon, 1996). In an intergroup situation affect may distract a perceiver from the behavior of the outgroup. This possibility is based on the premise that attention is a zero-sum game. The more affect saps attention, the less there is available to deal with other activities. As a result, persons rely on well-learned habits (e.g., stereotypes) in lieu of careful attention to their immediate environment.

A similar argument has been made in other literatures. Research on helping has shown that sad moods sometimes increase and sometimes decrease helping. One determinant appears to be the focus of the sad person's attention. When attention is focused inwardly, helping decreases, in part, because need for aid may be less noticed (e.g., Pyszczynski & Greenberg, 1987). In addition, Fiske and Morlin (1996) have argued that anxiety due to powerlessness can lead to a reduction of processing capacity. One way in which this may occur is that the anxiety allows intrusive thoughts that interfere with attention to the task at hand.

Applied to intergroup relations, the distraction hypothesis predicts that strong affect should enhance reliance on existing prejudice and stereotypes when evaluating members of an outgroup. Strong affect should increase perceptions of outgroup homogeneity and, consequently, should lessen the impact of atypical behavior in the outgroup. The distraction hypothesis seems to be most applicable to situations involving relatively "hot" affect such as anger or anxiety at the prospect of an imminent threat. Anxiety, for example, has been associated with a narrowing of one's focus of attention (Easterbrook, 1959; Kahneman, 1973). Distraction appears less relevant to the milder mood inductions used in the many happy–sad experiments (Bodenhausen, Kramer, & Susser, 1994). Nevertheless, a distraction explanation may partially account for the differential effects of happy versus sad moods predicted by the mood and general information hypothesis. Bless,

Schwarz, and Kemmelmeier (in press) point to evidence that more positive than negative information is stored in memory and that positive information is better connected than negative. Consequently, if a positive mood state activates similarly valenced cognitions, the potential for interference and distraction is greater for persons in a positive mood state. Consistent with a distraction prediction, being in a pleasant mood should decrease processing capacity and increase reliance on heuristics, such as stereotypes, when making judgments of others (Macrae, Milne, & Bodenhausen, 1994).

In a set of studies relevant to the distraction hypothesis, Bodenhausen and his colleagues (Bodenhausen & Kramer, 1990; Bodenhausen, Sheppard, & Kramer, 1994) looked at the relationship between negative moods and stereotyping. They reported that happiness and anger increased reliance on stereotypes but that sadness had no effect as compared to a neutral control. Both happy and angry subjects appeared to rely more on heuristic cues when making judgments and less on individuating or particular information. From the standpoint of the distraction hypothesis, anger and happiness are likely to be "hotter" emotions than sadness and, therefore, more likely to distract subjects from careful attention to the task, thereby increasing the likelihood of their making stereotypic judgments.

Baron, Burgess, Kao, and Logan (1990) examined the impact of anxiety on stereotyping in a dental setting. In the first of two experiments subjects completed a mood measure assessing their anxiety while waiting for a dentist appointment. Then they read a series of sentences involving members of occupational groups (e.g., "Sue, a librarian, is wise and gentle"). The statements systematically varied how stereotypic were the actors' behaviors. Anxious subjects significantly overestimated the correlation between stereotypic traits and members of the corresponding occupation.

In Baron et al.'s (1990) second study, subjects were provided with information about dental procedures that was designed to generate either high or low fear. Then they were exposed to a weak persuasive message that was presented with superficial cues suggesting a strong message (e.g., applauding audience). Baron et al. reasoned that subjects who examined the message carefully would rate it poorly whereas those who superficially examined the message would judge it to be more convincing. The latter subjects would be more affected by the peripheral cues and presentation style of the speaker. As expected, subjects in the high fear condition rated the message as more persuasive than subjects in the low fear condition. These findings suggest that high fear led to superficial processing of the message.

A set of experiments by Wilder and Shapiro (1989a, 1989b, 1991; Wilder, 1993a, 1993b) investigated the impact of anxiety on judgments of an outgroup member who behaved contrary to expectations about his group. Following Stephan and Stephan (1985), Wilder and Shapiro reasoned that intergroup contact may not improve relations between groups when anxiety is generated in anticipation of the contact. Such anxiety (and any attempts to cope with it) may poison the interaction, not only because the negative affect is associated with the outgroup, but also because it interferes with information processing in the contact setting. To the extent that anxiety distracts individuals, they should be more likely to interpret the contact experiences in terms of their expectations or stereotypes of the outgroup. In a series of experiments, subjects were made anxious at the prospect of either making an embarrassing speech, posing for some embarrassing pictures, or receiving a set of electric shocks. Then they viewed a tape of a group interaction in which one of the four group members behaved quite differently from the majority (e.g., he behaved incompetently while the other members behaved competently). Subjects who were anxious underestimated the degree to which the deviant differed from the majority. Thus, anxious subjects were more likely than nonanxious subjects to judge the deviant to be acting according to expectations about the group, based on the majority's behavior. (Note that the same findings were obtained whether the group's behavior was positive and the deviant's negative or vice versa.) Moreover, self-reported anxiety was significantly correlated with judgments that assimilated the deviant's behavior in the direction of the majority.

In one of these experiments, following the mood induction, subjects viewed a set of humorous cartoons designed to reduce anxiety. These subjects did not make more stereotypic judgments of the deviant outgroup member. This finding, coupled with the strong, positive correlations between self-reported anxiety and stereotypic judgments in these studies, suggests that anxiety was a causal factor in subjects' stereotypic evaluations of the outgroup member.

Overall, findings from research conducted by Baron, Wilder, and their associates have been largely consistent with the distraction hypothesis. When subjects were anxious, they were more likely to overlook counterstereotypic information and relied on stereotypes when making judgments of outgroup members.

In sum, each of the five hypotheses that various researchers have posed to explain affect–bias effects has generated some support. Much of the research looking at affect and bias has compared pleasant (happy) versus unpleasant (sad, angry) moods. In this literature the general finding has been that pleasant mood, anger, and anxiety encourage greater reliance on pre-existing stereotypes and attitudes toward the outgroup. In general, sad mood appears to have no impact beyond that of a no-mood manipulation. However, manipulations that increase perceivers' processing of target information result in stronger mood congruent effects on judgments. How might we account for this pattern of findings?

A Two-Step Model Linking Affect and Intergroup Bias

We have briefly reviewed five explanations of when and why affect may influence judgments of outgroups. Clearly, several of these hypotheses draw from each other and several make similar predictions. Collectively, the five hypotheses address two distinct issues: allocation of attention and infusion of affect. The distraction and mood and general knowledge hypotheses focus on how affect may influence perceivers' allocation of attention. The affect consistency, affect as information, and affect infusion hypotheses deal with the extent of influence affect has on judgments once attention has been directed. As a gambit for research, we suggest the following synthesis: Affect influences intergroup judgments by both influencing the direction of attention and the valence of subsequent cognitions about the outgroup.

1. *Allocation of attention.* Two variables determine how affect shapes what persons attend to and use as grist for judgments of outgroups: valence of affect and strength of affect.

(a) *Valence of affect.* Negative affect commands greater vigilance than does positive affect. As discussed by Bless et al. (in press), this may be due to the greater threat inherent in negative affect (especially anxiety and fear). It may also reflect greater informational value of negative events (e.g., Jones & Davis, 1965). In a broader sense, it may reflect the function of conscious thought as a problem-solving mechanism for humans. We tune to negative affect because that is precisely what our active thought processes are designed to address. Pleasant affect, while sought out, lulls us to bliss and dulls our attentiveness.

In addition, Isen and her colleagues (Isen & Daubman, 1984; Isen, Niedenthal, & Cantor, 1992) have shown that positive affect broadens cognitive categories so that nontypical exemplars are more readily included. Applied to the mood and bias literature, positive affect may encourage perceivers to see the similarities in their environment and, therefore, underestimate the differences between target persons and the group to which they belong. Simply put, happy perceivers will overlook (or underweight) individuating information in favor of their expectations about the group category to which the target belongs.

(b) *Strength of affect.* Strong, "hot" emotion grabs more attention than cooler moods. Although strength of affect has not been manipulated systematically in this research area, comparisons across studies support this argument. Studies involving anxiety and arousal (Baron et al., 1990; Wilder & Shapiro, 1989a, 1989b) have provided evidence that strong affect can distract subjects from careful attention to the behavior of outgroup members and increase reliance on stereotypic and biased beliefs. Outgroup members were judged to be more homogeneous and their behavior more consistent with stereotypes when subjects were under high arousal as a result of an anxiety manipulation. Moreover, distraction produced by anxiety was significantly related to bias. The more anxious and distracted subjects reported themselves to be, the more biased they were in their judgments of outgroup members.

Note that the Wilder and Shapiro experiments differed from others in the mood–bias literature in that affect was generated by the expectation of a forthcoming unpleasant or fearful interaction. Thus, when subjects attended to the stimulus persons they had no opportunity to compartmentalize or dissociate their anxiety from the task at hand because resolution of the anxiety was yet to come. On the other hand, in the typical studies in the Bodenhausen, Mackie, and Forgas research programs, mood induction was presented to subjects as part of a separate experiment that preceded exposure to outgroup members. It seems to us that any distraction that may have been created by subjects having to focus on their emotions and cope with them would be minimized under this "two experiment" paradigm. Consequently, we suspect that the emotions experienced in the Wilder and Shapiro procedures were more intense and likely to produce coping responses that distracted subjects from careful attention to the target outgroup.

2. *Infusion of affect.* The affect consistency, affect as information, and affect infusion hypotheses posit that more mood congruent cognitions should be made salient with more in-depth cognitive processing. Literature on affect and bias has identified at least three variables that may influence processing strategies and, therefore, degree of affect infusion: motivational demands, temporal demands, and target demands.

(a) Motivational demands. To the extent that perceivers are motivated to be accurate in their judgments, they will give greater weight to individuating information and less to general knowledge schemas such as stereotypes (Fiske & Neuberg, 1990; Kruglanski, 1989). In several studies, when happy persons were motivated to process stimulus information more carefully, they did not rely on stereotypes more than did neutral or sad perceivers (Bless et al., 1990; Bodenhausen et al., 1994). For instance, Queller, Mackie, and Stroessner (1994, cited in Mackie, Queller, Stroessner, & Hamilton, 1996) manipulated subjects' mood states (neutral or happy) and had subjects read descriptions of members of a group of "Big Brothers." Half of their subjects were asked to form a simple impression of the group. These subjects showed the typical mood effect: happy subjects perceived the Big Brothers as more homogeneous than did neutral subjects. The other subjects were asked to sort the descriptions into piles based on similarity and then form an impression of the group. Subjects who had attended more closely to the information by sorting the cards on the basis of similarity did not display the happy–neutral mood difference. Using a different manipulation, Bodenhausen, Kramer, and Susser (1994, experiment 4) also varied how accountable subjects were for their judgments. Increasing accountability resulted in happy subjects processing information more carefully and making less stereotypic judgments.

The motivational demands perceivers carry into a situation clearly affect where they will allocate their attention and what cognitive strategies they will adopt. Thus, motivation to be accurate is likely to lead to more meticulous consideration of specific individuating information about targets than is motivation for a quick judgment. The former should lead to greater affect infusion because of the longer time spent processing information in making the judgment (Forgas, 1995). A snap judgment, by contrast, is likely to be based more strongly on pre-existing bias. As Forgas (1995) has argued in his AIM model, processing strategies influence the amount of time spent making judgments and, therefore, the opportunity of affect to infuse on judgments by arousing affect-consistent cognitions. This leads us to our second variable: temporal demands.

(b) Temporal demands. The more time spent processing information, the greater is the opportunity for affect to infuse the judgment process (Forgas, 1995). On the other hand, under severe time constraint, judgments tend to be more heuristic and homogeneous. For example, Stroessner and Mackie (1992) varied how much time subjects had to look at descriptions of members of another group. When they had only three seconds between stimuli, they found that happy subjects perceived greater homogeneity in the outgroup than did neutral subjects. However, this difference was significantly reduced when time between stimulus presentations was increased to seven seconds. Their findings indicate that the relationship between mood and stereotyping may be affected by the time available for processing information. With less time to process stimuli, happy subjects were less attentive to variability and, by implication, more reliant on their expectation of similarity within the outgroup.

(c) Target demands. Judgments of an outgroup or of specific members are made in a social context. Context is provided by the presence of others (e.g., bystanders, other outgroup members), or, at minimum, by the expectations associated with the outgroup. In either case, evidence indicates that outgroup members who appear to be atypical or who engage in unexpected behavior elicit close inspection. As a result, their individuating

characteristics and behavior exercise greater impact on judgments than do simple group stereotypes (Bless et al., in press; Fiske & Neuberg, 1980).

In sum, to the extent perceivers are motivated to process information carefully and have sufficient time to do so, to the extent affect is not so strong as to distract them from attending to the actions of the target, and to the extent the target is atypical in word or deed, perceivers' judgments will be based more strongly on individuating information present in the situation and less on stereotypes and prejudice about the outgroup. Moreover, closer attention to the target will promote more affect infusion such that positive mood should lead to a more positive evaluation and negative mood to a more negative evaluation of the target.

Implications for Intergroup Contact

In closing, consider some implications that can be drawn from the affect–bias literature for that venerable solution to intergroup bias: the contact hypothesis. Although not always made explicit, the contact hypothesis is grounded in the supposition that contact between groups will more likely improve relations if the contact generates positive rather than negative affect. Certainly, reviews of the contact literature have concluded that a pleasant experience, while not sufficient, contributes to successful interactions (e.g., Allport, 1954; Amir, 1969; Brewer & Miller, 1984; Hewstone & Brown, 1986; Pettigrew, 1986, 1998; Stephan, 1987; Wilder, 1984). On the other hand, cooperative contact that is unsuccessful is less likely to improve intergroup relations (Worchel, 1986). Failure in the contact setting generates negative affect which, in turn, can poison the contact experience. Negative experiences can trigger affect-consistent cognitions, including memories of past unpleasantness with the outgroup. Failure, thereby, reinforces negative stereotypes and prejudice toward the outgroup.

The prospect of contact with members of a disliked or threatening outgroup can be a source of considerable anxiety (Islam & Hewstone, 1993; Pettigrew, 1998; Stephan & Stephan, 1985). Anxiety, in turn, can undermine any beneficial impact of a contact experience by causing persons to either avoid the contact, misconstrue the experience, or behave in a defensive manner that may poison the experience (Stephan & Stephan, 1985; Wilder & Simon, 1996). In a field study in Bangladesh, Islam and Hewstone (1993) reported that contact between Hindu and Muslim students resulted in more favorable attitudes toward the respective outgroups and a reduction of reported anxiety when the contact was of high quality (e.g., intimate rather than superficial). Interestingly, they also reported that anxiety was positively associated with contact with outgroup members who were viewed as more typical of their group. Evidently, the more typical the outgroup members, the more they possessed undesirable or threatening characteristics associated with existing prejudice. This finding gives pause to the recommendation that contact with typical outgroup members is most likely to result in the generalization of that experience to attitudes about the outgroup as a whole (Hewstone & Brown, 1981; Wilder, 1984). Contact with typical outgroup members may be of little benefit if it also generates anxiety that vitiates the contact experience. Given that anxiety may interfere with successful contact experiences, what other implications might be drawn from the literature on affect and bias that bear upon the contact hypothesis?

If we apply research on affect and bias to the contact situation, we immediately stumble. Much of the reviewed research indicates that happiness, anger, and anxiety foster superficial processing and reliance on existing prejudice and stereotypes. On the other hand, other research suggests that a sad or a neutral mood is more conducive to noticing and carefully processing information in a contact situation. This pattern of findings augurs poorly for the beneficial effects of pleasant contact with an outgroup.

Although it is tempting to infer that a good mood might be detrimental to reducing bias, that nonobvious "man bites dog" conclusion would be premature for two reasons. First, Stroessner, Hamilton, and Mackie (1992) have evidence that a positive mood can prevent the formation of stereotypes based on illusory correlations. In their experiment happy or neutral subjects were exposed to a standard illusory correlation paradigm (Hamilton & Gifford, 1976). They saw information about two groups (A and B): 24 descriptions of group A – 16 desirable and 8 undesirable behaviors; 12 descriptions of group B – 8 desirable and 4 undesirable behaviors. Thus, the proportion of desirable and undesirable descriptors were the same for both groups. In the neutral mood condition subjects rated group B less favorably than group A (illusory correlation effect). Thus, the less frequent and, therefore, more distinct negative behaviors had a greater impact for evaluations of group B. On the other hand, in the happy mood condition, both groups were rated equally. Stroessner et al. argued that the happy mood resulted in less careful processing of the information. Consequently, happy subjects were less attendant to the distinctive negative information about group B and less likely to form a negative stereotype.

Second, as the research on affect infusion (e.g., Forgas, 1995; Forgas & Fiedler, 1996) has demonstrated, the influence of mood on thoughts and actions tends to be affect-consistent and more pronounced with additional processing time. The key for successful contact, then, appears to be to encourage persons in a pleasant mood to attend closely to the actions of the outgroup in the positive contact setting. Close attention to the outgroup's actions should counter the superficial processing tendency associated with a positive mood, should provide opportunity for greater affect infusion, and should generate concrete positive experiences that prolong the positive mood state.

Close attention to the outgroup can be facilitated by the factors discussed above: motivational demands, temporal demands, and task demands. Prompting interactants for accuracy, allowing sufficient time for positive mood infusion, and presenting them with contact persons who clearly disconfirm biases should provide the opportunity both for maximum mood infusion and generation of positive cognitions that are inconsistent with existing biases (Hewstone & Lord, 1998; Wilder, 1984). This recommendation fits with what is known about successful contact (e.g., Amir, 1969). Past research has concluded that contact is most successful when it involves cooperative pursuit of shared goals, equal status, intimacy, and support from others. Moreover, as Pettigrew (1998) has pointed out, positive contact is more likely to be successful if it occurs frequently and if each experience is not so brief as to preclude the formation of friendship bonds across groups.

These are all conditions that are likely to lead to careful processing of information and the opportunity for infusion of positive affect.

Conclusions

The notion that affective states can influence judgments of groups is certainly not new (e.g., Allport, 1954). What is relatively recent, however, is a body of literature that has examined the impact of different affective states on judgments of outgroups using carefully controlled experiments. This chapter has focused on that literature and five hypotheses that have been offered to explain the role of affect in intergroup judgments. We have offered a two-component synthesis of those hypotheses: The influence of affect on intergroup judgments is mediated by how the affect influences allocation of attention and opportunity for infusion.

It should be noted that most of this literature has been generated by laboratory experiments in which affect is manipulated independently of the judged outgroup; that is, incidental to the outgroup (Bodenhausen, 1993). One may question whether the same findings would be observed were the affect integral; that is, caused by or attributed to the outgroup. One set of experiments (Wilder & Shapiro, 1989a) did employ integral affect by having the manipulation of affect linked to the behavior of members of the target outgroup. The results from this study were the same as when affect was manipulated incidental to the outgroup.

Finally, it should be noted that this literature has focused on judgments of outgroups. But certainly affect also exerts influence on judgments of ingroups. (In a recent chapter in this handbook series, Kelly (in press) has looked at mood and emotion within groups.) Affective relations among ingroup members may very likely contribute to affect directed toward an outgroup. (For example, see Allport's (1954) discussion of projection.) In a complementary fashion, affect generated by an outgroup may influence judgments of the ingroup. There is evidence that the mere salience of an outgroup is sufficient to make salient a perceiver's relevant ingroup (Wilder & Shapiro, 1986). Because outgroups and corresponding ingroups are linked, it is probable that affect associated with one has implications for affect and judgments toward the other. One direction that may prove fruitful is to expand the current research beyond examining how affect influences judgments of outgroups to a broader consideration of the influence of affect on judgments of ingroup–outgroup pairings.

References

Abelson, R. P., Aronson, E., McGuire, W. J., Newcomb, T. M., Rosenberg, M. J., & Tannenbaum, P. H. (1968). *Theories of cognitive consistency*. Chicago, IL: Rand McNally.

Adorno, T. W., Frenkel-Brunswick, E., Levinson, D., & Sanford, R. N. (1950). *The authoritarian personality*. New York: Harper.

Allport, G. W. (1954). *The nature of prejudice.* Cambridge, MA: Addison-Wesley.

Amir, Y. (1969). Contact hypothesis in ethnic relations. *Psychological Bulletin, 71,* 319–342.

Baron, R. S., Burgess, M. L., Kao, C. F., & Logan, H. (1990). *Fear and superficial social process-ing: Evidence of stereotyping and simplistic persuasion.* Paper presented at the annual convention of the Midwestern Psychological Association, Chicago, IL.

Berkowitz, L. (1990). On the formation and regulation of anger and aggression: A cognitive-neoas-sociationistic analysis. *American Psychologist, 45,* 494–503.

Berkowitz, L. (1993). *Aggression: Its causes, consequences, and control.* New York: McGraw-Hill.

Bies, R. J. (1987). The predicament of injustice: The management of moral outrage. In L. Cummings & B. M. Staw (Eds.), *Research in organizational behavior* (Vol. 9, pp. 289–319). Greenwich, CT: JAI.

Bies, R. J., Tripp, T. M., & Kramer, R. M. (1996). At the breaking point: Cognitive and social dynamics of revenge in organizations. In J. Greenberg & R. Giacalone (Eds.), *Antisocial behav-ior in organizations.* Thousand Oaks, CA: Sage.

Bless, H., & Fiedler, K. (1995). Affective states and the influence of activated general knowledge. *Personality and Social Psychology Bulletin, 21,* 766–778.

Bless, H., Mackie, D. M., & Schwarz, N. (1992). Mood effects on encoding and judgmental processes in persuasion. *Journal of Personality and Social Psychology, 63,* 585–595.

Bless, H., Schwarz, N., & Kemmelmeier, M. (in press). Mood and stereotyping: Affective states and the use of general knowledge structures. In W. Stroebe & M. Hewstone (Eds.), *European review of social psychology* (Vol. 7). New York: Wiley.

Bodenhausen, G. V. (1993). Emotions, arousal, and stereotypic judgments: A heuristic model of affect and stereotyping. In D. M. Mackie & D. L. Hamilton (Eds.), *Affect, cognition, and stereo-typing* (pp. 13–37). San Diego, CA: Academic Press.

Bodenhausen, G. V., & Kramer, G. P. (1990). *Affective states trigger stereotypic judgments.* Paper presented at the annual convention of the American Psychological Society, Dallas, TX.

Bodenhausen, G. V., Kramer, G. P., & Susser, K. (1994). Happiness and stereotypic thinking in social judgment. *Journal of Personality and Social Psychology, 66,* 621–632.

Bodenhausen, G. V., Sheppard, L. A., & Kramer, G. P. (1994). Negative affect and social judg-ment: The differential impact of anger and sadness. *European Journal of Social Psychology, 24,* 45–62.

Bower, G. H. (1981). Mood and memory. *American Psychologist, 36,* 129–148.

Brewer, M. B. (1981). Ethnocentrism and its role in interpersonal trust. In M. B. Brewer & B. E. Collins (Eds.), *Scientific inquiry and the social sciences* (pp. 345–360). San Francisco, CA: Josey-Bass.

Brewer, M. B. (1988). A dual-process model of impression formation. In T. K. Srull & R. S. Wyer (Eds.), *Advances in social cognition* (Vol. 1, pp. 1–36). Hillsdale, NJ: Erlbaum.

Brewer, M. B., & Miller, N. (1984). Beyond the contact hypothesis: Theoretical perspectives on desegregation. In N. Miller & M. B. Brewer (Eds.), *Groups in contact: The psychology of desegre-gation* (pp. 281–302). Orlando, FL: Academic Press.

Byrne, D., & Clore, G. L. (1970). A reinforcement model of evaluation responses. *Personality: An International Journal, 1,* 103–128.

Campbell, D. T. (1975). On the conflict between biological and social evolution and between psychology and moral tradition. *American psychologist, 30,* 1103–1126.

Clore, G. L., & Byrne, D. (1974). The reinforcement affect model of attraction. In L. Huston (Ed.), *Foundations of interpersonal attraction* (pp. 143–170). San Diego, CA: Academic Press.

Clore, G. L., Schwarz, N., & Conway, M. (1994). Cognitive causes and consequences of emotion. In R. S. Wyer & T. K. Srull (Eds.), *Handbook of social cognition* (2nd ed., pp. 323–417). Hillsdale, NJ: Erlbaum.

Dollard, J., Doob, L. W., Miller, N. E., Mowrer, O. H., & Sears, R. R. (1939). *Frustration and aggression*. New Haven, CT: Yale University Press.

Dovidio, J. F., Brigham, J., Johnson, B. T., & Gaertner, S. L. (1996). Stereotyping, prejudice, and discrimination. In N. Macrae, C. Stangor, & M. Hewstone (Eds.), *Foundations of stereotypes and stereotyping* (pp. 337–366). Hillsdale, NJ: Erlbaum.

Dovidio, J. F., Gaertner, S. L., Isen, A. M., & Lawrence, R. (1995). Group representations and intergroup bias: Positive affect, similarity, and group size. *Personality and Social Psychology Bulletin, 21*, 856–865.

Easterbrook, J. A. (1959). The effect of emotion on cue utilization and the organization of behavior. *Psychological Review, 66*, 183–201.

Fiedler, K. (1991). On the task, the measures and the mood in research on affect and social cognition. In J. P. Forgas (Ed.), *Emotion and social judgment* (pp. 83–104). Elmsford, NY: Pergamon Press.

Fiske, S. T., & Morlin, B. (1996). Stereotyping as a function of personal control motives and capacity constraints: The odd couple of power and anxiety. In R. M. Sorrentino & E. T. Higgins (Eds.), *Handbook of motivation and cognition: The interpersonal context* (Vol. 3, pp. 322–346). New York: Guilford.

Fiske, S. T., & Neuberg, L. (1990). A continuum of impression formation, from category-based to individuating processes: Influences of information and motivation on attention and interpretation. In M. Zanna (Ed.), *Advances in experimental social psychology* (Vol. 23, pp. 1–74). San Diego, CA: Academic Press.

Forgas, J. P. (1989). Mood effects on decision-making strategies. *Australian Journal of Psychology, 41*, 197–214.

Forgas, J. P. (1995). Mood and judgment: The affect infusion model (AIM). *Psychological Bulletin, 117*, 39–66.

Forgas, J. P., & Fiedler, K. (1996). Us and them: Mood effects on intergroup discrimination. *Journal of Personality and Social Psychology, 70*, 28–40.

Forgas, J. P., & Moylan, S. J. (1991). Affective influences on stereotype judgments. *Cognition and Emotion, 5*, 379–397.

Hamilton, D. L., & Gifford, R. K. (1976). Illusory correlation in interpersonal perception: A cognitive basis of stereotypic judgments. *Journal of Experimental Social Psychology, 12*, 392–407.

Hamilton, D. L., & Rose, T. L. (1980). Illusory correlation and the maintenance of stereotypic belief. *Journal of Personality and Social Psychology, 19*, 832–845.

Hewstone, M., & Brown, R. (1986). Contact is not enough: An intergroup perspective on the contact hypothesis. In M. Hewstone & R. Brown (Eds.), *Contact and conflict in intergroup encounters* (pp. 169–195). Oxford, UK: Blackwell.

Hewstone, M., & Lord, C. G. (1998). Changing intergroup cognitions and intergroup behavior: The role of typicality. In C. Sedikides, J. Schopler, & C. A. Insko (Eds.), *Intergroup cognition and intergroup behavior* (pp. 367–392). Mahwah, NJ: Erlbaum.

Hunter, J. A., Platow, M. J., Bell, L. M., & Kypri, K. (1997). Intergroup bias and self-evaluation: Domain-specific self-esteem, threats to identity and dimensional importance. *British Journal of Social Psychology, 36*, 405–426.

Hunter, J. A., Platow, M. J., & Howard, M. L. (1996). Social identity and intergroup evaluative bias: Realistic categories and domain specific self-esteem in a conflict setting. *European Journal of Social Psychology, 26*, 631–647.

Isen, A. (1984). Toward understanding the role of affect in cognition. In R. S. Wyer & T. K. Srull (Eds.), Handbook of social cognition (Vol. 20, pp. 179–236). Hillsdale, NJ: Erlbaum.

Isen, A. (1987). Positive affect, cognitive processes and social behavior. In L. Berkowitz (Ed.), *Advances in experimental social psychology* (Vol. 20, pp. 203–253). San Diego, CA: Academic Press.

Isen, A. M., & Daubman, K. A. (1984). The influence of affect on categorization. *Journal of Personality and Social Psychology, 47,* 1206–1217.

Isen, A. M., Niedenthal, P. M., & Cantor, N. (1992). An influence of positive affect on social categorization. *Motivation and Emotion, 16,* 65–78.

Islam, M. R., & Hewstone, M. (1993). Dimensions of contact as predictors of intergroup anxiety, perceived out-group variability, and out-group attitude: An integrative model. *Personality and Social Psychology Bulletin, 19,* 700–710.

Kahneman, D. (1973). *Attention and effort.* Englewood Cliff, NJ: Prentice-Hall.

Kelly, J. R. (in press). Mood and emotion in groups. In M. Hogg & S. Tindale (Eds.), *Blackwell handbook in social psychology, Vol. 3: Group Processes.* Oxford, UK: Blackwell.

Kramer, R. M., & Messick, D. M. (1998). Getting by with a little help from our enemies: Collective paranoia and its role in intergroup relations. In C. Sedikides, Schopler, & C. A. Insko (Eds.), *Intergroup cognition and intergroup behavior* (pp. 233–255). Mahwah, NJ: Erlbaum.

Jones, E. E., & Davis, K. E. (1965). A theory of correspondent inferences: From acts to dispositions. In L. Berkowitz (Ed.), *Advances in experimental social psychology* (Vol. 2). New York: Academic Press.

Kruglanski, A. W. (1989). *Lay epistemics and human knowledge: Cognitive and motivational bases.* New York: Plenum.

Lemyre, L., & Smith, P. M. (1985). Intergroup discrimination and self-esteem in the minimal group paradigm. *Journal of Personality and Social Psychology, 49,* 660–670.

LeVine, R. A., & Campbell, D. T. (1972). *Ethnocentrism: Theories of conflict, ethnic attitudes, and group behavior.* New York: Wiley.

Mackie, D. M., Hamilton, D. L., Schroth, H. A., Carlisle, C. J., Gersho, B. F., Meneses, M., Nedler, B. F., & Reichel, L. D. (1989). The effects of induced mood on expectancy-based illusory correlations. *Journal of Experimental Social Psychology, 25,* 524–544.

Mackie, D. M., Queller, S., & Stroessner, S. J. (1994). The impact of positive mood on perceptions of behavioral consistency and member typicality in social groups. Unpublished manuscipt, University of California, Santa Barbara.

Mackie, D. M., Queller, S., Stroessner, S. J., & Hamilton, D. L. (1996). Making stereotypes better or worse: Multiple roles for positive affect in group impressions. In R. M. Sorrentino & E. T. Higgins (Eds.), *Handbook of motivation and cognition* (Vol. 3, pp. 371–396). New York: Guilford Press.

Mackie, D. M., & Worth, L. T. (1989). Cognitive deficits and the mediation of positive affect in persuasion. *Journal of Personality and Social Psychology, 57,* 27–40.

Macrae, C. N., Milne, A. B., & Bodenhausen, G. V. (1994). Stereotypes as energy-saving devices: A peek inside the toolbox. *Journal of Personality and Social Psychology, 66,* 37–47.

Meindl, J. R., & Lerner, M. (1984). Exacerbation of extreme responses to an out-group. *Journal of Personality and Social Psychology, 47,* 71–84.

Messick, D. M., & Mackie, D. M. (1989). Intergroup relations. In M. R. Rosenzweig & W. Porter (Eds.), *Annual review of psychology* (Vol. 40, pp. 45–81). Palo Alto, CA: Annual Reviews.

Oakes, P. J., & Turner, J. C. (1980). Social categorization and intergroup behaviour: Does minimal intergroup discrimination make social identity more positive? *European Journal of Social Psychology, 10,* 295–301.

Paulhus, D. L., & Lim, T. K. (1994). Arousal and evaluative extremity in social judgments: A dynamic complexity model. *European Journal of Social Psychology, 24*, 89–100.

Pettigrew, T. F. (1986). The intergroup contact hypothesis reconsidered. In M. Hewstone & R. Brown (Eds.), *Contact and conflict in intergroup encounters* (pp. 169–195). Oxford, UK: Blackwell.

Pettigrew, T. F. (1998). Intergroup contact theory. *Annual review of psychology* (Vol. 49, pp. 65–85). Annual Reviews.

Petty, R. E., & Cacioppo, J. T. (1986a). The elaboration likelihood model of persuasion. In L. Berkowitz (Ed.), *Advances in experimental social psychology* (Vol. 19). New York: Academic Press.

Petty, R. E., & Cacioppo, J. T. (1986b). *Communication and persuasion: Central and peripheral routes to attitude change.* New York: Springer-Verlag.

Pyszczynski, T. A., & Greenberg, J. (1987). Depression, self-focused attention, and self-regulatory presevation. In C. R. Snyder & C. E. Ford (Eds.), *Coping with negative life events: Clinical and social psychological perspectives* (pp. 105–129). New York: Plenum Press.

Schachter, S., & Singer, J. (1962). Cognitive, social, and physiological determinants of the emotional state. *Psychological Review, 69*, 379–399.

Schwarz, N. (1990). Feelings as information: Informational and motivational functions of affective states. In R. M. Sorrentino & E. T. Higgins (Eds.), *Handbook of motivation and cognition: Foundations of social behavior* (Vol. 2, pp. 527–561). New York: Guilford.

Schwarz, N., & Bless, H. (1991). Happy and mindless, but sad and smart? The impact of affective states on analytic reasoning. In J. Forgas (Ed.), *Emotion and social judgments* (pp. 55–71). Oxford, UK: Pergamon.

Schwarz, N., Bless, H., & Bohner, G. (1991). Mood and persuasion: Affective states influence the processing of persuasive communications. In M. Zanna (Ed.), *Advances in experimental social psychology* (Vol. 24, pp. 161–197). New York: Academic Press.

Schwarz, N., & Clore, G. L. (1988). How do I feel about it? The informative function of affective states. In K. Fiedler & J. P. Forgas (Eds.), *Affect, cognition, and social behavior* (pp. 44–62). Göttingen, Germany: Hogrefe.

Sherif, M. (1966). *In common predicament: Social psychology of intergroup conflict and cooperation.* Boston, MA: Houghton-Mifflin.

Sinclair, R. C., Mark, M. M., & Clore, G. L. (1994). Mood-related persuasion depends on misattributions. *Social Cognition, 12*, 309–326.

Staats, A. W., & Staats, C. K. (1958). Attitudes established by classical conditioning. *Journal of Abnormal and Social Psychology, 57*, 37–40.

Stephan, W. G. (1987). The contact hypothesis in intergroup relations. In C. Hendrick (Ed.), *Review of personality and social psychology* (Vol. 9, pp. 13–40). Newbury Park, CA: Sage.

Stephan, W. G., & Stephan, C. W. (1985). Intergroup anxiety. *Journal of Social Issues, 41*, 157–175.

Stroessner, S. J., Hamilton, D. L., & Mackie, D. M. (1992). Affect and stereotyping: The effect of induced mood on distinctiveness-based illusory correlations. *Journal of Personality and Social Psychology, 62*, 564–576.

Stroessner, S. J., & Mackie, D. M. (1992). The impact of induced affect on the perception of variability in social groups. *Personality and Social Psychology Bulletin, 18*, 546–554.

Stroessner, S. J., & Mackie, D. M. (1993). Affect and perceived group variability: Implications for stereotyping and prejudice. In D. M. Mackie & D. L. Hamilton (Eds.), *Affect, cognition, and stereotyping: Interactive processes in group perception* (pp. 63–86). San Diego, CA: Academic Press.

Tajfel, H. (1982). *Social identity and intergroup behaviour.* Cambridge, UK: Cambridge University Press.

Trivers, R. L. (1971). The evolution of reciprocal altruism. *Quarterly review of Biology, 46*, 35–57.

Turner, J. C. (1987). *Rediscovering the social group: A self-categorization theory.* Oxford, UK: Basil Blackwell.

Wilder, D. A. (1984). Intergroup contact: The typical members and the exception to the rule. *Journal of Experimental Social Psychology, 20*, 177–194.

Wilder, D. A. (1993a). The role of anxiety in facilitating stereotypic judgments of outgroup behavior. In D. M. Mackie & D. L. Hamilton (Eds.), *Affect, cognition, and stereotyping: Interactive processes in group perception* (pp. 87–109). San Diego, CA: Academic Press.

Wilder, D. A. (1993b). Freezing intergroup evaluations: Anxiety fosters resistance to counter-stereotypic information. In M. A. Hogg & D. Abrams (Eds.), *Group motivation: Social psychological perspectives* (pp. 68–86). New York: Harvester/Wheatsheaf.

Wilder, D. A., & Shapiro, P. (1989a). Role of competition-induced anxiety in limiting the beneficial impact of positive behavior by an outgroup member. *Journal of . . .*

Wilder, D. A., & Shapiro, P. (1989b). Effects of anxiety on impression formation in a group context: An anxiety-assimilation hypothesis. *Journal of Experimental Social Psychology, 25*, 482–499.

Wilder, D. A., & Shapiro, P. (1991). Facilitation of outgroup stereotypes by enhanced ingroup identity. *Journal of Experimental Social Psychology, 27*, 431–452.

Wilder, D. A., & Simon, A. F. (1996). Incidental and integral affect as triggers of stereotyping. In R. M. Sorrentino & E. T. Higgins (Eds.), *Handbook of motivation and cognition: The interpersonal context* (Vol. 3, pp. 397–419). New York: Guilford Press.

Wills, T. A. (1981). Downward comparison principles in social psychology. *Psychological Bulletin, 90*, 245–271.

Worchel, S. (1986). The role of cooperation in reducing intergroup conflict. In S. Worchel & W. G. Austin (Eds.), *Psychology of intergroup relations* (2nd ed., pp. 288–304). Chicago, IL: Nelson-Hall.

Zillman, D. (1983). Transfer of excitation in emotional behavior. In J. T. Cacioppo & R. E. Petty (Eds.), *Social psychophysiology.* New York: Academic Press.

PART III

Prejudice

CHAPTER NINE

Implicit and Explicit Attitudes: Examination of the Relationship between Measures of Intergroup Bias

John F. Dovidio, Kerry Kawakami, and Kelly R. Beach

Attitudes serve a fundamental function by subjectively organizing people's environment and orienting them to objects and people in it. To operate in this functional way, particularly quickly and efficiently, attitudes would seem to need to convey a single, clear evaluation – positive or negative. Along these lines, theories of attitudes have typically defined them as "unidimensional summary statements" (Thompson, Zanna, & Griffin, 1995, p. 362). Evaluation is similarly central in Eagly and Chaiken's (1998) definition of an attitude as "a psychological tendency that is expressed by evaluating a particular entity with some degree of favor or disfavor" (p. 269).

Attitudes do not have to be consciously accessible to produce evaluative reactions to an object, however. The mere presence of the attitude object is often sufficient to activate the associated attitude automatically (Chen & Bargh, 1997; Fazio, Sanbonmatsu, Powell, & Kardes, 1986), often without awareness. In short, attitudes may be implicit as well as explicit. The present chapter examines evidence for the existence of implicit social attitudes, the reliability and validity of implicit attitudes, the relationship between implicit and explicit attitudes, and their respective influence on behavior (see also Devine, Plant, & Blair, this volume, chapter 10).

Implicit and Explicit Attitudes

The distinction between implicit and explicit memory processes has received substantial empirical attention (e.g., Schacter, 1990). Implicit memory processes involve lack of

Preparation of this manuscript was supported by NIMH Grant MH 48721 and facilitated by NSF support for the Construct Validity/Implicit Social Cognition Conference (Chicago, IL, organized by A. G. Greenwald and M. R. Banaji).

awareness and are unintentionally activated, whereas explicit processes are conscious, deliberative, and controllable. A similar distinction has emerged in the literature on attitudes and stereotyping (Greenwald & Banaji, 1995). Explicit attitudes and stereotyping operate in a conscious mode and are exemplified by traditional, self-report measures of these constructs (see Dovidio, Brigham, Johnson, & Gaertner, 1996). Implicit attitudes and stereotypes, in contrast, are evaluations and beliefs that are automatically activated by the mere presence (actual or symbolic) of the attitude object. They commonly function in an unconscious fashion. Implicit attitudes and stereotypes develop with repeated pairings, either through direct experience or social learning of the association, between the category or object and evaluative and semantic characteristics. They are typically assessed using response latency procedures, memory tasks, physiological measures (e.g., galvanic skin response, GSR), and indirect self-report measures (e.g., involving attributional biases). These techniques for assessing automatic activation offer conceptually and empirically different perspectives on both attitudes and stereotypes than traditional self-report measures.

Complex Attitudes

Despite empirical evidence that attitudes are typically positive *or* negative, it is also possible that people may hold more complex attitudes toward an object or a person. People's evaluative reactions toward an attitude can also be *simultaneously* mixed (Cacioppo, Gardner, & Berntson, 1997; Thompson et al., 1995). Ambivalence theory (Katz, Wakenhut, & Hass, 1986), for instance, proposes that people may have both positive and negative reactions (e.g., sympathy and aversion), which create psychological conflict, tension, and ultimately behavioral amplification.

In contrast to ambivalence models that posit a person's awareness of both the positive and negative aspects of the attitude, Wilson, Lindsey, and Schooler (2000) have presented an alternative model of attitudes representing different evaluations of the same object. In this model, however, people are not aware of their different evaluations of the attitudinal object. Specifically, Wilson et al. hypothesize that people may have "dual attitudes," which are defined as "different evaluations of the same attitude object, one of which is a habitual, implicit attitude and the other an explicit attitude" (Wilson et al., 2000, p. 104). Wilson and his colleagues hypothesize that the explicit and implicit components of dual attitudes can be acquired in either order or simultaneously. Dual attitudes, however, commonly arise developmentally. With experience or socialization, people change their attitudes. However, the original attitude is not replaced, but rather it is stored in memory and becomes implicit, whereas the newer attitude is conscious and explicit. In general, explicit attitudes can change and evolve relatively easily, whereas implicit attitudes, because they are rooted in overlearning and habitual reactions, are much more difficult to alter.

Because they may be a product of similar experience and learning history and may, in fact, form the basis for the development of implicit attitudes through repeated exposure or application (Shiffrin & Schneider, 1977; Smith, 1990), explicit and implicit attitudes may correspond with each other. Other times, they might not. One factor that may determine the evaluative correspondence of the implicit and explicit evaluations involved in dual attitudes is the normative context for the attitude object. For instance, people may initially acquire negative attitudes toward groups through socialization within a particular cultural or historical context. Later, when norms change or the person is exposed to new normative proscriptions that dictate that people should *not* have these negative feelings toward these groups, people adopt explicit unbiased or positive attitudes. Nevertheless, negative implicit attitudes linger.

This reasoning suggests that there may be greater correspondence between implicit and explicit attitudes for issues that are not socially sensitive than for those that are socially sensitive or are associated with norms that are inconsistent with historical norms or traditional socialization. Evidence from research by Fazio, Williams, and Sanbonmatsu (1990) supports this notion. Fazio et al. compared people's self-reported (explicit) and automatically activated (implicit) attitudes for attitude objects that did or did not involve socially sensitive issues. The correlation between explicit and implicit attitudes for objects that did not involve socially sensitive issues (e.g., snakes, dentists) was high ($r = .63$). In contrast, the correlation for objects associated with socially sensitive issues (e.g., pornography, Blacks) was weak and, in fact, negative ($r = -.11$).

In their model of dual attitudes, Wilson et al. (2000) further identify how and when implicit and explicit attitudes can influence behavior. Specifically, they propose, "When dual attitudes exist, the implicit attitude is activated automatically, whereas the explicit one requires more capacity and motivation to retrieve from memory" (p. 104). According to Wilson et al. (2000), the relative influence of explicit and implicit attitudes depends upon the type of response that is made. Explicit attitudes shape deliberative, well-considered responses in which the costs and benefits of various courses of action are weighed. Implicit attitudes influence "uncontrollable responses (e.g., some nonverbal behaviors) or responses that people do not view as an expression of their attitude and thus do not attempt to control" (p. 104).

In terms of behavioral consequences, this proposition is similar to aspects of Fazio's (1990) MODE model. The name MODE refers to motivation and opportunity as determinants of the processing mode by which behavioral decisions are made. The MODE model suggests that behavioral decisions may involve conscious deliberation or occur as spontaneous, unconscious reactions to an attitude object or issue. When people have the opportunity (e.g., sufficient time) and motivation (e.g., concern about evaluation) to assess the consequences of various actions, explicit attitudes primarily influence responses as people reflect upon their conscious attitudes that are relevant to the decision. When the opportunity is not permitted (e.g., because of time pressure) or the motivation is absent (e.g., because the task is unimportant), implicit attitudes are more influential. Thus the relative impact of implicit and explicit attitudes is a function of the context in which the attitudinal object appears, the motivation and opportunity to engage in deliberative processes, and the nature of the behavioral response.

Wilson et al.'s (2000) model of dual attitudes and Fazio's (1990) MODE model offer comprehensive and integrative frameworks for understanding the relationship between implicit and explicit attitudes and their consequences. In the next section of this chapter we explore the implications of these frameworks to a particular social attitude – the racial attitudes of Whites toward Blacks. We have selected this as a "case study" to illustrate the operation of implicit and explicit attitudes for several reasons. First, there has been considerable theorizing about the complex nature of the attitudes of Whites toward Blacks. Although much of this work speculates about the existence of dual attitudes, until recently the techniques for assessing implicit attitudes were unavailable. Current research, however, can help form a conceptual bridge between the general frameworks of Wilson et al. and Fazio to a specific type of social attitude. Second, because of the nature of contemporary racial attitudes, this is a phenomenon in which implicit and explicit attitudes are likely to diverge. Consequently, the separate effects of each are more easily observable. Third, although implicit and explicit attitudes have been studied for a variety of objects and groups, much of the empirical work that considers both implicit and explicit attitudes has been concentrated on this issue. Thus, there is a sufficient empirical basis for evaluating the relationship between implicit and explicit attitudes within this common domain.

The Case of Racial Attitudes

In this section we first describe theoretical perspectives on the contemporary racial attitudes of Whites toward Blacks, which suggests the existence and operation of dual attitudes – one attitude explicit and the other implicit. We then review the evidence on implicit racial attitudes and the reliability and validity of these measures. After that we explore, conceptually and empirically (through meta-analysis), the relationship between implicit and explicit racial attitudes. Next, we examine the relationship between implicit and explicit racial attitudes and interracial behavior. Finally, we consider the malleability of implicit attitudes. Although our focus is on the racial attitudes of Whites toward Blacks, we also discuss related work and findings in other domains.

Theoretical perspectives

Whereas the traditional, "red-neck" form of racial prejudice is considered to be direct and univalently negative, the contemporary racial attitudes of Whites, particularly White Americans, are hypothesized to be more complex – reflecting both negative and positive reactions. Two approaches exemplifying this complexity are the aversive racism framework and the symbolic racism framework.

According to the aversive racism perspective (Gaertner & Dovidio, 1986; see also Dovidio & Gaertner, 1998), many people who consciously, explicitly, and sincerely support egalitarian principles and believe themselves to be nonprejudiced also develop, through normal cognitive (e.g., social categorization), motivational (e.g., needs for group status), and sociocultural (e.g., social learning) processes, unconscious negative feelings and beliefs about Blacks and other historically disadvantaged groups (e.g., Latinos and women). The attitudes of aversive racists are consciously egalitarian but unconsciously negative. The aversive racism framework further suggests that contemporary bias is expressed in indirect ways that do not threaten the aversive racist's nonprejudiced self-image, such as when inappropriate behavior is not obvious or when a negative response can be justified on the basis of some factor other than race.

Symbolic racism theory (Sears, Van Laar, Carillo, & Kosterman, 1997) also proposes that racism is now more subtle, indirect, and less conscious than in the past. According to this theory, negative feelings toward Blacks, which Whites acquire early in life, are relatively stable across the life span and persist into adulthood. When primed, these implicit predispositions influence responses to racially associated attitudinal objects, such as race-related policies. However, because explicit beliefs change more fully and rapidly than these racial feelings and are more likely to conform to prevailing egalitarian norms, these negative attitudes are expressed indirectly, symbolically, or in rationalizable ways (as in terms of opposition to busing or resistance to preferential treatment) rather than directly or overtly (as in support for segregation).

In general, both aversive and symbolic racism theories propose that Whites may simultaneously hold egalitarian attitudes about Blacks while also harboring negative racial feelings. Although the aversive racism framework has its historical roots in psychodynamic principles (see Kovel, 1970), recent treatments (e.g., Dovidio, Kawakami, Johnson, Johnson, & Howard, 1997; Dovidio & Gaertner, 1998) have reconceptualized it in terms of dual attitudes, one explicit and egalitarian and the other implicit and negative. Similarly, symbolic racism posits that many Whites develop nonprejudiced explicit attitudes as a consequence of prevailing norms and may genuinely believe that discrimination is no longer a problem, but they continue to have implicit negative attitudes that are vestiges of earlier socialization and experience. Thus, both frameworks are compatible with Wilson et al.'s (2000) recent general model of dual attitudes. Also consistent with the dual attitudes model, aversive racism and symbolic racism perspectives propose that whereas explicit, nonprejudiced attitudes may govern overt and deliberative forms of interracial behavior, implicit negative attitudes are related to indirect, subtle, and less obvious racial biases. In the next section, we examine evidence for the activation of implicit negative racial attitudes of Whites toward Blacks.

Implicit attitudes

Evidence of implicit racial attitudes has been generally consistent and strong. Response latency procedures, in particular, have demonstrated that racial attitudes and stereotypes may operate like other stimuli to facilitate responses and decision making about related concepts (e.g., doctor–nurse). In general, the greater the associative strength between two stimuli, the faster people can make decisions about them (e.g., Gaertner & McLaughlin, 1983).

Convergent evidence has been obtained with a variety of different priming procedures. For example, a representation of Black and White racial categories is often presented for a short period of time before participants are asked to make a decision about a positive or negative word that follows. Faster response times are assumed to reflect stronger associations between the category and the evaluation. Dovidio, Evans, and Tyler (1986) and Judd, Park, Ryan, Brauer, and Kraus (1995) using semantic categories as primes;

Fazio, Jackson, Dunton, and Williams (1995) employing photographs of Blacks and Whites as primes; Dovidio et al. (1997) using subliminally presented schematic faces of Blacks and Whites as primes, and Wittenbrink, Judd, and Park (1997) using subliminal category labels as primes have found faster response latencies to negative traits after Black than White primes and faster response latencies to positive traits after White than Black primes.

The Implicit Association Test (IAT; Greenwald, McGhee, & Schwartz, 1998) represents another technique for assessing implicit attitudes.[1] The IAT is based on the assumption that it is more difficult, and thus takes longer, to produce evaluatively incompatible than compatible responses. Specifically, participants in the IAT are instructed to classify targets and attributes by pressing the appropriate key. In an IAT task, for example, participants' first two steps may involve practice classifying Black and White photographs and then positive and negative evaluative words using specified response keys on the left or right. In subsequent steps, participants respond to combinations of photographs and words using the same response key. It is assumed that when the target (e.g., a social group) and an attribute (e.g., pleasant) share the same response key, people will make the response more quickly when the evaluation of the target group and the attribute are congruent than when they are incongruent. Studies using the IAT (Dasgupta, McGhee, Greenwald, & Banaji, 2000; Greenwald, McGhee, & Schwartz, 1998, Experiment 3; Ottaway, Hayden, & Oakes, in press; Rudman, Ashmore, & Gary, 1999) have also reliably provided evidence of relatively negative implicit attitudes of Whites toward Blacks.

Other studies assessing implicit racial prejudice have employed indirect techniques for measuring intergroup bias more generally. For instance, research on the linguistic intergroup bias (Maass, Salvi, Arcuri, & Semin, 1989) has shown that undesirable actions of outgroup members are encoded at more abstract levels (e.g., she is hostile) whereas desirable behaviors are encoded at more concrete levels (e.g., she walked across the street holding the old man's hand) relative to the same behaviors of ingroup members. These biases produce a persistence of more positive cognitions and evaluations about ingroup than outgroup measures. Because behaviors encoded at concrete levels are individual instances that can be discounted, they do not necessarily affect more general beliefs – represented by abstract schematas. Thus, for example, positive stereotype-disconfirming behaviors of outgroup members, which are encoded at a concrete level, would leave the more abstract, dispositionally based, stereotypic schema undisturbed. Von Hippel, Sekaquaptewa, and Vargas (1997) found evidence of implicit prejudice of Whites toward Blacks on a measure of linguistic intergroup bias, as well as other measures of biased attributions.

Evidence for implicit social attitudes has not only been obtained for Whites toward Blacks, but also for ingroups and outgroups generally (Perdue, Dovidio, Gurtman, & Tyler, 1990, with subliminal priming), and for Blacks toward Whites (Judd et al., 1995; Fazio et al., 1995, with supraliminal priming), men and women toward women (Banaji & Greenwald, 1995, in judgments of fame), between Japanese and Korean students (Greenwald et al., 1998, using the IAT), between northern and southern Italians (Maass, Ceccarelli, & Rudin, 1996, with the linguistic intergroup bias), and between northern Germans and Bavarians (Newman et al., 1998, on the IAT).

Reliability and validity of implicit attitudes

If implicit measures are assumed to reflect actual attitudes, then it is also important to examine their psychometric properties. For instance, in their edited book, *Measures of Personality and Social Psychological Attitudes*, Robinson, Shaver, and Wrightsman (1991) outline basic evaluative criteria for these measures that include "reliability (both test-retest reliability and internal consistency), and validity (both convergent and discriminant)" (p. 2). These criteria have only rarely been applied to response latency measures of attitudes or stereotypes.

With respect to test-retest reliability, we were unable to locate any published studies for implicit racial attitudes. Unpublished data by Rudman et al. (1999), however, did reveal a test-retest correlation of .50 over a nine-week period for an IAT prejudice measure. Data for implicit stereotypes also suggest some stability over time. Using a variation of Banaji and Hardin's (1996) task, in which stereotype-related traits were used as primes that preceded trials on which participants were instructed to categorize photographs of people as either White or Black, Kawakami and Dovidio (in press, Study 2) found evidence of stereotypic biases. Participants responded faster to stereotype-consistent trait-photograph trials than to stereotype-inconsistent ones. The test-retest correlation of the extent to which each individual exhibited this stereotypic bias across two administrations of the task in a one-hour session was .42 ($p < .001$). Across a 5- to 15-day period, the correlation for an independent sample of White participants was comparable, and in fact somewhat higher, .60. Test-retest reliability over a three-week period using a subliminal priming task (see Dovidio et al., 1997) was .50 (Kawakami & Dovidio, in press, Study 3). Using an IAT procedure, Rudman et al. (1999) found test-retest correlations of .48 for negative racial stereotypes and .54 for positive racial stereotypes over nine weeks. For each of these four samples, participants showed significant evidence of implicit racial stereotyping for both the first and second administrations of the task, but individual differences in implicit stereotyping reflected only modest reliability. The reliability coefficients for implicit stereotyping were substantially lower than those for explicit prejudice. Over a three-week period Kawakami and Dovidio (in press, Study 3) found the reliability coefficient for the Modern Racism Scale (McConahay, 1986) was .64 and for the Attitudes Toward Blacks Scale (Brigham, 1993) was .98.

The test-retest reliability for implicit racial stereotyping obtained in these studies is similar to the level for other implicit measures. Kawakami and Dovidio (in press, Study 3) reported a test-retest correlation of .51 for two administrations of the Banaji and Hardin (1996) priming task for gender stereotypes within the same session. Pelham and Hetts (1999) found a test-retest correlation of .47 for a measure of implicit self-regard (based on a word-completion task) over a five-week period. A measure of implicit group regard was less stable, $r = .22$. Taken together, this line of research suggests that at an aggregate level evidence of implicit stereotypes and negative racial attitudes can be reliably obtained, but the stability of *individual differences* in these areas is modest – and substantially less than one would expect for established explicit measures.

Evidence for a correlation among different measures of implicit attitudes and stereotyping is also sparse. Dovidio and Kawakami (in press) obtained a moderate correlation,

.28, between responses on one measure of implicit racial stereotyping based on a Banaji and Hardin-type (1996) task and another measure from a subliminal priming procedure (Dovidio et al., 1997). This relationship is somewhat weaker than the correlation, .39, between implicit racial attitudes on the IAT when White and Black names were used as target stimuli and responses of the same participants when White and Black pictures were the target stimuli (Dasgupta et al., 2000). With respect to a different type of attitude object, attitudes toward cigarettes, Sherman, Presson, Chassin, Rose, and Koch (1999) found an overall correlation of .22 between a priming measure (based on Fazio et al., 1995) and the IAT in one study (Study 2) but a lower correlation, .06, in another (Study 3).

The modest relationship for implicit measures assessed with different techniques may initially be unsettling, but it is not altogether surprising given work in cognitive psychology. Methodologically, De Houwer (1999) has argued that techniques, such as Stroop and priming procedures, may share some superficial similarities in how participants are asked to make decisions but they differ in fundamental structural ways. As a consequence, they tap into somewhat different cognitive processes. Conceptually, research in cognitive science (Squire & Kandel, 1999) indicates that various forms of implicit memory can be largely dissociated from one another. Thus the relatively weak relationship among implicit measures of social attitudes and stereotypes is consistent with empirical and theoretical work in cognition more generally. In the next section, we explore the relationship between implicit and explicit measures of racial attitudes.

Relationship between implicit and explicit measures

Intuitively, one might expect that implicit attitudes and explicit measures would be directly related because they are likely to be rooted in the same socialization experiences. Moreover, at first glance one might consider this to represent a test of convergent validity. However, researchers in this area have argued that implicit and explicit measures involve different processes and thus are not necessarily expected to be highly correlated (see Dovidio et al., 1997; Greenwald & Banaji, 1995; Wilson et al., 2000). Theoretically, response latency measures and self-report measures may reflect the distinction between activation and application (Bargh, 1999; Devine, 1989; Gilbert & Hixon, 1991). The presentation of an attitude object may automatically activate an associated evaluation from memory (Fazio et al., 1995) which *may* influence its subsequent use in judgments. However, as Gilbert and Hixon (1991) argue, automatic activation "does not mandate such use, nor does it determine the precise nature of its use. It is possible for activated information to exert no effect on subsequent judgments or to have a variety of different effects" (p. 512; see also Fiske, 1989). Thus, it is quite possible that implicit attitude activation and explicit expressions of prejudice could be empirically unrelated.

As we noted earlier, a dissociation between implicit attitudes and self-reported attitudes may be likely to be observed generally for socially sensitive issues (Dovidio & Fazio, 1992; Fazio et al., 1990), and particularly for racial attitudes. Devine (1989; see also Devine, Plant, & Blair, this volume, chapter 10), for example, proposed that high- and low-prejudiced people are equally knowledgeable about cultural stereotypes about minority groups and similarly activate these stereotypes automatically with the real or symbolic presence of a member of that group. Low- and high-prejudiced individuals differ, however, in their personal beliefs and their motivations to control the potential effects of the automatically activated cultural stereotypes. Lower prejudiced people are more motivated to control, suppress, and counteract their initial, automatic, biased reactions. Thus unconscious associations, which are culturally shared and automatically activated, may be disassociated from expressions of personal beliefs that are expressed on self-report measures of prejudice and systematically vary.

Other theoretical perspectives on contemporary racism also imply a relatively weak relationship between implicit and explicit attitudes. The aversive racism framework, for example, focuses on three theoretically relevant cells representing the combinations of implicit and explicit attitudes: People who are low in self-reported prejudice and nonbiased on implicit measures (nonprejudiced); people who are high on both (traditional racists); and people who are low in self-reported prejudice but biased on implicit measures (aversive racists). This taxonomy of racial attitudes associated with the aversive racism framework – three of the four cells in an Explicit x Implicit Attitudes matrix – suggests a positive but weak empirical relationship. For instance, Dovidio, Gaertner, and Kawakami (1998) conducted a series of simulations based on the assumptions of the aversive racism framework and on the data from implicit and explicit measures to determine correlations between implicit and explicit measures. The resulting average correlation was .30, which is positive but modest. Thus weak correlations between explicit and implicit attitudes may not reflect weak measures, but may instead represent the nature of contemporary prejudice.

To summarize the empirical findings on the relationship between explicit and implicit racial attitudes, we conducted a meta-analytic review of studies using a range of different implicit measures of racial prejudice, including the physiological measure of GSR as well as response latency measures, by Whites toward Blacks. The results of these 27 tests involving 1562 participants are presented in Table 9.1. Overall, there was a significant, $Z = 7.44$, $p < .001$, but modest positive relationship, mean Fisher $Z = .249$, mean $r = .244$ (fail-safe number = 524). The magnitude of this effect approximated Dovidio et al.'s (1998) simulations. Although there was some variability in magnitude, the relationships between implicit and explicit attitudes were significant across 14 tests involving priming measures, $Z = 3.87$, $p < .001$, mean Fisher $Z = .156$, mean $r = .155$ (fail-safe number = 63); three tests using other latency measures (e.g., times for looking at pictures), $Z = 3.84$, $p < .001$, mean Fisher $Z = .500$, mean $r = .463$ (fail-safe number = 13); and four tests with physiological measures, $Z = 3.98$, $p < .001$, mean Fisher $Z = .388$, mean $r = .4370$ (fail-safe number = 19).

Blair (in press) also conducted a comprehensive, narrative review of the relationship between implicit and explicit attitudes, not only of Whites toward Blacks but of attitudes toward other groups as well. Blair's review indicates that the relationship between explicit and implicit attitudes toward women is variable and, on average, even lower than the relationship between implicit and explicit attitudes toward Blacks: Banaji and Greenwald (1995, Study 3), $r = -.10$; Moskowitz, Wasel, Gollwitzer, and Schaal (1998, Study 1), $r = +.31$; von Hippel et al. (1997), r = .01.

Table 9.1. Relationship between Implicit and Explicit Measures of Racial Prejudice

Study	Implicit prejudice measure	Explicit prejudice measure	Statistic (df, n, direction)	Effect size (r)
Best et al. (1976)	Color Meaning Test II	PRAM II	r(54) = .62 {56}{+}	0.62
Blascovich et al. (1997, study 1)	Latency for identification of Black and White faces	Modern Racism Scale	F(1,13) = 4.60 {15}{+}	0.51
Blascovich et al. (1997, study 2)	Latency for identification of Black and White faces	Modern Racism Scale	F(1,36) = 4.40 {38}{+}	0.33
Bray (1950)	Conformity in autokinetic judgments	Attitudes Toward Negroes Scale	r(48) = .108 {50}{+}	0.11
Dasgupta et al. (2000)	IAT using names and pictures	Overall effect	r(73) = .145 {75}{+}	0.15
		Feelings Thermometer	r(73) = .22	
		Semantic Differential	r(73) = .31	
		Modern Racism Scale	r(73) = −.055	
		Diversity Scale	r(73) = .06	
		Discrimination Scale	r(73) = .045	
Dovidio et al. (1997, study 1)	Evaluative race priming (Black vs. White faces; positive vs. negative adjectives)	Overall effect	r(22) = .215 {24}{+}	0.22
		Attitudes Toward Blacks Scale	r(22) = .28	
		Modern Racism Scale	r(22) = .15	
Dovidio et al. (1997, study 2)	Evaluative race priming (Black vs. White faces; positive vs. negative adjective)	Overall effect	r(31) = .55 {33}{+}	0.55
		Modern Racism Scale	r(31) = .60	
		Old-Fashioned Racism Scale	r(31) = .49	
Dovidio et al. (1997, study 3)	Evaluative race priming (Black vs. White faces; positive vs. negative adjectives)	Overall effect	r(31) = −.03 {33}{−}	−0.03
		Modern Racism Scale	r(31) = .01	
		Old-Fashioned Racism Scale	r(31) = −.07	
Fazio et al. (1995, study 1)	Evaluative race priming (Black vs. White faces; positive vs. negative adjectives)	Modern Racism Scale	r(51) = .15 (53}{−}	−0.15
Fazio et al. (1995, study 2)	Evaluative race priming (Black vs. White faces; positive vs. negative adjectives)	Modern Racism Scale	r(47) = .28 {49}{−}	−0.28
Fazio et al. (1995, study 4)	Evaluative race priming (Black vs. White faces; positive vs. negative adjectives)	Modern Racism Scale	NS {117}{0}	0

Table 9.1. *Continued*

Study	Implicit prejudice measure	Explicit prejudice measure	Statistic (df, n, direction)	Effect size (r)
Greenwald et al. (1998)	Implicit Race Association Test (Black vs. White names; positive vs. negative words)	Overall effect	r(24) = .144 {26}{+}	0.144
		Semantic Differential	r(24) = .21	
		Modern Racism Scale	r(24) = .07	
		Feelings Thermometer	r(24) = .13	
		Diversity Index	r(24) = .24	
		Discrimination Index	r(24) = .07	
Porier & Lott (1967)	GSR	Overall effect	r(58) = .25 {60}{+}	0.25
		E-scale	r(58) = .38	
		Opinionation Scale	r(58) = .13	
Rudman, Ashmore, & Gary (study 1)	Implicit Race Association Test (Black vs. White names; positive vs. negative words)	Overall effect	r(62) = .30 {64}{+}	0.30
		Modern Racism Scale	r(62) = .37	
		Feelings Thermometer	r(62) = .23	
Rudman, Ashmore, & Gary (study 2)	Implicit Race Association Test (Black vs. White names; positive vs. negative words)	Overall effect	r(45) = .295 {47}{+}	0.30
		Modern Racism Scale	r(45) = .36	
		Feelings Thermometer	r(45) = .23	
Schnake & Ruscher (1998)	Linguistic Intergroup Bias	Modern Racism Scale	F(1,62) = 3.97 {65}{+}	0.25
Sensening et al. (1973)	Examination times of pictures of Black and White students	Semantic Differential	F(1,22) = 8.6 {24}{+}	0.53
Thomsen (1991)	Evaluative race priming (Black vs. White faces; positive vs. negative adjectives)	Overall effect	r(45) = .191 {47}{+}	0.19
		Modern Racism Scale	r(45) = .16	
		Multifactor Racial Attitude Inventory	r(45) = .221	
Tognacci & Cook (1975)	GSR	Multifactor Racial Attitude Inventory	F(1,20) = 7.71 {24}{+}	0.53
Vanman et al. (1997, study 3)	Facial EMG in response to photos of Black vs. White students	Modern Racism Scale	F(1,23) = 7.485 {25}{+}	0.49
Vidulich & Krevanick (1966)	GSR	Attitudes Toward Negroes Scale	F(1,36) = .98 {40}{+}	0.16
von Hippel et al. (1997, study 1)	Linguistic Intergroup Bias	Modern Racism Scale	r(188) = −.05 {190}{−}	−0.05
von Hippel et al. (1997, study 2)	Linguistic Intergroup Bias	Modern Racism Scale	r(116) = .03 {118}{+}	0.03

Table 9.1. *Continued*

Study	Implicit prejudice measure	Explicit prejudice measure	Statistic (df, n, direction)	Effect size (r)
Williams (1969)	Color ratings on a semantic differential scale	Overall effect	*r*(49) = .30 {51}{+}	0.30
		Likert-type Scale	*r*(49) = .26	
		Semantic Differential	*r*(49) = .33	
		Multifactor Racial Attitude Inventory	*r*(49) = .31	
Wittenbrink et al. (1997)	Evaluative race priming (Black vs. White faces; positive vs. negative adjectives)	Overall effect	*r*(86) = .31 {88}{+}	0.31
		Modern Racism Scale	*r*(86) = .41	
		Pro-Black	*r*(86) = .33	
		Anti-Black	*r*(86) = .17	
		Diversity Scale	*r*(86) = .32	
		Discrimination Scale	*r*(86) = .32	
Wittenbrink et al. (1998, study 1)	Conceptual race priming (Black vs. White faces; positive vs. negative adjectives)	Overall effect	*r*(73) = .23 {75}{+}	0.23
		Modern Racism Scale	*r*(73) = .40	
		Pro-Black	*r*(73) = .17	
		Anti-Black	*r*(73) = .12	
		Diversity Scale	*r*(73) = .26	
		Discrimination Scale	*r*(73) = .24	
		Feelings Thermometer	*r*(73) = .19	
Wittenbrink et al. (1998, study 2)	Evaluative race priming (Black vs. White faces; positive vs. negative adjectives)	Overall effect	*r*(73) = .101 {75}{+}	0.10
		Modern Racism Scale	*r*(73) = .18	
		Pro-Black	*r*(73) = .13	
		Anti-Black	*r*(73) = −.14	
		Diversity Scale	*r*(73) = .14	
		Discrimination Scale	*r*(73) = .14	
		Feelings Thermometer	*r*(73) = .16	

Blair's (in press) review also examined the relationship between explicit prejudice and implicit stereotypes. Theoretically, prejudice and stereotypes are related but still distinct concepts: Attitudes are evaluative responses, whereas stereotypes are specific beliefs about a group. Consequently, the empirical relationship between measures of prejudice and stereotypes would be expected to be lower than between two measures of the same construct (either prejudice or stereotypes). Consistent with this reasoning, Dovidio et al.'s (1996) meta-analytic review of explicit racial prejudice and explicit stereotypes revealed a relatively weak overall relationship, mean effect = .26, much lower than relationships among different explicit measures of prejudice (e.g., Dovidio et al., 1997). This relationship between explicit prejudice and implicit stereotypes of Blacks is even lower. Based on the data reported by Blair (in press), the mean *r* is .14. Across two more recent studies by Rudman et al. (1999) modern racism and implicit negative stereotypes correlated .19. These effects are comparable (mean *r* = .18) to the relationship between explicit attitudes and implicit stereotypes about women (see Blair, in press, for details).

In terms of research on other groups, Bessenoff and Sherman (1999) found a weak relationship between implicit and explicit anti-fat attitudes ($r = .05$), Greenwald et al. (1998, Study 2) obtained a mean correlation of .31 for the relationship between implicit and explicit attitudes between Japanese and Korean students, and Hense, Penner, and Nelson (1995) found a weak relationship between implicit stereotypes and explicit attributions for the elderly ($r = .15$). In a different attitude domain, Sherman et al. (1999), in a series of studies about attitudes toward smoking, found generally weak and inconsistent correlations between explicit attitudes toward smoking and implicit priming ($rs = .07, .23,$ and $.04$) and responses on the IAT ($rs = .14$ and $.29$).

On the basis of her review and analysis of the literature on implicit and explicit intergroup attitudes more generally, Blair (in press) concluded, "Although more than 25 studies have examined the relation between implicit and explicit intergroup bias, a clear understanding of their relationship has not emerged" (p. 8). She also identified both theoretical and methodological explanations for the generally weak relationship. In particular, theoretically, Blair recognized that motivations to appear to be or to actually be nonprejudiced (see Devine, 1989; Gaertner & Dovidio, 1986) may produce a general dissociation between implicit and explicit measures of bias. Consistent with this reasoning, Fazio et al. (1995) found a more substantial correlation between implicit and explicit prejudice among people with weaker motivations to control their prejudice. In addition, Blair offers a measurement account: "As explicated by Campbell and Fiske (1959), careful attention must be given to methodological issues before conclusions can be drawn regarding the meaning of a new measure . . . the psychometric properties of implicit measures have been generally ignored" (Blair, in press).

Additional attention might also be given to the nature of the implicit and explicit measures. Implicit measures typically reflect global evaluations (positive vs. negative) of a group. In contrast, whereas some explicit measures (such as semantic differential ratings or feeling thermometers) also assess general favorability of attitudes, other measures (such as the Modern Racism Scale) involve more complex, policy-related endorsements. A closer correspondence between the types of implicit and explicit attitudes that are measured might produce stronger empirical relationships. For example, Dasgupta et al. (2000) found that two IAT measures of racial prejudice correlated more strongly with semantic differential ($rs = .24$ and $.38$) and feeling thermometer ($rs = .23$ and $.21$) measures than with the Modern Racism Scale ($rs = -.13$ and $.02$) and a diversity scale ($rs = -.02$ and $.14$). Across the independent tests represented in our meta-analyses,[2] the significance levels, $Z = 2.67$, $p < .01$, and effect sizes, $Z = 1.86$, $p < .062$, of the implicit–explicit prejudice relationship were weaker for the 18 tests involving issue-oriented prejudice measures, $Z = 4.63$, $p < .001$, mean Fisher $Z = .205$, than for the nine tests involving more general evaluations, $Z = 6.55$, $p < .001$, Fisher $Z = .325$.

In general, then, implicit and explicit measures of prejudice and stereotyping among Whites toward Blacks and other groups are only weakly related, and the effects are highly variable. We concur with Blair (in press): The relationship is not yet clearly understood. Although methodological factors are likely to be involved to some extent, theoretical perspectives on the nature of contemporary intergroup biases also imply that implicit and explicit prejudice may be largely dissociated. In the next section, we explore some of the implications of these perspectives for understanding the influence of implicit and explicit attitudes on behavior.

Attitudes and behavior

As described earlier, Fazio's (1990) MODE model and Wilson et al.'s (2000) dual attitudes model generally describe how implicit and explicit attitudes can influence behavior. In the MODE model, explicit attitudes are expected primarily to influence behavior when people have the opportunity and motivation to engage in deliberative processing for behavioral decisions. When the behavior is spontaneous, when the opportunity for reflection is limited, or when people are not motivated to deliberate in their decision, implicit attitudes are hypothesized to influence action. Wilson et al. also emphasize the importance of the type of response that is to be made, and further propose that implicit attitudes can influence not only "uncontrollable" behaviors but also responses that people do not see as expressions of their attitudes and thus do not attempt to control.

Consistent with these frameworks, but considering racial attitudes in particular, Dovidio et al. (1997) hypothesized that the relationship between racial attitudes and behavior may be affected by the way attitudes are measured and the type of behavior being examined. Theoretically, racial attitudes may be examined at three different levels. First, there may be *public* attitudes. Individuals may publicly express socially desirable (nonprejudiced) attitudes even though they are aware that they privately hold other, more negative attitudes. Second, there may be *personal*, conscious aspects of racial attitudes. In contrast to public attitudes that are related to impression management, these personal attitudes are influenced by an individual's private standards and ideals (Devine & Monteith, 1993; Gaertner & Dovidio, 1986). At a third level are unconscious feelings and beliefs, which are often different than personal or public attitudes (Greenwald & Banaji, 1995). Public and personal attitudes are explicit, whereas unconscious feelings and beliefs are implicit.

Which level represents a White person's "true" racial attitude? Dovidio et al. (1997) argued that each of these levels represents a "true" aspect of an attitude and that the central question should be instead, "Which aspect of an attitude best predicts which type of behavior?" Their general position, which was guided by Fazio's MODE model, was that implicit (unconscious) aspects of an attitude will best predict spontaneous behaviors (see also Chen & Bargh, 1997), personal attitudes will best predict private but controlled responses, and public aspects of attitudes will best predict behavior in situations in which social desirability factors are salient.

This framework is consistent with recent research demonstrating the predictive validity of implicit, response latency measures of racial attitudes. For instance, Fazio et al. (1995) showed that direct ratings concerning the legitimacy of the Rodney King verdict and the illegitimacy of the anger of the Black community were correlated mainly with self-reported prejudice (Modern Racism); these responses did not correlate with the implicit measure. However, the implicit measure in comparison to Modern Racism scores correlated more highly with the *relative* responsibility ascribed to Blacks and Whites for the tension and violence that ensued after the verdict as well as perceptions of participant friendliness by a Black interviewer, perhaps more subtle and indirect manifestations of racial bias.

Dovidio et al. (1997) reported two studies on the predictive validity of implicit and explicit measures for relatively spontaneous behaviors. One study (Study 2) involved two ostensibly unrelated parts: (1) measures of racial attitudes; and (2) race-related decisions. The measures of racial attitudes included a response latency task and two self-report measures, McConahay's (1986) Old-Fashioned Racism and Modern Racism Scales. The decision-making part of the present research included tasks that varied along a deliberative-spontaneous dimension (Fazio, 1990). The deliberative tasks involved juridic judgments of the guilt or innocence of Black male defendants. Spontaneous responses were measured in a variation of Gilbert and Hixon's (1991) word-completion task in which participants completed word fragments by pressing an appropriate key (e.g., an "a" or "u" to complete "B–D") after being primed with Black and White faces. The measure of racial bias was the extent to which participants created more negative words following Black than White primes. It was hypothesized that self-report measures of prejudice would significantly predict juridic judgments, for which motivations to comply with both social norms and personal standards of egalitarianism would be salient and there would be opportunity to consider these factors in formulating a response. In contrast, the response latency measure of implicit attitudes was expected to predict answers to the word-completion task.

Supportive of the hypotheses, explicit and implicit racial attitudes predicted race-related decisions – but different ones. Ratings of the guilt of a Black defendant were correlated most strongly with Old-Fashioned ratings ($r = .51$), but also significantly with Modern Racism ($r = .38$). As with Fazio et al.'s (1995) findings for ratings about the Rodney King verdict, ratings of guilt were not predicted by the implicit measure ($r = .02$). In contrast, bias in the word-completion task, a more spontaneous type of response, was significantly predicted by implicit attitudes ($r = .48$) and not by either self-report measure of prejudice ($rs = .10$ and $.14$).

Dovidio et al. (1997, Study 3) further investigated how implicit and explicit measures of racial attitudes may differentially predict the responses of White participants to Black and White partners during face-to-face interaction. As a measure of deliberative behavior, participants were asked to evaluate both other interactants on a series of rating scales. The nonverbal behaviors of eye contact and blinking were utilized as an index of more spontaneous forms of behavior. Higher levels of visual contact (i.e., time spent looking at another person) reflect greater attraction, intimacy, and respect. Higher rates of blinking have been demonstrated to be related to higher levels of negative arousal and tension. Both of these types of nonverbal behaviors are particularly difficult to monitor and control. It was predicted that explicit measures of prejudice would primarily relate to bias in the evaluations of Black relative to White interviewers by White participants. In contrast, the response latency measure of implicit negative racial attitude was expected to be the best predictor of nonverbal reactions – specifically higher rates of blinking and less visual contact with the Black relative to the White interviewer.

The results supported the predictions. Bias in terms of more negative judgments about Black than White interviewers was correlated with the two explicit measures of prejudice, Old-Fashioned Racism ($r = .37$) and Modern Racism ($r = .54$), but was uncorrelated with implicit prejudice ($r = .02$). In contrast, implicit prejudice predicted lower levels of visual contact ($r = -.40$) and higher rates of blinking ($r = .43$), but Old-Fashioned Racism ($rs = .02, -.04$) and Modern Racism ($rs = .20, .07$) did not.

Dovidio, Kawakami, and Gaertner (1997) further explored the interactive implications of the dissociation between implicit and explicit racial attitudes. In particular, consistent with the previous study, explicit attitudes of Whites predicted their verbal friendliness toward Black discussion partners (as judged by independent coders), whereas implicit attitudes related primarily to the perceived friendliness of their nonverbal displays. However, when the Black partners were asked to rate the friendliness of the White participant, their ratings were significantly related to the nonverbal displays (which were predicted by the implicit attitudes) but not to the verbal content (which was predicted by the explicit attitude). Because Whites may judge their actions based on the behaviors they can monitor (i.e., what they say) and Blacks may focus on the behaviors that Whites are less conscious of (i.e., nonverbal behaviors), the same interaction can produce different and conflicting impressions. This difference, which may not be apparent to either interactant, can ultimately contribute to intergroup tensions and distrust at both interpersonal and intergroup levels.

Although the data related to implicit and explicit attitudes and behavior are generally supportive of the frameworks of Fazio (1990), Wilson et al. (2000), and Dovidio et al. (1997; see also Dovidio & Fazio, 1992), we caution that this is an emerging line of research and the data are limited to date. Nevertheless, a number of studies using a variety of operationalizations do indicate that implicit racial attitudes are reliable predictors of subtle interracial behavior. Stabler, Zeig, and Rembold (1976) and Verna (1982) found modest relations between implicit measures (color evaluations) and children's interracial play ($r = .14$) and placement of Black and White figures ($r = .24$), respectively. In a study by Weitz (1972), evaluations of "coldness" in a White person's voice when talking to a Black person predicted measures of willingness to interact with the Black person ($r = .23$). Recently, Rudman et al. (1999) found that, in two studies, an IAT measure of prejudice significantly predicted engagement with verbal bias (e.g., telling racial jokes; $rs = .41$ and $.45$) but not with direct hostility toward Blacks ($rs = .12$ and $.08$). Although these relationships are not consistently strong, they are, on average, only slightly weaker than the magnitude of the relationship that Dovidio et al. (1996) obtained in their meta-analysis for explicit racial attitudes and interracial behavior ($r = .32$).

With respect to other attitudes, Bessenoff and Sherman (1999) demonstrated that an implicit measure of anti-fat attitudes, based on a priming task, significantly predicted greater seating distance from an overweight person ($r = .20$), whereas an explicit measure of attitude did not ($r = -.10$). In terms of stigmatized behaviors, Stacy (1997) found that an implicit, but not an explicit, measure of attitudes toward marijuana predicted college students' marijuana use. However, for a less stigmatized behavior, alcohol consumption, both explicit and implicit measures predicted use. Taken together, studies of the predictive validity of implicit attitudes indicate that they are reliably related to behaviors – particularly spontaneous ones – and that they may influence behavior in ways dynamically and empirically independent of explicit attitudes.

Malleability of implicit attitudes and stereotypes

Given evidence of the predictive validity of implicit measures, other questions of current interest involve whether implicit attitudes are changeable, and if so, what is needed to change them. The current evidence of whether the activation of implicit attitudes or stereotypes is controllable even in the short term, however, is controversial. Blair and Banaji (1996) reported that changing participants' expectancies from stereotypic ones to stereotype-inconsistent ones reduced automatic stereotype activation. However, Bargh's (1999) re-analyses of these data challenged Blair and Banaji's conclusions about the inhibition of stereotypic activation.

Direct attempts to control prejudiced responses and suppress stereotyping, rooted in automatic activation, may not only be limited and temporary in their effectiveness, but they can also have unintended consequences that make these attitudes and stereotypes subsequently more accessible. That is, attempting to suppress a thought can make that thought more accessible than if suppression was not attempted (Macrae, Bodenhausen, Milne, & Jetten, 1994; Wegner, 1994; see also Monteith, Sherman, & Devine, 1998). However, Monteith et al. (1998) concluded that although suppression may sometimes produce a "rebound effect" when suppression efforts are relaxed or overtaxed by competing demands, suppression does not necessarily produce these ironic effects, and even if implicit attitudes and stereotypes do become more accessible their expression may be limited by other motivations and goals.

Other research further suggests that changing implicit attitudes and stereotypes may be possible but it requires extensive retraining. Again, evidence comes mainly from research on stereotypes. Implicit stereotypes are hypothesized to reflect habitual ways of thinking (Devine, 1989). Consistent with this notion, work on individual differences in automatic racial stereotype activation as a function of exposure to a group (Kawakami, Dion, & Dovidio, 1998; Lepore & Brown, 1997) indicates that high prejudiced people, who are more likely to endorse cultural stereotypes and to apply them more frequently, show stronger activation of implicit racial stereotypes upon exposure to the category than do low prejudiced people. Kawakami, Dovidio, Moll, Hermsen, and Russin (in press) thus proposed that it may be possible to foster alternative ways of thinking to undermine cultural (typically habitual) associations. To test this proposal, participants across four studies received varying degrees of practice in negating stereotypes. They were instructed not to think about cultural associations and to respond "no" to traditional, stereotypic photograph-trait combinations related to skinheads or to Black and White racial categories. The subsequent automatic activation of stereotypes was measured utilizing either a primed Stroop task (Studies 1, 2, and 3) or a Banaji and Hardin (1996) categorization task (Study 4).

The results demonstrated that when they received no training, limited training, or training involving an irrelevant stereotype, participants continued to exhibit the spontaneous activation of implicit stereotypes. However, after they received an extensive amount of training (480 trials) involving negating specific stereotypic group-trait combinations, the activation of implicit stereotypes was significantly weakened and virtually eliminated for up to 24 hours. Although this research does not address the issue of whether explicit attitudes and stereotypes are easier to change than implicit ones (Wilson et al., 2000), the results do indicate that the activation of implicit stereotypes can be changed, but it involves concentrated practice and repetition (see also Monteith et al., 1998).

Conclusion

In summary, compelling evidence has accumulated on the existence of implicit attitudes and beliefs. Although this line of work has its roots in cognitive and neuropsychological research, social psychological perspectives help to place the issues in a broader conceptual context, produce a more complete understanding of the phenomenon, and identify productive avenues for future study. In particular, the empirical and theoretical interest in implicit social cognition within social psychology has moved the research from demonstrating the existence of these implicit processes and considering the implications for brain structure and function to considering their influence on personal functioning and interpersonal and intergroup relations. Perspectives such as Wilson et al.'s (2000) model of dual attitudes and Fazio's (1990) MODE model offer broad, integrative frameworks on the operation of implicit attitudes in social contexts. Other approaches, such as the aversive racism and symbolic racism positions, consider the influence of implicit attitudes and beliefs in a more circumscribed, intergroup domain.

However, once these types of implicit social cognitions are given the status of attitudes (and stereotypes), the psychometric properties of these measures invite closer scrutiny. But, as Blair (in press) observed, these properties have received little attention. The data that do exist, which we reviewed, indicate modest stability (in terms of test-retest reliability), but the level that is obtained is relatively consistent for durations of one hour to nine weeks. Tests of convergent validity are also rare and only moderately successful. Perhaps greater understanding of implicit processes and the relationship of different measurement techniques to these processes may eventually produce results more consistent with the standards for explicit measures. Nevertheless, these measures may still be theoretically and empirically useful at this time. For instance, some clinically based projective techniques have similar psychometric properties and also do not correlate with explicit measures, but they have provided valuable insights into personal functioning, such as achievement motives (McClelland, Koestner, & Weinberger, 1989). The implicit–explicit distinction may thus be a fundamental one for understanding the dynamics of cognitions, feelings, and motivations.

In conclusion, the study of implicit attitudes provides a unique bridge between research and theory across a broad range of levels of analysis, from neuropsychology to cognition to interpersonal and intergroup relations. It offers new techniques for assessing attitudes that complement self-reports and consequently can, conceptually, enhance an understanding of the nature of attitudes and, practically, improve the ability to predict behavior from attitudes. More fundamentally, the demonstration that people may be significantly influenced by implicit attitudes and beliefs expands the scope of the discipline for a serious reconsideration of the power of the unconscious.

Notes

1. For further information about the IAT and a demonstration of the test, see Anthony Greenwald's World Wide Web site: http://weber.u.washington.edu/~agg/ (e-mail:agg@u.washington.edu).
2. To provide independent samples, for studies with multiple explicit measures only one was included for this analysis. Details are available from the authors.

References

Banaji, M. R., & Greenwald, A. G. (1995). Implicit gender stereotyping in judgments of fame. *Journal of Personality and Social Psychology, 68*, 181–198.

Banaji, M. R., & Hardin, C. D. (1996). Automatic gender stereotyping. *Psychological Science, 7*, 136–141.

Bargh, J. (1999). The cognitive monster. In S. Chaiken & Y. Trope (Eds.), *Dual processes in social psychology*. New York: Guilford.

Bessenoff, G. R., & Sherman, J. W. (1999). *Automatic and controlled components of prejudice toward the overweight: Evaluation versus stereotype activation.* Unpublished manuscript, Northwestern University.

Best, D. L., Field, T., & Williams, J. E. (1976). Color bias in a sample of young German children. *Psychological Reports, 38*, 1145–1146.

Blair, I. V. (in press). Implicit stereotypes and prejudice. In G. Moskowitz (Ed.), *Future directions in social cognition.*

Blair, I., & Banaji, M. R. (1996). Automatic and controlled processes in gender stereotyping. *Journal of Personality and Social Psychology, 70*, 1142–1163.

Blascovich, J., Wyer, N. A., Swart, L. A., & Kibler, J. L. (1997). Racism and racial categorization. *Journal of Personality and Social Psychology, 72*, 1364–1372.

Bray, D. W. (1950). The prediction of behavior from two attitude scales. *Journal of Applied Social Psychology, 45*, 64–84.

Brigham, J. C. (1993). College students' racial attitudes. *Journal of Applied Social Psychology, 23*, 1933–1967.

Cacioppo, J. T., Gardner, W. L., & Berntson, G. G. (1997). Beyond bipolar conceptualizations and measures: The case of attitudes and evaluative space. *Personality and Social Psychology Review, 1*, 3–25.

Campbell, D., & Fiske, D. (1959). Convergent and discriminant validation by the multitrait-multimethod matrix. *Psychological Bulletin, 56*, 81–105.

Chen, M., & Bargh, J. (1997). Nonconscious behavioral confirmation processes: The self-fulfilling consequences of automatic stereotype activation. *Journal of Experimental Social Psychology, 33*, 541–560.

Dasgupta, N., McGhee, D. E., Greenwald, A. G., & Banaji, M. R. (2000). Automatic preference for White Americans: Eliminating the familiarity explanation. *Journal of Experimental Psychology, 36,* 316–328.

De Houwer, J. (1999, May). *A structural analysis of paradigms used to measure implicit attitudes: What's new?* Paper presented at the Construct Validity/Implicit Social Cognition Conference, Chicago, IL.

Devine, P. G. (1989). Stereotypes and prejudice: The automatic and controlled components. *Journal of Personality and Social Psychology, 56,* 5–18.

Devine, P. G., & Monteith, M. J. (1993). The role of discrepancy-associated affect in prejudice reduction. In D. M. Mackie & D. L. Hamilton (Eds.), *Affect, cognition, and stereotyping: Interactive processes in intergroup perception* (pp. 317–344). Orlando, FL: Academic Press.

Dovidio, J. F., Brigham, J. C., Johnson, B. T., & Gaertner, S. L. (1996). Stereotyping, prejudice, and discrimination: Another look. In N. Macrae, C. Stangor, & M. Hewstone (Eds.), *Foundations of stereotypes and stereotyping* (pp. 276–319). New York: Guilford.

Dovidio, J. F., Evans, N., & Tyler, R. B. (1986). Racial stereotypes: The contents of their cognitive representations. *Journal of Experimental Social Psychology, 22,* 22–37.

Dovidio, J. F., & Fazio, R. H. (1992). New technologies for the direct and indirect assessment of attitudes. In J. Tanur (Ed.), *Questions about survey questions: Meaning, memory, attitudes, and social interaction* (pp. 204–237). New York: Russell Sage Foundation.

Dovidio, J. F., & Gaertner, S. L. (1998). On the nature of contemporary prejudice: The causes, consequences, and challenges of aversive racism. In J. Eberhardt & S. T. Fiske (Eds.), *Confronting racism: The problem and the response* (pp. 3–32). Newbury Park, CA: Sage.

Dovidio, J. F., Gaertner, S. L, & Kawakami, K. (1998, October). *Multiple attitudes and contemporary racial bias.* Paper presented at the annual meeting of the Society for Experimental Social Psychology, Lexington, KY.

Dovidio, J. F., & Kawakami, K. (1999). *Relation between two priming measures of implicit racial attitudes.* Unpublished manuscript, Colgate University, Hamilton, NY.

Dovidio, J. F., Kawakami, K., & Gaertner, S. L. (1997, October). *Intergroup attitudes and implicit and explicit stereotypes.* Presentation at the annual meeting of the Society for Experimental Social Psychology, Toronto, Ontario, Canada.

Dovidio, J., Kawakami, K., Johnson, C., Johnson, B., & Howard, A. (1997). The nature of prejudice: Automatic and controlled processes. *Journal of Experimental Social Psychology, 33,* 510–540.

Eagly, A. H., & Chaiken, S. (1998). Attitude structure and function. *The handbook of social psychology* (4th ed., Vol. 1, pp. 269–322). New York: McGraw-Hill.

Fazio, R. H. (1990). Multiple processes by which attitudes guide behavior: The MODE model as an integrative framework. In M. P. Zanna (Ed.), *Advances in experimental social psychology* (Vol. 23, pp. 75–109). Orlando, FL: Academic Press.

Fazio, R. H., Jackson, J. R., Dunton, B. C., & Williams, C. J. (1995). Variability in automatic activation as an unobtrusive measure of racial attitudes: A *bona fide* pipeline? *Journal of Personality and Social Psychology, 69,* 1013–1027.

Fazio, R., Sanbonmatsu, D., Powell, M., & Kardes, F. (1986). On the automatic activation of attitudes. *Journal of Personality and Social Psychology, 50,* 229–238.

Fazio, R. H., Williams, C. J., & Sanbonmatsu, D. M. (1990). *Toward an unobtrusive measure of attitude.* Unpublished manuscript, Indiana University, Bloomington, IN.

Fiske, S. (1989). Examining the role of intent: Toward understanding its role in stereotyping and prejudice. In J. Uleman & J. Bargh (Eds.), *Unintended thought* (pp. 75–123). New York: Guilford.

Gaertner, S. L., & Dovidio, J. F. (1986). The aversive form of racism. In J. F. Dovidio & S. L. Gaertner (Eds.), *Prejudice, discrimination, and racism* (pp. 35–59). Orlando, FL: Academic Press.

Gaertner, S. L., & McLaughlin, J. P. (1983). Racial stereotypes: Associations and ascriptions of positive and negative characteristics. *Social Psychology Quarterly, 46,* 23–30.

Gilbert, D. T., & Hixon, J. G. (1991). The trouble of thinking: Activation and application to stereotypic beliefs. *Journal of Personality and Social Psychology, 60,* 509–517.

Greenwald, A., & Banaji, M. (1995). Implicit social cognition: Attitudes, self-esteem, and stereotypes. *Psychological Review, 102,* 4–27.

Greenwald, A., McGhee, D., & Schwartz, J. (1998). Measuring individual differences in implicit cognition: The implicit association test. *Journal of Personality and Social Psychology, 74,* 1464–1480.

Hense, R., Penner, L., & Nelson, D. (1995). Implicit memory for age stereotypes. *Social Cognition, 13,* 399–415.

Judd, C. M., Park, B., Ryan, C. S., Brauer, M., & Kraus, S. (1995). Stereotypes and ethnocentrism: Diverging interethnic perceptions of African American and White American youth. *Journal of Personality and Social Psychology, 69,* 460–481.

Katz, I., Wakenhut, J., & Hass, R. G. (1986). Racial ambivalence, value duality, and behavior. In J. F. Dovidio & S. L. Gaertner (Eds.), *Prejudice, discrimination, and racism* (pp. 61–89). Orlando, FL: Academic Press.

Kawakami, K., Dion, K. L., & Dovidio, J. (1998). Racial prejudice and stereotype activation. *Personality and Social Psychology Bulletin, 24,* 407–416.

Kawakami, K., & Dovidio, J. F. (in press). *Implicit stereotyping: How reliable is it? Personality and Social Psychology Bulletin.*

Kawakami, K., Dovidio, J. F., Moll, J., Hermsen, S., & Russin, A. (in press). Just say no (to stereotyping): Effects of training in trait negation on stereotype activation. *Journal of Personality and Social Psychology.*

Kovel, J. (1970). *White racism: A psychohistory.* New York: Pantheon.

Lepore, L., & Brown, R. (1997). Category and stereotype activation: Is prejudice inevitable? *Journal of Personality and Social Psychology, 72,* 275–287.

Maass, A., Ceccarelli, R., & Rudin, S. (1996). Linguistic intergroup bias: Evidence for ingroup-protective motivation. *Journal of Personality and Social Psychology, 71,* 512–526.

Maass, A., Salvi, D., Arcuri, L., & Semin, G. R. (1989). Language use in intergroup contexts: The linguistic intergroup bias. *Journal of Personality and Social Psychology, 57,* 981–993.

Macrae, N., Bodenhausen, G., Milne, A., & Jetten, J. (1994). Out of mind but back in sight: Stereotypes on the rebound. *Journal of Personality and Social Psychology, 67,* 808–817.

McClelland, D. C., Koestner, R., & Weinberger, J. (1989). How do self-attributed and implicit motives differ? *Psychological Review, 96,* 690–702.

McConahay, J. B. (1986). Modern racism, ambivalence, and the modern racism scale. In J. F. Dovidio & S. L. Gaertner (Eds.), *Prejudice, discrimination, and racism* (pp. 91–125). Orlando, FL: Academic Press.

Monteith, M., Sherman, J., & Devine, P. (1998). Suppression as a stereotype control strategy. *Personality and Social Psychology Review, 1,* 63–82.

Moskowitz, G., Wasel, W., Gollwitzer, P., & Schaal, B, (1998). *A model of habitual stereotyping: Stereotype activation and use is like a habit; silent and efficient, sometimes inappropriate, but under volitional control.* Unpublished manuscript, Princeton University, Princeton, NJ.

Newman, R., Ebert, M., Gabel, B., Guelsdorff, J., Krannich, H., Lauterbach, C., & Wiedl, K. (1998). Prejudice between Bavarians and north Germans: Applying a new method for assessing evaluative association within prejudice. *Zeitschrift für Experimentelle Psychologie, 45,* 99–108.

Ottaway, S. A., Hayden, C. D., & Oakes, M. A. (in press). Implicit attitudes and racism: Effects of word familiarity and frequency in the Implicit Association Test. *Social Cognition.*

Pelham, B. W., & Hetts, J. J. (1999). *Implicit self-evaluation.* Manuscript under editorial review.

Perdue, C. W., Dovidio, J. F., Gurtman, M. B., & Tyler, R. B. (1990). "Us" and "Them": Social categorization and the process of intergroup bias. *Journal of Personality and Social Psychology, 59,* 475–486.

Porier, G. W., & Lott, A. J. (1967). Galvanic skin responses and prejudice. *Journal of Personality and Social Psychology,* 5, 253–259.

Robinson, J. P., Shaver, P. R., & Wrightsman, L. S. (1991) (Eds.) *Measures of personality and social psychological attitudes.* San Diego, CA: Academic Press.

Rudman, L. A., Ashmore, R. D., & Gary, M. (1999). *Implicit and explicit prejudice and stereotypes: A continuum model of intergroup orientation assessment.* Unpublished data, Rutgers University, Piscataway, NJ.

Rudman, L. A., Greenwald, A. G., & McGhee, D. (1997). *Sex differences in gender stereotypes revealed by the Implicit Association Test.* Unpublished manuscript, Rutgers University, Piscataway, NJ.

Schacter, D. L. (1990). Introduction to "Implicit memory: Multiple perspectives." *Bulletin of the Psychonomic Society, 28(4),* 338–340.

Schnake, S. B., & Ruscher, J. B. (1998). Modern racism as a predictor of linguistic intergroup bias. *Journal of Language and Social Psychology, 17,* 484–491.

Sears, D. O., van Laar, C., Carillo, M., & Kosterman, R. (1997). Is it really racism? The origin of White Americans' opposition to race-targeted policies. *Public Opinion Quarterly, 61,* 16–53.

Sensening, J., Jones, R. A., & Varney, L. (1973). Inspection of faces of own and other race as a function of subjects' prejudice. *Representative Research in Social Psychology,* 4, 85–92.

Sherman, S. J., Presson, C. C., Chassin, L., Rose, J. S., & Koch, K. (1999). *Implicit and explicit attitudes toward cigarette smoking: The effects of context on motivation.* Unpublished manuscript, Indiana University.

Shiffrin, R., & Schneider, W. (1977). Controlled and automatic human information processing: Perceptual learning, automatic attending, and a general theory. *Psychological Review, 84,* 127–190.

Smith, E. (1990). Content and process specificity in the effects of prior experiences. In T. Srull & R. Wyer Jr. (Eds.), *Advances in social cognition* (Vol. 3, pp. 1–60). Hillsdale, NJ: Erlbaum.

Squire, L. R., & Kandel, E. R. (1999). *Memory: From mind to molecules.* New York: W. C. Freeman.

Stabler, J. R., Zeig, J. A., & Rembold, A. B. (1976). Children's evaluation of the colors Black and White and their interracial play behavior. *Child Study Journal, 6,* 191–197.

Stacy, A. W. (1997). Memory activation and expectancy as prospective predictors of alcohol and marijuana use. *Journal of Abnormal Psychology, 106,* 61–73.

Thompson, M. M., Zanna, M. P., & Griffin, D. W. (1995). Let's not be indifferent about (attitudinal) ambivalence. In R. E. Petty & J. A. Krosnick (Eds.), *Attitude strength: Antecedents and consequences* (pp. 361–386). Mahwah, NJ: Erlbaum.

Thomsen, C. J. (1991). *On the automatic activation of racial stereotypes and prejudice.* Unpublished doctoral dissertation, University of Minnesota.

Tognacci, L. N., & Cook, S. W. (1975). Conditioned automatic responses as bidirectional indicators of racial attitude. *Journal of Personality and Social Psychology, 31,* 137–144.

Vanman, E. J., Paul, B. Y., Ito, T. A., & Miller, N. (1997). The modern face of prejudice and structural features that moderate the effect of cooperation on affect. *Journal of Personality and Social Psychology, 73,* 941–959.

Verna, G. B. (1982). A study of the nature of children's race preferences using a modified conflict paradigm. *Child Development, 53,* 437–445.

Vidulich, R. N., & Krevanick, F. W. (1966). Racial attitudes and emotional response to visual representations of the Negro. *Journal of Social Psychology, 68,* 85–93.

Von Hippel, W., Sekaquaptewa, D., & Vargas, P. (1997). The linguistic intergroup bias as an implicit indicator of prejudice. *Journal of Experimental Social Psychology, 33,* 490–509.

Wegner, D. (1994). Ironic processes of mental control. *Psychological Review, 101,* 34–52.

Weitz, S. (1972). Attitude, voice, and behavior: A repressed affect model of interracial interaction. *Journal of Personality and Social Psychology, 24,* 14–21.

Williams, J. E. (1969). Individual differences in color-name connotations as related to measures of racial attitude. *Perceptual and Motor Skills, 29,* 383–386.

Wilson, T. D., Lindsey, S., & Schooler, T. Y. (2000). A model of dual attitudes. *Psychological Review, 107,* 101–126.

Wittenbrink, B., Judd, C., & Park, B. (1997). Evidence for racial prejudice at the implicit level and its relationship with questionnaire measures. *Journal of Personality and Social Psychology, 72,* 262–274.

Wittenbrink, B., Judd, C., & Park, B. (1998, October). *Spontaneous prejudice in context: Evaluative versus conceptual judgments in automatic attitude activation.* Paper presented at the annual meeting of the Society for Experimental Social Psychology, Lexington, KY.

CHAPTER TEN

Classic and Contemporary Analyses of Racial Prejudice

Patricia G. Devine, E. Ashby Plant, and Irene V. Blair

One of the most enduring challenges for social psychologists has been to understand the nature of intergroup prejudice. How social psychologists have conceptualized prejudice has changed over time. Perhaps more than any other social psychological phenomenon, the analysis of prejudice has been integrally linked to significant historical events which led both social scientists and lay people alike to ask different questions about the nature of prejudice and how to eradicate it. In early theorizing there was a fair amount of clarity about what prejudice was (e.g., negative intergroup attitude and correspondent discriminatory behavior). The focus of classic theories was to offer conceptual analyses of the origin of prejudice with the hope that understanding its origins would yield insights on how to eliminate its ill effects. As society became less approving of prejudiced attitudes and overt discriminatory behavior, expressions of prejudice changed and become more subtle and covert. More contemporary analyses have sought to conceptualize these changes in the expression of prejudice.

It is important to point out that our analysis focuses on racial prejudice, specifically Whites' prejudice toward Blacks. There are several reasons for this focus. First, racial prejudice is an important problem. Second, most of the theories concerning the origins and nature of prejudice, both historically and contemporarily, were developed in the context of efforts to understand racial prejudice, and, as such, provide the clearest context for contrasting classic and contemporary analyses of prejudice. Third, efforts to improve intergroup relations and reduce prejudice have similarly focused on racial prejudice. The emphasis on racial prejudice, however, is not meant to imply that prejudice directed toward other groups (e.g., women, Latinos, Jews, gays) is not important or worthy of study. Thus, although space limitations preclude a full analysis of other forms of intergroup bias, we encourage the reader to consider the adequacy and relevance of the various theories regarding the origins of racial prejudice and attempts to reduce racial prejudice for these other prejudices.

Our goal in this chapter is to provide a general, though non-exhaustive, overview of classic approaches to understanding racial prejudice as a backdrop to understanding the more contemporary theories. After reviewing the newer theories and the implications of these theories for both how to measure and to reduce prejudice, we consider the impact of distinct motivational forces as they may affect both reports of attitudes and people's racial behavior in the contemporary social and political climate.

Classic Theories of Prejudice

Classically, interest focused on understanding the origins of prejudice. A historical review of the research trends reveals decade-by-decade shifts in theoretical analyses and questions of interest about the origins of prejudice most popular during those periods. Duckitt (1992), in a comprehensive review of the historical developments in the study of prejudice, suggests that research in this area is shaped as much by historical events and social circumstances as by the ordinary evolution of knowledge. This progression led to many and varied theoretical and empirical approaches to the study of the origins of intergroup prejudice. Duckitt's review suggests that many research questions were abandoned when social circumstances drew attention to new, equally important issues.

For example, following the massive genocide of Jews perpetrated by the Nazis in World War II, the previously popular conception of prejudice as a universal and essentially normal process became threatening and unacceptable to people. Hence, the search began for a disturbed personality structure (i.e., the prejudice-prone personality or bigot) that could be held responsible for such heinous acts. This search resulted in the famous research program of Adorno, Frenkel-Brunswick, Levinson, and Sanford (1950) on the authoritarian personality. According to this approach, prejudice was conceptualized as a personality disorder characterized by rigid adherence to and fear of punishment for deviating from conventional values, generalized hostility, and intolerance for groups that differed from one's own. The authoritarian personality was thought to develop as a result of domineering and unaffectionate child-rearing techniques. As adults, children raised under these conditions were believed to displace their hostility toward their parents onto safe targets (i.e., minority groups).

In contrast to this individual difference approach, in the 1970s, following the Civil Rights movement, researchers looked for reasons why prejudice against Blacks persisted in the United States. For example, realistic conflict theory holds that direct competition for valuable but limited resources is responsible for the development of prejudice (Levine & Campbell, 1972). Group conflicts, which create differences in group status or power, help determine which groups are the disliked groups (Blauner, 1972; Bonacich, 1972; Cox, 1948; Sherif & Sherif, 1953). Thus, the nature of contact between groups can direct prejudice toward specific target groups and can lead to consensual agreement among the members of a group about which outgroups are targeted for prejudice. The designation of ingroups and outgroups is also critically important to Tajfel and Turner's (1986) social identity theory. According to their theory, important group memberships constitute a fundamental part of people's self-concept and in order to maintain a positive group identity people will engage in a motivated search for group differences that favor their ingroup over the outgroup.

In large measure, whatever the theoretical analysis preferred during the early years of study, prejudice was thought to involve negative attitudes which led to rather overt patterns of discrimination. Indeed, prior to the legislative changes making overt discrimination illegal and admitting to prejudice socially taboo, prejudice was not only normatively (and legally) acceptable, but encouraged. The legislative changes fundamentally altered the social and political landscape in significant ways. Consider that, prior to such changes, one could more readily expect disapproval from others for responding in positive ways toward Black people (e.g., having a Black as a roommate, friend, etc.) than for responding in negative ways (e.g., excluding Blacks from employment opportunities or as friends). This pattern of responding to Blacks in the United States was due, at least in part, to the historical legacy of slavery and the development of Jim Crow laws which legally sanctioned the "separate but equal" concept. In a nation founded on the fundamental principle of equality, such discriminatory patterns ultimately set the stage for a kind of collective moral uneasiness associated with these discriminatory patterns.

It was out of this moral uneasiness that the landmark legislative changes such as the 1954 Supreme Court ruling on school desegregation proclaiming that separate is inherently unequal and the Civil Rights laws of the 1960s arose. In short, the Civil Rights movement began the process of eroding traditional racist norms. These changes in the social milieu culminated in a rather pervasive social norm discouraging overt expressions of prejudice toward Blacks (Blanchard, Lily, & Vaughn, 1991; Monteith, Deneen, & Tooman, 1996; Plant & Devine, 1998). With these changes came new challenges for social scientists interested in understanding the nature of prejudice and how prejudice is expressed. Indeed, developing conceptual analyses concerning how people respond to prevailing norms that discourage overt expressions of prejudice forms the cornerstone of several contemporary theories of racial attitudes (e.g., Dovidio & Gaertner, 1986; Katz, Wackenhut, & Hass, 1986; McConahay, 1986; Sears & Kinder, 1985).

Contemporary Theories of Prejudice

In this section, we examine several of the influential contemporary theoretical models of prejudice. In contrast to classic theories exploring the origins of prejudice, many of the contemporary conceptions of prejudice have tried to understand the implications of the legal and normative changes on the modern face of prejudice. At the societal level, the changes have been dramatic. In many ways, overt discriminatory treatment of others based on race has been successfully eliminated (i.e., no longer are there separate water fountains, lunch counters, etc.). Changes at the individual level also appear to have occurred. Survey studies of racial and ethnic attitudes and beliefs suggest that racial prejudice is declining in the United States (e.g., Taylor, Sheatsley, & Greeley, 1978; Schuman, Steeh, & Bobo, 1985). Whereas a majority of Whites expressed overt racism in the 1950s, only a minority do today. The survey evidence suggests that over time White Americans have become more positive in attitudes toward integration of schools, housing, and jobs. Stereotypes about Blacks have also become more favorable, and fewer people endorse negative characteristics about Blacks (see Devine & Elliot, 1995; Dovidio & Gaertner, 1986, 1998). In the political arena, a smaller percentage of Whites say that they would not vote for a well-qualified Black presidential candidate. There also appears to be a decrease in racial stereotyping in the mass media (e.g., television programs, movies, advertisements) (Dovidio & Gaertner, 1986; Sears, 1998). In sum, overt, direct forms of prejudice (often labeled "old-fashioned" prejudice) have declined.

Despite the abandonment of old-fashioned prejudiced attitudes evident in survey studies, support for specific governmental policies that would promote racial equality (e.g., affirmative action, busing for integration) has remained weak over time (e.g., Jacobson, 1985; Kinder & Sears, 1981). In addition, in a number of experimental studies, subtle indicators (e.g., unobtrusive measures, nonverbal responses) continue to reveal negative treatment toward Blacks even among those who claim to have renounced prejudice (Crosby, Bromley, & Saxe, 1980; Dovidio, Kawakami, Johnson, Johnson, & Howard, 1997). How should these paradoxical reactions be understood? Any model developed to understand this paradox must address why negative (prejudiced) responses persist in the face of changes in attitudes or beliefs.

Several contemporary models have taken on this challenge. The contemporary theories have sought to explain how people cope with these cultural and normative changes and how these changes play out at the individual level in terms of attitude expression. That is, these theories focus less on the origins of prejudice than on reasons for the complex, often contradictory, nature of contemporary racial attitudes. As such, the contemporary theories are not to be considered alternatives to the classic theories regarding the origins of prejudice. A cornerstone of many recent models of prejudice is the assumption that, in response to normative expectations, there have been fundamental changes in the nature of people's attitudes. Specifically, people's attitudes have shifted from predominantly reflecting negativity to being more mixed or ambivalent in nature. A theme common in contemporary theories of prejudice is that Whites experience a conflict between two competing tendencies in their reactions toward Blacks. One tendency encourages positive or nonprejudiced responses; the other encourages negative or prejudiced responses. In some cases, theorists argue that, in response to normative prescriptions against overt bias, prejudice has gone underground or that it has been transformed into subtle and increasingly covert expressions of prejudice. In short, these more modern conceptions of prejudice suggest that contemporary racial attitudes are complex and expressed subtly. Our goals for this section of the chapter are to examine the nature of these more modern interpretations and delineate their implications for how prejudice is conceptualized, whether prospects for further reductions in prejudice are encouraging or dim, and how to best assess prejudice in these more modern times.

Overt vs. covert forms of racism

Several theorists have argued that overt or "old-fashioned racism" (e.g., overt hostility, derogatory beliefs, social distance) is no longer very widespread and has been replaced with a new, more covert form of racism.[1] A number of alternative theories have been advanced to account for the more covert expression of prejudice. At the core, these theories have in common the assumption that most people reject traditionally racist beliefs and embrace abstract principles of justice and fair treatment embodied in the American creed (Myrdal, 1944). Yet, because their negative feelings toward Blacks were learned early in socialization and persist into adulthood, they are considered ambivalent in their reactions to Blacks. The conflict is created by a desire to maintain a nonprejudiced image even though they dislike Blacks. Their prejudices, as a result, can only be expressed in subtle, indirect, or disguised ways.

In the United States, the more subtle form of racism has been referred to as modern racism (McConahay, 1986), symbolic racism (Kinder & Sears, 1981), and aversive racism (Gaertner & Dovidio, 1986). In Western Europe, subtle racism is the term used to capture the more covert forms of bias (Pettigrew & Meertens, 1995). Modern and symbolic racists, for example, are thought to cope with their ambivalence by rationalizing their negative feelings in terms of abstract political and social issues (e.g., opposition to policies such as affirmative action that are designed to promote racial equality). Their negative reactions to Blacks reflect their feelings that Blacks are violating cherished values and are making illegitimate demands for change in the racial status quo. Pettigrew and Meertens (1995) suggest that subtle racism is expressed in socially acceptable ways. Thus, negative feelings toward ethnic groups are expressed through defense of traditional (ingroup) values, exaggeration of cultural differences, and denial of positive emotional responses toward the outgroup. Pettigrew and Meertens argue that those high in subtle racism comply with egalitarian norms and "express their negative intergroup views only in ostensibly nonprejudiced ways that 'slip under the norm'" (p. 73).

Aversive racists similarly reject overt forms of prejudice, but possess unacknowledged negative feelings and beliefs which are the legacy of being socialized into a historically racist culture coupled with cognitive and motivational biases that promote ingroup favoritism (Gaertner & Dovidio, 1986). Aversive racists presumably alternate between positive and negative behaviors toward Blacks. Which type of response will occur is thought to depend on the normative structure within a situation and the potential for generating a nonracial justification for a prejudiced response. When normative prescriptions are weak or ambiguous, or when a justification is readily available, aversive racists' negative tendencies will be manifested. Their biased responses go unacknowledged by the self, however, so that their egalitarian self-image will not be threatened. This conflict between their prejudiced tendencies and egalitarian beliefs is supposedly not consciously recognized.

Ambivalence: Conflict between value and attitude structures

Katz and his colleagues' theory of ambivalence-induced behavior amplification (e.g., Katz, 1981; Katz & Hass, 1988; Katz et al., 1986) posits that many White Americans simultaneously hold two sets of conflicting values, egalitarianism and individualism, which affect their reactions to Blacks. Whereas egalitarianism is grounded in democratic and humanitarian principles, individualism is grounded in the Protestant work ethic and supports principles such as personal freedom, individualism, self-reliance, devotion to work, and achievement. According to Katz, the alternative value orientations encourage the development of specific attitudes regarding Blacks. Egalitarian values, for example, give rise to genuine pro-Black sentiments, including sympathy for and favorable stereotypes about Blacks. Individualism values, however, give rise to anti-Black sentiments, including beliefs that negative outcomes, such as unemployment, drug addiction, and criminal behavior, are rooted in the personal weakness of Blacks (e.g., lack of ambition) rather than in situational factors. This "attitude-duality" creates ambivalence, which helps to explain the persistence of prejudiced responses among people who sometimes appear to be low in prejudice.

The simultaneous existence of largely independent negative and positive cognitive structures has implications for White people's responses toward Black people. Specifically, Katz and colleagues maintain that ambivalent attitudes give rise to psychological discomfort and behavioral instability (Hass, Katz, Rizzo, Bailey, & Moore, 1992; Katz et al., 1986). Responses to Black people are either positive or negative, depending on which component of the ambivalent attitude is activated in a given situation. Furthermore, both positive and negative responses can threaten the ambivalent person's self-esteem because either response would discredit the opposing component of the ambivalent disposition. In order to reduce this threat, either the positive or negative response is amplified. That is, "the ambivalent subject's extreme evaluations of the black are viewed theoretically as an attempt to disavow the contradicted attitude and thereby restore positive self-regard" (Katz et al., 1986, p. 54).

Dissociation model: Conflict between stereotype-based responses and personal beliefs

Devine (1989), offering a somewhat different approach, argued that to understand the nature of contemporary forms of prejudice, one must distinguish between two types of stored information: (1) stereotypes and (2) personal beliefs (or attitudes) about group members. In the dissociation model, a stereotype is defined as *knowledge* of the attributes that are stereotypically associated with a particular group. Prejudiced personal beliefs are defined as the endorsement or acceptance of the content of a negative cultural stereotype. Importantly, being knowledgeable about the stereotype does not necessarily entail endorsement of the stereotype, so that the content of the stereotype would not be a part of the low-prejudice individual's personal beliefs about the target group (see Devine & Elliot, 1995).

Devine argued that this distinction is important because the activation of stereotypes and personal beliefs is governed by different cognitive processes: automatic and controlled processes, respectively. One implication of this analysis is that the two cognitive structures should provide the basis for responses under different circumstances. Because stereotypes typically have a long socialization history and have been frequently activated, Devine (1989) argued that they can be automatically activated, providing a "default" basis for responding in the presence of members of the stereotyped group or their symbolic equivalent. Thus, low-prejudice people (who renounce prejudice) and high-prejudice people (who do not) are equally susceptible to the automatic activation and use of stereotypes because they are equally knowledgeable about the cultural stereotype (Devine, 1989; Devine & Elliot, 1995).

In contrast to stereotypes, personal beliefs about a target group are often developed after the initial, early learning of the stereotype (see Allport, 1954; Proshansky, 1966). As a result, they are less accessible cognitive structures than stereotypes and rely on controlled processing for their activation. The important implication of this analysis is that the default response, even among low-prejudice people, is a stereotype-based response (Banaji & Greenwald, 1995; Bargh, 1999; Chen & Bargh, 1997). That is, low-prejudice people can inhibit stereotype-based responses only if they have the time and the cognitive capacity to initiate controlled processes so as to bring their personal beliefs to mind (Monteith, 1993). It should be noted that accumulating findings suggest that not all White people are equally vulnerable to the automatic activation of stereotype-based or negative evaluative responses (e.g., Fazio, Jackson, Dunton, & Williams, 1995; Lepore & Brown, 1997; Wittenbrink, Judd, & Park, 1997); the ever-burgeoning literature addressing these issues is reviewed later in the chapter. Nevertheless, Devine's analysis provides a contrasting viewpoint on the nature of conflict experienced by many who renounce prejudice and embrace nonprejudiced, egalitarian values.

In short, Devine and colleagues have argued that many experience discrepancies between how they believe they should respond to Blacks and how they actually would respond. They suggest the prejudice-related conflict arises because White people often respond in ways that are more prejudiced than their personal standards indicate is appropriate (e.g., feeling more uncomfortable when sitting next to a Black person than one believes one should). For those who renounce prejudice, these prejudice-related discrepancies give rise to feelings of guilt and self-criticism (Devine, Monteith, Zuwerink, & Elliot, 1991; Monteith, Devine, & Zuwerink, 1993; Monteith & Viols, 1998; Zuwerink, Monteith, Devine, & Cook, 1996). The goal for these low-prejudice people, then, becomes learning how to inhibit well-learned stereotype-based responses and replace them with belief-based responses, which likely takes considerable attention and time (see Devine & Monteith, 1993). This analysis suggests that subtle, contemporary forms of prejudice exist in part because many low-prejudice people have not progressed far enough in the prejudice reduction process to be efficient and effective at generating nonprejudiced responses that are consistent with their nonprejudiced beliefs.

Prospects for future change

Most of the contemporary models of prejudice take as their starting point that there has already been some change in racial attitudes. However, they also suggest that more change is needed (i.e., people still have some negative reactions to Blacks). What do each of these models suggest about the possibility for further reductions in prejudice? Consideration of these issues is important because Monteith (1996) demonstrated that these forms of contemporary prejudice-related conflict show very little overlap (e.g., measures of the distinct forms of contemporary conflict are not strongly correlated and they are differentially associated with specific affective consequences such as guilt and positive affect).[2] Monteith suggests that their distinctiveness implies that each form of conflict is likely to have different causal antecedents or roots. In this context, it is not surprising that each of the perspectives leads to different expectations regarding prospects for future change and likely strategies. As Monteith notes, "change strategies must be tailored to individuals, according to the types(s) of conflict present" (p. 472).

From both the modern racism and aversive racism perspectives, prospects for future change are dim. Neither modern nor aversive racists see themselves as racist and, thus, perceive no need to change. In addition, modern and aversive racists are not consciously aware of their conflicted reactions. Change would require, at minimum, first becoming aware of their subtle negative biases. Next, the salience of nonprejudiced norms would need to be enhanced to make clear how one should respond across a variety of situations. From the perspective of the ambivalence-amplification model, future change might be brought about by strengthening the egalitarian values to make the positive aspects of the attitudinal structure highly accessible (and more accessible than the negative aspect of their attitudinal structure). Katz and Hass (1988) specifically suggest an educational approach for reducing prejudice stemming from ambivalent attitudes. They suggest that it would be important to both stress egalitarian values and link them directly to Blacks' rights and encourage people to realize that the Protestant work ethic principles can only fairly be applied when all people have equal access to opportunities and incentives.

In the context of Devine and colleagues' analysis of origins of prejudice-related discrepancies, reducing prejudice would involve learning to inhibit prejudiced responses and making people's low-prejudiced beliefs highly accessible. In recent years, a great deal of attention has focused on identifying strategies, and the processes underlying the strategies, that may enable people to effectively avoid or otherwise control the use of stereotypes and prejudice in intergroup judgments and behavior. Some of this research suggests that intentional control is possible, though difficult and fraught with intrapersonal distress (e.g., Monteith, 1993). Other research suggests, however, that intentional control, through efforts at suppression (i.e., banishing stereotypic thoughts from consciousness), may backfire and produce unintended heightened activation and use of stereotypes (see Bodenhausen & Macrae, 1996). Although, the current evidence on the efficacy of alternative control mechanisms suggests a complex picture (e.g., individual differences in prejudice moderate the effectiveness of stereotype suppression; see Monteith, Sherman, & Devine, 1998, for a review), it seems clear that these theoretical and empirical efforts will yield a greater understanding of the processes involved in controlling stereotyping and prejudice and may lead to better methods for instructing people how to control their responses.

Changing norms and the assessment of prejudice: The need for implicit measures?

In one way or another, each of the contemporary theories suggests that the manifestations of prejudice are not deliberate and, indeed, in some cases are not consciously accessible. Such bias without intention, combined with prevailing concerns over whether verbal (overt) reports of attitudes can be trusted, fueled interest in developing measures that could assess such unintentional or hidden bias. That is, in the face of the social, political, and cultural changes that discouraged the overt expression of prejudice, many argued that straightforward measures of prejudice were inadequate to deal with the pressures to conform to emerging (and now prevalent) socially desirable nonprejudiced norms (Crosby et al., 1980; Dovidio & Fazio, 1992; Jones & Sigall, 1971; Sigall & Page, 1971).

Early efforts focused on devising assessment strategies that would circumvent the social desirability biases presumed to be associated with traditional self-report measures. Jones and Sigall (1971), for example, developed the now famous bogus pipeline technique, in which participants believe that a machine monitoring their implicit muscle responses can detect if their responses are veridical or misleading. The logic of the technique was to convince participants that it would be imprudent to conceal their true (presumably negative) racial beliefs. In many bogus pipeline studies, participants reported greater levels of racial prejudice in bogus pipeline than comparison conditions. In short, the bogus pipeline has been widely accepted as a useful, though cumbersome, way to reduce the social desirability biases that are presumed to contaminate traditional self-report measures (see Roese & Jamieson, 1993, for a review).

In more recent years, efforts to measure modern forms of racism have focused on developing items that would assess the more subtle or indirect manifestations of racism (e.g., McConahay, 1986; Kinder & Sears, 1981).[3] Modern racists' negative racial beliefs are expressed in terms of abstract ideology suggesting, for example, that Blacks are violating cherished values and making illegitimate demands for changes in the racial status quo. Thus, whereas modern racists would support laws against overt discrimination, they also endorse items suggesting that "Blacks are getting too demanding in their push for equal rights" or "Over the past few years, Blacks have gotten more economically than they deserve." Because people can agree with these types of items and rationalize their negative reactions in nonracial terms, McConahay, Hardee, & Batts, V. (1981) argued that the items were nonreactive and would therefore, be more likely to reveal racial bias that is typically concealed on old-fashioned racism items. There is, however, considerable debate in the literature concerning both the alleged nonreactive nature of the Modern Racism Scale and whether it is uniquely a measure of racial bias (Fazio et al., 1995).

In the continuing search for alternatives to explicit self-reported measures of racial attitudes, recently a great deal of attention has been devoted to developing implicit measures of racial bias. The purported strength of such measures is that they bypass self-reported beliefs altogether. These implicit measures are grounded on the basic principle that perceivers have cognitive representations of various social groups that include the attributes and evaluations associated with each group. For example, an average White American's representation of Black Americans probably includes traits such as lazy and hostile; roles such as entertainer and drug dealer; prototypical anatomical features such as kinky hair; and an overall negative evaluation (Devine, 1989; Devine & Elliot, 1995). Of importance is the idea that these associations can become activated (primed) by environmental cues, and, once activated, they influence subsequent information processing without the perceiver's awareness or intention (Bargh, 1997, 1999; Bodenhausen & Macrae, 1998; Devine, 1989; Greenwald & Banaji, 1995). For example, Devine (1989) and Chen and Bargh (1997) have shown that subliminal exposure to race cues can activate stereotypes of Black Americans and lead to exaggerated perceptions of a target's hostility and an increase in hostile interpersonal behavior.

The strategy of assessing implicit prejudice is fully within the contemporary *Zeitgeist* in social psychology, which has shown a fascination with automatic processes (see Bargh, 1997; Wegner & Bargh, 1998), and many researchers have turned their focus to issues of automatic assessment. Implicit measures may be particularly useful in assessing the more modern forms of prejudice, partly because they may reveal bias of which respondents may not be fully aware (e.g., aversive racism). Moreover, they ultimately may hold promise for facilitating the field's understanding of the complex and often conflicted nature of contemporary racial attitudes (i.e., presence of implicit racial bias in the absence of explicit negative attitudes).

Research on implicit stereotypes and prejudice has utilized a number of different measures, ranging from brain-wave activity and facial EMG (e.g., Vanman, Paul, Ito, & Miller, 1997) to interpersonal judgments (e.g., Devine, 1989) and behavior (e.g., Chen & Bargh, 1997). By far the most common method of studying automatic associations is the response-time (RT) latencies procedure (e.g., Dovidio, Evans, & Tyler, 1986; Dovidio et al., 1997; Fazio et al., 1995; Greenwald, McGhee, & Schwartz, 1998; Wittenbrink et al., 1997; see Blair, in press, for a review). These procedures focus on speeded response latencies as an indicator of strength of association between categories and evaluations (positive or negative) or stereotype characteristics. Over the past decade, a large and growing literature has provided strong evidence for implicit stereotypic and prejudicial associations. Implicit race and ethnic bias has received the greatest attention with over 30 studies showing that Whites have relatively strong automatic negative associations with Blacks (or other non-White groups) and positive associations with Whites (e.g., Bargh, Chen, & Burrows, 1996; Chen & Bargh, 1997; Devine, 1989; Dovidio et al., 1986, 1997; Fazio & Dunton, 1997; Fazio et al., 1995; Gaertner & McLaughlin, 1983; Greenwald et al., 1998; Lepore & Brown, 1997; Locke, MacLeod, & Walker, 1994; Spencer, Fein, Wolfe, Fong, & Dunn, 1998; Vanman et al., 1997; Wittenbrink et al., 1997).[4]

With the accumulation of evidence that stereotypes and prejudice can operate on an automatic level, many important questions have been raised about the nature of such effects and what they imply about modern conceptions of prejudice. One of the key questions taking center stage most recently among prejudice theorists concerns the extent to which there is correspondence between implicit and explicit measures of prejudice (see also Dovidio, Kawakami, & Beach, this volume, chapter 9). Interestingly, it was the lack of a relationship between self-reported attitudes and less controlled, indirect measures (e.g., Crosby et al., 1980) which led to the development of most of the modern theories of prejudice (i.e., overt expressions of prejudice have simply been replaced with more covert, subtle forms of prejudice). Concerns over this inconsistency also resulted in a clear preference for the more implicit or covert types of measures in the assessment of racial attitudes, arguing that the strength of such measures is that they do not involve careful, deliberate, and intentional thought (see also Dovidio & Fazio, 1992). In short, although the technology for assessing unintentional or nonthoughtful bias has become more sophisticated, the fundamental concern that there may be a disparity between the more and less thoughtful or controllable responses remains the same. And, the evidence concerning these issues continues to yield rather mixed findings.

A number of studies, for example, have shown that people exhibit relatively strong automatic racial stereotypes and prejudice, and these biases do not correspond to their personal endorsement or rejection of stereotypes and prejudice (Devine, 1989; Dovidio et al., 1997; Fazio et al., 1995; Gaertner & McLaughlin, 1983; Greenwald et al., 1998). Other research, however, has shown that the relation between implicit and explicit prejudice may be more complex. In particular, a number of studies have found moderate correspondence between participants' automatic responses and their personal beliefs and attitudes toward the social group (e.g., Devine, Plant, & Brazy, 2000; Kawakami, Dion, & Dovidio, 1998; Lepore & Brown, 1997; Locke et al., 1994; Moskowitz & Solomon, in press; Vanman et al., 1997; Wittenbrink et al., 1997; for a review, see Blair, in press). Theoretical analysis focuses on how to best interpret such findings. One interpretation is that automatic stereotypes and prejudice may reflect socialization experiences, but those experiences may not be as uniform as previously believed. That is, people who were socialized to be more accepting of outgroups, may not have developed strong automatic stereotypes and prejudice (Greenwald et al., 1998; Blair, 1999). An alternative account for the correspondence between implicit and explicit prejudice is the idea that personal beliefs and strategic processes can alter automatic stereotypes and prejudice, first temporarily, and then, with practice, more permanently (Devine & Monteith, 1993; Monteith, 1993). Research evidence for this idea is beginning to accumulate, and it suggests that automatic stereotypes and prejudice are more malleable and context-specific than previously believed (Blair & Banaji, 1996; Blair & Ma, 1999; Dasgupta, 1999; Kawakami, Dovidio, Moll, Hermsen, & Russin, 1999; Lowery, Hardin, & Sinclair, 1999; Wittenbrink, Judd, & Park, 1999; see Blair, in press, for a review).

Contemporary Focus on Motivations for Controlling Prejudice

The complexity of the interplay between explicit self-report measures and more indirect or implicit measures is an important issue in many of the contemporary theories of prejudice. For example, this lack of correspondence between implicit and explicit measures of prejudice, particularly for low-prejudice people, lies at the crux of Devine's (1989) dissociation model of prejudice. Recall that, according to Devine's model, low-prejudice people have stereotypes automatically activated by virtue of being socialized in a prejudiced culture; however, as indicated by their self-reported personal beliefs, low-prejudice people do not endorse these stereotypes. As a result, the challenge for low-prejudice people is to develop the ability (through controlled processes) to control the activation of stereotypes and prejudice or otherwise control the influence of such activation in order to respond consistently with their nonprejudiced personal beliefs. Consistent with other recent theorizing on the control of prejudiced responses, Devine's (1989) analysis emphasizes the importance of being motivated to control prejudice as a precursor to initiating control efforts (see also Bodenhausen & Macrae, 1998; Fazio, 1990; Fazio et al., 1995).

Although these models specify when control efforts are likely (e.g., when people are motivated and have the opportunity to implement controlled processes), they have not been particularly specific about what creates motivation to control prejudice. Most often, these researchers used traditional attitude measures as a surrogate for motivation, under the assumption that those who report low-prejudice attitudes would have high motivation to respond without prejudice (i.e., because they personally believe prejudice is wrong). However, a moment's reflection suggests that high-prejudice people could also be highly motivated to control their prejudiced responses, although probably for different reasons and under different circumstances (e.g., self-presentation considerations). In the recent literature, there has been growing recognition that attitude measures, which are most typically measures of evaluative propensity, are not sufficient to represent the diversity of reasons underlying people's motivation to respond without prejudice. To address these issues, some researchers have begun to develop measures that assess the extent to which people are motivated to control prejudice (e.g., the amount of motivation, Dunton & Fazio, 1997) and the reasons underlying people's motivation (e.g., why people are motivated to respond without prejudice, Plant & Devine, 1998). Conceptual developments addressing such issues are critically important for resolving key theoretical and measurement issues in the prejudice literature.

For example, over the last few decades, considerable debate has ensued in the prejudice literature concerning the extent to which professed nonprejudiced attitudes reflect internalized egalitarian values or mere compliance with emerging egalitarian norms discouraging expressions of prejudice (see Crosby et al., 1980; Devine, 1989; Dovidio & Fazio, 1992). Disentangling these possibilities is difficult precisely because responding without prejudice is socially desirable. And, indeed, because compelling social (external) norms proscribing prejudice are prevalent, internal reasons are often discounted (e.g., Crosby et al., 1980). This line of reasoning has led to a preference in the assessment of prejudice for more implicit measures and a corresponding belief that self-reported nonprejudiced attitudes reflect efforts to create a socially desirable impression in the eyes of others (e.g., Crosby et al., 1980) and, in some cases, in one's own eyes (e.g., Gaertner & Dovidio, 1986). It is our position that it is important to examine both personal (internal) and normative (external) sources of motivation to respond without prejudice if we are to understand the nature of people's contemporary efforts to control prejudice, as these alternative reasons for responding without prejudice are likely to have both theoretical and practical significance.

Kelman's (1958) classic theorizing on the characteristics of opinions suggests that there are important differences between the internalization of beliefs and compliance with normative standards. Whereas an internalized belief is entrenched in a person's value system and is likely to be drawn upon whenever relevant to a current issue, mere compliance is based on fear of punishment or desire for reward from the normative audience and occurs only when under direct surveillance (Bodenhausen & Macrae, 1998; Plant & Devine, 1998). Distinguishing between nonprejudiced responses that reflect commitment to personally significant, internalized egalitarian values versus simple compliance with normative pressure will likely have important implications for understanding when control over prejudice is exerted as well as exactly what people try to control (e.g., any form of bias vs. overt expressions of bias).

If the reason underlying control efforts is predominantly normative, then any method that removes blatantly prejudiced responses should prove to be adequate. That is, stereotypes and hostile feelings may be activated in this case, but only the overt responses need be adjusted or controlled to prevent the appearance of bias. In contrast, if the reason underlying control efforts arises from internalized nonprejudiced beliefs, then the goal is to remove bias from all forms of responses (e.g., thoughts, feelings, and behavior). Indeed, anything less would be a viewed a personal failure (Devine et al., 1991). Fundamentally, then, the distinction is between eliminating prejudice from one's response repertoire (e.g., overcoming prejudice) and effectively concealing (privately accepted) prejudice from others.

Clearly, personal and normative sources of motivation to respond without prejudice can be distinguished conceptually. Can they, however, be sensitively measured empirically? And, if so, do they differentially predict important outcomes? Recent work suggests that the answer to both questions is yes. Plant and Devine (1998) developed and validated separate measures of internal (personal) and external (normative) sources of motivation to respond without prejudice. The crucial difference between these sources of motivation is the evaluative audience (self or significant others) who sets the standard for appropriate behavior. When the motivation derives from internal standards, the self is the evaluative audience of importance and the motivation arises from internalized and personally important nonprejudiced beliefs. In contrast, when the motivation derives from external standards, others constitute the important evaluative audience and the motivation results from a desire to avoid condemnation or censure from others. Plant and Devine (1998) found that the measures of internal and external sources of motivation to respond without prejudice are largely independent such that people can be motivated to respond without prejudice primarily for internal reasons, primarily for external reasons, for both internal and external reasons, or for neither reason.

Plant and Devine (1998) further demonstrated that the measures of internal and external motivation to respond without prejudice were reliable and showed good convergent,[5] discriminant, and predictive validity. In a key test of the predictive validity of the measures, Plant and Devine (1998; Devine et al., 2000) showed that people's reports of their level of stereotype endorsement differed as a function of situational circumstances that would make self or other as audience salient (e.g., private or public reporting conditions, respectively) and the source of people's motivation to respond without prejudice. Specifically, only participants whose primary motivation for responding without prejudice was external (e.g., high external and low internal motivation) showed differences in their reported endorsement of the stereotype in private and public reporting conditions. Although in private when there was no need to be concerned about the social disapprobation of others, they reported high levels of stereotype endorsement; when under the watchful eyes of another, they strategically altered their responses to avoid revealing their true prejudiced attitudes. For none of the other groups did the level of stereotype endorsement vary as a function of whether they gave their responses privately or publicly, and the level of stereotype endorsement was determined by their level of internal motivation. That is, highly internally motivated participants, regardless of their level of external motivation, reported low levels of stereotype endorsement; participants low in both internal and external motivation reported fairly high levels of stereotype endorsement.

We have recently begun to examine the extent to which these alternative sources of motivation can help in addressing the interplay between implicit and explicit responses.

Our specific interest has focused on identifying the types of people for whom and the specific circumstances under which consistency or dissociation between implicit and explicit responses would be expected. In a recent study (Devine et al., 2000), we obtained explicit measures of prejudice (e.g., Brigham's, 1993 Attitude Toward Blacks or ATB scale) and an implicit measure of racial bias (Greenwald et al.'s 1998 Implicit Association Test or IAT), as well as measures of internal and external motivation to respond without prejudice. The explicit measure of prejudice and the measures of sources of motivation to respond without prejudice were collected in a large mass testing situation which strongly encouraged a sense of anonymity. The implicit measure was obtained several weeks later. The IAT measures people's implicit negativity toward Blacks by assessing the extent to which respondents automatically associate positive and negative evaluative words with White and Black people. In the IAT, participants provide timed responses to evaluatively congruent (e.g., Black – negative and White – positive) and incongruent (e.g., Black – positive and White – negative) pairs. Faster responses to congruent than incongruent pairings (i.e., the IAT effect) is used as a measure of implicit racial bias. Importantly, this implicit measure like other implicit measures is presumed to bypass strategic self-presentation concerns.

The findings from this study revealed that among those who were low in external motivation to respond without prejudice, regardless of their level of internal motivation, there was a strong correspondence between implicit prejudice and anonymous measures of self-reported prejudice. Specifically, for low internal, low external participants, both measures revealed negative attitudes; for high internal, low external participants, little racial bias was revealed on either the implicit or explicit measure. The findings for participants high in external motivation to respond without prejudice, revealed a more complex picture.

Specifically, for those high in external motivation whether consistency or dissociation was observed between implicit and explicit measures depended upon their level of internal motivation to respond without prejudice. For example, participants high in external motivation who were also highly internally motivated to respond without prejudice exhibited negative implicit racial attitudes, but nonprejudiced explicit racial attitudes. In contrast, people high in external but low in internal motivation responded with both negative implicit and explicit attitudes. However, the findings from Plant and Devine's (1998) study involving public and private self-reported attitudes suggest that whether these people's explicit responses are consistent with their biased implicit responses may depend on whether their explicit attitudes are reported publicly or privately. Recall that although low internal, high external people's privately reported explicit attitudes revealed prejudice, their publicly reported explicit attitudes did not (also see Devine et al., 2000).

When taken together, the findings across the recent program of research led us to believe that the nature of people's contemporary conflicts associated with prejudice may differ as a function of why they are motivated to respond without prejudice. For example, although the explicit responses of those who are high in external motivation to respond without prejudice very likely reflect controlled processes (i.e., they must overcome their automatic implicit biases), we argue that these control efforts are directed toward different ends depending on their level of internal motivation to respond without prejudice (e.g., approaching cherished values vs. concealing personally accepted prejudice). In short, though much more research is needed to elucidate these issues, we suggest that for some, the dilemma concerns appearing prejudiced to oneself (and possibly others), whereas for other people, the dilemma concerns appearing prejudiced to others.

Conclusions

It is quite striking that, although the role of normative prescriptions has been central in the development of most of the modern conceptions of prejudice (e.g., because prejudice is socially unacceptable, prejudice is expressed in subtle or covert ways), it is only very recently that there has been any systematic attempt to assess the extent to which people are responsive to such normative pressure (Plant & Devine, 1998). We would like to argue that our overall understanding of contemporary challenges associated with the control of prejudice (either implicit or explicit) would be greatly facilitated by exploring the independent and joint effects of the distinct internal and external sources of motivation to respond without prejudice.

Although it is not possible to fully delineate the possibilities here, considering the source of motivation to respond without prejudice may help to elucidate when efforts to respond without prejudice are likely (e.g., for high internals control is likely across situations because it is a personally important goal, for low internal, high externals situational specificity of control is likely) as well as what types of control strategies are likely to be initiated (e.g., individuation of targets, suppression of inappropriate reactions, correction for an already activated stereotype, adjustment of overt responses, see Devine & Monteith, 1999 and Monteith, Sherman, & Devine, 1998 for reviews). In subsequent research, it will be critically important to determine whether the control mechanisms engaged are similar or different when the motivation originates from within or without (or both) and whether these mechanisms lead to effective control.

Our research on internal and external sources of motivation to respond without prejudice brings into focus concerns that are important both theoretically and practically. For example, among those who have no personal convictions that prejudice is wrong, compliance with normative standards can easily be elicited, at least among those high in external motivation to respond without prejudice (Plant & Devine, 1998). That is, when concerned about how others may evaluate their prejudiced views, these people concealed their prejudice from others. However, the motivational nature of feeling compelled to meet standards imposed on one by others is not necessarily cost free. That is, complying with such standards can be construed as a restriction on one's freedom and may create resentment and reactance (Brehm, 1966). These feelings may ultimately fuel prejudice and increase the tendency to lash out against nonprejudiced norms, those exerting the social pressure, or outgroup members (Plant & Devine, 2000 for evidence supporting this possibility). To the extent backlash is likely, short-term gains (i.e., curtailing immediate expressions of prejudice) could lead to negative outcomes (i.e., resentment of imposed nonprejudiced norms and backlash).

Another issue that comes into focus in this context is that efforts to eliminate prejudice, a long-standing goal of prejudice theorists, are likely to require different strategies for those for whom the struggle to overcome prejudice involves learning to respond consistently with internalized nonprejudiced values (i.e., developing the ability to respond without prejudice) compared with the those for whom changing prejudiced attitudes is the more immediate goal (i.e., developing internal motivation). To the extent that we develop a better understanding of the unique challenges implied by these alternative goals, prejudice researchers will be in a better situation to develop and offer useful advice on how to accomplish these goals.

We conclude by arguing that it is not sufficient to suggest that contemporary racial attitudes are complex and ambivalent. That is, beyond these issues, it is important to recognize that there are motivational forces that stem from within and without that affect how people negotiate issues related to prejudice in their everyday lives. Efforts to systematically explore how personal and normative sources of motivation to respond without prejudice affect the expression of prejudice may lead to refinements in theorizing about the nature and measurement of prejudice in our contemporary social and political climate. Gordon Allport (1954) long ago cautioned students of intergroup relations that the story of intergroup prejudice would not be easily told. As the research reviewed in this chapter suggests, Allport's premonition was accurate. As a phenomenon that is inextricably linked with social, political, and cultural developments, the study of prejudice has confronted each generation of prejudice researchers with new and complex challenges. Over time the tale has taken some interesting turns and we eagerly anticipate subsequent developments in the ongoing efforts to understand the nature of prejudice.

Notes

1.   See Kleinpenning and Hagendoorn (1993) for an interesting attempt to array alternative theories of racism on a single continuum that runs from blatant racism (e.g., believes in genetic superiority of ingroup) through subtle racism (e.g., modern and aversive racism) to the absence of racism (e.g., egalitarianism).

2.   Monteith did not compare aversive racism with the other models because a scale for measuring aversive racism does not exist and hence could not be empirically compared with the other models.

3.   Similar efforts have been made to assess more modern or subtle forms of sexism (e.g., Swim, Aikin, Hall, & Hunter, 1995). Much of the logic underlying the development of the new sexism measures parallels the rationale for the development of the modern racism measures.

4.   Although space limitation precludes a detailed consideration of other target groups, accumulating evidence suggests that implicit measures are sensitive to gender bias, age bias, negative outgroup bias, as well as biases associated with a variety of occupational and social roles (see Blair, in press, for a comprehensive review).

5.   It is important to note that the internal motivation to respond without prejudice measure is strongly related to traditional measures of prejudice (e.g., Modern Racism Scale, McConahay, 1986; Attitude Toward Blacks Scale or ATB, Brigham, 1993), such that highly internally motivated people tend to report lower prejudiced attitudes toward Blacks than less internally motivated people. External motivation is much less strongly correlated with traditional prejudice measures; however, the relationship is such that highly externally motivated people tend to report somewhat higher levels of prejudice than their less externally motivated counterparts.

References

Adorno, T., Frenkel-Brunswick, E., Levinson, D., & Sanford, R. (1950). *The authoritarian personality.* New York: Harper & Row.

Allport, G. (1954). *The nature of prejudice.* Reading, MA: Addison-Wesley.

Banaji, M., & Greenwald, A. (1995). Implicit gender stereotyping in judgments of fame. *Journal of Personality and Social Psychology, 68,* 181–198.

Bargh, J. (1997). The automaticity of everyday life. In R. S. Wyer (Ed.), *Advances in social cognition* (Vol. 10, pp. 1–61), Mahwah, NJ: Erlbaum.

Bargh, J. (1999). The cognitive monster: The case against the controllability of automatic stereotype effects. In S. Chaiken & Y. Trope (Eds.), *Dual-process theories in social psychology* (pp. 361–383). New York: Guilford Press.

Bargh, J., Chen, M., & Burrows, L. (1996). Automaticity of social behavior: Direct effects of trait construct and stereotype activation on action. *Journal of Personality and Social Psychology, 71,* 230–244.

Blair, I. (1999). *Personal contact and community norms as predictors of explicit prejudice and automatic evaluation.* Unpublished manuscript, University of Colorado, Boulder, CO.

Blair, I. (in press). Implicit stereotypes and prejudice. In G. Moskowitz (Ed.), *Future directions in social psychology.*

Blair, I., & Banaji, M. (1996). Automatic and controlled processes in stereotype priming. *Journal of Personality and Social Psychology, 70,* 1142–1163.

Blair, I., & Ma, J. (1999). *Imagining stereotypes away: The moderation of automatic stereotypes through mental imagery.* Unpublished manuscript, University of Colorado, Boulder, CO.

Blanchard, F., Lilly, T., & Vaughn, L. (1991). Reducing the expression of racial prejudice. *Psychological Science, 2,* 101–105.

Blauner, R. (1972). *Racial oppression in America.* New York: Harper & Row.

Bodenhausen, G., & Macrae, C. (1996). The self-regulation of intergroup perception: Mechanisms and consequences of stereotype suppression. In C. Macrae, C. Stangor, & M. Hewstone (Eds.), *Stereotypes and stereotyping.* New York: Guilford Press.

Bodenhausen, G., & Macrae, C. (1998). Stereotype activation and inhibition. In R. Wyer (Ed.), *Advances in social cognition* (Vol. 11, pp. 1–52). Mahwah, NJ: Erlbaum.

Bonacich, E. (1972). A theory of ethnic antagonism: The split labor market. *American Sociological Review, 37,* 447–559.

Brehm, J. (1966). *A theory of psychological reactance.* New York: Academic Press.

Brigham, J. (1993). College Students' Racial Attitudes. *Journal of Applied and Social Psychology, 23,* 1933–1967.

Chen, M., & Bargh, J. (1997). Nonconscious behavioral confirmation processes: The self-fulfilling consequences of automatic stereotype activation. *Journal of Experimental Social Psychology, 33,* 541–560.

Cox, O. (1948). *Caste, class, and race: A study in social dynamics.* New York: Doubleday.

Crosby, F., Bromley, S., & Saxe, L. (1980). Recent unobtrusive studies of Black and White discrimination and prejudice: A literature review. *Psychological Bulletin, 87,* 546–563.

Dasgupta, N. (1999). *Combating implicit prejudice.* Presented at APS, Denver, CO.

Devine, P. (1989). Stereotypes and prejudice: Their automatic and controlled components. *Journal of Personality and Social Psychology, 56,* 5–18.

Devine, P., & Elliot, A. (1995). Are racial stereotypes really fading? The Princeton trilogy revisited. *Personality and Social Psychology Bulletin, 21,* 1139–1150.

Devine, P., & Monteith, M. (1993). The role of discrepancy associated affect in prejudice reduction. In D. Mackie & D. Hamilton (Eds.), *Affect, cognition, and stereotyping: Interactive processes in intergroup perception* (pp. 317–344). San Diego, CA: Academic Press.

Devine, P., & Monteith, M. (1999). Dual processes in stereotyping. In S. Chaiken & Y. Trope (Eds.), *Dual-process theories in social psychology* (pp. 339–360). New York: Guilford Press.

Devine, P., Monteith, M., Zuwerink, J., & Elliot, A. (1991). Prejudice with and without compunction. *Journal of Personality and Social Psychology, 60*, 817–830.

Devine, P., Plant, E., & Brazy, P. (2000). Exploring the relationship between implicit and explicit prejudice: The role of motivations to respond without prejudice. Manuscript under review.

Dovidio, J., Evans, N., & Tyler, R. (1986). Racial stereotypes: The contents of their cognitive representations. *Journal of Experimental Social Psychology, 22*, 22–37.

Dovidio, J., & Fazio, R. (1992). New technologies for the direct and indirect assessment of attitudes. In J. Tanur (Ed.), *Questions about questions: Inquiries into the cognitive bases of surveys* (pp. 204–237). New York: Russell Sage Foundation.

Dovidio, J., & Gaertner, S. (1986). Prejudice, discrimination, and racism: Historical trends and contemporary approaches. In J. Dovidio & S. Gaertner (Eds.), *Prejudice, discrimination, and racism* (pp. 1–34). San Diego, CA: Academic Press.

Dovidio, J., & Gaertner, S. (1998). On the nature of contemporary prejudice: The causes, consequences, and challenges of aversive racism. In J. Eberhardt & S. Fiske (Eds.), *Confronting racism: The problem and the response* (pp. 3–32). Thousand Oaks, CA: Sage.

Dovidio, J., Kawakami, K., Johnson, C., Johnson, B., & Howard, A. (1997). On the nature of prejudice: Automatic and controlled processes. *Journal of Experimental Social Psychology, 33*, 510–540.

Duckitt, J. (1992). *The social psychology of prejudice.* New York: Praeger.

Dunton, B., & Fazio, R. (1997). An individual difference measure of motivation to control prejudiced reactions. *Personality and Social Psychology Bulletin, 23*, 316–326.

Fazio, R. (1986). How do attitudes guide behavior. In R. Sorrentno & E. Higgins (Eds.), *Handbook of motivation and cognition: Foundations of social behavior* (pp. 204–243). New York: Guilford Press.

Fazio, R. (1990). Multiple processes by which attitudes guide behavior: The MODE model as an integrated framework. In M. Zanna (Ed.), *Advances in experimental social psychology* (Vol. 23, pp. 75–109). New York: Academic Press.

Fazio, R., & Dunton, B. (1997). Categorization by race: The impact of automatic and controlled components of racial prejudice. *Journal of Experimental Social Psychology, 33*, 451–470.

Fazio, R., Jackson, J., Dunton, B., & Williams, C. (1995). Variability in automatic activation as an unobtrusive measure of racial attitudes: A *bona fide* pipeline? *Journal of Personality and Social Psychology, 69*, 1013–1027.

Gaertner, S., & Dovidio, J. (1986). The aversive form of racism. In J. Dovidio & S. Gaertner (Eds.), *Prejudice, discrimination, and racism.* San Diego, CA: Academic Press.

Gaertner, S., & McLaughlin, J. (1983). Racial stereotypes: Associations and ascriptions of positive and negative characteristics. *Social Psychology Quarterly, 46*, 23–30.

Greenwald, A., & Banaji, M. (1995). Implicit social cognition: Attitudes, self-esteem, and stereotypes. *Psychological Review, 102*, 4–27.

Greenwald, A., McGhee, D., & Schwartz, J. (1998). Measuring individual differences in implicit cognition: The implicit association test. *Journal of Personality and Social Psychology, 74*, 1464–1480.

Hass, R., Katz, I., Rizzo, N., Bailey, J., & Moore, L. (1992). When racial ambivalence evokes negative affect, using a disguised measure of mood. *Personality and Social Psychology Bulletin, 18,* 786–797.

Jacobson, C. (1985). Resistance to affirmative action. *Journal of Conflict Resolution, 29,* 306–329.

Jones, E., & Sigall, H. (1971). The bogus pipeline: A new paradigm for measuring affect and attitude. *Psychological Bulletin, 76,* 349–364.

Katz, I. (1981). *Stigma: A social psychological analysis.* Hillsdale, NJ: Erlbaum.

Katz, I., & Hass, R. (1988). Racial ambivalence and American value conflict: Correlational and priming studies of dual cognitive structures. *Journal of Personality and Social Psychology, 55,* 893–905.

Katz, I., Wackenhut, J., & Hass, R. (1986). Racial ambivalence, value duality, and behavior. In J. Dovidio & S. Gaertner (Eds.), *Prejudice, discrimination, and racism* (pp. 35–60). San Diego, CA: Academic Press.

Kawakami, K., Dion, K., & Dovidio, J. (1998). Racial prejudice and stereotype activation. *Personality and Social Psychology Bulletin, 24,* 407–416.

Kawakami, K., Dovidio, J., Moll, J., Hermsen, S., & Russin, A. (1999). *Just say no (to stereotyping): Effects of training in trait negation on stereotype activation.* Unpublished manuscript. University of Nijmegen, The Netherlands.

Kelman, H. (1958). Compliance, identification, and internalization: Three processes of attitude change. *Journal of Conflict Resolution, 2,* 51–60.

Kinder, D., & Sears, D. (1981). Prejudice and politics: Symbolic racism versus racial threats to the good life. *Journal of Personality and Social Psychology, 40,* 414–431.

Kleinpenning, G., & Hagendoorn, L. (1993). Forms of racism and the cumulative dimension of ethnic attitudes. *Social Psychology Quarterly, 56,* 21–36.

Lepore, L., & Brown, R. (1997). Category and stereotype activation: Is prejudice inevitable? *Journal of Personality and Social Psychology, 72,* 275–287.

Levine, R., & Campbell, D. (1972). *Ethnocentrism: Theories of conflict, ethnic attitudes and group behavior.* New York: Wiley.

Locke, V., MacLeod, C., & Walker, I. (1994). Automatic and controlled activation of stereotypes: Individual differences associated with prejudice. *British Journal of Social Psychology, 33,* 29–46.

Lowrey, B., Hardin, C., & Sinclair, S. (1999). *Social tuning effects on automatic racial prejudice.* Presented at APS, Denver, CO.

McConahay, J. (1986). Modern racism, ambivalence, and the Modern Racism Scale. In J. Dovidio & S. Gaertner (Eds.), *Prejudice, discrimination, and racism* (pp. 91–125). Orlando, FL: Academic Press.

McConahay, J. B., Hardee, B. B., & Batts, V. (1981). Has racism declined? It depends on who's asking and what is asked. *Journal of Conflict Resolution, 25,* 563–579.

Monteith, M. (1993). Self-regulation of stereotypical responses: Implications for progress in prejudice reduction. *Journal of Personality and Social Psychology, 65,* 469–485.

Monteith, M. (1996). Contemporary forms of prejudice-related conflict: In search of a nutshell. *Personality and Social Psychology Bulletin, 22,* 416–473.

Monteith, M., Deneen, N., & Tooman, G. (1996). The effect of social norm activation on the expression of opinions concerning gay men and Blacks. *Basic and Applied Social Psychology, 18,* 267–288.

Monteith, M., Devine, P., & Zuwerink, J. (1993). Self-directed vs. other-directed affect as a consequence of prejudice-related discrepancies. *Journal of Personality and Social Psychology, 64,* 198–210.

Monteith, M., Sherman, J., & Devine, P. (1998). Suppression as a stereotype control strategy. *Personality and Social Psychology Review, 2,* 63–82.

Monteith, M., & Viols, C. (1998). Proneness to prejudiced responses: Toward understanding the authenticity of self-reported discrepancies. *Journal of Personality and Social Psychology, 75,* 901–916.

Moskowitz, G., & Salomon, A. (in press). Implicit control of stereotype activation through the preconscious operation of chronic goals. *Social Cognition.*

Myrdal, G. (1944). *An American dilemma.* New York: Harper & Row.

Pettigrew, T., & Meertens, R. (1995). Subtle and blatant prejudice in Western Europe. *European Journal of Social Psychology, 25,* 57–75.

Plant, E., & Devine, P. (1998). Internal and external motivation to respond without prejudice. *Journal of Personality and Social Psychology, 75,* 811–832.

Plant, E., & Devine, P. (1999). *Responses to social influence: Influence of motivation to respond without prejudice.* Manuscript in preparation.

Proshansky, H. (1966). The development of intergroup attitudes. In L. Hoffman & M. Hoffman (Eds.), *Review of child development research* (pp. 311–371). New York: Russell Sage.

Roese, N., & Jamieson, D. (1993). Twenty years of bogus pipeline research: A critical review and meta-analysis. *Psychological Bulletin, 114,* 363–375.

Schuman, H., Steeh, C., & Bobo, L. (1985). *Racial attitudes in America: Trends and interpretation.* Cambridge, MA: Harvard University Press.

Sears, D. (1998). Racism and politics in the United States. In J. L. Eberhardt & S. T. Fiske (Eds.), Confronting racism: The problem and the response (pp. 76–100). Thousand Oaks, CA: Sage.

Sears, D., & Kinder, D. (1985). Whites' opposition to busing: On conceptualization and operationalization group conflict. *Journal of Personality and Social Psychology, 48,* 1141–1147.

Sherif, M., & Sherif, C. (1953). *Groups in harmony and tension.* New York: Harper.

Sigall, H., & Page, R. (1971). Current stereotypes: A little fading, a little faking. *Journal of Personality and Social Psychology, 16,* 252–258.

Spencer, S., Fein, S., Wolfe, C., Fong, C., & Dunn, M. (1998). Automatic activation of stereotypes: The role of self-image threat. *Personality and Social Psychology Bulletin, 24,* 1139–1152.

Swim, J., Aikin, K., Hall, W., & Hunter, B. (1995). Sexism and racism: Old-fashioned and modern prejudices. *Journal of Personality and Social Psychology, 68,* 199–214.

Tajfel, H., & Turner, J. (1986). The social identity theory of intergroup behavior. In S. Worchel & W. Austin (Eds.), *Psychology of intergroup relations* (2nd ed., pp. 7–24). Chicago, IL: Nelson-Hall.

Taylor, D., Sheatsley, P., & Greeley, A. (1978). Attitudes toward racial integration. *Scientific American, 238,* 42–49.

Vanman, E., Paul, B., Ito, T., & Miller, N. (1997). The modern face of prejudice and structural features that moderate the effect of cooperation on affect. *Journal of Personality and Social Psychology, 73,* 941–959.

Wegner, D., & Bargh, J. (1998). Control and automaticity in social life. In D. Gilbert, S. Fiske, & G. Lindzey (Eds.), *The handbook of social psychology* (4th ed., Vol. 1, pp. 446–497), Boston, MA: McGraw-Hill.

Wittenbrink, B., Judd, C., & Park, B. (1997). Evidence for racial prejudice at the implicit level and its relationship with questionnaire measures. *Journal of Personality and Social Psychology, 72,* 262–274.

Wittenbrink, B., Judd, C., & Park, B. (1999). *Moving targets: The malleability of automatically activated attitudes.* Presented at APS, Denver, CO.

Zuwerink, J., Monteith, M., Devine, P., & Cook, D. (1996). Prejudice toward Blacks: With and without compunction? *Basic and Applied Social Psychology, 18,* 131–150.

CHAPTER ELEVEN

Sexism: Attitudes, Beliefs, and Behaviors

Janet K. Swim and Bernadette Campbell

Throughout the last century, the status of women in many societies has undergone enormous favorable changes. This includes changes in politics, with women gaining the right to vote, advances in education, with more women receiving degrees in areas previously denied to them such as law and medicine (U.S. Bureau of Labor Statistics, 1998), and changes in the workplace, where progressive gender discrimination laws have been enacted. Structural and legislative advances have also been accompanied by changes in personal attitudes. For instance, data from national polls illustrate great strides in people's acceptance of women in high status leadership positions. In 1974 about 80% of Americans reported being willing to vote for a qualified woman for president in comparison to just over 90% in 1996 (as cited in Eagly & Karau, 1999). Similarly, in 1953, 66% of respondents preferred to have a man as a boss, 5% preferred a woman, and 25% reported no preference. By 1995, however, this shifted to 46% of those surveyed preferring a man, 20% preferring a woman and 33% reporting no preference (as cited in Eagle & Karau, 1999). Finally, when differences in women's and men's status remain, such as the so-called glass ceiling effect where women are advanced to a level where they can see upper management but cannot be a part of upper management, arguments can be made that these differences are not a result of discrimination but instead a result of reasonable choices that women make (Furchtgott-Roth & Stolba, 1996).

Despite evidence to suggest decreasing gender inequality, concerns remain. Women are still much more likely to be living in poverty than are men in virtually every nation in the world including Western countries such as the United States (Lipps, 1999). Moreover, every year thousands of women across the globe are victims of physical and sexual abuse (Lipps, 1999). For example, the American Psychological Association reports that "a recent national survey found that 7.2 of every 1000 women each year are victims of rape . . . two decades of research indicates that at least two million women in the United States may be the victims of severe assaults by their male partners in an average 12-month period. At least 21% of all women are physically assaulted by an intimate male at least once during adulthood" (American Psychological Association, 1998). Turning to the workplace, the polls mentioned above indicate there remains a substantial number of people who prefer male to female bosses. Finally, arguments can also be made that the slow progress of women in academic, political, and business settings, such as illustrated by the glass ceiling effect, is fundamentally a result of gender-based expectations throughout women's lifetimes that influence the choices that women make (Valian, 1998).

One's opinion about women's status is likely a function of whether one sees the glass half empty or half full. Further, beliefs about the extent of gender inequality are likely a function of the conceptual boundaries placed on the attitudes, beliefs, and behaviors typically considered to be evidence of sexism. Narrower conceptualizations of sexism will likely lead to impressions that sexism is less of a problem than would more inclusive conceptualizations. A noteworthy theme in current psychological research on sexism has been the refinement and broadening of the construct. Indeed, as will be discussed below, conceptualizations of sexism are no longer limited to what might be considered obvious or old-fashioned indicators of sexism – endorsing traditional gender roles and stereotypes, and holding negative attitudes and beliefs about women (Glick & Fiske, 1996; Swim, Aikin, Hall, & Hunter, 1995; Tougas, Brown, Beaton, & Joly, 1995).

In the present chapter, we look at how social psychologists have refined and expanded their conceptualizations of sexism, resulting in a more precise understanding of the characteristics of present-day gender prejudice and discrimination. We illustrate how current research builds on and expands past research, addressing findings that could be interpreted as evidence of the lack of sexism in current Western societies.[1]

We place the social psychological research on sexism within a larger framework of attitudes, beliefs, and behaviors in order to impose a meaningful structure on the literature and to clarify some confusion that can result without these distinctions. Research on and definitions of sexism vary in terms of whether the primary focus is gender-based attitudes, beliefs, behaviors, or some combination of these factors. Sexism has variously been described as a form of prejudice (Rickabaugh, 1996), beliefs that women are inferior and should be subordinated to men (Anderson, 1997), and discrimination or unjust treatment based upon one's gender (Marshall, 1994). While these three definitions are at least conceptually linked, the distinctions can be lost in the research and cause confusion. In some cases people may be assessing beliefs about gender roles but call it attitudes toward women (Eagly & Mladinic, 1989) or researchers might be testing discriminatory judgments but call such responses an assessment of prejudice (e.g., Goldberg, 1968). Here we define sexism as attitudes, beliefs, or behaviors that support the unequal status of women and men.[2] We organize our review of the literature into these three domains as a way of illustrating similarities and differences among several lines of research on sexism.

Attitudes toward Women

Variations in definitions of attitudes over the last several decades may alter the way that attitudes toward women are conceived (Duckitt, 1992; Eagly & Chaiken, 1993). Here we are defining attitudes as evaluations of an attitude object. Thus, we are examining research that assesses evaluations of women as a group and not particular beliefs derived from scales that some might describe as attitudes toward women (Eagly & Mladinic, 1989).

Early research on evaluations of women as a group was largely focused on assessing the evaluative nature of gender-based stereotypes (Del Boca, Ashmore, & McManus, 1986). Despite assumptions that women were evaluated negatively relative to men, reviews of this research revealed mixed results in terms of which gender was evaluated more positively (Del Boca et al., 1986; Eagly & Mladinic, 1994). Current research assesses global evaluations of women with feeling or evaluation thermometers or ratings on semantic differential scales. Respondents are asked to indicate how warmly they feel about or how positively they evaluate women and men. Semantic differential scales employ ratings of women and men on a series of descriptors (e.g., positive vs. negative, pleasant vs. unpleasant). Findings from current research reveal that both women and men tend to evaluate women more favorably than men – a phenomenon Eagly has dubbed the "women-are-wonderful effect" (Eagly & Mladinic, 1989, 1994).

Further exploration of people's evaluations of women reveals that global evaluations alone may not be sufficient to capture the "nuances" involved in attitudes toward the larger category of women. Haddock and Zanna (1994) demonstrated, for example, that the "women-are-wonderful effect" is qualified by participants' construal of the term "women." Specifically, high right-wing authoritarians who construed women as feminists provided the least favorable evaluations of women on evaluation thermometers, while high right-wing authoritarians who construed women as housewives provided the most favorable evaluations. Clearly, the positivity of evaluations was dependent upon the subgroup of women being evaluated. Attitudes toward subgroups have implications for all women. For instance, prejudice against lesbians can affect heterosexual women's endorsement of feminism (Swim, Ferguson, & Hyers, 1999) and prejudice against heavy women supports restrictive prescriptive beliefs about women's physical appearance.

In addition to global evaluations being insufficient to tell the whole story about attitudes toward particular groups, they may also not fully capture the extent to which BOTH positive and negative evaluations coexist. Little, if any, research has assessed ambivalence using purely evaluative measures. Our understanding of ambivalent attitudes is largely based on studies that employ measures of beliefs about women. It has long been known that people hold both positive and negative stereotypes about both women and men (e.g., Spence, Helmreich, & Holahan, 1979). Eagly and Mladinic (1989, 1994) have argued that positive evaluations of women are a result of more positive than negative stereotypes about women than men. However, there may be a general tendency to stereotype, such that those who tend to attribute positive stereotypes to women may also tend to ascribe negative stereotypes to them (Swim & Thomsen, 1993). This illustrates that more positive stereotypes about women are not necessarily favorable for women because the more one endorses positive stereotypes, the more one also endorses the negative stereotypes. Moreover, the extent to which women are stereotyped may be as important as the valence of the stereotype.

Although the notion that both positive and negative beliefs about women coexist has long been realized (Del Boca et al., 1986), its importance has only recently been highlighted. Such coexistence can be seen in the tendency for people to like women but not necessarily respect them (Glick & Fiske, 1999; MacDonald & Zanna, 1998). Supporting this distinction, MacDonald and Zanna (1998) found that about 90% of their male participants tended to like traditional women more than they respected them. Further, studies using the Ambivalent Sexism Inventory have illustrated that positive and negative beliefs can, at a minimum, coexist and may actually foster each other (Glick & Fiske, 1996). Benevolent sexist beliefs include the endorsement of complementary gender differentiation, heterosexual intimacy, and paternalism. Although benevolent beliefs do not appear hostile, they can imply hostility when gender differentiation leads to a justification for men's social power, heterosexual intimacy leads to men fearing the dependency that they might have on women, and paternalism leads to perceiving women as incompetent adults.

In sum, despite early assumptions that people generally have negative evaluations of women, researchers found that people actually evaluate women more positively than men. A more inclusive and precise conceptualization of attitudes toward women, however, examines evaluations of subgroups of women and ambivalent attitudes, and evaluations in terms of respect as well as liking.

Beliefs about Women

Expanded conceptualizations of sexism can also be seen in recent measures of sexist beliefs. While the previously mentioned public opinion polls assessing preference for male leaders may be viewed as an example of old-fashioned, direct sexist beliefs, other aspects of the responses provide insight into more modern manifestations of sexism. Among the 1995 respondents to the leader preference question, men (44%) were more likely than women (24%) to indicate no preference for either gender. Further, women (54%) were more likely than men (37%) to indicate a preference for a male boss. Such differential responding may reflect a tendency for men to be more concerned than women about appearing sexist. Observations such as these were the impetus for developing measures such as the Modern Sexism and Neosexism scales (Swim et al., 1995; Tougas et al., 1995). These measures assess beliefs about whether discrimination is a problem, antagonism toward women who complain about discrimination, and resentment of initiatives designed to counter discrimination. One could argue that the content of the items in these scales represents an indirect assessment of traditional beliefs. Yet, these contemporary measures also represent an expansion of the beliefs that are considered to be sexist. That is, like modern racist beliefs (see Devine, Plant, & Blair, this volume, chapter 10), beliefs are defined as modern sexist if they support the maintenance of the status quo of gender inequality.

The Modern Sexism and Neosexism scales represent only a small fraction of scales that have been designed to measure beliefs about women. Beliefs about women generally fall into the psychological types outlined in Table 11.1 (cf. Mason, 1975; as cited by Brannon, 1978). Some scales focus on one of these four types of beliefs and others intermix these beliefs. Whereas the Attitudes Toward Women scale (Spence & Helmreich, 1972) primarily assesses prescriptive beliefs about characteristics and behaviors of women, the Ambivalent Sexism Inventory measures several of these dimensions. The use of this

Table 11.1. Examples of Four Types of Gender-Related Beliefs

	Descriptive beliefs	*Prescriptive beliefs*
Beliefs about women's characteristics and behaviors	Perceived stereotypes	Endorsement of traditional gender roles
Beliefs about the treatment of women	Perceived prevalence of discrimination	Endorsement of paternalistic behavior

framework also highlights sources of overlap between sexism measures. For instance, both the Modern Sexism scale (Swim et al., 1995) and the Hostile Sexism scale (from the Ambivalent Sexism Inventory, Glick & Fiske, 1996) include items assessing perceptions of the prevalence of gender discrimination. Rather than reviewing specific scales, we review issues that emerge from various scales designed to measure sexist beliefs. The organization presented in Table 11.1 allows us to integrate findings from this research, illustrate controversies within each type of belief, and contrast past and current conceptualizations of sexist beliefs.

Beliefs about women's characteristics and behaviors

Descriptive beliefs. Research concerned with the content of descriptive beliefs about women and men typically falls under the domain of gender stereotypes. Most of this research addresses perceived traits or abilities associated with women and men. Using an array of methods (e.g., open-ended questions, Sherriffs & McKee, 1957; checklists, Williams & Best, 1990; rating scales, Spence et al., 1979; diagnosticity ratios, Martin, 1987; implicit associations, Greenwald & Banaji, 1995), social psychologists have identified some commonalities in the content of gender stereotypes. One commonly cited trend is that stereotypes about women reflect communal and nurturant qualities, whereas stereotypes about men reflect agentic and instrumental qualities. This distinction has also been supported cross-culturally (Eagly, 1987; Spence et al., 1979; Williams & Best, 1990; see Ashmore, Del Boca, & Wohlers, 1986, for a compilation of characteristics).

Another trend in the stereotype literature is the growing recognition that many beliefs about gender differences reflect actual gender differences (e.g., Hall & Canter, 1999; Swim, 1994). Early research on gender differences, like research on race differences (Duckitt, 1992), was used to demonstrate women's inferiority (e.g., Shields, 1975). Research on gender differences in the last half of the 20th century, by contrast, was conducted with the goal of demonstrating small or nonexistent gender differences and variability within gender indicating that stereotypes delineating differences are inaccurate (Eagly, 1995). Research on gender differences has resulted in many important findings, yet has not fulfilled its promise of demonstrating small gender differences. Results from several decades of research and meta-analyses examining the strength of gender differences converge on the conclusion that gender differences are, in fact, not minimal (Eagly, 1995, but see also Hyde & Plant, 1995 and Marecek, 1995). Moreover, research on perceptions of gender differences does not reveal an average tendency of either women or men to uniformly overestimate the gender differences that have been reported in meta-analyses (Swim, 1994). In fact, the predominant tendency is either to be accurate or to underestimate the size of gender differences in areas such as mathematical abilities and influenceability.

None the less, a number of qualifications concerning the findings from research on the accuracy of gender stereotypes should be noted. Research on accuracy reflects average tendencies to be accurate about average differences between women and men. Accuracy about average differences does not mean that each individual is accurately predicted. Further, gender differences are not stable – contexts are very important for understanding when gender differences will emerge (Deaux & LaFrance, 1998) and people are likely to underestimate the impact of context on the size of gender differences (Swim, 1994). Moreover, there are likely individual differences in the tendency to be accurate (e.g., Hall & Carter, 1999) and the presence of accuracy on some attributes does not necessarily imply accuracy on all attributes. For example, people have been found to overestimate men's aggressiveness and women's verbal skills (Swim, 1994), and there are descriptive beliefs such as rape myths (Burt, 1980) that have specifically been identified as inaccurate. Finally, accuracy criteria and methods of assessing perceptions can influence one's conclusions about degree of accuracy (Swim, 1994).

Why the concern if beliefs are accurate? Despite the qualifications, it is true that there is some degree of accuracy in perceptions of the characteristics typically associated with women and men. As such, the question can rightly be raised as to whether descriptive beliefs about women and men should be considered sexist if they are accurate. There are at least three possible responses to this question. First, these beliefs may be misapplied to particular women because any generalization may not be appropriate for any particular woman. Second, although there are likely biological bases for gender differences,[3] the accuracy in people's beliefs can be attributed in part to these beliefs creating the gender differences or some third variable (such as traditional gender roles) causing both the beliefs and the gender differences (Eagly, 1987; Jussim, 1991). Third, descriptive beliefs can be sexist when they support prescriptive beliefs about women and men that result in gender inequality (Hoffman & Hurst, 1990). As Brannon (1978) notes, "For many traditional people, one suspects that the line between what is and what should be is less obvious than in the perceptions of reformers and social scientists" (p. 682). Descriptive and prescriptive stereotypes of low status groups tend to "work together," particularly when the dominant group's outcomes depend in some way on the low status group (Glick & Fiske, 1999; Jackman, 1994). For instance, in a traditional marriage, the husband benefits from his wife's deference to his authority. This description could easily lead to the prescription that women *should* be deferential to their husbands. The extent to which descriptive beliefs predict prescriptive beliefs may be a function of people's folk theories about gender differences or the attributions people make for the causes of such differences (Martin & Parker, 1995; Vescio, in press). For example, those who attribute gender differences primarily to biological factors may be more likely to prescribe differences in behaviors than would those who attribute the same gender differences to socialization or discrimination.

In sum, although past research reveals that some stereotypes may be accurate, it is insufficient to assess accuracy alone. One must also assess beliefs about the sources of gender differences, as well as the potential consequences of such beliefs. One such consequence is the association between prescriptive and descriptive beliefs.

Prescriptive beliefs. A large body of research that has historically been used to demonstrate sexism has been research on people's preference for traditional gender roles. These beliefs have been assessed in national polls and many scales have been designed to assess the extent to which people prescribe different behaviors for women and men (e.g., in marital, parental, employment, social-interpersonal-heterosexual, and educational domains, King & King, 1997). These measures often mention behaviors women or men should or should not engage such as "Women should worry less about their rights and more about becoming good wives and mothers," as noted in the Attitudes Toward Women scale (Spence & Helmreich, 1972). Early research demonstrated that a substantial number of women and men showed a preference for division of labor by gender, including a preference for males in leadership roles. Yet, the strength of these preferences seems to have diminished (Eagly & Karau, 1999; Twenge, 1997).

Why the concern if there has been a decrease in endorsement of traditional gender roles? One concern is that changes in self-reported beliefs do not necessarily mean that equality is uniformly preferred. In a 1990 Gallup poll, 37% of respondents preferred a traditional marital arrangement where the husband provides for family and the wife takes care of the house and children. Further, about half the women and men surveyed agreed that "it is much better for everyone involved if the man is the achiever outside the home and the woman takes care of the home and family." Moreover, contemporary gender prescriptions may be less centered on traditional gender roles, and more focused on issues such as women's self-presentation. People likely hold prescriptive beliefs about the way that women should present themselves verbally (e.g., as revealed in reactions to women versus men who self-promote, Rudman, 1998) and physically (e.g., as revealed in cosmetic alterations ranging from make-up to tummy tucks). The impact of such gendered prescriptions was illustrated in the Price-Waterhouse case where evaluations of the woman suing the accounting firm for discrimination included recommendations that she walk and talk more femininely (Fiske, Bersoff, Borgida, Deaux, & Heilman, 1991).

In sum, a complete understanding of people's prescriptive beliefs requires one to recognize the substantial number of people who *do* endorse traditional roles despite overall decreases in reported endorsement. Further, we must go beyond defining prescriptive beliefs simply as endorsement of traditional gender roles, toward a recognition of the importance of other prescriptive beliefs such as the way women should present themselves to others.

Beliefs about the treatment of women

Descriptive beliefs. Most of the research examining perceptions of the treatment of women and men has concentrated on perceptions of discrimination against women. Going beyond the traditional concern about the "proper" roles for women and men, recent measures of sexist beliefs incorporate perceptions of how women and men are treated (e.g., Glick & Fiske, 1996; Swim et al., 1995; Tougas et al., 1995). In these measures, the belief that "discrimination is no longer a problem" is explicitly used as one indicator of sexist beliefs. One assumption underlying contemporary measures of sexist beliefs is that discrimination against women is an ongoing problem and believing that it is not a problem is indicative of denial of discrimination.[4]

Why would beliefs about discrimination be sexist? Denial of discrimination can be a way for people to hide preferences for maintaining differential treatment and the status quo (Swim & Cohen, 1997; Tougas et al., 1995). In support of this argument, Tougas et al. (1995) have shown that their Neosexism scale is correlated with lack of support for affirmative action programs, presumably a mechanism to obtain gender equality. Beliefs that discrimination is not a problem may also be related to resistance to altering inequality not only at a societal level, but also at an interpersonal level (e.g., equalizing power in decision making, division of labor, and amount of time spent on leisure activities within marital relationships, Major, 1993). In addition to being related to prescriptive beliefs about the treatment of women, these descriptive beliefs are related to prescriptive beliefs about women's behavior. The more one believes that discrimination is not a problem, as assessed by the Modern Sexism scale, the more likely one is to endorse traditional gender roles (Swim & Cohen, 1997). Thus, like the connection between descriptive and prescriptive beliefs about women's characteristics and behaviors, descriptive beliefs about the treatment of women can be considered sexist when they are associated with prescriptive beliefs that result in gender inequality.

It should be noted that one can focus on the consequences of minimizing the occurrence of discrimination, without requiring an underlying desire for inequality. There may, in fact, be relatively benign reasons for this minimization, such as being unaware of the extent to which inequality exists, being unaware of the harm that accrues from current forms of inequality, or not believing that the harm that occurs is meaningful. A focus on the consequences of beliefs about the treatment of women redirects the emphasis from covert sexism, purposefully hiding sexist beliefs and behaviors, to subtle sexism, which is characterized by tolerating (and hence maintaining) sexist beliefs and behaviors in oneself and others because they are not recognized as being sexist (Benokraitis & Feagin, 1995; Swim & Cohen, 1997).

In sum, descriptive beliefs about women include beliefs about the way women are treated as well as the characteristics ascribed to women.[5] These beliefs may appear benign, especially when the underlying motives for holding the beliefs are benign. Yet, these beliefs can be sexist when they are associated with prescriptive beliefs that maintain inequality.

Prescriptive beliefs. There are at least three types of prescriptive beliefs about the treatment of women that can be considered sexist. One obvious, old-fashioned type is advocating behaviors that lead to traditional gender roles, such as encouraging men and not women to go to college or teaching girls and not boys about child care. A second type, noted above, is the lack of support for treatment that could arguably eliminate status differences such as changes in laws or interpersonal behavior. A third, perhaps not as obvious, type comes in the form of endorsement of paternalistic behavior.

Glick and Fiske (1996) discuss two forms of paternalism that support each other. Dominative paternalism involves the attribution of child-like qualities to women, who are deemed to be less than fully competent adults and therefore require a male figure to guide and make decisions for them. Benevolent paternalism is consistent with the notion of chivalry and reflects the belief that women should be loved, treasured, and protected. People who tend to support dominative paternalism also tend to support benevolent paternalism (Glick & Fiske, 1996). Most accounts of paternalism note that there is inter-dependence between those in low and high status positions and paternalism allows the high status person to maintain their status. As Jackman (1994) notes, the dominant group deems itself to be in a position to decide what is best for the subordinate group, allowing them to simultaneously dictate what is appropriate behavior for subordinates and to justify it as motivated by a concern for the subordinate's best interest. Understanding paternalistic behavior can be critical to understanding how dominant groups maintain their social power over subordinate groups because it maintains inequality while at the same time preventing resistance. Some of the costs of paternalistic behavior were illustrated as early as 1959 when Nadler and Marrow demonstrated that endorsement of chivalrous behaviors (such as protectiveness, stylized gestures of deference and politeness, and idealizing women as pure and honorable) was correlated with other prescriptive beliefs (supporting restrictive policies) and descriptive beliefs (believing women are naturally inferior, and viewing women as narrow minded, nagging, exploitative, and offensive) that support the subordination of women.

In sum, conceptualizations of sexist beliefs about how women should be treated have expanded beyond merely endorsing more favorable treatment of men than women. Sexist beliefs also include beliefs that on the surface appear to be egalitarian or favorable to women but result in maintaining the status quo or reinforcing women's subordinate position to men.

Treatment of Women

One type of research on the treatment of women examines actual differences in hiring, promotion, and wages. Results generally indicate that, after controlling for legitimate determinants of these outcomes, differential treatment of women and men remains (Eagly & Karau, 1999). These studies, however, are limited in that they cannot adjust for many legitimate determinants of outcomes such as self-presentation styles. In contrast to these studies, psychologists have taken an experimental approach by equating women's and men's performances and assessing judgments about the performances. In a prototypical study, participants read a description of a person's performance, with the name indicating the target's gender. Participants judge the quality of the work, make decisions about the target's future, or make attributions for the quality of the work. In a similar manner, stereotypical perceptions and treatment of children have also been assessed. Here, participants are asked to make judgments about or interact with a baby. Some are told the baby is female and others are told the same baby is male. They are then asked to make judgments about the baby's traits or to select toys for the baby.

It is not uncommon for qualitative reviews (e.g., Topp, 1991; Unger & Saundra, 1993; Valian, 1998) of the experimental approach to studying gender discrimination to indicate that: 1) work ascribed to a man was rated more favorably than the same work attributed to a woman; 2) attributions for work were affected by gender stereotypes, with successes on masculine tasks being attributed to stable causes for men (e.g., ability) and unstable causes for women (e.g., effort) and with failures on masculine tasks being attributed to stable causes for women (e.g., task difficulty) and unstable causes for men (e.g., lack of effort and bad luck); and 3) judgments and treatment of infants reflected gender stereotypes. The assumption that gender would have a strong impact on judgments can be seen in several early information processing models (see Operario & Fiske, this volume, chapter 2). These models assumed that category information, more so than other specific information about individuals, such as their physical appearance or qualifications, influences impressions of individuals, unless a series of conditions are met, such as a person being motivated to process the information. While supporting the general conclusion that category information influences judgments, several meta-analyses call into question the extent to which gender category influences judgments (Bowen, Swim, & Jacobs, 1999; Eagly, Makhijani, & Klonsky, 1992; Olian, Schwab, & Yitchak, 1988; Swim, Borgida, Maruyama, & Myers, 1989; Swim & Sanna, 1996).

The average effect sizes testing the effect of target gender on evaluations and attributions are often small (approximate $d \leq .10$). Similar small effects can be found in the perceptions of infants. For the present review, we calculated effect sizes based upon the studies reviewed in Stern and Karraker (1989) and found that the average effect sizes for the stereotypicality of the personality ratings and the manner in which participants interacted with children were very small and not significantly different from zero. The largest average effect size was found for the stereotypicality of adults' toy choice for the infant. This effect size was about .35 and was significantly different from zero. Further, Olian et al.'s (1988) meta-analysis revealed that the gender of a person being evaluated had considerably less impact on evaluations than did their actual qualifications. Similarly, Kunda and Thagard (1996) provide meta-analytic evidence to support the argument that individuating information has a greater impact on impressions than does category-based information. Moreover, even these small effect sizes may be artificially high because the evaluation effect sizes are at least partially a function of connotations associated with the names used to represent the evaluatees (Kasof, 1993) and the effect sizes for attributions to ability, luck, and task ease may be the result of a methodological artifact (Swim & Sanna, 1996). Finally, in contrast to the argument that the small effect sizes found in meta-analyses examining evaluations of women and men are primarily a function of participants' ratings of fictitious people, Bowen et al. (1999) found similarly small overall effect sizes in a meta-analysis of performance appraisals of actual women and men.

In contrast to the older information processing models, newer models such as Kunda and Thagard's (1996) Parallel Constraint Satisfaction model, can account for the weak effect of category information on judgments. In their model, category information has the same cognitive effects as other types of information in that both simultaneously result in activation or inhibition of other thoughts and feelings. Impressions are based upon associations that are activated in parallel such that category information is not given a special processing role. Further, the model assumes that category information has less of an impact on impressions than does other information about a person.

Why the concern if gender has little effect on judgments?

Meta-analyses and the newer processing models indicate that gender has inconsistent and weak effects on judgments, especially in comparison to the influence of specific individuating information about a person. Yet, a closer look reveals that gender can have a practically significant impact on judgments made about women and is important for a wide range of types of sexist treatment.

First, much of the research examining evaluations of and attributions for women's and men's performances has attempted to test possible moderators of the effects and in some cases gender biases within levels of moderators are relatively large (Bowen et al., 1999; Eagly & Karau, 1999). Hence, it is not necessarily surprising that there is a great deal of variability in the results across studies and that the average effect size is not large. Even if effect sizes within levels of the moderators are small, the additive effect of several moderators could be large. For instance, the difference between evaluating a woman or a man would be particularly large if they were not only performing a masculine task, but they were also being evaluated by a man who endorsed traditional gender roles. Because there have been several reviews of many of the moderators tested in these studies, we do not review them here (see Swim et al., 1989; Topp, 1991; Unger & Saundra, 1993). More recent research on stereotyping has highlighted moderators that influence the salience and relevance of category and individuating information on judgments and motivational processes that impact the effect of category information on judgments (Fiske, 1998; Macrae & Bodenhausen, in press; Rudman, 1998).

Second, even if category information does not have a special role and may even have less of a role than individuating information in impression formation, it is important to remember that specific information about people is often gendered. Gender stereotypes can influence impressions through other routes such as the stereotypicality of information about a person (Deaux & Lewis, 1984). For instance, the gender stereotypicality of individuating information (such as a person's physical appearance) is a stronger predictor of the stereotypicality of judgments about a person (e.g., their traits) than whether they are identified as male or female (Swim, 1994). Thus, judgments about women's and men's performances may not be specifically influenced by whether they are labeled as male or female, but may instead be influenced by gender stereotypic individuating information which is often confounded with gender in natural environments.

Third, even small average effect sizes can be meaningful and consequential (Abelson, 1985; Prentice & Miller, 1992; Rosenthal & Rubin, 1982). A small effect size in the direction favoring men could indicate that within the population at large, a large number of women are affected even though it is a small percent of women. Moreover, considering the number of times a person can be evaluated in a lifetime, small effect sizes can result in an accumulation of disadvantage for women. Agars (1994) demonstrated that a small effect size at an entry-level position could result in large disparities in upper level management over the course of several missed promotions. Similarly, the AFL-CIO demonstrated that the pay gap between women and men at the beginning of their careers can add up to huge discrepancies over their lifetimes (www.aflcio.org/women/equalpay.htm). Thus, the strength of gender category information on judgments may not be because the category information necessarily overrides or colors the individuating information as early information processing models suggest, but instead, the strength may be because of its frequent reccurrence.

Fourth, gender-based expectations can influence judgments in either an assimilative or a contrasting manner (Biernat & Kobrynowicz, 1999). Early processing models assumed that less favorable expectations would result in less favorable evaluations because the expectations would be assimilated into the judgments. Yet, gender-based expectations can also result in contrast effects such that a mediocre performance by a woman might exceed expectations while the same mediocre performance by a man might not meet expectations resulting in the woman receiving higher evaluations than the man. Biernat and Kobrynowicz (1997) argue that contrast effects occur when judgments are based upon subjective rather than common rule standards (i.e., scales with endpoints that allow people to form their own conceptualization of the endpoint values rather than scales where the endpoints are defined externally and applied the same to all groups). This has important implications for decisions that result from the evaluations. People may shift their standards for subjective evaluations of women but may not when making decisions in terms of concrete standards such as how much of a raise the person should get. As Biernat and Vescio (1999) note using a baseball analogy, a woman may be evaluated favorably because she may play well "for a girl" yet not be given the most desirable field positions in the game.

Fifth, it is important that conceptualizations of the treatment of women are not restricted solely to judgments of their performances. Indeed, judgment studies may not represent the best method of assessing the *prevalence* of sexist behavior. That is, while it is not uncommon for people to use this literature to illustrate that gender influences judgment processes (Topp, 1991; Unger & Saundra, 1993), large or small effect sizes do not illustrate the frequency with which gender influences judgments. This literature is better able to assess whether gender *can* influence judgments rather than whether or how often it *does* influence judgments.

Another problem with judgment studies is that they constrain the conceptualization of sexism, failing to reveal the variety of ways that men and women are treated differently. There seems to be an implicit assumption that discriminatory judgments are the best way to assess differential treatment of women and men. This, perhaps, reflects early concerns about barriers to women's entrance to and advancement in male-dominated occupations. It may also be one of the least ambiguous demonstrations of bias. However, judgment biases may not capture other potent forms of sexist treatment.

Research on the prevalence of sexual harassment is a useful break from the judgment literature in that it expands the conceptualization of unfair treatment in the workplace and in academic settings to include gender-based threatening and hostile treatment. This research suggests that sexism in the form of sexual harassment is prevalent (but see Arvey & Cavanaugh, 1995 for a critique of the assessment of the frequency of sexual harassment). One can also move outside of the workplace and academics to find examples of sexist behaviors. As noted in the introduction, statistics on the prevalence of rape and spouse abuse illustrate the prevalence of this particular form of sexism against women which has been identified as a form of "patriarchal terror" (Johnson, 1995).

Less violent, everyday forms of sexism are also prevalent. Everyday sexism includes discussions with friends that reveal endorsement of traditional gender roles, demeaning labels used to describe women or men, street remarks, and objectifying sexual comments (Swim, Hyers, Cohen, & Ferguson, 1998). One interesting illustration of the everyday nature of imbalance in power is documented gender differences in control over the television remote (Walker, 1996). Although this certainly reflects only one potential domain within a relationship, it does highlight the mundane and perhaps subtle nature of everyday sexism. Self-reported accounts of encounters with sexism from daily diary studies reveal that, on average, women and men report perceiving about one to two impactful sexist events per week directed at women as compared to less than one sexist event per week directed at men (Swim et al., 2000).

Mundane sexist events also include encounters with sexism in the media. Although sexism in advertisements has changed with women breaking out of traditional roles, media portrayals of women have become much more sexualized (Plous & Neptune, 1997). Sexualization of women in advertisements can alter the way that men treat women (Rudman & Borgida, 1995) and influence women's self-perceptions (Lavine, Wagner, & Sweeney, in press). The current media focus on women's appearance can contribute to women sexually objectifying their own bodies, potentially resulting in shame about not meeting cultural standards, distraction from other goals, and clinical issues of depression, eating disorders, and sexual dysfunction (Fredrickson & Roberts, 1997).

In sum, although meta-analyses reviewing research on the treatment of women reveal nearly negligible differences in the way that women and men are judged, a closer look reveals that gender can have meaningful influences on people's judgments. Further, it is important not to limit one's conceptualization of the treatment of women to judgment studies. Women experience sexist treatment in a wide range of situations and forms.

Comparisons with Other Forms of Prejudice and Discrimination

There are likely meaningful overlaps as well as important distinctions across domains of prejudice and discrimination. As such, it might be useful to make comparisons between research on sexism and other forms of prejudice and discrimination. First, the overlaps in attitudes include examining ambivalence (Devine, Plant, & Blair, this volume, chapter 10) and the evaluation of subgroups with some being evaluated more favorably than others are (e.g., African American sports figures versus criminals, Devine & Baker, 1991). Second, our framework for classifying descriptive and prescriptive beliefs about women is likely applicable for understanding beliefs about other groups, even though the specific content of the beliefs may differ. The similarities include recent research on the accuracy of stereotypes about many different groups (e.g., Lee, Jussim, & McCauley, 1995) and the inclusion of beliefs about the prevalence of discrimination in racism scales (e.g., Katz & Hass, 1988). It is also important to understand prescriptive beliefs for many social groups with some prescriptive beliefs maintaining dominant relationships (e.g., Blacks should not complain about discrimination) and others reflecting lack of tolerance for difference (e.g., not supporting homosexual behavior). Third, there are overlaps in the treatment of different groups. Paternalistic treatment can be a general strategy used by dominant group members to preempt or subvert conflict with subordinate groups (Jackman, 1994). Moreover, much research on the role of category information on information processing crosses many types of categories (see Operario & Fiske, this volume, chapter 2). Finally, there are parallels between everyday encounters with prejudice and discrimination (Swim, Cohen, & Hyers, 1998) and between violence against women and other forms of hate crimes, as is being recognized in a movement to include gender-biased crimes, such as rape, in assessments of the frequency of hate crimes (American Psychological Association, 1998).

Important distinctions between groups rest largely on the role of negative affect, interdependence, and intergroup contact. People's positive reactions to women relative to men may be a relatively unique phenomenon and may reflect the quality of many types of interrelationships with women including familial and sexual relationships (however, see Jackman, 1994). Evaluations of African Americans versus European Americans by European Americans differ from evaluations of women versus men in that there are not, on average, more positive ratings of African Americans than European Americans (Thomsen, 1991). This same pattern likely occurs with other groups where negativity is more socially acceptable (e.g., gays and lesbians or heavy individuals). A similar lack of parallel findings can be seen with measures that address racial segregation and interracial contact (cf. Biernat & Crandall, 1999). Given gender relationships between women and men it would seem unusual to measure prejudice against women through social distance measures. It would seem odd, for instance, for sexist people not to endorse women as close kin by marriage but accept them in employment settings. Thus, although there may be considerable overlap in some areas, research and theories on intergroup relationships may not always be directly applicable to gender relations. It may be most applicable to work situations where there remains substantial gender segregation (Jackman, 1994).

Finally, given the placement of this chapter in this section, the reader may have noted an ironic lack of emphasis on the intergroup nature of sexist attitudes, beliefs, and behaviors. In general, women and men are likely to hold different attitudes and beliefs about women and women are less likely to treat each other stereotypically. Yet, there may be more similarity between women's and men's attitudes, beliefs, and behavior than there is, for instance, between European American and African American attitudes, beliefs, and behaviors (e.g., Gurin, 1985). Thus, one might wonder whether sexism should be considered within the domain of intergroup relationships. We believe that it should because sexist attitudes, beliefs, and behaviors serve to define social, political, and economic relationships between women and men, even if some women's attitudes, beliefs and behaviors serve to support unequal relationships.

Several factors must be examined in order to understand why some women may endorse beliefs or act in ways that support unequal gender relationships. This includes understanding the interdependent relationships between women and men with women receiving benefits from such relationships. It also includes understanding variation within women and their perceptions of prejudice and discrimination against their own gender group. The latter can be seen within the research on the target's perspective on prejudice including research on variations in women's sensitivity to being a target of prejudice (Pinel, 1999; Stangor, Seichrist, & Swim, 1999), their willingness to label themselves targets of prejudice (Ruggerio & Major, 1998), and feelings of collective identity with other women (Branscombe, 1998).

Conclusions

The research reviewed here highlights why people may differ in their beliefs about the current extent of gender inequality and whether sexism is a source of this inequality. The positivity of people's evaluations and beliefs about women, the tendency for some beliefs to be accurate, the possible lack of intent to be prejudiced, historical changes, and the tendency for gender category information to have weak effects on judgments all lead to difficulty in concluding that sexism is a problem. However, these conclusions reflect a lack of precision about and recognition of the variety of gender-based attitudes, beliefs, and treatment. The research reviewed here reveals that negativity can emerge in sub-groups. Moreover, people do not only have positive evaluations and beliefs about women but instead have ambivalent evaluations and beliefs. Further, descriptive beliefs can lead to prescriptive beliefs that support inequality and prescriptive beliefs include domains where people still endorse double standards for women and men. Finally, gender can have a meaningful impact on judgments, and sexist treatment can take many forms and emerge in a variety of contexts. Thus, if one takes a restrictive and perhaps old-fashioned view of sexism, one might conclude that sexism is not much of a problem. However, broadening and refining one's conceptualization of prejudice and discrimination may help to elucidate the current social psychological manifestations of sexism. This breadth and refinement represents a more mature and well-developed understanding of the complexities associated with the manifestations of sexism.

Notes

1. Because most social psychological research on sexism has been conducted within Western cultures, our review primarily addresses findings from these cultures. Although there are likely overlapping cross-cultural themes in research on gender prejudice, including the importance of the cultivation of beauty, restrictions on movement and other freedoms, and subservience to one's husband (Lipps, 1999), more must be done to test the generalizability of the issues and findings presented here.
2. Whereas our definition includes men as well as women as potential targets of sexism, most definitions and research focus on sexism as it applies to women because of their lower social, economic, and political status. Accordingly, our review of the literature reflects this focus.
3. A discussion on the origins of gender differences is beyond the scope of this chapter.
4. These measures assume that not acknowledging discrimination is inaccurate. However, it is possible that people may overperceive the extent to which discrimination is a problem. This alternative form of inaccuracy can have important consequences such as for identification of particular events as sexist and for interpersonal relationships (Feldman Barrett & Swim, 1998).

5. Descriptive beliefs about the treatment of women also include beliefs about gender-based priv-
    ileges (e.g., Branscombe, 1998; Crawfoot & Chesler, 1996). Male privileges include: a) being
    the one favored when discrimination occurs; b) not having to fear threats of discrimination;
    and c) being assured that one is represented in discussions among political leaders. Recogni-
    tion of these privileges may be related to willingness to take actions to remove the privileges
    (Swim & Miller, 1999).

References

Abelson, R. P. (1985). A variance explanation paradox: When a little is a lot. *Psychological Bulletin,*
97, 128–132.
Agars, M. D. (1994, March). *The cumulative effect of gender stereotypes on selection and promotion*
decisions. Paper presented at the 15th Annual Industrial/Organizational and Organizational
Behavior Graduate Student Conference, Chicago, IL.
American Psychological Association (1998). *Hate crimes today: An age-old foe in modern dress.* Wash-
ington, DC: American Psychological Association.
Anderson, M. L. (1997). *Thinking about women: Sociological perspectives on sex and gender, Fourth*
edition. Boston, MA: Allyn and Bacon.
Arvey, R. D., & Cavanaugh, M. A. (1995). Using surveys to assess the prevalence of sexual harass-
ment: Some methodological problems. *Journal of Social Issues, 51,* 39–52.
Ashmore, R. D., Del Boca, F. K., & Wohlers, A. J. (1986). Gender stereotypes. In R. D. Ashmore
& F. K. Del Boca (Eds.), *The social psychology of female-male relations: A critical analysis of central*
concepts (pp. 69–119). Orlando, FL: Academic Press.
Benokraitis, N. V., & Feagin, J. R. (1995). *Modern sexism* (2nd ed.). Englewood Cliffs, NJ:
Prentice-Hall.
Biernat, M., & Crandall, C. S. (1999). Racial attitudes. In J. P. Robinson, P. R. Shaver, & L. S.
Wrightsman (Eds.), *Measures of political attitudes.* San Diego, CA: Academic Press.
Biernat, M., & Kobrynowicz, D. (1999). A shifting standards perspective on the complexity of
gender stereotypes and gender stereotyping. In W. B. Swann, J. H. Langlois, & L. A. Gilbert
(Eds.), *Sexism and stereotypes in modern society: The gender science of Janet Taylor Spence* (pp.
75–106). Washington, DC: American Psychological Association.
Biernat, M., & Vescio, T. K. (1999). *She swings, she hits, she's great, she's benched: The effects of gender*
on subjective praise and the allocation of limited resources. Unpublished manuscript.
Bowen, C. C., Swim, J. K., & Jacobs, R. R. (1999). *Evaluating gender biased appraisals: A meta-*
analysis. Manuscript submitted for publication.
Brannon, R. (1978). Measuring attitudes toward women (and otherwise): A methodological
critique. In J. A. Sherman & F. L. Denmark (Eds.), *The psychology of women: Future directions*
in research. New York: Psychological Dimensions.
Branscombe, N. R. (1998). Thinking about gender privilege or disadvantage: Consequences for
well being in women and men. *British Journal of Social Psychology, 37,* 167–184.
Burt, M. (1980). Cultural myths and support for rape. *Journal of Personality and Social Psychology,*
38, 217–230.
Crawfoot, J. E., & Chesler, M. A. (1996). White men's roles in multicultural coalitions. In B. P.
Bowser & R. G. Hunt (Eds.), *Impacts of racism on White Americans* (2nd ed., pp. 202–229).
Thousand Oaks, CA: Sage.
Deaux, K., & LaFrance, M. (1998). Gender. In D. T. Gilbert, S. T. Fiske, & G. Lindzey (Eds.),
The handbook of social psychology (4th ed., Vol. 1, pp. 788–827). New York: McGraw-Hill.

Deaux, K., & Lewis, L. L. (1984). The structure of gender stereotypes: Interrelationships among components and gender label. *Journal of Personality and Social Psychology, 46*, 991–1004.

Del Boca, F. K., Ashmore, R. D., & McManus, M. A. (1986). Gender-related attitudes. In R. D. Ashmore & F. K. Del Boca (Eds.), *The social psychology of female-male relations: A critical analysis of central concepts* (pp. 121–161). Orlando, FL: Academic Press.

Devine, P. G., & Baker, S. M. (1991). Measurement of racial stereotype subtyping. *Personality & Social Psychology Bulletin, 17*, 44–50.

Duckitt, J. H. (1992). *The social psychology of prejudice*. New York: Praeger.

Eagly, A. H. (1987). *Sex differences in social behavior: A social-role interpretation*. Hillsdale, NJ: Erlbaum.

Eagly, A. H. (1995). The science and politics of comparing women and men. *American Psychologist, 50*, 145–158.

Eagly, A. H., & Chaiken, S. (1993). *The psychology of attitudes*. Fort Worth, TX: Harcourt Brace Jovanovich.

Eagly, A. H., & Karau, S. J. (1999). *Few women at the top: Is prejudice a cause?* Manuscript under review.

Eagly, A. H., Makhijani, M. G., & Klonsky, B. G. (1992). Gender and the evaluation of leaders: A meta-analysis. *Psychological Bulletin, 111*, 3–22.

Eagly, A. H., & Mladinic, A. (1989). Gender stereotypes and attitudes toward men and women. *Personality and Social Psychology Bulletin, 15*, 543–558.

Eagly, A. H., & Mladinic, A. (1994). Are people prejudiced against women? Some answers from research on attitudes, gender stereotypes, and judgments of competence. In W. Stroebe & M. Hewstone (Eds.), *European review of social psychology* (Vol. 5., pp. 1–35). New York: Wiley.

Feldman Barrett, L., & Swim, J. K. (1998). Appraisals of prejudice and discrimination. In J. K. Swim & C. Stangor (Eds.), *Prejudice: The target's perspective* (pp. 11–36). San Diego, CA: Academic Press.

Fiske, S. T. (1998). Stereotyping, prejudice, and discrimination. In D. T. Gilbert, S. T. Fiske, & G. Lindsey (Eds.), *The handbook of social psychology* (4th ed., Vol. 2, pp. 357–411). New York: McGraw-Hill.

Fiske, S. T., Bersoff, D. N., Borgida, E., Deaux, K., & Heilman, M. E. (1991). Social science research on trial: Use of sex stereotyping research in Price Waterhouse vs. Hopkins. *American Psychologist, 46*, 1049–1060.

Fredrickson, B. L., & Roberts, T. (1997). Objectification theory: Toward understanding women's lived experiences and mental health risks. *Psychology of Women Quarterly, 21*, 173–206.

Furchtgott-Roth, D., & Stolba, C. (1996). *Women's figures: The economic progress of women in America*. Washington, DC: American Enterprise Institute.

Gallup, G. (1990). *The Gallup poll: Public opinion 1990*. Wilmington, DE: Scholarly Resources.

Glick, P., & Fiske, S. T. (1996). The Ambivalent Sexism Inventory: Differentiating hostile and benevolent sexism. *Journal of Personality and Social Psychology, 70*, 491–512.

Glick, P., & Fiske, S. T. (1999). Sexism and other "isms": Independence, status, and the ambivalent content of stereotypes. In W. B. Swann, J. H. Langlois, & L. A. Gilbert (Eds.), *Sexism and stereotypes in modern society: The gender science of Janet Taylor Spence* (pp. 193–222). Washington, DC: American Psychological Association.

Goldberg, P. (1968, April). Are women prejudiced against women? *Transaction*, 28–30.

Greenwald, A. G., & Banaji, M. R. (1995). Implicit social cognition: Attitudes, self-esteem, and stereotypes. *Psychological Review, 102*, 4–27.

Gurin, P. (1985). Women's gender consciousness. *Public Opinion Quarterly, 49*, 143–163.

Haddock, G., & Zanna, M. P. (1994). Preferring "housewives" to "feminists": Categorization and the favorability of attitudes toward women. *Psychology of Women Quarterly, 18*, 25–52.

Hall, J. A., & Carter, J. D. (1999). Gender stereotypes as an individual difference. *Journal of Personality and Social Psychology, 77*, 350–359.

Hoffman, C., & Hurst, N. (1990). Gender stereotypes: Perception or rationalization? *Journal of Personality and Social Psychology, 58*, 197–208.

Hyde, J. S., & Plant E. A. (1995). Magnitude of psychological gender differences: Another side to the story. *American Psychologist, 50*, 159–161.

Jackman, M. R. (1994). *The velvet glove, paternalism and conflict in gender, class, and race relations.* Berkeley, CA: University of California Press.

Johnson, M. P. (1995). Patriarchal terrorism and common couple violence: Two forms of violence against women in U.S. families. *Journal of Marriage and the Family, 57*, 283–294.

Jussim, L. (1991). Social perception and social reality: A reflection-construction model. *Psychological Review, 98*, 54–73.

Kasof, J. (1993). Sex bias in the naming of stimulus persons. *Psychological Bulletin, 113*, 140–163.

Katz, I., & Hass, R. G. (1988). Racial ambivalence and value conflict: Correlational and priming studies of dual cognitive structures. *Journal of Personality and Social Psychology, 55*, 893–905.

King, L. A., & King, D. W. (1997). Sex-Role Egalitarianism scale: Development, psychometric properties, and recommendations for future research. *Psychology of Women Quarterly, 21*, 71–87.

Kunda, Z., & Thagard, P. (1996). Forming impression from stereotypes, traits, and behaviors: A parallel-constraint-satisfaction theory. *Psychological Review, 103*, 284–308.

Lavine, H., Wagner, S. H., & Sweeney, D. (in press). Depicting women as sex objects in television advertising: Effects on body dissatisfaction and attitudes toward women. *Personality and Social Psychology.*

Lee, Y., Jussim, L. J., & McCauley, C. R. (1995). *Stereotype accuracy: Toward appreciating group differences.* Washington, DC: American Psychological Association.

Lipps, H. M. (1999). *A new psychology of women: Gender, culture, and ethnicity.* Mountain View, CA: Mayfield.

MacDonald, T. K., & Zanna, M. P. (1998). Cross-dimension ambivalence toward social groups: Can ambivalence affect intentions to hire feminists? *Personality and Social Psychology Bulletin, 24*, 427–441.

Macrae, C. N., & Bodenhausen, G. V. (in press). Social cognition: Thinking categorically about others. *Annual Review of Psychology.*

Major, B. (1993). Gender, entitlement, and the distribution of family labor. *Journal of Social Issues, 49*, 141–160.

Marecek, J. (1995). Gender, politics, and psychology's ways of knowing. *American Psychologist, 50*, 162–163.

Marshall, G. (1994). *The concise Oxford dictionary of sociology.* Oxford, UK: Oxford University Press.

Martin, C. L. (1987). A ratio measure of sex stereotyping. *Journal of Personality and Social Psychology, 52*, 489–499.

Martin, C. L., & Parker, S. (1995). Folk theories about sex and race differences. *Personality and Social Psychology Bulletin, 21*, 45–57.

Nadler, E. B., & Morrow, W. R. (1959). Authoritarian attitudes toward women and their correlates. *Journal of Social Psychology, 49*, 113–123.

Olian, J. D., Schwab, D. P., & Yitchak, H. (1988). The impact of gender compared to qualifications on hiring recommendations: A meta-analysis of experimental studies. *Organizational & Human Decision Processes, 41*, 180–195.

Pinel, E. C. (1999). Stigma consciousness: The psychological legacy of social stereotypes. *Journal of Personality and Social Psychology, 76*, 114–128.

Plous, S., & Neptune, D. (1997). Racial and gender biases in magazine advertising: A content-analytic study. *Psychology of Women Quarterly, 21*, 627–644.

Prentice, D. A., & Miller, D. T. (1992). When small effects are impressive. *Psychological Bulletin, 112*, 160–164.

Rickabaugh, C. A. (1996). Sexism. In F. N. Magill (Ed.), *International encyclopedia of psychology, 2*, London: Fitzroy Dearborn.

Rosenthal, R., & Rubin, D. B. (1982). A simple, general-purpose display of magnitude of experimental effect. *Journal of Educational Psychology, 74*, 166–169.

Rudman, L. A. (1998). Self-promotion as a risk factor for women: The costs and benefits of counterstereotypical impression management. *Journal of Personality and Social Psychology, 74*, 629–645.

Rudman, L., & Borgida, E. N. (1995). The afterglow of construct accessibility: The behavioral consequences of priming men to view women as sexual objects. *Journal of Experimental Social Psychology, 6*, 493–517.

Ruggerio, K. M., & Major, B. N. (1998). Group status and attributions to discrimination: Are low or high status group members more likely to blame their failure on discrimination? *Personality and Social Psychology Bulletin, 24*, 821–838.

Sherriffs, A. C., & McKee, J. P. (1957). Qualitative aspects of beliefs about men and women. *Journal of Personality, 18*, 247–255.

Shields, S. A. (1975). Functionalism, Darwinism, and the psychology of women: A study in social myth. *American Psychologist, 30*, 739–754.

Spence, J. T., & Helmreich, R. (1972). The Attitudes Toward Women scale: An objective instrument to measure attitudes toward the rights and roles of women in contemporary society. *Catalog of Selected Documents in Psychology, 66*–67.

Spence, J. T., Helmreich, R. L., & Holahan, C. K. (1979). Negative and positive components of psychological masculinity and femininity and their relationships to self-reports of neurotic and acting out behaviors. *Journal of Personality and Social Psychology, 37*, 1673–1682.

Stangor, C., Sechrist, G. B., & Swim, J. K. (1999). *Gender prejudice accessibility and its effects on perceiving sexism.* Manuscript under review.

Stern, M., & Karraker, K. H. (1989). Sex stereotyping of infants: A review of gender labeling studies. *Sex Roles, 20*, 501–521.

Swim, J. K. (1994). Perceived versus meta-analytic effect sizes: An assessment of the accuracy of gender stereotypes. *Journal of Personality and Social Psychology, 66*, 21–36.

Swim, J. K., Aikin, K. J., Hall, W. S., & Hunter, B. A. (1995). Sexism and racism: Old-fashioned and modern prejudices. *Journal of Personality and Social Psychology, 68*, 199–214.

Swim, J., Borgida, E., Maruyama, G., & Myers, D. G. (1989). Joan McKay versus John McKay: Do gender stereotypes bias evaluations? *Psychological Bulletin, 105*, 409–429.

Swim, J. K., & Cohen, L. L. (1997). Overt, covert, and subtle sexism: A comparison between the Attitudes Toward Women and Modern Sexism scales. *Psychology of Women Quarterly, 21*, 103–118.

Swim, J. K., Cohen, L. L., & Hyers, L. L. (1998). Experiencing everyday prejudice and discrimination. In J. K. Swim & C. Stangor (Eds.), *Prejudice: The target's perspective.* New York: Academic Press.

Swim, J. K., Hyers, L. L., Cohen, L. L., & Ferguson, M. J. (in press). Everyday sexism: Evidence of its incidence, nature, and psychological impact from three diary studies. *Journal of Social Issues.*

Swim, J. K., Ferguson, M. J., & Hyers, L. L. (1999). Avoiding stigma by association: Subtle prejudice against lesbians in the form of social distancing. *Basic and Applied Social Psychology, 21*, 61–68.

Swim, J. K., & Miller, D. (1999). White guilt: Its correlates and relationship to attitudes about affirmative action. *Personality and Social Psychology Bulletin, 25,* 500–514.

Swim, J. K., & Sanna, L. J. (1996). He's skilled, she's lucky: A meta-analysis of observers' attributions for women's and men's successes and failures. *Personality and Social Psychology Bulletin, 22,* 507–519.

Swim, J. K., & Thomsen, C. T. (1993). *Stereotypes of black and white women and men.* Unpublished raw data.

Thomsen, C. J. (1991). *On the automatic activation of racial stereotypes and prejudice: I and II.* Unpublished dissertation. University of Minnesota.

Topp, T. J. (1991). Sex bias in the evaluation of performance in the scientific, artistic, and literary professions: A review. *Sex Roles, 24,* 73–106.

Tougas, F., Brown, R., Beaton, A. M., & Joly, S. (1995). Neosexism: Plus ça change, plus c'est pareil. *Personality and Social Psychology Bulletin, 21,* 842–849.

Twenge, J. M. (1997). Attitudes Toward Women, 1970–1995: A meta-analysis. *Psychology of Women Quarterly, 21,* 35–52.

Unger, R., & Saundra (1993). Sexism: An integrated perspective. In F. L. Denmark & M. A. Paludi (Eds.), *Psychology of women: A handbook of issues and theories.* Westport, CN: Greenwood Press.

U.S. Bureau of Labor Statistics (1998). The law at work. *Monthly Labor Review, 121* (July, 1998).

Valian, V. (1998). *Why so slow? The advancement of women.* Cambridge, MA: MIT Press.

Vescio, T. K. (in press). The attributional underpinnings of prejudice. *Journal of Personality and Social Psychology.*

Walker, A. J. (1996). Couples watching television: Gender, power, and the remote control. *Journal of Marriage and Family, 58,* 813–823.

Willams, J. E., & Best, D. L. (1990). *Measuring sex stereotypes: A multination study* (Vol. 6). Newbury Park, CA: Sage.

CHAPTER TWELVE

Psychological Consequences of Devalued Identities

Jennifer Crocker and Diane M. Quinn

The person who is stigmatized is a person whose social identity or membership in some social category calls into question his or her full humanity – the person is devalued, spoiled, or flawed in the eyes of others (Goffman, 1963; Jones et al., 1984). The stigmatized are often the targets of negative stereotypes (Jones et al., 1984), and elicit emotional reactions such as pity, anger, anxiety, or disgust (e.g., Katz, 1981; Weiner, Perry, & Magnusson, 1988; Weiner, 1995), but the central feature of social stigma is devaluation and dehumanization by others (Goffman, 1963; Crocker, Major, & Steele, 1998). In nearly every culture, some groups are devalued or stigmatized, although the particular social identities considered to be flawed differ across cultures and historical eras (see Archer, 1985; Becker & Arnold, 1986; Jones et al., 1984; and Solomon, 1986, for reviews).

In this chapter, we contrast the traditional social science assumption that the psychological consequences of social stigma are deeply internalized with an alternative view, that the consequences of social stigma emerge in the situation, as a function of the meaning that situation has for people with valued and devalued identities. Due to space limitations, we focus on the consequences of devalued identities for self-esteem and performance on intellectual tests, two areas in which recent research has led to dramatically new understandings of these phenomena. For other perspectives on devalued identities, see Simon, Aufderheide, and Kampmeier (this volume, chapter 15), Ellemers and Barreto (this volume, chapter 16), and Schofield and Eurich-Fulcer (this volume, chapter 23).

Preparation of this manuscript was supported by an NIMH predoctoral traineeship to Diane M. Quinn, and by NIMH grant 1 R01 MH58869-01 to Jennifer Crocker.

The Psychological Consequences of Stigma: Internalized or Situationally Constructed?

Most discussions of stigma assume that the psychological and behavioral consequences of stigmatization result from internalization of devaluing images and stereotypes, or from other effects that stigmatization has on the personality, character, and values of the stigmatized. This view was expressed by Allport (1954) when he asked, ". . . what would happen to your personality if you heard it said over and over again that you are lazy and had inferior blood?" (p. 42). Consistent with Allport's view, differences associated with race, gender, and other valued or devalued social identities are typically explained in terms of inherent or internalized characteristics of the stigmatized themselves. Explanations tend to focus on biological differences, differences in access to resources such as good schools or safe neighborhoods, differences in exposure to prejudice and discrimination, or differences in socialization experiences. Each of these explanations suggests that differences between people with valued and devalued social identities reflect deeply internalized and stable characteristics, and that these group differences are exceedingly difficult, if not impossible, to eliminate. For example, research on race differences in performance on tests of intellectual abilities has tended to attribute such differences to genetic differences, or to socialization experiences and differential access to high quality schooling (see Steele, 1992, 1997, for discussions). Recently, African Americans' poor school achievement has been attributed to an oppositional identity that devalues the importance of school (Ogbu, 1986; Osborne, 1995), or to inferiority feelings that result from internalizing negative stereotypes about the intellectual abilities of African Americans (e.g., S. Steele, 1990). Women's poor math achievement has been linked to poor academic self-concepts and devaluation of mathematics as a consequence of negative stereotypes about women's math ability (Frome & Eccles, 1998; Jacobs & Eccles, 1992), as well as genetic male superiority in mathematical reasoning ability (Benbow & Stanley, 1980). Research on gender differences in vulnerability to a variety of psychological disorders such as depression and eating disorders has often attributed such differences to biological processes that increase the vulnerability of girls and women to these disorders, to personality characteristics that make them vulnerable, or to socialization experiences (e.g., Nolen-Hoeksema, 1987 for a review).

We argue that existing psychological models of group differences place undue emphasis on internalized and relatively immutable differences, and fail to recognize the extent to which differences between those with valued and devalued identities are highly dependent on the social context and features of the immediate situation in which the stigmatized find themselves. Thus, research indicates that the consequences of stigma have a "now you see it, now you don't" quality that is unacknowledged in most analyses.

In its essence, our argument is that to understand why stigmatized and nonstigmatized people behave or feel differently, we must understand both the unique meanings of situations for the stigmatized and the nonstigmatized, and how features of the situation, often very subtle features, can alter those meanings. Although these differences may be stable across similar situations that have the same meaning, and hence may appear to be internalized, it is often possible to alter the features of the situation and attenuate or eliminate those differences. In some respects, this is a very social psychological analysis, recognizing the power of the situation to affect self-esteem, performance on standardized tests, and other psychological experiences and behavior. However, most social psychological analyses of the power of the situation have assumed that a particular situation means the same thing for everyone in it. In contrast, recent research suggests that the same situation can have very different meanings, implications, and consequences for people with different social identities.

Collective Representations and the Meaning of Situations

One strategy for understanding what meanings might be important for particular situations is to examine the collective representations significant to a particular situation or context. Collective representations are shared beliefs, values, ideologies, or systems of meaning. Collective representations that affect the meaning of situations for the stigmatized may take the form of awareness of cultural stereotypes about one's group, understandings of why one's group occupies the position it does in the social hierarchy, and ideologies such as belief in a just world or belief in the Protestant ethic. These collective representations may lead the same situation to have different meanings, and different implications for self-worth, for stigmatized and nonstigmatized people. Thus, to understand the effects of having a devalued identity, we must understand both the collective representations that stigmatized individuals bring to situations, and how features of the situation, often very subtle features, make those collective representations relevant in that situation, or irrelevant.

Cultural values and ideologies

Most often, those who have valued versus devalued identities will have shared collective representations, as a result of living in a society in which those meanings are widely shared, and widely represented in popular culture. Many ideologies, for example, are endorsed broadly both by those who have valued and those who have devalued identities. In highly individualistic cultures, such as North America and many northern European cultures, the values of individualism, including independence, self-reliance, and personal responsibility for one's outcomes in life constitute a core ideology (Kleugel & Smith, 1981, 1986). Although these values are widely shared, they have unique implications for people with devalued identities (Jost & Banaji, 1994; Sidanius & Pratto, 1993). In particular, these ideologies suggest that the negative outcomes of people with devalued identities are under their control, and often deserved. For example, Crandall (1994) found that conservative political values, endorsement of the Protestant ethic, and belief in a just world all were related to the belief that being overweight is under one's control. Overweight and normal-weight Americans are equally likely to endorse this ideology (Crandall, 1994; Quinn & Crocker, 1999), but the ideology has different implications for these two groups. Specifically, belief in the Protestant ethic is associated with low levels of psychological well being in the overweight, but high levels of psychological well being in the normal weight (Quinn & Crocker, 1999, Study 1).

Beliefs about prejudice and discrimination

One collective representation shared by members of many stigmatized groups is the belief that others are prejudiced against them. This belief may affect the meaning that positive and negative events have for the stigmatized and the implications of those events for the self (Crocker & Major, 1989; Major & Crocker, 1994). In general, stigmatized individuals seem to be aware of prejudice against people with their social identity. For example, Rosenberg (1979) found that African Americans past the age of 14 are generally aware that others are prejudiced against their group. Most women believe that women are discriminated against (Crosby, 1982). Mentally retarded persons are aware of the negative consequences of their label (Gibbons, 1981), as are the blind (Scott, 1969), the obese (Harris, Waschull, & Walters, 1990; Jarvie, Lahey, Graziano, & Framer, 1983; Millman, 1980) the mentally ill (Link, 1987), and homosexuals (D'Emilio, 1983). People with different devalued identities differ in their beliefs about prejudice and discrimination against their group. For example, South Asian and Haitian women in Montreal believe that their group is discriminated against more than do Inuit people (Taylor, Wright, & Porter, 1994). Furthermore, individuals who share a devalued social identity differ in their beliefs about discrimination against their group. For example, Taylor et al. (1994) showed that undergraduate women at a university are more likely to believe that women are targets of discrimination than are non-university women.

Although many stigmatized people believe that others are prejudiced against their group, they do not always believe that they personally have experienced prejudice and discrimination. In general, people believe that their group is discriminated against more than they personally are discriminated against (see Taylor et al., 1994, for a review). For example, Crosby (1984) found that employed women tended to believe that women in general are discriminated against, but did not believe that they personally had been discriminated against, a phenomenon she labeled "denial of discrimination." Denial of personal discrimination is not always found in members of stigmatized groups, however (Taylor et al., 1994).

Black students' collective representations include the belief that Blacks are frequently the targets of racial discrimination. Crocker and her colleagues (Crocker, Luhtanen, Blaine, & Broadnax, 1994; Crocker, Luhtanen, Broadnax, & Blaine, 1999) investigated self-esteem and collective representations about prejudice and discrimination in a sample of 91 Black and 96 White college students at a large public university. African American students were more likely to believe that they personally had been discriminated against than were Whites. In results from the same study reported elsewhere (Crocker et al., 1999), they also found that Black students had very different understandings of the plight of Black Americans than did White students: They were higher in system blame (i.e., more likely to believe that problems confronting the Black community are caused by prejudice and discrimination) and more likely to believe that the U.S. government conspires to harm Black Americans, than were Whites. Thus, the collective representations of Black students clearly include the beliefs that Blacks in general, and they personally, are targets of racial prejudice. These beliefs are not widely shared by White students, regarding either their own experiences with racial prejudice, or their understanding of Blacks' experiences with racial prejudice.

Awareness of stereotypes

A related collective representation that the stigmatized may bring to situations is awareness of specific stereotypes about their group. Because these stereotypes are often pervasive in the culture, it may be inevitable that members of stigmatized groups know the content of those stereotypes (Devine, 1989; Gaertner & Dovidio, 1986). That is not to say that stigmatized individuals inevitably accept the validity of these stereotypes, although some do (see Jost & Banaji, 1994, for a discussion). Rather, stigmatized individuals are aware of the accusations against them that are contained in those stereotypes. African Americans, for example, are likely to be well aware that stereotypes accuse them of being intellectually inferior and aggressive; women are well aware that stereotypes accuse them of being emotional, bad at math, and lacking in leadership aptitude; gay men are aware that stereotypes accuse them of being flamboyant, effeminate, and promiscuous; the overweight are aware that stereotypes accuse them of lacking self-control and being inwardly miserable (Allon, 1982; Jones et al., 1984).

Contingencies of self-esteem

Another collective representation that people bring with them to situations is beliefs about what makes a person worthwhile – beliefs that Crocker and Wolfe (1998) have called contingencies of self-esteem. Self scholars have long noted that individuals differ in the value or importance they place on doing well in a particular domain (e.g., Steele, 1992; Tesser, 1988). Of course, domains may be important for a variety of reasons – because they are instrumentally useful for achieving one's goals, because they are important to significant others such as parents or in the larger culture, and of most interest here, because they form the basis of one's self-esteem. When self-esteem is at stake in situations that are relevant to one's contingencies of worth, emotional reactions, thoughts, and behavior are likely to be affected (Baumeister, 1998; Crocker & Wolfe, 1998; Kernis & Waschull, 1995; Steele, 1988).

Typically, research on the importance of various domains focuses on specific arenas of competence, such as school competence, athletic competence, attractiveness, and so on (e.g., Harter, 1986). Crocker and Wolfe (1999) have expanded the focus of this work to include contingencies of self-esteem not directly related to competence. They argue that self-esteem can also be based on such contingencies as having power over others, receiving approval or regard from others, being virtuous or moral, and being loved by God. These contingencies of self-esteem may determine the meaning of particular situations for people. For example, a student whose self-esteem is based on others' approval may be more personally distressed by prejudice directed against her than a student whose self-esteem is based mainly on God's love.

Are contingencies of self-esteem collective, rather than merely personal, representations? Gender scholars have suggested that women and men differ in the basis of their self-esteem. For example, women's self-esteem is more strongly correlated with their perceived physical attractiveness, whereas men's self-esteem is more strongly correlated with their perceived physical effectiveness (Harter, 1986; Lemer, Orlos, & Knapp, 1976). Given the pervasive cultural messages that women are objectified, and evaluated in terms of their physical appearance (Fredrickson & Roberts, 1997), it is not surprising that women's self-esteem would be more strongly linked to their appearance than is men's. Because of differences in the degree to which self-esteem is based on appearance, situations such as speaking in public may have different meanings for men and women.

Josephs, Markus, and Tafarodi (1992) argued that the self-esteem of men "is derived, in part, from fulfilling the goals ascribed to their gender – being independent autonomous, separate, and better than others" (p. 392), whereas the self-esteem of women is derived, at least in part, from "being sensitive to, attuned to, connected to, and generally interdependent with others" (p. 392; see also Cross & Madson, 1997; Markus & Oyserman, 1989; Wood, Christensen, Hebl, & Rothgerber, 1997, for reviews). In a series of studies, Josephs et al. (1992) showed that the tendency to see oneself as superior to others is more strongly associated with self-esteem among men than among women. In a second study, encoding words with reference to close others (a group or one's best friend) facilitated recall for high self-esteem women more than for high self-esteem men, or low self-esteem subjects of either gender. In a third study, women responded with more defense of self-esteem when threatened with failure on a test of "interdependent thinking" than on a test of "independent thinking," whereas men showed the reverse pattern. These results suggest that self-esteem is linked more to interdependence in women and independence in men.

Two studies by Wood and her colleagues (Wood et al., 1997) also suggest that there are gender differences in the standards that people use in evaluating the self, but only for people who aspire to meet society's gender ideals. In one of their studies (Wood et al., Study 2), men and women viewed slides depicting communal relationships or dominant relationships, and imagined themselves in the scene depicted. Participants for whom traditional gender ideals were personally important had more positive affect, and fewer discrepancies between their actual and ideal selves when imagining themselves in the gender congruent relationships (dominant relationships for men and communal relationships for women). Participants for whom traditional gender ideals were of only moderate or low relevance generally did not show these effects.

Evidence of racial or ethnic differences in the bases of self-esteem has also appeared from time to time. For example, White Americans' self-esteem is more strongly correlated with self-efficacy than is the case among African Americans, whereas African Americans' self-esteem is more strongly correlated with religiousness than is the case among White Americans (Blaine & Crocker, 1995; St. George & McNamara, 1984). The self-esteem of African Americans may be based less on approval and regard from others than is the case for European Americans. In a study of collective self-esteem among Black,

White, and Asian college students, Crocker et al. (1994) found that feelings of regard for one's racial group were strongly correlated with beliefs about how others regard one's racial group for both White and Asian college students, but were uncorrelated among Black college students, consistent with the idea that Black students' self-esteem is less likely to depend on the approval or regard they receive from others.

Wolfe, Crocker, Coon, and Luhtanen (1999) directly measured the degree to which students base their self-esteem on others' approval. European American students were most likely to base their self-esteem on approval from others, followed by Asian American students, and African American students were least likely to base their self-esteem on approval from others. These group differences in basing self-esteem on others' approval have now been replicated in a number of college student samples (Wolfe et al., 1999). Similar effects were found in a sample of women ranging in age from 18 to 90 recruited at a downtown mall in Buffalo, NY (Kerr, Crocker, & Broadnax, 1995). Again, African American women scored significantly lower on a three-item version of the Wolfe et al. (1999) scale than did the European American women.

These collective representations about what makes a person worthwhile influence the meaning of events for stigmatized and nonstigmatized individuals. For example, for those whose self-esteem is based on God's love rather than others' approval, situations in which others are prejudiced may have very different meaning than they do for people whose self-worth is highly contingent on others' approval. For those whose self-esteem is based on school competency, testing situations may have very different meaning than they do for people whose self-esteem is less contingent on school competency.

Constructing the Consequences of Devalued Identities

How do these various collective representations shape the experience and behavior of the stigmatized in particular situations? In the next sections of this chapter, we consider research on self-esteem, performance on academic tests, and self-objectification, that illustrates that these collective representations interact with subtle features of situations to create, or eliminate, psychological differences between stigmatized and nonstigmatized individuals.

Self-esteem

Self-esteem refers to a global judgment about the worth or value of the self (Rosenberg, 1979). To many people who do not have a negative social identity conferred by a stigma, it can seem obvious, even inevitable, that the stigmatized are low in self-esteem (Jones et al., 1984). This assumption is shared by many psychologists. For example, Cartwright (1950) argued that, "The group to which a person belongs serves as a primary determinant of his self-esteem. To a considerable extent, personal feelings of worth depend on the social evaluation of the group with which a person is identified. Self-hatred and feelings of worthlessness tend to arise from membership in underprivileged or outcast groups" (p. 440).

Yet, empirical research on the consequences of having a devalued identity has been inconsistent. Comparisons of average levels of self-esteem among stigmatized and nonstigmatized groups have yielded conflicting results (Crocker & Major, 1989). For example, studies comparing the self-esteem of African Americans to that of Americans of European descent typically report either no difference, or higher self-esteem in African Americans (Gray-Little & Hafdahl, 2000; Porter & Washington, 1979; Rosenberg, 1965). Studies of gender differences in self-esteem typically find no differences, or very small differences favoring males (Maccoby & Jacklin, 1974; Major, Barr, Zubek, & Babey, 1999). Studies comparing self-esteem in obese and nonobese populations also typically find no differences or very small differences (Friedman & Brownell, 1995; Miller & Downey, 1999).

In almost all of these studies, self-esteem is conceptualized as a stable trait that is consistent across situations, rather than as a psychological state. Consistent with some other self-esteem researchers (e.g., Heatherton & Polivy, 1991; Leary & Downs, 1995), we (Crocker, 1999; Crocker & Quinn, in press; Crocker & Wolfe, 1999) have argued that self-esteem is not a stable characteristic that individuals bring with them to situations, but rather that feelings of self-worth, self-regard, and self-respect are constructed in the situation. People bring a set of beliefs, values, and standards to the situations in which they find themselves. When positive or negative events happen, self-esteem depends on the meaning those events have for the self, which depends, in turn, on the individual's chronically accessible beliefs, attitudes, and values (see Schwarz & Strack, 1999, for a discussion).

Attributions to prejudice and self-esteem. A study illustrating this situational construction of self-esteem in the stigmatized was conducted by Crocker and her colleagues (Crocker, Voelkl, Testa, & Major, 1991, Study 2). In that study, African American and European American students received information that another student (always European American and the same sex as the participant) either was or was not interested in becoming friends with them. Participants believed that the European American student either was or was not aware of their race, because the blinds on a one-way mirror were either up (other aware of race) or down (other unaware of race). The feedback had little impact on the self-esteem of European American students. For African American students, however, the effect of the feedback on self-esteem depended on whether students believed the other person (the evaluator) was aware of their race or not. When the blinds were down (other unaware of race), the self-esteem of African American students went up following positive feedback and down following negative feedback, as expected. When the blinds were up, however, self-esteem was unaffected by negative feedback, and went down following positive feedback. Examination of the degree to which the students thought the other's reactions to them reflected prejudice and racism suggested why this was the case. The feedback was more likely to be attributed to prejudice when it was negative, and when the blinds were up. Thus, self-esteem was buffered when negative feedback was received, if the blinds were up and the feedback could be attributed to prejudice rather than one's own flaws. The typical boost in self-esteem from positive feedback, however, was reversed when it was attributed to prejudice, rather than one's own qualities.

In the present context, two points can be made about this study. First, it is clear from this and other research that African Americans have collective representations about the prejudice and racism of White Americans, and these beliefs affect the meaning and implications for self-esteem of positive and negative feedback from Whites. Second, a rather subtle variation in the situation (whether the blinds on the mirror were up or down), rendered these beliefs about prejudice relevant (blinds up) or irrelevant (blinds down) for interpreting the meaning of the positive and negative feedback.

Not all researchers have found that attributing negative feedback to an evaluator's prejudice is self-protective. For example, Ruggiero and Taylor (1997) found that women who received a negative evaluation from a man showed higher performance self-esteem, but lower social self-esteem when they attributed the evaluation to his prejudice against women. Again, however, these results are likely dependent on the collective representations that participants bring with them to this situation. For example, many women (and men) endorse gender stereotypes (Swim, 1995), so the women in the Ruggiero and Taylor study may have believed that the man's prejudice was justified. Furthermore, the women likely had self-esteem that was based more on others' approval than did the African American students in Crocker et al.'s study. These explanations for the discrepant results suggest that the collective representations that the stigmatized bring to situations are multidimensional and complex, and predicting the responses of the stigmatized to these situations requires a full understanding of these complexities.

Beliefs about biased tests and self-esteem. Similar to beliefs about individual prejudice and discrimination are beliefs about institutional bias, such as testing instruments that are biased against Blacks. A series of studies by Major and her colleagues (Major, Spencer, Schmader, Wolfe, & Crocker, 1998) demonstrates the influence of subtle contextual features on self-esteem among African American students taking a test. In one study (Major et al., 1998, Study 2), Black and White students took an intellectual test. For students in one condition of the experiment, race was never mentioned by the experimenter. For the other half of the students, the experimenter mentioned that one purpose of the research was to find out if the test was racially biased. Students then received information that they had done poorly on the test, and their self-esteem was measured. In the condition in which race was never mentioned by the experimenter, Black students' self-esteem following failure was lower than was that of White students. When the possibility that the test could be biased had been mentioned by the experimenter, however, the Black students' self-esteem was higher than was that of White students. Thus, the impact of poor test performance on self-esteem depended on the collective representations about biased tests that Black students brought with them to the testing situation, and features of the situation that made the beliefs salient or not.

Ideology and self-esteem. Another type of collective representation that may affect the meaning of situations for the stigmatized and nonstigmatized is ideologies, or widely shared cultural values. The values may be so widely shared and unquestioned that people are not even aware that they represent ideologies, or are not shared by people in different cultures. None the less, these ideologies and cultural values provide an important standard against which the self is evaluated, and hence can be a source of high or low self-esteem (Greenberg, Pyszczynski, & Solomon, 1986; Greenberg et al., 1993). The stigmatized are particularly likely to fall short when evaluated in the context of these ideologies and cultural values – indeed, people with particular social identities may be stigmatized *because* they are perceived as not measuring up to these ideologies and shared values (see Crocker et al., 1998, for a discussion).

As noted previously, one of the dominant ideologies in the United States is individualism (Kleugel & Smith, 1981, 1986). Individualism encompasses a variety of beliefs and values, all focused on personal responsibility, freedom, and the power of individuals to work autonomously and achieve their goals. Although this ideology, on the face of it, has nothing to do with body shape or size, endorsement of the Protestant ethic and related notions of personal responsibility are associated with attitudes toward the overweight. Crandall (1994) demonstrated that the belief that being fat results from a lack of willpower is part of a larger system of beliefs about personal responsibility, including conservative political leanings, belief in a just world, and endorsement of the Protestant ethic. This link between individualistic ideology and anti-fat attitudes, especially willpower beliefs, suggests that individualistic ideologies may provide a frame by which the overweight evaluate themselves, and consequently affects their self-esteem. Although endorsement of individualism may be positively related to self-esteem among those who are relatively successful, it may be negatively related to self-esteem in the overweight. Indeed, a study of 257 female undergraduates at the University of Michigan revealed exactly this pattern (Quinn & Crocker, 1999, Study 1).

Although ideologies such as the Protestant ethic may be endorsed by many people in our culture, competing ideologies, such as egalitarianism, are also widely endorsed (e.g., Katz, 1981). Consequently, whether the Protestant ethic is used as a standard against which the stigmatized evaluate themselves may depend on features of the situation that make the Protestant ethic, or competing, more inclusive ideologies salient. We investigated this hypothesis in the context of the stigma of being overweight (Quinn & Crocker, in press, Study 2).

In this study, women who rated themselves as overweight or normal weight in a pretest at the beginning of the semester were recruited for a study of comprehension and mood effects of media messages (Quinn & Crocker, in press, Study 2). The salience of the Protestant ethic was manipulated by having women read a political speech. For half of the women, the speech emphasized the values of the Protestant ethic (e.g., "America is a country where people can stand proud on their accomplishments. Self-reliance and self-discipline are the cornerstones of this country"). For the remaining women, the speech emphasized inclusiveness (e.g., "America is a country in which we strive to combine our differences into unity . . . A country whose divergent but harmonizing communities are a reflection of our deeper community values . . .") which was taken from Ronald Reagan's 1988 State of the Union address. After reading the speech, women rated it on a number of measures included to support the cover story. Then, all women read a "newspaper article" about the negative social experiences of the overweight. This latter message was included to ensure that all women were focused on their weight and the negative consequences of being overweight. Dependent measures included several state measures of psychological well-being, including the Rosenberg (1965) self-esteem inventory modified to reflect momentary feelings about the self. The results showed that in the Protestant ethic condition, overweight women had lower self-esteem than did normal weight women, whereas in the inclusive message condition, the difference between overweight and normal weight women did not approach significance. Taken together, these studies on ideology and the psychological well-being of overweight women indicate that the self-esteem of women who are overweight, or think they are, depends on the collective representations that are salient.

In sum, research on self-esteem in people with devalued identities has tended to assume that self-esteem is a trait that is consistent across situations and social contexts, and that being devalued necessarily results in low self-esteem. In contrast, the very recent studies reviewed here indicate that self-esteem is best conceived as a psychological state, and that self-esteem in the stigmatized depends jointly on the collective representations they bring to situations, and features of the situation that make those collective representations relevant or not. Whether the stigmatized are high or low in self-esteem will depend greatly on the situations in which they find themselves.

Note that in this view some stigmatized people may have consistently low (i.e., trait-like) self-esteem across time, if they have internalized ideologies that devalue their worth, or if they chronically find themselves in situations that devalue them. However, in our view these individuals could experience high self-esteem if alternative, more accepting ideologies were made highly salient, or if they were able to escape the devaluing situation.

Test performance

Members of stigmatized groups, particularly ethnic minorities and women, consistently tend to underperform on tests of at least some types of academic abilities. As noted, differences in test performance have been explained in terms of genetics and socialization, and both of these explanations view testing differences as relatively stable. However, until recently the testing situation itself was rarely seen as differentially affecting stigmatized and nonstigmatized groups. Stereotypes about stigmatized groups remain well known in the culture (Devine, 1989). Even though no overt act of discrimination or stereotyping may take place, those who are devalued bring their collective representations of stereotypes into testing situations with them. Knowledge of the stereotypes – and whether they could be applied to the self – may affect performance when the stereotypes are salient and/or applicable. A testing situation may have very different meanings for the stigmatized and non-stigmatized.

Stereotype threat. Recently, Claude Steele and his colleagues (Steele, 1997; Steele & Aronson, 1995; Spencer, Steele, & Quinn, 1999) have described a type of situation or "predicament" in which a member of a stereotyped group is in a situation in which he or she could confirm the negative stereotype through personal behavior. They have called this type of situation a "stereotype threat" situation. Stereotype threat theory predicts that although members of stigmatized and nonstigmatized groups may be in the same situation, such as taking a standardized test, the situation has different meaning for the stigmatized and nonstigmatized, and, consequently, different outcomes.

Recent research has examined the consequences of stereotype threat for test performance. Steele and Aronson (1995) gave a standardized test to African American and European American college students. Half of the students were told that the purpose of the test was to gauge verbal ability (diagnostic condition), whereas the other half were told the purpose was simply to better understand problem solving (nondiagnostic condition). When the participants believed the test to be diagnostic, African American students performed worse than European American students – just as is seen on standardized tests such as the SAT and GRE. However, when the same test was described as nondiagnostic, African American and European American students performed equally well on the test. Using similar methods, Quinn and Spencer (1996) altered the perceived diagnosticity of a math test for men and women students with equal math backgrounds. When the test was perceived as diagnostic, women underperformed. When the same test was perceived as nondiagnostic, women and men performed equally. Brown and Josephs (1999) manipulated whether a diagnostic test was described as diagnosing whether a student was exceptionally strong or exceptionally weak at math. Brown and Josephs hypothesized that if women were most concerned with the possibility of confirming the negative stereotype about their math ability, they should perform worse when the test was described as diagnostic of weakness at math, than when it was described as diagnostic of strength. This is exactly what was found. Men, however, showed a reverse pattern of effects. The effects of describing a test to be diagnostic or nondiagnostic of intellectual ability have also been shown to affect those of low socio-economic status in France (Croizet & Claire, 1998).

These studies demonstrate that it is not immutable differences in ability, but rather something about the testing situation, in this case, the threat of one's ability being judged, that affects group differences in performance. In order to show that it is the devalued identity that is interacting with the situation, a variety of studies have manipulated the salience of the stereotyped identity. Steele and Aronson (1995) gave African Americans and European Americans a standardized test, which was described as nondiagnostic for all participants. Immediately before the test, participants answered several demographic questions. For half of the participants, the final demographic question concerned their race, whereas for the other half of the participants this question was omitted. With just this small change in the situation, this subtle reminder of identity, the African Americans performed worse than the European Americans.

Research on women, who are stereotyped to be inferior at math, has shown that gender differences in performance can be eliminated when a test is described as gender-fair – thereby removing the applicability of the stereotype to a particular testing situation (Spencer et al., 1999). Research by Levy (1996) found that when the elderly were primed with a negative stereotype about the elderly they performed worse on a memory test than if primed with a positive stereotype. Shih, Pittinsky, and Ambady (1999) have nicely demonstrated that it is the particular social identity that is salient in a situation that affects test performance. Although most studies have concentrated on the one identity that is devalued, Shih et al. examined participants who had both an identity connected with a positive stereotype about math ability – Asian Americans – and a negative stereotype about math ability – women. Shih et al. had Asian American women take a quantitative test. Before the test participants completed a questionnaire which made their female identity salient, their Asian identity salient, or neither identity salient. Results showed that the women scored the highest on the test when their Asian identity was salient, intermediate when no identity was salient, and the lowest when their female identity was made salient.

These dramatic effects on performance with just small changes in the situation show that the consequences of having a devalued identity are constructed within the situation. The fact that performance differences can so easily be eradicated demonstrates that differences in performance on tests of intellectual ability are not caused by genetic or deeply internalized differences. Instead, it seems that the testing situation has different meanings for those in stigmatized and nonstigmatized groups.

Research on stereotype threat has examined the meaning of the testing situation by assessing some of the cognitions accessible in stereotype threat situations. For example, using the diagnostic paradigm described above, Steele and Aronson (1995) gave participants a word fragment completion task in which fragments could be completed either with words related to the African American stereotype or not. Results showed that African Americans in the diagnostic condition had more stereotypical completions than any other group. Because this was a situation in which they could be judged in the light of a negative stereotype, the meaning of the situation – literally what was on their mind – was quite different for the African American and European American students. Spencer et al. (1999), in a study described previously, found that women felt more anxiety than men in the stereotype threat condition. Stangor, Carr, and Kiang (1998) showed that when women were told that they were about to work on a task in which men performed better than women, earlier positive feedback about their performance was undermined, and their task expectations were lowered. Taken together, these studies suggest that in situations in which a negative stereotype could be used to judge one's performance, members of stigmatized groups experience the situation quite differently than nonstigmatized people – in such a situation, stereotypes about their group can be activated, they may feel more anxious, previous positive experiences in the domain may be undermined, and their performance may suffer.

One might wonder how individual members of groups that are the targets of negative ability stereotypes ever learn to do well on academic tasks, if they are constantly exposed to stereotype threatening testing contexts. However, research on stereotype threat indicates that it takes a toll on performance only under very specific circumstances: When the individual is highly identified with the domain being tested (e.g., Aronson, Lustina, Keough, Steele, & Brown, 1999); when the content of the test is at the very limits of the person's ability, as when college freshmen take the advanced GRE exam in mathematics (e.g., Spencer et al., 1999), and when the negative stereotype is salient (e.g., Steele & Aronson, 1995). Thus, stereotype threat is not likely to be a constant in the lives of stigmatized groups. Rather, it is likely to occur when one moves to a new level of difficulty in some domain, as in the transition from high school to college, or the transition from college to graduate school.

Self-objectification. In addition to the activation of stereotypes related to ability, women's test performance may be affected by their devalued identity in a different way. One way women are devalued is through sexual objectification. Objectification theory, proposed by Fredrickson and Roberts (1997), argues that in American culture there is a very strong and constant focus on women's bodies. In the media and in face-to-face contact, women are often objectified – that is they are reduced to being just their bodies. Fredrickson and Roberts hypothesize that because of this focus on bodies, girls and women learn to self-objectify, or to view their own bodies from a third-person perspective. That is, women learn to monitor their outward appearance, to be especially concerned with others' perceptions of their appearance, and to be more preoccupied with how their body looks than what it can do. Maintaining this third-person perspective on the body may have a number of negative consequences, including increased body shame, restrained eating, and disrupted attention. If women are distracted by thoughts about how they appear to others, they cannot devote their full attention to the task at hand. Although there are differences at the trait level to the extent that people, both men and women, self-objectify (Fredrickson, Roberts, Noll, Quinn, & Twenge, 1998), some situations may also induce self-objectification. Because the negative consequences of objectification are particularly strong for women, a self-objectifying situation will have very different meanings for men and women, and one consequence of those different meanings may be disrupted performance for women.

Fredrickson et al. (1998) brought men and women into a lab and had them try on either a swimsuit or sweater, in private. While wearing either the swimsuit or the sweater, participants were asked to look at themselves in a full-length mirror and to think about how they would feel about wearing the garment in public. They were also asked to take a math test while wearing the garment. It was hypothesized that all participants in the swimsuits would view themselves in a self-objectifying manner, but that this would have a very different meaning and different consequences for the women compared to men. Results showed that although both men and women described themselves more in terms of their bodies when in the swimsuit compared to the sweater, only the women in the swimsuit felt increased body shame, revulsion, and disgust with themselves. In addition, women in the swimsuit performed worse on the math test than any of the other three groups. Thus, although both men and women were in the same situation – trying on either a swimsuit or a sweater – this situation had very different meanings and consequences for women and men. For women, feeling objectified led to increased feelings of shame about their bodies, and decreased cognitive resources available to devote to the math test, resulting in worse performance.

In order to demonstrate that self-objectification disrupts performance by consuming cognitive resources, Fredrickson and Quinn (1999) conducted a second study in which participants – in this case all women – were again asked to try on a swimsuit or a sweater. Instead of taking a math test, participants performed a modified Stroop task in which they pronounced the color of words that appeared on a computer screen. Their reaction times to pronounce the words were recorded. Results showed that when wearing the swimsuit, as compared to the sweater, participants were slower to pronounce the words – regardless of whether the words were body related or neutral. Based on these results, it seems that for women being in a state of self-objectification leads to having fewer cognitive resources to devote to the task at hand. Thus, in this case, the consequences of having a devalued identity are unrelated to the content of the devalued identity, but none the less are situationally detrimental.

Implications and Conclusions

The studies described here were not designed to test the notion that the effects of stigma on self-esteem depend on the collective representations that the stigmatized bring to the situation, and features of the situation that make those collective representations relevant or not. None the less, the pattern of results across these studies seems very consistent with this view. The consequences of social stigma for self-esteem and performance on intellectual tests are not deeply internalized and immutable, but rather depend on features of the situation – sometimes very subtle features – that alter the meaning of that situation. Furthermore, they demonstrate that what appears to be the same situation in an objective sense may be subjectively experienced very differently, and have very different meanings, implications for self-esteem, and consequences for intellectual performance, for people with valued and devalued identities. Some important implications for the study of social stigma follow from this perspective.

First, understanding the experience of the stigmatized requires that we understand the collective representations that the stigmatized bring with them to situations. Research on the experience of the stigmatized should not only document the collective representations that the stigmatized and nonstigmatized bring with them to situations, but should also explore how those collective representations affect the meaning of situations for the stigmatized and nonstigmatized. We cannot assume that the same situation will mean the same thing for stigmatized and nonstigmatized people.

Second, our analysis suggests that the experience of disadvantaged, devalued, or stigmatized groups cannot be understood by creating stigmatized identities or minimal groups in the laboratory. Such studies strip away the shared beliefs and values that the stigmatized bring with them that give situations their meaning. In the present analysis, the effects of stigma are crucially dependent on those collective representations.

Third, this analysis suggests that stigmatization and its consequences do not require the immediate presence of prejudiced individuals. Because collective representations are widely known and shared among the stigmatized, it is not necessary for a prejudiced person to communicate the devaluation of the stigmatized for that devaluation to be felt. The stigmatized bring with them to situations collective representations that may devalue them, as the Protestant ethic devalues the overweight, or deflect devaluation, as awareness of prejudice and system blame may for African American students.

Recursive effects. We also want to emphasize that there is a recursive aspect to the consequences of stigma that is not captured by the laboratory experiments described here. Specifically, although the consequences of stigma are constructed in the situation as a joint function of the collective representations the stigmatized bring to bear in those situations and features of the situation that make those collective representations relevant or irrelevant, it is also true that experiences the stigmatized have in these situations can affect their collective representations. Thus, there is a loop from collective representations to meaning of situations back to collective representations. For example, when stigmatized individuals attribute a rejection to prejudice against them, this may in turn inform the individual's beliefs about the degree of prejudice against their group among nonstigmatized individuals.

Long-term consequences of stigma. Our analysis has emphasized the temporary consequences of social stigma that are constructed in the immediate social situation, as a function of the meaning that situation has for the stigmatized person. We believe that this perspective remedies a tendency in the social sciences to assume that the experience of having a devalued identity necessarily leads to internalization of that devaluation and to distortions in the character of the stigmatized. However, it is crucially important to recognize that these transient consequences may ultimately have important long-term consequences. For example, as Steele (1997) has noted, the effects of stereotype threat on performance on intellectual tests may lead talented students to disidentify with school, or with a domain of academic such as mathematics. This disidentification may, in turn, increase the likelihood that these students will drop out of their major, or drop out of school altogether. Thus, to say that these consequences are constructed in the situation in no way suggests that they are trivial.

References

Allon, N. (1982). The stigma of overweight in everyday life. In B. Wolman (Ed.), *Psychological aspects of obesity: A handbook* (pp. 130–174). New York: Van Nostrand Reinhold.

Allport, G. (1954). *The nature of prejudice.* New York: Doubleday Anchor Books.

Archer, D. (1985). Social deviance. In G. Lindzey & E. Aronson (Eds.), *Handbook of social psychology* (3rd ed., Vol. 2, pp. 743–804). New York: Random House.

Aronson, J., Lustina, M. J., Keough, K., Steele, C. M., & Brown, J. (1999). When White men can't do math: Necessary and sufficient factors in stereotype threat. *Journal of Experimental Social Psychology, 35,* 29–46.

Baumeister, R. F. (1998). The self. In D. Gilbert, S. T. Fiske, & G. Lindzey (Eds.), *Handbook of social psychology* (4th ed., Vol. 2, pp. 680–740). Boston, MA: McGraw-Hill.

Becker, G., & Arnold, A. (1986). Stigma as a social and cultural construction. In S. C. Ainlay, G. Becker, & L. Coleman (Eds.), *The dilemma of difference: A multidisciplinary view of stigma* (pp. 39–57). New York: Plenum.

Benbow, C. P., & Stanley, J. C. (1980). Sex differences in mathematical ability: Fact or artifact? *Science, 210,* 1262–1264.

Blaine, B., & Crocker, J. (1995). Religiousness, race, and psychological well being: Exploring social psychological mediators. *Personality and Social Psychology Bulletin, 21,* 1031–1041.

Brown, R. P., & Josephs, R. A. (1999). A burden of proof: Stereotype relevance and gender differences in math performance. *Journal of Personality and Social Psychology, 76*(2), 246–257.

Cartwright, D. (1950). Emotional dimensions of group life. In M. L. Raymert (Ed.), *Feelings and emotions* (pp. 439–447). New York: McGraw-Hill.

Crandall, C. S. (1994). Prejudice against fat people: Ideology and self-interest. *Journal of Personality and Social Psychology, 66*(5), 882–894.

Crocker, J. (1999). Social stigma and self-esteem: Situational construction of self-worth. *Journal of Experimental Social Psychology, 35*(1), 89–107.

Crocker, J., Luhtanen, R., Blaine, B., & Broadnax, S. (1994). Collective self-esteem and psychological well being among White, Black, and Asian college students. *Personality and Social Psychology Bulletin, 20,* 502–513.

Crocker, J., Luhtanen, R., Broadnax, S., & Blaine, B. (1999). Belief in U.S. government conspiracies against Blacks: Powerlessness or system blame. *Personality and Social Psychology Bulletin, 25,* 941–953.

Crocker, J., & Major, B. (1989). Social stigma and self-esteem: The self-protective properties of stigma. *Psychological Review, 96,* 608–630.

Crocker, J., Major, B., & Steele, C. (1998). Social stigma. In D. Gilbert, S. T. Fiske, & G. Lindzey (Eds.), *The handbook of social psychology* (4th ed., Vol. 2, pp. 504–553). New York: McGraw Hill.

Crocker, J., & Quinn, D. M. (in press). Social stigma and the self: Meanings, situations, and self-esteem. To appear in T. Heatherton, R. Kleck, & J. Hull (Eds.), *Stigma.* New York: Guilford Press.

Crocker, J., & Wolfe, C. T. (1999). *Contingencies of self-esteem.* Manuscript under review, University of Michigan, Ann Arbor.

Crocker, J., Voelkl, K., Testa, M., & Major, B. (1991). Social stigma: The affective consequences of attributional ambiguity. *Journal of Personality and Social Psychology, 60,* 218–228.

Croizet, J., & Claire, T. (1998). Extending the concept of stereotype threat to social class: The intellectual underperformance of students from low socioeconomic backgrounds. *Personality and Social Psychology Bulletin, 24*(6), 588–594.

Crosby, F. (1982). *Relative deprivation and working women.* New York: Oxford University Press.

Crosby, F. (1984). The denial of personal discrimination. *American Behavioral Scientist, 27,* 371–386.

Cross, S. E., & Madson, L. (1997). Models of the self: Self-construals and gender. *Psychological Bulletin, 122*(1), 5–37.

D'Emilio, J. (1983). *Sexual politics, sexual communities: The making of a homosexual minority in the United States: 1940–1979.* Chicago, IL: University of Chicago Press.

Devine, P. G. (1989). Stereotypes and prejudice: Their automatic and controlled components. *Journal of Personality and Social Psychology, 56,* 5–18.

Fredrickson, B. L., & Quinn, D. M. (1999). *Sex differences in self-objectification and use of cognitive resources.* Manuscript in preparation. University of Michigan.

Fredrickson, B. L., & Roberts, T. (1997). Objectification theory: Toward understanding women's lived experiences and mental health risks. *Psychology of Women Quarterly, 21,* 173–206.

Fredrickson, B. L., Roberts, T., Noll, S. M., Quinn, D. M., & Twenge, J. M. (1998). That swimsuit becomes you: Sex differences in self-objectification, restrained eating, and math performance. *Journal of Personality and Social Psychology, 75*(1), 269–284.

Friedman, M. A., & Brownell, K. D. (1995). Psychological correlates to obesity: Moving to the next research generation. *Psychological Bulletin, 117*(1), 3–20.

Frome, P. M., & Eccles, J. S. (1998). Parents' influence on children's achievement-related perceptions. *Journal of Personality and Social Psychology, 74*(2), 435–452.

Gaertner, S. L., & Dovidio, J. F. (1986). The aversive form of racism. In J. F. Dovidio & S. L. Gaertner (Eds.), *Prejudice discrimination, and racism* (pp. 61–89). San Diego, CA: Academic Press.

Gibbons, F. X. (1981). The social psychology of mental retardation: What's in a label? In S. S. Brehm, S. M. Kassin, & F. X. Gibbons (Eds.), *Developmental social psychology* (pp. 249–270). New York: Oxford University Press.

Goffman, E. (1963). *Stigma: Notes on the management of spoiled identity.* Englewood Cliffs, NJ: Prentice-Hall.

Gray-Little, B., & Hafdahl, A. R. (2000). Factors influencing racial comparisons of self-esteem: A quantitative review. *Psychological Bulletin, 126*, 26–54.

Greenberg, J., Pyszczynski, T., & Solomon, S. (1986). The causes and consequences of a need for self-esteem: A terror management theory. In R. F. Baumeister (Ed.), *Public self and private self*. New York: Springer-Verlag.

Greenberg, J., Pyszczynski, T., Solomon, S., Pinel, E. et al. (1993). Effects of self-esteem on vulnerability-denying defensive distortions: Further evidence of an anxiety-buffering function of self-esteem. *Journal of Experimental Social Psychology, 29*, 229–251.

Harris, M. B., Waschull, S., & Walters, L. (1990). Feeling fat: Motivations, knowledge, and attitudes of overweight women and men. *Psychological Reports, 67*, 1191–1202.

Harter, S. (1986). Processes underlying the construction, maintenance, and enhancement of the self-concept in children. In J. Suls & A. G. Greenwald (Eds.), *Psychological perspectives on the self* (Vol. 3, pp. 136–182). Hillsdale, NJ: Erlbaum.

Heatherton, T. F., & Polivy, J. (1991). Development and validation of a scale from measuring state self-esteem. *Journal of Personality and Social Psychology, 60*, 895–910.

Jacobs, J. E., & Eccles, J. S. (1992). The impact of mothers' gender-role stereotypic beliefs on mothers' and children's ability perceptions. *Journal of Personality and Social Psychology, 63(6)*, 932–944.

Jarvie, G. J., Lahey, B, Graziano, W., & Framer, E. (1983). Childhood obesity and social stigma: What we know and what we don't know. *Developmental Review, 3*, 237–273.

Jones, E. E., Farina, A., Hastorf, A. H., Markus, H., Miller, D. T., & Scott, R. A. (1984). *Social stigma: The psychology of marked relationships*. New York: Freeman.

Josephs, R. A., Markus, H. R., & Tafarodi, R. W. (1992). Gender and self-esteem. *Journal of Personality and Social Psychology, 63*, 391–402.

Jost, J. T., & Banaji, M. R. (1994). The role of stereotyping in system-justification and the production of false consciousness. *British Journal of Social Psychology, 33*, 1–27.

Katz, I. (1981). *Stigma: A social-psychological perspective*. Hillsdale, NJ: Erlbaum.

Kemis, M. H., & Waschull, S. B. (1995). The interactive roles of stability and level of self-esteem: Research and theory. In M. P. Zanna (Ed.), *Advances in experimental social psychology* (Vol. 27, pp. 93–141). San Diego, CA: Academic Press.

Kerr, K., Crocker, J., & Broadnax, S. (1995, August). *Feeling fat and feeling depressed: The stigma of overweight in Black and White women*. Paper presented at the annual meeting of the American Psychological Association, New York.

Kluegel, J. R., & Smith, E. R. (1981). Beliefs about stratification. *Annual Review of Sociology, 7*, 29–56.

Kluegel, J. R., & Smith, E. R. (1986). *Beliefs about inequality: Americans' view of what is and what ought to be*. Hawthorne, NJ: Aldine de Gruyer.

Leary, M. R., & Downs, D. L. (1995). Interpersonal functions of the self-esteem motive: The self-esteem system as sociometer. In M. Kernis (Ed.), *Efficacy, agency, and self-esteem* (pp. 123–144). New York: Plenum.

Lerner, R. M., Orlos, J. B., & Knapp, J. R. (1976). Physical attractiveness, physical effectiveness, and self-concept in late adolescents. *Adolescence, 11(43)*, 313–326.

Levy, B. (1996). Improving memory in old age through implicit self-stereotyping. *Journal of Personality and Social Psychology, 71*, 1092–1107.

Link, B. G. (1987). Understanding labeling effects in the area of mental disorders: An assessment of the effects of expectations of rejection. *American Sociological Review, 52*, 96–112.

Maccoby, E. E., & Jacklin, C. N. (1974). *The psychology of sex differences*. Stanford, CA: Stanford University Press.

Major, B., Barr, L., Zubek, J., & Babey, S. H. (1999). Gender and self-esteem: A meta-analysis. In W. B. Swan, J. H. Langlois, & L. A. Gilbert (Eds.), *Sexism and stereotypes in modern society: The gender science of Janet Taylor Spence* (pp. 223–253). Washington, DC: American Psychological Association.

Major, B., & Crocker, J. (1994). Social stigma: The affective consequences of attributional ambiguity. In D. M. Mackie & D. L. Hamilton (Eds.), *Affect, cognition, and stereotyping: Interactive processes in intergroup perception* (pp. 345–370). New York: Academic Press.

Major, B., Spencer, S. J., Schmader, T., Wolfe, C. T., & Crocker, J. (1998). Coping with negative stereotypes about intellectual performance: The role of psychological disengagement. *Personality and Social Psychology Bulletin, 24*(1), 34–50.

Markus, H., & Oyserman, D. (1989). Gender and thought: The role of the self-concept. In M. Crawford & M. Gentry (Eds.), *Gender and thought: Psychological perspectives* (pp. 100–127). New York: Springer-Verlag.

Miller, C., & Downey, K. T. (1999). A meta-analysis of heavyweight and self-esteem. *Personality and Social Psychology Review, 3*, 68–84.

Millman, M. (1980). *Such a pretty face: Being fat in America.* New York: Norton.

Nolen-Hoeksema, S. (1987). Sex differences in unipolar depression: Evidence and theory. *Psychological Bulletin, 101*(2), 259–282.

Ogbu, J. (1986). The consequences of the American caste system. In U. Neisser (Ed.), *The school achievement of minority children: New perspectives.* Hillsdale, NJ: Erlbaum.

Osbourne, J. W. (1995). Academics, self-esteem, and race: A look at the underlying assumptions of the disidentification hypothesis. *Personality and Social Psychology Bulletin, 21*, 449–455.

Porter, J. R., & Washington, R. E. (1979). Black identity and self-esteem: A few of studies of Black self-concept, 1968–1978. *Annual Review of Sociology, 5*, 53–74.

Quinn, D. M., & Crocker, J. (1999). When ideology hurts: Effects of feeling fat and the Protestant ethic on the psychological well being of women. *Journal of Personality and Social Psychology, 77*, 402–414.

Quinn, D. M., & Spencer, S. J. (1996, August). *Stereotype threat and the effect of test diagnosticity on women's math performance.* Paper presented at the annual American Psychological Association conference, Toronto, Canada.

Rosenberg, M. (1965). *Society and the adolescent self-image.* Princeton, NJ: Princeton University Press.

Rosenberg, M. (1979). *Conceiving the self.* New York: Basic Books.

Ruggiero, K. M., & Taylor, D. M. (1997). Why minority group members perceive or do not perceive the discrimination that confronts them: The role of self-esteem and perceived control. *Journal of Personality and Social Psychology, 72*(2), 373–389.

Schwarz, N., & Strack, F. (1999). Reports of subjective well being: Judgmental processes and their methodological implications. In E. D. D. Kahneman & N. Schwarz (Eds.), *Well-being: Foundations of hedonic psychology.* New York: Russell Sage.

Scott, R. A. (1969). *The making of blind men: A study of adult socialization.* New York: Russell Sage Foundation.

Shih, M., Pittinsky, T. L., & Ambady, N. (1999). Stereotype susceptibility: Identity salience and shifts in quantitative performance. *Psychological Science, 10*(1), 80–83.

Sidanius, J., & Pratto, F. (1993). The inevitability of oppression and the dynamics of social dominance. In P. M. Sniderman & P. E. Tetlock (Eds.), *Prejudice, politics, and the American dilemma* (pp. 173–211). Stanford, CA: Stanford University Press.

Solomon, H. M. (1986). Stigma and western culture: A historical approach. In S. C. Ainlay, G. Becker, & L. Coleman (Eds.), *The dilemma of difference: A multidisciplinary view of stigma* (pp. 59–76). New York: Plenum.

Spencer, S. J., Steele, C. M., & Quinn, D. M. (1999). Stereotype threat and women's math performance. *Journal of Experimental Social Psychology, 35*(1), 4–28.

St. George, A., & McNamara, P. H. (1984). Religion, race, and psychological well being. *Journal for the Scientific Study of Religion, 23*, 351–363.

Stangor, C., Carr, C., & Kiang, L. (1998). Activating stereotypes undermines task performance expectations. *Journal of Personality and Social Psychology, 75*(5), 1191–1197.

Steele, C. M. (1988). The psychology of self-affirmation: Sustaining the integrity of the self. In L. Berkowitz (Ed.), *Advances in experimental social psychology* (Vol. 21, pp. 261–302). San Diego, CA: Academic Press.

Steele, C. M. (1992, April). Race and the schooling of Black Americans. *The Atlantic Monthly.*

Steele, C. M. (1997). A threat in the air: How stereotypes shape intellectual identity and performance. *American Psychologist, 52*, 613–629.

Steele, C. M., & Aronson, J. (1995). Stereotype vulnerability and the intellectual test performance of African Americans. *Journal of Personality and Social Psychology, 69*, 797–811.

Steele, S. (1990). *The content of our character.* New York: St. Martin's press.

Swim, J. K., Aikin, K. J., Hall, W. S., & Hunter, B. A. (1995). Sexism and racism: Old-fashioned and modern prejudices. *Journal of Personality and Social Psychology, 68*, 199–214.

Taylor, D. M., Wright, S. C., & Porter, L. E. (1994). Dimensions of perceived discrimination: The personal/group discrimination discrepancy. In M. P. Zanna & J. M. Olson (Eds.), *The psychology of prejudice: The Ontario symposium* (Vol. 7, pp. 233–255). Hillsdale, NJ: Erlbaum.

Tesser, A. (1988). Toward a self-evaluation maintenance model of social behavior. In L. Berkowitz (Ed.), *Advances in experimental social psychology* (Vol. 21, pp. 181–227). San Diego, CA: Academic Press.

Weiner, B. (1995). *Judgments of responsibility: A foundation for a theory of social conduct.* New York: Guilford Press.

Weiner, B., Perry, R. P., & Magnusson, J. (1988). An attributional analysis of reactions to stigmas. *Journal of Personality and Social Psychology, 55*, 738–748.

Wolfe, C. T., Crocker, J., Coon, H., & Luhtanen, R. (1998). Manuscript in preparation, University of Michigan, Ann Arbor.

Wood, W., Christensen, N., Hebl, M. R., & Rothgerber, H. (1997). Conformity to sex-typed norms, affect, and the self-concept. *Journal of Personality and Social Psychology, 73*, 523–535.

PART IV

Language and Influence

CHAPTER THIRTEEN

How Language Contributes to Persistence of Stereotypes as well as other, more general, Intergroup Issues

Klaus Fiedler and Jeannette Schmid

The title of the present chapter provides a neat example for the various subtle ways in which language can induce beliefs and expectations. It uses several rhetorical devices that can have quite strong influences on communication partners, for they typically go unnoticed and thereby evade conscious control. The title uses *presupposition* and *nominalization* – two most prominent devices for reification and elimination of critical thought. Nominalizations like "persistence of stereotypes" take it for granted that stereotypes tend to persist, rather than being updated, and almost exclude the possibility of calling this premise into question (Bolinger, 1973). The same nominal phrase silently induces a restrictive theory which states that language contributes to stereotype persistence, as opposed to stereotype formation, or change. According to Grice's (1975) maxim of quantity, using a restrictive term can be taken as evidence that this restriction is substantive. Moreover, the title presupposes that language does contribute to stereotypes which in turn have to be conceived as a subcategory of other, more general, intergroup issues. All these linguistically induced assumptions are more likely to be encoded as veridical facts than to be discovered as potentially unjustified suggestions.

Language as a powerful symbol system offers such a rich repertoire of lexical terms and grammatical forms that virtually every utterance reflects a choice for this utterance, and against others. Moreover, language entails a gradient of connotative, evaluative meanings, such that any utterance conveys to some degree acceptance or rejection, approach or avoidance. It is thus no surprise that utterances about people and groups can have a potentially strong impact on social stereotypes.

The present chapter is organized as follows: An introductory section is devoted to illustrating the common social-interactional origin of both language acquisition and stereotyping, from a developmental or social-learning perspective. The methods and findings reviewed afterwards address two different but related topics: Language as a system and language as a toolbox to be used in social encounters or cultures. With respect to De Saussure's (1915) famous distinction, the former refers to "la langue" whereas the latter part is concerned with contextualized language use, or "le parole."

Language and Stereotyping from a Social-Learning Perspective

Although language is not given a systematic status in textbooks, monographs, and reviews of stereotype research (cf. Dovidio & Gaertner, 1986; Mackie & Hamilton, 1993), both representational systems, language and stereotypes, originate in the same process of social learning and interaction. Decades ago, pioneers in the psychology of stereotyping noted that ethnic stereotypes are often acquired during childhood, with little direct contact to the target groups (Brigham, 1971; Gardner, Taylor, & Feenstra, 1970). Such stereotypes are not based on first-hand experience but on second-hand information which is typically conveyed in humans' most effective symbol system, language. From an ontogenetic perspective, stereotypes are obviously encoded in language before they are encoded in children's memories.

Granting this central role of language in the learning and cultural sharing of stereotypes, the question arises whether language is only a medium for transferring cognitive representations from one person (parents, peers) to others (children, novices), or whether language adds something beyond the intended communication. As our starting example has shown, it is hardly possible to communicate without adding (actual or erroneously inferred) intentions, evaluations, interpretations, and simplifications. The essential need to be concise and informative rather than circumstantial, serves to simplify and accentuate original information in verbal communication. Thus, the Western European mother who never lived in a Turkish family but merely read a journal article about Turkish gender rules will presumably convey this knowledge to her daughter in a simplified and polarized fashion. The way in which she discourages her daughter from engaging in a close relationship with a Turk will leave little latitude for differentiation and cultural adaptation, and will induce more fear or xenophobia than when the daughter establishes a direct contact with Turks.

Without exaggeration, the acquisition of language and stereotypes not only coincides but also is identical in terms of basic learning processes. Learning the meaning of any word, such as "table," requires the (one-year-old) child to abstract from specific stimulus patterns elicited by particular objects and to acquire object constancy. Different tables produce different images on the retina and even the same table (perceived from varying angles, distances, illumination conditions, etc.) never reproduces the same sensory input. But the child has to understand all these different manifestations as belonging to the same abstract category, "table." This object constancy also converges in other sensory or operational modalities, such as touching the table surface, hearing knocking on table wood, lifting the table, using it as a place for eating and working, etc. Once this abstract word meaning is acquired different exemplars of the category can be recognized as "the same," or at least as more similar than before.

An analogous process can be assumed for the acquisition of generic word meanings, such as ethnic or national group labels (Japanese, Hispanics, Jews, Aboriginals), vocational categories (lawyers, professors, prostitutes), or groups defined by behavioral or habitual criteria (soccer players, homosexuals, juvenile delinquents). Learning of these categories involves abstracting from specific instances and ascribing the prototype or ideal type of that category to newly encountered exemplars. From a learning-theoretical point of view, there is basically no difference between language learning in general and learning of stereotype labels in particular.

A central defining feature of language (cf. Glucksberg & Danks, 1975), besides its generic infinity, is its reliance on arbitrary symbols that need not resemble the reference object. The sound pattern or graphical contour of the word "table" has no intrinsic similarity to the object table. It is this symbolic independence that creates the virtually unrestricted flexibility of verbal communication. Symbols used for denoting objects do not obey restrictive rules; any symbol will suffice, and human intelligence is flexible enough to figure out some resemblance between any two objects given the same arbitrary label. This arbitrariness points to a particularly intriguing aspect of social stereotypes. For any two persons, there are numerous ways of classifying them as same and different: Dagmar and Joshua may belong to different religions, sex groups, age groups, and professional groups, but they may be members of the same sports club, share the same hobbies, ethical and political values, and they may even be married. Treating Dagmar and Joshua differently or alike depends on the arbitrary choice of one categorization, perhaps dependent on which linguistic label happens to be activated. Categorization effects can even be obtained when meaningless fantasy terms are used to create artificial categories (e.g., "overestimators"), as evident from research on minimal groups (Tajfel, 1970).

Social learning does not take place in a vacuum, but in dynamic social interaction. It is learning by doing and instrumental learning. A young child who is only exposed to a radio receiver rather than to social interaction would hardly succeed in language acquisition. The same point holds, presumably, for stereotype acquisition. Just like the child uses words (table, ball, puppy) to get, express, avoid, or search something, stereotype terms are usually embedded in behavioral contexts. They come along with evaluations, behavioral intentions, approach or avoidance goals, specific topics or tasks, and local or temporal boundary conditions. This contextualized meaning of stereotypes constitutes their *surplus meaning* that often evades conscious awareness and is therefore hard to control or correct.

How Language as a System Affects Stereotype Maintenance

Language as a system has its own structural properties, independent of the language users' goals, perspectives, or personal styles. The constraints on information transmission imposed by these structural properties are relatively stable and inevitable. They include, among others, lexical, morphological, syntactical, semantical, and pragmatical constraints.

The role of sexist language in promoting anti-female stereotypes may illustrate this point. The lexicon supports the maintenance and reproduction of sexist attitudes in that it includes, for instance, many more terms applicable to promiscuous women than comparable terms for males. Thus, the lexicon makes lascivious, sexist talk about females a likely language game. A related example of morphological constraints would be the suffixes used to mark female expressions in many languages. While the generic, default terms are normally male, female forms are typically marked and thereby highlight the femininity of the person as an essential aspect (e.g., governor–governess; master–mistress).

An obvious manifestation of syntactic structure is the attention focus placed on the sentence subject – an almost inevitable consequence of the canonical order of sentence parts, from subject to predicate to object. The differentiation between active and passive voice has special importance in the possibility of shifting responsibilities for personal mishaps or interpersonal violence. This method has been investigated in the area of psychological accounts, for example in the context of rape trials (Henley, Miller, & Beazley, 1995). In the passive form "she was raped," the female target, rather than the male agent, is in the focal position, leading to decreased attribution of responsibility to the assailant and increased victim blame.

One pervasive source of semantic constraints is the associative network of word meanings. Numerous priming experiments demonstrate that conscious or unconscious priming effects can activate sexist knowledge in memory. This quasi-automatic influence is hard to control voluntarily (Blair & Banaji, 1996; Fazio, Sanbonmatsu, Powell, & Kardes, 1986; Wittenbrink, Judd, & Park, 1997). The greatest part of the present section will be devoted to semantic constraints.

Finally, the impact of pragmatic rules on the persistence of stereotypes can be illustrated with sexist jokes. The extent to which disparaging humor and culturally shared joke repertoires can contribute to gender stereotypes affords an intriguing research question (Hobden & Olson, 1994). One pragmatic reason why females are so vulnerable to anti-female jokes is that there is no way of disconfirming or objecting to the contents of a joke. Objections would only render things worse and increase the malicious effect of the joke.

The systematic distortion hypothesis

Central to the study of social stereotypes are the semantic constraints of trait adjectives, because stereotypes relate groups to traits, or traits to traits. (Virtually any trait category, like extrovert, can be reframed as a group, extrovert people). By definition, a stereotype states that some attribute or trait is more likely within a given group (or category) than in general (McCauley & Stitt, 1978). Stereotype research is thus about the learning and cognitive representations of trait contingencies. According to Shweder's (1975, 1982) systematic distortion hypothesis, this process is seriously biased toward the semantic similarities that exist between trait terms. People systematically confuse "likelihood" and "likeness"; they believe in correlations among those attributes that appear semantically similar. For instance, the correlation between *extroversion* and *leadership ability*, which is in fact close to zero, is drastically over-estimated just because the semantic meaning of the two terms, "extroversion" and "leadership ability," is rather similar. Shweder (1982) has made a strong point for his systematic distortion hypothesis, extrapolating from singular examples to whole arrays of trait terms. The general conclusion is that semantic similarities between traits constitute a much better predictor of subjective trait correlations than actually observed correlations.

A study conducted by D'Andrade (1974) illustrates the power of similarity-based illusory correlations. Observers of classroom interactions used the Bales (1950) categories to code the pupils' behavior over an extended period. These included behavioral categories like *asks for opinion, gives information, shows tension, agrees*, etc. Later on, observers were asked to judge the degree to which these behaviors correlated with each other. Judgments more clearly reflected the pairwise semantic similarities between the behavioral categories than the actually observed and encoded intercorrelations. Convergent evidence for this phenomenon comes from countless other studies on expectancy-based illusory correlations (Hamilton & Rose, 1980).

One interesting way in which illusory correlations can support stereotypes is through role labels. When the number of typical male and female attributes observed in two stimulus groups is the same, but the majority of members in both groups are labeled with different social roles (breadwinners vs. child raisers) associated with gender, observers believe they have seen more male traits in the group with the male label and more female traits in the female label group (Hoffman & Hurst, 1990).

To understand the underlying process, it is important to recognize the constructive nature of social perception. Most meaningful traits (emotionality, attraction, ability, hostility, credibility) are not amenable to immediate perception but have to be inferred or construed on the basis of fallible cues. That somebody is *emotional* is typically inferred from such cues as expressive voice, mimic reactions, crying and smiling, or disclosure of intimate states. As the symbolic meaning of these cues is much closer to *femininity* than masculinity, the stereotype that females are more emotional than males arises as a natural consequences of such cue overlap.

Verification and falsification of trait attributes

The semantic meaning of trait adjectives restricts the amount of evidence necessary to verify or falsify a stereotypical attribute. It takes more evidence to confirm that somebody is *honest* than to confirm that the same person is *dishonest*. As a general rule, evaluatively negative traits are often easier to verify than positive traits in the domain of morality-related social behavior, as Reeder and Brewer (1979), Skowronski and Carlston (1989), and others have shown. This asymmetry reflects the quantifiers that are implicit in the semantics of trait terms (Gidron, Koehler, & Tversky, 1993). To be honest means to act honestly most of the time, whereas to be dishonest means to cheat or to lie a few times, perhaps only once. Different confirmation thresholds can thus have obvious consequences for the likelihood with which positive versus negative stereotypes are inferred. Whereas negative stereotypes are easier to verify in the morality domain, positive inferences are more likely in the ability domain (Reeder & Brewer, 1979). Thus, a single observation of somebody juggling with seven balls is sufficient to infer juggling ability.

Other semantic components of trait terms concern the breadth of the behavioral domain within which a stereotype can be verified or falsified, and the frequency distribution of corresponding behaviors in social ecology (Hampson, John, & Goldberg, 1986; Rothbart & Park, 1986). As the stereotype "females are talkative" refers to a more specified class of behaviors than the stereotype "females are emotional," the latter should be more vague to test and falsify than the former, because of the unequal behavioral domains. Likewise, a stereotype referring to an infrequent, abnormal class of behaviors, such as "females are hysterical," is hard to correct because of the paucity of relevant occasions.

Linguistic categories and attribution

Semin and Fiedler's (1988) linguistic category model offers a comprehensive approach to understanding the lexical constraints imposed on interpersonal language. This model applies to verbs and adjectives that can serve the predicate role in sentences. Research in this framework has shown that semantic influences on stereotyping are not confined to trait similarities. Rather, it appears that entire implicit attribution theories are built into the semantics of particular word classes.

The linguistic category model (LCM) distinguishes four levels of abstractness that language offers to describing people and their behavior. *Adjectives* (friendly, dishonest) convey the highest abstractness; they abstract from particular behavioral episodes and from specific object persons and situations. At the second-most abstract level, *state verbs* (trust, detest) still refer to rather enduring states and therefore abstract from single, enumerable acts, but their meaning is already attached to specific object persons (i.e., the persons trusted or detested). Most state verbs refer to covert emotional states, but they can as well refer to cognitive states, or changes of states. *Interpretive action verbs* (to help, to insult) point to intentional actions with a clearly defined beginning and end. Unlike state verbs, the behavioral referents of action verbs are manifest and accessible to direct observation. *Descriptive action verbs* (to look at, to call) constitute the lowest level of abstractness and the highest dependence on contextual information. Whether looking at somebody reflects distrust, interest, or merely attraction, cannot be deduced from the linguistic term but has to be inferred from the context. Unlike interpretative action verbs, descriptive action verbs are defined by at least one physically invariant attribute (e.g., the voice for calling, a pen for writing), and they carry much less dispositional meaning and evaluation.

A summary of the semantic implications of these four classes is given in Table 13.1. When describing the behavior of a target person, abstract terms have stronger implications than specific terms about the subject person's personality, abstract terms suggest more temporal stability over time, but abstract statements suggest less voluntary control than specific statements, and less clear-cut situational references. Abstract statements are therefore more difficult to verify or falsify, and more likely to cause disagreement than specific statements. For example, the same dyadic behavior between Walter and Paul could be described as "Walter shouts at Paul" (specific, descriptive action verb) or "Walter is impulsive" (abstract, adjective). Clearly, the abstract term impulsive appears more informative about Walter, suggests a more stable disposition that exists independently of the situation, but implies less voluntary control (the imperative "Be impulsive!" sounds anomalous) than the former description. In contrast, the meaning of the specific term to shout depends on the concrete situational context. Once the specific term is contextualized (e.g.,

Table 13.1. Taxonomy and Cognitive-Semantic Properties of Linguistic Categories (after Semin & Fiedler, 1988)

Verb class:	Descriptive action verbs	Interpretive action verbs	State verbs	Adjectives
Examples:	• Hit • Look at • Escort	• Attack • Monitor • Guard	• Hate • Distrust • Care	• Aggressive • Suspicious • Protective
Semantic implications:	Contextualized Local, unstable Reference to concrete action	Contextualized Local, evaluative Reference to action category	Decontextualized Stable, enduring Reference to internal state	Decontextualized Stable, general Reference to trait or disposition
Stereotyping implications:	Localization Highly verifiable Non-diagnostic Neutral	Internal causation Verifiable Intentionality Evaluative	External causation Difficult to verify Uncontrollability Emotional	Generalization Hardly verifiable Highly diagnostic Categorical

"Walter shouts at Paul on the soccer field"), the resulting statement becomes clearly verifiable or falsifiable, unlike abstract statements.

Because of these semantic implications, abstract descriptions of social behavior are more likely to suggest strong and stable dispositions in persons and groups than specific descriptions. However, since adjectives and abstract states are detached from specific situations and too vague to be tested critically, they do not invite verification attempts and reality tests. Relative to specific verbs, adjectives are thus relatively immune from falsification and therefore more suitable for inducing and communicating social stereotypes.

Semin and Fiedler (1992) have factor-analyzed the semantic ratings of linguistic categories on the semantic dimensions summarized in Table 13.1. Two dimensions were extracted that can account for the differences between abstract and specific terms. The first dimension contrasts abstract (adjectives) versus specific terms (descriptive action verbs) and represents a *dispositionality factor*, with highest loadings on subject informativeness, temporal stability, and a slightly negative loading on verifiability. The second dimension is *locus of causality*. The extreme poles on this dimension are represented by the two middle categories; interpretive action verbs (e.g., hurt, help) imply a cause within the sentence subject, whereas state verbs (e.g., admire, abhor) imply a cause within the sentence object or situation. This phenomenon of implicit verb causality (Brown & Fish, 1983; Fiedler & Semin, 1988; Rudolph & Försterling, 1997) generalizes over more than 80% of the entire lexicon and over many languages. It is primarily mediated by two semantic properties, emotion and controllability, which receive the highest loadings on the locus of causality dimension. The meaning of action verbs (prevent, influence) implies little emotion but high control in the sentence subject. In contrast, the semantics of state words (fear, desire), entail high subject emotion and little control.

Thus, with regard to social stereotypes, the two dimensions offer two ways in which verbs and adjectives can be used to convey attributions to persons and groups (see empirical evidence in the next section). On the dispositionality dimension, the two extreme categories, adjectives and descriptive action verbs, can be used to highlight either the stable, dispositional nature of some attribute (aggressive, jealous), or its local, unstable, neutral, situational character (to raise hands, to call). And on the locus of causality dimension, action verbs versus state verbs serve to convey the impression that social behavior originates in the sentence subject or object, respectively. Without overtly committing oneself to prejudice and group stereotypes, communicators can use these subtle tools to blame outgroups and excuse ingroup behavior (see next section) or to communicate evaluations without appearing partial (Hamilton, Gibbons, Stroessner, & Sherman, 1992; Maass, Milesi, Zabbini, & Stahlberg, 1995; Maass, Salvi, Arcuri, & Semin, 1989). Conversely, receivers can infer communicated attitudes from the words used to describe target persons (Von Hippel, Sekaquaptewa, & Vargas, 1997).

Since language users are hardly aware of the silent implications of linguistic categories, the stereotype-maintaining function of language is particularly hard to control. Indeed, there is evidence to suggest that the reasons underlying an abstract, adjectival language style are systematically misunderstood. As Wicklund and Braun (1990) have shown, people resort to static, dispositional descriptors suggesting predictability when they feel insecure or incomplete. For instance, when professional lawyers are compared with law students in their beginning semesters, the novices rather than the experts tend to ascribe static (stereo-)typical person descriptors to lawyers – a symptom of immaturity or incompleteness. However, when people are asked to infer others' expertise from their language style, the same static descriptors are mistakenly associated with experts rather than novices.

Consistent findings have been reported by other researchers showing that global, abstract language increases when people are high in need for closure (Rubini & Kruglanski, 1997; Webster, Kruglanski, & Pattison, 1997) or threatened by lethal symbols (Solomon, Greenberg, & Pyszczynski, 1991) and decreases with the familiarity and security of long-term close relationships (Fiedler, Semin, Finkenauer, & Berkel, 1995).

Two word classes serve to convey internal attributions to persons or groups, although for different reasons. *Adjectives* imply maximal dispositionality (stability and globality of attributes), whereas *action verbs* imply internal causation (personal control as opposed to emotional reactions). There is an intriguing analogy between the semantic properties of these two word classes and two major attribution theories. The manner in which adjectives mediate internal attributions reflects Kelley's (1967) attribution model. As indicated in Table 13.1, adjectives imply low consensus (high information about the sentence subject that cannot be generalized over other subjects), low distinctiveness (independence of situations), and high consistency (stability over time). In contrast, the manner in which interpretive action verbs induce internal attributions can be easily explained by Jones and Davis' (1965) correspondent inference model. The semantic properties of interpretive action verbs (hurt, encourage) include ability and intentionality (voluntary control) and an informative effect that is directed at specific goals or objects and cannot be generalized to many other objects (Brown & Fish, 1983). Given this almost perfect congruence with two major attribution theories, the attributional consequences of adjectives and action verbs are hardly surprising.

Evaluative language and accentuation

Stereotyping not only means to attribute dispositions but also to discriminate between different persons or groups. Accordingly, language not only serves an important function in the attribution paradigm but also in the categorization paradigm (Bruner & Goodman, 1947; Eiser & Stroebe, 1972; Tajfel, 1969). As a general rule, two stimuli tend to appear more different if they are associated with different category labels than if they belong to the same category. For example, the difference between permissive versus restrictive educational attitude statements is accentuated (Eiser, 1971) when associated with different newspapers (fictitious labels: *The Messenger* vs. *The Gazette*). Likewise, political attitudes will appear more different when associated with different rather than same party labels, or the same behaviors will appear different when ascribed to different group labels.

Theoretically, this accentuation effect can be explained in terms of informational redundancy. When the task is to rate attitude positions on a judgment scale x, feminism (see Figure 13.1), the discrimination is enhanced when the relevant variable x (i.e., pro-feminist vs. anti-feminist attitudes) is correlated with another variable, y, that can result from a fully irrelevant classification (e.g., by age, race, or arbitrary groups). Consequently, statements not only differ in their attitude toward feminism (pro vs. anti) but also on the correlated dimension (e.g., association with different groups). The redundancy gained from such a superimposed categorization, y, facilitates the discrimination on the judgment dimension x, even when y is fully neutral or nonsensical.

An intriguing and almost universal source of accentuation is evaluation (cf. Eiser & Stroebe, 1972). Thus, for a woman who is herself a decided feminist, pro- and anti-feminist statements (dimension x) will be inevitably correlated with acceptance versus rejection on the valence dimension y, thus leading to accentuation. Therefore, involved feminists discriminate more between pro- and anti-feminist attitudes than people with a neutral attitude (Judd & Johnson, 1981). Accentuation of this kind is clearly relevant to understanding intergroup discrimination.

Most relevant to the role of language is that accentuation is moderated by semantic connotations. Discrimination on the judgment scale increases when the evaluative connotations of the scale labels are compatible with the judge's own attitude (Eiser & Mower-White, 1975; Oakes, Turner, & Haslam, 1991). For example, a pro-feminist judge should polarize more on a scale labeled "tolerant" (pro/positive) versus "narrow-minded" (anti/negative) than on a scale labeled "disloyal" (pro/negative) and "dutiful" (anti/positive). On the latter scale, a feminist's judgment would be deaccentuated. Evaluative language can thus be used, again in a subtle and hardly noticeable fashion, to accentuate or blur behavioral discrimination.

Methods of language analysis and diagnostic tools

The methods of language analysis differ in the unit of analysis as well as in the aspect of language they intend to assess. Some of them originate in straight linguistics while others owe more to social psychology.

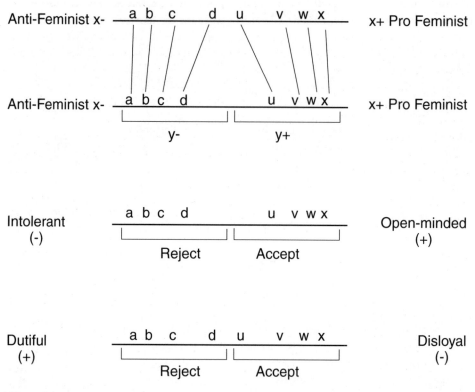

Figure 13.1. Graphical illustration of attitude accentuation. As pro-feminist statements (a, b, c, d) and anti-feminist statements (u, v, w, x) are correlated with different category labels (y− vs. y+), the difference between pro and anti positions is accentuated (upper part). When the judge is herself a feminist (middle part), pro and contra statements are correlated with acceptance vs. rejection. However, the resulting accentuation effect is reduced when the connotations of the judgment scale (+ vs. −) are incompatible with the judge's evaluative reactions (reject vs. accept; see bottom part).

A major part of language research uses content analytic methods (Holsti, 1968). Categories are developed that capture formal or thematic aspects of texts. One of the smallest possible text unit is individual words. If a lexicon of relevant words can be established beforehand, computer programs can be used to scan a text corpus, thus lightening the burden of the investigator, increasing coding objectivity and, due to the opportunity to scan large samples, enhancing the statistical power and reliability. Content-analytic methods can be used to establish contingencies, as for example between the co-occurrence of ingroup and outgroup references and evaluative adjectives. Such methods are often used to analyze samples from news media reports or TV shows. Their scope also encompasses long-term changes in language use, operationalized as an increase or decrease of relative frequencies of instances.

Greenwald, McGhee, and Schwartz (1998) have recently proposed the Implicit Association Test (IAT), a measure of stereotypes that is also located at the word level but that is sensitive to stereotypical word meanings in memory rather than the manifestation of words in text. It utilizes the compatibility principle that was already introduced in the above section on accentuation. The aim is to assess the latencies required to categorize stimulus words, using two response keys. For example, when applying the IAT to sexist stereotypes, respondents first have to assign female Christian names to the left response key and male names to the right response key. Then they have to assign negative attributes to the left key (previously associated with female) and positive attributes to the right key (previously associated with male). Then the respondents are presented with combined lists including female and male names as well as negative and positive attributes in alternating order. Assuming an anti-female stereotype, sorting response latencies should be faster in the compatible condition, when female names and negative attributes as well as male and positive terms have to be assigned to the same response key, than in an incompatible condition, where female and positive terms and male and negative terms have to be assigned to the same response keys. The IAT has been applied to measure sexist and ethnic stereotypes (see Greenwald et al., 1998). Its heuristic appeal arises from the fact that it assesses an implicit aspect of stereotypical language (Lepore & Brown, 1997) rather than overt attitudes that can be controlled and corrected voluntarily.

Other language-analytic methods are not confined to lexical units but also use syntactical and pragmatical information. The linguistic category model (LCM; Semin & Fiedler, 1988) described previously is still based on words (predicates), but it classifies these words by syntactical categories rather than semantic meaning. Categorization by thematic rather than syntactic units is characteristic of Vallacher and Wegner's (1987) action identification theory. In this method of content analysis, descriptions of actions on a low level (giving the mechanical details) are distinguished from behaviors identified on a high level (the action's effect and implications).

Firmly in opposition to frequency analytic methods is discourse analysis. It treats language as reflexive, performative, and constructive (Edwards & Potter, 1992; Potter & Wetherell, 1987). Language is seen as not purely descriptive but as goal-directed. To understand discourse, expectations and interventions of the listener have to be taken into account. As discourse is strongly dependent on the context and the interaction goals, large intersituational as well as intraindividual variance must be expected.

These selected methods can be arranged on several dimensions: From word analysis to discourse, the recording unit size increases, as well as the control attributed to the sender over his/her language production. Also, the anticipated expectations of the recipient play an increasing role. The more complex the recording unit gets, the more interpretative effort is needed on the part of the researcher. This disadvantage is partly compensated by the advantage that larger recording units allow for richer and more context-sensitive coding.

How Rules of Language Use Affect the Stereotyping Process

The connection of language use and stereotypes can be constructed from two vantage points: (1) Stereotypes have implications for the way social groups communicate with each other. (2) Taking language as a starting point, communication rules can strengthen existing stereotypes.

The linguistic intergroup bias

When people describe the behavior of ingroup and outgroup members, systematic differences can be observed. The most prominent findings regarding implicit attributions of dispositionality come from Maass' and her colleagues' research on the linguistic intergroup bias (LIB; Maass, Salvi, Arcuri, & Semin, 1989). Their analyses demonstrate a tendency to describe positive ingroup behaviors and negative outgroup behaviors in more abstract terms than negative ingroup and positive outgroup behaviors. Similar results were obtained by Fiedler, Semin, and Finkenauer (1993) in males' and females' descriptions of male and female behavior. These findings lend themselves to an explanation in terms of an ingroup serving bias, or striving for positive ingroup identity (Tajfel & Turner, 1986). A global negative evaluation keeps the outgroup at its (inferior) place and ensures the necessary distance, while discounting negative ingroup behavior as local and context-dependent.

Apart from ingroup–outgroup differences, cooperative and informative communication is characterized by a general tendency to abstract from concrete details and to provide interpretations and evaluations beyond mere descriptions (Fiedler, Semin, & Bolten, 1989). The degree of this general abstraction tendency increases with the amount of shared knowledge. A related result is reported by Maass, Montalcini, and Biciotti (1998): The earlier in history a stereotype came into being, the more abstract is its description. A shift toward concreteness should occur, however, when the validity of statements is challenged (thus questioning the common ground) or when concrete language helps to communicate personal interests (Rubini & Kruglanski, 1997).

The tendency to communicate expected, commonly shared knowledge in abstract terms raises an alternative interpretation of the LIB. Most of the time, positive ingroup behavior and negative outgroup behavior are more in line with prior expectations than negative ingroup and positive outgroup behavior. However, when expectedness and group-serving biases are pitted against each other, the former overrides the latter. That is, when describing ingroups on negative but stereotypically expected dimensions, descriptions tend to be abstract rather than concrete. Thus, the basic variant of the LIB can be understood as a completely normal instance of cooperative language use, without any discriminative intention: What is already known can be said in general terms, but the unexpected and surprising must be particularized.

Intergroup perspective and actor-observer biases

In accordance with the general phenomenon of an actor-observer bias (Jones & Nisbett, 1972; Watson, 1982), behavior is more readily attributed to stable dispositions or traits from the perspective of an outgroup observer than from the actor's own ingroup perspective (Fiedler et al., 1993). This finding holds for the intergroup as well as the interpersonal domain, as evident in attributions of one's own and one's partner's behavior (Fiedler, Semin, & Koppetsch, 1991; Fiedler et al., 1995).

Mass communication

The mass media have been credited with an important role in the process of socialization and political attitude formation. Especially in magazines and TV, stereotypical depictions of minority groups and women have for a long time been an issue of heated discussions. It is feared that particularly children and adolescents are susceptible to these influences. Many content analytic studies have addressed the stereotypic contamination of media information. For instance, in an analysis of Italian newspapers, Maass, Corvino, and Arcuri (1994) have shown that the description of an anti-Semitic episode during a basketball game differed markedly between Jewish and non-Jewish newspapers. Non-Jewish newspapers used less abstract words to describe anti-Semitic aggression (implying less internal, dispositional attributions).

Language use in the legal system

The attribution of guilt (or innocence) is part of the professional work of lawyers in court. Whereas the prosecution does argue from an outgroup position when referring to the defendant, the defense closes ranks with the defendant with the ultimate goal to influence the jury to see this person as a person much like themselves, as a member of the ingroup. Examining a witness gives attorneys unique opportunities to discredit witnesses and plant impressions in the jury. Closing speeches are the last chance of the two parties, prosecution and defense, to sway the jury or to immunize them against the arguments of the legal adversary. Keeping the semantic properties of word classes in mind, several strategies suggest themselves: (a) The causality-dimension (viz., the choice between interpretive action verbs and state verbs) can be used to attribute blame to other agents or even the victim. (b) Using the abstractness-dimension (adjectives), the behavior of the alleged perpetrator can be attributed to stable traits or situational pressures. (c) The abstractness-dimension also controls the attribution of credibility of the argument, for dispositional statements are hard to verify and may reduce a communication's credibility. When talking about linguistic strategies in the legal context, it is important not to misunderstand the word "'strategy'" as implying consciousness. It only denotes a systematic use of linguistic categories that can be linked with attributional consequences.

An analysis of protocols of the Nuremberg Trials (Schmid & Fiedler, 1996) and an experimental study with lawyers-in-training giving closing speeches for the defense and for the prosecution (Schmid & Fiedler, 1998) support these expectations. The defendant is on trial because of assumed negative actions that can be described concretely (e.g., defendant took victim's purse, descriptive action verb). The prosecution can try to imply dispositionality (the defendant is greedy, adjective), but since abstract statements are hard to verify, they prefer to apply the alternative strategy to induce internal attributions using interpretative action verbs (defendant stole from victim), suggesting intentionality and voluntary control. In comparison, the defense must try to downplay and distract from the typically negative behavior of the defendant in a criminal trial. As concrete positive terms are not applicable, they have to resort either to rather abstract, vague positive predicates (defendant is a responsible citizen) or to negative state verbs which suggest external causes or excuses for negative behavior (defendant detested victim). Moreover, the subject phrases of defense attorneys' statements often avoid direct references to the defendant and instead refer to co-defendants or fuzzy groups as a means of shifting blame and attributional focus.

The videotapes of the final speeches given by the lawyers-in-training were shown to laypersons who had to act in the capacity of a jury member. Their subsequent decisions were significantly influenced by language features (Schmid & Fiedler, 1998).

Stereotypes and the verbal interaction process

Someone who reads a paper or watches a TV show has only limited possibilities to interact with the sender, and a jury member has to listen to the arguments put forth by the lawyers. In contrast to this one-sided information flow, intergroup affairs are normally embedded in a dynamic interaction process that conveys symbolic meaning and emotional signs in multiple ways.

Speech accommodation. It is a well-known phenomenon that speakers adjust their speech style to converge with or to diverge from their communication partners' style. The more effort they put in converging, the more favorably are they evaluated so that the listeners also start to converge (communication accommodation theory; Giles & Coupland, 1991). Accommodation takes place not only in speech, but also in paralinguistic and extralinguistic behavior. One of the functions of accommodation is identity maintenance. If someone converges with an outgroup member, he/she demonstrates a desire for integration, whereas divergence underscores social distance. In a similar vein, dialects and accents can improve or worsen the evaluation of the speaker. Nonstandard dialects may lead to the inference of incompetence and low social status (Ng & Bradac, 1993).

In the first part of this chapter, sexist language was introduced as an example of the way language as a system can further stereotypes. The socialization of gender roles not only consists of the learning of connotations and denotations of gender related vocabulary, but also includes gender differences in communicative behavior. Communication styles of men and women are expected to differ and exceptions may not be tolerated and may lead to negative impressions of the speaker (Mulac, Lundell, & Bradac, 1986). So-called female speech patterns have strong similarities to powerless speech, which not only gives the speaker a lesser chance to hold her own in an argument, but also raises a general impression of indecisiveness and weakness (O'Barr, 1982). Both the lexical and the conversational features of gender-related language can be interpreted as routinely used measures of intergroup control (Ng, 1990).

The communication game. In contrast to communication approaches that focus on the encoding and decoding of message contents, other theories propose that the meaning of a message is negotiated between participants in conversation. Communication can be described as a game with rules, roles, and goals (communication game; Higgins, 1981). The rules reflect conventions of language use that have to be followed to achieve the desired effect. Of major importance is the tuning to the audience's expectations. An already familiar example of social tuning is that information that is quite well known to the audience will be conveyed on an abstract level.

Of course, skillfully excluding an audience to indicate distance is also an option in this game. Here the communication game approach converges with communication accommodation theory. However, communication game theory has a distinct link to social cognition: What and how speakers communicate not only determines the information conveyed to recipients but also affects the speakers' own memory (Wyer & Gruenfeld, 1995). Higgins and Rholes (1978) demonstrated that senders who were asked to convey a description of a target person to an audience that either liked or disliked the target not only tuned their message in a way that fit the evaluative expectations, but the senders' own subsequent impressions of the target person reflected the evaluative bias.

The question-answering paradigm. In verbal interaction, the answers (given by politicians, patients, or applicants) are determined to a considerable degree by the questions asked (of journalists, diagnosticians, or personnel managers). This is the empirical message of the question-answering paradigm (Rubini & Kruglanski, 1997; Semin & Marsman, 1994; Semin, Rubini, & Fiedler, 1995). For instance, a teacher might ask a female student "Why did you *choose* physics as a major?" (using an action verb) or, alternatively, "Why do you *like* physics as a major?" (using a state verb). As noted above, action verbs trigger knowledge structures that induce internal attributions to the subject whereas state verbs induce external attributions. These knowledge structures give rise to systematically different answers. Answers to the "choose" question will typically refer to the respondent's own internal motives, goals, or talents. In contrast, answers to the "like" question will point to external factors, such as assets of the discipline, physics. Moreover, as state verbs are more abstract than action verbs, answers to state-verb questions will tend to be more abstract than answers to action-verb questions. The answers then can strengthen the attributions that already shaped the questions.

What are the psychological processes underlying this self-fulfilling circle? On the one hand, verbal interaction is generally affirmative (Snyder, 1984; Zuckerman, Knee, Hodgins, & Miyake, 1995), that is, conversation relies on a silent contract to cooperate with conversation partners' goals, which means to acquiesce most of the time. Thus, whether the question refers to advantages or disadvantages of a political party, either question will elicit a tendency to comply with the language game (i.e., let's talk about assets vs. deficits), and to find an affirmative answer for both suggestions.

On the other hand, the respondent may take the very fact that the question asks for advantages rather than disadvantages as conjectural evidence (Snyder, 1984) that the interviewer has relevant background information. And similarly, the response alternatives offered in questionnaires or interviews may serve as cues or demands as to appropriate answers (Schwarz, 1996).

Automatic processes. Language forces people to step into the shoes of their predecessors and even walk a bit in the direction they took. Language use is partly routinized, without conscious effort or intent on the part of the individual, and the processes as well as their results are sometimes beyond the individual's control. In particular, trait inferences from behaviors occur spontaneously and independently of explicit goals or intentions (Newman & Uleman, 1989; Uleman, 1987).

Inference processes start with observed behavior and (sometimes) end up with stereotypes. These stereotypical concepts can in turn induce manifest behavior. Simple words presented incidentally or even subliminally can elicit subsequent actions, as many recent priming studies show. For example, priming the social category of the elderly can reduce the walking speed of people who are fully unaware of this influence (Bargh, Chen, & Burrows, 1996), and priming of the stereotype "professor" can increase performance on general knowledge tasks (Dijksterhuis & Van Knippenberg, 1998). Even the priming of ingroup or outgroup pronouns ("us" vs. "them") can be used to influence evaluative judgments (Perdue, Dovidio, Gurtman, & Tyler, 1990).

The priming paradigm attempts to quantify stereotypes as reaction time gains. It is not exactly clear, though, what is measured with such instruments. Their proponents hold that automatic associations are implicit indicators of stereotypical knowledge and prejudices. A more skeptical account would be that these methods assess associative strength of concepts, but not necessarily the individual's belief in those stereotypes nor their behavioral dispositions.

Summary and Conclusion

The first part of this chapter was concerned with the various constraints that language as a system places on the way in which stereotype-relevant information can be conveyed in verbal communication. Apart from lexical, morphological, syntactic, and pragmatic constraints, the present section was mainly concerned with semantic influences on social stereotypes. Semantic similarities between trait terms lead to an overestimation of the actual correlation between traits, and the breadth of the related behavioral domain as well as the valence of the attribute have an impact on the possibility to verify and falsify a stereotype. Several techniques for the investigation of such semantic constraints on interpersonal language were presented.

The second part of this chapter dealt with the impact of language use on the stereotyping process. Several language approaches to stereotype formation and consolidation were introduced that can be ordered along a dimension of controllability. Theories of automatic processes in stereotype formation are located at the low-controllability end of this dimension, which is of central importance for understanding stereotype maintenance and change (see Brewer & Gaertner this volume, chapter 22; Rothbart, this volume, chapter 3). Subtle language effects are so important because they evade the conscious attention and control of language users.

The enhanced accessibility of stereotypical word meanings and associations constitutes an essential aspect of semantic knowledge. However, this knowledge should be neither confused with the belief that a stereotype is true nor with actual discriminating behavior toward the target group or person. Nevertheless, as the present chapter has shown, there is a growing body of evidence which suggests that semantic, syntactic, and pragmatic factors can have notable influences on attitudes, judgments, and manifest behaviors.

References

Bales, R. F. (1950). A set of categories for the analysis of small group interactions. *American Sociological Review, 15*, 257–263.

Bargh, J. A., Chen, M., & Burrows, L. (1996). Automaticity of social behavior. Direct effects of trait construct and stereotype activation on action. *Journal of Personality and Social Psychology, 71*, 230–244.

Blair, I. V., & Banaji, M. R. (1996). Automatic and controlled processes in stereotype priming. *Journal of Personality and Social Psychology, 70*, 1142–1163.

Bolinger, D. (1973). Truth is a linguistic question. *Language, 49*, 539–550.

Brigham, J. C. (1971). Ethnic stereotypes. *Psychological Review, 76*, 15–38.

Brown, R., & Fish, D. (1983). The psychological causality implicit in language. *Cognition, 14*, 233–274.

Bruner, J. S., & Goodman, C. D. (1947). Value and need as organizing factors in perception. *Journal of Abnormal and Social Psychology, 42*, 33–44.

D'Andrade, R. L. (1974). Memory and the assessment of behavior. In H. M. Block, Jr. (Ed.), *Measurement in the social sciences*. Chicago, IL: Aldine.

De Saussure, F. (1915). *Cours de linguistique générale*. Paris: Payot.

Dijksterhuis, A., & van Knippenberg, A. (1998). The relation between perception and behavior, or how to win a game of Trivial Pursuit. *Journal of Personality and Social Psychology, 74*, 865–877.

Dovidio, J. F., & Gaertner, S. L. (1986) (Eds.), *Prejudice, discrimination, and racism*. San Diego, CA: Academic Press.

Edwards, D., & Potter, J. (1992). *Discursive psychology*. Newbury Park, CA: Sage.

Eiser, J. R. (1971). Enhancement of contrast in the absolute judgment of attitude statements. *Journal of Personality and Social Psychology, 17*, 1–10.

Eiser, J. R., & Mower-White, C. J. (1975). Categorization and congruity in attitudinal judgment. *Journal of Personality and Social Psychology, 31*, 769–775.

Eiser, J. R., & Stroebe, W. (1972). *Categorization and social judgment*. London: Academic Press.

Fazio, R. H., Sanbonmatsu, D. M., Powell, M. C., & Kardes, F. R. (1986). On the automatic activation of attitudes. *Journal of Personality and Social Psychology, 50*, 229–238.

Fiedler, K., & Semin, G. R. (1988). On the causal information conveyed by different interpersonal verbs. *Social Cognition, 6*, 21–39.

Fiedler, K., Semin, G. R., & Bolten, S. (1989). Language use and reification of social information: Top-down and bottom-up processing in person cognition. *European Journal of Social Psychology, 19*, 271–295.

Fiedler, K., Semin, G. R., & Finkenauer, C. (1993). The battle of words between gender groups: A language-based approach to intergroup processes. *Human Communication Research 19*, 409–441.

Fiedler, K., Semin, G. R., Finkenauer, C., & Berkel, I. (1995). Actor-observer bias in close relationships: The role of self-knowledge and self-related language. *Personality and Social Psychology Bulletin, 21*, 525–538.

Fiedler, K., Semin, G. R., & Koppetsch, C. (1991). Language use and attributional biases in close personal relationships. *Personality and Social Psychology Bulletin, 17*, 147–155.

Gardner, R. C., Taylor, D. M., & Feenstra, H. J. (1970). Ethnic stereotypes: Attitudes or beliefs? *Canadian Journal of Psychology, 24*, 321–334.

Gidron, D., Koehler, D. J., & Tversky, A. (1993). Implicit quantification of personality traits. *Personality and Social Psychology Bulletin, 19*, 594–604.

Giles, H., & Coupland, N. (1991). *Language: Contexts and consequences.* Oxford, UK: Open University Press.

Glucksberg, S., & Danks, J. H. (1975). *Experimental psycholinguistics: An introduction.* Hillsdale, NJ: Erlbaum.

Greenwald, A. G., McGhee, D. E., & Schwartz, J. L. K. (1998). Measuring individual differences in implicit cognition: The implicit association test. *Journal of Personality and Social Psychology, 74*, 1464–1480.

Grice, H. P. (1975). Logic of conversation. In P. Cole & J. L. Morgan (Eds.), *Syntax and semantics* (Vol. 3: Speech acts, pp. 41–58). New York: Academic Press.

Hamilton, D. L., Gibbons, P. A., Stroessner, S. J., & Sherman, J. W. (1992). Stereotypes and language use. In G. R. Semin & K. Fiedler (Eds.), *Language, interaction, and social cognition* (pp. 102–128). London: Sage.

Hamilton, D. L., & Rose, R. L. (1980). Illusory correlation and the maintenance of stereotypic beliefs. *Journal of Personality and Social Psychology, 39*, 832–845.

Hampson, S. E., John, O. P., & Goldberg, L. R. (1986). Category breadth and hierarchical structure in personality: Studies of asymmetries in judgments of trait implications. *Journal of Personality and Social Psychology, 51*, 37–54.

Henley, N. M., Miller, M., & Beazley, J.-A. (1995). Syntax, semantics, and sexual violence: Agency and the passive voice. *Journal of Language and Social Psychology, 14*, 60–84.

Higgins, E. T. (1981). The "communication game": Implications for social cognition and persuasion. In E. T. Higgins, C. P. Herman, & M. P. Zanna (Eds.), *Social cognition: The Ontario symposium* (pp. 343–392). Hillsdale, NJ: Erlbaum.

Higgins, E. T., & Rholes, W. J. (1978). "Saying is believing": Effects of message modification on memory and liking for the person described. *Journal of Experimental Social Psychology, 14*, 363–378.

Hobden, K. L., & Olson, J. M. (1994). From jest to antipathy: Disparagement humor as a source of dissonance-motivated attitude chance. *Basic and Applied Social Psychology, 15*, 239–249.

Hoffman, C., & Hurst, N. (1990). Gender stereotypes: Perception or rationalization? *Journal of Personality and Social Psychology, 58*, 197–208.

Holsti, O. R. (1968). Content analysis. In G. Lindzey & E. Aronson (Eds.), *The handbook of social psychology* (2nd ed., Vol. 2, pp. 596–692). Reading, MA: Addison-Wesley.

Jones, E. E., & Davis, K. E. (1965). From acts to dispositions: The attribution process in person perception. In L. Berkowitz (Ed.), *Advances of experimental social psychology* (Vol. 2). New York: Academic Press.

Jones, E. E., & Nisbett, R. E. (1972). The actor and the observer: Divergent perceptions of the causes of behavior. In E. E. Jones et al. (Eds.), *Attribution: Perceiving the causes of behavior* (pp. 79–94). Morristown, NJ: General Learning Press.

Judd, C. M., & Johnson, J. T. (1981). Attitudes, polarization, and diagnosticity: Exploring the effect of affect. *Journal of Personality and Social Psychology, 41*, 26–36.

Kelley, H. H. (1967). Attribution theory in social psychology. In D. Levine (Ed.), *Nebraska symposium on motivation* (Vol. 15, pp. 192–238). Lincoln: University of Nebraska Press.

Lepore, L., & Brown, R. (1997). Category and stereotype activation: Is prejudice inevitable? *Journal of Personality and Social Psychology, 72*, 275–287.

Mackie, D. M., & Hamilton, D. L. (1993). *Affect, cognition, and stereotyping: Interaction processes in group perception.* New York: Academic Press.

Maass, A., Corvino, P., & Arcuri, L. (1994). Linguistic intergroup bias and the mass media. *Revue de Psychologie Sociale, 1*, 31–43.

Maass, A., Milesi, A., Zabbini, S., & Stahlberg, D. (1995). Linguistic intergroup bias: Differential expectancies or in-group protection? *Journal of Personality and Social Psychology*, *68*, 116–126.

Maass, A., Montalcini, F., & Biciotti, E. (1998). On the (dis)-confirmability of stereotypic attitudes. *European Journal of Social Psychology*, *28*, 383–402.

Maass, A., Salvi, D., Arcuri, L., & Semin, G. R. (1989). Language use in intergroup contexts: The linguistic intergroup bias. *Journal of Personality and Social Psychology*, *57*, 981–993.

McCauley, C., & Stitt, C. L. (1978). An individual and quantitative measure of stereotypes. *Journal of Personality and Social Psychology*, *36*, 929–940.

Mulac, A., Lundell, T. L., & Bradac, J. J. (1986). Male/female language differences and attributional consequences in a public speaking setting: Toward an explanation of the gender-linked language effect. *Communication Monographs*, *53*, 115–129.

Newman, L. S., & Uleman, J. S. (1989). Spontaneous trait inference. In J. S. Uleman & J. A. Bargh (Eds.), *Unintended thought* (pp. 155–188). New York: Guilford Press.

Ng, S. H. (1990). Language and control. In H. Giles & W. P. Robinson (Eds.), *Handbook of language and social psychology* (pp. 271–285). Chichester, UK: Wiley.

Ng, S. H., & Bradac, J. J. (1993). *Power in language*. Newbury Park, CA: Sage.

Oakes, P. J., Turner, J. C., & Haslam, S. A. (1991). Perceiving people as group members: The role of fit in the salience of social categorizations. *British Journal of Social Psychology*, *30*, 125–144.

O'Barr, W. M. (1982). *Linguistic evidence: Language, power, and strategy in the courtroom*. New York: Academic Press.

Perdue, C. W., Dovidio, J. F., Gurtman, M. B., & Tyler, R. B. (1990), Us and them: Categorization and the process of intergroup bias. *Journal of Personality and Social Psychology*, *59*, 475–486.

Potter, J., & Wetherell, M. (1987). *Discourse and social psychology: Beyond attitudes and behaviour*. London: Sage.

Reeder, G. D., & Brewer, M. B. (1979). A schematic model of dispositional attribution in interpersonal perception. *Psychological Review*, *86*, 61–79.

Rothbart, M., & Park, B. (1986). On the confirmability and disconfirmability of trait concepts. *Journal of Personality and Social Psychology*, *50*, 131–142.

Rubini, M., & Kruglanski, A. W. (1997). Brief encounters ending in estrangement: Motivated language use and interpersonal rapport in the question-answer paradigm. *Journal of Personality and Social Psychology*, *72*, 1047–1060.

Rudolph, U., & Försterling, F. (1997). The psychological causality implicit in verbs: A review. *Psychological Bulletin*, *121*, 192–218.

Schmid, J., & Fiedler, K. (1996). Language and implicit attributions in the Nuremberg trials: Analyzing prosecutors' and defense attorneys' final speeches. *Human Communications Research*, *22*, 371–398.

Schmid, J., & Fiedler, K. (1998). The backbone of closing speeches: The impact of prosecution versus defense language on juridical attributions. *Journal of Applied Social Psychology*, *28*, 1140–1172.

Schwarz, N. (1996). Survey research: Collecting data by asking questions. In G. R. Semin & K. Fiedler (Eds.), *Applied social psychology* (pp. 65–90). London: Sage.

Semin, G. R., & Fiedler, K. (1988). The cognitive functions of linguistic categories in describing persons: Social cognition and language. *Journal of Personality and Social Psychology*, *54*, 558–568.

Semin, G. R., & Fiedler, K. (1992). The inferential properties of interpersonal verbs. In G. R. Semin & K. Fiedler (Eds.), *Language, interaction and social cognition* (pp. 58–78). London: Sage.

Semin, G. R., & Marsman, G. (1994). On the information mediated by interpersonal verbs: Event precipitation, dispositional inference, and implicit causality. *Journal of Personality and Social Psychology*, *67*, 836–849.

Semin, G. R., Rubini, M., & Fiedler, K. (1995). The answer is in the question: The effect of verb causality on locus of explanation. *Personality and Social Psychology Bulletin, 21*, 834–841.

Shweder, R. A. (1975). How relevant is an individual difference theory of personality? *Journal of Personality, 43*, 455–484.

Shweder, R. A. (1982). Fact and artifact in trait perception: The systematic distortion hypothesis. In B. A. Maher & W. B. Maher (Eds.), *Progress in experimental personality research* (Vol. 2). New York: Academic Press.

Skowronski, N. J., & Carlston, D. E. (1989). Negativity and extremity biases in impression formation: A review of explanations. *Psychological Bulletin, 105*, 131–142.

Snyder, M. (1984). When belief creates reality. *Advances in Experimental Social Psychology, 18*, 247–305.

Solomon, S., Greenberg, J., & Pyszczynski, T. (1991). A terror management theory of social behavior: The psychological functions of self-esteem and cultural world views. In M. P. Zanna (Ed.), *Advances in Experimental Social Psychology, 24*, 93–157.

Tajfel, H. (1969). Cognitive aspects of prejudice. *Journal of Social Issues, 25*, 79–97.

Tajfel, H. (1970). Experiments in intergroup discrimination. *Scientific American, 223*, 96–102.

Tajfel, H., & Turner, C. J. (1986). The social identity theory of intergroup behavior. In S. Worchel & W. G. Austin (Eds.), *Psychology of intergroup relations*. Chicago, IL: Nelson-Hall.

Uleman, J. S. (1987). Consciousness and control: The case of spontaneous trait inferences. *Personality and Social Psychology Bulletin, 13*, 337–354.

Von Hippel, W., Sekaquaptewa, D., & Vargas, P. (1997). The linguistic intergroup bias as an implicit indicator of prejudice. *Journal of Experimental Social Psychology, 33*, 490–509.

Vallacher, R., & Wegner, D. M. (1987). What do people think they're doing? Action identification and human behavior. *Psychological Review, 94*, 3–15.

Watson, D. (1982). The actor and the observer: How are their perceptions of causality divergent? *Psychological Bulletin, 92*, 682–700.

Webster, D. N., Kruglanski, A. W., & Pattison, D. A. (1997). Motivated language use in intergroup context: Need-for-closure effects on the linguistic intergroup bias. *Journal of Personality and Social Psychology, 72*, 1122–1131.

Wicklund, R. A., & Braun, O. L. (1990). Creating consistency among pairs of traits: A bridge from social psychology to trait psychology. *Journal of Experimental Social Psychology, 26*, 545–558.

Wittenbrink, B., Judd, C. M., & Park, B. (1997). Evidence for racial prejudice at the implicit level and its relationship with questionnaire measures. *Journal of Personality and Social Psychology, 72*, 262–274.

Wyer, R. S. Jr., & Gruenfeld, D. H. (1995). Information processing in social contexts: Implications for social memory and judgment. *Advances in Experimental Social Psychology, 27*, 49–91.

Zuckerman, M., Knee, C. R., Hodgins, H. S., & Miyake, K. (1995). Hypothesis confirmation: The joint effect of positive test strategy and acquiescence response set. *Journal of Personality and Social Psychology, 68*, 52–60.

CHAPTER FOURTEEN

Social Influence in an Intergroup Context

Diane M. Mackie and Crystal L. Wright

Thirty, forty, or fifty years ago, a chapter on this topic would never have had this chapter's title. As the discipline of social psychology was first taking shape, persuasion, attitude change, and influence were all considered so inherently social that to specify the group context for such activity would have been to state the obvious. The earliest social psychology research on these issues had its roots in the concept of suggestion, the acceptance of influence based on social and emotional ties (LeBon, 1896). From Allport's (1924) concept of conformity as submission to the group, through Sherif's (1936) description of social norms, to Hyman's (1942) notion of the reference group, attitude and opinion change were seen as firmly rooted in the nexus of social relationships. Today, however, specifying the intergroup context of social influence in the title of this chapter may have more added value.

First, the study of influence in the intervening decades has moved away from a concern with its social determinants toward a concern with its cognitive determinants. Keeping the intergroup context in focus thus reminds us that cognitive processing cannot occur in a social vacuum. Even when researchers are unconcerned with such issues, message recipients no doubt make assumptions about the group membership of message sources.

Second, such a focus may highlight the need to explore the differences, if any, that occur in persuasion as a function of salience of an *intragroup* versus an *intergroup* context. If message recipients with no information about a source assume his or her shared group membership, the study of persuasion without regard for the intergroup context is in fact the study of intragroup persuasion. As we note below, much to the credit of social identity theories of social influence, there is now some empirical base from which to draw conclusions about influence in an intergroup context.

In discussing influence in an intergroup context, we are concerned with the processes mediating the private *acceptance* of attitudes or opinions. Intragroup and intergroup

We acknowledge the support of award SBR 9507628 from the National Science Foundation to Diane M. Mackie and a National Science Foundation Graduate Fellowship to Crystal L. Wright.

processes that produce mere *compliance* (advocacy-consistent action unmatched by advocacy-consistent attitude change) are not our focus (Asch, 1951; Deutsch & Gerard, 1955; Festinger, 1953; Moscovici, 1980). Instead we focus on the variety of mechanisms that cause privately accepted change in attitudes or opinions as a result of receiving a communication from either an ingroup or an outgroup member. We use the general term "group-mediated influence" for situations in which the social relationship between the source and recipient plays a significant role in attitudinal outcomes. Of course, as the literature on reference groups taught us many decades ago, an individual's social psychological identification may not correspond to his or her actual group memberships (Hyman, 1942; Tajfel & Turner, 1986; Turner, 1982). That is, relationships between the perceiver and source are in the eye of the recipient.

This chapter has six main sections. In the second section, we briefly review the history of research and theories that focus on the importance of group membership for effecting influence. In reviewing these early theories, we note a strange irony. Most of this early work was solidly grounded in the assumption that influence was absolutely dependent upon social identifications. The impact of social group memberships had to be understood, therefore, as a precursor to understanding influence, regardless of the nature of more proximal determinants of such change. At the same time, however, the contemporary theories of group influence that underpinned this early work encouraged distinctions between types of influence that encouraged almost total neglect during the 1960s and 1970s of the mechanisms responsible for group-based attitude or opinion change.

Thus, it was not until some two decades later that theorists and researchers returned to a more explicit investigation of group-mediated influence. They were spurred on in this enterprise by the development of cognitive paradigms that allowed the assessment of mediational processes, as well as by the growth and acceptance of social identity theory, which re-asserted the centrality of membership concerns to social influence. Research spawned by these two approaches has provided the most systematic view thus far of the mechanisms that underlie intragroup and intergroup influence. This is the research reviewed in the third, fourth, and fifth sections of the chapter. We will review first processing approaches that have focused explicitly on manipulations of ingroup and outgroup membership and measures of the mechanisms by which any resultant change occurred. Second, self-categorization approaches to intergroup influence will be discussed, as these approaches extended social identity theory to focus on the influential effects of categorization itself and of ingroups as compared to outgroups. As noted above, studies in this tradition have also been most likely to assess the impact of manipulations of the salience of the intergroup context on social influence. Third, we will comment on the burgeoning interest in majority and minority influence processes provoked by Moscovici's (1980) conversion theory, which produced a body of research with clear implications for influence in an intergroup context.

Finally, in the sixth section, we draw some conclusions about the nature of privately accepted change in attitudes and opinions that occurs in an intergroup context, and, on the basis of this review, comment on influence more generally. In particular, we argue that this body of literature makes very clear the need to return to more explicit consideration of the social context of all influence processes, even those processes that appear cognitive in nature. As Eugene Hartley (1950–51, p. 670) put it more than 40 years ago, "attitudes and opinions . . . can only be fully understood if we explore the relation of the individual to the group represented by the opinion. . . ."

Intergroup Influence in Historical Perspective

In 1936, Muzafer Sherif demonstrated the powerful effect of social standards of reference on an individual's perception of the world. Participants converged on, and retained, a judgment about the illusory movement of a single point of light (an autokinetic effect) that reflected the views expressed by others also exposed to the light. The substantial persuasive impact of membership groups as social standards of reference was confirmed in 1943, when Theodore Newcomb demonstrated the powerful effect that fellow students had on the politics of the freshman class at Bennington College. Of particular importance was Newcomb's finding that the students' attitudes reflected the opinion of groups they *psychologically* identified with rather than demographically belonged to (Sherif, 1948).

Newcomb's results were nicely consistent with reference group theory (Hyman, 1942; Merton, 1957), a concept that had been invoked to help explain why people did not always assimilate to the opinions of groups to which they apparently belonged. Instead, attitudes seemed to be a function of the groups with which individuals "affiliated" and with the "degree and permanence of that affiliation" (Murphy, Murphy, & Newcomb, 1937). For reference group theorists, the important point – a point repeated by social identity theorists much more recently (Turner, 1982) – was that the groups with which an individual identified (his or her social standards of reference) could not be imputed arbitrarily.

With the concept of reference groups gaining popularity, theorists turned to the question of what mechanisms might underlie the persuasive power of such groups. Several approaches are relevant and had particular impact: the concept of group attraction (Festinger, 1950, 1953, 1954), further development of reference group concepts (Kelley, 1952; Siegel & Siegel, 1957), and Deutsch and Gerard's (1955) analysis of social influence. Despite theoretical differences, these dual process approaches were remarkably similar in postulating two routes by which ingroups might effect change.

Festinger (1950, 1954), for example, suggested that relevant groups could achieve conformity because they helped define social reality, providing a gauge for the appropriateness of their members' responses. But he also argued that groups exercise pressure toward conformity to reach group goals, and that conformity resulting from this pressure often reflected change in the *expression* of beliefs and behaviors unaccompanied by their actual *acceptance*.

Kelley (1952) drew a similar distinction about the function of reference groups. According to Kelley, reference groups can fulfill either a comparative function that helps the individual to evaluate his or her attributes and environment or a normative function through which the individual merely aligns his or her own values and beliefs with those of the reference group. Such a distinction was soon echoed by Deutsch and Gerard (1955). They contrasted informational influence, in which the desire for accuracy leads individuals to rely on groups for information about objective reality, with normative influence, in which group members comply with social pressure to achieve rewards or avoid punishments (see also informational and effect dependence, Jones & Gerard, 1967).

One important conclusion that might have been drawn from this remarkable similarity among theories was that group membership could effect influence through multiple mechanisms. In fact, the theoretical and empirical legacy of these dual process approaches was quite different. More and more frequently, group influence became associated with pressure toward compliant or "apparent" influence, the "normative" route postulated by these models. At the same time, this "group" influence was contrasted to the mechanisms that produced "true" or "real" attitude change about reality based on the careful and thorough evaluation of information.

Some theories did allow for the possibility that group influence resulted in privately accepted rather than merely public change. Even in these cases, however, such influence was often accorded a status that was conceptually distinct from that of influence based on careful and thoughtful consideration of different points of view. Kelman's (1958, 1961) views illustrate best this shift. In addition to compliance, Kelman presumed the existence of two mechanisms that might produce private acceptance. Identification produces privately accepted change that depends upon a positive relation of identity between source and recipient. Because of its role-defined nature, such change is regarded as situation specific, involving little effort or thought, and transitory in that it typically does not outlast the relationship (for a similar mechanism, see also referent power, French & Raven, 1959). And because of its role-defined nature, this mechanism seemed to capture particularly well the influence demonstrated by membership groups. Internalization, in contrast, involves the thoughtful and thorough integration of new material into a broad framework of cognitive associations.

Thus, by the 1970s, group-induced influence was depicted primarily, although not necessarily intentionally, as producing context-specific public compliance or, at best, superficial and/or transitory attitude change. At the same time, as the concern of the discipline turned toward cognitive processes mediating social behavior, theory and research focused on the mechanisms that produced "true persuasion" via careful consideration, evaluation, and acceptance of arguments and evidence. Interest was inevitably drawn away from the more social antecedents of influence.[1]

One literature that proved the exception to this rule was the group polarization literature. In 1961, James Stoner reported that group discussion of issues led groups to make riskier decisions than individuals. Further research soon showed that if their members favored caution to begin with, groups made more cautious decisions than their individual members did. Thus group discussion apparently polarizes the initial tendencies of group members (Moscovici & Zavalloni, 1969). The basis of this extremitization effect became the focus of hot debate during the 1970s.

On the one side, social comparison theorists (Myers, 1982; Sanders & Baron, 1977) attempted to show that polarization occurred because people are motivated to adopt a more extreme socially valued position that positively differentiates them from fellow group members. This view had much of the flavor of normative influence with a component of intragroup competition as well. On the other side, proponents of the persuasive arguments view (Burnstein & Vinokur, 1977) suggested that group discussion exposed individuals to novel arguments that predominantly supported the side of the issue initially taken by the majority of group members. Exposure to such arguments then extremitized opinions through informational mechanisms.

A comprehensive review of the literature on group polarization is beyond the scope of this chapter (see Turner, Hogg, Oakes, Reïcher, & Wetherell, 1987). Suffice it to say, however, that the results of a decade of creative empirical tests could basically be described as a draw. While neither the social comparison nor the persuasive arguments positions seemed independently sufficient, neither could either be wholly rejected as a possible explanation. The difficulty in explaining group polarization seemed to reflect in microcosm the debate over the nature of the influence effected by groups. Like that larger debate, further resolution depended on later developments in theory and methods.

Processing Approaches to Intergroup Influence

Although the cognitive revolution in social psychology drew interest away from group-mediated influence, it had the benefit of further developing theories and paradigms capable of distinguishing the mechanisms by which privately accepted change occurred. Interestingly, contemporary models of persuasion continue to be dual process models, but the distinctions they draw (because of their focus on private acceptance alone) are more parallel to Kelman's contrast of internalization and identification than to the earlier theories.

Both the Heuristic-Systematic Model (HSM; Chaiken, 1987) and the Elaboration Likelihood Model (ELM; Petty & Cacioppo, 1986) have suggested that attitude change can result from two different strategies for processing persuasive messages. While the two models differ in their preferred terminology, the processing strategies proposed are largely similar in nature. Both systematic processing (Chaiken, 1987) and central route processing (Petty & Cacioppo, 1986) involve extensive evaluation, elaboration, and integration of information relevant to the advocated position. Such processing typically allows recipients to assess the quality of arguments presented in support of the advocated position, and thus results in considerable attitude change in response to strong arguments and little attitude change in response to weak arguments. Such content-focused processing requires both motivation and capacity on the part of the message recipient (for reviews, see Chaiken, Liberman, & Eagly, 1989; Petty & Cacioppo, 1986).

In contrast, heuristic processing (Chaiken, 1987) or peripheral route processing (Petty & Cacioppo, 1986) involves little cognitive effort. When subjects are processing heuristically, attitude change depends upon the presence or absence of persuasion cues (e.g., source attributes) in the communication context. The use of such cues can replace extensive processing of message content as a means of assessing message validity if motivation or capacity is low.

The development of paradigms to test these dual process models provided an opportunity to investigate the question of whether group membership produced change via the systematic/central or peripheral/heuristic route. In the original formulation of the ELM, source characteristics such as shared group membership were seen as operating via the peripheral route and thus as producing change because of mechanisms other than the careful processing of available topic-relevant information. In this view, change that occurs through the peripheral route is also implied to have less to do with the true validity of the advocated position, and thus group-mediated attitude change is presumed to be tainted with a certain lack of objectivity. More recently, source characteristics such as expertise have also been considered as informational items and as factors increasing message processing (Hass, 1981; Kruglanski & Thompson, 1999; Puckett, Petty, Cacioppo, & Fisher, 1983).

Source characteristics such as expertise and attractiveness have also been studied in their role as persuasion cues within the framework of the heuristic model of attitude change (Chaiken, 1986). Category membership may operate as a heuristic because of the attractiveness of the source to recipients (Kelman, 1958, 1961; Pallak, 1983) or because subjects can rely on an ingroup member's views as appropriately defining reality (Festinger, 1950; Kelman, 1958, 1961). Although the impact of shared category membership has not been featured in either the heuristic model or the elaboration likelihood model, these approaches echo Kelman's intimation that group-mediated change may be rooted in less content-focused and less extensive information processing than the attitude change brought about by true internalization.

On the other hand, there are equally plausible motivational and cognitive reasons to believe that exposure to a message from an ingroup source or about an ingroup could invoke more extensive processing. First, a communication from a same-category source might be persuasive for the simple fact that it is seen as reflecting and defining social reality for people similar to the recipient (Festinger, 1950). Turner (1982, Turner et al., 1987) has argued (following Kelley, 1967) that the subjective validity of our views (the extent to which we think our views accurately reflect reality) is a function of the extent to which similar others agree with those views. In focusing on similar others, Turner is interested not so much in demographic group membership as in psychological identification with those assumed to have the relevant attributes for making the judgment at hand (true reference group membership). Thus, assuming accuracy is the perceiver's goal, the views of such fellow group members thus provide information of high interest and diagnosticity for the recipient, presumably increasing processing motivation.

Second, increases in the ability to process category-relevant messages may result from the activation of category-relevant information induced by the recognition of shared group membership (for examples of this effect in specific knowledge domains see Bargh & Thein, 1985; Markus, 1977). From this perspective, then, ingroup membership may not only serve as a source characteristic that motivates the recipient to engage in systematic processing but may also foster the capacity to do so.

Finally, exposure to ingroup views that differ from one's own opinions violates the expectation that our opinions are widely held (Heider, 1958; Ross, Greene, & House, 1977), especially by similar others (Allen & Wilder, 1978, 1979; Turner, 1982). Violation of such expectancies is likely to induce active processing of relevant information (Baker & Petty, 1994; Petty & Cacioppo, 1986).

For any or all of these reasons, then, same-category sources could bring about attitude change that is based on extensive processing of presented information as well as or instead of attitude change achieved via group identity as a heuristic cue. Since the 1980s a small research literature has developed which assesses the processing mechanisms underlying group-mediated persuasion. In addition to investigating whether or not groups produce privately accepted rather than compliant change, these studies provide evidence regarding the mechanism by which such change occurs – heuristic or peripheral processes as compared to extensive or elaborative processing.

In an early attempt to assess the processing mechanisms underlying group-mediated influence, we (Mackie, Gastardo-Conaco, & Skelly, 1992) gauged the impact of receiving an ingroup or outgroup message on the use of heuristic versus systematic or elaborative processing strategies. Male and female University of California, Santa Barbara (UCSB) undergraduates were first asked their opinions on a variety of issues. Responses indicated that they were generally in favor of legalization of euthanasia and opposed to generalized handgun possession. In a purportedly unrelated task, participants were asked to report their own views on several issues.

Presumably in order to familiarize themselves with the task, participants were told that they would first read another participant's responses. They then learned about the source of the message in the form of a code number and the source's school affiliation. All participants were then exposed to a two-part message from the source. In the *position statement*, the source expressed his or her own position on one of the key issues. This position was always counter-attitudinal to the participant's own view on the issue, in that it either opposed euthanasia or supported handgun possession. That is, the source stated clear opposition to euthanasia or support of handgun possession. In the *argument statement*, the source presented three arguments supporting and three arguments opposing the position taken. The balance of arguments was either strong (three strong supporting arguments plus three weak opposing arguments) or weak (three weak supporting arguments plus three strong opposing arguments). After each source's presentation was complete, participants reported their own views on the issue.

There were three key manipulations. First, before message presentation, all participants learned the source's group membership. The source was either a UCSB student (ingroup) or a University of Manitoba, Canada student (outgroup). Second, participants read the source's position statement either *before* or *after* argument presentation. Consequently, in only some conditions could a source heuristic (i.e., this is my group's position) be used to effect influence without message processing. Third, half of the participants read arguments that, on balance, strongly supported the advocated position whereas the other half read arguments that weakly supported the position. This design allowed us to see if and how the source heuristic was used when it was available and how participants processed ingroup versus outgroup communications when it was not possible to use the source as a heuristic cue.

Analysis indicated that the extent to which participants were persuaded on the two issues depended on the source's group membership, when the source's position became known, and the quality of the arguments supporting the source's position. When the source's position was announced before arguments were presented, participants were more likely to accept an ingroup member's position than an outgroup member's opinion, regardless of argument quality. Such unqualified acceptance of the ingroup position thus appeared to reflect heuristic processing, particularly of counter-attitudinal positions.

When the source's position statement was delayed until after argument presentation, the quality of the arguments influenced attitude change, but only when the source was an ingroup member. Participants were significantly more accepting of the ingroup member's opinion when it was accompanied by strong rather than weak arguments. Argument quality had no impact on reactions to an outgroup member's views. Measures of the time spent reading each argument before moving on to the next paralleled attitude change results. When participants knew the source's position beforehand, ingroup arguments were processed more rapidly than outgroup arguments, but when announcement of the source's position was delayed, participants spent more time processing ingroup than outgroup arguments. These results suggest that a message received from an ingroup member was systematically processed when it was not possible to use the source's group membership as a heuristic cue.

Thus both attitude change and processing indices suggested that ingroup status can operate as a heuristic cue, leading to the acceptance of ingroup messages with little content-focused processing. When participants were unaware of the source's position beforehand, however, they showed considerable content-focused processing of the ingroup message, as evidenced by the considerable amount of time they spent processing arguments, presumably to ascertain the ingroup source's position. This extra processing meant that persuasion was dictated largely by argument quality. Although recipients were persuaded by an ingroup position backed by strong arguments, they rejected an ingroup position backed by weak ones. Finally, in contrast to the evidence for both heuristic and systematic processing of ingroup messages, outgroup messages produced no attitude change and showed fast reading times, suggesting the absence of systematic processing.

These results suggested that private acceptance of ingroup messages is routinely heuristic unless the ingroup position is ambiguous, in which case systematic processing might occur. We were aware, however, that issues like euthanasia or gun control were unrelated to subjects' group membership as UCSB students, which might reduce processing motivation on these topics. As reductions in processing motivation are often associated with increased reliance on heuristic cues, it seemed possible that ingroup sources produced heuristic change because of issue non-relevance rather than as a default means of dealing with ingroup messages.

Assessing this possibility required monitoring processing reactions to messages from ingroup and outgroup sources on a group-relevant issue. Thus in a separate experiment (Mackie, Worth, & Asuncion, 1990, Experiment 1), participants read a message about standardized testing, an issue that was particularly relevant to our predominantly freshman participants' status as UCSB students. Having ascertained participants' initial attitudes on the issue of continued use of the SAT as a criterion for college admissions, we presented them with a message that advocated abolishing the use of SAT scores. After reading the speech, participants answered questions about the speech and the source, including items re-assessing their attitudes toward the SAT exam.

Two manipulations were important in this study. First, the experimenter identified the source either as a UCSB student representing the views of UCSB students (the ingroup) or as a University of New Hampshire (UNH) student said to be representing UNH students (the outgroup). Second, participants read a message comprising arguments that had been pretested to be either strong and valid or weak and specious. In all cases, the first sentence in the message stated the source's position that the use of SAT scores should be discontinued.

If receiving a message from an ingroup member initiated heuristic processing, we expected both strong and weak ingroup messages to lead to significant attitude change. If, on the other hand, receiving a message from an ingroup source triggered systematic processing, we expected to find that participants would be persuaded by a strong message from the ingroup source, but not by a weak one. Receiving a message from an outgroup member was predicted to be less persuasive than receiving a message from an ingroup member.

Assessment of changes in participants' attitudes revealed two clear effects. First, participants exposed to a message from the ingroup source showed significant change toward the advocated position, whereas those exposed to the outgroup source moved slightly, but nonsignificantly, in the direction opposite that advocated in the message. Thus overall, ingroup sources were more persuasive than outgroup sources. Second, tests of the simple effect of argument quality for the ingroup source condition revealed that the ingroup's persuasive superiority derived largely from the condition in which the message was strong rather than when it was weak, a pattern consistent with increased content processing of ingroup messages. This pattern of differentiation between strong and weak messages was not present when the source was a member of another group: the outgroup source was largely ineffective regardless of message quality.

Three additional measures bolstered these conclusions. First, participants recalled a slightly greater number of arguments from ingroup than outgroup messages. Second, the valence of elaborations made about message content and source expertise differed quite dramatically depending on the source's group membership, with strong ingroup messages receiving more favorable than unfavorable responses and weak ingroup messages receiving more unfavorable than favorable responses. When the message was attributed to an outgroup source, however, argument quality had no impact on elaborations. Finally, the favorability of the message elaborations was a significant predictor of attitude change when participants read ingroup messages but not when they were exposed to messages from an outgroup source. These results suggested that messages relevant to group-definitional issues delivered by an ingroup member received considerable scrutiny relative to messages attributed to an outgroup source.

As we had suspected, then, the relevance of the issue at hand to the salient ingroup influenced how persuasive appeals were processed. The results of these two studies combined suggested that when messages are not relevant to the ingroup, the ingroup source acts as a heuristic cue prompting acceptance unqualified by careful processing of message content. When the issue at hand is relevant and group defining, on the other hand, ingroup messages may be processed more systematically. However, as these conclusions were inferred from comparisons across studies, we manipulated issue relevance, group membership of the source, and message quality in a single experiment in order to better assess the impact of issue relevance on the processing of ingroup messages (Mackie et al., 1990, Experiment 2).

We selected two issues that participants rated in a pretest as being equally important but of differential relevance to a salient ingroup. One week later, participants listened to two two-minute speeches, one on each issue, while viewing a slide of the source, ostensibly delivered by either an ingroup (UCSB) or an outgroup (UNH) delegate at a student-initiated environmental conference. The source's group identification was mentioned by the experimenter and was made salient by the T-shirt the source wore. Issue relevance was also manipulated such that all participants heard one speech discussing an issue relevant to the ingroup (oil drilling off the southwestern coast of the United States) and one less relevant to the ingroup (acid rain problems in the northeastern United States). Finally, messages were composed of either strong or weak arguments. After listening to each speech, participants reported their own attitude on the issue.

Analysis of the extent of change toward the position advocated in the message revealed the combined impact of source status, issue relevance, and argument quality. When participants received a message on an ingroup relevant issue (oil drilling) from an ingroup source, they accepted the advocated position more when the message was strong than when it was weak. This pattern of attitude change suggested an increase in content-focused, systematic processing of the ingroup relevant message from the ingroup source. When the issue was not ingroup relevant, however, participants showed moderate and significant amounts of change toward the position advocated by the ingroup source regardless of message quality. This acceptance of the ingroup position without careful processing of content suggested that source status acted mainly as a heuristic cue when the issue was not ingroup relevant. In sharp contrast, the manipulations had little impact in the outgroup source condition. Outgroup members were much less persuasive than ingroup members, and attitude change was not significantly greater than zero in any condition.

Thus messages that are not especially group-relevant from ingroup members may be accepted on the basis of heuristic processing. On the other hand, messages from ingroup members about group-definitional issues appear to receive systematic, elaborative processing. McGarty, Haslam, Hutchinson, and Turner (1994) confirmed these results in a study assessing processing mediators of the acceptance of ingroup and outgroup appeals. Their participants were exposed to a videotaped persuasive communication on brain damage from an attitudinal ingroup or outgroup source (the attitudinal nature of the categorization made the message group-relevant). When this group membership was made directly salient, participants were more persuaded by the ingroup, and this effectiveness was mediated by greater recall of ingroup than outgroup arguments.

Even clearer support for and extension of the conclusion that ingroup relevant appeals receive systematic, elaborative processing comes from a series of studies in which argument strength and relevance of argumentation to the ingroup were manipulated (van Knippenberg & Wilke, 1991, 1992). Subjects were presented with arguments that were either prototypical of the ingroup or not. Once again, attitudes reflected argument quality when received from the ingroup but not when received from the outgroup. Importantly, evidence for elaboration and higher ratings of argument quality were most prevalent when prototypical ingroup arguments were presented.

Self-Categorization Approaches to Intergroup Influence

The main impetus for a renewed interest in group-mediated influence in the 1980s was the development of the social identity-based self-categorization model of influence

(Turner, 1982, 1985, 1991; Turner et al., 1987). According to self-categorization theory, people may categorize themselves as members of social groups (a categorization that may vary with the social context). As such social identities become salient, people perceive themselves more in terms of the shared features that define that membership. This process includes the adoption of group-defining attitudes and norms. To the extent that people categorize themselves as similar to others, they expect to agree with those others. This presumed agreement provides subjective validity because it implies that such consensus arises from the objective state of the world (after Kelley, 1967). As a stimulant to research, self-categorization theory thus re-asserted the powerfully persuasive private acceptance effect that social psychological ingroups should have. In addition, highly identified group members are more likely to adopt ingroup positions and to process ingroup arguments in a biased manner, leading to acceptance (Fleming & Petty, 1999).

Research generated by this approach has established that categorization into and psychological identification with groups plays a crucial role in influence processes. Their importance has been verified by evidence that influence occurs only when information or positions are attributed to members of groups, and not when the same information or positions are presented by uncategorized individuals (Hogg & Turner, 1987; Mackie, 1986). Hogg and Turner (1987), for example, showed that when categorized into groups, participants were more likely to move toward an incorrect ingroup response and away from their previously favored correct response, compared to when they were not categorized. Wilder (1990) also confirmed that views attributed to an ingroup were much more persuasive than outgroup views compared to when the same positions were said to be held by uncategorized individuals. Consistent with self-categorization theory, McGarty et al. (1994) report that their participants were more persuaded by ingroup than outgroup only when explicitly and directly reminded of their shared membership with the source of the persuasive appeal.

Research from the social identity/self-categorization perspective also illustrates the contribution of the intergroup context to persuasion. It has done so in two different ways. First, studies in this tradition have compared the effects of ingroup and outgroup views. A substantial body of research confirms greater influence by ingroups than by outgroups and suggests that such influence is privately accepted rather than a result of compliance (Abrams, Wetherell, Cochrane, Hogg, & Turner, 1990; Hogg & Turner, 1987; Mackie, 1986; Mackie & Cooper, 1984; Turner, Wetherell, & Hogg, 1989).

Many of these studies found effects in the context of establishing the crucial role of social identity in producing group polarization effects. For example, Turner et al. (1989) showed that the categorization processes inherent in ingroup membership made the ingroup position appear more extreme (in the initially favored direction) and also demonstrated that acceptance of this extremitized ingroup norm produced group polarization. Others (Hogg & Turner, 1987; Van Knippenberg & Wilke, 1988) have used a modified Asch paradigm to demonstrate both the persuasive power of exposure to ingroup rather than outgroup dissenting views and to illustrate that acceptance of such views occurred when self-presentational concerns were carefully minimized.

It has long been known that when group concerns are salient people conform more to ingroup norms (Sherif, 1967). Research in the social identity tradition provided more systematic confirmation of this greater acceptance of ingroup norms both when identity concerns are enhanced and when comparisons between ingroups and outgroups are possible. Salience of ingroup and outgroup categorization produces self-stereotyping, in which ingroup members assume the qualities and characteristics of the ingroup, including their attitudes (Hogg & Turner, 1987; Mackie, 1986; Ullah, 1987).

For example, heightened social identification has been determined to cause the conformity to group norms typically found in deindividuation paradigms (Reicher, 1984; Spears, Lea, & Lee, 1990). In a recent meta-analysis of 60 studies, Postmes and Spears (1998) found that deindividuation (heightened, almost exclusive, group identification) increased normative behavior.

In one study illustrating this point, Johnson and Downing (1979) varied the group norms and group members' anonymity. Some groups of participants dressed in robes and hoods designed to activate negative associations (with executioners, for example), whereas others dressed in nurses' uniforms, outfits that activated positive associations. In addition, some groups in each of these conditions were anonymous – their outfits cloaking their faces – whereas others were identifiable. All participants had to decide the level of shock to deliver to another person for failing a task. Anonymous participants in the negative costumes delivered higher levels of shock than those who were identifiable, whereas anonymous participants in nurses' uniforms delivered *lower* levels of shock when they were highly categorized than when individuated.

Ingroup views are particularly persuasive when comparisons between ingroups and outgroups are possible. Doise (1969), for example, demonstrated greater acceptance of ingroup norms among Parisian students when they were confronted with the ostensible opinions of a rival student group. Wilder and Shapiro (1984) examined the role of outgroup salience in adherence to an ingroup norm. Participants' judgments in mock legal suits were biased in the direction of the norm of an ingroup that was associated with an outgroup that had been made salient. An earlier experiment indicated that this effect was related to an increase in the activation of ingroup relevant material in the presence of cues about an outgroup (see also Turner et al., 1988, 1989).

Contributions to Intergroup Influence from the Majority/Minority Literature

By definition, influence from a majority or minority source has identity and thus intergroup implications. The centrality of these implications to a majority's or minority's goal of bringing about attitude change was recognized by Moscovici (1980, 1985) and has received extensive treatment by Turner (1991; David & Turner, 1996), Wood (Wood, Lundgren, Ouellette, Busceme, & Blackstone, 1994), Clark and Maass (1988a, 1988b), and Nemeth (1986). Although a thorough review of the relevant literature is beyond the scope of this chapter, there are some studies that have explicitly assessed the contribution of group membership to majority and minority influence.

With few exceptions, minorities categorized as outgroups are less effective than minorities categorized as ingroups (Clark & Maass, 1988a, 1988b; Martin, 1988a, 1988b, 1988c; Mugny, 1984; Mugny, Kaiser, Papastamou, & Perez, 1984; Mugny & Papastamou, 1982).[2] Clark and Maass (1988a), for example, found that ingroup minorities have more impact than outgroup minorities in both public and private contexts. Participants in their experiment were simultaneously exposed to opposing majority and minority views on abortion. The majority was always portrayed as consisting of ingroup members, whereas the minority was portrayed as consisting of either ingroup (same university) or outgroup (different university) members. Regardless of their majority or minority status, ingroup members were seen as more credible. When the minority were outgroup members, participants shifted away from the outgroup position and toward ingroup opinion in both public and private contexts, compared to when the minority were ingroup members. The ingroup minority was perceived to be more credible than the outgroup minority and effected significantly more private influence than the outgroup minority.

Similarly, David and Turner (1996) independently manipulated the group membership (ingroup or outgroup) and majority or minority status of a source who made a persuasive appeal on a group-relevant environmental topic. When exposed to both majority and minority outgroup sources, their Australian participants moved away from the advocated position toward a more extreme ingroup position, on both public and private and immediate and delayed measures. Both ingroup majorities and minorities produced significant change.

Consistent with the reasoning that social identity concerns are central to the occurrence of majority and minority influence, Wendy Wood and her colleagues (Pool, Wood, & Leck, 1998; Wood, Pool, Leck, & Purvis, 1996) have demonstrated the attitudinal impact of the motivation to move toward valued majorities and away from devalued minorities. In one set of studies, participants who learned that a majority group had an opinion different from their own moved to agree with the group if they considered it relevant to their self-definition (but not if it was irrelevant). Participants who judged a minority group as (negatively) self-relevant moved away from their initial position on an issue upon learning that the minority group shared it. A second set of studies indicated that self-esteem mediated such effects, since non-alignment with a valued group and alignment with a derogated group produced reductions in self-esteem. Because these studies exposed participants to positions rather than arguments, message-processing measures could not be assessed. However, other measures showed that the identity concerns raised by disagreeing with a valued group and agreeing with a devalued group triggered motivated interpretation of the attitude issues that aided the desired attitude change.

Conclusions: On the Nature of Influence in an Intergroup Context

What general conclusions about intergroup influence can be drawn from the relevant literature? First, it is readily apparent that ingroup communications very typically result in private acceptance. Recent research confirms earlier assertions of such an effect (Allen, 1965; Insko, Smith, Alicke, Wade, & Taylor, 1985; Kiesler & Kiesler, 1969; Wilder & Allen, 1977).

Second, it is clear that this influence is the result of self-categorization as an ingroup member. Exposure to similar positions or arguments that are attributed to uncategorized or irrelevant sources does not lead to private acceptance. In fact, when a message is delivered by an outgroup source, significant change away from the source's position may occur. It is important to note that while categorization is critical, self-categorization is even more crucial. As the early reference group theorists and researchers claimed and as social identity proponents more recently confirmed, ingroup mediated private acceptance depends on the social psychological relevance of the group to the target. Groups with which individuals identify, groups that are self-relevant or self-definitional for them, groups on whom their self-esteem depends – these are the modern definitions of reference groups.

Third, ingroups can produce private acceptance via a number of mechanisms. As long as the term "normative influence" is not tainted by its earlier association with unthinking compliance, both normative and informational mechanisms have been demonstrated to increase acceptance of ingroup views (Turner, 1991). Discovering that they disagree with valued others obviously provokes both mastery and connectedness concerns for individuals that engender motivations intended at once to both discover the truth and realign with those who should know what that truth is. Such motivations to accept or reject certain positions can then translate under different circumstances into biased interpretation of issues, heuristic evaluation of issues, or systematic and elaborative evaluation of issues and of arguments accompanying the issues. There is some evidence that the processing mode activated depends at least somewhat on the self-definitional relevance of the issue under consideration. However, a fuller understanding of the factors that control this process requires further empirical work.

Empirical questions about the consequences of change engendered by these various mechanisms also remain. Because change brought about by systematic or elaborative processing makes the resultant attitudes well embedded in other cognitive structures and highly accessible, it is assumed to be more resistant, more persistent, and a more effective guide for behavior. But the kind of heuristic change provoked by groups may well operate because of associations to important, complex, and long-lived mental representations: the self, for example. Such connections should ensure some resistance, persistence, and accessibility for guiding behavior in the case of this kind of change as well (Mackie, 1987; Petty & Wegener, 1998).

Fourth, group-mediated change can be triggered by exposure to the group's position, with or without accompanying argumentation. This does not imply, however, that exposure to norms alone entails change caused only by interpretive or heuristic means. Information about a position alone can generate extensive thinking, just as an extensive message can generate heuristic change. More empirical attention needs to be focused on the subprocesses that make ingroup mediated, elaborative processes possible. In addition to the motivational processes noted above, the self-categorization processes crucial to these effects may contribute to biased perceptions of norms, biased perceptions of the meaning of the normative positions, and enhanced accessibility of group-relevant information. All of these factors may also, for example, contribute to individuals' greater ability to process ingroup relevant information.

Fifth, as should already be clear, any factors that make salient the intergroup context in which influence occurs heighten the acceptance of ingroup positions and the rejection of outgroup opinions. Thus, making the outgroup salient, making relations between the ingroup and outgroup salient, and making relations between the ingroup and outgroup hostile should all enhance the persuasive advantage of the ingroup source over the outgroup source.

Perhaps the most far-reaching conclusion that can be drawn from this literature is that influence is defined by as well as mediated by the social relations between source and recipient. This is not simply to say that 50 years of research has confirmed, as Kelley (1952) argued, that consensus information is a powerful determinant of informational validity, leading as it does to external attributions. This is neither just to confirm, as Moscovici (1985) argued, that social ambiguity, disagreement in the face of expected unanimity, was more unsettling than ambiguity in the physical world. It is to say, in addition, that social processes are essential to conferring validity on information and thus to effecting influence. Even when message variables appear to determine persuasion, the cognitive processes that mediate their effectiveness often presuppose, assume, and depend on an appropriate social context. It is the social conferring of validity resulting from agreement among ingroup members that turns information into knowledge.

Notes

1.   There was some interest in source similarity during this time. For the most part, it comprised a nontheoretical proliferation of possible dimensions of source/recipient similarity (Huston & Levinger, 1978; Simons, Berkowitz, & Moyer, 1970), followed by debates over whether similarity effects could be explained by the impact of expertise and liking (Berscheid, 1985; Byrne, 1969; Wagner, 1984). In this literature, similarity at first seemed to promise increased persuasive effectiveness but was later regarded as having inconclusive effects (e.g., Brock, 1965; Goethals & Nelson, 1973; Leavitt & Kaigler-Evans, 1975; Mills & Kimble, 1973).
2.   Outgroup minorities appear to have more influence than ingroup minorities when the positions adopted by the former oppose the outgroup majority (Perez & Mugny, 1987; Volpato, Maass, Mucchi-Faina, & Vitti, 1990). This opposition may make such minorities seem less like the outgroup and more like the ingroup.

References

Abrams, D., Wetherell, M. S., Cochrane, S., Hogg, M. A., & Turner, J. C. (1990). Knowing what to think by knowing who you are: Self-categorization and the nature of norm formation, conformity, and group polarization. *British Journal of Social Psychology, 29,* 97–119.

Allen, V. L. (1965). Situational factors in conformity. In L. Berkowitz (Ed.), *Advances in experimental social psychology* (Vol. 2, pp. 133–175). New York: Academic Press.

Allen, V. L., & Wilder, D. (1978). Perceived persuasiveness as a function of response style: Multi-issue consistency over time. *European Journal of Social Psychology, 8,* 289–296.

Allen, V. L., & Wilder, D. (1979). Group categorization and attribution of belief similarity. *Small Group Behavior, 10,* 73–80.

Allport, F. L. (1924). The group fallacy in relation to social science. *Journal of Abnormal Psychology and Social Psychology, 19,* 60–73.

Asch, S. (1951). Effects of group pressure upon the modification and distortion of judgments. In H. Guetzkow (Ed.), *Groups, leadership, and men* (pp. 177–190). Pittsburgh, PA: Carnegie Press.

Baker, S. M., & Petty, R. E. (1994). Majority and minority influence: Source-position imbalance as a determinant of message scrutiny. *Journal of Personality and Social Psychology, 67,* 5–19.

Bargh, J. A., & Thein, R. D. (1985). Individual construct accessibility, person memory, and the recall-judgment link: The case of information overload. *Journal of Personality and Social Psychology, 49,* 1129–1146.

Berscheid, E. (1985). Interpersonal attraction. In G. Lindzey & E. Aronson (Eds.), *Handbook of social psychology* (3rd ed., Vol. 2, pp. 413–484). New York: Random House.

Brock, T. C. (1965). Communicator-recipient similarity and decision change. *Journal of Personality and Social Psychology, 1,* 650–654.

Burnstein, E., & Vinokur, A. (1977). Persuasive argumentation and social comparison as determinants of attitude polarization. *Journal of Experimental Social Psychology, 13,* 315–332.

Byrne, D. (1969). Attitudes and attraction. In L. Berkowitz (Ed.), *Advances in experimental social psychology* (Vol. 4, pp. 35–89). New York: Academic Press.

Chaiken, S. (1986). Physical appearance and social influence. In C. P. Herman, M. P. Zanna, & E. T. Higgins (Eds.), *Physical appearance, stigma, and social behavior: The Ontario symposium* (Vol. 3, pp. 143–177). Hillsdale, NJ: Erlbaum.

Chaiken, S. (1987). The heuristic model of persuasion. In M. P. Zanna, J. M. Olson, & C. P. Herman (Eds.), *Social influence: The Ontario symposium* (Vol. 5, pp. 3–39). Hillsdale, NJ: Erlbaum.

Chaiken, S., Liberman, A., & Eagly, A. H. (1989). Heuristic and systematic information processing within and beyond the persuasion context. In J. S. Uleman & J. A. Bargh (Eds.), *Unintended thought* (pp. 212–252). New York: Guilford Press.

Clark, R. D., & Maass, A. (1988a). The role of social categorization and perceived source credibility in minority influence. *European Journal of Social Psychology, 18,* 381–394.

Clark, R. D., & Maass, A. (1988b). Social categorization in minority influence: The case of homosexuality. *European Journal of Social Psychology, 18,* 347–364.

David, B., & Turner, J. C. (1996). Studies in self-categorization and minority conversion: Is being a member of the out-group an advantage? *British Journal of Social Psychology, 35,* 179–199.

Deutsch, M., & Gerard, H. B. (1955). A study of normative and informational social influences upon individual judgment. *Journal of Abnormal and Social Psychology, 51,* 629–636.

Doise, W. (1969). Intergroup relations and polarization of individual and collective judgements. *Journal of Personality and Social Psychology, 12,* 136–143.

Festinger, L. (1950). Informal social communication. *Psychological Review, 57,* 271–282.

Festinger, L. (1953). An analysis of compliant behavior. In M. Sherif & M. O. Wilson (Eds.), *Group relations at the crossroads* (pp. 232–256). New York: Harper.

Festinger, L. (1954). A theory of social comparison processes. *Human Relations, 7,* 117–140.

Fleming, M. A., & Petty, R. E. (1999). Identity and persuasion: An Elaboration Likelihood Model. In D. J. Terry & M. A. Hogg (Eds.), *Attitudes, behavior, and social context: The role of norms and group membership.* Mahwah, NJ: Erlbaum.

French, J. R. P., & Raven, B. H. (1959). The bases of social power. In D. Cartwright (Ed.), *Studies in social power* (pp. 150–167). Ann Arbor, MI: Institute of Social Research.

Goethals, G. R., & Nelson, R. E. (1973). Similarity in the influence process: The belief-value distinction. *Journal of Personality and Social Psychology, 25,* 117–122.

Hartley, E. L. (1950–51). The social psychology of opinion formation. *Public Opinion Quarterly, Winter,* 668–674.

Hass, R. G. (1981). Effects of source characteristics on cognitive responses and persuasion. In R. E. Petty, T. M. Ostrom, & T. C. Brock (Eds.), *Cognitive responses in persuasion* (pp. 141–172). Hillsdale, NJ: Erlbaum.

Heider, F. (1958). *The psychology of interpersonal relations.* New York: Wiley.

Hogg, M. A., & Turner, J. C. (1987). Social identity and conformity: A theory of referent information influence. In W. Doise & S. Moscovici (Eds.), *Current issues in European social psychology* (Vol. 2, pp. 139–182). Cambridge, UK: Cambridge University Press.

Huston, T. L., & Levinger, G. (1978). Interpersonal attraction and relationships. *Annual Review of Psychology, 29,* 115–156.

Hyman, H. (1942). The psychology of subjective status. *Psychological Bulletin, 39,* 473–474.

Insko, C. A., Smith, R. H., Alicke, M. D., Wade, J., & Taylor, S. (1985). Conformity and group size: The concern with being right and the concern with being liked. *Personality and Social Psychology Bulletin, 11,* 41–50.

Johnson, R. D., & Downing, L. L. (1979). Deindividuation and valence of cues: Effects on prosocial and antisocial behavior. *Journal of Personality and Social Psychology, 37,* 1532–1538.

Jones, E. E., & Gerard, H. B. (1967). *Foundations of social psychology.* New York: Wiley.

Kelley, H. H. (1952). Two functions of reference groups. In G. E. Swanson, T. M. Newcomb, & E. L. Hartley (Eds.), *Readings in social psychology* (2nd ed., pp. 410–414). New York: Holt, Rinehart, and Winston.

Kelley, H. H. (1967). Attribution theory in social psychology. In D. Levine (Ed.), *Nebraska symposium on motivation* (Vol. 15, pp. 192–238). Lincoln, NE: University of Nebraska Press.

Kelman, H. C. (1958). Compliance, identification, and internalization: Three processes of attitude change. *Journal of Conflict Resolution, 2,* 51–60.

Kelman, H. C. (1961). Processes of attitude change. *Public Opinion Quarterly, 25,* 57–78.

Kiesler, C. A., & Kiesler, S. B. (1969). *Conformity.* Reading, MA: Addison-Wesley.

Kruglanski, A. W., & Thompson, E. P. (1999). Persuasion by a single route: A view from the unimodel. *Psychological Inquiry, 10,* 83–109.

Leavitt, C., & Kaigler-Evans, K. (1975). Mere similarity versus information processing: An exploration of source and message interaction. *Communication Research, 2,* 300–306.

LeBon, G. (1896). *The crowd: A study of the popular mind.* London: Unwin.

Mackie, D. M. (1986). Social identification effects in group polarization. *Journal of Personality and Social Psychology, 50,* 720–728.

Mackie, D. M. (1987). Systematic and nonsystematic processing of majority and minority persuasive communications. *Journal of Personality and Social Psychology, 53,* 41–52.

Mackie, D. M., & Cooper, J. (1984). Attitude polarization: The effects of group membership. *Journal of Personality and Social Psychology, 46,* 575–585.

Mackie, D. M., Gastardo-Conaco, M. C., & Skelly, J. J. (1992). Knowledge of the advocated position and the processing of in-group and out-group persuasive messages. *Personality and Social Psychology Bulletin, 18,* 145–151.

Mackie, D. M., Worth, L. T., & Asuncion, A. G. (1990). Processing of persuasive in-group messages. *Journal of Personality and Social Psychology, 58,* 812–822.

Markus, H. (1977). Self-schemata and processing information about the self. *Journal of Personality and Social Psychology, 35,* 63–78.

Martin, R. (1988a). Ingroup and outgroup minorities: Differential impact on public and private responses. *European Journal of Social Psychology, 18,* 39–52.

Martin, R. (1988b). Minority influence and social categorization: A replication. *European Journal of Social Psychology, 18,* 369–373.

Martin, R. (1988c). Minority influence and "trivial" social categorization. *European Journal of Social Psychology, 18,* 465–470.

McGarty, C., Haslam, A. S., Hutchinson, K. J., & Turner, J. C. (1994). The effects of salient group memberships on persuasion. *Small Group Research, 25*, 267–293.

Merton, R. K. (1957). *Social theory and social structure* (Rev. ed.). Glencoe, IL: Free Press.

Mills, J., & Kimble, C. E. (1973). Opinion change as a function of perceived similarity of the communicator and subjectivity of the issue. *Bulletin of the Psychonomic Society, 2*, 35–36.

Moscovici, S. (1980). Toward a theory of conversion behavior. In L. Berkowitz (Ed.), *Advances in experimental social psychology* (Vol. 13, pp. 209–239). New York: Academic Press.

Moscovici, S. (1985). Social influence and conformity. In G. Lindzey & E. Aronson (Eds.), *The handbook of social psychology* (Vol. 2, 3rd ed., pp. 347–412). New York: Random House.

Moscovici, S., & Zavalloni, M. (1969). The group as a polarizer of attitudes. *Journal of Personality and Social Psychology, 12*, 365–380.

Mugny, G. (1984). The influence of minorities: Ten years later. In H. Tajfel (Ed.), *The social dimension: European development in social psychology* (Vol. 2, pp. 498–517). Cambridge, UK: Cambridge University Press.

Mugny, G., Kaiser, C., Papastamou, S., & Perez, J. A. (1984). Intergroup relations, identification, and social influence. *British Journal of Social Psychology, 23*, 317–322.

Mugny, G., & Papastamou, S. (1982). Minority influence and psycho-social identity. *European Journal of Social Psychology, 12*, 379–394.

Murphy, G., Murphy, L. B., & Newcomb, T. M. (1937). *Experimental social psychology* (2nd ed.). New York: Harper and Brothers.

Myers, D. G. (1982). Polarizing effects of social interaction. In H. Brandstatter, J. H. Davis, & G. Stocker-Kreichgauer (Eds.), *Group decision making* (pp. 125–161). London: Academic Press.

Nemeth, C. J. (1986). Differential contributions of majority and minority influence. *Psychological Review, 93*, 1–10.

Newcomb, T. M. (1943). *Personality and social change: Attitude formation in a student community.* New York: Dryden Press.

Pallak, S. R. (1983). Salience of a communicator's physical attractiveness and persuasion: A heuristic versus systematic processing interpretation. *Social Cognition, 2*, 158–170.

Perez, J. A., & Mugny, G. (1987). Paradoxical effects of categorization in minority influence: When being an outgroup is an advantage. *European Journal of Social Psychology, 17*, 157–169.

Petty, R. E., & Cacioppo, J. (1986). The Elaboration Likelihood Model of persuasion. In L. Berkowitz (Ed.), *Advances in experimental social psychology* (Vol. 19, pp. 123–205). New York: Academic Press.

Petty, R. E., & Wegener, D. T. (1998). Attitude change: Multiple roles for persuasion variables. In D. T. Gilbert, S. T. Fiske, & G. Lindzey (Eds.), *Handbook of social psychology* (4th ed., pp. 323–390). Boston, MA: McGraw-Hill.

Pool, G. J., Wood, W., & Leck, K. (1998). The self-esteem motive in social influence: Agreement with valued majorities and disagreement with derogated minorities. *Journal of Personality and Social Psychology, 75*, 967–975.

Postmes, T., & Spears, R. (1998). Deindividuation and antinormative behavior: A meta-analysis. *Psychological Bulletin, 123*, 1–22.

Puckett, J., Petty, R. E., Cacioppo, J. T., & Fisher, D. (1983). The relative impact of age and attractiveness stereotypes on persuasion. *Journal of Gerontology, 38*, 340–343.

Reicher, S. D. (1984). Social influence in the crowd: Attitudinal and behavioral effects of de-individuation in conditions of high and low group salience. *British Journal of Social Psychology, 23*, 341–350.

Ross, L., Greene, D., & House, P. (1977). The "false consensus effect": An egocentric bias in social perception and attribution processes. *Journal of Experimental Social Psychology, 13*, 279–301.

Sanders, G. S., & Baron, R. S. (1977). Is social comparison irrelevant for producing choice shifts? *Journal of Experimental Social Psychology, 13*, 303–314.

Sherif, M. (1936). *The psychology of social norms.* New York: Harper and Brothers.

Sherif, M. (1948). *An outline of social psychology.* New York: Harper.

Sherif, M. (1967). *Group conflict and cooperation: Their social psychology.* London: Routledge and Kegan Paul.

Siegel, A. W., & Siegel, S. (1957). Reference groups, membership groups, and attitude change. *Journal of Abnormal and Social Psychology, 55*, 360–364.

Simons, H. W., Berkowitz, N. N., & Moyer, R. J. (1970). Similarity, credibility, and attitude change: A review and a theory. *Psychological Bulletin, 73*, 1–16.

Spears, R., Lea, M., & Lee, S. (1990). De-individuation and group polarization in computer-mediated communication. *British Journal of Social Psychology, 29*, 121–134.

Stoner, J. A. F. (1961). *A comparison of individual and group decisions involving risk.* Unpublished Master's thesis, School of Industrial Management, Massachusetts Institute of Technology.

Tajfel, H., & Turner, J. C. (1986). The social identity theory of intergroup behavior. In S. Worchel & W. G. Austin (Eds.), *Psychology of intergroup relations* (2nd ed., pp. 7–24). Chicago, IL: Nelson-Hall.

Turner, J. (1982). Toward a cognitive redefinition of the social group. In H. Tajfel (Ed.), *Social identity and intergroup behavior* (pp. 15–40). Cambridge, UK: Cambridge University Press.

Turner, J. C. (1985). Social categorization and the self-concept: A social cognitive theory of group behavior. In E. J. Lawler (Ed.), *Advances in group processes* (Vol. 2, pp. 77–122). Greenwich, CN: JAI Press.

Turner, J. C. (1991). *Social influence.* Pacific Grove, CA: Brooks/Cole.

Turner, J. C., Hogg, M. A., Oakes, P. J., Reicher, S. D., & Wetherell, M. S. (1987). *Rediscovering the social group: A self-categorization theory.* Oxford, UK: Basil Blackwell.

Turner, J. C., Wetherell, M. S., & Hogg., M. A. (1988). *Referent informational influence and group polarization. Experiment 1.* Unpublished paper, Macquarie University, Sydney.

Turner, J. C., Wetherell, M. S., & Hogg., M. A. (1989). Referent information influence and group polarization. *British Journal of Social Psychology, 28*, 135–147.

Ullah, P. (1987). Self-definition and psychological group formation in an ethnic minority. *British Journal of Social Psychology, 26*, 17–23.

Van Knippenberg, A., & Wilke, H. (1988). Social categorization and attitude change. *European Journal of Social Psychology, 18*, 395–406.

Van Knippenberg, A., & Wilke, H. (1991). Social categorization and attitude change. *European Journal of Social Psychology, 18*, 395–406.

Van Knippenberg, A., & Wilke, H. (1992). Prototypicality of arguments and conformity to ingroup norms. *European Journal of Social Psychology, 22*, 141–155.

Volpato, C., Maass, A., Mucchi-Faina, A., & Vitti, E. (1990). Minority influence and social categorization. *European Journal of Social Psychology, 20*, 119–132.

Wagner, W. (1984). Social comparison of opinions: Similarity, ability, and the value-fact distinction. *Journal of Psychology, 117*, 197–202.

Wilder, D. A. (1990). Some determinants of the persuasive power of in-groups and out-groups: Organization of information and attribution of independence. *Journal of Personality and Social Psychology, 59*, 1202–1213.

Wilder, D. A., & Allen, V. L. (1977). Veridical social support, extreme social support, and conformity. *Representative Research in Social Psychology, 8*, 33–41.

Wilder, D. A., & Shapiro, P. N. (1984). Role of out-group cues in determining social identity. *Journal of Personality and Social Psychology, 47*, 342–348.

Wood, W., Lundgren, S., Ouellette, J. A., Busceme, S., & Blackstone, T. (1994). Minority influence: A meta-analytic review of social influence processes. *Psychological Bulletin, 115,* 323–345.

Wood, W., Pool, G. J., Leck, K., & Purvis, D. (1996). Self-definition, defensive processing, and influence: The normative impact of majority and minority groups. *Journal of Personality and Social Psychology, 71,* 1181–1193.

PART V

Social Comparison

CHAPTER FIFTEEN

The Social Psychology of Minority–Majority Relations

Bernd Simon, Birgit Aufderheide, and Claudia Kampmeier

Groups are a fact and a medium of social life. The evolution of humankind as well as the development of each single individual took and still takes place within social groups. Physical as well as social existence critically depends on, and is shaped by, coordinated human action within and between social groups. In turn, groups are embedded in a structured context of intergroup relations characterized by a number of parameters such as goal interdependence, relative power, size, status, prestige, etc. An adequate analysis of human perception and behavior must therefore take into account social group memberships as well as the wider intergroup context.

The focus in this chapter is on the effect of group membership in the context of minority–majority relations. Many, if not most, real-life intergroup contexts consist of groups that hold either a minority or majority position vis-à-vis each other (Farley, 1982; Tajfel, 1981). A common definition of minority or majority group membership rests on numbers. Groups with fewer members are then defined as minorities and numerically larger groups as majorities (e.g., Brewer, 1991; Moscovici & Paicheler, 1978; Simon, 1992). In addition, relative power or social status is sometimes used as a criterion for defining minority and majority group membership (e.g., Tajfel, 1981). That definition assigns oppressed groups a minority position and dominant groups a majority position even when the numerical relation is balanced or reversed. For instance, in most societies, women would then be considered a (social) minority and men a (social) majority. Similarly, during apartheid in South Africa, Whites would have been considered a majority and Blacks a minority, even though the former group was numerically smaller than the latter (Tajfel, 1978). In this chapter, however, we start from a numerical definition of

Our own research reported in this chapter was supported by grants from the Deutsche Forschungsgemeinschaft (Si 428/2-1,2,3).

minority and majority group membership. This approach is in line with the bulk of research on minority–majority relations conducted by experimental social psychologists (e.g., Brewer, 1991, 1998; Mullen, 1991; Simon, 1992, 1998a). Also, in real life, numerical asymmetries often, though not necessarily, co-vary with power or status asymmetries such that the numerical minority is also a low-status or oppressed minority, and the numerical majority a high-status or dominant majority. This appears to be the case especially in Western democratic societies with their ideological emphasis on majority rule (Sachdev & Bourhis, 1984; Sherif, 1966). However, this correlation also implies that the effects of relative group size and status or power are often confounded in real life. Consequently, although relative group size constitutes the central independent variable in the research discussed in this chapter, power and status dimensions are not ignored in our analysis. In particular, we also try to disentangle the effects of relative group size and status (see also Ellemers & Barreto, this volume, chapter 16).

In line with our basic premise that group memberships and the corresponding intergroup relations have a profound influence on social life, we examine a wide spectrum of possible consequences, or in other words, dependent variables. These fall into four broad classes, namely, (1) self-definition, (2) information processing, (3) well-being, and (4) behavior. This classification is not meant to suggest a mutual independence of the underlying psychological processes, nor is it intended as a conceptually exhaustive list. Rather, it is viewed as a helpful ordering scheme for reviewing the pertinent literature and structuring this chapter. More specifically, we examine whether membership in a minority group and membership in a majority group each constitute a distinct social psychological situation for the particular group member which elicits distinct reactions from her or him related to each of these four classes of dependent variables. In the next four major sections of this chapter, we therefore deal in turn with each class and discuss, in an exemplary, non-exhaustive fashion, typical minority–majority differences. In the final section, we then attempt to integrate these four parts and present a first outline of a more comprehensive theory of the social psychology of minority–majority relations.

Self-definition in Minority–Majority Contexts

There is wide agreement among social psychologists that our perception of other people is strongly influenced by our knowledge of their group memberships. For example, we readily perceive outgroup members as relatively similar to one another and attribute rather extreme and negative characteristics to them (e.g., Messick & Mackie, 1989; Tajfel, 1982). However, it is not just other people who are group members. We ourselves also belong to social groups or categories which may influence how we see ourselves. Self-categorization theorists have therefore suggested distinguishing between two basic forms of self-definition, namely between the individual self (or personal identity) and the collective self (or social identity) (Turner, Hogg, Oakes, Reicher, & Wetherell, 1987). Following self-categorization theory, the individual self stands for self-definition as a unique individual ("me") and the collective self for self-definition as an interchangeable group member ("we"). Relative to the individual self, the collective self is a cognitive representation of oneself at a higher level of abstraction or inclusiveness that implies depersonalization of individual self-perception.

Elaborating on the distinction between the individual self and the collective self, Simon (1997, 1998a) has proposed a self-aspect model (SAM) which should be particularly helpful in understanding minority—majority differences in self-definition. According to that model, the collective self emerges when self-definition centers on a single self-aspect that the person shares with other, but not all other people in the relevant social context (e.g., "First and foremost, I am a Christian."). The individual self, on the other hand, emerges when self-definition is based on a more comprehensive set or configuration of different, nonredundant self-aspects (e.g., "I am female, Christian, musical, a lawyer, have brown hair, like French cuisine, etc.").

Numerical distinctiveness

According to the self-aspect model, the collective self is predicated on focused self-definition. It follows that factors which facilitate this focusing or concentration process should also facilitate the collective self. One factor that could play such a facilitating role is the numerical distinctiveness of a social-categorical self-aspect. This may be so because novel or rare features generally tend to move in the perceptual foreground and thus become particularly salient (Fiske & Taylor, 1991; Mullen, 1991). By virtue of its numerical distinctiveness membership in a (numerical) minority should thus facilitate the collective self. There is indeed a growing body of evidence indicating that minority group membership may possess a particular "attention-grabbing power" so that it figures prominently in self-definition. For example, McGuire and McGuire (1988) found that children tended to think of themselves in terms of their gender and ethnicity to the extent that their respective group membership (e.g., being a boy or a girl) held a minority position in their usual social milieu. Laboratory research conducted in more controlled social environments points in the same direction. Simon and Hamilton (1994, Experiment 1) found that members of laboratory-created minority groups self-stereotyped more strongly than members of laboratory-created majority groups. In self-descriptions, minority members more strongly endorsed positive and negative ingroup attributes and more strongly rejected negative outgroup attributes. They also indicated more perceived similarity between themselves and their ingroup as well as more perceived homogeneity of the ingroup as a whole. Similarly, Brewer and Weber (1994) showed that minority members aligned their self-perceptions more strongly with a portrait of another ingroup member than did majority members. And again in line with Simon and Hamilton (1994, Experiment 1), this minority—majority difference was observed even when it implied the incorporation of negative ingroup characteristics into one's self-definition on the part of minority members (see also Ellemers, Kortekaas, & Ouwerkerk, 1999).

Meaningful social categorization

Oakes and colleagues (Oakes, 1987; Oakes & Turner, 1986) questioned that it is numerical distinctiveness per se that facilitates the collective self and instead emphasized the role of meaningful social categorization. Thus, being one of two men in an otherwise all-female psychology class should not matter with regard to self-definition unless the discussion shifts to relevant topics such as abortion or affirmative action policies. That is, any potential salience advantage of numerically distinct self-aspects may not translate into increased collective self-definition until possession or nonpossession of the critical self-aspect (e.g., being male) can systematically be related to the current social context (e.g., a discussion about affirmative action policies). Given such a relationship, however, social categorization into ingroup and outgroup based on the particular self-aspect becomes meaningful because it now fits the current social context. Then, minority group membership should indeed "benefit" from its salience advantage. Direct evidence for the hypothesized role of meaningful social categorization in minority–majority contexts was obtained by Simon, Hastedt, and Aufderheide (1997). In addition to relative ingroup size (minority vs. majority), we manipulated meaningfulness of the underlying social categorization (low vs. high) as a second independent variable by either weakening or strengthening the perceived correlation between group membership and performance on the alleged experimental task. As expected, the two independent variables had an interactive effect on several indicators of the collective self (e.g., self-ascribed typicality relative to self-ascribed individual uniqueness). The collective self was significantly stronger for minority members than for majority members, but only when the social categorization was meaningful. Otherwise, minority and majority members did not differ from each other. Moreover, the minority–majority difference in the high-meaningfulness condition was mainly due to an increase in the collective self among minority members. A second experiment replicated these findings and showed that a stronger meaningfulness manipulation led to an even stronger effect on minority members, but remained ineffectual with regard to majority members.

Note that in real-life minority–majority contexts the role of meaningfulness typically remains implicit. That is, people tend to focus mostly on minority–majority categorizations for which they have seemingly "good" reasons to presume the necessary social contextual fit or meaningfulness. They may do so either on the basis of actually observed correlations between minority–majority membership and important dimensions of the social context (e.g., actual correlations between ethnicity and religious practices) or on the basis of collectively shared belief systems (e.g., racist ideologies or myths). However, even in experimental research the role of meaningfulness often remains implicit because, in the attempt to construct a credible cover story, research participants are typically also provided with a meaningful link between social categorization and the current social context. In the Simon and Hamilton (1994) research, for example, participants were told that group membership was correlated with the introversion–extroversion dimension of personality. As all ratings relating to self-definition had to be made with reference to that personality dimension, social categorization was indeed highly meaningful in that research context. As a consequence, meaningfulness is often taken for granted as a given constant, and its critical role is overlooked. To progress in our understanding of minority–majority differences, we have to avoid this "taken-for-granted fallacy," however. In the Simon et al. (1997) research, we did so by explicitly increasing or decreasing the meaningfulness of social categorization in minority–majority contexts. Therefore, the major contribution of that research was to have made explicit the role of meaningful social categorization in minority–majority contexts thereby guarding against an overestimation of the role of numerical distinctiveness.

Relative group status

Another complication regarding the interpretation of minority–majority differences in self-definition concerns the role of status or power.[1] As indicated in the introduction, a numerical asymmetry may often co-vary with a status or power asymmetry such that the numerical minority is also a low-status or oppressed group and the numerical majority also a high-status or dominant group. However, the existence of many high-status, powerful numerical minorities or elites (e.g., the aristocracy in England, Brahmins in India, or – at least for many decades – Whites in South Africa) proves that this is not necessarily so. Simon and Hamilton (1994, Experiment 2) experimentally disentangled relative ingroup size (minority vs. majority) and ingroup status (low vs. high) by creating low- and high-status minority and majority groups in the laboratory. It was predicted that collective self-definition would be a direct function of the attractiveness of the respective ingroup (Tajfel & Turner, 1986). Ingroup attractiveness in turn was expected to vary according to the "scarcity principle" (Ditto & Jemmott, 1989) which postulates that the attractiveness of positively valenced and negatively valenced characteristics (i.e., high- and low-status group membership) is more polarized when the perceived frequency of these characteristics is low rather than high (i.e., when the ingroup is a minority rather than a majority) (Ellemers, Doosje, Van Knippenberg, & Wilke, 1992). The results were in line with these predictions. Overall, minority members were more willing to see themselves in terms of their collective self when ingroup status was high as opposed to low, whereas ingroup status was mostly ineffectual for majority members.

It should be noted, however, that these interactive effects are also compatible with a somewhat different perspective. The self-aspect model suggests that, given a meaningful social categorization (such as in Simon & Hamilton's research), numerical minority members' self-definition is much more centered or focused on group membership than numerical majority members' self-definition. Consequently, ingroup status is much more likely to "hit the heart" of minority members' self-definition. It should thus have a much more powerful impact on minority members' than on majority members' self-definition.

Although it is impossible at this point to draw any definite conclusions as to whether the original *scarcity account* or the latter *centrality account* (or some combination of both) provides a superior explanation, there is some indirect evidence that supports the centrality account. For example, Simon, Aufderheide, and Hastedt (2000) found that, when questioned immediately after the experimental manipulation of relative ingroup size, members of numerical minorities seemed to pay less attention to alternative self-aspects as they produced significantly less complex self-descriptions than members of numerical majorities. (But this effect disappeared when self-complexity was measured toward the end of the experimental session [see also Simon, 1998a, pp. 12–14].) Another potentially relevant pattern of results was observed in a real-life minority–majority context (Simon, Glässner-Bayerl, & Stratenwerth, 1991). In that field study, we found that members of a low-status, oppressed minority (gay men) showed greater awareness of their group membership than did members of the corresponding high-status, dominant majority (heterosexual men). At the same time, however, minority members also tended to be less glad to belong to their ingroup than were majority members. In line with our self-aspect model, this pattern thus points to an interesting ambivalence of members of low-status minorities toward their group membership. On the one hand, group membership appears to take a central and therefore particularly salient position in the cognitive self-definitions of members of low-status minority groups, while on the other hand, its negative value connotations make it an unattractive self-aspect. We will return to this cognitive-affective crossfire later in this chapter.

Information Processing in Minority–Majority Contexts[2]

Several social psychological approaches to social perception distinguish between two major levels or types of information processing, namely between individual-level or person-based processing, on the one hand, and group-level or category-based processing, on the other hand (Brewer, 1988, 1998; Fiske & Neuberg, 1990; Turner et al., 1987). Group-level processing is characterized, among other things, by the accentuation of perceived interchangeability of all members belonging to the same group, whereas accentuation of interpersonal differences is characteristic of individual-level processing. Following self-categorization theory (Turner et al., 1987), self-definition and information processing are closely interrelated such that the individual self underlies, and is itself reinforced by, individual-level processing, whereas the collective self underlies, and is reinforced by, group-level processing. Consequently, it can be assumed that the level of information processing is determined by variables similar to those that influence the level of self-definition. In light of the minority–majority differences in self-definition discussed in the preceding section, we should therefore also expect minority–majority differences in information processing.

Perception of ingroup and outgroup homogeneity

Taking perceived ingroup and outgroup homogeneity as an indicator of group-level information processing, it appears that there are indeed interesting minority–majority differences. Whereas members of (numerical) majorities tend to perceive more homogeneity in the outgroup than in the ingroup, members of (numerical) minorities often show the opposite tendency (Simon, 1992). Thus majority members seem to engage in group-level processing primarily regarding information about outgroup members, whereas minority members may engage in group-level processing also regarding information about ingroup members, and perhaps even more so than regarding information about outgroup members.

These differences nicely correspond to the minority–majority differences in self-definition discussed in the preceding section. However, this correspondence might not be too surprising given that measures of perceived group homogeneity tend to overlap with measures of self-definition as both are often based on ratings of perceived similarities and differences within the ingroup (e.g., Simon & Hamilton, 1994). It is therefore also necessary to review research which employed alternative methodologies to gauge information processing.

Recognition errors

A more sophisticated experimental paradigm which examines group-level relative to individual-level information processing is the recognition confusion task developed by Taylor and her colleagues, in which research participants have to remember who of a number of alleged ingroup and outgroup members made which statement (Taylor, Fiske, Etcoff, & Ruderman, 1978; Brewer, 1998; Lorenzi-Cioldi, 1998; Simon, 1998a; for a critical review, see Klauer & Wegener, 1998). In a first presentation stage, participants are typically presented with a number of statements each of which is identified as being made by either an ingroup member or an outgroup member. Statements are carefully pretested to avoid confounding variables (e.g., differential attractiveness of ingroup and outgroup statements), and their total number usually varies between 6 and 16 across studies. Statements are presented on audio or videotape or simply as written sentences on a computer screen, and each alleged speaker is identified by photographs or written information. In a second (recognition) stage, participants are presented with each statement once again. But this time, information as to who was the speaker is left out. Instead, participants are provided with lists of the names or photographs of all former speakers and are instructed to remember "who said what" and to match statements and faces or names accordingly. Three types of confusion errors can be distinguished: (1) within-ingroup errors resulting from attributing a statement allegedly made by a particular ingroup member erroneously to another ingroup member; (2) within-outgroup errors resulting from attributing a statement allegedly made by a particular outgroup member erroneously to another outgroup member; (3) intergroup errors resulting from attributing a statement allegedly made by an ingroup member erroneously to an outgroup member and vice versa. To anticipate a general result, the latter error type appears to be rather insensitive to experimental variations of relative ingroup size so that the following discussion focuses on intragroup errors (i.e., within-ingroup errors and within-outgroup errors). High numbers of such errors indicate the degree to which group members are seen or remembered as interchangeable exemplars of their respective groups or, in other words, the degree to which the perceiver engages in group-level as opposed to individual-level information processing.

Research on minority–majority differences in information processing using the recognition confusion task yielded mixed results. Thus Brewer, Weber, and Carini (1995, Experiment 3) found no minority–majority differences in the processing of information about outgroup members, but observed that, relative to majority members, minority members tended toward *less* group-level processing, or at least additional individual-level processing, when information about ingroup members was concerned. The latter finding is particularly surprising in light of the preceding discussions of minority–majority differences in self-definition and perceived group homogeneity which seemed to suggest that minority members should be particularly likely to engage in group-level, but not individual-level, processing of ingroup information. One obvious way to reconcile this apparent contradiction is to look for possible moderator variables. Recent research by Simon et al. (2000) indeed points to the existence of such variables. As a first step, we experimentally designed a standard minority–majority context in which group member-ship was highlighted at the expense of participants' individuality. The recognition con-fusion task was administered, and confusion errors served as the main dependent variable. As expected, minority members showed more group-level information processing than majority members. This standard minority–majority context was then contrasted with another minority–majority context which differed from the first in only one aspect. In this new context, we administered an individualizing self-description task before mea-suring the dependent variables. We predicted and found that this individualization process undermined the minority–majority difference in group-level information processing. It should be noted that, as in the Brewer et al. research (1995, Experiment 3), effects were observed only for within-ingroup errors, whereas within-outgroup errors were again insensitive to the experimental manipulations. However, the critical interaction effect was replicated in a second experiment with different measures of information processing (e.g., participants' use of abstract vs. concrete information), and this time the effect was obtained for processing of both ingroup and outgroup information (although the effect was somewhat weaker for the latter). More importantly, in this second experiment, the interaction effect involved a significant reversal. When individualization was fostered, group-level information processing decreased for minority members, but increased for majority members so that minority members showed less group-level information pro-cessing than majority members. Our tentative explanation was that individualization is compatible with majority group membership because, unlike minorities, majorities are typically construed as consisting of unique individuals (Mullen, 1991). In a seemingly paradoxical fashion, individualized self-perception may thus reinforce majority members' group membership and their group-level perspective. Although the pattern of results obtained in our individualized minority–majority context closely resembles that observed by Brewer et al. (1995, Experiment 3), it remains an open question at this point whether or exactly how such a moderator variable may have been operating in those authors' exper-iment. One possibility is that individualization processes were inadvertently fostered through the assignment of individual ID numbers, even though that assignment was apparently arbitrary. It is a well-established social psychological phenomenon that arbi-trary category labels foster group formation processes (Tajfel, 1982). By the same token, even arbitrary ID numbers may foster individualization processes.

Relative group status

So far, we have focused in this section on minority and majority groups that were defined in purely numerical terms. But what about intergroup contexts in which ingroup and outgroup differ not only in size, but also in status? There is some research that addresses this issue as well. Lorenzi-Cioldi (1998, Study 7) manipulated relative group size and group status as orthogonal experimental factors and examined their effects on informa-tion processing using the recognition confusion task. He found that relative ingroup size did not influence information processing. Instead, there was only a general effect of group status. Participants showed more group-level information processing (i.e., more within-group errors) regarding low-status groups than regarding high-status groups, irrespective of whether these groups were minority or majority ingroups or minority or majority out-groups. The author interpreted these processing differences in terms of socially shared, stable, and generalized conceptions about low-status and high-status groups which, for various cognitive (e.g., attributional) and social (e.g., normative and ideological) reasons, should involve more differentiated mental representations of high-status groups relative to low-status groups (see also Sedikides, 1997).

However, such a static view may underestimate the role of motivated and strategic cognition in information processing (Fiske & Taylor, 1991; Kunda, 1990). For example, research by Doosje, Ellemers, and Spears (1995) as well as by Simon and Hastedt (1997, Experiment 1) suggests that members of low-status or otherwise unattractive groups prefer group-level information processing as part of a group-level strategy to cope with their collective predicament, whereas they tend more toward individual-level information processing when individual escape seems possible or acceptable. Simon and Hastedt (1997, Experiment 2) examined this motivational or strategic approach also in a minority–majority context. In addition to relative ingroup size, we manipulated two other independent variables. As an analogue of ingroup status, we varied ingroup attractiveness by highlighting either positive or negative ingroup characteristics. Although this manipulation differs from the standard manipulation of ingroup status (e.g., Simon & Hamilton, 1994; Lorenzi-Cioldi, 1998), it still captures the central social psychological component of the concept of ingroup status, namely its (positive or negative) implications for group members' self-evaluations (Tajfel & Turner, 1986). Individualization of the self was manipulated as a third independent variable as it was directly relevant to testing the role of motivated and strategic cognition in information processing. Whereas half of the participants worked on the dependent measures immediately after the manipulation of relative ingroup size and ingroup attractiveness, the remaining participants were additionally administered an individualizing self-description task between the manipulation of the two other independent variables and the measurement of the dependent variables. Within-ingroup errors derived from the recognition confusion task served again as the main dependent variable. (There were no effects on within-outgroup errors in this experiment.) It was predicted and found that our third independent variable served as an important moderator of the combined influence of relative ingroup size and ingroup attractiveness. When individualization of the self was difficult (i.e., in a standard intergroup context without an individualizing self-description task), ingroup attractiveness had opposite effects on minority and majority members: Minority members showed more group-level information processing when the ingroup was attractive as opposed to unattractive, whereas majority members showed more group-level information processing when the ingroup was unattractive. However, when individualization of the self was facilitated by way of a self-description task, ingroup attractiveness had identical effects on minority and majority members: Irrespective of relative ingroup size, group-level information processing was stronger when the ingroup was attractive as opposed to unattractive.

Taken together, these results suggest that high status of the minority ingroup motivates group-level information processing, and low status of the minority ingroup motivates individual-level information processing. Most likely, this is so because, depending on whether ingroup status is high or low, either group-level or individual-level perspectives are most conducive to the achievement or maintenance of positive self-evaluations (Tajfel & Turner, 1986). For majority members, however, the relationship between ingroup status and information processing seems to depend on an additional strategic consideration. As indicated above, group-level information processing can be part of a group-level strategy to cope collectively with a shared predicament such as low ingroup status (Doosje et al., 1995; Simon, 1998b). Moreover, large ingroup size can be an important resource in the collective struggle for social change (Klandermans, 1997). In light of their numerical superiority, members of low-status majority groups may therefore consider a group-level strategy including group-level information processing a viable option, but only as long as there is no easier individual way out of the predicament such as distancing oneself from the ingroup through individualization (see also Lalonde & Silverman, 1994; Wright, Taylor, & Moghaddam, 1990). Conversely, for minority members, who do not have such a resource at their disposal, a group-level strategy to cope with low ingroup status would generally be too risky.

Well-being in Minority–Majority Contexts

Our group memberships do not only influence how we define ourselves and how we process social information, they should also have an influence on our emotions or feelings (Turner et al., 1987). In this section, we examine whether there are systematic differences in minority and majority members' well-being. Because neither the quantity nor the quality of the research available for this purpose allows a more fine-grained differentiation, we look at well-being in a rather broad sense including a variety of temporary emotional states or moods (e.g., happiness, anxiety, depression) as well as more stable positive or negative feelings about oneself and one's situation (e.g., self-respect, self-acceptance, self-esteem).

"There is safety in numbers?"

From a theoretical point of view, there is some reason to assume that membership in a minority group, even when defined in purely numerical terms, may be associated with less positive feelings or well-being than membership in a majority group. For example, based on Festinger's (1954) theory of social comparison processes, it could be argued that members of relatively small groups are at a disadvantage, compared with members of larger groups, when it comes to soliciting consensual validation from many similar others. As a consequence, members of (numerical) minorities may feel less secure than members of (numerical) majorities. This minority–majority difference may be further accentuated for two reasons. First, because group membership tends to be a more central self-aspect for minority members than for majority members (McGuire & McGuire, 1988), consensual validation concerning characteristics related to one's group membership should be a more salient task for minority members than for majority members. Second, at least in Western cultures with their ideological emphasis on majority rule, numerical inferiority is likely to be associated with error, deviance, and weakness (Sherif, 1966, p. 111: "There is safety in numbers"; see also Sachdev & Bourhis, 1984, pp. 37–39). Unfortunately, empirical evidence on differences in (numerical) minority and majority members' well-being is sparse. In fact, we know of only one experiment in which the researchers looked at group members' well-being in purely numerically defined minority–majority contexts. Using a mood adjective checklist, Bettencourt, Charlton, and Kernahan (1997, Study 1) found no overall differences between minority and majority members, although separate analyses of each item indicated that minority members felt indeed less relaxed than majority members.

Relative group status and power

A few researchers have looked at aspects of minority and majority members' well-being in laboratory contexts in which, in addition to relative ingroup size, ingroup status and/or ingroup power were manipulated as well. Sachdev and Bourhis (1991) found that well-being was influenced by relative ingroup size irrespective of ingroup status and ingroup power. In keeping with our theoretical analysis, minority members felt less comfortable, less satisfied and less happy about their group membership than majority members. However, this minority–majority difference was not replicated by Ellemers et al. (1992). They found that relative ingroup size and ingroup status interacted such that members of high-status minority groups felt most pride, while members of low-status minority and low- and high-status majority groups did not differ from each other.

Another category of research focused on real-life minority–majority contexts in which numerical asymmetries were confounded with status and/or power asymmetries. Typically, that research examined whether members of low-status (oppressed or stigmatized) minority groups had lower self-esteem than members of high-status (dominant) majority groups. In light of our preceding theoretical discussion of the well-being implications of membership in a numerical minority as well as several other theoretical perspectives that predict lower self-esteem among members of low-status groups (Crocker & Major, 1989), one would expect that members of low-status minority groups should suffer from deficient self-esteem compared with members of high-status majority groups. Yet, after reviewing relevant research conducted over a time span of more than 20 years, Crocker and Major (1989) had to conclude that such self-esteem deficits seemed rather rare. That review spurred many efforts to account for this discrepancy between theory and data. Thus subsequent research provided valuable insights into several psychological mechanisms by which members of low-status minority groups may protect their self-esteem (e.g., attributional externalization, selective social comparisons), but it also identified possible harmful effects of such self-protective mechanisms (Crocker & Quinn, this volume, chapter 12; Major & Crocker, 1993; see also Branscombe, Schmitt, & Harvey, 1999).

However, there is also new evidence which confirms that, at least under some conditions, members of low-status minority groups differ in well-being from members of high-status majority groups as originally expected. Thus Hewstone, Islam, and Judd (1993, Experiment 2) found lower self-esteem for members of a low-status minority group (Hindus in Bangladesh) than for members of a high-status majority group (Muslims in Bangladesh). Research conducted by Islam and Hewstone (1993) in a similar context further indicates that in direct intergroup encounters members of low-status minority groups may suffer from increased intergroup anxiety. In addition, Frable, Platt, & Hoey (1998) found that members of low-status minority groups whose group membership or stigma was concealable as opposed to visible experienced lower self-esteem and more negative affect than members of high-status majority groups. Frable et al.'s (1998) observation that the well-being of members of low-status minority groups was negatively affected only when their stigma was concealable is in line with other research which points to the positive or compensatory role of intragroup support and collective identification in the well-being of members of low-status minority groups (Branscombe et al., 1999; Phinney, 1990; Verkuyten, 1995). For these compensatory resources should be less easily available when it is not immediately clear (i.e., visible!) who is one of "us." Similarly, Simon et al. (1991) observed that members of a low-status minority group with a concealable stigma (gay men) tended to be less happy with their group membership than members of the corresponding high-status majority group (heterosexual men).

Intergroup Behavior in Minority–Majority Contexts

The socially undesirable phenomenon of intergroup discrimination is widely regarded as the paradigmatic case of intergroup behavior (Sumner, 1906; Allport, 1954; Tajfel, 1982). Our discussion of minority–majority differences in intergroup behavior therefore focuses primarily on minority–majority differences in intergroup discrimination. Currently the most prominent social psychological explanation of intergroup discrimination is provided by social identity theory (Tajfel & Turner, 1986). It holds that, from a social psychological perspective, intergroup discrimination can be understood as an attempt to establish a positively valued distinctiveness for one's ingroup in order to achieve or maintain a positive social identity or, in other words, a positive collective self. Although there are still many open questions concerning this phenomenon and its adequate explanation (e.g., Mummendey & Otten, this volume, chapter 6), there is nevertheless wide consensus among social psychologists that social identity theory provides a very helpful framework for a better understanding of intergroup discrimination in general (Smith & Mackie, 1995) and in minority–majority contexts in particular (e.g., Mullen, Brown, & Smith, 1992).

Salience or threat?

Most researchers who examined the effect of relative ingroup size on intergroup discrimination started with the expectation that members of (numerical) minorities would show stronger intergroup discrimination than members of (numerical) majorities (but see also Moscovici & Paicheler, 1978, for a notable exception). There are two typical arguments as to why this should be the case. For one, it is argued that, due to its numerical distinctiveness or salience, minority group membership engenders a "heightened sense of kindredness" (Gerard & Hoyt, 1974) or, in other words, is more "identifying" than majority group membership (also Mullen et al., 1992). As a consequence, minority group membership arouses stronger social identity concerns (i.e., a stronger motivation to achieve or maintain a positive social identity or collective self) which then translate into more discriminatory behavior. Note that this argument corresponds directly to the centrality account derived from our self-aspect model (Simon, 1997; 1998a) which we discussed in the section on self-definition. The second argument centers on possible threatening implications of being in the numerically smaller group. As reviewed in the preceding section on well-being, there is good theoretical reason to assume that members of (numerical) minorities feel more insecure than members of (numerical) majorities. To compensate for this insecurity, minority members should therefore strive to strengthen their positive social identity by discriminating against the majority outgroup, when given the opportunity (e.g., Sachdev & Bourhis, 1984). As both the salience argument as well as the threat argument predict stronger intergroup discrimination on the part of minority members, we will first review the relevant research and then examine which of them provides a better account of the empirical evidence.

In a meta-analysis of research findings secured over a time span of 15 years, Mullen et al. (1992) found that their index of intergroup discrimination decreased as a function of the proportionate size of the ingroup (i.e., the size of the ingroup divided by the sum of the size of the ingroup and the size of the outgroup). However, their index of intergroup discrimination was derived primarily from ingroup and outgroup ratings on evaluative attribute dimensions which are rather indirect or remote indicators of actual intergroup behavior. Fortunately, other research has employed more direct measures of intergroup behavior. Following Tajfel, Billig, Bundy, & Flament (1971), researchers have used various types of resource-allocation tasks in which research participants are requested to distribute meaningful resources (e.g., money, course credit) between ingroup and outgroup members. Using such a task with laboratory-created (numerical) minorities and majorities, Sachdev and Bourhis (1984) obtained a complex pattern of results. They found some evidence that, unlike majority members, minority members were more concerned with their ingroup's absolute outcome than with intergroup fairness. But majority members also showed discriminatory tendencies. Although they did not appear particularly interested in maximizing their ingroup's absolute outcome, majority members seemed concerned about maintaining or establishing outcome differentials between the ingroup and the outgroup in favor of the ingroup. More recent experimental research by Bettencourt et al. (1997) yielded results more in line with the expected minority–majority difference in intergroup discrimination. In the context of forced intergroup cooperation, they found that when participants' attention was not experimentally focused on particular aspects of the cooperative setting (control condition), members of (numerical) minorities showed more intergroup discrimination against the outgroup than members of (numerical) majorities. The latter even tended toward reversed discrimination in favor of the minority outgroup. In two additional experimental conditions, participants were instructed by the experimenter to focus their attention either on interpersonal aspects of the cooperation (individual-focus condition) or on each group's contribution to the overall task (task-focus condition). While the interpersonal focus did not eliminate the minority–majority difference in intergroup discrimination, the task focus did. In fact, there was even a slight reversal in the task-focus condition such that majority members now seemed to show more intergroup discrimination than minority members. Note that Bettencourt et al.'s (1997) results do not support a salience account of increased intergroup discrimination on the part of minority members compared with majority members, because such a minority–majority difference was observed even when minority members' attention was experimentally redirected away from their group memberships to interpersonal aspects. On the other hand, the reversal toward more intergroup discrimination on the part of majority members in the task-focus condition supports a *threat account* of intergroup discrimination. As suggested by Bettencourt et al. (1997, p. 653), the task-focus instructions which requested all participants to acknowledge each group's contributions to the cooperative endeavor might have strengthened especially the minority group who would have received less recognition otherwise. Thus rendered on more equal footing with majority members, minority members should feel less threatened and therefore less motivated to discriminate against the majority outgroup. In contrast, for majority members, this equal footing might have lessened their otherwise perceived superiority and might thus have strengthened their motivation to discriminate against the minority outgroup.

Relative group status and power

Other research has examined intergroup discrimination in laboratory contexts in which, in addition to relative ingroup size, ingroup status and/or ingroup power were manipulated as well. For example, Mummendey, Simon, Dietze, Grünert, Haeger, Kessler, Lettgen, and Schäferhoff (1992, Experiment 2) varied both relative ingroup size and ingroup status and found main effects of both variables, but no interaction effect.[3] That is, members of (numerical) minorities showed more intergroup discrimination than members of (numerical) majorities, and members of low-status groups showed more intergroup discrimination than members of high-status groups (see Otten, Mummendey, & Blanz, 1996, for similar findings). As a result of the compound effects of relative ingroup size and ingroup status, members of low-status minority groups were most discriminatory (see also Espinoza & Garza, 1985).

Sachdev and Bourhis (1991) also manipulated relative ingroup size and ingroup status and even added ingroup power as a third independent variable. Unfortunately, they used the same criterion (i.e., creativity) for both the status manipulation and the resource-allocation task. This confound renders the status effects inconclusive because it is impossible to decide whether allocation decisions in favor of a high-status ingroup are to be considered a true effect (i.e., intergroup discrimination) or simply a manipulation check (i.e., a reproduction of the experimentally created status differential). We therefore limit our discussion here to the effects of relative ingroup size and ingroup power including their interactive effects. Sachdev and Bourhis (1991) again found a complex pattern of results. More specifically, their results indicated that members of (numerical) minorities were generally less fair than members of (numerical) majorities, although the latter also appeared to be concerned about maintaining or establishing some intergroup differentials in favor of the ingroup (see Sachdev & Bourhis, 1984). Moreover, members of powerful minorities tended to be more discriminatory than members of powerful majorities, while the opposite tendency was observed for members of powerless minorities and majorities. This interactive effect of relative ingroup size and ingroup power points to an interesting explanation as to why the evidence of increased intergroup discrimination on the part of minority members compared with majority members is often weak or inconsistent. Due to their numerical inferiority, minority members may often suffer from insufficient self-confidence or insufficient trust in their collective efficacy which then prevents them from engaging in assertive intergroup behavior.

Thus threat may play a dual, and perhaps contradictory, role in minority–majority relations (see also Ng & Cram, 1988). On the one hand, the threatening implications of the numerical inferiority of one's ingroup may lead to feelings of insecurity and an increased need for a positive social identity which in turn increases the willingness to discriminate against outgroups. On the other hand, however, numerical inferiority may threaten minority members' self-confidence and feelings of collective efficacy which are necessary preconditions of assertive intergroup behavior (Klandermans, 1997; Moscovici & Paicheler, 1978). In other words, minority members may often feel the need for discriminatory behavior in favor of the ingroup, but at the same time they may lack the necessary confidence to put this desire into action.

Integration and Conclusions

Thus far we have reviewed research on four important aspects of social life in intergroup contexts, namely self-definition, information processing, well-being, and intergroup discrimination. The particular focus was on the effect of minority and majority group membership on each of these four aspects. The empirical findings reveal a high degree of complexity both between and within these aspects, and this complexity is further magnified when, in addition to the size asymmetry, status and power asymmetries between ingroup and outgroup are taken into account as well. Nevertheless, there are also common themes in the observed minority–majority differences which provide a starting point for an integrative perspective. In the remainder of this chapter we will try to pull these themes together in an attempt to form the first building blocks of a more comprehensive theory of the social psychology of minority–majority relations. Though informed by the research findings reviewed in this chapter, these building blocks should not be taken as proven empirical generalizations, but as informed conjectures or hypotheses which can be, and should be, tested empirically.

The cognitive-affective crossfire

Our basic premise it that membership in a minority group and membership in a majority group each constitute a distinct social psychological situation for the particular group member which elicits distinct cognitive, affective, and behavioral reactions. Most importantly, it appears that, unlike majority members, minority members typically find themselves in a *cognitive-affective crossfire*. On the one hand, being a small figure against a large background, it is very likely that their group membership is particularly salient to others as well as to themselves. It is therefore very difficult for minority members to forget or ignore their group membership. There are always many more other people who do not forget minority members' group membership and continually remind them of it by word and deed. In this way, their respective group membership becomes a much more central self-aspect for minority members than for majority members. On the other hand, minority membership entails specific risks and stressful experiences which may be largely unknown to majority members. These risks range from insecuring deficits in consensual validation to personal persecution and extermination because of one's alleged deviance from the norm. These risks and the negative affective consequences are further exacerbated when numerical inferiority is also associated with status and/or power inferiority. In other words, compared with majority members, there are stronger cognitive forces pushing minority members toward their group (or keeping them in it), while at the same time there are also stronger affective forces pulling them away from it (or keeping them out of it). As a consequence, minority members should develop strategies to escape from, or at least cope with, this cognitive-affective crossfire. Depending on the perceived affordances or opportunity structure of the social context (e.g., the permeability of group boundaries), they may opt for individualistic strategies involving psychological dis-identification or actual exit from their group or for collective strategies involving assertive intergroup behavior, or for a combination of both (Simon, 1998b; Simon, Loewy, Stürmer, Weber, Freytag, Habig, Kampmeier, & Spahlinger, 1998; Tajfel & Turner, 1986).

Mindful minorities and mindless majorities

It also appears that, relative to majority members, minority members are more likely to be *mindful of the intergroup dimension* of their life space (Azzi, 1992; Frable, Blackstone, & Scherbaum, 1990). Whatever strategy minority members opt for in order to escape from, or cope with, the cognitive-affective crossfire discussed above, it is difficult for them to ignore the intergroup dimension. Assertive intergroup behavior directed against the majority group as well as assimilation attempts to become one of "them" presuppose an intergroup perspective with the majority group as a point of reference (Moscovici & Paicheler, 1978). In particular, minority members need to be mindful of the intergroup differences and intragroup similarities, be it in order to overcome them individually by assimilation or mimicry or in order to restructure them and the associated value hierarchy by collective action. Conversely, majority members can be more mindless in this respect, at least as long as they don't feel threatened by an assertive minority. As there are, by definition, more majority members than minority members, majority members are likely to interact most of the time with their own kind so that for them interpersonal similarities and differences are more relevant behavioral guidelines than intergroup differences and intragroup similarities. To illustrate this differential mindfulness in minority–majority contexts, the relationship between proponents of minority positions and adherents of majority or mainstream positions in science can serve as an instructive example. In order to be recognized in the scientific community (e.g., get their work published), proponents of minority positions need to be very knowledgeable about the mainstream, its strengths and weaknesses, as well as about the differences between the minority and the mainstream positions and how these differences could be bridged. Conversely, adherents of the mainstream, whose rules typically rule the community, do not need to pay too much attention to the minority. They can ignore it much longer and garnish this ignorance with occasional displays of "*se montrer bon prince*" (Moscovici & Paicheler, 1978, p. 253).

Assertive and defensive intergroup behavior

As indicated above, majority members usually tend toward an interpersonal perspective because the status quo is typically structured in such a way that this perspective works for them and in favor of them (Apfelbaum, 1979; Tajfel, 1978). If, under such conditions, they perceive group members at all, and not just "people," it is outgroup members, not ingroup members they perceive. At best, they then adopt a quasi-intergroup perspective in that they construe "them," the minority, as an odd group that differs from ordinary people (Simon, 1993). However, truly intergroup situations with both minority and majority members adopting an intergroup perspective can arise as well. This is most likely to be the case when minority members show assertive intergroup behavior in order to escape from or cope with the cognitive-affective crossfire (or worse) because such assertiveness may incite defensive intergroup behavior on the part of majority members. Then, "the empire strikes back." Note that, on the surface, assertive and defensive intergroup behavior may take the same form such as intergroup discrimination. From a theoretical point of view, however, the underlying meaning is different because such phenotypically similar behavior serves different purposes for minority and majority members. The *assertive-defensive distinction* could thus be another important building block for a better understanding of minority–majority relations (Moscovici & Paicheler, 1978).

Notes

1. Given the limited scope of this chapter, we do not attempt to systematically disentangle the effects of status and power, although we acknowledge the importance of such an endeavor (e.g., Sachdev & Bourhis, 1991).
2. In addition to the work discussed in this section, other research has also investigated effects of relative group size on information processing (e.g., Biernat & Vescio, 1993; Taylor et al., 1978; Van Twuyver & Van Knippenberg, 1999). However, that research focused on the effects of the relative sizes of the stimulus groups about which research participants had to process information, whereas the relative size of the participants' ingroup was not systematically varied. That research is therefore not included in this review.

320   *Bernd Simon, Birgit Aufderheide, and Claudia Kampmeier*

3. Unlike most prior work, Mummendey et al. (1992) requested participants to distribute neg-
    ative, rather than positive, outcomes between ingroup and outgroup (i.e., negative auditory
    stimulation and meaningless syllables to memorize). In this context, intergroup discrimina-
    tion therefore means allocating less negative outcomes to the ingroup.

References

Allport, G. W. (1954). *The nature of prejudice.* Cambridge, MA: Addison-Wesley.

Apfelbaum, E. (1979). Relations of domination and movements for liberation: An analysis of power between groups. In W. G. Austin & S. Worchel (Eds.), *The social psychology of intergroup relations* (pp. 188–204). Monterey, CA: Brooks/Cole.

Azzi, A. E. (1992). Procedural justice and the allocation of power in intergroup relations: Studies in the United States and South Africa. *Personality and Social Psychology Bulletin, 18,* 736–747.

Bettencourt, B. A., Charlton, K., & Kernahan, C. (1997). Numerical representation of groups in cooperative settings: Social orientation effects on ingroup bias. *Journal of Experimental Social Psychology, 33,* 630–659.

Biernat, M., & Vescio, T. K. (1993). Categorization and stereotyping: Effects of group context on memory and social judgment. *Journal of Experimental Social Psychology, 29,* 166–202.

Branscombe, N. R., Schmitt, M. T., & Harvey, R. D. (1999). Perceiving pervasive discrimination among African Americans: Implications for group identification and well-being. *Journal of Personality and Social Psychology, 77*(1), 135–149.

Brewer, M. B. (1988). A dual process model of impression formation. In T. Srull & R. Wyer (Eds.), *Advances in social cognition* (Vol. 1, pp. 1–36). Hillsdale, NJ: Erlbaum.

Brewer, M. B. (1991). The social self: On being the same and different at the same time. *Personality and Social Psychology Bulletin, 17,* 475–482.

Brewer, M. B. (1998). Category-based vs. person-based perception in intergroup contexts. In W. Stroebe & M. Hewstone (Eds.), *European review of social psychology* (Vol. 9, pp. 77–106). Chichester, UK: Wiley.

Brewer, M. B., & Weber, J. G. (1994). Self-evaluation effects of interpersonal versus intergroup social comparison. *Journal of Personality and Social Psychology, 66,* 268–275.

Brewer, M. B., Weber, J. G., & Carini, B. (1995). Person memory in intergroup contexts: Categorization versus individuation. *Journal of Personality and Social Psychology, 69,* 29–40.

Crocker, J., & Major, B. (1989). Social stigma and self-esteem: The self-protective properties of stigma. *Psychological Review, 96,* 608–630.

Ditto, P. H., & Jemmott, J. B. I. (1989). From rarity to evaluative extremity: Effects of prevalence information on evaluations of positive and negative characteristics. *Journal of Personality and Social Psychology, 57,* 16–26.

Doosje, B., Ellemers, N., & Spears, R. (1995). Perceived intragroup variability as a function of group status and identification. *Journal of Experimental Social Psychology, 31,* 410–436.

Ellemers, N., Kortekaas, P., & Ouwerkerk, J. W. (1999). Self-categorization, commitment to the group and group self-esteem as related but distinct aspects of social identity. *European Journal of Social Psychology, 29,* 371–389.

Ellemers, N., Doosje, B., Van Knippenberg, A., & Wilke, H. (1992). Status protection in high status minority groups. *European Journal of Social Psychology, 22,* 123–140.

Espinoza, J. A., & Garza, R. T. (1985). Social group salience and interethnic cooperation. *Journal of Experimental Social Psychology, 21,* 380–392.

Farley, J. (1982). *Majority–minority relations.* Englewood, NJ: Prentice-Hall.

Festinger, L. (1954). A theory of social comparison processes. *Human Relations, 7,* 117–140.

Fiske, S. T., & Neuberg, S. L. (1990). A continuum of impression formation, from category-based to individuating processes: Influences of information and motivation on attention and interpretation. In M. P. Zanna (Ed.), *Advances in experimental social psychology* (Vol. 23, pp. 1–74). New York: Random House.

Fiske, S. T., & Taylor, S. E. (1991). *Social cognition* (2nd ed.). New York: McGraw-Hill.

Frable, D. E. S., Blackstone, T., & Scherbaum, C. (1990). Marginal and mindful: Deviants in social interactions. *Journal of Personality and Social Psychology, 59,* 140–149.

Frable, D. E. S., Platt, C., & Hoey, S. (1998). Concealable stigmas and positive self-perceptions: Feeling better around similar others. *Journal of Personality and Social Psychology, 74,* 909–922.

Gerard, H., & Hoyt, M. F (1974). Distinctiveness of social categorization and attitude toward ingroup members. *Journal of Personality and Social Psychology, 29,* 836–842.

Hewstone, M., Islam, M. R., & Judd, C. M. (1993). Models of crossed categorization and intergroup relations. *Journal of Personality and Social Psychology, 64,* 779–793.

Islam, M. R., & Hewstone, M. (1993). Dimensions of contact as predictors of intergroup anxiety, perceived outgroup variability, and outgroup attitude: An integrative model. *Personality and Social Psychology Bulletin, 19,* 700–710.

Klandermans, B. (1997). *The social psychology of protest.* Oxford, UK: Blackwell.

Klauer, K. C., & Wegener, I. (1998). Unraveling social categorization in the "Who said what?" paradigm. *Journal of Personality and Social Psychology, 75,* 1155–1178.

Kunda, Z. (1990). The case for motivated reasoning. *Psychological Bulletin, 108,* 480–498.

Lalonde, R. N., & Silverman, R. A. (1994). Behavioral preferences in response to social injustice: The effects of permeability and social identity salience. *Journal of Personality and Social Psychology, 66,* 78–85.

Lorenzi-Cioldi, F. (1998). Group status and perceptions of homogeneity. In W. Stroebe & M. Hewstone (Eds.), *European review of social psychology* (Vol. 9, pp. 31–75). Chichester, UK: Wiley.

Major, B., & Crocker, J. (1993). Social stigma: The consequences of attributional ambiguity. In D. M. Mackie & D. L. Hamilton (Eds.), *Affect, cognition, and stereotyping: Interactive processes in group perception* (pp. 345–370). San Diego, CA: Academic Press.

McGuire, W. J., & McGuire, C. V. (1988). Content and process in the experience of self. In L. Berkowitz (Ed.), *Advances in experimental social psychology* (Vol. 21, pp. 97–144). New York: Academic Press.

Messick, D. M., & Mackie, D. M. (1989). Intergroup relations. *Annual Review of Psychology, 40,* 45–81.

Moscovici, S., & Paicheler, G. (1978). Social comparison and social recognition: Two complementary processes of identification. In H. Tajfel (Ed.), *Differentiation between social groups* (pp. 251–266). London: Academic Press.

Mullen, B. (1991). Group composition, salience, and cognitive representations: The phenomenology of being in a group. *Journal of Experimental Social Psychology, 27,* 297–323.

Mullen, B., Brown, R., & Smith, C. (1992). Ingroup bias as a function of salience, relevance, and status: An integration. *European Journal of Social Psychology, 22,* 103–122.

Mummendey, A., Simon, B., Dietze, C., Grünert, M., Haeger, G., Kessler, S., Lettgen, S., & Schäferhoff, S. (1992). Categorization is not enough: Intergroup discrimination in negative outcome allocation. *Journal of Experimental Social Psychology, 28,* 125–144.

Ng, S. H., & Cram, F. (1988). Intergroup bias by defensive and offensive groups in majority and minority conditions. *Journal of Personality and Social Psychology, 55,* 749–757.

Oakes, P. J. (1987). The salience of social categories. In J. C. Turner, M. A. Hogg, P. J. Oakes, S. D. Reicher, & M. S. Wetherell (Eds.), *Rediscovering the social group. A self-categorization theory* (pp. 117–141). Oxford, UK: Basil Blackwell.

Oakes, P. J., & Turner, J. C. (1986). Distinctiveness and the salience of social category member-ships: Is there a perceptual bias towards novelty? *European Journal of Social Psychology, 16*, 325–344.

Otten, S., Mummendey, A., & Blanz, M. (1996). Intergroup discrimination in positive and neg-ative outcome allocations: Impact of stimulus valence, relative group status, and relative group size. *Personality and Social Psychology Bulletin, 22*, 568–581.

Phinney, J. S. (1990). Ethnic identity in adolescents and adults: Review of research. *Psychological Bulletin, 108*, 499–514.

Sachdev, I., & Bourhis, R. Y. (1984). Minimal majorities and minorities. *European Journal of Social Psychology, 14*, 35–52.

Sachdev, I., & Bourhis, R. Y. (1991). Power and status differentials in minority and majority group relations. *European Journal of Social Psychology, 21*, 1–24.

Sedikides, C. (1997). Differential processing of ingroup and outgroup information: The role of relative group status in permeable boundary groups. *European Journal of Social Psychology, 27*, 121–144.

Sherif, M. (1966). *The psychology of social norms.* New York: Harper Torchbook.

Simon, B. (1992). The perception of ingroup and outgroup homogeneity: Re-introducing the intergroup context. In W. Stroebe & M. Hewstone (Eds.), *European review of social psychology* (Vol. 3, pp. 1–30). Chichester, UK: Wiley.

Simon, B. (1993). On the asymmetry in the cognitive construal of ingroup and outgroup: A model of egocentric social categorization. *European Journal of Social Psychology, 23*, 131–147.

Simon, B. (1997). Self and group in modern society: Ten theses on the individual self and the col-lective self. In R. Spears, P. J. Oakes, N. Ellemers, & S. A. Haslam (Eds.), *The social psychology of stereotyping and group life* (pp. 318–335). Oxford, UK: Blackwell.

Simon, B. (1998a). The self in minority–majority contexts. In W. Stroebe & M. Hewstone (Eds.), *European review of social psychology* (Vol. 9, pp. 1–31). Chichester, UK: Wiley.

Simon, B. (1998b). Individuals, groups, and social change: On the relationship between individ-ual and collective self-interpretations and collective action. In C. Sedikides, J. Schopler, & C. Insko (Eds.), *Intergroup cognition and intergroup behavior* (pp. 257–282). Mahwah, NJ: Lawrence Erlbaum.

Simon, B., Aufderheide, B., & Hastedt, C. (2000). The double negative effect: The (almost) para-doxical role of the individual self in minority and majority members' information processing. *British Journal of Social Psychology, 39*, 73–93.

Simon, B., Glässner-Bayerl, B., & Stratenwerth, I. (1991). Stereotyping and self-stereotyping in a natural intergroup context: The case of heterosexual and homosexual men. *Social Psychology Quarterly, 54*, 252–266.

Simon, B., & Hamilton, D. L. (1994). Self-stereotyping and social context: The effects of relative ingroup size and ingroup status. *Journal of Personality and Social Psychology, 66*, 699–711.

Simon, B., & Hastedt, C. (1997). When misery loves categorical company: Accessibility of the individual self as a moderator in category-based representation of attractive and unattractive in-groups. *Personality and Social Psychology Bulletin, 23*, 1254–1264.

Simon, B., Hastedt, C., & Aufderheide, B. (1997). When self-categorization makes sense: The role of meaningful social categorization in minority and majority members' self-perception. *Journal of Personality and Social Psychology, 73*, 310–320.

Simon, B., Loewy, M., Stürmer, S., Weber, U., Freytag, P., Habig, C., Kampmeier, C., & Spahlinger, P. (1998). Collective identification and social movement participation. *Journal of Personality and Social Psychology, 74*, 646–658.

Smith, E. R., & Mackie, D. M. (1995). *Social psychology.* New York: Worth.

Sumner, W. C. (1906). *Folkways.* Boston, MA: Ginn.

Tajfel, H. (1978). *The social psychology of minorities.* London: Minority Rights Group (No. 7).

Tajfel, H. (1981). *Human groups and social categories: Studies in social psychology.* Cambridge, UK: Cambridge University Press.

Tajfel, H. (1982). Social psychology of intergroup relations. *Annual Review of Psychology, 33,* 1–39.

Tajfel, H., & Turner, J. C. (1986). The social identity theory of intergroup behavior. In S. Worchel & W. G. Austin (Eds.), *Psychology of intergroup relations* (pp. 7–24). Chicago, IL: Nelson-Hall.

Tajfel, H., Billig, M. G., Bundy, R. P., & Flament, C. (1971). Social categorization and intergroup behaviour. *European Journal of Social Psychology, 1,* 149–178.

Taylor, S. E., Fiske, S. T., Etcoff, N. L., & Ruderman, A. J. (1978). Categorical and contextual bases of person memory and stereotyping. *Journal of Personality and Social Psychology, 36,* 778–793.

Turner, J. C., Hogg, M. A., Oakes, P. J., Reicher, S. D., & Wetherell, M. S. (1987). *Rediscovering the social group. A self-categorization theory.* Oxford, UK: Basil Blackwell.

Van Twuyver, M., & Van Knippenberg, A. (1999). Social categorization as a function of relative group size. *British Journal of Social Psychology, 38*(2), 135–156.

Verkuyten, M. (1995). Self-esteem, self-concept stability, and aspects of ethnic identity among minority and majority youth in the Netherlands. *Journal of Youth and Adolescence, 24,* 155–173.

Wright, S. C., Taylor, D. M., & Moghaddam, F. M. (1990). Responding to membership in a disadvantaged group: From acceptance to collective protest. *Journal of Personality and Social Psychology, 58,* 994–1003.

CHAPTER SIXTEEN

The Impact of Relative Group Status: Affective, Perceptual and Behavioral Consequences

Naomi Ellemers and Manuela Barreto

1 Introduction

The present chapter takes a social identity approach to examine the effects of group status on the feelings, beliefs, and behaviors of individual group members. We first consider how group status is likely to affect individual group members, and which psychological processes might play a role in this. Then we provide an overview of relevant empirical evidence, indicating that straightforward effects of group status are moderated by various factors such as the socio-structural characteristics of the intergroup situation, the degree of ingroup identification, and the nature of the social context. Data on ingroup identification, satisfaction, and self-esteem inform us about group members' affective responses. Turning to perceptual effects of group status, we take into consideration that these may include various strategic judgments and attributional biases. Finally, we describe how biased reward allocations and attempts at self- and group improvement may be seen as behavioral consequences of differential group status.

2 The Meaning of Status for Group Members

Looking at historical developments in the study of social status, it is striking that this issue was originally addressed from a sociological perspective. Status was usually defined in terms of social class, and the main concern of scientists in this area was to address the socio-political consequences of social inequality and social injustice (see Tyler & Smith, 1998 for a review). During the past two decades, however, the study of inequalities between social groups has also moved into the realm of social psychology, with the aim of assessing the implications of social status for individual group members (e.g., Dovidio & Gaertner, 1986; Major, 1994).

Over the years, empirical evidence has accumulated to document the sometimes-severe consequences of social group membership for individual well-being. Specifically, members of stigmatized or otherwise disadvantaged groups report higher levels of depression than members of advantaged groups (Crocker, Major, & Steele, 1998). More generally, rejection from desirable social groups can lead to alienation and psychological disturbance (e.g., Kobrynowicz & Branscombe, 1997). Obviously, the self-perceived standing of one's group does not necessarily correspond to externally determined status differences. Nevertheless, to the extent that one is continually approached by others in terms of one's externally defined group status, this is inevitably internalized, and in due time it becomes irrelevant whether it is subjectively or objectively based (Tajfel, 1978).

While the term "status" is commonly used to indicate that groups may differ from each other in terms of their relative prestige, the root of such differences may vary widely from (beliefs about) the relative performances of the groups on some experimental task, to group memberships that are severely stigmatizing in daily life. Broad as this conceptualization may be, in the present chapter we want to focus on the effects of group status per se. That is, we will not extend our discussion to include a specification of how the implications of group status may differ, depending on whether this is based on power differences, on differential access to material resources, or on the nature of interdependence and goal relations between groups.

In line with commonsense conceptualizations, the terms minority or majority group are often used to denote differences in social standing (as is usually the case with ethnic minorities), instead of more narrowly referring to the numerical representation of group members. While in some cases these two aspects may coincide, we think it is important to keep in mind that this is not the case as a matter of principle. Indeed recent studies aiming to orthogonally manipulate numerical size and group status have revealed that they have different and independent effects (see Simon, Aufderheide, & Kampmeier, this volume, chapter 15). To avoid similar confusions in the present chapter, we will focus on the effects of group status per se.

Psychological processes

When we consider the processes that may lead people to think about their group memberships in terms of the social standing these accord them, social comparisons play a central role (see Tajfel, 1978; Tajfel & Turner, 1979). The original focus of social comparison theory was on the establishment of relative competence through performance comparisons (Festinger, 1954). Research within this theory has mostly concentrated on the investigation of affective and perceptual consequences of social comparison information regarding individual performances. Relative deprivation theory expanded this theorizing to address outcome comparisons, having to do with relative power, or economic success. In addition, the focus of relative deprivation theory was also enlarged, encompassing both individual and group level comparisons, although the latter has constituted a privileged object of research (Kawakami & Dion, 1993). Our choice to conduct the present review from a social identity perspective reflects the fact that this theory subsumes both kinds of comparisons (i.e., regarding performances and outcomes), assuming that either may feed into the comparative prestige of different social groups. Moreover, social identity theory incorporates different psychological processes, specifying the consequences of social comparison at both the individual and the group level.

When considering whether results from studies on (interpersonal) social comparisons are relevant to explain the effects of intergroup differences in social standing, it is important to keep in mind that people may have different comparison goals, that guide their comparison preferences in different situations (Major, Testa, & Bylsma, 1991). Thus, to the extent that research on interpersonal comparisons has revealed a preference for upward comparison, this is likely to be motivated by self-improvement considerations (Levine & Moreland, 1989). By contrast, a preference for downward comparison targets in intergroup comparisons may stem from self-enhancement motives (Wills, 1981). Despite the general desire to make comparisons from which the ingroup emerges favorably, we argue that groups that have a perspective for performance improvement may choose to engage in upward comparison, and acknowledge their group's current inferiority as a first step in the pursuit of collective improvement (Ouwerkerk, Ellemers, & de Gilder, 1999).

Multi-level and crossed-categories

In addition to these different goals or motivational considerations there are also other, more structural factors that may determine the target of comparison, such as (physical) proximity, salience, or perceived similarity (Levine & Moreland, 1989). This issue is particularly important when we consider that, in most real-life situations, social perceivers are confronted with a full constellation of different social groups, which may cross-cut each other, or be related at different levels of inclusiveness, while they are likely to include various comparative dimensions (Turner, 1987). Some categories such as race, gender, or social class prove to be basic, in the sense that information concerning these categories is automatically processed. Nevertheless, more often than not, people may choose from different alternative frames of reference, according to which the relative standing of a particular group can be judged. As a result, group status is not given, but largely context dependent, and empirical research has established that different comparison contexts may influence the perceived status position of an identical target group (Ellemers & Van Knippenberg, 1997).

Intra- and intergroup status

Although there are situations in which individuals consider themselves and others as interchangeable elements of the same social category, group members may also differ from each other in important ways. Thus intragroup differences in (perceived) competence, prototypicality, respect, or liking may moderate the way individual group members respond to identical circumstances. For instance, the extent to which someone is seen as a prototypical group member affects how well he or she is liked by fellow group members (Hogg & Hains, 1996). As a result, nonprototypical or otherwise peripheral group members may be primarily concerned with improving their personal image within the group, rather than anything else (Noel, Wann, & Branscombe, 1995). A converse effect is that individual group members seem less vulnerable to the threat of low group status, when they compare positively to other ingroup members (Major, 1994) as we will explain in more detail below.

3   Affective Responses to Group Status

Identification

While relatively few studies have examined affective responses in a strict sense (i.e., by asking group members to report the intensity and nature of the specific emotions they experience), it is important to consider that people's affective responses to existing inter-group differences are moderated by the strength of their ties with this particular group. This was illustrated in a study by Wann and Branscombe (1990) among sports specta-tors, showing that spectator enjoyment was more dependent on the outcome of the game as people identified more strongly with one of the teams involved. That is, compared to low identifiers, high identifiers showed more enjoyment after group success and less after group failure (Tougas & Veilleux, 1988).

A review of experimental work on the effects of relative group status on the degree to which individuals identify with their group reveals that low group status generally results in lower levels of identification than high group status (see Ellemers, 1993, for an overview). This has been explained from a social identity perspective, by arguing that people are likely to resist involvement with a lower status group because this may dimin-ish their possibilities to achieve a positive social identity (Tajfel, 1978; Tajfel & Turner, 1979). In other words, decreasing the level of identification may help individuals to avoid the negative emotions that may ensue from membership in a lower status group.

While minority/majority groups are sometimes taken to represent differential group status, we again want to emphasize that the relative size of the group does not necessar-ily inform us of its perceived standing. In fact, people generally identify more strongly with minority than majority groups (see Mullen, Brown, & Smith, 1992, for a meta-analysis), which is in line with the assumption that the association with a minority group is likely to enhance the distinctiveness of one's group membership (see Brewer, 1991). Thus, the smaller the relative size of the group, the stronger the connection between the group's fate and the emotions this evokes in individual group members. In other words, the relative size of the group is likely to affect the extent to which people *cognitively* perceive themselves as members of a particular group, while the relative status primarily impacts the *affective* consequences of this group membership (see Ellemers, Kortekaas, & Ouwerkerk, 1999; Simon, Glässner-Bayerl, & Stratenwerth, 1991). As a result, relative group size can intensify the (positive or negative) effects of (high or low) group status.

Satisfaction

Experiments in which overall levels of satisfaction were compared have generally revealed greater satisfaction with the group's relative standing, as well as with one's group membership, as the ingroup had a higher status position (e.g., Ellemers, Van Knippenberg, De Vries, & Wilke, 1988). At a more specific level, Sachdev and Bourhis (1987) observed that high and equal status group members report more positive feelings (being comfortable, satisfied, and happy) than lower status group members (see also Ouwerkerk et al., 1999).

While these effects of group status seem rather straightforward, a perhaps more interesting issue is that they may either be undermined or intensified, depending on the further implications of the group status difference, as well as the importance of the group for the individual. That is, to the extent that current differences in group status are seen as transitory or otherwise unstable, their influence on the affective responses of group members is less pronounced as this may engender hopes of status improvement (increasing satisfaction) among members of lower status groups (Ellemers, Van Knippenberg, & Wilke, 1990), while higher status group members have to cope with the prospect of position loss, which may depress satisfaction. As a result, enduring disadvantage, as when women or African Americans are discriminated against, is much more consequential than temporary disadvantage, that is, when men or Whites consider ways in which they are discriminated against (Branscombe, 1997).

Additionally, while people generally tend to perceive their outcomes as less legitimate as they are less favorable (distributive justice, Deutsch, 1985), the perceived legitimacy of an identical status position may differ, depending on the procedures that resulted in the current state of affairs (procedural justice, Tyler & Smith, 1998), as well as the attributions people make for their own outcomes (Major, 1994). Thus, the perceived history underlying current outcomes may also moderate the effects of differences in group status. For instance, to the extent that membership in a lower status group results from rejection by those in the higher status group, feelings of resentment, dissatisfaction, and frustration are quite strong (see Wright, Taylor, & Moghaddam, 1990). In a similar vein, the effects of group status on overall satisfaction are more pronounced when people think intergroup status differences result from illegitimate treatment of their group, while they tend to resign to legitimate low status (Ellemers, Wilke, & Van Knippenberg, 1993; Kawakami & Dion, 1993). In sum, aside from the current relative standing of their group, people's affective responses also depend on the historical development of these differences, as well as their future perspectives.

Self-esteem

In an early theoretical analysis of the possible consequences of group status differences, Cartwright (1950) argued that the evaluation of the groups to which one belongs is the primary determinant of self-esteem. Accordingly, over the years, research evidence has accumulated to show that comparisons with better-off others (upward comparisons) generally decrease positive affect and self-esteem, while comparisons with worse-off others increase positive affect and self-esteem (e.g., Wills, 1981).

At first sight, this seems consistent with social identity theory: When one's group compares negatively to relevant other groups, this may constitute a threat to positive social identity, and hence limit the extent to which membership in this group can contribute to positive self-esteem (Tajfel & Turner, 1979). This has been taken to predict that membership in a low-status group should result in depressed self-esteem (Hinkle & Brown, 1990; Hogg & Abrams, 1990). However, research on the relation between relative group status and self-esteem has yielded inconsistent results.

Methodological issues. In their research review, Crocker and Major (1989) show that membership in low-status groups is not associated with low personal self-esteem. Likewise, reported levels of collective self-esteem are not systematically related to membership in a disadvantaged group (see Crocker, Luhtanen, Blaine, & Broadnax, 1994). Overall, it seems that stigmatized and disadvantaged individuals are not particularly dissatisfied with their lives, as has been observed with respect to women (Major, 1994) as well as African Americans (Diener, 1984).

In the literature, considerable discussion has been devoted to the question of why this may be the case. In relation to this, an important problem is that various studies in this area of research have methodological flaws that may account for the lack of a relationship between group status and self-esteem (see Long & Spears, 1997; Rubin & Hewstone, 1998, for an extensive discussion of this issue). For instance, sometimes personal self-esteem was assessed instead of group-based self-esteem, or measures of general or stable self-esteem were taken, instead of specific or momentary self-esteem. Addressing this issue, Long and Spears (1997) argue that interactive effects of personal and collective levels of self-esteem should be taken into account, because only the combination of the two can inform us of whether the way people think of themselves corresponds to the standing awarded to them on the basis of their group membership.

Coping strategies. More interesting from a theoretical point of view is that the experience of threat may elicit various coping responses that can serve to protect and/or bolster self-esteem. That is, under some circumstances research participants may perceive the self-esteem measure as providing them with an opportunity to communicate their perceived self-worth to the researcher as the representative of some wider audience. Accordingly, when the standing of their group is called into question, this may elicit strategic and perhaps even reactive answering patterns, which may help group members cope with the threat they experience (Ellemers, Barreto, & Spears, 1999). This is likely to be an important reason why no straightforward relation between group status and self-esteem could be obtained in research. When we examine such strategic responses more specifically, we can distinguish between certain classes of responses. In social identity theory, different strategies have been described that may be employed to address a negative social identity (Tajfel & Turner, 1979).

From different perspectives it has been argued that in addition to the different courses of action people may undertake to improve the actual outcomes or performance of their group (problem-focused coping, see Folkman & Lazarus, 1990), they may also try to come to terms with the situation without actually changing it (i.e., engage in emotion-focused coping). The latter type of strategy might entail de-emphasizing the connection of the individual to the group, which may result in decreased ingroup identification, as we have seen above. Alternatively, group members may cope with their predicament as a group, by reducing the perceived importance of the unfavorable comparative dimension. Indeed there is now a substantial body of empirical evidence demonstrating that members of lower status groups might downplay the implications of their inferior standing by challenging or denying the relevance of the status criterion (Ellemers, Van Rijswijk, Roefs, & Simons, 1997; Spears & Manstead, 1989).

Another way of coping with inferior group status is by changing the level of comparison (Turner, 1987), and trying to ensure that one's personal standing within the group is esteem-enhancing, despite the fact that the group does not compare favorably to other groups (see Ellemers et al., 1990; Marsh & Parker, 1984). Thus, focusing on the way one's personal situation compares to that of others within the same social group, may serve to protect the self-esteem of those who belong to stigmatized groups (see Crocker & Major, 1989 for a review). The validity of this argument is underlined by empirical evidence showing that women who compare their jobs and wages to other women report higher self-esteem than those who compare their own situation to that of men (Major, 1994). Consequently, when opportunities to distinguish the individual self from a group that is discriminated are limited, for instance because the individual has committed him/herself to the group (Barreto & Ellemers, in press; Ellemers & Van Rijswijk, 1997) or because group boundaries are closed (Ellemers et al., 1988; Lalonde & Silverman, 1994), the self-esteem threat is intensified and feelings of collective deprivation are more pronounced. This again illustrates that the nature of the social situation may determine which level of identity is salient, and hence whether interpersonal or intergroup comparisons will be made (Brewer & Weber, 1994).

4   Perceptual Consequences

When we turn to the perceptual consequences of group status, the main question is how group perceptions may differ, depending on the relative status position of the group to which people belong. From a social identity perspective, we may argue that group members' general motivation to achieve positive distinctiveness is likely to guide their evaluations, in the sense that they should generally be predisposed to view their own group in a more positive light than other groups (see Tajfel, 1978; Tajfel & Turner, 1979). In other words, social identity theory would predict that people may hold differential perceptions of an identical intergroup comparison, depending on their own perspective as members of one of these groups.

Previous efforts to review empirical evidence to this effect have mainly pointed to the inconsistent nature of the relationship between relative group status and ingroup favoring perceptions (Hinkle & Brown, 1990; Mullen, Brown, & Smith, 1992). That is, although sometimes more bias was displayed by members of lower status groups, sometimes they showed less bias, or relative group status had no effect. Researchers investigating the evaluative consequences of group status with artificially created laboratory groups have often reported stronger biases in high status compared to lower status groups (e.g., Sachdev & Bourhis, 1987), and this is consistent with observations among various natural groups, that lower status group members evaluate the other group more positively than their own group (e.g., Mlicki & Ellemers, 1996).

In this section we will focus on strategic perceptions of current group characteristics, in the sense that we will consider how group status affects the perceived average standing of the group, the perceived importance of group characteristics, the perceived homogeneity of the group, and the occurrence of various attributional biases.

Strategic judgments

In order to understand why such diverse aspects of intergroup perception may be affected, we have to consider the implications of group status in greater detail. As we have seen in the previous section of this chapter, compared to high-status group membership, belonging to a lower status group can be identity threatening, and is likely to elicit coping responses. Again, it is important to consider that *different kinds of strategies* may be employed to this end, and favoring the ingroup in evaluative judgments is only one possibility among a range of responses that may be displayed. Furthermore, we have to keep in mind that, aside from these motivational consequences, relative group status also refers to consensually defined aspects of social reality, and this may limit the interpretational freedom people may have to depict their group positively in important ways (see Ellemers et al., 1997).

This may at least partly explain why results from laboratory investigations seem to be inconsistent with observations in field settings (Mullen, Brown, & Smith, 1992). When we consider that laboratory studies commonly employ experimental groups, where group status is usually based on a single (performance) criterion, this implies that intergroup differences are not rooted in historical developments, nor do they have much predictive value for people's prospects outside the laboratory context. Even though such group-status manipulations appear to be highly involving and evoke strong responses from research participants, the actual implications of group status manipulated in this way are quite modest, compared to the consequentiality of more long-standing status differences in natural groups, and this may explain at least part of the ease with which they are challenged in biased judgments. In a similar vein, we have to consider that group members' responses in laboratory simulations usually remain anonymous, and that there is no need to justify or account for one's private perceptions. Recent empirical evidence has demonstrated that under such anonymous conditions members of lower status groups feel relatively free to claim ingroup superiority and will do so, if they identify strongly with the group and its standing. However, they are likely to refrain from doing so when publicly accountable for their group ratings (see Ellemers, Barreto, & Spears, 1999). In sum, we can point to various features of experimentally simulated intergroup status differences that render it more likely that members of lower status groups challenge or limit the implications of the status manipulation by displaying ingroup favoring judgments. Also, as we have argued in the previous section, this general tendency may be more pronounced for those group members who derive the confidence to do this from more long-standing sources of esteem, such as the fact that in the "real" world they belong to a group with superior social standing (Branscombe, 1997; see also Long & Spears, 1997).

This is not to say that laboratory experimentation is useless for predicting actual responses of group members in real social situations. Instead, the above argument is intended to illustrate that any laboratory simulation can only capture a specific sample of conditions, while there are real-life situations that are characterized by other or additional features. Thus, the results of laboratory experiments primarily attest to the fact that membership in a group with low status elicits the *motivation* to perceive one's group in a positive way. However, the extent to which such motivation is actually translated into ingroup favoring judgments (or other behavioral responses) also depends on the further implications of current status differences, as well as group members' opportunities to protect their group's image in alternative ways.

Group-level strategies. Indeed, those who have suggested that empirical research fails to support predictions from social identity theory (e.g., Hinkle & Brown, 1990) have neglected the original claim of social identity theory that people may resort to different strategies in order to deal with a negative social identity (Turner, 1999). Group members do not necessarily engage in ingroup bias when their group is threatened, but may use various alternative strategies instead.

When people aim to depict their group in a favorable light, more subtle strategies may be used to address a negative social identity. That is, while taking into account the above-described social reality constraints, members of lower status groups may nevertheless challenge the predictive value of mean differences between groups (Doosje & Ellemers, 1997), question the importance of the comparative dimension involved (Ellemers & Van Rijswijk, 1997), or propose alternative status dimensions (Lalonde, 1992). Likewise, while members of a devalued group may acknowledge their inferior standing vis-à-vis the higher status group, they may nevertheless perceive their own group relatively positively when comparing to a second outgroup (Spears & Manstead, 1989, Study 2).

Importantly, the very social features that motivate group members to engage in identity-enhancing group perceptions may also restrict the interpretational freedom they have in doing so, and hence delimit the possibilities to display ingroup favoring biases. As a result, how relative group status translates into group perceptions depends on the salient social context (Oakes, Haslam, & Turner, 1990). Given the fact that in real-life situations multiple comparison groups and multiple comparative dimensions are available, members of different groups may engage in what has been labeled "social coopera-tion," as opposed to "social competition," in the sense that they mutually acknowledge each other's value by perceiving the ingroup as superior in some specific respects, while deferring to outgroup superiority on other comparative dimensions. Notwithstanding this cooperative pattern, some competition might still emerge in establishing the relative importance of different comparative dimensions, when each party emphasizes that those features or abilities that characterize the ingroup are actually more relevant, and should therefore determine overall group standing (e.g., Mummendey & Schreiber, 1984).

Individual-level strategies. If identification with the group is lacking, indicating that membership in this particular group is relatively unimportant for the people involved, they may willingly acknowledge the inferior standing of their group overall. At the same time, however, they are likely to emphasize intragroup differences, which enables them to detach themselves from the group (i.e., engage in individual mobility) and to protect or improve their individual position in the social system (see Branscombe & Ellemers, 1998). Thus, while it has been proposed that outgroups are generally seen as more homogeneous than ingroups (e.g., Park & Judd, 1990), we think there is sufficient empirical evidence to attest to the moderating role of relative group status on perceived group homogeneity (e.g., Fiske, 1993; Simon, 1992). Thus, members of lower status groups strategically accentuate the heterogeneity of their group, while intragroup similarities are emphasized when the ingroup compares positively to relevant other groups (Doosje, Spears, & Koomen, 1995). Again, however, given that such strategic perceptions mainly serve to protect the personal self-image at the expense of the rest of the group, they are only displayed when commitment to the group is relatively low (see Spears, Ellemers, & Doosje, 1999, for an overview).

Attributions

Self-serving attributions. As is the case with other consequences of intergroup differences in social standing, group members may strategically use attributions of current differences in group status to protect the self-perceived worth of themselves or their group. First, people may differ in the extent to which they attribute group outcomes to particular group members, or more specifically, in the extent to which they take personal responsibility for group outcomes. When feedback regarding the group's performance is provided, people generally take personal credit for the group's success and reject responsibility for its failure (e.g., Mynatt & Sherman, 1975), and this self-serving pattern is more pronounced as groups are less cohesive (e.g., Schlenker & Miller, 1977). In line with the idea that people may use attributions strategically to protect their personal self-image, Schlenker, Soraci, & McCarthy (1976) showed that after failure group members tended to admit that the group had performed poorly while maintaining that they themselves had performed well. In successful groups, by contrast, group members are more willing to attribute the responsibility of success to the "average group member" than in failing groups.

Group-serving attributions. While these self-serving attributions have been observed in response to intergroup status differences, attributional biases may also emerge at the group level (Pettigrew, 1979). That is, laboratory experiments on the attributions of group performance as well as natural group members' accounts of spontaneously occurring group behavior show a systematic difference with respect to the perceived causes of positive and negative behavior, depending on whether an ingroup or an outgroup is involved (see Hewstone, 1990, for a review), as is also apparent from the linguistic terms they select to describe these behaviors (i.e., the linguistic intergroup bias, Maass, Salvi, Arcuri, & Semin, 1989). People are generally inclined to make internal attributions for positive acts of ingroup members, and negative acts of outgroup members (e.g., Winkle & Taylor, 1979). By contrast, outgroup success and ingroup failure are more often ascribed to (good or bad) luck, (high or low) effort, or the difficulty of the task (Hewstone, 1990). However, in line with what we have seen above with respect to group perceptions more generally, in some cases intergroup status differences may seem so deeply rooted that with the attributions they make, lower status group members end up favoring the outgroup or derogating the ingroup, instead of challenging the current state of affairs (e.g., Yarkin, Town, & Wallston, 1982). Internal attributions for unfavorable group outcomes or for status differences between groups may serve to legitimize the status quo and thus undermine the possibilities of status improvement.

Attributions to prejudice. One form of external attribution that has more recently been the focus of much attention is the attribution (of either group outcomes or personal treatment) to discrimination. Hewstone and Jaspars (1982) showed that information concerning differences between Whites and Blacks in Britain (rate of arrest, unemployment, educational achievement, and occupational status) were attributed less to internal characteristics and more to discrimination by Blacks than by Whites. Recent research has suggested that people are actually rather reluctant to engage in this sort of attribution (Crosby, 1984). Ruggiero and Taylor (1997) showed that participants were only willing to attribute a judge's negative evaluation of themselves to discrimination when they were told that there was a very high probability that the judge would discriminate (above 90%). While attributions to discrimination may alleviate a sense of personal inadequacy, they at the same time decrease people's feeling of control over their outcomes, which is associated with a decrease in self-esteem (see also Branscombe & Ellemers, 1998). Indeed, Ruggiero and Taylor observed positive correlations of attributions to discrimination with performance self-esteem, but negative correlations with social self-esteem and perceived control.

   While attributions to prejudice may therefore not be the primary choice of lower status group members, if they do occur they can help to promote collective action. For instance, Gurin, Gurin, Lao, and Beattie (1969) showed that as Blacks attributed their social position more to discrimination than to personal causes, they aspired more to nontraditional Black jobs and were more likely to engage in collective action. Attributions to discrimination should, however, not prevent group members from searching for other possible causes for their poor outcomes. In fact, making internal attributions for failure may help to identify problems and difficulties and may importantly contribute to the improvement of the situation of the group.

5   Behavioral Consequences

Ingroup bias in reward allocations

In addition to expressing a more positive evaluation of the ingroup than of the outgroup, group members may display ingroup favoritism in more consequential ways, by allocating more rewards to the ingroup than to the outgroup. Research with the minimal group paradigm, developed by Tajfel and his colleagues, has shown that the mere categorization of individuals into groups can be sufficient to elicit biased allocations of rewards favoring the ingroup (see Brewer & Brown, 1998; Diehl, 1990). Overall, such ingroup biases in reward allocations have been shown to be stronger for high-status groups than low-status groups (see Mullen, Brown, & Smith, 1992, for a meta-analysis). However, there are specific conditions under which low-status group members may be the ones who display the strongest ingroup bias.

One class of situations in which ingroup favoring allocations may occur among lower status group members, is when they are highly motivated to improve the fate of the ingroup. This may be the case when the threat associated with inferior status is aggravated, by the fact that negative (e.g., an unpleasant noise) instead of positive (money or points) rewards have to be allocated (see Mummendey & Otten, 1998, for an overview). Alternatively, members of low-status groups may be especially motivated to favor their group in reward allocations if they identify strongly with the group (Perreault & Bourhis, 1999). However, stronger ingroup identification does not automatically result in greater bias, as this depends on the contextually salient ingroup norm. That is, if the group norm prescribes fairness, this may lead those who identify strongly with the group to show *less* (rather than more) bias in reward allocations (Jetten, Spears, & Manstead, 1997).

A second source of variation in the responses of lower status group members, is the extent to which their inferior status position may seem to delimit their behavioral options (see Ellemers, Barreto, & Spears, 1999, for an overview). This may be the case when reward allocations are closely related to the status criterion. As a result, among lower status group, ingroup favoritism in reward allocations is significantly stronger when the measure that is used is not related to current status differentials (e.g., Reichl, 1997). In a more general sense, to the extent that the status system is considered as legitimate or fair, this may prevent lower status group members from making biased allocations. By contrast, illegitimate status differences imply that the current distribution of resources is in itself wrong, and allocating more rewards to the ingroup than to the outgroup may seem a direct way to redress this injustice. Consequently, low status group members generally discriminate more in favor of the ingroup as status differences seem less legitimate (e.g., Ellemers, Wilke, & Van Knippenberg, 1993).

Attempts at self- and group improvement

While reward allocations may constitute attempts at manipulating the relative gains of the group in a specific situation, the fact that they do not change the actual social standing of the group may imply that these gains are merely temporary. In later situations, the opportunity for allocating resources may not exist and low-status group members are thus likely to remain disadvantaged. As Steele and co-workers have shown, the improvement of one's social standing may constitute a rather daunting endeavor, as members of disadvantaged groups may confirm their disadvantaged position by underperforming on status-relevant tasks in which their group is stereotypically believed to be inferior, thereby contributing to the legitimization and stability of the status quo (see Crocker, Major, &

Steele, 1998 for a review). However difficult such attempts may be, members of disadvantaged groups do seem to be concerned with the improvement of their social status. An actual improvement of one's current standing may either be achieved by leaving the low-status group and attempting individual upward mobility, or by joining the group in a collective attempt to change the social system (Tajfel & Turner, 1979). While both status improvement strategies may be equally effective, they are fundamentally different, and therefore often incompatible (Branscombe & Ellemers, 1998). Therefore, it is important to consider under which circumstances group members engage in active efforts to improve the position of the group, or rather work at their individual status improvement (see Mackie & Wright, this volume, chapter 14).

While membership in a lower status group may give rise to feelings of discontent and deprivation, the locus of concern, and therefore the target of improvement efforts, may differ, depending on the salient level of identity (see Kawakami & Dion, 1993, for a review). As social identity theory and self-categorization theory argue, group identification is accompanied by internalization of group norms and goals, and is thus likely to result in pro-group behavior (Hogg & Turner, 1987). Consistent with this view, level of identification with the group has been shown to determine concern with its social position, willingness to engage in effort to improve the group (Barreto & Ellemers, in press; Ouwerkerk et al., 1999), involvement in pro-group activities (Ethier & Deaux, 1994), and desire for individual mobility (Ellemers, Spears, & Doosje, 1997). Consequently, involvement in collective protest has only been observed among those who are highly identified and therefore feel deprived as a group (see Kelly & Breinlinger, 1996, for a review).

Moreover, degree of identification has been found to modify the relation between other relevant variables and pro-group behavior. That is, besides being differentially motivated to engage in pro-group behavior, low and high identifiers also differ in what motivates them to do so at all. In particular, Barreto and Ellemers (in press) observed that, while high identifiers were internally motivated to strive at collective improvement, low identifiers showed similar behavior when this helped them avoid the social disapproval that individualistic forms of action may entail. More generally, it would seem that the specific activity or form of behavior high identifiers display while aiming at group status improvement will depend on what the group defines as the valued form of action while low identifiers seem to be primarily guided by what is instrumental to their personal goals (Barreto & Ellemers, in press).

People may perceive their group to be disadvantaged and still not engage in collective status enhancement strategies. In fact, other characteristics of the social structure seem to play an important role in determining personal or collective level responses to social disadvantage. It has been shown that for group members to be mobilized into a collective protest, their disadvantage has to be felt as illegitimate (e.g., Klandermans, 1997).

In a similar Vein, Ellemers, Van Knippenberg, and Wilke (1990) showed that group members were willing to direct themselves at group status improvement when the status structure was perceived as unstable. Importantly, this was the case irrespective of group members' individual chances of gaining access to a higher status group. This may also help explain why privileged members of a disadvantaged group would be willing to engage in collective protest, despite possible opportunities to improve their fate individually (Gurin & Epps, 1975). In short, it seems that when changing the group's status seems justified or feasible, group members may focus on the situation of the group, irrespective of their opportunities for personal improvement.

6   Conclusions and Directions for Future Research

In this chapter we have reviewed empirical evidence attesting to the profound implications group status may have for the emotions individuals experience, the way they judge their group in relation to other groups, and the social behavior this may elicit. Gaining an overall picture is all the more difficult, given that various other features of the group and the social system more generally may feed into perceived group prestige. To address the confusion this can and has resulted in, we have specified how important additional group characteristics, such as its relative size or its power position, may sometimes modify or obscure the consequences of group status per se. Additionally, particularly in more complex and rich natural group settings, group members may selectively choose to consider themselves in terms of one particular group membership instead of another, or they may emphasize intragroup differences, focusing on personal features instead of on characteristics they share with other group members.

We have argued throughout this chapter that the various indicators that have been used in empirical research to examine how relative group prestige impinges upon the life of individual group members should not always be taken at face value. That is, while we sometimes may be able to infer how group members actually perceive or experience the relative standing of their group, more often research measures tap into the next stage in this process, by revealing how group members attempt to *deal with* the feelings that ensue from their group's relative standing, for example, by denying or attempting to change current intergroup differences. While this perspective may help us understand why seemingly inconsistent findings are reported in the literature, critics are likely to argue that our stance would seem to imply that empirical research in this area is quite uninformative. To counter this possible criticism, we have aimed to specify the conditions and measures that are likely to inform us of internalized convictions about one's group, differentiating these from situations where group members may more easily use different coping strategies. In so doing, we have consistently focused on a limited set of variables that moderate group members' responses.

In this context, we have emphasized that intergroup differences in group status may motivate group members to enhance or protect the current standing of their group. However, this general motivation may give rise to different responses, depending on the importance of the group for the individual (identification or group commitment), the perceived origin of current intergroup differences (as is evident from legitimacy ratings and attributions), and prospects for future change at the individual (group boundary permeability), or group level (stability of intergroup status differences). Together, these factors determine: (a) whether the main goal is to cope with intergroup status differences individually or as a group, (b) which aspects of the group's status position offer scope to maintain self- or group-enhancing perceptions, and (c) what attempts group members are likely to make to improve or protect their group's current standing.

The assumption that responses to group status differences should be seen as indicators of various strategies raises a host of novel theoretical and empirical questions. *First,* it would seem essential to gain more insight into the specific goals group members are likely to pursue, as well as the factors that may lead them to prefer particular goals over others. For this purpose, we should uncover more about the likely consequences of different strategic responses for the individual, the group, and the greater social system in which they find themselves.

A *second* important direction for future research would entail a more systematic consideration of the way in which different classes of responses group members may show are related to each other in a meaningful way. Research to date has usually focused on one central outcome variable (e.g., group members' self-esteem, or degree of ingroup bias), assuming that different kinds of responses can be seen as complementary and interchangeable indicators of the perceived worth of the group. However, we think that this is perhaps too reductionist an approach to gain insight into the psychological implications of these responses. That is, while different responses may be related to each other, the strategy group members choose to cope with current status differences may also cause them to display a particular combination of responses which at first sight seems inconsistent. For instance, when hoping to improve their group's position, group members may report dissatisfaction with the group's current status, but refuse to admit that this threatens their self-esteem. In other words, we think it is important to consider how affect, perceptions, and behaviors are linked to each other. In this context, the previously made distinction between problem-focused and emotion-focused coping may play a crucial role.

A *third* question that emerges from our review concerns the strategic nature of social category activation. While it has been repeatedly pointed out that theoretical accounts and empirical investigations of intergroup relations should pay more attention to the issue of multiple categorization, this has so far only yielded a modest amount of studies, which mostly focus on the reduction of intergroup discrimination through cross-categorization (e.g., Vanbeselaere, 1991). Additionally, we have summarized some empirical work attesting to the possibility that people focus on within-group instead of intergroup comparisons. However, in order to predict people's responses in natural group settings, it seems mandatory to acquire a better insight into the extent to which people are likely to strategically focus on an alternative categorization, or switch to a higher or lower level of category inclusiveness when this may help them cope with the categorization that is spontaneously salient.

Finally, we have to acknowledge that a major part of the empirical work we reviewed, as well as the greatest theoretical elaboration, concerns the plight of lower status group members. Obviously, the confrontation with an unfavorable intergroup comparison is most likely to elicit a variety of coping responses, which are an intriguing object of study, both from a theoretical and from an applied point of view. However, the lack of explicit attention for the way high group status may influence the way people feel, perceive, and behave (except as a "contrast" condition to compare the responses of those with low group status), should not be taken as a sign that this is a less interesting or important issue. In fact, even a concern with the possibilities of lower status groups to achieve status improvement should imply that high-status groups merit closer attention, if only because they are often the ones that determine the success or failure of such status improvement attempts. Additionally, in line with a relative deprivation approach, the psychological implications for people in an objectively different situation might be quite similar, and high-status group members may be equally concerned with maintaining or protecting their current standing. The interesting question then is to what extent this concern gives rise to similar or different strategies, depending on whether current group status is high instead of low (see Ellemers & Bos, 1998).

To conclude, we hope that this chapter has illustrated that a strategic approach may both enable us to subsume a large body of seemingly inconsistent research findings into a single theoretical framework, and offer challenging prospects for further development of this important area.

References

Barreto, M., & Ellemers, N. (in press). You can't always do what you want: Social identity and self-presentation determinants of the choice to work for a low status group. *Personality and Social Psychology Bulletin.*

Branscombe, N. R. (1997). Thinking about one gender group's privileges or disadvantages: Consequences for well-being in women and men. *British Journal of Social Psychology, 37*(2), 167–184.

Branscombe, N. R., & Ellemers, N. (1998). Coping with group-based discrimination: Individualistic versus group level strategies. In J. K. Swim & C. Stangor (Eds.), *Prejudice: The target's perspective.* New York: Academic Press.

Brewer, M. B. (1991). The social self: On being the same and different at the same time. *Personality and Social Psychology Bulletin, 17*, 475–482.

Brewer, M. B., & Brown, R. J. (1998). Intergroup relations. In D. Gilbert, S. Fiske, & H. Lindzey (Eds.), *Handbook of social psychology* (4th ed.). New York: Erlbaum.

Brewer, M. B., & Weber, J. G. (1994). Self-evaluation effects on interpersonal versus intergroup social comparisons. *Journal of Personality and Social Psychology, 66*, 268–275.

Cartwright, D. (1950). Emotional dimensions of group life. In M. L. Reymert (Ed.), *Feelings and emotions* (pp. 439–447). New York: McGraw-Hill.

Crocker, J., Luhtanen, R., Blaine, B., & Broadnax, S. (1994). Collective self-esteem and psychological well-being among White, Black, and Asian college students. *Personality and Social Psychology Bulletin, 20*, 502–513.

Crocker, J., & Major, B. (1989). Social stigma and self-esteem: The self-protective properties of stigma. *Psychological Review, 96*, 608–630.

Crocker, J., Major, B., & Steele, C. (1998). Social stigma. In D. Gilbert, S. Fiske, & H. Lindzey (Eds.), *Handbook of social psychology* (4th ed.). New York: Erlbaum.

Crosby, F. (1984). The denial of personal discrimination. *American Behavioral Scientist, 27*, 371–386.

Deutsch, M. (1985). *Distributive justice.* New Haven, CN: Yale University Press.

Diehl, M. (1990). The minimal group paradigm: Theoretical explanations and empirical findings. In W. Stroebe & M. Hewstone (Eds.), *European review of social psychology* (Vol. 1, pp. 263–292). Chichester, UK: Wiley.

Diener, E. (1984). Subjective well-being. *Psychological Bulletin, 95,* 542–575.

Doosje, B., & Ellemers, N. (1997). Stereotyping under threat: The role of group identification. In R. Spears, P. Oakes, N. Ellemers, & A. Haslam (Eds.), *The social psychology of stereotyping and group life* (pp. 257–272). Oxford, UK: Blackwell.

Doosje, B., Spears, R., & Koomen, W. (1995). When bad isn't all bad: Strategic use of sample information in generalization and stereotyping. *Journal of Personality and Social Psychology, 69,* 642–655.

Dovidio, J. F., & Gaertner, S. L. (1986). Prejudice, discrimination, and racism: Historical trends and contemporary approaches. In J. F. Dovidio & S. L. Gaertner (Eds.), *Prejudice, discrimination, and racism.* New York: Academic Press.

Ellemers, N. (1993). The influence of socio-structural variables on identity management strategies. In W. Stroebe & M. Hewstone (Eds.), *European review of social psychology* (Vol. 4, pp. 27–58). Chichester, UK: Wiley.

Ellemers, N., Barreto, M., & Spears, R. (1999). Commitment and strategic responses to social context. In N. Ellemers, R. Spears, & B. Doosje (Eds.), *Social identity: Context, commitment, content* (pp. 127–146). Oxford, UK: Blackwell.

Ellemers, N., & Bos, A. (1998). Individual and group level responses to threat experienced by Dutch shopkeepers in East-Amsterdam. *Journal of Applied Social Psychology, 28,* 1987–2005.

Ellemers, N., Kortekaas, P., & Ouwerkerk, J. (1999). Self-categorisation, commitment to the group and group self-esteem as related but distinct aspects of social identity. *European Journal of Social Psychology, 29,* 371–389.

Ellemers, N., Spears, R., & Doosje, B. (1997). Sticking together or falling apart: Ingroup identification as a psychological determinant of group commitment versus individual mobility. *Journal of Personality and Social Psychology, 72*(3), 417–426.

Ellemers, N., & Van Knippenberg, A. (1997). Stereotyping in social context. In R. Spears, P. Oakes, N. Ellemers, & S. A. Haslam (Eds.), *The social psychology of stereotyping and group life.* Oxford, UK: Blackwell.

Ellemers, N., Van Knippenberg, A., De Vries, N. K., & Wilke, H. (1988). Social identification and permeability of group boundaries. *European Journal of Social Psychology, 18,* 497–513.

Ellemers, N., Van Knippenberg, A., & Wilke, H. (1990). The influence of permeability of group boundaries and stability of group status on strategies of individual mobility and social change. *British Journal of Social Psychology, 29,* 233–246.

Ellemers, N., & Van Rijswijk, W. (1997). Identity needs versus social opportunities: The use of group-level and individual-level identity management strategies. *Social Psychology Quarterly, 60*(1), 52–65.

Ellemers, N., Van Rijswijk, W., Roefs. M., & Simons, C. (1997). Bias in intergroup perceptions: Balancing ingroup identity with social reality. *Personality and Social Psychology Bulletin, 23*(2), 186–198.

Ellemers, N., Wilke, H., & Van Knippenberg, A. (1993). Effects of the legitimacy of low group or individual status on individual and collective identity enhancement strategies. *Journal of Personality and Social Psychology, 64,* 766–778.

Ethier, K. A., & Deaux, K. (1994). Negotiating social identity when contexts change: Maintaining identification and responding to threat. *Journal of Personality and Social Psychology, 67*(2), 243–251.

Festinger, L. (1954). A theory of social comparison processes. *Human Relations, 7,* 117–140.

Fiske, S. T. (1993). Controlling other people: The impact of power on stereotyping. *American Psychologist, 48,* 621–628.

Folkman, S., & Lazarus, R. S. (1990). Coping and emotion. In N. L. Stein, B. Leventhal, et al. (Eds.), *Psychological and biological approaches to emotion.* Hillsdale, NJ: Erlbaum.

Gurin, P., & Epps, E. (1975). *Black consciousness, identity, and achievement: A study of students in historically Black colleges.* New York: Wiley.

Gurin, P., Gurin, D., Lao, R., & Beattie, H. (1969). Internal–external control in the motivational dynamics of Negro youth. *Journal of Social Issues, 25,* 29–53.

Hewstone, M. (1990). The "ultimate attribution error"? A review of the literature on intergroup causal attribution. *European Journal of Social Psychology, 20,* 311–335.

Hewstone, M., & Jaspars, J. (1982). Intergroup relations and attribution processes. In H. Tajfel (Ed.), *Social identity and intergroup relations.* Cambridge, UK/Paris: Cambridge University Press/Maison des Sciences de l'Homme.

Hinkle, S., & Brown, R. (1990). Intergroup comparisons and social identity: Some links and lacunae. In D. Abrams & M. A. Hogg (Eds.), *Social identity theory: Constructive and critical advances.* London: Harvester Wheatsheaf.

Hogg, M. A., & Abrams, D. (1990). Social motivation, self-esteem, and social identity. In D. Abrams & M. A. Hogg (Eds.), *Social identity theory: Constructive and critical advances.* London: Harvester Wheatsheaf.

Hogg, M. A., & Hains, S. C. (1996). Intergroup relations and group solidarity: Effects of group identification and social beliefs on depersonalized attraction. *Journal of Personality and Social Psychology, 70*(2), 295–309.

Hogg, M. A., & Turner, J. C. (1987). Social identity and conformity: A theory of referent informational influence. In W. Doise & S. Moscovici (Eds.), *Current issues in European social psychology* (Vol. 2). Cambridge, UK: Cambridge University Press.

Jetten, J., Spears, R., & Manstead, A. S. R. (1997). Strength of identification and intergroup differentiation: The influence of group norms. *European Journal of Social Psychology, 27,* 816–817.

Kawakami, K., & Dion, K. L. (1993). The impact of salient self-identities on relative deprivation and action intentions. *European Journal of Social Psychology, 23,* 525–541.

Kelly, C., & Breinlinger, S. (1996). *The social psychology of collective action: Identity, injustice, and gender.* London: Taylor & Francis.

Klandermans, B. (1997). *The social psychology of protest.* Oxford, UK: Blackwell.

Kobrynowicz, D., & Branscombe, N. R. (1997). Who considers themselves victims of discrimination? Individual difference predictors of perceived gender discrimination in women and men. *Psychology of Women Quarterly, 21*(3), 347–363.

Lalonde, R. N. (1992). The dynamics of group differentiation in the face of defeat. *Personality and Social Psychology Bulletin, 18*(3), 336–342.

Lalonde, R. N., & Silverman, R. A. (1994). Behavioral preferences in response to social injustice: The effects of group permeability and social identity salience. *Journal of Personality and Social Psychology, 66,* 78–85.

Levine, J. M., & Moreland, R. L. (1989). Social values and multiple outcome comparisons. In N. Eisenberg, J. Reykowski, et al. (Eds.), *Social and moral values: Individual and societal perspectives.* Hillsdale, NJ: Erlbaum.

Long, K., & Spears, R. (1997). The self-esteem hypothesis revisited: Differentiation and the disaffected. In R. Spears, P. J. Oakes, N. Ellemers, & S. A. Haslam (Eds.), *The social psychology of stereotyping and group life.* Oxford, UK: Blackwell.

Maass, A., Salvi, D., Arcuri, L., & Semin, G. (1989). Language use in intergroup contexts: The linguistic intergroup bias. *Journal of Personality and Social Psychology, 57,* 981–993.

Major, B. (1994). From social inequality to personal entitlement: The role of social comparisons, legitimacy appraisals, and group membership. In L. Berkowitz (Ed.), *Advances in experimental social psychology* (Vol. 12). New York: Academic Press.

Major, B., Testa, M., & Bylsma, W. H. (1991). Responses to upward and downward social comparison: The impact of esteem-relevance and perceived control. In J. Suls & T. A. Wills (Eds.), *Social comparison: Contemporary theory and research* (pp. 237–260). Hillsdale, NJ: Erlbaum.

Marsh, H. W., & Parker, J. (1984). Determinants of student self-concept: Is it better to be a relatively large fish in a small pond even if you don't learn to swim as well? *Journal of Personality and Social Psychology, 47,* 213–231.

Mlicki, P., & Ellemers, N. (1996). Being different or being better? National stereotypes and identifications of Polish and Dutch students. *European Journal of Social Psychology, 26,* 97–114.

Mullen, B., Brown, R., & Smith, C. (1992). Ingroup bias as a function of salience, relevance, and status: An integration. *European Journal of Social Psychology, 22,* 103–123.

Mummendey, A., & Otten, S. (1998). Positive–negative asymmetry in social discrimination. In W. Stroebe & M. Hewstone (Eds.), *European review of social psychology* (Vol. 9). Chichester, UK: Wiley.

Mummendey, A., & Schreiber, H.-J. (1984). "Different" just mean "better": Some obvious and some hidden pathways to ingroup favoritism. *British Journal of Social Psychology, 23,* 363–368.

Mynatt, C., & Sherman, S. J. (1975). Responsibility attributions in groups and individuals: A direct test of the diffusion of responsibility hypothesis. *Journal of Personality and Social Psychology, 32,* 1111–1118.

Noel, J. G., Wann, D. L., & Branscombe, N. R. (1995). Peripheral ingroup membership status and public negativity toward outgroups. *Journal of Personality and Social Psychology, 68*(1), 127–137.

Oakes, P. J., Haslam, S. A., & Turner, J. C. (1990). *Stereotyping and social reality.* Oxford, UK: Blackwell.

Ouwerkerk, J. W., Ellemers, N., & De Gilder, D. (1999). Group commitment and individual effort in experimental and organizational contexts. In N. Ellemers, R. Spears, & B. Doosje (Eds.), *Social identity: Context, commitment, content.* Oxford, UK: Blackwell.

Park, B., & Judd, C. M. (1990). Measures and models of perceived group variability. *Journal of Personality and Social Psychology, 59,* 173–191.

Perreault, S., & Bourhis, R. Y. (1999). Ethnocentrism, social identification, and discrimination. *Personality and Social Psychology Bulletin, 25(1),* 92–103.

Pettigrew, T. F. (1979). The ultimate attribution error: Extending Allport's cognitive analysis of prejudice. *Personality and Social Psychology Bulletin, 5,* 461–476.

Reichl, A. J. (1997). Ingroup favouritism and outgroup favouritism in low status minimal groups: Differential responses to status-related and status-unrelated measures. *European Journal of Social Psychology, 27,* 617–633.

Rubin, M., & Hewstone, M. (1998). Social identity theory's self-esteem hypothesis: A review and some suggestions for clarification. *Personality and Social Psychology Review, 2*(1), 40–62.

Ruggiero, K. M., & Taylor, D. M. (1997). Why do minority group members perceive or do not perceive the discrimination that confronts them: The role of self-esteem and perceived control. *Journal of Personality and Social Psychology, 72,* 373–389.

Sachdev, I., & Bourhis, R. Y. (1987). Status differentials and intergroup behaviour. *European Journal of Social Psychology, 17*(3), 277–293.

Schlenker, B. R., & Miller, R. S. (1977). Group cohesiveness as a determinant of egocentric perceptions in cooperative groups. *Human Relations, 30,* 1039–1055.

Schlenker, B. R., Soraci, J., & McCarthy, B. (1976). Self-esteem and group performance as determinants of egocentric perceptions in cooperative groups. *Human Relations, 29,* 1163–1176.

Simon, B. (1992). The perception of ingroup and outgroup homogeneity: Reintroducing the intergroup context. In W. Stroebe & M. Hewstone (Eds.), *European review of social psychology* (Vol. 3, pp. 1–30). Chichester, UK: Wiley.

Simon, B., Glässner-Bayerl, B., & Stratenwerth, I. (1991). Stereotyping and self-stereotyping in a natural intergroup context: The case of heterosexual and homosexual men. *Social Psychology Quarterly, 54,* 252–266.

Spears, R., Ellemers, N., & Doosje, B. (1999). Commitment and the context of social perception. In N. Ellemers, R. Spears, & B. Doosje (Eds.), *Social identity: Context, commitment, content* (pp. 59–83). Oxford, UK: Blackwell.

Spears, R., & Manstead, A. S. R. (1989). The social context of stereotyping and differentiation. *European Journal of Social Psychology, 19,* 101–121.

Tajfel, H. (1978). *Differentiation between social groups: Studies in the social psychology of intergroup relations.* London: Academic Press.

Tajfel, H., & Turner, J. (1979). An integrative theory of intergroup conflict. In W. G. Austin & S. Worchel (Eds.), *The social psychology of intergroup relations.* Monterey, CA: Brooks Cole.

Tougas, F., & Veilleux, F. (1988). The influence of identification, collective relative deprivation, and procedure implementation on women's response to affirmative action: A causal modeling approach. *Canadian Journal of Behavioural Science, 20,* 15–28.

Turner, J. C. (1987). A self-categorization theory. In J. C. Turner, M. A. Hogg, P. J. Oakes, S. Reicher, & M. S. Wetherell (Eds.), *Rediscovering the social group: A self-categorization theory* (pp. 42–67). Oxford, UK: Blackwell.

Turner, J. C. (1999). Some current themes in research on social identity and self-categorization. In N. Ellemers, R. Spears, & B. Doosje (Eds.), Social identity: context, commitment, and content. Oxford, UK: Blackwell.

Tyler, T. R., & Smith, H. J. (1998). Social justice and social movements. In D. Gilbert, S. Fiske, & H. Lindzey (Eds.), *Handbook of social psychology* (4th ed.). New York: Erlbaum.

Vanbeselaere, N. (1991). The different effects of simple and crossed categorizations: A result of the category differentiation process or of differential category salience? *European Review of Social Psychology, 2,* 247–278.

Wann, D. L., & Branscombe, N. R. (1990). Die-Hard and Fair-Weather fans: Effects of identification on BIRGing and CORFing tendencies. *Journal of Sport and Social Issues, 14*(2), 103–117.

Wills, T. A. (1981). Downward comparison principles in social psychology. *Psychological Bulletin, 90,* 245–271.

Winkle, J. D., & Taylor, S. E. (1979). Preference, expectation, and attributional bias: Two field studies. *Journal of Applied Social Psycholoy, 9,* 183–197.

Wright, S. C., Taylor, D. M., & Moghaddam, F. M. (1990). Responding to membership in a disadvantaged group: From acceptance to collective protest. *Journal of Personality and Social Psychology, 58,* 994–1003.

Yarkin, K. L., Town, J. P., & Wallston, B. S. (1982). Blacks and women must try harder. *Personality and Social Psychology Bulletin, 8,* 21–24.

CHAPTER SEVENTEEN

Social Justice

Tom R. Tyler

Studies in the field of social justice make clear that when people interact with other people, groups, or organizations, their judgments, feelings, and behaviors are influenced by their evaluations of what is "fair" or "unfair," "just" or "unjust." These fairness concerns are distinct from people's self-interested desires to gain as much as they can for themselves and/or for their groups. The justice literature shows both that people have conceptions about what is just, and that those conceptions shape their judgments, feelings, and behaviors (Tyler, Boeckmann, Smith, & Huo, 1997; Tyler & Smith, 1997).

This review first examines justice as an individual-level issue. It identifies three key literatures that explore the role of individual justice judgments in shaping people's reactions to their experiences. This is followed by an examination of the relationship between two key forms of justice – distributive and procedural – by an examination of the meaning of procedural justice; and by a consideration of evidence concerning the role that justice plays in shaping people's reactions to the situation of others.

Justice is also considered from a group-level perspective. The individual versus group levels of injustice are distinguished, and the antecedents and consequences of thinking of justice on these different levels for intergroup relations are considered. This is followed by an examination of how people respond to injustice and of the role of group boundaries in shaping the "scope" within which people care about justice.

Justice and Individuals' Reactions to their Personal Experiences

Relative deprivation

Relative deprivation research shows that people's subjective satisfaction is not closely linked to the objective quality of their personal or group outcomes (Merton & Kitt, 1950;

Walker & Pettigrew, 1984). Instead, satisfaction is determined through comparisons of one's own outcomes to other outcomes. The same objective outcomes can either satisfy or upset a person depending upon their comparison processes. The choices of both comparison target and comparison standards are key to this process.

The lack of a close connection between the objective and subjective worlds raises the question of what shapes the subjective world. Justice studies demonstrate that judgments of justice or entitlement play a key role in shaping subjective feelings. Two types of justice judgments matter: assessments of the fairness of allocations (distributive justice) and of evaluations of the fairness of processes (procedural justice).

Distributive justice

One aspect of people's concern for justice is shown by their reactions to the fairness of personally received allocations. The importance of distributive justice has been compellingly demonstrated in the equity literature, which shows that people are most satisfied when they receive fair wages at work (Adams, 1965; Adams & Freedman, 1976; Deutsch, 1965; Greenberg, 1988, 1990; Pritchard, Dunnette, & Jorgenson, 1972; Schmitt & Marwell, 1972; Walster, Walster, & Berscheid, 1978). They similarly seek fair allocations in interpersonal relationships (Hatfield & Traupmann, 1981; Van Yperen & Buunk, 1994).

While studies provide widespread support for the importance of distributive justice judgments in shaping people's feelings and behaviors, research in this area suggests that distributive justice may not provide a useful approach for resolving social conflicts. A key problem is that people are found to make self-serving judgments about what they deserve (Messick, Bloom, Boldizar, & Samuelson, 1985; Thompson & Loewenstein, 1992). For example, in work settings, people overestimate their performance and, consequently, their entitlements (Schlenker & Miller, 1977). This makes it difficult to provide people with the level of rewards that they regard as fair. The tendency to make self-serving judgments about what one deserves is exacerbated in ambiguous situations, where people are especially likely to overallocate resources to themselves (Allison, McQueen, & Schaerfl, 1992; Allison & Messick, 1990; Herlocker, Allison, Foubert, & Beggan, 1997; Messick & Sentis, 1979).

A reaction to the overestimation of entitlement is the frequent use of the equality heuristic for reward allocation in situations where interpersonal harmony is important (Messick, 1995). Since the equal division of rewards does not require that relative contributions be assessed, it avoids subjective enhancement problems.

Studies also suggest that distributive justice models are limited because they do not speak to people's central justice concerns. People's dissatisfactions, even in work settings, are not typically linked to issues of reward allocation (Messick et al., 1985; Mikula, 1986, 1987, 1993; Mikula, Petri, & Tanzer, 1990). Instead, people more often complain about the manner in which they are treated, for example about "inconsiderate, impolite, or aggressive conduct," and about actions that "violate a person's dignity" and "indicate lack of loyalty from close people" (Mikula, 1993, p. 228).

Procedural justice

Justice research demonstrates the independent importance of people's judgments about the justice of allocation or decision-making procedures. Thibaut and Walker (1975) present the first systematic set of experiments examining the impact of procedures on satisfaction and acceptance. These experiments demonstrate that people's assessments of the fairness of third-party decision-making procedures shape their satisfaction with their outcomes. Their findings have been widely confirmed in subsequent laboratory and field studies on procedural justice (Lind & Tyler, 1988; Tyler & Smith, 1997).

Procedural justice judgments are found to have especially robust effects on adherence to agreements over time (Pruitt, Peirce, McGillicuddy, Welton, & Castrianno, 1993). Pruitt and his colleagues found that the procedural fairness of an initial mediation session was an important determinant of whether people were adhering to the agreement reached six months later. Other studies show that procedural justice is especially important in gaining deference to social rules over time (Paternoster, Brame, Bachman, & Sherman, 1997).

The implications of these findings are hopeful and optimistic. They demonstrate that providing people with procedural justice can be an important and viable mechanism for gaining decision acceptance. People do not need to depend on promised rewards and/or threatened punishments to gain acceptance of rules and decisions. Hence, conflict resolution efforts can gain viability by using fair decision-making procedures. These findings suggest the potential of social justice to help people manage the problems of cooperation with others by both helping to define fair ways to resolve conflicts and by helping to gain acceptance for their outcomes (Mikula & Wenzel, in press). In addition, since injustice is often a trigger for conflict, knowledge of justice principles can minimize the likelihood that conflicts will develop (Mikula & Wenzel, in press).

Procedural justice is especially important because it is central to creating and maintaining internal values that support voluntary cooperative behavior on the part of the members of groups. The importance of developing and maintaining such values is increasingly being recognized, as social scientists identify the limited ability of rewards/punishment mechanisms to foster cooperation (Tyler, 1999). Fair decision-making procedures lead to loyalty and commitment toward those groups (Taylor, Tracy, Renard, Harrison, & Carroll, 1995). Similarly, procedural justice promotes deference to social rules because it promotes the belief that authorities are legitimate and ought to be obeyed (Tyler, 1990, 1997, 1999).

As has been noted, the potential benefits of distributive justice based approaches to social coordination are decreased by people's tendency to make distributive justice judgments in self-serving ways. The value of procedural justice would be similarly diminished if there were evidence of self-serving biases in judgments about the criteria defining procedural fairness, that is, if people thought that procedures in which they felt they would win were fairer. Thibaut and Walker (1975) show that people's assessments of fairness are not simply an effort to choose procedures through which they believe that they will prevail. Similarly, research generally suggests that neither social background, that is, ethnicity, gender, education, and/or income, nor ideology have much impact upon the way people define the fairness of a procedure (Bierbrauer, 1997; Peterson, 1994; Tyler, 1988, 1994).

On the other hand, self-interest does influence, but does not define, procedural preferences (see Leung & Lind, 1986; Lind, Huo, & Tyler, 1994; Tyler, Huo, & Lind, 1999). Further, Azzi (1992, 1993a, 1993b) consistently finds that group-level self-interest shapes people's definitions of procedural justice criteria in their judgments about political decision-making procedures.

The Relationship of Distributive and Procedural Justice

When psychologists first distinguished between distributive and procedural justice, they viewed procedures as a tool that people evaluated by the degree to which procedures produced fair outcomes (Leventhal, 1976; Leventhal, Karuza, & Fry, 1980; Thibaut & Walker, 1978). However, much of the subsequent research conducted on justice has either: (1) studied only one type of justice or (2) studied both, but treated distributive and procedural justice as distinct issues that are assessed and considered separately.

Research findings suggest that, while both forms of justice have an important role in shaping personal satisfaction, the willingness to accept decisions, and turnover intentions, procedural justice is especially central to people's relationships to society and social authorities – that is, to commitment to a group, views about the legitimacy of an authority, the willingness to follow social rules, and to engagement in voluntary helping behavior (Alexander & Ruderman, 1987; Casper, Tyler, & Fisher, 1988; Gilliland & Beckstein, 1996; Tyler, Casper, & Fisher, 1989).

Brockner and Wiesenfeld (1996) review a number of studies that assess both distributive and procedural justice and find that there is a typical interaction pattern in the effects produced by these two forms of justice. When people experience a procedure to be unfair, they are more strongly influenced by whether or not their outcome is fair. Conversely, when people judge their outcome to be unfair, they are more strongly influenced by whether or not the procedure is fair. Hence, experiencing either type of unfairness heightens the impact of judgments about the fairness of the other type of unfairness. A fair procedure can mitigate the impact of an unfair outcome, and a fair outcome can mitigate the impact of an unfair procedure.

In natural settings, procedural justice concerns are typically found to dominate people's reactions to their experiences. This may occur because procedures are usually in place and are normally encountered first. Only after experiencing a procedure do people typically learn the outcome of the procedure. At that point the influence of the outcome information is found be "cushioned" by the prior judgments about procedural fairness. Further, people do not typically re-evaluate their views about procedural fairness once they have information about outcome fairness (Tyler, 1996), even after several experiences of distributive unfairness (Paese, 1985).

Lind's fairness heuristic theory (Lind, 1995a, 1995b, 1997, 1998) argues that either outcome or procedural information can potentially be used to evaluate social situations, with the actual importance of each form of justice in a particular setting depending upon features of the situation. When fairness judgments are being initially formed, people take whatever fairness-relevant information is available from procedures and outcomes to make general-fairness judgments, which then influence subsequent judgments about the experience. If procedural information is available first, as it generally is, it will most strongly influence general-fairness judgments. If outcome-fairness information is available first, it will most strongly influence general-fairness judgments.

The fairness heuristic model has been supported by a series of experiments that manipulate features of the situation. For example, people are found to rely more heavily upon whichever type of information is available first (Van den Bos, Vermunt, & Wilke, 1997). Further, when people lack comparison information that would allow them to evaluate the fairness of their own outcomes they rely more heavily on procedural information (Van den Bos, Lind, Vermunt, & Wilke, 1997; Van den Bos, Wilke, Lind, & Vermunt, 1998). Similarly, when people know in advance whether or not an authority is trustworthy, they are less concerned about procedural information, so they focus more upon information about outcomes (Van den Bos, Wilke, & Lind, 1998). Hence, it seems clear that people can potentially evaluate the fairness of situations using either distributive or procedural information.

The Meaning of Procedural Justice

Early procedural justice research framed the meaning of procedural justice in terms of direct or indirect control over the exchange of resources. People were viewed as focusing upon issues of control (Thibaut & Walker, 1975). This view of justice flows from a social exchange view of social interaction in which people's primary concern is with the resources they obtain from others.

While research on control supports the argument that people want to have control, it does not support the outcome-based model of control proposed by Thibaut and Walker (1975). People are found to value control because they value the opportunity to address authorities, irrespective of whether their arguments change the decisions made (Lind, Kanfer, & Earley, 1990). For control to have a positive influence people need only feel that their arguments are listened to and considered by the decision maker (Tyler, 1987). Hence, control has a "value-expressive" function, which is linked to concerns about identity and status.

Tyler (1989; Tyler & Lind, 1992) argues that people's primary concerns when dealing with groups and group authorities are with information about the quality of their relationship with the group, information that helps them to define their identities and status. He distinguishes three "relational" concerns: neutrality, trustworthiness, and status recognition. Neutrality refers to decision making that is factual, evenhanded, and free of personal bias. Trustworthiness refers to the belief that the authority is benevolently motivated, that is, caring and concerned about the best interests of group members. Status recognition refers to treatment with dignity and respect. Such treatment confirms the status of those involved in social relationships or with society more generally, reaffirming their entitlement to the rights and protections of group membership when dealing with others.

Studies suggest that relational judgments are the primary factors shaping judgments about the fairness of decision-making procedures (Tyler & Lind, 1992). Interestingly, the effects of control are found to occur because control has an influence upon relational judgments. Control has no independent influence upon reactions to experiences once relational issues are taken into account (Lind, Tyler, & Huo, 1997; Tyler & Blader, 2000).

These findings suggest that an important role of fair decision-making procedures is to affirm people's feelings that the group to which they belong is a valuable and high-status group, inclusion in which conveys high status (pride in the group). Fair treatment also tells people that they are valued members of that group, entitled to its rights, protections, and status (respect from the group). Both of these status judgments are linked to procedural justice judgments (Tyler, Degoey, & Smith, 1996).

These findings about the meaning of procedural justice provide strong support for an identity-based view of justice. While justice was originally conceived as a tool for regulating social exchanges and resolving social conflicts, subsequent studies suggest that justice plays a much broader role in people's social interactions with other people, groups, and societies. People use the procedural justice that they experience from others, as well as their more general evaluations of the fairness of group procedures, to evaluate both the status of the groups and societies of which they are members and their status within these social entities. These status evaluations then shape people's social identities and their sense of their own self-worth and self-esteem (Koper, Van Knippenberg, Bouhuijs, Vermunt, & Wilke, 1993; Tyler & Blader, 2000; Tyler, Degoey, & Smith, 1996).

Justice and People's Reactions to Harm Done to Others

Recent justice research suggests another important area in which fairness judgments may be important. This is in people's willingness to help others when they observe others experiencing injustice. Thibaut and Walker (1975) demonstrate that people are upset when they observe unfairness to others, and studies show that people are motivated to help others whom they view as the victims of injustice (see Lind, Kray, & Thompson, 1998).

A key distributive justice question is when those who are advantaged are willing to redistribute resources to the disadvantaged (Montada, 1995, 1997). Montada and Schneider (1989) found that people are willing to engage in redistributive behaviors that are not in their self-interest when they feel that others are entitled to help. Recent research also demonstrates that guilt over having personal advantages leads to lower mental health among the advantaged (Maes, Schmitt, Lischetzke, & Schmiedemann, 1998).

Smith & Tyler (1996) similarly find that procedural justice judgments shape the willingness to help others. They find that people are more willing to defer to a policy that redistributes resources to the disadvantaged when they feel that the procedures used to enact the policy are fair. Research suggests that people in groups are generally more likely to voluntarily help others when they think that group decisions are being made through fair procedures (Moorman, 1991; Moorman, Niehoff, & Organ, 1993; Tyler, 1999).

Individual versus Group Levels of Conceptualizing Justice

Early research on both distributive and procedural justice focuses primarily upon the feelings of the individuals who experience justice or injustice. On this level, there is widespread evidence that justice plays a central role in shaping people's feelings and behaviors. Further, people both react to their own experiences of justice or injustice and act to provide justice to other people when they observe injustice.

Justice can also be conceptualized and responded to on the level of groups, not individuals. This crucial insight is contained in the early distinction between egoistical and fraternal deprivation (Runciman, 1966). Instead of being concerned with personally receiving fairness, people can judge the fairness received by groups. Psychologists have increasingly recognized that group memberships are an important element in people's self-definitions (Hogg & Abrams, 1988). This has heightened attention to people's reactions to the experiences of groups, as well as to their own personal experiences. Hence, justice for groups is a distinct and increasingly important justice concern.

An example of group-level research on justice is the work of Azzi on procedural justice in multigroup decision-making bodies. Azzi explores the understanding of justice among the members of majority and minority social groups (Azzi, 1992, 1993a, 1993b; Azzi & Jost, 1997). He finds that majority group members are more likely to judge "one person, one vote" procedures to be fair, while minority group members are more likely to view "one group, one vote" procedures to be fair. His work suggests that procedures providing mutual control are generally viewed as procedurally fairest by the members of all groups. For example, the United States government has a Senate, which gives each political group (i.e., the 50 states) equal representation, and a House of Representatives, which gives each citizen equal representation. The combination of these two bodies provides mutual control to both political groups and to citizens.

The important role that group membership plays in defining people's feelings and behaviors suggests that group-level injustice is an important area for future justice research. The ability of group membership to shape people's justice-related behavior is shown by Doosje, Branscombe, Spears, and Manstead (1998). Their study demonstrates that people who identify with a group that has harmed another group in the past are more willing to support compensating the injured group. This is true even when the group with which the person identifies committed the harms before the person was connected with that group.

In general, the implications of group-based justice are underexplored. Research in this area could build upon the interesting suggestion from relative deprivation research that social movements and collective actions, such as riots, are especially likely to be the result of believing that the groups to which one belongs are being treated unfairly. Building on this observation, future research should explore the role that group-based justice judgments play in minimizing or exacerbating intergroup conflict. Justice researchers need to first identify the circumstances under which people's social behavior is shaped by judgments about personal and/or group-level injustice and then explore the impact of judgments about group-level injustice.

One theoretical framework that might be applied to understanding the role of justice in intergroup relations is social identity theory (Platow, McClintock, & Liebrand, 1990). That theory demonstrates that people behave in ways that favor their own group and discriminate against other groups. This would seem to suggest that distributive injustice governs intergroup relations. However, the motivations underlying such behavior might or might not reflect injustice. People may exaggerate their group's value, making unequal distributions fair under the principle of equity. What is needed is an exploration of the justice motives that shape people's behavior in intergroup situations.

Responding to Injustice

The research outlined makes clear that people become troubled when they feel that injustice has occurred. However, psychologists frequently observe that particular objective social conditions or experiences that might be described as objectively unfair are not experienced as unfair. To understand this seeming failure to recognize injustice, we need to consider a conflict between two types of motivation: the motivation to respond to injustice behaviorally versus the motivation to respond to injustice psychologically.

Behavioral versus psychological responses to injustice

Behavioral responses to injustice involve efforts to correct injustice by changes in what people do, that is, by altering the distribution of effort, resources, and/or treatment. People can change how many resources they have by taking more or giving some back; they can work harder, or slow down; and they can quit or join organizations advocating change in an effort to either receive or give others justice.

Psychological responses to injustice involve efforts to justify one's outcomes or treatment psychologically by changing one's judgments or beliefs to be consistent with one's situation. Instead of taking more or giving some back, people can change their thinking to be consistent with the resources they have or the treatment they receive.

The advantaged

Justice theory suggests that the unfairly advantaged should feel guilt, and should be motivated to eliminate that guilt. From a self-interest perspective, the unfairly advantaged are most strongly motivated to eliminate their guilt psychologically (Taylor & Moghaddam, 1994). If they do so, they need not redistribute resources, make more effort, or treat those around them more fairly, to re-establish justice. An example of psychological justification is found in a recent study of people's attitudes toward affirmative action (Bobocel, Son Hing, Davey, Stanley, & Zanna, 1998). The attitudes studied were influenced by prejudice, with people viewing policies that help people they do not like as unjust. In other words, people rationalized their prejudice-based policy preferences by viewing them as

consistent with justice principles. Many studies find evidence that such self-serving distortions occur when people interpret their social experiences (Keltner & Robinson, 1997;
Stillwell & Baumeister, 1997), and justice studies show clearly that such distortions can
involve judgments about what is deserved (Walster, Walster, & Berscheid, 1978).

Of course, if the advantaged only engaged in psychological justifications, justice would
have no independent influence upon people's policy positions or behaviors. Research suggests that this is not the case, since feelings of unjust advantage do motivate efforts to
help the disadvantaged. For example, in the previously outlined study of attitudes toward
affirmative action, people are also influenced by "genuine beliefs" about justice that are
not linked either directly or indirectly to their prejudices. Research suggests that while
the unfairly advantaged clearly justify their advantages to some extent, their responses are
also shaped by conceptions of justice that are not simply rationalizations for their position, and they make real efforts to alter the objective world to restore actual justice (see
Montada & Schneider, 1989). The question is what factors determine the balance
between these two opposing approaches to dealing with one's advantage.

The disadvantaged

The unfairly disadvantaged are those who receive too little. They would initially seem to
be primarily motivated by the desire to label disadvantage as injustice and to re-establish
objective fairness through mechanisms such as restitution and compensation. After all,
why would people want to psychologically justify their own disadvantage? Justice
researchers find, however, that the motivations of the disadvantaged are more complex.

The disadvantaged are often found to be reluctant to label their experiences as disadvantage and injustice. For example, women who are paid less than men often do not label
their lower wages as "unfairly" low (Crosby, 1982). The failure to label their experiences
as injustice may be an effort by the disadvantaged to protect their feelings of self-worth
and self-esteem from the impact of feeling like a victim of injustice (Crosby, 1982). They
may also represent an effort to maintain feelings of control over the world (Ruggiero &
Taylor, 1995, 1997).

Research on the interpretation of their experience by the disadvantaged illustrates the
difficulties they face. If the disadvantaged interpret their poor outcomes as due to discrimination, they can maintain the belief that, in a fair competition, they would receive
better outcomes, thus maintaining their performance self-esteem (Ruggiero & Taylor,
1997). However, their social self-esteem suffers, since they must recognize that they are
not valued by the other members of society who have discriminated against them. On
the other hand, if the disadvantaged interpret their poor outcomes as not being due to
discrimination, they must believe that they performed poorly, and their performance self-
esteem will decline. However, they need not feel that other members of society do not
respect them, since they do not view themselves as discriminated against, so their social
self-esteem can remain high. The disadvantaged face complex and conflicting psychological pressures when trying to interpret whether their experience reflects injustice.

When they do decide that injustice has occurred, the predominant behavioral reaction
of the disadvantaged is to do nothing. In part, this inaction reflects the real risks associ-

ated with confronting powerful others, and an objective recognition of the low likelihood of success (Mikula, 1986; Rusbult, 1987). On the other hand, risk is not enough of an explanation for the behavior of the disadvantaged. For example, although the willingness to engage in collective action is influenced by the likelihood of success (Klandermans, 1989, 1997; Van Knippenberg, 1989), studies of collective action suggest that people often engage in collective actions against injustice even when the likelihood of success is small (Klandermans, 1989, 1997).

The failure to act may protect the disadvantaged from negative social experiences with powerful others. However, it clearly has psychological costs, including depression and other symptoms of psychological distress (Abrams, 1990; Hafer & Olson, 1993; Keith & Schafer, 1985; Walker & Mann, 1987). Further, it may encourage the advantaged to derogate the victim to justify their actions in an effort to restore justice, something which becomes less psychologically important when the disadvantaged take even unsuccessful action (Walster, Walster, & Berscheid, 1978). Retaliation, for example, does not restore resources to the disadvantaged, but it does obviate the need for the advantaged to derogate their victims. On the other hand, retaliation may have real costs in an objective sense because the advantaged may have the ability to deprive the disadvantaged of resources such as a job.

Many of the behavioral options available to the disadvantaged involve retaliatory actions that cause damage to the advantaged, rather than restoring resources to the disadvantaged, and which violate social rules ("nonnormative" behaviors). For example, stealing from one's employer (Greenberg, 1990, 1993), sabotaging the workplace (Hafer & Olson, 1993), or trying to embarrass or damage the reputation of harmdoers (Bies & Tripp, 1996). These actions may also take collective form, as when mobs destroy property or attack the advantaged.

The disadvantaged may also seek to leave the setting or relationship within which injustice has occurred (Rusbult, 1987; Valenzi & Andrew, 1971). Again, these actions may also occur collectively. Disadvantaged groups may become involved in separatist movements that reflect a group desire to exit from the larger society (Taylor & Moghaddam, 1994). They may also join cults or live in segregated communities that exit from society via isolation rather than through confrontation.

Societies' reaction to injustice

Other members of society who observe injustice may also become involved in efforts to restore justice. For example, the courts seek to compel harmdoers to restore unjust gains. Less formally, mobs and vigilante gangs chase down, detain, and even rough up criminals (Shotland & Goodstein, 1984).

A second view of society's reaction to injustice develops from the recognition that the advantaged typically have a dominant position within society, and can shape social values and attitudes. This perspective suggests that dominant groups and institutions use their influence to create a set of justifications, or "legitimizing" myths, that present existing injustices in outcomes or treatment as fair. These legitimizing myths are accepted by both the advantaged and the disadvantaged, creating a situation in which the bulk of those within a society accept its values and institutions as fair. In such a situation "existing social arrangements are legitimized, even at the expense of personal and group interest" (Jost & Benaji, 1994, p. 2). If existing society is legitimized, the advantaged have an investment in maintaining this psychological justification of injustice, rather than in trying to encourage actual "objective" justice.

One legitimizing myth is the "belief in a just world" (Lerner, 1980). This ideology reflects the belief that people generally get what they deserve, and deserve what they get. A similar legitimizing myth is the belief in "group dominance" (Sidanius & Protto, 1999). According to this set of beliefs, hierarchy and dominance by some social groups is inevitable. Not surprisingly, the members of dominant groups believe that dominance is natural and inevitable and oppose the redistribution of resources, opportunities, and status. However, the group dominance approach suggests that the members of nondominant groups often also accept this ideology, leading to a stable social system. The effectiveness of these justifying ideologies is linked to the broad acceptance within a given society of "ideologies" and of "stereotypes" of the disadvantaged that justify their receipt of unfair outcomes or treatment (Jost & Benaji, 1994; Crocker, Major, & Steele, 1997).

Levels of behavioral response to injustice

When people experience injustice, they can potentially respond in a variety of ways. The central distinction among types of responses is between individual and collective or group-level behaviors. A second distinction is between constructive actions, which occur within the context of social rules, and destructive, nonnormative, actions that break social rules.

Individual behaviors are those engaged in to benefit an individual, usually oneself. They can be constructive. For example, people who feel underpaid might potentially go to school or work harder. They can also be destructive – that is, drinking or using drugs. In contrast, collective behaviors are engaged in by individuals or groups to benefit groups, typically by those who perceive injustice as occurring to people because they are the members of a group. For example, a person might feel that they or some other group member are underpaid because they are a woman or a minority. As with individual actions, collective actions can also be constructive or destructive. People can work for groups within the context of social rules in the political process to get their candidate elected. They can also step outside of socially acceptable actions to engage in riots or separatist movements.

What determines whether people respond to injustice in individual or collective terms? A key issue is how people interpret experiences – that is, the reason for injustice they experience or observe. If people feel that the injustice is occurring to someone as an individual person, and is due to their personal actions, they will respond personally. If they feel that the injustice is occurring to someone due to their membership in particular groups, or to all the people who share a common group membership, they will respond collectively (Dube & Guimond, 1986; Hafer & Olson, 1993; Olson & Hafer, 1994; Tougas & Veilleux, 1988; Walker & Mann, 1987).

Social identity theory argues that the way people interpret their experience is determined by how they think about people, in particular, the degree to which people construct their sense of self in terms of the groups to which people belong (Hogg & Abrams, 1988). To the degree to which people think of themselves or others in personal terms, they interpret experiences as reflecting unique personal characteristics and behaviors, and they think about fairness in personal terms. To the degree that people think of people in terms of the group(s) to which they belong, and have self-definitions dominated by the social self as opposed to the personal self, they interpret experiences as reflecting treatment as a member of groups and think about justice in group terms.

Studies confirm that those with strong social selves are more likely to (1) interpret experiences as reflecting attitudes toward the groups to which they and others belong and to (2) respond to injustice by engaging in collective behavior (Grant and Brown, 1995; Kelly & Kelly, 1994; Lalonde & Silverman, 1994; Simon, Loewy, Sturmer, Weber, Freqtag, Habig, Kampmeier, & Spahlinger, 1998).

Of course, the salience of different group memberships in the framing of issues of injustice is shaped by society, as well as by individuals. Social ideologies provide people with particular ways of thinking about their societies and their social experiences. For example, Americans think about injustice in terms of ethnic group memberships and Europeans focus more strongly upon injustice linked to social class (Aalberg, 1998; Lipset, 1996).

Similarly, the manner in which people think about justice is to some degree socially constructed and people can be encouraged to conceptualize justice in particular ways. For example, Martin, Scully, and Levitt (1990) look at the speeches of revolutionary leaders and suggest that they show a deliberate effort to encourage people to reframe their thinking about the nature of injustice in ways that encourage support for social change. Conversely, social authorities encourage people to frame their thinking in ways that discourage the motivation for social change, for example, viewing their own success and failure in life as a result of individual effort and ability (Kluegel & Smith, 1986).

The decisions of the disadvantaged about whether to respond to injustice individually or collectively are not only shaped by their judgments about why injustice is occurring. Choices among possible behavioral responses are also influenced by people's judgments about the intergroup situation (Ellemers, 1993; Tajfel, 1982). For example, people are influenced by their assessments of the permeability of group boundaries. If people believe that it is possible for individuals to move from low-status groups to higher status groups, they are more likely to act as individuals. If people believe that the group's boundaries are not permeable, they are more likely to act collectively to raise the status of their group. Interestingly, studies suggest that very few low-status group members need to be successful for people to view the group's boundaries as sufficiently permeable to justify individual, as opposed to collective, action (Wright, Taylor, & Moghaddam, 1990).

People are also influenced by the perceived stability of group status. When group status can change, people are more likely to act collectively on behalf of the group. If group status is fixed, people are more likely to try to escape a low-status group. Finally, people are influenced by their views about the legitimacy of the status of existing groups. If people view current social arrangements as illegitimate, they are more likely to engage in collective action to change them (Major, 1994).

Justice and Intergroup Relations

Is concern about justice universal?

If we think of justice as a ubiquitous social motive, we would expect to find people concerned about justice in all of their interactions (Lerner, 1980, 1981, 1982). This would suggest that justice might be important in efforts to manage conflict between groups. The key question is the degree to which justice is, in fact, a universal human concern.

An alternative view of justice is that the degree to which people are concerned about justice when dealing with others varies depending upon the nature of their social interaction, that is, upon whom they are dealing with and/or the type of social situation in which they are involved. Deutsch (1985) coined the term "the scope of one's moral community" (p. 4) to describe the idea that there might be a range of situations outside of which people would be less concerned about extending justice to others.

If justice is not applied universally, what shapes the boundaries within which people feel that they should utilize morality and justice in their dealings with others? One clear possibility is that people care more about justice within the boundaries of the groups to which they belong. Recent research shows that people are more concerned about justice and injustice when they are dealing with the members of their own group (Tyler, Lind, Ohbuchi, Sugawara, & Huo, 1998). This suggests that justice will more effectively facilitate social interactions within the boundaries of a common group.

How are group boundaries defined?

Since group boundaries influence the scope of justice, it is important to understand how people define group boundaries. One way that people might define group boundaries is by defining the framework of their resource exchanges with others (Deutsch, 1985). An alternative, identity-based, approach to justice suggests that people feel they are in groups with those with whom they share a sense of common identity. In either case, the boundaries established should shape the role of justice in people's interactions with others.

Recent research provides evidence that identification with others frames the scope of distributive justice concerns. Wenzel (July, 1997; 2000) shows that East and West Germans who identify with the overall category "German" apply distributive justice norms of equality to the entitlements of all citizens within that society. That is, they are concerned that everyone they define as within their group receives equal economic and social resources.

Tyler and colleagues similarly find that identification shapes the willingness of people to defer to authorities who are acting in procedurally fair ways. People are more willing to defer to authorities because those authorities follow fair decision-making rules if they identify with the group or organization that those authorities represent (Huo, Smith, Tyler, & Lind, 1996; Smith & Tyler, 1996; Tyler & Degoey, 1995). Similarly, Van Vugt and De Cramer (1998) found that when people identify with a group the fairness of group authorities governs how much they will contribute to a public good that helps their group.

Platow and colleagues have also compared distributive and procedural justice effects in intergroup and intragroup settings (Bruins, Platow, & Ng, 1995). Their findings suggest less concern for the distributive and procedural fairness of authorities in intergroup settings (Platow, Hoar, Reid, Harley, & Morrison, 1997; Platow, O'Connell, Shave, & Hanning, 1995; Platow, Reid, & Andrew, 1998).

These findings suggest that issues of identification have an important role in shaping the scope of people's justice concerns. Why is this true? From an identity perspective, the key point is that people's sense of identity is influenced by their belief that justice principles apply within the groups or societies that define their sense of self and self-worth. To see *injustice* occurring within groups that define oneself diminishes the status of those groups and damages the identities of those within them. Hence, either experiencing unfairness or observing it is upsetting. However, this principle applies primarily to experiences involving those with whom one shares group membership. How one is treated by outsiders, or how one treats outsiders, has lesser implications for one's views about either one's own status or the group's status.

Given that the degree to which people care about justice is influenced by the boundaries of identification with others, a key question is how such identification is formed, maintained, and changed. A variety of factors may shape the degree to which people naturally identify with groups, for example their size (Brewer, 1999) and the degree to which they share a common history, common customs, and common values (Azzi, 1994).

Summary

The findings of social justice research provide a striking and important confirmation that people's judgments, feelings, and behaviors are not simply a reflection of their estimates of their own self- or group interests. Research within the areas of distributive and procedural justice clearly demonstrates that justice matters in social situations. People both respond to their sense of what is just when they are dealing with others and act when they see injustice occurring to others. The power of justice in social settings makes clear that it provides an important mechanism for coordinating social interactions and resolving social conflicts.

The findings of social justice research have important implications for our image of how social interactions occur. They suggest that people in social settings are motivated by principles of morality and justice that depart fundamentally from their conceptions of their personal or group self-interest. People's willingness to respond to such principles has an important role in the effective coordination of social behavior and the ability of social authorities to resolve social conflicts.

Most past justice research has focused on the dynamics of justice within groups. It is clear, however, that future justice research should expand to explore the role of justice and injustice in encouraging or helping to resolve intergroup conflicts. Such intergroup conflicts are key to the issues and problems that dominate the concerns of most societies. It is not currently clear, however, whether the strong findings of support for the importance of justice in shaping intragroup behavior extend to intergroup settings.

Past social justice research compellingly demonstrates the importance of justice in social settings. More recent social justice research has focused on trying to develop theoretical models that explain why justice is important. Early psychological models of justice emphasize the role of justice in coordinating resource exchanges. More recent models, such as the group-value model, link concerns about justice to issues of identity and status. They suggest that people use fairness, in particular procedural fairness, to evaluate the status of the groups to which they belong and to indicate their status within those groups. This identity-based view of justice is widely support by the findings of recent justice research.

References

Aalberg, T. (May, 1998). *Welfare regimes and public beliefs: Distributive justice and the state.* Paper delivered at the International Society for Justice Research 7th Biennial Conference. Denver, Colorado.

Abrams, D. (1990). *Political identity: Relative deprivation, social identity, and the case of Scottish nationalism.* Economic and Social Research Council 16–19. Initiative – Occasional Papers.

Adams, J. S. (1965). Inequity in social exchange. In L. Berkowitz (Ed.), *Advances in experimental social psychology* (Vol. 2, pp. 267–299). New York: Academic Press.

Adams, J. S., & Freedman, S. (1976). Equity theory revisited. In L. Berkowitz & E. Walster (Eds.), *Advances in experimental social psychology* (Vol. 9, pp. 43–91). New York: Academic Press.

Alexander, S., & Ruderman, A. (1987). The role of procedural and distributive justice in organizational behavior. *Social Justice Research, 1,* 177–198.

Allison, S. T., McQueen, L. R., & Schaerfl, L. M. (1992). Social decision-making processes and the equal partitionment of shared resources. *Journal of Experimental Social Psychology, 28,* 23–42.

Allison, S. T., & Messick, D. M. (1990). Social decision heuristics in the use of shared resources. *Journal of Behavioral Decision Making, 3,* 195–204.

Azzi, A. (1992). Procedural justice and the allocation of power in intergroup relations. *Personality and Social Psychology Bulletin, 18,* 736–747.

Azzi, A. (1993a). Group representation and procedural justice in multigroup decision-making bodies. *Social Justice Research, 6,* 195–217.

Azzi, A. (1993b). Implicit and category-based allocation of decision-making power in majority-minority relations. *Journal of Experimental Social Psychology, 29,* 203–228.

Azzi, A. (1994). From competitive interests, perceived injustice, and identity needs to collective action. In B. Kapferer (Ed.), *Nationalism, ethnicity, and violence.* Oxford, UK: Oxford University Press.

Azzi, A., & Jost, J. T. (1997). Votes without power: Procedural justice as mutual control in majority-minority relations. *Journal of Applied Social Psychology, 27,* 124–155.

Bierbrauer, G. (July, 1997). *Political ideology and allocation preferences: What do Turkish immigrants in Germany deserve?* Paper delivered at the International Network for Social Justice Research, 6th Biennial Meeting. Potsdam, Germany.

Bies, R. J., & Tripp, T. M. (1996). Beyond distrust: "Getting even" and the need for revenge. In R. Kramer & T. R. Tyler (Eds.), *Trust in organizations.* Thousand Oaks, CA: Sage.

Bobocel, D. R., Hing, L. S. S., Davey, L. M., Stanley, D. J., & Zanna, M. P. (1998). Justice-based opposition to social policies: Is it genuine? *Journal of Personality and Social Psychology, 75,* 653–669.

Brewer, M. B. (1999). Distinctiveness motives as a source of the social self. In T. R. Tyler, R. Kramer, & O. P. John (Eds.), *The psychology of the social self.* Hillsdale, NJ: Erlbaum.

Brockner, J., & Wiesenfeld, B. M. (1996). An integrative framework for explaining reactions to decisions. *Psychological Bulletin, 120,* 189–208.

Bruins, J., Platow, M. J., & Ng, S. H. (1995). Distributive and procedural justice in interpersonal and intergroup situations. *Social Justice Research, 8,* 103–121.

Casper, J. D., Tyler, T. R., & Fisher, B. (1988). Procedural justice in felony cases. *Law and Society Review, 22,* 483–507.

Crocker, J., Major, B., & Steele, C. (1997). Social stigma. In D. T. Gilbert, S. T. Fiske, & G. Lindzey (Eds.), *Handbook of social psychology* (Vol. 2, pp. 504–553). New York: Erlbaum.

Crosby, F. (1982). *Relative deprivation and working women.* New York: Oxford University Press.

Deutsch, M. (1965). *Distributive justice: A social-psychological perspective.* New Haven, CT: Yale University Press.

Deutsch, M. (1985). *Distributive justice.* New Haven, CT: Yale University Press.

Doosje, B., Branscombe, N., Spears, R., & Manstead, A. S. R. (1998). Guilty by association: When one's group has a negative history. *Journal of Personality and Social Psychology, 75,* 872–886.

Dube, L., & Guimond, S. (1986). Relative deprivation and social protest. In J. Olson, C. P. Hermann, & M. Zanna (Eds.), *Relative deprivation and social comparison.* Hillsdale, NJ: Erlbaum.

Ellemers, N. (1993). The influence of socio-structural variables on identity management strategies. In W. Stroebe & M. Hewstone (Eds.), *European review of social psychology* (Vol. 4). Chichester, UK: Wiley.

Greenberg, J. (1988). Equity and workplace status: A field experiment. *Journal of Applied Psychology, 73,* 606–613.

Greenberg, J. (1990). Employee theft as a reaction to underpayment inequity. *Journal of Applied Psychology, 75,* 561–568.

Greenberg, J. (1993). Stealing in the name of justice: Informational and interpersonal moderators of theft reactions to underpayment inequity. *Organizational Behavior and Human Decision-Making Processes, 54,* 81–103.

Gilliland, S. W., & Beckstein, B. A. (1996). Procedural and distributive justice in the editorial review process. *Personnel Psychology, 49,* 669–691.

Grant, P. R., & Brown, R. (1995). From ethnocentrism to collective protest. *Social Psychology Quarterly, 58,* 195–211.

Hafer, C., & Olson, J. (1993). Beliefs in a just world, discontent, and assertive actions by working women. *Personality and Social Psychology Bulletin, 19,* 30–38.

Hatfield, E., & Traupmann, J. (1981). Intimate relationships: A perspective from equity theory. In S. Duck & R. Gilmour (Eds.), *Compatible and incompatible relationships.* New York: Springer-Verlag.

Herlocker, C. E., Allison, S. T., Foubert, J. D., & Beggan, J. K. (1997). Intended and unintended overconsumption of physical, spatial, and temporal resources. *Journal of Personality and Social Psychology, 73,* 992–1004.

Hogg, M. A., & Abrams, D. (1988). *Social identifications: A social psychology of intergroup relations and group processes.* New York: Routledge.

Huo, Y. J., Smith, H. J., Tyler, T. R., & Lind, E. A. (1996). Superordinate identification, subgroup identification, and justice concerns. *Psychological Science, 7,* 40–45.

Jost, J., & Benaji, M. (1994). The role of stereotyping in system-justification and the production of false consciousness. *British Journal of Social Psychology, 33,* 1–27.

Keith, P. M., & Schafer, R. B. (1985). Role behavior, relative deprivation, and depression in one- and two-job families. *Family Relations, 34,* 227–233.

Kelly, C., & Kelly, J. (1994). Who gets involved in collective action? *Human Relations, 47,* 63–88.

Keltner, D., & Robinson, R. J. (1997). Defending the status quo: Power and bias in social conflict. *Personality and Social Psychology Bulletin, 23,* 1066–1077.

Klandermans, B. (1993). A theoretical framework for comparisons of social movement participation. *Sociological Forum, 8,* 383–402.

Klandermans, B. (1997). *The social psychology of protest.* Oxford, UK: Blackwell.

Kluegel, J. R., & Smith, E. R. (1986). *Beliefs about inequality: Americans' views about what is and what ought to be.* New York: Aldine.

Koper, G., Van Knippenberg, D., Bouhuijs, F., Vermunt, R., & Wilke, H. (1993). Procedural fairness and self-esteem. *European Journal of Social Psychology, 23,* 313–325.

Lalonde, R. N., & Silverman, R. A. (1994). Behavioral preferences in response to social injustice. *Journal of Personality and Social Psychology, 66,* 78–85.

Lerner, M. J. (1980). *The belief in a just world.* New York: Plenum.

Lerner, M. J. (1981). The justice motive in human relations: Some thoughts on what we know and need to know about justice. In M. J. Lerner & S. C. Lerner (Eds.), *The justice motive in social behavior.* New York: Plenum.

Lerner, M. J. (1982). The justice motive in human relations and the economic model of man. In V. J. Derlega & J. Grzelak (Eds.), *Cooperation and helping behavior: Theories and research.* New York: Academic.

Leung, K., & Lind, E. A. (1986). Procedural justice and culture. *Journal of Personality and Social Psychology, 50,* 1134–1140.

Leventhal, G. S. (1976). What should be done with equity theory? New approaches to the study of fairness in social relationships. In K. J. Gergen, M. S. Greenberg, & R. H. Willis (Eds.), *Social exchange: Advances in theory and research.* New York: Plenum.

Leventhal, G. S., Karuza, J., & Fry, W. R. (1980). Beyond fairness: A theory of allocation preferences. In G. Mikula (Ed.), *Justice and social interaction.* New york: Springer-Verlag.

Lind, E. A. (1995a). *Social conflict and social justice: Some lessons from the social psychology of justice.* Leiden, The Netherlands: Leiden University Press.

Lind, E. A. (1995b). Justice and authority in organizations. In R. Cropanzano & K. M. Kacmar (Eds.), *Politics, justice, and support: Managing the social climate of work organizations* (pp. 83–96). Westport, CT: Quorum.

Lind, E. A. (1997). Litigation and claiming. In R. Giacalone & J. Greenberg (Eds.), *Antisocial behavior in organizations* (pp. 150–171). Beverly Hills, CA: Sage.

Lind, E. A. (1998). Procedural justice, disputing, and reactions to legal authorities. In A. Sarat, M. Constable, D. Engel, V. Hans, & S. Lawrence (Eds.), *Everyday practices and problem cases* (pp. 177–198). Evanston, IL: Northwestern University Press.

Lind, E. A., Huo, Y. J., & Tyler, T. R. (1994). And justice for all: Ethnicity, gender, and preferences for dispute resolution procedures. *Law and Human Behavior, 18,* 269–290.

Lind, E. A., Kanfer, R., & Earley, P. C. (1990). Voice, control, and procedural justice. *Journal of Personality and Social Psychology, 59,* 952–959.

Lind, E. A., Kray, L., & Thompson, L. (1998). The social construction of injustice: Fairness judgments in response to own and others' unfair treatment by authorities. *Organizational Behavior and Human Decision Processes, 75,* 1–22.

Lind, E. A., & Tyler, T. R. (1988). *The social psychology of procedural justice.* New York: Plenum.

Lind, E. A., Tyler, T. R., & Huo, Y. J. (1997). Procedural context and conflict: Variation in the antecedents of procedural justice judgments. *Journal of Personality and Social Psychology, 73,* 767–780.

Lipset, S. M. (1996). *American exceptionalism: A double-edged sword.* New York: W. W. Norton & Company.

Maes, J., Schmitt, M., Lischetzke, T., & Schmiedemann, V. (1998). *Effects of experienced injustice in unified Germany on well-being and mental health.* Unpublished manuscript, Fachbereich-I-Psychologie, Universität Trier, Germany.

Major, B. (1994). From social inequality to personal entitlement: The role of social comparisons, legitimacy appraisals, and group membership. In M. Zanna (Ed.), *Advances in experimental social psychology* (Vol. 26, pp. 293–355). New York: Academic Press.

Martin, J., Scully, M., & Levitt, B. (1990). Injustice and the legitimation of revolution. *Journal of Personality and Social Psychology, 59,* 281–290.

Merton, R. K., & Kitt, A. S. (1950). Contributions to the theory of reference group behavior. In R. K. Merton & P. F. Lazersfeld (Eds.), *Continuities in social research* (pp. 40–105). Grencoe, IL: Free Press.

Messick, D. M. (1995). Equality, fairness, and social conflict. *Social Justice Research, 8,* 153–173.

Messick, D. M., Bloom, S., Boldizaar, J. P., & Samuelson, C. D. (1985). Why we are fairer than others. *Journal of Experimental Social Psychology, 21,* 480–500.

Messick, D. M., & Sentis, K. P. (1979). Fairness and preference. *Journal of Experimental Social Psychology, 15,* 418–434.

Mikula, G. (1986). The experience of injustice. In H. W. Bierhoff, R. L. Cohen, & J. Greenberg (Eds.), *Justice in social relations* (pp. 103–123). New York: Plenum.

Mikula, G. (1987). Exploring the experience of injustice. In G. R. Semin & B. Krahe (Eds.), *Issues in contemporary German social psychology* (pp. 74–96). London: Sage.

Mikula, G. (1993). On the experience of injustice. *European Review of Social Psychology, 4,* 223–244.

Mikula, G., Petri, B., & Tanzer, N. (1990). What people regard as unjust. *European Journal of Social Psychology, 20,* 133–149.

Mikula, G., & Wenzel, M. (in press). Justice and social conflict: The impact of ideas of justice, perceptions of injustice, and justice arguments on the emergence, course, and resolution of social conflicts. *International Journal of Psychology.*

Montada, L. (1995). Applying social psychology: The case of redistributions in unified Germany. *Social Justice Research, 8,* 73–90.

Montada, L. (July, 1997). *Justice: Just a rational choice?* Paper delivered at the International Network for Social Justice Research, 6th Biennial Meeting. Potsdam, Germany.

Montada, L., & Schneider, A. (1989). Justice and emotional reactions to the disadvantaged. *Social Justice Research, 3,* 313–344.

Moorman, R. H. (1991). The relationship between organizational justice and organizational citizenship behaviors: Do fairness perceptions influence employee citizenship? *Journal of Applied Psychology, 76,* 845–855.

Moorman, R. H., Niehoff, B. P., & Organ, D. W. (1993). Treating employees fairly and organizational citizenship behavior. *Employee Responsibilities and Rights Journal, 6,* 209–225.

Olson, J. M., & Hafer, C. (1996). Affect, motivation, and cognition in relative deprivation research. In R. M. Sorrentino, & E. T. Higgins (Eds.), *Handbook of motivation and cognition* (Vol. 3, pp. 85–117). New York: Guilford Press.

Paese, P. (1985). *Procedural fairness and work group responses to performance evaluation procedures.* Unpublished Masters thesis. University of Illinois, Champaign-Urbana.

Paternoster, R., Brame, R., Bachman, R., & Sherman, L. W. (1997). Do fair procedures matter? *Law and Society Review, 31,* 163–204.

Peterson, R. (1994). The role of values in predicting fairness judgments and support of affirmative action. *Journal of Social Issues, 50,* 95–116.

Platow, M. J., Hoar, S., Reid, S., Harley, K., & Morrison, D. (1997). Endorsement of distributively fair and unfair leaders in interpersonal and intergroup situations. *European Journal of Social Psychology, 27*, 465–494.

Platow, M. J., McClintock, C. G., & Leibrand, W. B. G. (1990). Predicting intergroup fairness and ingroup bias in the minimal group paradigm. *European Journal of Social Psychology, 20*, 221–239.

Platow, M. J., O'Connell, A., Shave, R., & Hanning, P. (1995). Social evaluations of fair and unfair allocators in interpersonal and intergroup situations. *British Journal of Social Psychology, 34*, 363–381.

Platow, M. J., Reid, S., & Andrew, S. (1998). Leadership endorsement: The role of distributive and procedural behavior in interpersonal and intergroup contexts. *Group Processes and Intergroup Relations, 1*, 35–47.

Pritchard, D., Dunnette, M. D., & Jorgenson, D. O. (1972). Effects of perceptions of equity and inequity on worker performance and satisfaction. *Journal of Applied Psychology, 56*, 75–94.

Pruitt, D. G., Peirce, R. S., McGillicuddy, N. B., Welton, G. L., & Castrianno, L. M. (1993). Long-term success in mediation. *Law and Human Behavior, 17*, 313–330.

Ruggiero, K. M., & Taylor, D. M. (1995). Coping with discrimination: How disadvantaged group members perceive the discrimination that confronts them. *Journal of Personality and Social Psychology, 68*, 826–838.

Ruggiero, K. M., & Taylor, D. M. (1997). Why minority group members perceive or do not perceive the discrimination that confronts them. *Journal of Personality and Social Psychology, 72*, 373–389.

Runciman, W. G. (1966). *Relative deprivation and social justice.* Berkeley, CA: University of California Press.

Rusbult, C. (1987). Responses to dissatisfaction in close relationships. In D. Perlman & S. Duck (Eds.), *Intimate relationships* (pp. 209–237). Newbury Park, CA: Sage.

Schlenker, B. R., & Miller, R. S. (1977). Egocentrism in groups. *Journal of Personality and Social Psychology, 35*, 755–764.

Schmitt, D. R., & Marwell, G. (1972). Withdrawal and reward allocation as responses to inequity. *Journal of Experimental Social Psychology, 8*, 207–221.

Shotland, R. L., & Goodstein, L. I. (1984). The role of bystanders in crime control. *Journal of Social Issues, 40*, 9–26.

Sidanius, J., & Protto, F. (1999). *Social dominance: An intergroup theory of social hierarchy and oppression.* New York: Cambridge University Press.

Simon, B., Loewy, M., Sturmer, S., Wever, U., Freytey, P., Habig, C., Kampmeier, C., & Spahlinger, P. (1998). Collective identification and social movement participation. *Journal of Personality and Social Psychology, 74*, 646–658.

Smith, H. J., & Tyler, T. R. (1996). Justice and power. *European Journal of Social Psychology, 26*, 171–200.

Stillwell, A. M., & Baumeister, R. F. (1997). The construction of victim and perpetrator memories: Accuracy and distortion in role-based accounts. *Personality and Social Psychology Bulletin, 23*, 1157–1172.

Tajfel, H. (1982). *Human groups and social categories.* New York: Cambridge University Press.

Taylor, D. M., & Moghaddam, F. M. (1994). *Theories of intergroup relations.* New York: Praeger.

Taylor, M. S., Tracy, K. B., Renard, M. K., Harrison, J. K., & Carroll, S. J. (1995). Due process in performance appraisal. *Administrative Science Quarterly, 40*, 495–523.

Thibaut, J., & Walker, L. (1975). *Procedural justice.* Hillsdale, NJ: Erlbaum.

Thibaut, J., & Walker, L. (1978). A theory of procedure. *California Law Review, 66*, 541–566.

Thompson, L., & Loewenstein, G. (1992). Egocentric interpretations of fairness and interpersonal conflict. *Organizational Behavior and Human Decision Processes, 51,* 176–197.

Tougas, F., & Veilleux, F. (1988). The influence of identification, collective relative deprivation, and procedure of implementation on women's response to affirmative action. *Canadian Journal of Behavioral Science, 20,* 15–27.

Tyler, T. R. (1987). Conditions leading to value-expressive effects in judgments of procedural justice. *Journal of Personality and Social Psychology, 52,* 333–344.

Tyler, T. R. (1988). What is procedural justice? Criteria used by citizens to assess the fairness of legal procedures. *Law and Society Review, 22,* 103–135.

Tyler, T. R. (1989). The psychology of procedural justice. *Journal of Personality and Social Psychology, 57,* 830–838.

Tyler, T. R. (1990). *Why people obey the law.* New Haven, CT: Yale University Press.

Tyler, T. R. (1994). Governing amid diversity: Can fair decision-making procedures bridge competing public interests and values? *Law and Society Review, 28,* 701–722.

Tyler, T. R. (1996). The relationship of outcome and procedural fairness: How does knowing the outcome influence judgments about the procedure. *Social Justice Research, 9,* 311–325.

Tyler, T. R. (1997). The psychology of legitimacy. *Personality and Social Psychology Review, 1,* 323–344.

Tyler, T. R. (1999). Why do people cooperate in organizations? In B. Staw & R. Sutton (Eds.), *Research in organizational behavior.* Greenwich, CT: JAI Press.

Tyler, T. R., & Blader, S. (2000). *Cooperation in groups: Procedural justice, social identity, and behavioral engagement.* Philadelphia, PA: Psychology Press.

Tyler, T. R., Boeckmann, R. J., Smith, H. J., & Huo, Y. J. (1997). *Social justice in a diverse society.* Boulder, CO: Westview.

Tyler, T. R., Casper, J. D., & Fisher, B. (1989). Maintaining allegiance toward political authorities: The role of prior attitudes and the use of fair procedures. *American Journal of Political Science, 33,* 629–652.

Tyler, T. R., & Degoey, P. (1995). Collective restraint in a social dilemma situation. *Journal of Personality and Social Psychology, 69,* 482–497.

Tyler, T. R., Degoey, P., & Smith, H. J. (1996). Understanding why the justice of group procedures matters: A test of the psychological dynamics of the group-value model. *Journal of Personality and Social Psychology, 70,* 913–930.

Tyler, T. R., Huo, Y. J., & Lind, E. A. (1999). The two psychologies of conflict resolution: Differing antecedents of pre-experience choices and post-experience evaluations. *Group Processes and Intergroup Relations, 2,* 99–118.

Tyler, T. R., & Lind, E. A. (1992). A relational model of authority in groups. *Advances in Experimental Social Psychology, 25,* 115–191.

Tyler, T. R., Lind, E. A., Ohbuchi, K., Sugawara, I., & Huo, Y. J. (1998). Conflict with outsiders: Disputing within and across group boundaries. *Personality and Social Psychology Bulletin, 24,* 137–146.

Tyler, T. R., & Smith, H. J. (1997). Social justice and social movements. In D. T. Gilbert, S. T. Fiske, & G. Lindzey (Eds.), *Handbook of social psychology* (Vol. 2, pp. 595–632). New York: Erlbaum.

Valenzi, E. R., & Andrews, I. R. (1971). The effect of overpay and underpay inequity when tested with a new induction procedure. *Journal of Applied Psychology, 55,* 22–27.

Van den Bos, K., Lind, E. A., Vermunt, R., & Wilke, H. A. M. (1997). How do I judge my outcome when I do not know the outcome of others? *Journal of Personality and Social Psychology, 72,* 1034–1046.

Van den Bos, K., Vermunt, R., & Wilke, H. A. M. (1997). Procedural and distributive justice. *Journal of Personality and Social Psychology, 72,* 95–104.

Van den Bos, K., Wilke, H. A. M., & Lind, E. A. (1998). When do we need procedural fairness? The role of trust in authority. *Journal of Personality and Social Psychology, 74*, 1449–1458.

Van den Bos, K., Wilke, H. A. M., Lind, E. A., & Vermunt, R. (1998). Evaluating outcomes by means of the fair process effect. *Journal of Personality and Social Psychology, 74*, 1493–1503.

Van Knippenberg, A. (1989). Strategies for identity management. In J. P. Van Oudenhoven & T. M. Wilemsen (Eds.), *Ethnic minorities*. Amsterdam: Swets & Zeitlinger.

Van Vugt, M., & De Cramer, D. (May, 1998). *Collective action in social dilemmas: The effects of group identification on the acceptance of leadership in public goods*. Paper presented at the International Society for Justice Research, 7th Conference. Denver, Colorado.

Van Yperen, N. W., & Buunk, B. P. (1994). Social comparison and social exchange in marital relationships. In M. J. Lerner & G. Mikula (Eds.), *Entitlement and the affectionate bond: Justice in close relationships*. New York: Plenum.

Walker, I., & Mann, L. (1987). Unemployment, relative deprivation, and social protest. *Personality and Social Psychology Bulletin, 13*, 275–283.

Walker, I., & Pettigrew, T. F. (1984). Relative deprivation theory. *British Journal of Social Psychology, 23*, 301–310.

Walster, E., Walster, G. W., & Berscheid, E. (1978). *Equity: Theory and research*. Boston, MA: Allyn & Bacon.

Wenzel, M. (July, 1997). *Levels of identity and distributive justice*. Paper delivered at the International Network for Social Justice Research, 6th Biennial Meeting. Potsdam, Germany.

Wenzel, M. (2000). Justice and identity: The significance of inclusion for perceptions and entitlement and the justice motive. *Personality and Social Psychology Bulletin, 26*, 157–176.

Wright, S. C., Taylor, D. M., & Moghaddam, F. M. (1990). Responding to membership in a disadvantaged group. *Journal of Personality and Social Psychology, 58*, 994–1003.

PART VI

Cultural Influence

CHAPTER EIGHTEEN

Culture and its Implications for Intergroup Behavior

Harry C. Triandis and David Trafimow

This chapter describes some dimensions of cultural variation and examines their effects on intergroup behavior. One of the important attributes of cultural differences is that members of different cultures sample the environment differently. Members of collectivist cultures sample ingroup norms, the context, and the history of an event more than members of individualist cultures; conversely, members of individualist cultures sample internal attributes of individuals, such as attitudes, beliefs, and personality more than do members of collectivist cultures (Morris & Peng, 1994). Such sampling differences result in different definitions of the ingroup and outgroup, different definitions of the self (e.g., as interdependent or independent of the ingroup), and different pressures to conform with ingroup norms, which have major implications for intergroup relations. Furthermore, as intergroup relations are shaped, for example, cooperatively or competitively, these relations in their turn influence the sampling of information from the environment. In cooperative situations negative stereotypes of the ingroup are sampled less than in competitive situations (Sherif, 1966). Thus, for instance, if the norms of the ingroup require aggression against the outgroup conformity to those norms will be larger in the case of collectivist than individualist cultures.

To develop these points, the organization of this chapter will be as follows. First, we will provide some definitions of the key concepts. We will then discuss some dimensions of cultural differences, but with an emphasis on individualism–collectivism, which has been researched to a much greater extent than other cultural syndromes. Finally, we will complete this section with a discussion of the implications of the foregoing points for acculturation.

In the second part of the chapter, we will focus more specifically on determinants of intergroup relations. This includes a discussion of social identity theory, as well as other determinants (e.g., beliefs about the ingroups, social distance, history, and others). Finally, we will discuss the implications that individualism–collectivism has for intergroup relations.

Definitions

Culture has been defined in numerous ways. For our purpose it consists of "a set of human-made objective and subjective elements that in the past have increased the probability of survival and resulted in satisfaction for participants in an ecological niche, and thus became *shared* among those who could communicate with each other because they had a common language and they lived in the same time and place" (Triandis, 1994a, p. 22).

Thus, culture is what has worked in the past and has become incorporated in the cognitions of people who can communicate with each other, and thus transmit tools, standard operating procedures, unstated assumptions, categorizations, definitions, norms, and values to others. There are as many cultures as there are languages and ways of life within each language (e.g., physicians have a somewhat different culture than lawyers do).

An *ingroup* is a set of people who perceive each other as having something in common. Social psychologists are not in full agreement about its definition (e.g., Turner, 1988 vs. Rabbie & Horwitz, 1988). However, in cross-cultural work we are interested in definitions that reflect the way our research participants define our concepts. When that is done, we realize that there are cultural differences in the way ingroups are defined. In many traditional cultures the ingroup is defined as family, village of one's residence, tribe, co-religionists, etc. In modern cultures it is often defined as people who are like me, especially in their attitudes and values (Triandis, 1972). In short, the basis for judging other people as ingroup members can be different. In Western cultures, where people tend to be monotheists, "beliefs" are important, and there is an emphasis on "truth." This is not to say that what Westerners believe is necessarily true, only that they believe they have the truth, and it is important for ingroup members to share beliefs about what is true (Rokeach, 1960). In contrast, East Asian cultures emphasize "virtue," which means that people are evaluated as being good or bad on the basis of their behavior (Hofstede, 1982); what people actually believe is their own business and is much less important than actual behavior (Kashima, Siegel, Tanaka, & Kashima, 1992).

There are also degrees of being an ingroup member. The more people perceive each other as interdependent, the more they see each other as ingroup members. Typically, they perceive themselves as belonging together, because they experience common fate, common ancestry, are similar in their gender, age, ethnicity, geographic origins, language, religion, social class, occupation, way of life, attitudes, beliefs, norms, role definitions and/or values. In each culture a different combination of such attributes is emphasized when ingroups are defined (Triandis, 1967). Also, ingroups are dynamic constructs; people change their perceptions of ingroups and outgroups according to the situation. For example, two groups of workers may see each other as belonging to outgroups when they compete for a highly desirable group job assignment, and as belonging to an ingroup when they confront the management to establish a wage that will apply to all workers. Seeing another group as an ingroup ensures good intergroup relations.

Ingroup goals can influence the definition of the ingroup. Sometimes ingroup members have the goal of being more inclusive. Consequently, they may change their definition of the ingroup so as to include other groups. Such "recategorization" has been studied by Gaertner and his colleagues (e.g., Gaertner, Mann, Murrell, & Dovidio, 1989; Gaertner, Dovidio, Anastasio, et al., 1993).

An *outgroup* consists of a set of people who are not members of the ingroup. Members of the ingroup are likely to refer to outgroup members as "them" and to other ingroup members as "us." In addition to ingroups and outgroups some cultures use "neutral groups." Collectivist cultures (see below) tend to have minimal neutral groups, so that the other person is either "in" or "out," whereas individualist cultures have substantial neutral groups.

Intergroup behavior refers to the behavior of one group toward another group. A crucial distinction is whether this behavior is *interpersonal* or *intergroup*. When it is interpersonal the members of the group perceive primarily the personal attributes of the members of the other group. When it is intergroup, they react to all members of the other group as if they are the same.

Dimensions of Cultural Variation

Individualist cultures, such as the cultures found in Western societies, are defined by certain tendencies. First, people see the self as independent of groups whereas in collectivist cultures, such as those that are found in Asia, Latin America, and most traditional societies, the self is an aspect of one or more groups (Markus & Kitayama, 1991). The independent self is associated with self-enhancement, self-assertion, high self-esteem, well-being, and optimism. The interdependent self is primarily concerned with fitting in, being a good member of the group, and is associated with modesty and with only moderate levels of well-being.

Second, personal goals usually have priority over the goals of ingroups in individualist cultures (Triandis, 1990; Yamaguchi, 1994). Thus if a person wants to do something which is not favored by an ingroup, it is considered legitimate to ignore the desires of the ingroup. In contrast, the goals of individuals and groups tend to be consistent in collectivist cultures, and when they are inconsistent, it is not considered legitimate for the individual goals to have priority over the goals of ingroups.

Third, social behavior is determined primarily by attitudes and only slightly by norms in individualist cultures (Bontempo & Rivero, 1992; Davidson, Jaccard, Triandis, Morales, & Diaz-Guerrero, 1976; Kashima et al., 1992) whereas norms are slightly more important than attitudes in collectivist cultures. In short, in individualist cultures people do what they would like more than what they must; in collectivist cultures people do what they must more than what they would like to do.

Fourth, in individualist cultures exchange theory (Mills & Clark, 1982) provides a good account of social behavior (Triandis, 1995a). Thus, people compute the advantages and disadvantages of relationships and stay in relationships only if the advantages exceed the disadvantages. In collectivist cultures communal relationships are common (Mills &

Clark, 1982). People usually stay in relationships even when they are not "profitable." Consequently, divorce rates are quite different in the two kinds of cultures.

Triandis and Gelfand (1998) showed that the four facets of these constructs are interrelated, thus constituting a syndrome. Furthermore, the contrast between individualist and collectivist cultures has implications for every aspect of psychology. This impact can be seen in the review of Markus, Kitayama, and Helman (1996) who provided an extensive discussion of the way culture impacts biological, cognitive, personal motivation, intergroup, and group processes.[1]

Kinds of Collectives

There are many kinds of collectives. The nation is an important collective, and patriotism is a subcategory of collectivism. It is possible to make further distinctions, for example, patriotism can range from chauvinism (extravagant glorification of own country) to constructive patriotism (working hard for the benefit of the country) (Bar-Tal & Staub, 1997). Constructive patriotism may be helpful to intergroup relations, while chauvinism is often associated with tensions in intergroup relations. Similarly, Feshbach and Sakano (1997) distinguished patriotism, which is an intense attachment to a nation, from nationalism, which implies feelings of superiority toward other nations. By this definition nationalism is likely to result in poor intergroup relations. Worchel and Coutant (1997) disentangle the meanings of nationalism, patriotism, and ethnocentrism.

Maria Jarymowicz (discussed by Reykowski, 1997, pp. 122–123) studied the meaning of the "we" concept by examining people's self-descriptions. She found that people use two definitions of "we." The "we" that corresponds to "group identity" is reflected in concrete entities, such as family, nation, church, or professional organization. The "we" that corresponds to "attributive identity" focuses on relatively abstract attributes, such as "we who hate racism" or "we who want justice." Group identity is linked to collectivism, while attributive identity is something different. She found that those who use group identity disvalued the achievements of outgroup nations, whereas those who used attributive identity did not do so.

In addition, she found that those who showed little differentiation between "I" and "we" (an attribute of interdependent selves [Markus & Kitayama, 1991], linked to collectivism) showed a sharp differentiation between ingroup and outgroup (a typical finding in the collectivism literature, Triandis, 1972) and were more prone to stereotypic perception of national ingroups.

The Importance of Personalities and Situations

Individuals in different cultures include in their cognitive systems both individualist (e.g., is this going to be fun for me?) and collectivist elements (e.g., is this my duty towards this group?) in different mixtures. Depending on the situation they sample more of the individualist or collectivist cognitions, and that influences their behavior (Trafimow & Finlay, 1996; Ybarra & Trafimow, 1998). In addition to the four dimensions mentioned above, many more dimensions are important in defining *types* of individualism and collectivism (Triandis, 1994b; Triandis, 1995a, pp. 68–80). Two important types are the horizontal and vertical varieties of these constructs. Horizontal individualism emphasizes the uniqueness of individuals; vertical individualism stresses in addition that the individual is "better" than others, thus it is associated with competitiveness. Horizontal collectivism includes the merging of the self in the group; vertical collectivism includes in addition sacrificing for the group, and unquestioned obedience to ingroup authorities.

Corresponding to individualist cultural behavioral patterns there are personalities that are called *idiocentric*; corresponding to the collectivist behavioral patterns there are personalities called *allocentric*. In every culture there are both idiocentrics and allocentrics (Triandis, 1995a). However, their ratio is different in different cultures, for example, collectivist cultures may have 60% allocentrics and 40% idiocentrics, while individualist cultures may have the reverse ratio. Furthermore, any individual is likely to have both collectivist and individualist cognitions, and use either type of cognition, depending on the situation.

Chatman and Barsade (1995) showed the importance of the situation as a determinant of behavior in addition to allocentrism and idiocentrism. They randomly assigned idiocentrics and allocentrics to organizational simulations that constituted situations that were individualist or collectivist and studied their level of cooperation. Those assigned to the individualist situation were very low in cooperation; those who were assigned to the collectivist situation were cooperative. The allocentrics assigned to the collectivist situation were extremely cooperative; the idiocentrics assigned to the collectivist situation were moderately cooperative. There was an interaction between personality and situation, reflecting the extreme cooperativeness of the allocentrics in the collectivist situation. Thus, the situation accounted for more variance than the personality of the participants. But extremely high cooperation occurred only in the cell where allocentrics worked in a collectivist situation.

A prime (a stimulus that increases the cognitive accessibility of a concept) can be considered as providing a distinct situation. It can increase or decrease an individual's tendency toward one of the personality attributes. Trafimow, Triandis, and Goto (1991, Experiment 1) asked participants, randomly assigned to two conditions, to think for two minutes of what they have in common with their family and friends or what makes them different from their family and friends. These instructions shifted the scores of the participants toward the allocentric or idiocentric direction, depending on the instructions. A measure of allocentrism is the percentage of the time a person uses social aspects of the self (e.g., group memberships, roles) to describe the self. U.S. participants in the "what you have in common" condition gave 21% social content; in the "what makes you different" condition 6% social content; Chinese American participants in the former condition gave 34% and in the latter condition 19% social content. In Experiment 2, Trafimow et al. replicated these findings using a much more subtle prime, thereby eliminating demand characteristics as a plausible explanation. Trafimow, Silverman, Fan, and Law (1997) replicated these findings in Hong Kong and Trafimow and Smith (1998) replicated them using Native Americans. Thus, they seem to have considerable generality.

Priming has also been demonstrated to affect whether people base their decisions to perform behaviors on their attitudes or on their subjective norms (subjective norms refer to what people's "most important others" think they should do). Trafimow and Finlay (1996) suggested that an idiocentric prime should increase the use of attitudes in determining people's behaviors whereas an allocentric prime should increase the use of subjective norms. Ybarra and Trafimow (1998) tested this idea and obtained strong support in three experiments, despite the fact that the actual content of the primes had nothing to do with the behavior.

In addition to individualism–collectivism, Triandis (1989) described two other cultural syndromes and suggested how the three syndromes are related. Cultures can vary on their *complexity* (e.g., hunters and gatherers vs. information societies) and on their *tightness* (some cultures are less tolerant to deviations from social norms than are others). Collectivism is found in cultures that are relatively simple and tight; individualism is found in cultures that are relatively complex and loose. Individualism increases with affluence (both between and within cultures), and within cultures with social class, leadership roles, social mobility, migration, and level of exposure to the mass media. For example, most dictators, even in very collectivist cultures, are highly individualistic. Collectivism is high among the lower social classes, and among those of fixed residence who do not participate in the modern mass culture. Religious upbringing, threat to the ingroup by outsiders, and low access to resources making survival dependent on the group, enhance collectivism.

Greenwald and Pratkanis (1984) distinguished between the private, public, and collective self. Triandis (1989) argued that the private self is sampled more frequently in individualistic cultures; the public self and the collective self are sampled more frequently in collectivist cultures. When the collective self is sampled it is more likely that individuals will perceive intergroup rather than interpersonal relations. In social identity theory (Tajfel & Turner, 1986) two levels are considered: the personal and the social identity levels. Personal identity reflects the unique attributes of the individual; social identity reflects the attributes of the group that are internalized by the individual. Thus, in collectivist cultures the attributes of ingroups and outgroups are more salient than in individualist cultures.

Priming the private self induces people to think of others, even outgroup members, as individuals; priming the collective self induces people to think of outgroup members as a generic "them." Finlay and Trafimow (1998) found that when the private self was primed, people volunteered to help those who had AIDS (an outgroup) and actually spent more hours at this activity than in the no-prime condition.

Because the distinction between ingroup and outgroup is very accessible to collectivists (Triandis, 1972), such a person, upon meeting another person, is likely to ask: "What is my relationship to that person?" If an ingroup relationship is perceived, the individual is inclined to help, support, cooperate, and even self-sacrifice. If an outgroup relationship is perceived distrust, competition, and hostility can be the typical responses. Individualists do not show such strong differences in behavior when they deal with ingroup and outgroup members.

In fact, collectivist ingroups are relatively rigid, so that people may have some difficulty in joining them; individualist ingroups are less difficult to penetrate (Landis &
Bhagat, 1996). Lewin (1936) was an early observer of this difference.

Acculturation, Identity, and Intergroup Behavior

To understand intergroup behavior we need to consider the kinds of identities that
persons use. Consider, for example, a Chinese American male, living in London. This
person might sample the identities Chinese, American, male, or Londoner. Furthermore,
different identities might be primed depending on the situation at hand (e.g., the
American identity might be primed when watching an American movie whereas the
"male" identity might be primed when this person is in a room full of females). Such
"identity negotiation" is an important aspect of intercultural contact (Ting-Toomey,
1999). The identity that is selected affects intergroup behavior.

In the modern world most humans are influenced by more than one culture. In
our example, both the Chinese and American identities may or may not be sampled.
Berry (1980) identified four kinds of acculturation: where one samples both, one,
the other, or none of these two identities. The Tajfel and Turner (1986) theory of social
identity suggests that people will select identities that will result in the most positive
self-evaluations. In addition, people may sample identities that reflect gender, age,
social class, religion, nationality, occupation, region of the country, race, etc. The
combinations of sampled identities may interact with each other to produce a unique
personality.

Because collectivists have an accessible collective self, they are likely to mention groups
and roles within those groups when asked to describe themselves (Altocchi & Altocchi,
1995; Ma & Schoeneman, 1997; Trafimow et al., 1991, 1997; Trafimow & Smith,
1998). This benefits self-esteem if the outgroup is disvalued. However, if one of a person's
own identities is unfavorable, this person may try to change group membership,
and acquire a more favorable identity – a process that is more likely in individualist
cultures (Cinnirella, 1998). Thus, people absorb idiosyncratic combinations of
attributes, depending on the cultures that influence the individual, how much they
are favored, the possibilities for change, and the identities that are salient in particular
situations.

Members of minority cultures have the dilemma of becoming assimilated by rejecting
their own culture, or segregated by rejecting the culture of the majority. Involuntary
minorities (such as African Americans and Native Americans) are especially likely to reject
the culture of the majority (Ogbu, 1990, 1992).

The strength of the identification with a particular group must also be taken into
account. When minority members join a social environment that is dominated by another
culture, those with strong identifications with the minority culture increase their identification with it (ethnic affirmation), while those with a weak identification show decreased
identification with their own culture, that is, they tend toward assimilation (Ethier &
Deaux, 1994). Thus, there are many processes that shape the self.

Determinants of Intergroup Relations

Social identity theory

Social identity theory has been used to account for intergroup behavior (Tajfel & Turner, 1986). In the process of maximizing self-esteem people identify with various social groups. Social categorization results in intergroup discrimination and ingroup favoritism. Individuals pick the groups with which they can compare their ingroup, and the dimensions for comparison, in such a way as to maximize the favorability of the judgment of their ingroup. In judging whether or not an attribute of their group is favorable they use the values of their culture. Thus, for instance, in individualist cultures they may judge a group favorably if its members are autonomous from their parents, while in a collectivist culture they may judge it favorably if people are close to their parents.

When social identity is salient people deal with outgroups in intergroup rather than interpersonal ways. This is especially the case when there is a history of conflict between ingroup and outgroup. When the conflict is intense, there is often a strong attachment to the ingroup, there is anonymity of group membership, and there is a small possibility of changing membership from the ingroup to other groups (Sherif, 1966).

In self-categorization theory, self-conception varies in level of inclusiveness from personal to social identity, and salient social identity both reflects and makes possible emergent group phenomena (Turner & Oakes, 1997). However, Hinkle, Brown, and Ely (1992) reviewed literature that suggests that social identity theory has limiting conditions. They proposed a group taxonomy based on the individualism/collectivism constructs and a distinction between autonomous and relational group orientations. Relational groups exist in comparison to other groups. Specifically, for political parties, business organizations, and sports teams, comparison is an essential aspect of identity. In contrast, autonomous groups are freestanding. For example, hobbyists' groups do not have to compare themselves to others. Thus, autonomous groups have no reason to think in "us versus them" terms.

The situation determines if a group will use a relational or autonomous orientation at a particular point in time. Hinkle et al. (1992) hypothesized that the predictions of social identity theory will be well supported in the case of collectivist/relational orientation groups, and less well supported when the other three cells of their two-by-two typology are examined. They found that the collectivist/relational cell differed significantly from the other three cells. Specifically, the correlations between (i) ingroup identification and intergroup differentiation, and (ii) self-esteem and intergroup differentiation, were higher in the collectivist/relational cell than in the other cells. Further support for this position was obtained by Brown, Hinkle, Ely, Fox-Cardamore, Maras, & Taylor (1992) who found high positive identification/ingroup favoritism correlations among collectivists with a relational orientation, but zero correlations among individualists with an autonomous orientation.

Recent work suggests that there are several aspects of social identity, and the relationship between social identity and intergroup behavior depends on which aspect is stressed. Jackson and Smith (1999) updated social identity theory by emphasizing four variables that are presumed to affect social identity. First, there are perceptions of the intergroup context in which the ingroup may be more or less salient, and may be perceived to have competitive or cooperative relations with the outgroup. A second variable is the person's attraction to the ingroup. This is really an affective construct that can be measured by responses to items such as "How well do you like the group you are in?" A third variable is interdependence beliefs. These can be measured by responses to items such as "My fate and my future are bound with that of my group." Fourth, depersonalization can affect social identity. A person may think of herself and others as group members (high depersonalization) or as unique individuals (low depersonalization). Of course, all of these variables should be thought of as being continuous rather than as being dichotomous.

According to Jackson and Smith (1999), inconsistent findings concerning the relationship between measured social identity and intergroup bias (e.g., Brown, Condor, Mathews, Wade, & Williams, 1986; Hinkle, Taylor, Fox-Cardamone, & Cook, 1989; and Karasawa, 1991) are due to the fact that different studies emphasized different aspects of social identity. The inconsistencies would be cleared up if the separate aspects of social identity were measured. In general, a strong social identity will be related to intergroup bias and discrimination, but there are two broad types of social identity, which they called "secure" and "insecure." Secure social identity will be related to less intergroup bias than insecure social identity. It occurs when there is strong attraction to the group, but no especially high levels of common fate, depersonalization, or intergroup competition and conflict. By contrast insecure social identity occurs where there are competitive intergroup relations, common fate, and depersonalization.

In two studies, with the second replicating the results of the first, Jackson and Smith (1999) found support for their conception. While both kinds of social identity were related to intergroup bias, the insecure identity was more strongly related to intergroup bias than was the secure identity. Insecure identity was also related to ". . . elevated perceptions of ingroup homogeneity, whereas a higher degree of secure identity predicted favorable evaluations of outgroups, less intergroup bias, and fewer perceptions of ingroup homogeneity" (p. 132). Thus, secure and insecure identities had distinct consequences.

Ellemers, Kortekaas, and Ouwerkerk (1999) also argued that there are various aspects to social identity. They suggested that there is a self-categorization component (an awareness of one's membership in the group), an evaluative component (a positive or negative value is attached to the group membership), and an emotional component (commitment to the group). A complicated set of findings supported their distinctions and, with respect to ingroup favoritism, only the status of the ingroup was found to be relevant (higher status meant more ingroup favoritism). Thus, a good deal of recent research seems to indicate that there are several aspects of social identity, and these must be disentangled to provide a valid picture of how social identity affects intergroup bias.

Other Determinants of Intergroup Behavior

There are other determinants of intergroup behavior that should be mentioned before we discuss them later in the context of individualism and collectivism. They include norms, beliefs, behavioral intentions, feelings, and stereotypes (Boyanowsky & Allen, 1973; Fishbein & Ajzen, 1975; Triandis, 1980; Triandis & Triandis, 1962). These may be both the result of the history of previous intergroup contact and the cause of future intergroup behavior. However, they may also be affected by factors other than previous intergroup history such as hearsay. Sometimes it is in the interest of certain members of a group to induce other members of that group to have negative thoughts about a different group. For example, Hitler's ability to fan Germans' hatred of Jews was largely responsible for his rise to political power in Germany in the 1930s. More generally, a variety of situational factors (e.g., relative power of the ingroup and outgroup; zero-sum conflict resulting in competition, domination, or scapegoating) affect norms (e.g., antagonism, paternalism, persecution, submission, rebellion, repression, conciliation), stereotypes (threatening, inferior, superior, oppressive, powerful, weak), feelings (accepting, rejecting), and behavioral intentions (to hurt, to derogate, to punish, to submit, ambivalence). Discussion of these relationships is beyond the limits of this chapter, but see Duckitt (1992).

An additional variable that affects intergroup behavior was suggested by Stephan and Stephan (in press). According to these researchers, intergroup relations can be poor because people experience "symbolic threat" (feel that an outgroup will threaten their values) as well as "realistic threat" (e.g., they may see the outgroup taking their jobs). An example of symbolic threat would be the crusades in the Middle Ages, where people felt it was important to liberate Jerusalem from the "unbelievers" (who were supposed to be a threat to Christianity), and even convert them to believing in Christ. In general, it seems likely that when the two cultures that are in contact are very different from each other there will be much symbolic threat, and when there is a zero-sum situation there will be much realistic threat.

History, Cultural Norms, and Perceptions of Dissimilarity

In general people in collectivist cultures pay more attention to norms than people in individualist cultures (Suh, Diener, Oishi, & Triandis, 1998; Triandis, 1995a). They conform more in Asch paradigm experiments than individualists do (R. Bond & Smith, 1996). Thus, when ingroup norms call for social distance or aggression toward the outgroup, collectivists are more likely to behave as required by their ingroups (Triandis & Triandis, 1962). Also, people in collectivist cultures define the self in terms of social categories to a larger extent than people in individualist cultures (Altocchi & Altocchi, 1995; Triandis, McCusker, & Hui, 1990), and they are more likely to pay attention to stereotypes. Therefore, we expect that there will be more intergroup bias in collectivist than individualist cultures.

The history of intergroup conflict has generally been neglected in the social psychological literature, because most of the writers come from individualist cultures where history is less crucial in shaping interpersonal and intergroup behavior. But in collectivist cultures history is often a major factor in intergroup relations (e.g., consider modern Yugoslavia). In particular, a history of intergroup conflict may cause cultural distance.

The norms of two cultures or groups are likely to be very different when there is much cultural distance between the two groups. The more different the languages (e.g., Indo-European vs. a tonal language), family structures (e.g., monogamy vs. polygamy), religion, standard of living, and values of the two groups, the greater is the cultural distance between them (Triandis, 1994a). The greater the cultural distance the more the norms are likely to be different, and the more difficult it is for the two groups to develop good intergroup relations.

Cultural distance results in perceived dissimilarity. Dissimilarity together with frequent contact results in conflict. But if cultural distance is not too large, the more one group knows about the other group, the more people perceive each other as similar, which can make contact rewarding. When contact is rewarding it increases the frequency of interaction between the two groups (Homans, 1974). The more interactions, the greater the chances that commonalities between the members of the groups will be discovered (common friends, common feelings, and common reactions to events). The more one group knows about the other, the more they can make "isomorphic attributions" about the behavior of members of the other group (Triandis, 1975). That is, when a member of the other group performs a behavior the attributions that the observer and the actor make about that behavior are similar and thus the behavior has a similar meaning in the two groups. Consequently, people feel that they understand what the other group is doing, and even if they do not like what it is doing, the behavior is not as threatening as it is when they do not understand it (Triandis, Kurowski, & Gelfand, 1994).

The more one group knows about the other group, particularly if members of each group know each other's language, the more they see each other as similar. This perceived similarity increases if there are common goals or if one group cannot reach its goals without the help of the other group (which Sherif, 1965, called superordinate goals). Similarity also increases if people have about the same status, and they have many common friends. The more perceived similarity the greater the liking of one group for the other (Byrne, 1961; Brewer & Campbell, 1976) and the more interaction between the groups which, in turn, increases the accuracy of the stereotypes that each group has of the other group (Triandis & Vassiliou, 1967).

Although increased accuracy can improve relationships when there is little cultural distance, it can lead to conflict if there are different goals, interests, and a large cultural distance. Accurate stereotypes result in attributions that are more isomorphic, hence one can predict the behavior of the other group. Correct predictions of the other group's behavior result in a sense of control over the intergroup situation, and thus one feels less threat in that situation.

Stereotypes reflect, in part, attributes that contrast one's own group with other groups (Campbell, 1967; Triandis & Vassiliou, 1967), especially if the attributes are distinctive (Nelson & Miller, 1995). The sampling of attributes to be included in the stereotypes is biased in the direction of sampling those attributes that increase the positive evaluation of the ingroup (Tajfel & Turner, 1986). Thus, stereotypes have an important function in improving the sense of self-worth of the ingroup. Favorable stereotypes increase liking and decrease social distance (Homans, 1974). Liking is a more important factor in determining behavioral intentions in individualist than in collectivist cultures (Bontempo & Rivero, 1992).

A Closer Examination of Culture and Intergroup Relations

We will discuss next some details about the way collectivism is related to intergroup relations. However, most empirical findings were obtained from comparisons of East Asians
and Western samples. We need to be careful in generalizing to all collectivist cultures since
we do not have research from other collectivist cultures, and so we do not know if what
has been found with East Asians applies to all collectivists.

Collectivists have a stronger sense of "us versus them" than individualists (Kim,
Triandis, Kagitcibasi, Choi, & Yoon, 1994). For individualists the self is the figure and
others, including many groups, are the background. Thus, ingroups and outgroups are not
perceived as extremely different from each other because they perform similar functions as
background. Collectivists define themselves as aspects of their ingroups (Altocchi &
Altocchi, 1995; Triandis, McCusker, & Hui, 1990). Cooperation and even self-sacrifice for
the ingroup are "natural." But investing so much energy in one group makes reactions to
other groups sharply less positive, because individuals have limited energy. When relations
are less positive, they can easily become hostile, especially if resources are limited. Thus,
collectivists focus on their ingroups, and find negative stereotypes of outgroups natural,
that is, to be expected (Triandis & Triandis, 1962). Disliking outsiders is often a normal
state of the world. Large social distance from outgroups is exactly what is to be expected
(Triandis & Triandis, 1962). Norms that specify that one should avoid outgroups are seen
as desirable. In short, sometimes groups have strong norms about avoiding other groups
and reject members of these groups from workplaces, neighborhoods, schools, religious
establishments, and so on (Triandis & Triandis, 1962; Triandis, 1972).

Given this framework of hostility toward outgroups, collectivists are especially likely
to commit the ultimate attribution error. This error, first identified by Taylor and Jaggi
(1974; see Hewstone 1990 for a review), consists of perceiving positive behaviors of the
ingroup as due to internal factors (e.g., that is our nature); positive behaviors of the outgroup as due to external factors (e.g., they were forced to do that); negative behaviors of
the ingroup as due to external factors; and negative behaviors of the outgroup as due to
internal factors.

Individualists make trait-like attributions more frequently than context-dependent
attributions; conversely, collectivists are more likely than individualists to attribute
behavior to situational factors (Fiske, Kitayama, Markus, & Nisbett, 1998). Thus,
collectivists should be more likely to shift from positive to negative intergroup behaviors
when the situation changes.

Individualists are especially personally self-enhancing, thus they are also likely to see
their ingroup as especially deserving and "correct," and thus may appear to other groups
as "arrogant." In the nineteenth century members of individualist cultures were especially
likely to see those of other cultures as "savages" requiring the intervention of members of
their ingroup to "civilize" them. Thus, the colonial powers were especially likely to impose
their cultures on the regions they dominated.

Individualists are also likely to see themselves as unique and free to choose their own
behavior (Triandis & Gelfand, 1998). They have a strong sense that they control outcomes. Collectivists see themselves as bound by other people and norms, as under the

control of "fate," and think that they are quite ordinary members of their groups (Markus & Kitayama, 1991). In situations where members of the two kinds of cultures work together, or confront each other, the individualists will appear as arrogant, and the collectivists may appear to the other group as too rigid (Landis & Bhagat, 1996).

Individualists respond to praise and self-affirmation, and tend to compliment each other for good behavior, while collectivists see their behavior as ordinary and not deserving of special comment (Kitayama, 1996). That can produce misunderstandings and resentment when the two kinds of groups are working together, or are in a confrontation. Furthermore, individualists are more likely to become angry and show their anger, while collectivists control their negative emotional expressions (Matsumoto, Takeuchi, Andayani, Kouznetsova, & Krupp, 1998; Stephan, Stephan, & De Vargas, 1996). Similarly, East Asian collectivists avoid confrontation, and prefer mediation for conflict resolution (Leung, Au, Fernandez-Dols, & Iwawaki, 1992; Leung, 1997).

Collectivists are motivated to avoid criticism from ingroup members, and shame is a frequent emotion when they do not behave optimally (Triandis, 1995b). This contrasts sharply with the motivation of individualists who often use internal standards for judging good behavior, and feel guilty when they do not manage to behave optimally. The result of using different standards is that collectivists and individualists may evaluate outcomes differently. Collectivists stress "what will my ingroup say?" while individualists emphasize "how well does this group meet my goals?"

Individualists emphasize the uniqueness of individuals and so they see their ingroups as heterogeneous and their outgroups as relatively homogeneous (Triandis, McCusker, & Hui, 1990). This would increase their tendency toward intergroup behavior rather than interpersonal behavior, because they do not pay attention to the differences among outgroup members. On the other hand, they tend to use personal attributes in perceiving others, which will increase their interpersonal behavior. Thus, there are two contradictory tendencies that will result in different outcomes depending on the situation. If the situation is very tense, and there is a strong physical difference between ingroup and outgroup, individualists are perfectly able to commit atrocities.

Collectivists see their ingroups as relatively homogeneous (Triandis, McCusker, & Hui, 1990), but they also see their outgroups as homogeneous. Thus they tend to pay little attention to the personal attributes of members of any group. These tendencies result in intergroup rather than interpersonal behaviors.

When communicating, collectivists pay much attention to the situation, and to paralinguistic cues, and very little attention to the content of the message, whereas individualists pay attention to the exact words, but neglect the paralinguistic cues (Triandis, 1994a, chapter 7). Thus, miscommunications are very likely because each group neglects to pay attention to the most important channel of communication of the other group.

Individualists have the illusion of specialness in relation to their ingroup; collectivists have this illusion with respect to their group being special in relation to other groups. The notion of the "chosen people" is common among collectivists. Ethnocentrism is present in all cultures (Triandis, 1994a), but it is higher among collectivists than it is among individualists (Lee & Ward, 1998).

The literature has distinguished "primary control," where individuals change their environment in order to fit in, from "secondary control," where individuals change themselves to fit in the environment. Primary control is high among individualists and secondary control among collectivists (Weisz, Rothbaum, & Blackburn, 1984; Seniger, Trommsdorff, & Essau, 1993). Thus, the high self-determination of individualists is likely to result in attempts to change the situation. Collectivists are more likely to accept the situation the way it is. The implication is that in intergroup situations where the individual has a different opinion from the ingroup authorities, individualists will try to change the views of the authorities – by writing letters of protest, forming new political parties, etc. Collectivists are more likely to accept the view of the authorities, try to convince themselves that the authorities are correct, and do what they must even if it does not agree with what they would like done.

Conclusion

Culture shapes the kind of information that people sample from their environment. In individualist cultures people sample mostly internal processes, and focus on what happens to individuals. In collectivist cultures people sample norms, social influences, and external factors as well as what happens to groups. Different sampling of information results in different perceptions of reality, and intergroup behaviors. Individualists see fewer differences between ingroups and outgroups than do collectivists. Collectivists see more of a difference between "we" and "they" than do individualists. While both individualists and collectivists are capable of most undesirable intergroup behaviors, the factors that influence these behaviors are different, and depend on culture. Collectivists are more ethnocentric than individualists; they are more likely to change from positive to negative intergroup behaviors and from negative to positive intergroup behaviors when ingroup authorities suggest that they do so, than are individualists. When individualists confront collectivists the former are likely to be perceived as especially arrogant and the latter as especially rigid.

Intergroup conflict would become less problematic if we realized how dependent we are on the sampling of the tremendously rich information in our past and present environment. For example, historians usually write the histories of their own countries. Because they have an interest in selling copies of their books, and sales are larger when the history compliments the readers' own country, most histories provide samples of information that are biased in favor of that country, ignoring crucial unflattering information, such as the rape of Nanking in Japanese textbooks, or the genocide of Armenians in Turkish textbooks. Histories of the world do a better job, but they have so much material to cover that they cannot dwell very much on any one incident. If intergroup conflict is to be reduced we need to train historians and other social studies writers to become more objective. We also need to train readers to be suspicious of anything they read that presents only one side of the argument, especially if it favors their own group. People who glorify their own cultures, or their own cultural type (e.g., individualism or collectivism), should be trained to see the advantages of the other cultural patterns. Triandis (1995a, chapter 7) argued, among other points, that collectivism is especially desirable in small group situations, such as the family, and individualism is especially desirable in large group situations, such as the relationships of citizens to the state. Understanding that each cultural pattern has weaknesses is very likely to reduce the glorification of the cultural pattern. Understanding that we are all ethnocentric and need to become less ethnocentric by becoming exposed to the good features of other cultures is likely to reduce our ethnocentrism and improve intergroup relations. An ability to imagine oneself as a member of the other group in intergroup situations is an obvious need if intergroup relations are to improve.

Note

1. Interested readers may wish to consult the extensive literature on these constructs, for instance, the references in reviews by Kagitcibasi (1997) or M. H. Bond and Smith (1996). Smith and Bond (1999) organized their review of social psychology around the individualism and collectivism constructs.

References

Altocchi, J., & Altocchi, L. (1995). Polyfaceted psychological acculturation in Cook islanders. *Journal of Cross-Cultural Psychology, 26*, 426–440.

Bar-Tal, D., & Staub, E. (1997). *Patriotism: In the lives of individuals and nations*. Chicago, IL: Nelson-Hall.

Berry, J. W. (1980). Acculturation as varieties of adaptation. In A. Padilla (Ed.), *Acculturation: Theory, models, and some new findings* (pp. 9–25). Boulder, CO: Westview Press.

Bond, M. H., & Smith, P. B. (1996). Cross-cultural social and organizational psychology. *Annual Review of Psychology, 47*, 205–235.

Bond, R., & Smith, P. B. (1996). Culture and conformity: A meta-analysis of studies using Asch's (1952b, 1956) line judgment task. *Psychological Bulletin, 119*, 111–137.

Bontempo, R., & Rivero, J. C. (1992, August). *Cultural variation in cognition: The role of self-concept in the attitude-behavior rink*. Paper presented at the meetings of the American Academy of Management, Las Vegas, NV.

Boyanowsky, E. O., & Allen, V. L. (1973). In-group norms and self-identity as determinants of discriminatory behavior. *Journal of Personality and Social Psychology, 25*, 408–418.

Brewer, M., & Campbell, D. T. (1976). *Ethnocentrism and intergroup attitudes: East African evidence*. New York: Halstead/Wiley.

Brown, R. J., Condor, F., Mathews, A., Wade, G., & Williams, J. A. (1986). Explaining intergroup differentiation in an industrial organization. *Journal of Occupational Psychology, 22*, 78–92.

Brown, R., Hinkle, S., Ely, P. G., Fox-Cardamore, L., Maras, P., & Taylor, L. A. (1992). Recognizing group diversity: Individualist-collectivist and autonomous-relational social orientations and their implications for intergroup processes. *British Journal of Social Psychology, 31*, 327–342.

Byrne, D. (1961). Interpersonal attraction and attitude similarity. *Journal of Abnormal and Social Psychology, 62*, 713–715.

Campbell, D. T. (1967). Stereotypes and the perception of group differences. *American Psychologist, 22*, 817–829.

Chatman, J. A., & Barsade, S. G. (1995). Personality, organizational culture, and cooperation: Evidence from a business simulation. *Administrative Science Quarterly, 40*, 423–443.

Cinnirella, M. (1998). Exploring temporal aspects of social identity – the concept of possible social identities. *European Journal of Social Psychology, 28*, 227–248.

Davidson, A. R., Jaccard, J. J., Triandis, H. C., Morales, M. L., & Diaz-Guerrero, R. (1976). Cross-cultural model testing: Toward a solution of the etic-emic dilemma. *International Journal of Psychology, 11*, 1–13.

Duckitt, J. (1992). Patterns of prejudice: Group interests and intergroup attitudes. *South African Journal of Psychology, 22*, 147–156.

Ellemers, N., Kortekaas, P., & Ouwerkerk, J. W. (1999). Self-categorization, commitment to the group and group self-esteem as related but distinct aspects of social identity. *European Journal of Social Psychology, 29*, 371–389.

Ethier, K. A., & Deaux, K. (1994). Negotiating social identity when contexts change: Maintaining identification and responding to threat. *Journal of Personality and Social Psychology, 67*, 243–251.

Feshbach, S., & Sakano, N. (1997). The structure and correlates of attitudes toward one's nation in samples of United States and Japanese college students: A comparative study. In D. Bar-Tal & E. Staub (Eds.), *Patriotism: In the lives of individuals and nations* (pp. 91–107). Chicago, IL: Nelson-Hall.

Finlay, K. A., & Trafimow, D. (1998). The relationship between private self and helping victims of AIDS. *Journal of Applied Social Psychology, 28*, 1800–1811.

Fishbein, M., & Ajzen, I. (1975). *Belief, attitude, intention, and behavior: An introduction to theory and research.* Reading, MA: Addison-Wesley.

Fiske, A. P., Kitayama, S., Markus, H. R., & Nisbett, R. E. (1998). The cultural matrix of social psychology. In D. T. Gilbert, S. T. Fiske, & G. Lindzey (Eds.), *The handbook of social psychology* (Vol. 2, pp. 915–981). New York: Oxford University Press.

Gaertner, S. L., Mann, J., Murrell, A., & Dovidio, J. F. (1989). Reducing intergroup bias: The benefits of recategorization. *Journal of Personality and Social Psychology, 57*, 239–249.

Gaertner, S. L., Dovidio, J. F., Anastasio, P. A. et al. (1993). The common ingroup identity model: Recategorization and the reduction of intergroup bias. In W. Stoebe & M. Hewston (Eds.), *European Review of Social Psychology, 4*, 1–26.

Greenwald, A. G., & Pratkanis, A. R. (1984). The self. In R. S. Wyer & T. K. Srull (Eds.), *Handbook of social cognition* (Vol. 3, pp. 129–178). Hillsdale, NJ: Erlbaum.

Hewstone, M. (1990). The "ultimate attribution error"? A review of the literature on intergroup causal attribution. *European Journal of Social Psychology, 20*, 311–335.

Hinkle, S., Brown, R., & Ely, P. G. (1992). Social identity theory processes: Some limitations and limiting conditions. *Revista de Psicologia Social, 7*, 99–111.

Hinkle, S. W., Taylor, L. A., Fox-Cardamone, D. L., & Cook, S. (1989). Intragroup identification and intergroup differentiation: A multi-component approach. *British Journal of Social Psychology, 28*, 305–317.

Hofstede, G. (1982). *Cultural pitfalls for Dutch expatriates in Indonesia.* Maastricht, The Netherlands: Institute for Research on Intercultural Cooperation.

Homans, G. C. (1974). *Social Behavior: Its elementary forms.* New York: Harcourt Brace Jovanovich.

Jackson, J. W., & Smith, E. R. (1999). Conceptualizing social identity: A new framework and evidence for the impact of different dimensions. *Personality and Social Psychology Bulletin, 25*, 120–135.

Kagitcibasi, C. (1997). Individualism and collectivism. In J. W. Berry, M. H. Segall, & C. Kagitcibasi (Eds.), *Handbook of cross-cultural psychology: Social behavior and applications* (Vol. 3, pp. 1–50). Boston, MA: Allyn & Bacon.

Karasawa, M. (1991). Toward an assessment of social identity: The structure of group identification and its effects on ingroup evaluations. *British Journal of Social Psychology, 30*, 293–307.

Kashima, Y., Siegel, M., Tanaka, K., & Kashima, E. (1992). Do people believe behaviors are consistent with attitudes? Toward a cultural psychology of attribution processes. *British Journal of Social Psychology, 31*, 111–124.

Kim, U., Triandis, H. C., Kagitcibasi, C., Choi, S. C., & Yoon, G. (1994). Introduction. In U. Kim, H. C. Triandis, C. Kagitcibasi, S. C. Choi, & G. Yoon (Eds.), *Individualism and collectivism: Theory, method, and applications.* Thousand Oaks, CA: Sage.

Kitayama, S. (1996). *The mutual constitution of culture and self: Implications for emotion.* Paper presented to the meetings of the American Psychological Society, June, 1996.

Landis, D., & Bhagat, R. (1996). *Handbook of cross-cultural training.* (2nd ed.). Thousand Oaks, CA: Sage.

Lee, L., & Ward, C. (1998). Ethnicity, idiocentrism-allocentrism, and intergroup attitudes. *Journal of Applied Psychology, 28*, 109–123.

Leung, K. (1997). Negotiation and reward allocations across cultures. In P. C. Earley & M. Erez (Eds.), *New perspectives on I/O psychology* (pp. 640–675). San Francisco, CA: Jossey-Bass.

Leung, K., Au, Y-F., Fernandez-Dols, J. M., & Iwawaki, S. (1992). Preference for methods of conflict processing in two collectivist cultures. *International Journal of Psychology, 27*, 195–209.

Lewin, K. (1936). *Principles of topological psychology.* New York: McGraw-Hill.

Ma, V., & Schoeneman, T. J. (1997). Individualism versus collectivism: A comparison of Kenyan and American self-concepts. *Basic & Applied Social Psychology, 19*, 261–273.

Markus, H., & Kitayama, S. (1991). Culture and self: Implications for cognition, emotion, and motivation. *Psychological Review, 98*, 224–253.

Markus, H., Kitayama, S., & Helman, R. J. (1996). Culture and "basic" psychological principles. In T. Higgins & A. Kruglanski (Eds.), *Social psychology: A handbook of basic principles* (pp. 857–913). New York: Guilford Press.

Matsumoto, D., Takeuchi, S., Angayani, S., Kouznetsova, N., & Krupp, D. (1998). The contribution of individualism vs. collectivism to cross-national differences in display rules. *Asian Journal of Social Psychology, 1*, 147–165.

Mills, J., & Clark, M. S. (1982). Exchange and communal relationships. In L. Wheeler (Ed.), *Review of personality and social psychology* (Vol. 3, pp. 121–144). Beverly Hills, CA: Sage.

Morris, M. W., & Peng, K. (1994). Culture and cause: American and Chinese attributions for social and physical events. *Journal of Personality and Social Psychology, 67*, 949–971.

Nelson, L. J., & Miller, D. T. (1995). The distinctiveness effect in social categorization: You are what makes you unusual. *Psychological Science, 6*, 246–249.

Ogbu, J. U. (1990). Minority status and literacy in comparative perspective. *Daedalus, 119*, 141–168.

Ogbu, J. U. (1992). Understanding cultural diversity and learning. *Educational Researcher, 21*, 5–14.

Rabbie, J. M., & Horwitz, M. (1988). Categories versus groups as explanatory concepts in intergroup relations. *European Journal of Social Psychology, 18*, 117–123.

Reykowski, J. (1997). Patriotism and the collective system of meanings. In D. Bar-Tal & E. Staub (Eds.), *Patriotism: In the lives of individuals and nations* (pp. 108–128). Chicago, IL: Nelson-Hall.

Rokeach, M. (1960). *The open and closed mind.* New York: Basic Books.

Seniger, R., Trommsdorff, G., & Essau, C. (1993). Adolescent control beliefs: Cross-cultural variations of primary and secondary orientations. *International Journal of Behavioral Development, 16*, 243–260.

Sherif, M. (1965). Superordinate goals in the reduction of intergroup conflict: An experimental evaluation. In M. Schwebel (Ed.), *Behavior, science, and human survival.* Palo Alto, CA: Science and Behavior Books.

Sherif, M. (1966). *Group conflict and cooperation: Their social psychology.* London: Routlege & Kegan Paul.

Smith, P. B., & Bond, M. H. (1999). *Social psychology across cultures.* Boston, MA: Allyn & Bacon.

Stephan, W. G., & Stephan, C. W. (in press). An integrated threat theory of prejudice. In S. Oskamp (Ed.), *Claremont symposium on applied social psychology.* Hillsdale, NJ: Erlbaum.

Stephan, W. G., Stephan, C. W., & De Vargas, M. C. (1996). Emotional expression in Costa Rica and the United States. *Journal of Cross-Cultural Psychology, 27,* 147–160.

Suh, E., Diener, E., Oishi, S., & Triandis, H. C. (1998). The shifting basis of life satisfaction judgments across cultures: Emotions versus norms. *Journal of Personality and Social Psychology, 74,* 482–493.

Tajfel, H., & Turner, J. (1986). The social identity theory of intergroup relations. In S. Worchel & W. Austin (Eds.), *Psychology of intergroup relations* (2nd ed., pp. 7–24). Chicago, IL: Nelson-Hall.

Taylor, D. M., & Jaggi, V. (1974). Ethnocentrism and causal attribution in a South Indian context. *Journal of Cross-Cultural Psychology, 5,* 162–171.

Ting-Toomey, S. (1999). *Communicating across cultures.* New York: Guilford Press.

Trafimow, D., & Finlay, K. A. (1996). The importance of subjective norms for a minority of people. *Personality and Social Psychology Bulletin, 22,* 820–828.

Trafimow, D., & Smith, M. D. (1998). An extension of the "two baskets" theory to Native Americans. *European Journal of Social Psychology, 28,* 1015–1019.

Trafimow, D., Triandis, H. C., & Goto, S. (1991). Some tests of the distinction between the private self and the collective self. *Journal of Personality and Social Psychology, 60,* 649–655.

Trafimow, D., Silverman, E. S., Fan, R. M., & Law, J. S. F. (1997). The effects of language and priming on the relative accessibility of the private self and the collective self, *Journal of Cross-Cultural Psychology, 28,* 107–123.

Triandis, H. C. (1967). Toward an analysis of the components of interpersonal attitudes. In Carolyn & Muzafer Sherif (Eds.), *Attitudes, ego involvement, and change* (pp. 227–270). New York: Wiley.

Triandis, H. C. (1972). *The analysis of subjective culture.* New York: Wiley.

Triandis, H. C. (1975). Cultural training, cognitive complexity, and interpersonal attitudes. In R. W. Brislin, S. Bochner, & W. J. Lonner (Eds.), *Cross-cultural perspectives on learning* (pp. 39–77). Beverly Hills, CA: Sage.

Triandis, H. C. (1980). Values, attitudes, and interpersonal behavior. In H. E. Howe & M. M. Page (Eds.), *Nebraska symposium on motivation, 1979* (pp. 195–260). Lincoln, NE: University of Nebraska Press.

Triandis, H. C. (1989). The self and social behavior in differing cultural contexts. *Psychological Review, 96,* 269–289.

Triandis, H. C. (1990). Cross-cultural studies of individualism and collectivism. In J. Berman (Ed.), *Nebraska symposium on motivation, 1989* (pp. 41–133). Lincoln, NE: University of Nebraska Press.

Triandis, H. C. (1994a). *Culture and social behavior.* New York: McGraw-Hill.

Triandis, H. C. (1994b). Theoretical and methodological approaches to the study of collectivism and individualism. In U. Kim, H. C. Triandis, C. Kagitcibasi, S-C. Choi, & G. Yoon (Eds.), *Individualism and collectivism: Theory, method, and applications* (pp. 41–51). Thousand Oaks, CA: Sage.

Triandis, H. C. (1995a). *Individualism and collectivism.* Boulder, CO: Westview Press.

Triandis, H. C. (1995b). Motivation and achievement in collectivist and individualist cultures. In M. L. Maher & P. R. Pintrich (Eds.), *Advances in motivation and achievement: Culture, motivation, and achievement* (pp. 1–30). Greenwich, CT: Jai Press.

Triandis, H. C., & Gelfand, M. (1998). Converging measurement of horizontal and vertical individualism and collectivism. *Journal of Personality and Social Psychology, 74*, 118–128.

Triandis, H. C., Kurowski, L., & Gelfand, M. (1994). Workplace diversity. In H. C. Triandis, M. Dunnette, & L. Hough (Eds.), *Handbook of industrial and organizational psychology* (2nd ed., Vol. 4, pp. 769–827). Palo Alto, CA. Consulting Psychologists Press.

Triandis, H. C., McCusker, C., & Hui, C. H. (1990). Multimethod probes of individualism and collectivism. *Journal of Personality and Social Psychology, 59*, 1006–1020.

Triandis, H. C., & Triandis, L. M. (1962). A cross-cultural study of social distance. *Psychological Monographs, 76*(21) (whole of No. 540).

Triandis, H. C., & Vassiliou, V. (1967). Frequency of contact and stereotyping. *Journal of Personality and Social Psychology, 7*, 316–328.

Turner, J. C. (1988). Comments on Doise's individual and social identities in intergroup relations. *European Journal of Social Psychology, 18*, 113–116.

Turner, J. C., & Oakes, P. J. (1997). The socially structured mind. In C. McGarty & S. A. Haslam (Eds.), *The message of social psychology* (pp. 355–373). Oxford, UK: Blackwell.

Weisz, J. R., Rothbaum, F. M., & Blackburn, T. C. (1984). Standing out and standing in: The psychology of control in America and Japan. *American Psychologist, 39*, 955–969.

Worchel, S., & Coutant, D. (1997). The tangled web of loyalty: Nationalism, patriotism, and ethnocentrism. In D. Bar-Tal & E. Staub (Eds.), *Patriotism: In the lives of individuals and nations* (pp. 190–210). Chicago, IL: Nelson-Hall.

Yamaguchi, S. (1994). Collectivism among the Japanese: A perspective from the self. In U. Kim, H. C. Triandis, C. Kagitcibasi, S-C. Choi, & G. Yoon (Eds.), *Individualism and collectivism: Theory, method, and applications* (pp. 175–188). Thousand Oaks, CA: Sage.

Ybarra, O., & Trafimow, D. (1998). How priming the private self or collective self affects the relative weights of attitudes and subjective norms. *Personality and Social Psychology Bulletin, 24*, 362–370.

CHAPTER NINETEEN

Acculturation

Karmela Liebkind

1   Introduction

In the classical definition of acculturation, the concept refers to "those phenomena which result when groups of individuals having different cultures come into continuous first-hand contact, with subsequent changes in the original cultural pattern of either or both groups" (Redfield, Linton, & Herskovits, 1936, p. 149). This definition refers to groups in contact, thereby explicitly placing acculturation within the realm of intergroup relations. In its seminal article on acculturation, the Social Science Research Council (SSRC, 1954) clearly viewed intergroup relations as part of the acculturation process, although within anthropology, culture itself remained the main unit of analysis (SSRC, 1954). The original definition also encompassed bidirectionality, that is, changes can occur within both groups.

Cultural differences are tied to historical experiences, some of which are based on socio-economic stratification of a relatively recent nature, while others are rooted in a distant path of which nobody is conscious. This historically older culture is sometimes called "deep culture" as it is embedded in language, ethnicity, religion, and/or nationality. For the purpose of this chapter, culture is conceptualized as shared patterns of belief and feeling toward issues such as child-rearing practices, family systems, and ethical values or attitudes (Fernando, 1991; Liebkind, 1996). These are elements of what Triandis (1995) has called "subjective culture," created by interaction between people. Some researchers may use countries as the equivalent of cultures, but this equivalence is very approximate; while there are fewer than 200 countries in the world, the number of distinct cultures has been estimated to ca. 10,000 (Triandis, 1995, p. 3).

Acculturation research has been mostly conducted within cross-cultural psychology. Much of this research is relevant for the social psychology of intergroup relations, but traditionally, research on acculturation within social psychology on the one hand and cross-cultural psychology on the other have largely tended to ignore each other. It is therefore encouraging that several attempts have lately been made to combine the two fields of research. The literature reviewed in this chapter is selected from the immense body of existing research with the aim of identifying crucial dimensions to be acknowledged in future research on the social psychology of acculturation. The reader should, however, be prepared for a "bumpy road." The diverse literatures in the field of acculturation tackle a plethora of different issues and often seem to constitute a set of independent areas of inquiry, paying no more than lip service to each other in passing. However, an attempt is made at the end of this chapter to summarize the dimensions of acculturation that seem most relevant for a social psychology of intergroup relations.

2   Different Models of Acculturation

Acculturation can be viewed as a state or a process. As a process, acculturation implies changes over time in beliefs, emotions, attitudes, values, behavior, identification patterns, etc. of persons in first-hand contact with persons representing another culture. This perspective encompasses a range of different conceptual frameworks and includes the antecedents, mediators, moderators, and adaptational outcomes of the dynamic acculturation process (Ward, 1996; Berry, 1997). In contrast, researchers may conceptualize acculturation as a state and concern themselves with the measurement of the amount or extent of acculturation at a given moment, that is, the behavioral, affective, and attitudinal characteristics of the acculturated individual (Ward, 1996). The state approach dominates the field. As the empirical measurement of change is very difficult, acculturation is most often conceptualized as a matter of degree in relation to culture-specific markers (Ward, 1996). Change per se can only be noted and assessed when two sets of data, gathered at different points in time, are compared. While this is the ideal, in practice such longitudinal studies are seldom feasible. Instead, a common alternative is cross-sectional research in which a time-related variable, such as length of residence or generational status is employed, for example, among immigrants. The problem with this approach is that it assumes acculturation to be a linear process (Berry, Trimble, & Olmedo, 1986).

There are two main perspectives among the numerous theories of acculturation. One emphasizes a linear process of assimilation, and the other emphasizes cultural plurality (Berry, 1997; Nguyen, Messé, & Stollak, 1999; Sayegh & Lasry, 1993). In the first perspective, the term *acculturation* is often equated with assimilation, and it more commonly refers to the linear process of acquiring the host society's values and behaviors (Nguyen et al., 1999). The assimilationist model posits a unidirectional change toward the mainstream society and implies, then, an eventual disappearance of the original ethnic/cultural identity (Laroche, Kim, Hui, & Tomiuk, 1998; Sayegh & Lasry, 1993). In contrast, the second model emphasizes cultural pluralism. It is two-dimensional in the sense that it recognizes that ethnic groups and their members preserve, albeit in varying degrees, their heritage cultures while adapting to the mainstream society. It holds that a variety of cultures can and do exist in the same geographical region and maintain a part or the whole of the ethnic/cultural backgrounds while functioning successfully within a host society (Laroche et al., 1998).

As with culture shock and other processes of cultural transitions (Searle & Ward, 1990; Nguyen et al., 1999), the operationalization of acculturation has been fraught with several pitfalls (Ward, 1996). Nguyen and her colleagues (1999) have noted that past work has operationalized acculturation in divergent ways; with either a single index (e.g., generation status, language preference, years of residence in host society, etc.), with unidimensional bipolar scales (e.g., the ARSMA/Acculturation Rating Scale for Mexican Americans, Cuellar, Harris, & Jasso, 1980) or with bidimensional modes of acculturation (e.g., Berry, 1997). Single indexes are only proxy measures in which acculturation is implied. The main problem with the bipolar approach is its assumption of mutual exclusion. It assumes a perfect inverse relationship between the ethnic and host cultures. Unidimensional acculturation scales often involve language use, friendship patterns, media sources, occupational status, individual and parental birthplace, and values, ranging from "traditional" at one end of the scale to "mainstream" at the other (Palinkas & Pickwell, 1995).

In contrast, bidimensional models hold that cultural involvements in ethnic background and host society can and should be measured separately. However, the models differ in their assumptions on the relationship between these two orientations. Some assume the relationship to be orthogonal (e.g., Der-Karabetian, 1980; Hutnik, 1986; Sayegh & Lasry, 1993; Zak, 1973), while others assume a moderately inverse correlation (e.g., Laroche et al., 1998; Nguyen et al., 1999). Within cross-cultural psychology, there is at the conceptual level a clear tendency to move toward a two-dimensional model of acculturation, although empirical studies may still employ unidimensional acculturation scales. Social psychologists, however, have tended both theoretically and empirically to rely predominantly on the unidimensional model of acculturation, which casts home and host cultures as competing and mutually exclusive domains (Ward, 1996). In addition, social psychologists have traditionally tended to ignore research on acculturation within cross-cultural psychology more than vice versa. As a result, acculturation has, within social psychology, often been equated with social mobility.

3   Acculturation as Social Mobility

3.1   *The mobility model of cultural integration*

The so-called *mobility model of cultural integration* (Moghaddam, 1988) is based almost exclusively on *social identity theory* (SIT; Tajfel & Turner, 1986). For this model, acculturation is not a central concept, and it views cultural or ethnic minorities as no different from other socially and economically disadvantaged groups. Consequently, it examines the strategies such groups use to "get ahead," that is, to better their economic conditions and social status. According to SIT, reactions of disadvantaged groups to their disadvantage will vary according to the permeability of group boundaries and the stability and legitimacy of the intergroup status differential (Duckitt, 1992; Tajfel & Turner, 1979, 1986). Moghaddam (1988) applied these premises to the area of acculturation (cf. Lalonde & Cameron, 1993; Lalonde, Taylor, & Moghaddam, 1992). Following the so-called *five-stage model (FSM) of intergroup relations* by Taylor and McKirnan (1984), and *elite theory* (Pareto, 1935), Moghaddam (1988) assumed that "individuals will attempt first to achieve mobility on an individual basis, and only resort to collective action when they perceive the system to be closed and the way up to the advantaged group to be blocked" (p. 74).

According to this model, the alternative strategies available to such groups, notably immigrants, are determined by two dimensions, one of which is a unidimensional heritage cultural maintenance–assimilation continuum. The extreme poles of the other dimension are "total normative and total nonnormative behavior," where "normative behavior includes all activities that are endorsed by the majority group as being appropriate behavior for minority group members and explicitly or implicitly support the existing intergroup power hierarchy" (Moghaddam, 1988, p. 71). As Moghaddam (1988) notes that "assimilation is probably the most normative integration strategy for immigrants, because in terms of consequences, it leads to minimal threat to status quo" (p. 72), it becomes evident that the two dimensions are, in most cases, only one; the more the immigrant endorses assimilation as a strategy, the more normative this choice is. Only in the case of societies that are officially committed to multiculturalism is this relationship reversed, although it still exists. In this analysis, then, acculturation is treated as synonymous to assimilation, and assimilation, in turn, as totally determined by the host society's approval of attempts on the part of the minority group to enhance its social and economical position.

Moghaddam (1988) derived from his bidimensional model four strategies for immigrants to "get ahead" in society: *normative/assimilation, normative/heritage culture maintenance, nonnormative/assimilation,* and *nonnormative/heritage culture maintenance.* However, the interdependence of the two dimensions causes some difficulties in defining the strategies. For example, a nonnormative/assimilation is adopted when an immigrant attempts to "achieve social mobility within mainstream society, an acceptable goal," but does not "abide by the means to achieve these goals that are acceptable to the majority group" (Moghaddam, 1988, p. 73).

3.2   Empirical studies on acculturation as social mobility

While experimental studies within this framework often have nothing to do with acculturation (e.g., Boen & Vanbeselaere, 1998; Wright, Taylor, & Moghaddam, 1990), they nevertheless constitute empirical tests of the basic assumptions behind the social mobility model. These assumptions have not been well supported. The FSM of intergroup relations (Taylor & McKirnan, 1984) is built upon the conditions SIT proposes to be necessary for disadvantaged group members to move from apparent acceptance to some form of active response. Although there is some supportive experimental evidence for these conditions, this evidence is marred by inconsistencies and is by no means conclusive (Duckitt, 1992). For example, in an experimental study on 114 male teenagers trying to gain access into a high-status group, Boen and Vanbeselaere (1998) failed to replicate the results of Wright et al. (1990) on the general preference for individual mobility among members of disadvantaged groups. In fact, the main effect of the individual-collective factor in Boen and Vanbeselaere's (1998) study even went in the opposite direction, since their subjects endorsed collective action more than the individual action. This preference for collective action did not interact with the normative–nonnormative factor, and was not influenced by any of the experimentally manipulated variables, despite the fact that the experimental procedure was copied from the one used by Wright et al. (1990) (Boen & Vanbeselaere, 1998, p. 695).

Those studies within this framework which do involve acculturating groups operationalize acculturation using a variety of unidimensional scales ranging from total assimilation to total heritage culture maintenance (Lalonde & Cameron, 1993; Lambert, Mermigis, & Taylor, 1986; Lalonde, Taylor, & Moghaddam, 1992; Moghaddam, Ditto, & Taylor, 1990). The results generally show that there is more support for maintenance of the heritage culture than for assimilation (Moghaddam, Taylor, & Lalonde, 1987), particularly with regard to child-rearing values and heritage language (Lambert et al., 1986; Moghaddam & Taylor, 1987). However, some researchers have raised the question of the voluntariness of this preference and studied the degree to which it is an entirely "self"-driven choice (Ruggiero, Taylor, & Lambert, 1996). Lalonde and Cameron (1993) perceived a preference for the heritage culture as a direct consequence of a disadvantaged position, which "does not permit them easily to adopt an individual acculturation orientation, i.e., assimilation" (Lalonde & Cameron, 1993, p. 70).

One important aspect of disadvantage is the pervasive presence of negative attitudes and discrimination toward one's group. However, according to Ruggiero et al. (1996), these aspects of disadvantage do not motivate a preference for heritage culture. On the contrary, Ruggiero et al. (1996) found a strong, negative effect of perceived personal discrimination on ethnic group members' attitudes toward the importance of maintaining the heritage culture; the more African American and Hispanic American respondents had experienced personal discrimination, the less importance they assigned to heritage culture maintenance.

According to Tajfel and Turner (1979), the awareness of negative stereotypes and discrimination against one's group is likely to result in negative self-evaluations among the group members. Empirical evidence for this hypothesis is, however, remarkably scarce (Brown, 1998; Crocker & Major, 1989). The reason for this has been attributed to the self-protecting properties of stigma; members of stigmatized/disadvantaged groups can attribute personal failure externally (to discrimination) and thereby protect their self-esteem (Crocker & Major, 1989). However, no such tendency was found in an experimental study where subjects reacted to negative feedback after information about the probability of discrimination (Ruggiero & Taylor, 1997). Instead, both Blacks and Asians tended to minimize the perceived discrimination, choosing instead to blame their failure on themselves. The reason for not making external attributions to protect self-esteem is, according to Ruggiero and Taylor (1997), that the internal attribution implies more psychological benefits; while lowering self-esteem in relation to a specific performance, internal attribution increases the sense of personal control over the performance and especially over the social relations involved. Also self-esteem related to the latter is maintained (Ruggiero & Taylor, 1997).

Although Ruggiero and Taylor (1997) conclude that "the tendency of minority group members to attribute negative outcomes internally may provide members of majority groups with justifications for ongoing victimization of minority group members" (p. 387), it is not clear to what extent the experimental results they obtained can be generalized to long-term acculturation processes in society. It is true that the experiences of prejudice and discrimination have systematically been shown to negatively influence the well-being of ethnic minority members (Liebkind, 1996; Liebkind & Jasinskaja-Lahti, 2000a; Moghaddam et al., 1990). However, this effect seems to be dependent both on the specific ethnic group and the specific intergroup context in question (Liebkind & Jasinskaja-Lahti, 2000b). External attribution of personal drawbacks may be easier for small, visible and culturally more distant groups than for less visible and culturally proximal groups. As a consequence, perceived discrimination may be more directly related to psychological distress in the latter than the former kind of groups (Liebkind & Jasinskaja-Lahti, 2000b). Furthermore, the use of external attribution to protect self-esteem may fluctuate situationally; Brown (1998) found that Black students envisioned less positive views of themselves when imagining a semester-long interaction, but not when imagining a one-time interaction in which they were evaluated by a European American instructor.

4 Acculturation as Coping with Stress and Learning New Skills

4.1 *Definitions of successful acculturation*

The outcome variables used in acculturation research vary greatly. The characteristics of successful acculturation have been defined in terms of mental and physical health, psychological satisfaction, good self-esteem, competent work performance, and good grades (Ward, 1996). Within cross-cultural psychology, theoretical frameworks in relation to acculturation have been borrowed from different areas of mainstream psychology, notably the stress and coping literature on the one hand and research on social learning and skills acquisition on the other (Smith & Bond, 1998; Ward, 1996). In both perspectives, acculturation is primarily seen as individual adjustment and adaptation to a new culture. Searle and Ward (1990) have argued that adaptive outcomes of acculturation are meaningfully divided into psychological (emotional/affective) and sociocultural (behavioral) domains. The former has traditionally been the focus of study for the stress and coping framework, and the latter for the social learning framework (Ward, 1996). Individuals who are exposed to acculturative demands are motivated to maintain psychological well-being and to acquire culturally appropriate knowledge and skills (Ward, 1996). This division, however, does not account for distinctly social psychological factors like identity, attitudes, and values, which are spuriously called the "uniquely cognitive domain of adaptive outcomes" and which "may be better understood as mediators of the affective and behavioral outcomes" (Ward, 1996, p. 127).

The stress and coping tradition has been a very popular approach to the study of acculturation and has increased our knowledge of the psychological outcomes of cultural relocation (for reviews, see Berry, 1997; Ward, 1996). Within this framework, both unidimensional and bidimensional models of acculturation have been applied. Both kinds of models conceptualize the acculturation process as potentially stressful because of language problems, perceived discrimination, perceived cultural incompatibilities, identity conflicts, and the like (Berry, 1997). Negative outcomes occur when stressors of this kind exceed the individual's coping resources, or protecting mediators. In contrast to the stress and coping perspectives, social learning approaches emphasize the role of learning in the acquisition of culturally appropriate skills. Also within this framework, both unilinear and bidimensional models have been applied. There is a host of studies within cross-cultural psychology which explicitly adopts the social learning and skills acquisition approach to acculturation (for a review, see Ward, 1996).

4.2   Acculturation as unilinear adaptation to a new culture

Studies using bipolar acculturation scales have provided very diverse predictions, and this line of research has been rather controversial (Ward, 1996). Acculturation has been assumed to relate to mental health directly, indirectly, or in a curvilinear fashion (Rogler, 1994). A rudimentary meta-analysis of 30 studies of mental health among Hispanics (Rogler, Cortes, & Malgady, 1991) found support for all of the predictions in an overall pattern of inconsistent findings. Twelve studies supported a positive relationship between acculturation and mental health, thirteen supported a negative relationship, three suggested a curvilinear relationship, and two produced both positive and negative effects (Rogler et al., 1991). Often, in studies applying unidimensional scales, the empirical scale values obtained range only from the heritage end to the midpoint of the scale, which actually reflects empirical variation from monoculturalism (in the heritage culture) to biculturalism (e.g., Rivera-Sinclair, 1997). This could partly explain the inconsistent findings obtained.

A different perspective on the mental health outcomes of acculturation has been adopted by Halpern (1993). He tested the hypothesis that the mental health of minority members is fostered by higher group concentration: A generalized "group density effect." He found that the reasons for local group density to covary with lower levels of psychiatric admission are twofold: The relative density of ingroup members protects the group members from frequent and direct prejudice and provides them with social support to cope with their disadvantage. Elevation of psychiatric admissions in areas of low group density are thus, according to Halpern (1993), due to the dual influences of increased exposure to prejudice and the absence of group support.

In the cultural learning tradition, Smith and Bond (1998) follow Anderson (1994) in their view on cross-cultural adaptation as "just one type of "transition experience" (p. 269). It refers, in short, to the level of adoption of the predominant culture by an outsider or minority group. The greater the acculturation, the more the language, customs, values, identity, attitudes, and behaviors of the predominant culture are adopted (Dawson, Carno, & Burgoon, 1996). In this perspective, the role of the host society is simple: It is involved in the acculturation process by either "rewarding or punishing the cultural learner" (Smith & Bond, 1998, p. 269).

Many social scientists regard values as the fundamental variable distinguishing one cultural group from another, and study gradual value change as a measure of acculturation. Those applying unilinear models of acculturation often use universal value dimensions (e.g., collectivistic vs. individualistic) and assumed cultural differences on these (e.g., Triandis, Kashima, Shimada, & Villareal, 1986) as a basis for assessing acculturation. Phalet and Hagendoorn (1996) studied the effect of adherence to heritage culture values (collectivism) on levels of general emotional disturbance among Turkish youth in Belgium. They found that Turkish youngsters with collectivistic value orientations have fewer adjustment problems (Phalet & Hagendoorn, 1996). Georgas, Berry, Shaw, Christakopoulou, and Mylonas (1996) found, however, that Greek family values are partly lost when Greeks emigrate, but that the loss is less in Canada where multiculturalism is a more explicit policy than in Europe where assimilationist ideologies dominate.

It follows that acculturation is clearly influenced by both social and political factors in the host society. Bierbauer and Pedersen (1996) have noted that there are many unclear and uncharted areas in the experience of acculturation which, when projected against the myriad of its social psychological dimensions, appear to be so unexplored and diffuse as to be daunting. Various acculturation scales based on the bipolar model have been criticized because they constrain what they ought to enable research to examine: The actual complex patterns of change in cultural involvements and cultural disengagements (Rogler, 1994).

4.3   Acculturation as a multilinear process

To overcome the limitations of the single-index and unidimensional-bipolar approaches to acculturation, various culturally plural, two-dimensional frameworks and scales have been developed (Nguyen et al., 1999). Proponents of these models maintain that ethnic group members can have either strong or weak identifications with both their own and the mainstream cultures and that a strong relationship with one's heritage culture does not necessarily imply low involvement with the dominant culture (Phinney, 1990). The most impressive example of research among those who have, at least in part, relied on this approach, is John Berry's work on acculturation and acculturative stress (for a review, see Berry, 1997). Berry (1990, 1997) developed and validated a bidimensional model of acculturation, in which acculturation attitudes or strategies form the central variables. Individuals differ in the ways they orient themselves in the acculturation process. Acculturation attitudes are based on the individual's responses to two focal questions, the first of which pertains to the maintenance and development of one's ethnic/cultural distinctiveness and identity in society ("are my own ethnic/cultural identity and customs of value and should they be retained?"). The second question involves the desirability of intergroup contact and participation ("should I seek a positive relationship/get involved with the larger society?") (Berry, 1997; Nguyen at al., 1999).

These two dimensions allow for a fourfold classification of acculturation strategies. If an individual answers yes to both of the two questions, the *integration* option is chosen, implying that some degree of cultural integrity is maintained while the individual simultaneously seeks to participate as an integral part of the larger society. If an individual answers no to the first question and yes to the second, the *assimilation* option is chosen, whereby the individual does not wish to maintain his or her cultural identity while moving into the larger society. If the answer is yes to the first question and no to the second, *separation* is the preferred strategy, where the individual wants to hold on to his or her original culture but avoids interaction with the larger society. Finally, *marginalization* results from answering no to both questions, as there is little possibility for or interest in cultural maintenance or intergroup relations (Berry, 1997; Sayegh & Lasry, 1993). Acculturation may be "uneven" across different domains of behavior and social life: For example, one may seek economic assimilation (in work), linguistic integration (by way of bilingualism), and marital separation (by endogamy) (Berry, 1990, p. 217).

It has to be stressed, however, that these two dimensions are not orthogonal. One dimension assesses cultural maintenance and identification, implicitly assuming total maintenance of heritage culture in one end of the continuum and total rejection of heritage culture in the other. Although nothing is explicitly assumed about the replacement of the heritage culture with the dominant culture, it is possible to equate this dimension with a unidimensional acculturation scale. Berry (1997) himself equates a high degree of cultural maintenance with Gordon's (1964) conceptualization of a low degree of behavioral assimilation. The other dimension includes contacts with members of the host culture as well as participation in the larger society more generally. A high degree of contact and participation is equivalent to a high degree of structural assimilation in Gordon's (1964) terminology (Berry, 1997). Strictly speaking, then, integration means in this framework a middle position on the linear cultural maintenance–total assimilation scale, combined with structural assimilation, that is, participation in the social and occupational structure and the political, social, and cultural organizations of the dominant society. What makes this model distinct from other models of acculturation within cross-cultural psychology is that it explicitly distinguishes between the cultural and the social dimensions and acknowledges their relative independence of each other.

Preferences for different acculturation strategies have been measured in a number of studies with Likert-type scales covering both contact/participation and cultural maintenance items in various areas of life, for example, media usage, political participation, religious practices, language use, and preferences in daily practices (dress, food) and social relations (marriage partner, leisure time activities, work, etc.) (Berry et al., 1986, 1987). It has sometimes appeared difficult to maintain a clear separation between contact and participation measures on the one hand and cultural maintenance and identification measures on the other, with concomitant methodological difficulties (Berry et al., 1986). In all cases, however, the integration option has turned out to be the most preferred acculturation strategy, and this alternative also shows the strongest relationship with positive adaptation. Marginalization is the least beneficial strategy for adaptation, while assimilation and separation are intermediate. This pattern has been found in virtually every study, and is present for all types of acculturating groups (Berry, 1997). For example, Phinney, Chavira, and Williamson (1992) found in a study on high school and college students of mixed ethnic backgrounds that the students strongly favored integration and that assimilation attitudes were negatively correlated with self-esteem in both samples and all subgroups, while integration attitudes were related to higher self-esteem. Phinney et al. (1992) conclude that there appears to be some support for the prediction from social identity theory (Tajfel & Turner, 1986), that giving up one's ethnic culture can have a negative impact on the self-concept.

Also other bidimensional models of acculturation have been developed (e.g., Hutnik, 1986, 1991; Laroche et al., 1998; Padilla, 1980; Szapocznik & Kurtines, 1993). Hutnik's

(1986) two-dimensional model is based on two orthogonal identifications, one with the ingroup and one with the outgroup. An equivalent orthogonal bidimensional model has been suggested by Bourhis, Moise, Perreault, and Senecal (1997). Bourhis et al. (1997) set out to resolve the "possible inconsistencies" in Berry's (1990, 1997) model by substituting the dimension of contact and participation with a dimension pertaining to host culture adoption: "Is it considered to be of value to adopt the culture of the host community?" (Bourhis et al. 1997, p. 378). In this way, the unidimensional heritage cultural maintenance–assimilation scale is eliminated. Empirical tests of this model are not yet available.

It has been found that biculturally oriented activities are significant positive mediators of life satisfaction among Chinese in the United States (Ying, 1996), that identification with the heritage group significantly predicts high self-esteem among Vietnamese in Australia, and that self-esteem, in turn, significantly predicts low psychological distress in the same group (Nesdale, Rooney, & Smith, 1997). Correspondingly, Rivera-Sinclair (1997) found that biculturalism was strongly related to reduction of anxiety scores in respondents of Cuban origin in the United States. Laroche et al. (1998) found that the acquisition of the dominant culture and the retention of heritage culture were empirically distinct but somewhat interrelated dimensions. Similar results were obtained by Nguyen et al. (1999).

In contrast to numerous studies suggesting the adaptiveness of biculturality, Nguyen et al. (1999) found in their study that only the U.S. cultural dimension was related to better outcomes for the different indices of adjustment used. The results obtained by Sanchez and Fernandez (1993) point in the same direction. They applied the two-dimensional framework of Berry to the realm of ethnic identification and found that identification with the U.S. culture was related to lower levels of acculturative stress and perceived discrimination, while the Hispanic identification was related to neither (Sanchez & Fernandez, 1993). Nguyen et al. (1999) conclude, however, that for their Vietnamese respondents who lived in a predominantly Anglo-American community with only 703 Vietnamese inhabitants, it is not ethnic involvement as such which is maladaptive but the inconsistency between the individual's skills and the demands of his or her context.

Within the social learning perspective on acculturation, this inconsistency has been called lack of "cultural fit." Cultural fit reflects a high degree of fit between sojourners' personality and values on the one hand and the host society's norms on the other (Ward & Chang, 1997). Ward and Chang (1997) found that, among American sojourners in Singapore, those whose personality characteristics (level of extroversion) differed significantly from "host culture norms" (level of extroversion in a sample of Singaporeans) had significantly higher levels of depression. Cultural fit resembles the notion of cultural distance, that is, the extent of differences between culture of origin and culture of contact. Cultural distance, general knowledge about the new culture, length of residence in the new country, and amount of contact with host nationals are among the most obvious factors facilitating the learning of new cultural skills (Ward, 1996).

Ward and Kennedy (1993) found that sociocultural and psychological adaptation in cross-cultural transitions are largely predicted by different types of variables. They conclude that the host national group provides the avenue for the acquisition of culturally appropriate skills in that host national contacts are indispensable for culture learning. In contrast, the co-national group forms the important social support network as it is satisfaction with these relations that underpins psychological adjustment (Ward & Kennedy, 1993). Ward and Kennedy (1993) failed, however, to substantiate the proposed association of sociocultural adjustment with general cultural knowledge and with cultural identity.

4.4   Acculturation as situational shifts between cultures

A number of researchers (e.g., Clément & Noels, 1992; LaFromboise, Coleman, & Gerton, 1993; Noels, Pon, & Clément, 1996) have shown that the salience of cultural identity varies as a function of situational factors. LaFromboise and her colleagues (1993) propose an *alternation model* of second culture acquisition which, like other bidimensional models, assumes that it is possible for an individual to have a sense of belongingness in two cultures without compromising his or her sense of cultural identity. The model implies that individuals who learn to alternate their behavior to fit into the cultures in which they are involved will be less stressed and less anxious than those who are undergoing a process of linear acculturation. The model views biculturalism in essence as *bicultural competence.* It is an additive model of cultural acquisition parallel to the code-switching theories found in the research on bilingualism (LaFromboise et al., 1993).

Building on situated identity theory, Clément and Noels (1992) have proposed a similar model, where ethnolinguistic identity is viewed as dynamic and situationally dependent, and the ability to develop and maintain competence in both cultures and to shift between them as required by contextual demands as crucial for psychological well-being. It has been found that feelings of ethnic group belonging vary among Francophones and Anglophones in Canada across a variety of relevant situations (Clément & Noels, 1992) and that Chinese students in Canada feel either Chinese or Canadian – but not both simultaneously – in most situations (Noels et al., 1996). As individuals are motivated to maintain positive self-regard, they will, when confronted with alternative courses of action, choose the one that enhances self-presentation given the particular context (Noels et al., 1996). The authors conclude that the attitudes toward acculturation assessed, for example by Berry and his colleagues (Berry, 1997), may not be consistent with actual behavior and that identity may not necessarily follow the same acculturation pattern as attitudes (Noels et al., 1996). These discrepancies and the role of situational factors on self-representation are crucial for a genuinely social psychological study of acculturation.

5   Acculturation, Ethnic Identity, and Intergroup Relations

5.1   The relationship between ethnic/cultural identity and acculturation

It seems that the relationship between the constructs of acculturation and ethnic/cultural identity is both unexplored and ambiguous (Nguyen et al., 1999). Yet from a social psy-

chological point of view, the importance to individuals of their identification with particular social groups has a crucial impact on their intra- and intergroup cognitions, attitudes, and behavior (Hurtado, Gurin, & Peng, 1994; Tajfel & Turner, 1986). A central
question is whether ethnic identity is directly related to the degree of acculturation or
whether, conversely, it is independent (Phinney, 1990). Often the two concepts are used
almost interchangeably (Nguyen et al., 1999). If acculturation is understood as change
in cultural values, there is some support for this practice. Gaines et al. (1997) found that
minority members scored higher than majority members on a single-factor scale of ethnic
identity. Ethnic identity, in turn, was positively related to scores on measures of psychological individualism, collectivism, and familism. In addition, all significant differences
in cultural value orientations between ethnic minority and majority members disappeared
when ethnic identity was controlled for (Gaines et al., 1995). Similarly, Rhee, Uleman,
Roman, and Lee (1995) found predicted associations between cultural values (collectivistic or individualistic) and spontaneous ethnic self-categorizations among Asian
Americans; those who spontaneously identified themselves by ethnicity displayed more
collectivistic, spontaneous self-descriptions than those who did not. However, there was
no relationship between the degree of ethnic self-identifications or cultural values and a
linear degree of acculturation measured by generation status, degree of bilingualism, and
use of English (Rhee et al., 1995).

Other studies suggest that ethnic identity and acculturation are independent constructs. For example, Hutnik (1986, 1991) found no correlation between ethnic identification patterns (Indian and/or British) on the one hand and cultural attitudes and
behavior on the other among young Asians in Britain. She concludes that, for minority
individuals, ethnic identification may lag behind or run ahead of cultural adaptation and
that there is only a very moderate relationship between the two (Hutnik, 1991). Similarly, Phinney and Devich-Navarro (1997) found no relationship between self-ascribed
ethnic categories on the one hand and extent of pride and involvement in original ethnic
group and/or American society on the other among students from ethnically diverse high
schools in the United States.

Empirically, ethnic identity has been treated as the ethnic component of social identity, as ethnic self-identification, as feelings of belongingness and commitment, as a sense
of shared values and attitudes, or as attitudes toward one's own group (Liebkind, 1996).
Studies in ethnic and cultural identity reveal complexities which go beyond social identity theory as well as beyond simple adherence to cultural values (Laroche et al., 1998;
Liebkind, 1992; Phinney, 1990). For example, mere ethnic/cultural self-identification or
self-categorization fails to tell us what attitudes the individual holds toward his or her
heritage culture or how much he or she actually identifies with the self-applied category.
Yet the strength and nature of actual identification with the ingroup will determine much
of the individual's response to acculturation. However, the strength of ingroup identification should not be confused with cultural orientation in terms of endorsement of heritage culture and/or adoption of host culture. In many studies on acculturation, cultural
identity is simply equated with the degree of cultural heritage maintenance. However,
one may identify strongly with one's cultural ingroup and also have a positive attitude
toward maintenance of one's heritage culture, yet fail to endorse that culture oneself
(Liebkind, 1993, 1994, 1996; Phinney, 1990). The extent to which migrants endorse

heritage and host cultural values has been shown to influence psychological well-being more systematically than their attitudes toward these cultures (Liebkind, 1996).

In sum, then, ethnic minority members may acculturate to some degree, that is, acquire a certain level of competence in the ways of the dominant culture, yet possess the freedom to maintain, explore, rediscover, or reject their ethnic identity (Hutnik, 1986). Generally, however, maintenance of a strong ethnic identity has proved to improve adjustment among members of acculturating groups (Liebkind, 1996; Nesdale et al., 1997; Phinney, Cantu, & Kurtz, 1997).

One problem with theories of and empirical studies on ethnic identity is that they generally assume ethnic identity to derive from membership in one group only. For example, the so-called multigroup measure of ethnic identity (MEIM) developed by Phinney (1992) actually measures self-identification, sense of belonging, and ethnic behaviors with regard to the group the respondent initially has defined as his or her own ("In terms of ethnic group, I consider myself to be . . .") (Phinney, 1992, p. 172). Although Phinney (1992) included six items in her questionnaire assessing "other-group orientation" (p. 164), these are not included in the MEIM score. The term "multigroup" in the name of the scale simply refers to the fact that MEIM can be used as such with different ethnic groups. However, for the ethnic minority individual, multiple categories are readily available. Depending on the outcomes of their intra- and intergroup interactions and the resulting auto- and heterostereotypes, ethnic minority individuals will place themselves at a self-chosen distance from the ethnic minority group and the ethnic majority group (Hutnik, 1991). As we have seen earlier in this chapter, this placing can shift situationally. Focusing on a performative mode of social identity and emphasizing its dynamic nature in communication, Carbaugh (1996) claims that people enact different social identities depending not only on the intrinsic salience of these identities, but also on where the individual is, with whom he or she is, and what he or she can ably do in that particular situation.

5.2   *Acculturation and power differentials*

Ethnic/cultural groups can be majorities as well as minorities. Ethnic minorities are often subordinate segments of complex societies, and they often experience discrimination and social disadvantage. Social disadvantage as such may be a source of negative social identity. However, intergroup behavior related to societal inequality and power/status differentials should be distinguished from that pertaining to ethnic and/or cultural distinctiveness. In accordance with Berry's (1990, 1997) notion of integration, an immigrant may desire a change in his or her social status, that is, express a wish to individually or collectively participate in the larger society, yet may not want to change his or her cultural identity or orientation. The social dimension of Berry's (1990, 1997) model needs, however, a clear distinction between the two relatively independent aspects of social contact on the one hand and societal participation (e.g., in work life) on the other.

Even in cases where status differences between groups or social categories are relatively uncontaminated by direct conflicts of interest (e.g., urban and rural persons, occupational groups, and academic tracks in schools), they seem to be invariably associated with prejudice against the low-status group. The pervasiveness of prejudice against low-status and not high-status groups seems better explained in terms of the operation of attributional processes such as victim blaming rather than by tendencies to seek positive social identities (Duckitt, 1992). Social identity effects may moderate this such that the pervasive prejudice against low-status groups becomes intensified when the high-status group's advantage is threatened ("insecure"), and such that the low-status group comes to express prejudice against the high-status group when its advantage is seen as illegitimate and unstable (Duckitt, 1992, p. 113). Victim-blaming tendencies with concomitant prejudice have to be accounted for also in an intergroup perspective on acculturation. Hewstone (1989) has pointed out that there may exist a systematic pattern of misattributions shaped by prejudice when favorable ingroup behavior is attributed to dispositional factors and favorable outgroup behavior to external factors. Van Oudenhoven, Prins, and Buunk (1998) refer to this kind of misperception when explaining the discrepancy of perceptions between Dutch and immigrant respondents regarding immigrants' efforts to make contact with the Dutch; the Dutch may not perceive immigrants' behavior as intrinsically driven or sincere.

5.3   The interactive and intergroup nature of acculturation

By now it is very clear that acculturation does not take place in a social vacuum, rather, it unfolds itself within the context of intra- and intergroup relations that provide both support and challenges for the reconstruction of ethnic/cultural identity. The identity of an individual is formed, developed, changed, and preserved throughout life in numerous identity negotiations, involving self-presentation and alter-casting. Ethnic minority members calibrate their identities in interaction with others (Horenczyk, in press; Liebkind, 1992). The main contribution of Bourhis et al.'s (1997) *interactive acculturation model* (IAM) is its emphasis on the intergroup nature of the acculturation process. The IAM acknowledges, as others have done before (Berry, 1990, 1997; Horenzcyk, 1992), that acculturating minority groups are not always free to choose their acculturative strategies; both state policies and public opinion can have a substantial impact on the acculturation orientations of ethnic minorities. The state can influence public attitudes concerning the legitimacy of the ideological position it has adopted, but, in democracies, state policies can also be influenced by the acculturation orientation found to be most prevalent among members of the dominant group(s) in society (Bourhis et al., 1997, p. 375).

Bourhis et al. (1997) present a very useful typology of the different types of ideologies that underlie the policies adopted by the state to deal with immigration and integration issues. According to *pluralism ideology* (e.g., in Canada), immigrants should adopt the public values of the host country, but the state has no mandate in defining or regulating the private values of citizens. In addition, the state is willing, upon the request of interested parties, to support financially and socially the private activities related to maintenance of heritage cultures and languages. *Civic ideology* (e.g., in Great Britain) differs from the pluralism ideology mainly in its principle that only the cultural interests of the dominant majority are state funded, although individuals have the right to organize collectively in order to maintain or promote their respective group distinctiveness based on cultural, linguistic, ethnic, or religious affiliation. The *assimilation ideology* (e.g., in the United States, at least up till the 1960s, and in France) expects the state to interfere in some domains of private values, for example, the cultural and linguistic distinctiveness of immigrant groups, sometimes even forcefully through specific laws and regulations. Finally, *ethnist ideology* (e.g., in Germany, at least until recently) shares some of the features of assimilation ideology but sometimes does not expect immigrants to assimilate culturally because the host majority has no intention of ever accepting immigrants as rightful members of the host society (Bourhis et al., 1997).

While others have assessed host community attitudes as they are perceived by the immigrants themselves (Horenzcyk, in press) or through projective methods (Van Oudenhoven et al., 1998), Bourhis et al. (1997), argue for a host community acculturation scale, which assesses the acculturation orientations actually preferred by members of the host society. The aim of the IAM is to identify particular forms of intergroup relations resulting from different combinations of attitudes and strategies preferred by the two cultural groups in contact (Bourhis et al., 1997). Although it still has to be empirically validated, this model represents a more social psychological perspective on acculturation in that it brings back the intergroup nature of the process. Van Oudenhoven et al. (1998) have demonstrated, however, that consensual attitudes are not enough. Although both immigrant and host communities may have positive attitudes toward integration, host community members may still believe that separation, which is the least liked strategy by them, is the one most frequently chosen by the immigrants. Thus, prejudice and discrimination may continue on the basis of negative stereotyping, irrespective of the acculturation strategies actually preferred by the immigrants (Van Oudenhoven et al., 1998). Stereotypes, prejudice, and discrimination, in turn, are crucial elements of all intergroup relations, yet rarely accounted for in acculturation research (for exceptions, see Lalonde et al., 1992; Liebkind & Jasinskaja-Lahti, 2000b; Ruggiero et al., 1996).

5.4   *Toward a social psychology of acculturation*

On the basis of the reviewed literature, it can be concluded that future social psychological research on acculturation should distinguish at least the following aspects of ethnic/cultural identity:

1. *Subjective and "objective" (or self-recognized and alter-ascribed) identity.* Only self-recognized ingroup devaluation can result in negative ethnic/cultural identity (Liebkind, 1992). Even subjective perceptions of the ingroup as devalued do not necessarily threaten global self-esteem, if this devaluation is not attributed internally. Only internalized devaluation results in negative identity. Externally attributed ingroup devaluation may, in fact, contribute to positive identity (Crocker & Major, 1989).
2. *Social and cultural/ethnic identity.* Devaluation which derives from specific ethnic or cultural characteristics differs from that which derives from socio-economic disadvantage. Only the former can, under conditions outlined in (1) above,

become an incentive to cultural assimilation. The latter can be an incentive to individual or collective social mobility, but is relatively independent of the former kind of devaluation (Liebkind, 1984, 1989, 1992; Weinreich, 1989).

Social psychological studies on intergroup strategies used by members of acculturating groups should thus ideally encompass at least the following dimensions:

1. *Intergroup relations (A): power and status differentials.*
   (a) Power and status differentials or the extent to which an individual member of a socially disadvantaged ethnic/cultural group perceives his or her group or him- or herself personally to be socially disadvantaged.
   (b) The extent to which an individual member of a socially disadvantaged ethnic/cultural group attributes this disadvantage internally (to personal or ingroup characteristics) or externally (to prejudice and discrimination).
   (c) The extent to which an individual member of a socially disadvantaged ethnic/cultural group endorses an individual or a collective social mobility strategy.
2. *Intergroup relations (B): intergroup attitudes and behavior.*
   (a) Negative stereotypes, prejudice, hostility, and discrimination directed by the dominant group or society toward the ethnic/cultural minority. The extent/degree of the dominant group's in- and outgroup contacts and favoritism.
   (b) Negative stereotypes, prejudice, and hostility directed by the ethnic/cultural minority toward the dominant group. The extent/degree of the minority group's in- and outgroup contacts and favoritism.
3. *Ethnic/cultural identity.*
   (a) Degree and nature of the identification with the ethnic/cultural ingroup, including self-categorization, strength of identification with the ingroup, and ethnic/cultural pride, that is, the degree to which the individual considers the ingroup to be a desirable membership group.
   (b) Degree and nature of the identification with the ethnic/cultural outgroup, including self-categorization, strength of identification with the outgroup and the degree to which the individual considers the outgroup to represent a desirable membership group.
4. *Cultural orientation (A): Attitudes towards culture.*
   (a) The degree to which the individual values/devalues the heritage culture.
   (b) The degree to which the individual values/devalues the dominant culture.
5. *Cultural orientation (B): Adoption/endorsement of culture.*
   (a) Degree of actual endorsement or adoption of the heritage culture, including beliefs, values, and behavior.
   (b) Degree of actual endorsement or adoption of the dominant culture, including beliefs, values, and behavior.

For particular acculturating groups and individuals, the empirical content of the various dimensions presented above can differ in numerous ways, at a particular moment, in different situations, and over time. However, there is no reason to assume that the acculturation process should be less complex than one single cell in the human body or a modern computer. Most people cannot single out more than a few rules of grammar of the language they speak, but they are none the less able to formulate correct sentences according to the rules they cannot explain. The different dimensions of acculturation could well be operating in an equivalent manner. Ironically, the distinction and separation of all the numerous dimensions of acculturation may be a necessary first step toward achieving a more integrative understanding of this process and its consequences (Nguyen et al., 1999).

References

Anderson, L. E. (1994). A new look at an old construct: Cross-cultural adaptation. *International Journal of Intercultural Relations, 18*, 293–328.

Berry, J. W. (1990). Psychology of acculturation. In J. J. Berman (Ed.), *Cross-cultural perspectives* (pp. 201–234). Nebraska Symposium on Motivation 1989, University of Nebraska, Lincoln.

Berry, J. W. (1997). Immigration, acculturation, and adaptation. *Applied Psychology: An International Review, 46*(1), 5–68.

Berry, J. W., Kim, U., Minde, T., & Mok, D. (1987). Comparative studies of acculturative stress. *International Migration Review, 21*(3), 491–511.

Berry, J. W., Trimble, J., & Olmedo, E. (1986). Assessment of acculturation. In W. Lonner & J. W. Berry (Eds.), *Field methods in cross-cultural research* (pp. 291–324). Beverly Hills, CA: Sage.

Bierbauer, G., & Pedersen, P. (1996). Culture and migration. In G. S. Semin & K. Fiedler (Eds.), *Applied social psychology* (pp. 399–422). London: Sage.

Boen, F., & Vanbeselaere, N. (1998). Reactions upon a failed attempt to enter a high status group: An experimental test of the five-stage model. *European Journal of Social Psychology, 28*, 689–696.

Bourhis, R. Y., Moise, L. C., Perreault, S., & Senecal, S. (1997). Towards an interactive acculturation model: A social psychological approach. *International Journal of Psychology, 32*(6), 369–386.

Brown, L. M. (1998). Ethnic stigma as a contextual experience: A possible selves perspective. *Personality and Social Psychology Bulletin, 24*(2), 163–172.

Carbaugh, D. (1996). *Situating selves. The communication of social identities in American scenes.* New York: State University of New York Press.

Clément, R., & Noels, K. A. (1992). Towards a situated approach to ethnolinguistic identity: The effects of status on individuals and groups. *Journal of Language and Social Psychology, 11*(2), 203–232.

Crocker, J., & Major, B. (1989). Social stigma and self-esteem: the self-protective properties of stigma. *Psychological Review, 96*(4), 608–630.

Cuellar, I., Harris, L. C., & Jasso, R. (1980). An acculturation scale for Mexican American normal and clinical populations. *Hispanic Journal of Behavioral Sciences, 2*, 199–217.

Dawson, E. J., Carno, W. D., & Burgoon, M. (1996). Refining the meaning and measurement of acculturation: Revisiting a novel methodological approach. *International Journal of Intercultural Relations, 20*(1), 97–114.

Der-Karabetian, A. (1980). Relation of two cultural identities of Armenian-Americans. *Psychological Reports, 47*, 123–128.

Duckitt, J. (1992). *The social psychology of prejudice.* New York: Praeger.

Fernando, S. (1991). *Mental health, race and culture.* Basingstoke, UK: Macmillan in association with Mind publications.

Gaines, S. O. Jr., Marelich, W. D., Bledsoe, K. L., Steers, W. N., Henderson, M. C., Granrose, C. S., Barájas, L., Hicks, D., Lyde, M., Takahashi, Y., Yum, N., Ríos, D. I., García, B. F., Farris, K. R., & Page, M. S. (1997). Links between race/ethnicity and cultural values as mediated by racial/ethnic identity and moderated by gender. *Journal of Personality and Social Psychology, 72*(6), 1460–1476.

Georgas, J., Berry, J. W., Shaw, A., Christakopoulou, S., & Mylonas, K. (1996). Acculturation of Greek family values. *Journal of Cross-Cultural Psychology, 27*(3), 329–338.

Gordon, M. (1964). *Assimilation in American life*. London: Oxford University Press.

Halpern, D. (1993). Minorities and mental health. *Social Science and Medicine, 36*(5), 597–607.

Hewstone, M. (1989). Intergroup attribution: Some implications for the study of ethnic prejudice. In J. P. Van Oudenhoven & T. M. Willemsen (Eds.), *Ethnic minorities: Social psychological perspectives* (pp. 25–42). Amsterdam: Swets & Zeitlinger.

Horenczyk, G. (1992). Migrant identities in conflict: Attitudes and perceived acculturation ideologies. In G. Breakwell (Ed.), *Social psychology of identity and the self-concept* (pp. 241–250). London: Surrey University Press/Academic Press.

Horenczyk, G. (in press). Acculturation conflicts and the migrants' constructions of their social worlds. In E. Olshtain & G. Horenczyk (Eds.), *Language, identity, and immigration*. Jerusalem: Magnes Press.

Hurtado, A., Gurin, P., & Peng, T. (1994). Social identities: A framework for studying the adaptations of immigrants and ethnics: The adaptations of Mexicans in the United States. *Social Problems, 41*, 129–151.

Hutnik, N. (1986). Patterns of ethnic minority identification and modes of social adaptation. *Ethnic and Racial Studies, 9*(2), 150–167.

Hutnik, N. (1991). *Ethnic minority identity. A social psychological perspective*. Oxford, UK: Clarendon Press.

LaFromboise, T., Coleman, H. L. K., & Gerton, J. (1993). Psychological impact of biculturalism: Evidence and theory. *Psychological Bulletin, 114*(3), 395–412.

Lalonde, R. N., & Cameron, J. E. (1993). An intergroup perspective on immigrant acculturation with a focus on collective strategies. *International Journal of Psychology, 28*(1), 57–74.

Lalonde, R. N., Taylor, D. M., & Moghaddam, F. H. (1992). The process of social identification for visible immigrant women in a multicultural context. *Journal of Cross-Cultural Psychology, 23*(1), 25–39.

Lambert, W. E., Mermigis, L., & Taylor, D. M. (1986). Greek Canadians' attitudes toward own group and other Canadian ethnic groups: A test of the multiculturalism hypothesis. *Canadian Journal of Behavioral Science, 18*, 35–51.

Laroche, M., Kim, C., Hui, M. K., & Tomiuk, M. A. (1998). Test of nonlinear relationships between linguistic acculturation and ethnic identification. *Journal of Cross-Cultural Psychology, 29*(3), 418–433.

Liebkind, K. (1984). *Minority identity and identification processes: A social psychological study*. Maintenance and Reconstruction of Ethnolinguistic Identity in Multiple Group Allegiance. Commentationes Scientiarum Socialium 22, the Finnish Society of Sciences and Letters, Helsinki.

Liebkind, K. (1989). Conceptual approaches to ethnic identity. In K. Liebkind (Ed.), *New identities in Europe* (pp. 25–40). Aldershot, UK: Gower.

Liebkind, K. (1992). Ethnic identity: Challenging the boundaries of social psychology. In G. Breakwell (Ed.), *Social psychology of identity and the self-concept* (pp. 147–185). London: Surrey University Press/Academic Press.

Liebkind, K. (1993). Self-reported ethnic identity, depression, and anxiety among young Vietnamese refugees and their parents. *Journal of Refugee Studies, 6*(1), 25–39.

Liebkind, K. (1994). Ethnic identity and acculturative stress: Vietnamese refugees in Finland. *Migration, 23–24*, 155–177.

Liebkind, K. (1996). Vietnamese refugees in Finland – Changing cultural identity. In G. M. Breakwell & E. Lyons (Eds.), *Changing European identities* (pp. 227–240). Oxford, UK: Butterworth-Heinemann.

Liebkind, K., & Jasinskaja-Lahti, I. (2000a). Acculturation and psychological well-being among immigrant adolescents in Finland: A comparative study of adolescents from different cultural backgrounds. *Journal of Adolescent Research, 15*(4), 446–469.

Liebkind, K., & Jasinskaja-Lahti, I. (2000b). The influence of experiences of discrimination on psychological stress among immigrants: A comparison of seven immigrant groups. *Journal of Community and Applied Social Psychology, 10*(1), 1–16.

Moghaddam, F. M. (1988). Individualistic and collective integration strategies among immigrants. Toward a mobility model of cultural integration. In J. W. Berry & R. C. Annis (Eds.), *Ethnic psychology: Research and practice with immigrants, refugees, ethnic groups, and sojourners* (pp. 69–79). Lisse, The Netherlands: Swets & Zeitlinger.

Moghaddam, F. M., Ditto, B., & Taylor, D. M. (1990). Attitudes and attribution related to psychological symptomatology in Indian immigrant women. *Journal of Cross-Cultural Psychology, 21*(3), 335–350.

Moghaddam, F. M., & Taylor, D. M. (1987). The meaning of multiculturalism for visible minority immigrant women. *Canadian Journal of Behavioral Science, 19*, 121–136.

Moghaddam, F. M., Taylor, D. M., & Lalonde, R. N. (1987). Individualistic and collective integration strategies among Iranians in Canada. *International Journal of Psychology, 22*, 301–313.

Nesdale, D., Rooney, R., & Smith, L. (1997). Migrant ethnic identity and psychological distress. *Journal of Cross-Cultural Psychology, 28*(5), 569–588.

Noels, K. A., Pon, G., & Clément, R. (1996). Language, identity, and adjustment. The role of linguistic self-confidence in the acculturation process. *Journal of Language and Social Psychology, 15*(3), 246–264.

Nguyen, H. H., Messé, L. A., & Stollak, G. E. (1999). Toward a more complex understanding of acculturation and adjustment. Cultural involvements and psychosocial functioning in Vietnamese youth. *Journal of Cross-Cultural Psychology, 30(1)*, 5–31.

Nguyen, L., & Peterson, C. (1993). Depressive symptoms among Vietnamese-American college students. *Journal of Social Psychology, 133*(1), 65–71.

Padilla, A. M. (1980). The role of cultural awareness and ethnic loyalty in acculturation. In A. M. Padilla (Ed.), *Acculturation: Theory models and some new findings* (pp. 47–84). Boulder, CO: Westview.

Palinkas, L. A., & Pickwell, S. M. (1995). Acculturation as a risk factor for chronic disease among Cambodian refugees in the United States. *Social Science and Medicine, 40*(12), 1643–1653.

Pareto, V. (1935). *The mind and society: A treatise on general sociology* (Vols. 1–4). New York: Dover.

Phalet, K., & Hagendoorn, L. (1996). Personal adjustment to acculturative transitions: The Turkish experience. *International Journal of Psychology, 31*(2), 131–144.

Phinney, J. S. (1990). Ethnic identity in adolescents and adults: Review of research. *Psychological Bulletin, 108*(3), 499–514.

Phinney, J. S. (1992). The multigroup ethnic identity measure. A new scale for use with diverse groups. *Journal of Adolescent Research, 7*(2), 156–176.

Phinney, J. S., Cantu, C. L., & Kurtz, D. A. (1997). Ethnic and American identity as predictors of self-esteem among African American, Latino, and White adolescents. *Journal of Youth and Adolescence, 26*(2), 165–185.

Phinney, J. S., Chavira, V., & Williamson, L. (1992). Acculturation attitudes and self-esteem among high school and college students. *Youth and Society, 23*(3), 299–312.

Phinney, J. S., & Devich-Navarro, M. (1997). Variations in bicultural identification among African American and Mexican American adolescents. *Journal of Research on Adolescence, 7*(1), 3–32.

Redfield, R., Linton, R., & Herskovits, M. (1936). Memorandum on the study of acculturation. *American Anthropologist, 38*, 149–152.

Rhee, E., Uleman, J. S., Lee, H. K., & Roman, R. J. (1995). Spontaneous self-descriptions and ethnic identities in individualistic and collectivistic cultures. *Journal of Personality and Social Psychology, 69*(1), 142–152.

Rivera-Sinclair, E. A. (1997). Acculturation/biculturalism and its relationship to adjustment in Cuban-Americans. *International Journal of Intercultural Relations, 21*(3), 379–391.

Rogler, L. H. (1994). International migrations: A framework for directing research. *American Psychologist, 49*(8), 701–708.

Rogler, L. H., Cortes, D. E., & Malgady, R. G. (1991). Acculturation and mental health status among Hispanics: Convergence and new directions for research. *American Psychologist, 46*, 585–597.

Ruggiero, K. M., & Taylor, D. M. (1997). Why minority group members perceive or do not perceive the discrimination that confronts them: The role of self-esteem and perceived control. *Journal of Personality and Social Psychology, 72*(2), 373–389.

Ruggiero, K. M., Taylor, D. M., & Lambert, W. E. (1996). A model of heritage culture maintenance: the role of discrimination. *International Journal of Intercultural relations, 20*(1), 47–67.

Sanchez, J. I., & Fernandez, D. M. (1993). Acculturative stress among Hispanics: A bidimensional model of ethnic identification. *Journal of Applied Social Psychology, 23*(8), 654–668.

Sayegh, L., & Lasry, J-C. (1993). Immigrants' adaptation in Canada: Assimilation, acculturation, and orthogonal identification. *Canadian Psychology, 34*(1), 98–109.

Searle, W., & Ward, C. (1990). The prediction of psychological and socio-cultural adjustment during cross-cultural transitions. *International Journal of Intercultural Relations, 14*, 449–464.

Smith, P. B., & Bond, M. H. (1998). *Social psychology across cultures* (2nd ed.). Boston, MA: Allyn & Bacon.

Social Science Research Council (1954). Acculturation: An exploratory formulation. *American Anthropologist, 56*, 973–1002.

Szapocznik, J., & Kurtines, W. M. (1993). Family psychology and cultural diversity. Opportunities for theory, research, and application. *American Psychologist, 48*(4), 400–440.

Tajfel, H., & Turner, J. (1979). An integrative theory of intergroup conflict. In W. G. Austin & W. C. Worchel (Eds.), *The social psychology of intergroup relations* (pp. 33–47). Monterey, CA: Brooks/Cole.

Tajfel, H., & Turner, J. (1986). The social identity theory of intergroup behavior. In W. C. Worchel & W. G. Austin (Eds.), *Psychology of intergroup relations* (pp. 7–24). Chicago, IL: Nelson.

Taylor, D. M., & McKirnan, D. J. (1984). A five-stage model of intergroup relations. *British Journal of Social Psychology, 23*, 291–300.

Triandis, H. C. (1995). *Individualism and collectivism.* Boulder, CO: Westview.

Triandis, H. C., Kashima, Y., Shimada, E., & Villareal, M. (1986). Acculturation indices as a means of confirming cultural differences. *International Journal of Psychology, 21*, 43–70.

Van Oudenhoven, J. P., Prins, K. S., & Buunk, B. P. (1998). Attitudes of minority and majority members towards adaptation of immigrants. *European Journal of Social Psychology, 28*, 995–1013.

Ward, C. (1996). Acculturation. In D. Landis & B. Bhagat, *Handbook in intercultural training* (2nd ed., pp. 124–147). Newbury Park, CA: Sage.

Ward, C., & Chang, W. C. (1997). Cultural fit: a new perspective on personality and sojourner adjustment. *International Journal of Intercultural Relations, 21*(4), 525–533.

Ward, C., & Kennedy, A. (1993). Where is the "culture" in cross-cultural transition? Comparative studies of sojourner adjustment. *Journal of Cross-Cultural Psychology, 24*(2), 221–249.

Weinreich, P. (1989). Variations in ethnic identity: Identity structure analysis. In K. Liebkind (Ed.), *New identities in Europe* (pp. 41–76). Aldershot, UK: Gower.

Wright, S. C., Taylor, D. M., & Moghaddam, F. M. (1990). Responding to membership in a disadvantaged group: From acceptance to collective protest. *Journal of Personality and Social Psychology, 58*(6), 994–1003.

Ying, Y. W. (1996). Immigration satisfaction of Chinese Americans: An empirical examination. *Journal of Community Psychology, 24*(1), 3–16.

Zak, I. (1973). Dimensions of Jewish-American identity. *Psychological Reports, 33*, 891–900.

PART VII

Changing Intergroup Relations

CHAPTER TWENTY

Strategic Collective Action: Social Psychology and Social Change

Stephen C. Wright

A dominant feature of most intergroup relations is inequality in the distribution of resources, status, and power. The result is stratification into relatively advantaged and disadvantaged groups. Groups occupying a dominant or advantaged position are motivated to maintain their collective privilege. To this end, they are unlikely to engage in actions that threaten their position of power (Tajfel, 1982). In the words of Martin Luther King Jr., "Privileged groups rarely give up their privileges without strong resistance." Instead, they construct social institutions that protect their privilege, and they discriminate and legitimate violence against the disadvantaged outgroup (e.g., Jackman, 1998; Sachdev & Bourhis, 1991). Thus, stability or change in the intergroup hierarchy depend primarily on the actions of the disadvantaged group. Further, popular thinking and social science theory agree that social change is usually the result of people acting together. As suggested by the slogan "United we stand. Divided we fall" social change is most dependent on the propensity of the disadvantaged group's members to engage in disruptive *collective actions* (see Gamson, 1990; Tarrow, 1994).

This chapter presents a model that attempts to integrate the complex set of variables that interact to produce collective action, with specific attention to members of disadvantaged groups. The model (illustrated in Figure 20.1) proposes a sequence of psychological processes, including: (a) self-representation; (b) social comparison, and assessments of; (c) the permeability of intergroup boundaries; (d) the legitimacy of the intergroup context; (e) the controllability of the intergroup context; and (f) the availability of normative channels for collective change. At each step, a variety of intrapersonal, group, and societal forces can either enhance or undermine the potential for collective action.

Additionally, a dominant theme is the many impediments to collective action. Given the near universality of intergroup inequality, it is perhaps surprising that protest and rebellion are not a more dominant feature of human societies. When the frequency of

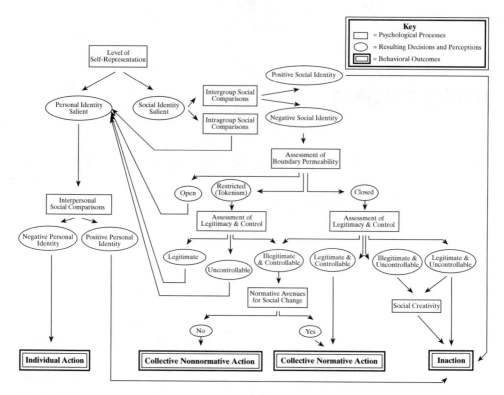

Figure 20.1. A model of collective action.

these incidents is compared with the amount of tranquility in intergroup relations, disruptive collective action appears relatively rare. The present model provides a partial explanation by pointing to the numerous obstacles that can derail the processes necessary to produce interest in disruptive collective action.

Defining Collective Action

The term collective action has been used in a variety of ways. However, I adopt a decidedly psychological perspective, defining collective action in terms of the actor's intentions and perceptions. *A group member engages in collective action any time that she or he is acting as a representative of the group and the action is directed at improving the conditions of the entire group* (Wright, Taylor, & Moghaddam, 1990a). This definition, consistent with Sherif's (1967) and Tajfel's (1978a) definitions of intergroup behavior, recognizes that actions are often not based on the person's unique personal identities, but rather are guided by social identities – the person's valued group memberships. Intergroup behavior involves depersonalized action (Hogg, 1992; Turner, Hogg, Oakes, Reicher, & Wetherell, 1987) resulting from the individual self-identifying as a group member and engaging in what he or she understands to be prototypical group behavior. Collective action, then, is a specific case of intergroup behavior that is strategic in that it is intended to improve the circumstance of the ingroup.

Collective action is perhaps best understood in contrast to its alternatives. In contrast to acting on behalf of the group, disadvantaged group members can attempt to improve their personal situation; they can take *individual action*. In this case, one focuses on one's personal identity and acts in ways that distance oneself from the disadvantaged ingroup, while attempting to acquire a more advantaged position. This distinction between individual action and collective action is consistent with the distinction made in social identity theory (SIT) between *individual mobility* and *social change*. Tajfel and Turner (1979) proposed that members of low-status groups can either attempt to leave their group in favor of a higher status outgroup (individual mobility), or attempt to raise the relative status of the disadvantaged ingroup (social change). Thus, the basis of the individual/collective action distinction is the intended target of the status change, me or my group (see also Branscombe & Ellemers, 1998).

A third alternative is inaction. Disadvantaged group members can do nothing to improve their personal or collective position. Disadvantage can be associated with a wide range of cognitive and affective responses. Relative deprivation theory has focused on feelings of resentment, frustration, and outrage, as well as stress symptoms, depression, and resignation (see Crosby, 1976; Olson, Herman, & Zanna, 1986; Walker & Pettigrew, 1984). Equity theory (Adams, 1965; Tyler, Boeckmann, Smith, & Huo, 1997) holds that feelings of inequity can be corrected by direct action (behavioral) or by manipulation of one's perceptions of the situation (psychological). Similarly, SIT describes several cognitive strategies for creating a positive image of the ingroup referred to as "social creativity." Although these cognitive and emotional outcomes of group deprivation may serve as mediators, moderators, or substitutes for action, in and of themselves they do not represent behavioral responses. In short, inaction may reflect a variety of underlying perceptions and affect, including cognitive revision of the intergroup situation, passive acceptance, hopeful patience that things will soon improve, angry resignation, etc. However, from a behavioral perspective the result of all of these is inaction.

The present conception of collective action differs from a number of other definitions and related concepts. Some discussions of collective action have focused on a group of people acting in concert (e.g., Turner & Killian, 1957). This emphasis on similar or joint action by a large number of people differs from the present focus on the intentions of individual group members. By the present definition, collective action is not determined by the number of participants, or by the specific content or eventual outcome of the action. It can be engaged in by a single individual. For example, a hunger strike undertaken by a lone prisoner demanding improvements in the treatment of all prisoners is collective action because the intent is to improve the conditions of the whole group. Conversely, many group members engaging in the same behavior may not be collective action. For example, a large group of students congregating outside a professor's office to complain about an "unfair" exam may appear like collective action. However, if each would agree to leave quietly if only his or her own test score were raised, this group/crowd behavior is not a collective action.

The present discussion of collective action also differs from many sociological perspectives which have tied collective action to *social movements*. From the present perspective, a social movement is a specific form of collective action, marked by sustained, disruptive, and organized action by a fairly large group of people (McAdam, McGarthy, & Zald, 1996; Tarrow, 1994). Although relevant to an understanding of social movement participation, the present analysis of collective action is broader in scope in that it considers episodic, normative, and spontaneous actions, as well as those engaged in by single individuals or small groups. At the same time, the present analysis is narrower, as it does not consider the additional specific conditions and resources necessary to build and sustain a social movement.

Completing a Framework for Action in Response to Disadvantage

In addition to the distinctions between collective action, individual action, and inaction, two additional distinctions are necessary to situate collective action in a more complete behavioral framework. The first is the distinction between strategic and reactive behaviors. When faced with severe frustration, disadvantaged groups' members may lash out. While important in their own right, reactive outbursts that lack strategic intent are not considered collective actions by this definition. However, actions which may appear to be reactive, such as violent riots, may actually be much more strategic than they appear (Reicher, Spears, & Postmes, 1995).[1]

Finally, Wright et al. (1990a) propose the normative/nonnormative distinction that differentiates actions that conform to the rules of the social system from actions that violate these rules (see also Martin, 1986). Like the distinction between collective and individual action, this distinction is psychological. If the actor is aware that an action violates societal expectations/conventions, it is nonnormative. Notice, this does not involve the actor's perception of the appropriateness, legitimacy, or morality of the action.[2] Thus, there are two forms of collective action – normative and nonnormative – which are contrasted with inaction and individual action.

Recent History and Background

For the most part, social psychological research on intergroup relations has stopped short of studying direct action. While most of the dominant models in the 1960s, 1970s, and 1980s described behavioral outcomes, the dependent measures in most of the research were not behaviors, but perceptions of justice and/or feelings of anger, resentment, and dissatisfaction. There are a number of potential explanations for this lack of focus on behavior (see Reicher, 1996; Wright, Taylor, & Moghaddam, 1990b), but whatever the cause, the result has been that, until recently, the study of collective action had been left primarily to sociology. And, unfortunately for psychology, the dominant sociological perspectives all but dismissed psychological variables as irrelevant. The resource mobilization approach (e.g., McGarthy & Zald, 1977) held that structural and organizational variables determine the likelihood of collective action, and that incorporating psychological variables added little to the model. Although sociological perspectives have since expanded to become more psychological (e.g., Gamson, 1992; McAdam, McGarthy, & Zald, 1996), mainstream social psychology has made few direct contributions to these expansions.

Fortunately, we are in the midst of a revitalization of the social psychology of collective action. SIT (Tajfel, 1982; Tajfel & Turner, 1979) presented the general concept of "social identity" and a fresh perspective on the self that formed the basis for a new perspective on groups and intergroup relations. Recently, the initial model has been strengthened by ideas from sociology and more traditional theories of intergroup relations, such as relative deprivation theory and equity theory (e.g., Hinkle, Fox-Cardamone, Haseleu, Brown, & Irwin, 1996; Kawakami & Dion, 1995; Kelly & Breinlinger, 1996; Klandermans, 1997; Simon, 1998). Creative laboratory and field research (e.g., Kawakami & Dion, 1993; Petta & Walker, 1992; Simon et al., 1998; Smith, Spears, & Oyen, 1994) have tested, and in some cases integrated, aspects of these theoretical perspectives. The model presented in this chapter draws on several of these new approaches.

The Road to Collective Action

Activation of the social self: When "I" becomes "We"

It is simply obvious that in order to engage in collective action the individual must recognize his or her membership in the relevant collective. Thus, the starting point for our analysis (and the foremost process in the model depicted in Figure 20.1) involves considering what leads individuals to consider themselves members of a social category and when that membership will become the foundation for thought and action. At the heart of this question is the distinction between the individual self (*personal identity*) and the collective self (*social identity*). The distinction between these two levels of self-conception is the cornerstone of SIT (Tajfel & Turner, 1979), and other recent theoretical accounts of the self (e.g., Brewer, 1991; Taylor & Dubé, 1986; Turner et al., 1987). Personal identity involves those aspects of the self that make one unique from others, while social identity involves those aspects of the self that connect one to others through shared memberships in social groups. The personal identity is the basis for thoughts and actions in interactions between oneself and other individuals. The social identity provides the basis for thoughts and actions in interactions between group members. When a group membership becomes the salient self-representation a process of depersonalization occurs, such that the self is perceived not as an independent individual but as an interchangeable exemplar of the social group. The individual's thoughts and actions are now based on his or her understanding of prototypic group attitudes and actions (i.e., ingroup norms).

From this perspective, the first roots of collective action are found in the self-representation of the individual group members, raising a twofold question: (a) When will social identity eclipse personal identity, and (because all of us belong to an array of specific groups) (b) how does a specific group membership form the basis for self-representation?

Collective self-representation 1: Activating "we". The first of these questions makes apparent one of many impediments to collective action. Although there may be no theoretical basis for assuming the supremacy of either personal or social identity (Oakes, Haslam, & Turner, 1994), there is some evidence that in practice the personal self may be primary (L. Gaertner, Sedikides, & Graetz, 1999). At the most macro/societal level, the general cultural orientation influences the availability of collective self-representations. Much has been written about the strength of the individualistic orientation in "Western" societies (e.g., Markus & Kitayama, 1991; Triandis & Trafimow, this volume, chapter 18). Independence and self-reliance are the cornerstones on which Western political, economic, and social institutions are built. The dominance of this ideology may reduce the potential for social categories to become the central self-representations (Tajfel, 1982). This does not, of course, preclude the possibility that an aspect of the social identity can become the primary basis of self-representation in Western individualistic contexts. However, these collective self-representations must overcome an a priori propensity for individual self-representation. Consistent with this, Oyerserman (in press) argues that the strength of engagement in collective action is associated with a "collectivist world view."

Collective self-representation 2: Activating the "right" we. Each of us belongs to an array of social groups and, thus, has many potential collective self-representations. Self-categorization theorists (e.g., Turner et al., 1987) and researchers investigating stereotype activation (e.g., Macrae, Bodenhausen, & Milne, 1995) both argue that, despite this larger available set, in any given situation, one primary categorization will dominate. Thus, we must consider the rather complex process by which a specific group becomes the basis for self-representation (see Oakes, this volume, chapter 1). Not only are there numerous relevant domains of self-categorization (e.g., ethnicity, political, national, geographical, occupational, etc.), within each domain there are numerous levels of self-categorization, including smaller *subcategories* and more inclusive *superordinate* categories (Brewer, 1991; Turner et al., 1987). Some of these subcategories can enhance interest in collective action, while others reduce it. For example, Simon et al. (1998) showed that while identification with the gay community was associated with participation in gay rights activities, identification with the smaller subgroup of "gay activists" was a stronger predictor of action. Conversely, Condor (1986) found that a group of women whose gender identification was with the subgroup of "traditional" women accepted the gender status quo and showed little interest in collective action. Thus, the specific subcategory that becomes the dominant self-representation can influence the propensity for collective action.

Self-representation as a member of a larger superordinate group that includes both the disadvantaged and advantaged groups can also reduce interest in collective action. For example, Gaertner, Dovidio, Anastasio, Bachman, and Rust (1993) have advocated for a *common group identity model* as a means of reducing intergroup bias. In this case, a super-ordinate identity replaces old "us" and "them" group boundaries with a more inclusive "we." For example, African American and White students are encouraged to focus on their shared membership in the larger student body, rather than their ethnic group. While this strategy can be very effective at reducing intergroup prejudice, it is also likely to reduce collective action by members of the disadvantaged group. Identification with the superordinate category reduces self-representations as a member of the subordinate ingroup and obscures the intergroup inequalities between groups at this "lower" level of categorization.

This point raises an important broader issue for the study of intergroup relations. An enormous amount of research has investigated conditions and practices that might reduce intergroup bias. Since most of this work focuses on reducing prejudice and discrimina-tion by members of powerful groups, this approach appears to make sense. However, from the perspective of disadvantaged groups, the same mechanism that serves to reduce the problems associated with advantaged group prejudice also weaken the impetus for members of the disadvantaged group to take collective action designed to reduce exist-ing intergroup inequalities. *Cross-cutting categorization* effects (e.g., Brown & Turner, 1979), *superordinate goals* (e.g., Sherif, 1967), *intergroup contact* effects (e.g., Pettigrew, 1998), and many other strategies improve intergroup attitudes in part by changing the degree of differentiation between the groups and, thus, each of these might also reduce collective action by disadvantaged group members.

What, then, determines when a specific social group becomes the primary self-representation. Tajfel (1978a) proposed the interaction of two factors: The chronic acces-sibility of the group membership for the particular individual, and the situational/contextual cues that focus the individual's attention on that group membership. Self-categorization theorists (see Oakes, this volume, chapter 1) expand on this idea by refer-ring to the combination of *accessibility* of the category (the "readiness" of a perceiver to use a particular category) and the *fit* of the category (the level to which the category simplifies and organizes the social context). Generally, accessibility is determined by elements of the individual, and fit is determined by relevant cues in the present environment.

Accessibility: Individual differences affect ingroup salience. Accessibility of a category can be temporarily increased by frequent use (e.g., Macrae et al., 1995), or when the category becomes relevant to one's immediate goals or needs. However, accessibility of a given group membership is heightened on a relatively permanent basis to the degree that the individual *identifies* with that group. Identification can be defined as the degree to which a group holds enduring psychological significance for the individual, or as the degree to which the group is included in the self (Tropp & Wright, 1999). Thus, ingroup iden-tification is an individual difference variable that the person "brings with him/her" to the situation.

Ingroups for which the group/self overlap (identification) is the greatest will be most chronically accessible. Greater accessibility of the group increases the likelihood that it will become the prominent self-representation and the impetus for action. Evidence of an association between ingroup identification and collective action has been found in research among religious groups in Israel (Struch & Schwartz, 1989), ethnic minorities in the United States (Wright & Tropp, in press), on support for affirmative action (Tougas & Veilleux, 1988), on pro- and anti-abortion lobbies (Hinkle et al., 1996), on participation in unions (Kelly & Kelly, 1994), the women's movement (Kelly & Breinlinger, 1996), the Gray Panthers (Simon et al., 1998, Study 1), the gay rights movement (Simon et al., 1998, Study 2), and in laboratory created groups (Branscombe & Ellemers, 1998). Doosje and Ellemers (1997) summarize that "'die-hard' members are more predisposed to act in terms of the group, and make sacrifices for it, than are 'fair-weather' members" (p. 358).

Fit: Situational cues affect ingroup salience. In addition to the accessibility of the category, a collective self-representation depends on environmental cues that make that aspect of identity salient. The power of local cues has been reviewed extensively by self-categorization theorists (see Oakes, this volume, chapter 1; Oakes et al., 1994), who propose two aspects of the fit. *Comparative fit* is the extent to which differences between the categories are greater than differences within the categories (i.e., does imposing this category maximize distinctions between ingroup and outgroup members?). *Normative fit* refers to the degree to which members of the two groups conform to expectations about category differences (i.e., does imposing this category provide an explanation for the actions of those present?). Thus, the degree to which the situation makes a category *apparent* and *useful* will determine the likelihood that the category will become salient and, thus, become a possible self-representation.

Specific events can also heighten the salience of collective self-representations. Some of the most publicized examples of disruptive collective action have followed an apparent trigger event. These events themselves should not be considered the *cause* of the subsequent large-scale collective action (see Klandermans, 1997). However, when these events are successfully *framed* (by group leaders, the media, etc.) as examples of collective injustice (Gamson, 1992), they may make more salient the relevant collective identity and heighten the chance of a collective self-representation. More broadly, influential others can frame the social context and specific events in terms of the relevant group identity. This process is a part of what has been called *consciousness raising* (Taylor & McKirnan, 1984) or *identity framing* (Gamson, 1992).

Fit × accessibility: Situational cues affect group salience through ingroup identification. While the distinction between accessibility and fit is conceptually useful, the two are clearly interrelated. Ingroup identification is not independent of the situational context in which the group and the individual are embedded. Clearly, present ingroup identification is the result of past experiences related to that group membership. For strong ingroup identification to develop, one must find oneself, relatively frequently, in contexts in which that group membership "fits." In addition, some situational factors not only make the category more immediately salient, they also increase the ability of the category to attract the identification of its members. Thus, some situational factors increase the salience of the relevant group membership by raising long-term identification with the group. Here, the distinction between relatively local immediate cues and more enduring systemic features of the environment becomes important. While cues in the immediate context may impact directly on the salience of a given category, the more enduring systemic features of the environment can impact on the salience of a category by increasing or decreasing its ability to attract ingroup identification. For instance, numerical representation of one's group in the immediate context impacts on the salience of that category. When the ingroup is underrepresented, the relevant category distinction will become more salient. So, the lone woman in a room full of men will likely become aware of her gender (e.g., Lord & Saenz, 1985). However, the relative size of the ingroup in the broader/societal environment can impact on the ability of that group to attract more long-term ingroup identification (e.g., Brewer, 1991). For example, McGuire, McGuire, Child, and Fujioka (1978) measured the spontaneous self-concepts of ethnic minority and majority children, and found that minority children were more likely to state ethnicity as a relevant social identity.

In addition, the nature of the existing relationship between two groups can impact on their ability to attract members' identification. The classic "Robbers Cave" studies (see Sherif, 1967) showed dramatically that intergroup conflict heightens cohesion and identification with the ingroup and increases the importance of category distinction in self-definition and interactions with others. Cooperative interdependence between groups, on the other hand, can reduce cross-group differentiation (e.g., Brewer & Miller, 1984) and, thus, reduce the attractiveness of the ingroup as a source of identification.

The relative status of the ingroup compared to the salient outgroup also affects the likelihood that the ingroup will become the dominant self-representation (Brewer, 1991; Ellemers, 1993; Simon, 1998). Groups that hold relatively low status will contribute negatively to their members' social identity and are likely to attract less identification. Conversely, high-status groups contribute positively to members' social identities and attract stronger identification (Tajfel & Turner, 1979). This pattern presents a dilemma. The groups most in need of disruptive collective actions to improve their relative position are less able to attract the necessary identification from their members. As mentioned earlier, the relative group size affects identification, such that group membership is more salient for members of minority groups. However, in addition to this main effect of size, size and status appear to interact such that it is high-status minority groups that are most able to attract strong identification (Simon, 1998; Wilder & Simon, this volume, chapter 8). Again, this has negative implications for the probability of collective action by disadvantaged minority groups.

The nature of the intragroup relations (relations among ingroup members) can also affect the group's ability to attract identification. Rabbie and Horwitz (1988) argue that when group members depend on each other to obtain common outcomes, the group will attract greater identification. However, the more crucial issue may be that the group has a history of "shared fate" (i.e., members share similar treatment or outcomes). Gurin and Townsend (1986), for example, found that the perception of common treatment and outcomes as a function of group membership was the strongest predictor of gender identity and political activism in a sample of women. Although there is some evidence that the effects of shared fate are stronger when the shared experience involves unjust treatment or common failure (Ellemers, 1993), there is also evidence that the shared experience need not be negative (Simon et al., 1995).

Experiencing Negative Social Identity: Making Intergroup Social Comparisons

SIT and self-categorization theory propose that when a group membership becomes salient, there is a qualitative shift in social perception such that attention is focused on collective outcomes and group status, rather than personal status and outcomes. The individual now makes intergroup comparisons to determine the relative position of the ingroup. When this comparison leads to the recognition that the ingroup occupies a disadvantaged position, the result is a negative social identity. This negative social identity serves as the impetus for further analysis of the intergroup context and continued progress on the road to collective action.

There are a number of theoretical perspectives which have considered how social comparison affects the thoughts, feelings, and actions of disadvantaged groups. The most notable, perhaps, is relative deprivation theory (see Olson et al., 1986; Walker & Pettigrew, 1984), which claims that it is not the objective deprivation of the ingroup, but rather the individual's perception of group deprivation resulting from comparisons with another group that determines how deprived one feels. Thus, it is important that social comparisons be made with a higher status outgroup. If members of an objectively disadvantaged group make comparisons with an even worse-off outgroup, they will not experience collective deprivation, and will be unlikely to consider actions to improve their situation. However, the feelings of collective deprivation that arise from comparisons with a better-off outgroup are strongly associated with support for collective action (Abrams, 1990; Walker & Pettigrew, 1984; Wright & Tropp, in press).

On the other hand, it appears that the model of a direct and straightforward relationship between a collective self-representation and a preference for intergroup comparisons may be too simple. Raising the general salience of a group membership not only increases attention to intergroup processes, it also increases attention to intragroup processes (Hogg, 1992). In other words, focusing on "self as group member" can lead to greater attention to structures and interaction *within* the group. For example, research by Smith et al. (1994) found that priming a disadvantaged group identity led to a reduction in feelings of deprivation among those group members who were satisfied with their personal position. They argue that the group prime, instead of focusing attention on the lower status of the ingroup, focused attention on participants' privileged personal position *within* the ingroup. Similarly, both Wright and Taylor (1998) and Lalonde and Silverman (1994) found that under some conditions increasing the general salience of group membership did not increase endorsement of collective action.

In answering the question "when will heightened ingroup salience lead to intergroup rather than intragroup (self/other) comparisons?" Wright (1997) argues that the key is whether the ingroup is made salient *within the context of a clearly defined intergroup rela-*

tionship. Only when collective self-focus is combined with an awareness that the ingroup stands in contrast (even opposition) to a relevant outgroup, will there be a preference for intergroup comparisons. Heightening group salience *without an expressly intergroup focus* will lead to individual-level intragroup comparisons. This view is consistent with the argument that collective action requires the isolating of a particular villain (the "them" that is set in contrast to the "us") who is blamed for the ingroup's disadvantaged position (Gamson, 1992; Klandermans, 1997). With this in mind, Figure 20.1 shows that a salient social identity can lead either to intragroup comparisons or intergroup comparisons, and it is only intergroup comparisons that continue the process toward collective action.

Compared to whom: Determining the target of intergroup social comparisons. Given the multitude of possible outgroup comparisons, what determines which of these outgroups will become the target of comparison? Self-categorization theorists (e.g., Oakes et al., 1994; Turner et al., 1987), suggest that many of the same variables that determine which of our many potential self-categorizations will become salient also determine the salient comparison outgroup, that is, accessibility and fit factors. While clarification of the mechanisms and processes that determine the choice of intergroup comparisons remains in need of more research (see Taylor & Moghaddam, 1994; Tyler et al., 1997), Pettigrew (1978) makes two interesting points related to the target of social comparison, arguing that: "when groups are the referent, as opposed to individuals, the number of possibilities are sharply reduced. And reference groups tend to be reciprocally paired in the manner of social roles: White–Black; native–immigrant; blue collar–white collar" (p. 36). The potential comparison targets for an ethnic group are almost certainly less numerous than the potential targets for a single individual, and the social history, and the present social structures, will very likely define the most relevant comparison target. Thus, Whites may be the "default" comparison for Blacks in America. Germans may be the default comparison for Turkish immigrants in Germany. However, there are good reasons why the default may not always be activated. Blacks in Miami may have reason to compare themselves to Cubans, and Turkish immigrants in Germany may compare themselves to Turks in Turkey.

In contrast to Pettigrew's position, Taylor, Moghaddam, and Bellerose (1989) argue for the flexibility of intergroup comparisons, focusing on the individual's immediate needs and motives as determinants of outgroup comparison target. They show that when one is motivated to see the ingroup in a positive light, lower status outgroups become the preferred target. However, when members of the same group need to appeal for sympathy for their plight, they prefer comparisons with more advantaged outgroups.

Proximity and *similarity* may also play a role. Some groups are more likely to find themselves sharing the same environment, and mere presence makes that outgroup a likely comparison target. Also, a preference for comparisons with similar others will make groups that are relatively similar to the ingroup more likely comparison targets (Brown & Haeger, 1999; Major, 1994; Taylor & Moghaddam, 1994). Finally, vivid incidental events (trigger events) involving cross-group interactions, can make apparent intergroup inequalities and focus attention on that intergroup comparison. For example, the beating of Rodney King (a Black motorist) by a group of White police officers brought intergroup comparisons with Whites into sharp focus for African Americans. In addition, these trigger events will have the greatest impact when they are "framed" by other ingroup members as examples of intergroup behavior (i.e., the event is characterized so that ingroup/outgroup distinctions are most clear). This process of influence is a part of what has been called "consciousness raising" (Taylor & McKirnan, 1984) or "identity framing" (Gamson, 1992).

In summary, while predicting what outgroup will be "selected" as the comparative other remains a problem, the selection is likely to be influenced by a combination of broader structural/societal factors (e.g., social history and present structures that define the default outgroup), local situational factors (e.g., propinquity, recent salient intergroup events, referent informational influence), and the present motivation of the individual (e.g., group-enhancement, group-deprecation).

Individual Mobility or Social Change: Assessing Boundary Permeability

To this point, we have examined psychological processes that focus on the individual and his or her relationship with the relevant ingroup. The next level of analysis considers the individual's understanding and interpretation of the existing social structure. SIT (Tajfel & Turner, 1979) proposes three assessments as crucial determinants of collective action: (a) The *permeability* of the intergroup boundaries (i.e., can the individual move from the lower to higher status group?); (b) the *legitimacy* of the status hierarchy (i.e., is the low-status position of the ingroup appropriate/deserved?); and (c) the *stability* of the status hierarchy (i.e., is the low-status position of the ingroup open to change?). Our earlier discussion of relative deprivation foreshadowed the importance of legitimacy assessments; feeling dissatisfied and angry requires not only recognition that the ingroup is disadvantaged, but also feelings of entitlement and illegitimacy (see Major, 1994). Also, work in sociology (e.g., Gamson, 1992; Klandermans, 1997) has described the need for disadvantaged group members to believe that the position of their group can be changed and that they have the resources to produce that change (see also Bandura, 1997; Kelly & Breinlinger, 1996). However, Wright (1997, in press), has argued, in a manner consistent with Tajfel (1982), that the assessment of boundary permeability may be the primary of these three assessments in determining disadvantaged group behavior.

Once the individual recognizes that the ingroup holds a relatively disadvantaged position, he or she must evaluate the degree to which his or her own membership in the group is immutable (Tajfel & Turner, 1979; Taylor & McKirnan, 1984). For collective action to occur, the disadvantaged group member must believe that, regardless of talents and effort, individual movement from the disadvantaged ingroup to the advantaged outgroup is impossible. In other words, collective action requires that the boundaries between the groups are seen to be *impermeable* (closed).

Perceiving boundary impermeability can lead to increased ingroup identification, enhanced motivation to improve the ingroup's position, and a preference for collective action. On the other hand, believing that movement into a more advantaged position is possible can lead to dissociation from the disadvantaged ingroup, and a preference for individual actions (Ellemers, 1993; Lalonde & Silverman, 1994; Wright & Taylor, 1998; Wright et al., 1990a).

Internal and external barriers to boundary permeability. The relative simplicity of this basic model is appealing. However, additional considerations increase the complexity of the process. Broadly speaking, assessments of boundary permeability consider two types of barriers to leaving the disadvantaged ingroup. *External* barriers include physical and structural factors that establish group boundaries, such as ascribed characteristics (e.g., race, gender), or social norms or institutions (e.g., discrimination practiced by the advantaged group) that prevent disadvantaged group members from leaving their group and/or from joining the outgroup. Additionally, there are *internal* barriers to leaving the group. One can be tied to the ingroup because of moral obligation, personal commitments, or high ingroup identification. For example, Ellemers, Spears, and Doosje (1997) found that compared to those with low levels of ingroup identification, high identifiers remain more committed to the ingroup and were less likely to pursue opportunities to improve their personal position, even when individual mobility was actually possible. Similarly, individuals' perceptions of their relative status within the ingroup, or their personal competence in status-relevant domains, can influence their assessment of boundary permeability (Wright et al., 1990a, 1990b).

In summary, the individual considers both the structural barriers to leaving the ingroup as well as internal barriers imposed by his or her own relationship with, or position in, the ingroup. As shown in Figure 20.1, when the boundaries between the groups are perceived to be open, relevant personal identities will become salient and individual action ensues. However, when the group boundaries are thought to be closed, the process toward collective action continues.

Restricted group boundaries: Responding to tokenism. While most theorists represent boundary permeability as a continuum, most empirical studies have characterized this perception as a dichotomous distinction between an "open" and a "closed" condition. Wright and his colleagues (see Wright, in press) argue that in contemporary North American society (and many other intergroup contexts), individual mobility is neither impossible (closed) nor is it entirely meritocratic (open). Instead, group boundaries are often restricted (Martin, 1986; Pettigrew & Martin, 1987), such that a small number of disadvantaged group members are accepted into advantaged positions, while access is systematically blocked for the rest of the group. This restricted context has been labeled "tokenism." A number of studies (see Wright, in press) have shown that, while entirely closed intergroup contexts produce strong endorsement of collective action, when as few as 2% of the qualified members of the disadvantaged group are allowed access to advantaged positions individual actions become the response of choice. The slightest hint of permeability appears to undermine interest in collective action. There is some evidence that tokenism may have this effect by focusing attention on personal identities and encouraging interpersonal social comparisons with the few successful tokens. However, there is also evidence that tokenism obfuscates subsequent assessments of the legitimacy and stability of the disadvantaged group's low-status position (Wright, 1997). I will discuss the impact of tokenism on these two assessments in some detail later, but first I will consider assessments of legitimacy and stability in more general terms.

Cognitive Alternatives/Collective Action Frames: Assessing Legitimacy and Collective Control

When disadvantaged group members cannot (or will not) abandon their membership in the disadvantaged group, individual action is no longer an option, and they must choose between collective action and inaction. The decision to take collective action rests on the individual's ability to imagine a situation where the relative positions of the groups are different. In SIT terms (Tajfel & Turner, 1979), the individual must recognize "cognitive alternatives" to the present status relationship. The recognition of cognitive alternatives depends on two assessments: *legitimacy*, the degree to which the groups' status differences are seen to be fair; and *stability*, the degree to which the status relationship is perceived to be immutable.

Legitimacy. Issues of legitimacy and justice play a central role in many perspectives in intergroup relations (e.g., Jost & Major, in press; Major, 1994; Olson et al., 1986; Tajfel, 1982; Tyler et al., 1997), and theories of social movements (e.g., Gamson, 1992; Klandermans, 1997). As described earlier in the discussion of relative deprivation, the perception that one's group is disadvantaged relative to another group is not sufficient to produce collective action. Rather, group members must also feel *dissatisfied* with the position of their group. Feelings of dissatisfaction indicate a sense of *entitlement* (Major, 1994), in that the group members feel that they (or the ingroup as a whole) deserve more. To the extent that group members feel their group is deprived, and entitled to more, they will perceive the status hierarchy as illegitimate (Major, 1994). These feelings of illegitimacy represent an essential step on the road to collective action (Abrams, 1990; Grant & Brown, 1995), because they provide the motivation and justification for collective actions that may be socially disruptive, and potentially costly and dangerous.

Stability and agency: The role of collective control. When disadvantaged group members consider the relative positions of the groups to be part of a fixed social order, an immutable reality (stable), they will not be inclined to engage in collective action. However, when they believe that the positions of the groups can change (unstable), collective action is much more likely (Tajfel, 1982). In related discussions, recent sociological theories of social movements have examined perceptions of the potential for change in the social structure, in terms of *agency* frames (Gamson, 1992). Agency refers to the extent to which group members feel capable of producing collective action that can reduce or remove the injustice they face. This concept of *agency* parallels Bandura's (1997) notion of *collective efficacy*, which is defined as "the group's shared belief in its conjoint capability to organize and execute the courses of action required to produce given levels of attainment" (p. 477).

Although clearly related, Gamson's (1992) *agency*, and Bandura's (1997) *collective effi-cacy*, do not correspond directly to Tajfel and Turner's (1979) *stability*. The distinction between the two may be understood best with reference to theories of *perceived control* (e.g., Abramson, Seligman, & Teasdale, 1978). According to this perspective, percep-tions of control require two simultaneous judgments. First, the individual must believe that relevant outcomes are contingent on behavior (i.e., the situation can be modified through appropriate action). At the group level, this judgment corresponds with the concept of *stability* as described in SIT. Second, the individual must believe that the rel-evant agent (oneself or the group) can execute the behaviors necessary to produce the desired change. This second judgement corresponds with the concepts of *agency* or *col-lective efficacy*. Thus, a lack of *collective control* may result from either a belief that the intergroup context is unresponsive to actions, or from a perception that the ingroup does not have the requisite resources or abilities to effect change. Although it would be inter-esting to consider the possible significance of the distinction between the two assessments, in the discussions that follow, we will refer to collective control as a unitary concept.

Assessing illegitimacy and control when group boundaries are impermeable. The combina-tion of the assessments of legitimacy and control leads to four alternatives.[3] At one extreme, the situation is understood to be both legitimate and uncontrollable. In this case, status differences are based on mutually accepted principles and neither group questions its place in the hierarchy. Under these circumstances, collective action is not considered and the resulting inaction reflects "true acceptance of inferiority." The relationship between men and women at particular times in history, or the traditional Indian caste system might be examples of this.

At the other extreme, the situation can be seen as illegitimate and controllable. Here, neither the principles that support the status inequalities nor the immutability of the intergroup hierarchy are accepted. Disadvantaged group members see their present status as unfairness, can envision their group holding a higher status position, and believe they have the necessary resources and capabilities to produce change. The result should be col-lective action. Whether this collective action will be normative or nonnormative will depend primarily on the availability of a normative option. In most cases, normative actions involve considerably less risk. Thus, where possible, disadvantaged group members are likely to try normative strategies first. If, however, normative channels are unavailable or prove unsuccessful, the combination of perceived illegitimacy and collective control provide the basis for collective nonnormative action.

In between these two extremes are two "mixed" situations: (1) Where the status hier-archy is considered legitimate but controllable; and (2) where the status hierarchy is con-sidered illegitimate but uncontrollable. Controllability and illegitimacy are likely correlated, such that conditions that undermine the stability of the status hierarchy are also likely to raise doubts about its legitimacy. Similarly, perceiving the status hierarchy as illegitimate will motivate one to consider and perhaps even seek evidence of its con-trollability (Tajfel, 1978b). Alternatively, clear evidence that the situation will not change could alter perceptions so that the situation appears increasingly legitimate (see Pettigrew, 1961 for a discussion of the "psychology of the inevitable"). Thus, "mixed" situations may create pressures that can move perceptions toward the illegitimate/controllable or the legitimate/uncontrollable extremes.

Despite these pressures, some mixed situations can be relatively enduring. Take, for example, the American two-party political system. Members of the party not in power (the disadvantaged group) usually accept that because they did not receive the necessary votes, their low-status position is legitimate. However, they also believe that the situation is controllable; that in the next election they will garner the necessary votes to change the status hierarchy. Thus, perceptions of legitimacy and controllability co-exist, because the principles that determine group status (democratic elections) and the instability of present positions are accepted by both groups. In this case, perceived control inspires collective action, but only normative collective actions. This is because, imbedded in the assessment that the situation is legitimate is an acceptance of the normative rules by which group status is determined.

In the other "mixed" case, the principles or beliefs that sustain intergroup inequalities are challenged (illegitimacy is perceived), but the relative status of the groups is seen as unchangeable. Take, for example, a nation ruled by a strong military dictatorship. Most of the poor may perceive the status differences between rich and poor as unfair, but may also see little chance that the distribution will become more equitable. Here, strategic collective action is unlikely. Of course, the resulting inaction does not reflect "acceptance" of the situation, but angry/discontented admission that things cannot be changed. However, when anger and resentment are not expressed in actions, observers from both the advantaged and disadvantaged groups may interpret this inaction as de facto acceptance. The advantaged group may believe that disadvantaged group members accept the myths that legitimize their high-status position. Other disadvantaged group members may also fall prey to this misinterpretation. Research on "pluralistic ignorance" (e.g., Miller & McFarland, 1987) shows that even when most disagree with the direction taken by the group, when others fail to act on their misgivings, each individual can mistakenly assume that he or she alone disagrees. The result, everyone conforms despite privately disagreeing. Pluralistic ignorance provides a partial explanation for why inaction persists when collective actions, if suggested, might be supported by many in the disadvantaged group.

Assessing legitimacy and control under conditions of tokenism. When the boundaries between groups are not entirely closed but are highly restricted (tokenism), efforts to improve one's personal position remain possible. Thus, in this context, the question is "when will the apparent preference for individual action (Wright, in press) be abandoned in favor of collective action?". Tokenism resembles a completely closed context in that group membership is used to deny access to advantaged positions. On the other hand, like an open context, merit remains a partial criterion for advancement (for a very few individuals, merit results in success). Thus, tokenism mingles elements of discrimination and meritocracy, and in so doing, creates uncertainty about the legitimacy of the intergroup status hierarchy (Wright, 1997).

Tokenism may also obfuscate judgments of collective control. In this restricted context, collective action is likely to be perceived as especially costly and/or dangerous (Martin, 1986). First, collective action under any circumstances exposes one to social disapproval and possible retaliation by the advantaged group. Thus, relatively clear perceptions of collective control are needed to outweigh these potential costs. Perceived controllability hinges on the belief that the ingroup has the necessary resources to succeed, and one of the key resources is the capacity to secure support from and to mobilize other ingroup members (Kelly & Breinlinger, 1996; Klandermans, 1997; McCarthy & Zald, 1977). If tokenism leads to uncertainty about illegitimacy, it should also lead to uncertainty about how other ingroup members will respond. Thus, by reducing confidence that other disadvantaged group members will approve of and support collective action, tokenism may heighten feelings of uncontrollability and reduce interest in collective action.

Thus, tokenism not only focuses attention on personal identity by cueing interpersonal comparisons with successful tokens, it can undermine assessments of illegitimacy and control. As illustrated in Figure 20.1, the result is a strong tendency for tokenism to produce individual action. Wright (1997) concludes that only when there are very strong messages that clarify the injustice and the potential controllability of the intergroup context, and when attention is focused on collective injustice, will collective action be the response to tokenism.

Summary and Conclusions

Why do clear intergroup inequalities go unaddressed and even unnoticed? When will members of socially disadvantaged groups choose to take action designed to improve their group's situation? Clearly, these questions have important societal implications, as they address issues of the stability of the social order and the correction of social injustices. Additionally, these are basic questions relevant to a number of prominent theoretical perspectives in social psychology. At their core, these questions involve the prediction and explanation of collective action.

While understanding and predicting collective action remains a significant challenge, the available literature provides considerable insight and the foundation for a complex and comprehensive model. The present sequential model proposes that the roots of collective action can be found in: (a) The individual's self-representations as a group member; (b) intergroup comparisons that lead to perception of disadvantage; (c) rejection of the possibility for individual upward mobility; (d) assessment that the ingroup's low-status position is illegitimate; and (e) the beliefs that the intergroup status hierarchy can change and that the ingroup has the capacity to produce that change. When we consider the complexity of this process, and the variety of influences that can derail the process and lead members of a disadvantaged group to take individual action or to do nothing at all, it is perhaps not surprising that collective actions are relatively rare.

Notes

1. This is not synonymous with the "rational/irrational" action distinction (Gamson, 1992). Strategic action need not result from a rational cost/benefit analysis, nor is it void of strong emotion as cause or affiliate.

2. This is not synonymous with the violent/nonviolent distinction. Civil disobedience, for example, can be nonviolent but nonnormative. Alternatively, some intergroup contexts (e.g., a football game) accept violence as part of the interaction.
3. While assessments of stability and legitimacy are likely continuous, action and inaction represent discrete categories. There needs to be a relatively discrete point where assessments of legitimacy and stability initiate a qualitative switch in behavioral strategy.

References

Abrams, D. (1990). *Political identity: Relative deprivation, social identity, and the case of Scottish nationalism.* Economic and Social Research Council 16–19 Initiative Occasional Paper no. 24. Social Statistics Research Unit, City University, London.

Abramson, L., Seligman, M., & Teasdale, J. (1978). Learned helplessness in humans: Critique and reformulation. *Journal of Abnormal Psychology, 87,* 49–74.

Adams, J. S. (1965). Inequity in social exchange. In L. Berkowitz (Ed.), *Advances in experimental social psychology* (Vol. 2, pp. 267–299). New York: Academic Press.

Bandura, A. (1997). *Self-efficacy: The experience of control.* New York: Freeman.

Branscombe, N. R., & Ellemers, N. (1998). Coping with group-based discrimination: Individualistic versus group-level strategies. In J. K. Swim & C. Stangor (Eds.), *Prejudice: The target's perspective* (pp. 243–266). San Diego, CA: Academic Press.

Brewer, M. B. (1991). The social self: On being the same and different at the same time. *Personality and Social Psychology Bulletin, 17,* 475–482.

Brewer, M. B., & Miller, N. (1984). Beyond the contact hypothesis: Theoretical perspectives on desegregation. In N. Miller & M. B. Brewer (Eds.), *Groups in contact: The psychology of desegregation* (pp. 281–302). New York: Academic Press.

Brown, R., & Haeger, G. (1999). "Compared to what?" Comparison choice in an international context. *European Journal of Social Psychology, 29,* 31–42.

Brown, R. J., & Turner, J. C. (1979). The criss-cross categorization effect in intergroup discrimination. *British Journal of Social and Clinical Psychology, 18,* 371–383.

Condor, S. (1986). Sex role beliefs and "traditional women": Feminists and intergroup perspectives. In S. Wilkinson (Ed.), *Feminist social psychology: Developing theory and practice.* Milton Keynes, UK: Open University Press.

Crosby, F. J. (1976). A model of egoistical relative deprivation. *Psychological Review, 83,* 85–113.

Doosje, B., & Ellemers, N. (1997). Stereotyping under threat: The role of group identification. In R. Spears & P. J. Oakes (Eds.), *The social psychology of stereotyping and group life* (pp. 257–272). Oxford, UK: Blackwell.

Ellemers, N. (1993). The influence of socio-structural variables on identity management strategies. In W. Stroebe & M. Hewstone (Eds.), *European review of social psychology* (Vol. 4, pp. 27–57). Chichester, UK: Wiley.

Ellemers, N., Spears, R., & Doosje, B. (1997). Sticking together or falling apart: Ingroup identification as psychological determinant of group commitment versus individual mobility. *Journal of Personality and Social Psychology, 72,* 617–626.

Gaertner, L., Sedikides, C., & Graetz, K. (1999). In search of self-definition: Motivational primacy of the individual self, motivational primacy of the collective self, or contextual primacy? *Journal of Personality and Social Psychology, 76,* 5–18.

Gaertner, S. L., Dovidio, J. F., Anastasio, P. A., Bachman, B. A., & Rust, M. C. (1993). The common ingroup identity model: Recategorization and the reduction of intergroup bias. In W. Stroebe & M. Hewstone (Eds.), *European review of social psychology* (Vol. 4, pp. 1–26). Chichester, UK: Wiley.

Gamson, W. A. (1990). *The strategy of social protest.* Belmont, CA: Wadsworth.

Gamson, W. A. (1992). The social psychology of collective action. In A. D. Morris & C. McClurg Mueller (Eds.), *Frontiers in social movement theory* (pp. 53–76). New Haven, CT: Yale University Press.

Grant, P. R., & Brown, R. (1995). From ethnocentrism to collective protest: Responses to relative deprivation and threats to social identity. *Social Psychology Quarterly, 58,* 195–211.

Gurin, P., & Townsend, A. (1986). Properties of gender identity and their implications for gender consciousness. *British Journal of Social Psychology, 25,* 139–148.

Hinkle, S., Fox-Cardamone, L., Haseleu, J. A., Brown, R., & Irwin, L. M. (1996). Grassroots political action as an intergroup phenomenon. *Journal of Social Issues, 52,* 39–51.

Hogg, M. A. (1992). *The social psychology of group cohesiveness: From attraction to social identity.* New York: New York University Press.

Jackman, M. R. (1998, August). *Violence and legitimacy in expropriative intergroup relations.* Paper presented at The Psychology of Legitimacy: Emerging Perspectives on Ideology, Justice, and Intergroup Relations, Stanford, CA.

Jost, J., & Major, B. (Eds.) (in press). *The psychology of legitimacy: Emerging perspectives on ideology, justice, and intergroup relations.*

Kawakami, K., & Dion, K. L. (1993). The impact of salient self-identities on relative deprivation and action intentions. *European Journal of Social Psychology, 23,* 525–540.

Kawakami, K., & Dion, K. L. (1995). Social identity and affect as determinants of collective action: Toward an integration of relative deprivation and social identity theories. *Theory and Psychology, 5,* 551–577.

Kelly, C., & Breinlinger, S. (1996). *The social psychology of collective action: Identity, injustice, and gender.* Washington, DC: Taylor & Francis.

Kelly, C., & Kelly, J. (1994). Who gets involved in collective action? Social psychological determinants in individual participation in trade unions. *Human Relations, 47,* 63–88.

Klandermans, B. (1997). *The social psychology of protest.* Oxford, UK: Blackwell.

Lalonde, R. N., & Silverman, R. A. (1994). Behavioral preferences in response to social injustice: The effects of group permeability and social identity salience. *Journal of Personality and Social Psychology, 66,* 78–85.

Lord, C. G., & Saenz, D. S. (1985). Memory deficits and memory surfeits: Differential cognitive consequences of tokenism for token and observers. *Journal of Personality and Social Psychology, 49,* 918–926.

Macrae, C. N., Bodenhausen, G. V., & Milne, A. B. (1995). The dissection of selection in person perception: Inhibitory processes in social stereotyping. *Journal of Personality & Social Psychology, 69,* 397–407.

Major, B. (1994). From social inequality to personal entitlement: The role of social comparisons, legitimacy appraisals, and group membership. *Advances in Experimental Social Psychology, 26,* 293–355.

Markus, H. R., & Kitayama, S. (1991). Culture and the self: Implications for cognition, emotion, and motivation. *Psychological Review, 98,* 224–253.

Martin, J. (1986). The tolerance of injustice. In J. M. Olson, C. P. Herman, & M. P. Zanna (Eds.), *Relative deprivation and social comparison: The Ontario symposium* (Vol. 4., pp. 217–242). Mahwah, NJ: Erlbaum.

McAdam, D., McGarthy, J. D., & Zald, M. N. (Eds.) (1996). *Comparative perspectives on social movements: political opportunities, mobilizing structures, and cultural framings.* New York: Cambridge University Press.

McGarthy, J. D., & Zald, M. N. (1977). Resource mobilization and social movements: A partial theory. *American Journal of Sociology, 82,* 1212–1241.

McGuire, W. J., McGuire, C. V., Child, P., & Fujioka, T. (1978). Salience of ethnicity in the spontaneous self-concept as a function of one's ethnic distinctiveness in the social environment. *Journal of Personality and Social Psychology, 36,* 511–520.

Miller, D. T., & McFarland, C. (1987). Pluralistic ignorance: When similarity is interpreted as dissimilarity. *Journal of Personality and Social Psychology, 53,* 298–305.

Oakes, P. J., Haslam, S. A., & Turner, J. C. (1994). *Stereotyping and social reality.* Oxford, UK: Blackwell.

Olson, J. M., Herman, C. P., & Zanna, M. P. (Eds.) (1986). *Relative deprivation and social comparison: The Ontario symposium,* (Vol. 4). Mahwah, NJ: Erlbaum.

Oyserman, D. (in press). Contextualizing culture: What can a cultural psychological perspective add to the study of social movements? In T. J. Owens, S. Stryker, & R. W. White (Eds.), *Self, identity, and social movements.* American Sociological Association Press.

Petta, G., & Walker, I. (1992). Relative deprivation and ethnic identity. *British Journal of Social Psychology, 31,* 285–293.

Pettigrew, T. F. (1961). Social psychology and desegregation research. *American Psychologist, 16,* 1045–1112.

Pettigrew, T. F. (1978). Three issues in ethnicity: Boundaries, deprivations, and perceptions. In J. M. Yinger & S. J. Cutler (Eds.), *Major social issues: A multidisciplinary view* (pp. 25–49). New York: Free Press.

Pettigrew, T. F. (1998). Intergroup contact theory. *Annual Review of Psychology, 49,* 65–85.

Pettigrew, T. F., & Martin, J. (1987). Shaping the organizational context for Black American inclusion. *Journal of Social Issues, 43,* 41–78.

Rabbie, J. M., & Horwitz, M. (1988). Categories versus groups as explanatory concepts in intergroup relations. *European Journal of Social Psychology, 18,* 117–123.

Reicher, S. D. (1996). Social identity and social change: Rethinking the context of social psychology. In W. P. Robinson (Ed.), *Social groups and identities: Developing the legacy of Henri Tajfel.* Oxford, UK: Butterworth-Heinemann.

Reicher, S. D., Spears, R., & Postmes, T. (1995). A social identity model of deindividuation phenomena. In W. Stroebe & M. Hewstone (Eds.), *European review of social psychology* (Vol. 6, pp. 161–198). Chichester, UK: Wiley.

Sachdev, I., & Bourhis, R. Y. (1991). Power and status differentials in minority and majority group relations. *European Journal of Social Psychology, 21,* 1–24.

Sherif, M. (1967). *Group conflict and cooperation: Their social psychology.* London: Routledge and Kegan Paul.

Simon, B. (1998). Individuals, groups, and social change: On the relationship between individual and collective self-interpretations and collective action. In C. Sedikides & J. Schopler (Eds.), *Intergroup cognition and intergroup behavior* (pp. 257–282). Mahwah, NJ: Erlbaum.

Simon, B., Loewy, M., Stuermer, S., Weber, U., Freytag, P., Habig, C., Kampmeier, C., & Spahlinger, P. (1998). Collective identification and social movement participation. *Journal of Personality and Social Psychology, 74,* 646–658.

Simon, B., Pantaleo, G., & Mummendey, A. (1995). Unique individual or interchangeable group member? The accentuation of intragroup differences versus similarities as an indicator of the individual self versus the collective self. *Journal of Personality and Social Psychology, 69,* 106–119.

Smith, H., Spears, R., & Oyen, M. (1994). "People like us": The influence of personal deprivation and group membership salience on justice evaluations. *Journal of Experimental Social Psychology*, 30, 277–299.

Struch, N., & Schwartz, S. H. (1989). Intergroup aggression: Its predictors and distinctness from ingroup bias. *Journal of Personality and Social Psychology*, 56, 363–373.

Tajfel, H. (1978a). Interindividual behavior and intergroup behavior. In H. Tajfel (Ed.), *Differentiation between social groups: Studies in the social psychology of intergroup relations*. London: Academic Press.

Tajfel, H. (1978b). *The social psychology of minorities* (Report No. 38). London: Minority Rights Group.

Tajfel, H. (Ed.) (1982). *Social identity and intergroup relations*. Cambridge, UK: Cambridge University Press.

Tajfel, H., & Turner, J. C. (1979). An integrative theory of intergroup conflict. In W. G. Austin & S. Worchel (Eds.), *The social psychology of intergroup relations* (pp. 33–48). Monterey, CA: Brooks/Cole.

Tarrow, S. G. (1994). *Power in movement: Social movements and contentious politics*. New York: Cambridge University Press.

Taylor, D. M., & Dubé, L. (1986). Two faces of identity: The "I" and the "We". *Journal of Social Issues*, 42, 81–98.

Taylor, D. M., & McKirnan, D. J. (1984). A five-stage model of intergroup relations. *British Journal of Social Psychology*, 23, 291–300.

Taylor, D. M., & Moghaddam, F. M. (1994). *Theories of intergroup relations: International and social psychological perspectives* (2nd ed.). Westport, CT: Preager.

Taylor, D. M., Moghaddam, F. M., & Bellerose, J. (1989). Social comparison in an intergroup context. *Journal of Social Psychology*, 129, 499–515.

Tougas, F., & Veilleux, F. (1988). The influence of identification, collective relative deprivation, and procedure of implementation on women's response to affirmative action: A causal modeling approach. *Canadian Journal of Behavioural Sciences*, 20, 15–28.

Tropp, L. R., & Wright, S. C. (1999). *Inclusion of ingroup in the self*. Paper submitted for publication.

Turner, J. C., Hogg, M. A., Oakes, P. J., Reicher, S. D., & Wetherell, M. S. (1987). *Rediscovering the social group: A self-categorization theory*. New York: Blackwell.

Turner, R. H., & Killian, L. M. (1957). *Collective behavior*. Englewood Cliff, NJ: Prentice-Hall.

Tyler, T. R., Boeckmann, R., Smith, H., & Huo, Y. (1997). *Social justice in a diverse society*. Boulder, CO: Westview Press.

Walker, I., & Pettigrew, T. F. (1984). Relative deprivation theory: An overview and conceptual critique. *British Journal of Social Psychology*, 23, 301–310.

Wright, S. C. (1997). Ambiguity, shared consensus, and collective action: Generating collective protest in response to tokenism. *Personality and Social Psychology Bulletin*, 23, 1277–1290.

Wright, S. C. (in press). Restricted intergroup boundaries: Tokenism, ambiguity, and the tolerance of injustice. In J. Jost & B. Major (Eds.), *The psychology of legitimacy: Emerging perspectives on ideology, justice, and intergroup relations*.

Wright, S. C., & Taylor, D. M. (1998). Responding to tokenism: Individual action in the face of collective injustice. *European Journal of Social Psychology*, 28, 647–667.

Wright, S. C., Taylor, D. M., & Moghaddam, F. M. (1990a). Responding to membership in a disadvantaged group: From acceptance to collective action. *Journal of Personality and Social Psychology*, 58, 994–1003.

Wright, S. C., Taylor, D. M., & Moghaddam, F. M. (1990b). The relationship of perceptions and emotions to behavior in the face of collective inequality. *Social Justice Research, 4,* 229–250.

Wright, S. C., & Tropp, L. R. (in press). Collective action in response to disadvantage: Intergroup perceptions, social identification and social change. In I. Walker & H. Smith (Eds.), *Relative deprivation: Specification, development, and integration.* Boulder, CO: Westview Press.

CHAPTER TWENTY-ONE

Trust and Intergroup Negotiation

Roderick M. Kramer and Peter J. Carnevale

The problem of managing interdependence between groups has been a central and consistent theme in the study of intergroup relations (Sherif, 1966; Sumner, 1906). Whether they are minimal groups created in a laboratory setting (Tajfel, 1970), groups of boys at a summer camp (Sherif, Harvey, White, Hood, & Sherif, 1961), groups within organizations (Blake & Mouton, 1986), or even nation-states (Kahn & Zald, 1990), intergroup behavior has been viewed as a reflection of the myriad and inescapable forms of interdependence that bind together the fate of groups.

Negotiation is a primary mechanism by which groups cope with interdependence. It is effective in addressing two common intergroup problems. First, when groups are embroiled in conflict regarding contested resources or issues, negotiation can help the parties forge mutually acceptable agreements, thereby avoiding costly stalemates or destructive escalation (Carnevale & Pruitt, in press; Pruitt & Rubin, 1986). Second, when groups perceive an opportunity for mutual gain, but lack a set of shared understandings and/or decision rules for structuring a productive collaboration, negotiation may be useful (Davis, Kahn, & Zald, 1990).

Researchers have long recognized the central role trust plays in negotiation (Pruitt & Kimmel, 1977; Ross & Lacroix, 1998; Webb & Worchel, 1986). Trust facilitates the attainment of more satisfactory bargaining outcomes, and the absence of trust impedes such results (Butler, 1995; Larson, 1997; Lewicki & Bunker, 1995). Despite the frequent assertion of its importance, however, surprisingly little attention has been afforded to explicating the impact of trust on intergroup negotiation processes and outcomes. Recent reviews of the intergroup relations literature (e.g., Messick & Mackie, 1996; Stephan & Stephan, 1996; Taylor & Moghaddam, 1987), for example, devote relatively little space to articulating the benefits of trust or how those benefits can be achieved. Similarly, many negotiation texts (e.g., Neale & Bazerman, 1991; Thompson, 1998) afford only cursory

The authors gratefully acknowledge the contributions of Marilynn Brewer, Sam Gaertner, Russell Hardin, Dave Messick, and Dean Pruitt to the development of these ideas.

attention to trust. The topic of trust, it seems, has fallen largely between the cracks of these important literatures.

This lack of attention to the role of trust in intergroup negotiation strikes us as unfortunate for at least two reasons. First, the benefits of trust are not easy to come by. Even a cursory survey of research on intergroup negotiation is sufficient to illustrate how difficult it is to create and sustain mutual trust. Second, there has been an enormous resurgence of interest in the study of trust in the social sciences (see Barber, 1983; Fukuyama, 1995; Hardin, 1992; Kramer, 1999 for recent reviews). As a consequence, we possess today a much deeper understanding of both the origins of trust and the myriad and often subtle benefits trust confers.

Despite these substantial conceptual strides, the intergroup negotiation literature has yet to engage this important and emerging body of research. A primary aim of our chapter, accordingly, is to review and assess the literature on trust as it pertains to intergroup negotiation. Our chapter focuses on several fundamental questions regarding the relationship between trust and negotiation in intergroup contexts. First, how should trust be conceptualized in the context of intergroup negotiation? Second, what are the benefits that have been ascribed to trust? Third, what are the barriers to the development of trust? Finally, how is trust created, especially in situations where a climate of distrust and suspicion already prevails? The latter question leads us to consider the important role of third parties in intergroup negotiation.

Conceptualizing Trust and Negotiation in Intergroup Contexts

Carnevale and Pruitt (in press) described negotiation as a process involving "discussion between two or more parties with the apparent aim of resolving a divergence of interest and thus escaping social conflict" (p. 2). When applied to intergroup contexts, negotiation can be defined more narrowly in terms of the distinctive character of the relationship between the negotiating parties. In his classic analysis of intergroup relations, Sherif (1966) proposed that "whenever individuals belonging to one group interact, collectively or individually, with another group or its members in terms of their group identification, we have an instance of intergroup behavior" (p. 12). Integrating these two definitions, we propose that when two or more individuals negotiate with each other as representatives of groups, and in terms of their group identification, we have an instance of intergroup negotiation.

This simple definition conceals many layers of complexity. Intergroup negotiation assumes many forms, ranging from the relatively simple situation where two individuals negotiate on behalf of their respective groups, to more complex negotiation involving multiple, large negotiating teams whose members have diverse expertise (Kramer, 1991). Moreover, the broader social, organizational, and institutional contexts within which such negotiations are embedded can exert a profound influence on the dynamics of a bargaining process (Allison, 1971; Barley, 1991).

Providing a crisp and compelling characterization of trust in intergroup negotiation presents some difficulties. Although social scientists have afforded considerable attention to the problem of defining trust (e.g., Barber, 1983; Hardin, 1992; Lewis & Weigert, 1985), a concise and universally accepted definition has remained elusive. As a consequence, the term *trust* is used in a variety of distinct, and not always compatible, ways within the social sciences.

At one extreme are formulations that highlight the explicit beliefs and tacit understandings that comprise trust in social systems (Barber, 1983; Lewis & Weigert, 1985). For example, Barber (1983) characterized trust as the set of "socially learned and socially confirmed expectations that people have of each other, of the organizations and institutions in which they live, and of the natural and moral social orders that set the fundamental understandings for their lives" (pp. 164–165). At the other end of the spectrum are conceptions that emphasize the strategic or calculative dimensions of trust. For example, Pruitt and Rubin (1986) defined trust as simply the belief that another is positively concerned about our interests. This concern need not be a result of genuine positive feeling, but might stem from the belief that the other is dependent on us or has sufficient incentives to perform in a trustworthy fashion. Along similar lines, Burt and Knez (1996) posited that trust can be defined as simply "anticipated cooperation" (p. 70), arguing that the "issue isn't moral . . . It is office politics" (p. 70).

Researchers have also differed in terms of whether they portray trust primarily as an individual cognition, or as an aspect of the relationship between two or more interdependent parties. Thus, trust has been treated by some researchers primarily as a dispositional variable or personality characteristic (Rotter, 1971; Sato, 1988; Wrightsman, 1991; Yamagishi & Yamagishi, 1994). However, others have construed trust as an emergent relation between interdependent parties (Granovetter, 1985; Lewis & Weigert, 1985). Whether viewed as a dispositional property of social actors or an emergent feature of their relationship, these diverse conceptions converge with regard to the fact that, whatever else it encompasses, trust can be viewed as a psychological state or orientation of a social actor (a truster) toward other people (prospective trustees) and the situations in which they find themselves (Hardin, 1992).

When conceptualized as a psychological state or orientation, trust has been further defined in terms of several interrelated cognitive processes. First and foremost, trust entails a state of perceived vulnerability or risk that is derived from individuals' uncertainty regarding the motives, intentions, and prospective actions of others with whom they are interdependent. As Lewis and Weigert (1985) observed, trust can be characterized as the "undertaking of a risky course of action on the confident expectation that all persons involved in the action will act competently and dutifully" (p. 971).

In the context of intergroup negotiation, trust entails a variety of perceptions, including the belief that the other party is expected to cooperate, is motivated to coordinate, and is open-minded and prepared to engage in earnest and constructive problem solving (Carnevale & Pruitt, in press). Thus, when trust of this sort is present, the presumption is that one negotiating party is ready to engage in cooperative behavior if the other party manifests a like readiness. This type of trust does not refer narrowly to a perception of the other's character or enduring attitude toward oneself but only of the other's orientation in the current situation. The perception that the other has benevolent intentions either toward the negotiator or the world in general is a possible source of trust, but is not trust itself.

Extrapolating from these various distinctions, we conceptualize trust in intergroup negotiation contexts as the set of assumptions, beliefs, and expectations held by a negotiator (or negotiators) from one group regarding the likelihood that the actions of a negotiator (or negotiators) from another group will be beneficial, favorable, or at least not detrimental to one's interests.

Benefits of Trust in Intergroup Negotiation

As noted earlier, numerous studies suggest that trust facilitates the achievement of integrative, mutually beneficial outcomes (Butler, 1985; Larson, 1997). Negotiation scholars have long been cognizant of the fact that integrative *potential* is inherent in many conflict situations, and have identified numerous strategies that negotiators can utilize to reach integrative solutions (Pruitt, 1981). Trust is often important in these strategies. For example, in the strategy of compensation, which can be employed when one party suffers as a result of the other party's demands or actions, the party which suffers is indemnified for its loss by the other. However, the success of the strategy requires the trust that the compensation will actually be delivered.

To fully realize the integrative potential within a negotiation, it is essential that negotiators exhibit considerable cognitive and behavioral flexibility (Carnevale & Probst, 1998). Among other things, they often must be willing to seek useful information about the other party's interests, preferences, and concerns (Thompson, 1998). As well, they often must be willing to reveal information regarding their own interests, preferences, and concerns. Finding the integrative potential in a negotiation depends, therefore, on negotiators' willingness to assume personal risks themselves, as well as their effectiveness at persuading the other party to incur such risks as well.

Support for the general proposition that trust facilitates both integrative bargaining processes and outcomes comes from a variety of studies. There is evidence that trust encourages the exchange of information about negotiators' respective values and priorities (Kimmel, Pruitt, Magenau, Konar-Goldband, & Carnevale, 1980). Trust also makes it easier to reach agreements on proposed offers (Lindskold & Han, 1988). Other research has demonstrated that individuals are much more likely to engage in cooperative behavior when they trust others with whom they are interdependent to reciprocate such cooperation (Deutsch, 1986). Such expectations are related to negotiators' beliefs about the other party's motives and intentions, and also their predictions about the probable behavior of the other party.

Trust can also affect behavior during negotiation. To see how, it is helpful to recognize that negotiation is a form of social influence, in which each party attempts to shape or modify the attitudes, goals, values, feelings, beliefs, preferences, and/or behaviors of the other. The term *strategic choice* refers to the specific influence strategies and tactics that negotiators use when trying to exert such influence (Greenhalgh & Kramer, 1990; Solomon, 1960). Such influence strategies vary considerably along such dimensions as their positivity or negativity. Rothbart and Hallmark (1988), for example, drew a distinction between conciliatory and coercive bargaining strategies used in intergroup

negotiation. Conciliatory strategies entail the use of positive inducements to elicit cooperative responses from a negotiation opponent. Coercive strategies, in contrast, entail the
use of threats and deterrents and are aimed at inducing compliance from a presumably
recalcitrant opponent.

Negotiators' trust in the other party plays an important role in strategic choice because
the selection of an influence strategy will be affected by a negotiator's assumptions regarding the other party's receptiveness or responsiveness to a given influence strategy. Negotiators are likely to employ positive influence strategies, for example, when trust in the
other's responsiveness is high. In contrast, they are likely to resort to more coercive strategies if their trust is so low that they believe the other party will exploit cooperative or
conciliatory gestures (Lindskold, 1978), or when punitive capability is high (De Dreu,
Giebels, & Van de Vliert, 1998).

Other social psychological research suggests that trust can affect not only negotiators'
expectations prior to negotiation and behavior during negotiation, but also the attributions they make about a negotiation after it is complete. When trust is high, individuals
are more likely to give the other party the benefit of the doubt (cf., Brewer, 1996). In
contrast, when trust is low, they are likely to construe the same behaviors and outcomes
in very different, and more sinister terms (Brewer & Brown, 1998; Kramer, 1994, 1998).

Barriers to Trust in Intergroup Negotiation

Social psychologists have recognized that substantial difficulties attend the creation and
maintenance of trust in intergroup contexts (Lindskold, 1986; Sherif et al., 1961; Webb
& Worchel, 1986). Why is trust between group negotiators so difficult to produce and
sustain? Researchers interested in this general question have focused on a variety of factors
that impede trust development. For our purposes, these factors can be grouped in terms
of psychological processes that undermine trust and social impediments to trust.

Psychological barriers to trust in intergroup negotiation

Behavioral scientists have afforded considerable attention to identifying psychological
processes that impair negotiator performance. Some recent work on this topic has
attempted to demonstrate the existence of cognitive and decision processes, and biases,
that adversely impact integrative bargaining (e.g., Neale & Bazerman, 1991; Thompson,
1998). In terms of identifying basic cognitive processes that undermine trust development between groups, perhaps the most extensive research to date has examined the deleterious effects of *social categorization* on social perception and judgment in intergroup
situations (see Brewer & Brown, 1998; Messick & Mackie, 1989 for reviews). Early
ethnographic research on ingroup bias demonstrated the existence of a robust and pervasive tendency for individuals to display favoritism toward other ingroup members (see
Brewer, 1981 and Brewer & Brown, 1998 for reviews). Individuals tend, for example, to
hold relatively positive views of their own group and its members (the ingroup) and

comparatively negative views of other groups and their members (outgroups). Subsequent laboratory research showed that even the process of "mere" categorization of individuals into arbitrary but distinct groupings resulted in systematic judgmental effects (Tajfel, 1970). Brewer and her associates (Brewer, 1979; Brewer & Silver, 1978), for example, demonstrated that categorization of a set of individuals into two distinct groups resulted in individuals viewing others outside the group boundary as less cooperative, honest, and trustworthy compared to members of their own group.

On the basis of such evidence, Messick and Mackie (1989) concluded that this phenomenon of *intergroup bias* seems well established. There is little doubt, they argue, that "the trivial or random classification of groups of people into two subgroups is sufficient to induce people in one of the subgroups to favor others in that group relative to those in the other group" (p. 59). Several recent studies provide direct support for these effects of "mere categorization" on intergroup negotiation (Polzer, 1996; Thompson, Valley, & Kramer, 1995) and for social identity-based arguments (Kramer, Pommerenke, & Newton, 1993; Probst, Carnevale, & Triandis, 1999; Robert & Carnevale, 1997).

Research by Insko, Schopler, and their associates on the *discontinuity effect* (reviewed in Insko & Schopler, 1997) points to a similar conclusion. Insko and Schopler have provided evidence regarding the existence of a negative *outgroup schema*, which, in negotiation contexts, can lead negotiators to be distrustful and suspicious of outgroup members and also to expect competitive behavior from them. According to Brewer and Brown (1998), this outgroup schema has two important components. The first is schema-based distrust which represents "the learned belief or expectation that intergroup relations are competitive and therefore the outgroup is not to be trusted and the ingroup's welfare must be protected" (p. 569). Second, this anticipated competition generates a self-fulfilling dynamic. As Brewer and Brown note, "when one believes that the other party has competitive intent, the only reasonable action is to compete oneself in order to avoid potential loss" (p. 569).

One implication is that negotiators may have diminished expectations regarding the other party's willingness to reciprocate concessions or respond in kind to unilateral trust-building initiatives. This may result in greater inhibition about initiating cooperation, and may also enhance negotiators' vigilance about failure to reciprocate. As a result, negotiators may react strongly to the hint or even mere suspicion that the other side is not reciprocating fully (Axelrod, 1984; Bendor, Kramer, & Stout, 1991).

Another manifestation of diminished expectations surrounds the negotiating parties' beliefs about the responsiveness of the other party to specific cooperative or conciliatory gestures. Rothbart and Hallmark (1988) found that one consequence of "mere" social categorization processes is that individuals tend to believe that ingroup members will be more responsive to conciliatory influence strategies, whereas outgroup members will be more responsive to coercive strategies. Such presumptions are likely to lead negotiators in intergroup contexts to opt for overly coercive strategies when trying to influence a presumably resistant opponent. Since the other side is judging this negotiator's motives and intentions by his or her actions, the result is a cycle of destructive action–reaction as each side responds in what it construes as a justified, defensive way to the threatening and provocative actions of the other side (Jervis, 1976; Kramer, 1989).

All else equal, it might seem as if these various judgmental distortions would be difficult to sustain, especially as disconfirming evidence becomes available to negotiators. A considerable body of theory and research on history-based forms of trust suggests that, when making judgments about others' trustworthiness, people act much like intuitive Bayesian statisticians who recalibrate or update their judgments on the basis of their personal experiences. From this perspective, one might expect that such misperceptions and errors should, over time, be self-correcting. Unfortunately, there are a number of psychological dynamics that may contribute to difficulties in correcting such misperceptions, especially in intergroup negotiation. These self-sustaining characteristics of distrust and suspicion arise, arguably, from both the distrustful perceiver's difficulty in learning from trust-related experiences, as well as their difficulty in generating useful (diagnostic) experiences.

One problem that the suspicious negotiator confronts is that, because of the presumption that the other party is untrustworthy and that things may not be what they seem, the perceived diagnostic value of any particular bit of evidence regarding the other's putative trustworthiness is, from the outset, tainted. As Weick (1979) noted in this regard, all diagnostic cues are inherently corruptible. He cites an interesting historical example to illustrate this problem. The day before the Japanese attack on Pearl Harbor, an American naval attaché had informed Washington that he did not believe a surprise attack by the Japanese was imminent because the fleet was still stationed at its home base. As evidence for this conclusion, he noted that large crowds of sailors could be observed casually walking the streets of Tokyo. What the attaché did not know was that these "sailors" were in actuality Japanese soldiers disguised as sailors to conceal the fact that the Japanese fleet had already sailed. From the perspective of the Japanese, this ruse was a brilliant example of what military intelligence experts call *strategic disinformation*. Such strategic misrepresentations can be used in negotiation and other conflict situations to mislead an adversary about one's capabilities or intentions (Kramer, Meyerson, & Davis, 1990).

In elaborating on the implications of this incident, Weick noted that the very fact that the attaché had searched for a fool-proof cue made him, ironically, more vulnerable to exploitation. Quoting a passage from Goffman (1969), Weick reasoned that

> the very fact that the observer finds himself looking to a particular bit of evidence as an incorruptible check on what is or might be corruptible, is the very reason he should be suspicious of this evidence; for the best evidence for him is also the best evidence for the subject to tamper with . . . when the situation seems to be exactly what it appears to be, the closest likely alternative is that the situation has been completely faked. (pp. 172–173)

For the already suspicious or distrustful negotiator, of course, the attaché's experience dramatically illustrates what happens when one is too relaxed about others' presumed trustworthiness.

In a climate in which trust is already low, even the *nonexistence* of diagnostic evidence can be construed as a compelling source of "data" that the other side should not be trusted. Dawes (1988) provides a nice illustration of this possibility in his discussion of the debate over internment of Japanese Americans at the beginning of World War II. When then California governor Earl Warren testified before a Congressional hearing regarding this policy, one of his interrogators noted that absolutely no evidence of espionage or sabotage on the part of any Japanese Americans had been presented or was available to the committee. Warren's response about how to construe this fact is revealing:

> I take the view that this lack [of evidence] is the *most ominous sign* in our whole situation. It convinces me more than perhaps any other factor that the sabotage we are to get, the Fifth Column activities we are to get, are timed just like Pearl Harbor was timed . . . *I believe we are just being lulled into a false sense of security.* (p. 251, emphases added)

Other research suggests additional cognitive barriers to trust that may plague intergroup negotiators. Slovic (1993) has noted, for example, that it is easier to destroy trust than create it. To explain this fragility of trust, he suggested that a variety of cognitive factors contribute to asymmetries in the trust-building versus trust-destroying process. First, he proposed that negative (trust-destroying) events are more visible and noticeable than positive (trust-building) events. Second, he proposed that trust-destroying events carry more weight in judgment than trust-building events of comparable magnitude. To provide evidence for this general *asymmetry principle*, Slovic evaluated the impact of hypothetical news events on people's trust judgments. In support of his general thesis, he found that negative events had more impact on trust judgments than positive events. Slovic noted further that asymmetries between trust and distrust may be reinforced by the fact that sources of bad (trust-destroying) news tend to be perceived as more credible than sources of good news. In the context of intergroup negotiation, and especially those in which a climate of distrust or suspicion already exists, good news (evidence of the other side's trustworthiness) is likely to be discounted, whereas bad news (confirmatory evidence that distrust is warranted) augments distrust (Rothbart & John, 1985).

In addition to impairing negotiators' ability to learn directly from their experience, situations that induce distrust may also impede their ability to generate the kind of diagnostic information needed to accurately calibrate the other party's trustworthiness. Learning about trustworthiness entails risk-taking (Hardin, 1992; Pruitt, 1981). People must engage in appropriate interpersonal "experiments" if they are to generate the diagnostic data necessary to learn who among them can be trusted and how much. Such experiments require that individuals expose themselves to the prospect of misplaced trust and misplaced distrust. Any systematic bias in the generation of data samples can, of course, influence the inferences that result from these experiments. Along these lines, trust theorists such as Hardin (1992) and Gambetta (1988) have argued that asymmetries in the presumptive trust of individuals who begin with low or high trust levels may differentially impact the frequency with which they generate useful learning opportunities. These asymmetries can also affect their ability to extract reliable cues from those opportunities that they do generate. As Gambetta (1988) noted in this regard, distrust is very difficult to invalidate through experience, because it either "prevents people from engaging in the appropriate kind of social experiment, or, worse, it leads to behavior which bolsters the validity of distrust itself" (p. 234). Similar to the differential difficulties that competitors and cooperators have when trying to learn about others' cooperativeness and competitiveness (Kelley & Stahelski, 1970), those who expect distrust tend to engender distrust. Consequently, presumptive distrust tends to become perpetual distrust.

Because of their heightened suspicion of the other party's motives and intentions, distrustful negotiators approach negotiation situations with an orientation of presumptive distrust. An instructive parallel can be drawn from research on the dynamics of hostile attribution among aggressive children (see Dodge, 1985). Such children approach social interactions prepared for the worst. They are, in a sense, almost "pre-offended." They thus elicit, through their own anticipation-driven behaviors the very outcomes they most dread. Much like the stance of these overly aggressive boys, who are perceptually vigilant when it comes to detecting hostility, so the presumptively distrustful negotiator is prepared for distrust (Kramer, 1998).

Social barriers to trust in intergroup negotiation

In addition to these psychological factors, there are a number of social dynamics that can contribute to asymmetries in judgments regarding trust and distrust in intergroup negotiation. For example, several intragroup dynamics may impede trust development. Insko and his associates investigated the effects of ingroup discussion on trust-related judgments (Insko, Schopler, Hoyle, Dardis, & Graetz, 1990). They had judges code tape-recorded discussions for both explicit and implicit statements of distrust. The results showed that there were significantly more distrust statements in discussions between groups compared to discussions between individuals. There was also a strong negative correlation between the level of distrust recorded in these conversations and subsequent cooperative behavior.

Third parties involved in intergroup negotiation may further exacerbate such tendencies. In the same study described earlier, Burt and Knez (1995) examined how social network structures, and the social dynamics they create, affect the diffusion of distrust information and its effects of trust judgments within the managers' networks. They found that, although both trust and distrust were amplified by third-party disclosures, distrust was amplified to a greater extent than trust. As a result, judgments about distrust had, as Burt and Knez put it, a "catastrophic" quality to them. In explaining these findings, Burt and Knez posited that third parties are more attentive to negative information and often prefer negative gossip to positive information and gossip. Consequently, indirect connections amplify the distrust associated with weak relations much more than they amplify trust among strong relations.

Another potential social barrier to generating trust-building experiences derives from various self-presentational predicaments that negotiators, as representatives for their groups, face. As Kressel (1981) noted, "negotiators may be pressured by their constituents into presenting the constituents' demands vehemently and without backing down, while their opposite numbers across the bargaining table may expect these same negotiators to adhere to norms of moderation and compromise" (p. 227). Thus, when individuals feel accountable to others, they are more likely to be concerned not only about the objective outcomes they obtain, but also about how those outcomes are perceived and evaluated by those to whom they feel accountable (Carnevale, 1985). Negotiators are accountable to constituents to the extent that their constituents are perceived to have power over them. If the other party is viewed as being accountable to a tough constituency, the other is unlikely to be trusted. Kimmel et al. (1980) found that trust and information exchange were both lower when negotiators did not know what instructions the other had received than when they knew that the other had received problem-solving instructions.

Research on the effects of perceived accountability on negotiator judgment and decision shows that such self-presentational concerns exert an important influence on negotiator judgment and behavior. Carnevale, Pruitt, and Seilheimer (1981) reported that accountability to constituents engenders a competitive atmosphere in between-group negotiation, which then diminishes the use of explicit information exchange and increases the likelihood of poor agreements. Interestingly, under high accountability, negotiators who did well tended to rely on indirect information exchange, such as the use of heuristic trial and error tactics (e.g., making and then remaking offers within a close range of value).

The interactive or dynamic complexity between trust and constituent accountability is further illustrated by Adams (1976). Adams noted that representatives who are trusted by constituents are frequently given considerable autonomy by their constituents, and thus are freer to develop good relations with outsiders with whom they must negotiate. However, if those same constituents observe their representative cooperating with the other side, they may become suspicious and concerned that their interests are not being vigorously defended or represented. Accordingly, they will engage in greater monitoring of their negotiator's behavior. This may be seen by the representative as a signal to stop cooperating with outsiders. In more complex intergroup negotiation situations, where negotiators are representing multiple constituencies with diverse concerns, these self-presentational predicaments become even more difficult to navigate (see Ginzel, Kramer, & Sutton, 1991).

Untying the Knot: Creating and Sustaining Trust in Intergroup Negotiation

The numerous psychological and social barriers to trust identified in the previous section, especially when viewed as operating in concert, might seem to militate against the prospects of trust ever gaining a toehold, let alone flourishing, in intergroup negotiation. To be sure, the problem of creating and sustaining trust, especially against the backdrop of a history of mutual enmity or wariness, has proven daunting both in practice and theory. The difficulty, as experienced by negotiators themselves, was nicely captured in a personal communiqué sent by Soviet Premier Nikita Khruschev to President John F. Kennedy at the height of tensions during the Cuban Missile Crisis. Khruschev cautioned Kennedy that the escalating conflict between their countries could be likened to a rope with a knot in the middle of it, ". . . the harder you and I pull, the tighter this knot [of war] will become," he suggested. "And a time may come when this knot is tied so tight that the person who tied it is no longer capable of untying it" (cited in Kennedy, 1969, p. 81).

Although formidable, there is evidence that the barriers to trust are not insurmountable. Accordingly, we turn now to a discussion of the literature that addresses the question of how trust can be created and the knot of distrust, if not untied completely, can at least be loosened. We organize our discussion of these approaches in terms of 1) unilateral initiatives that can be undertaken by the negotiating parties themselves, 2) interventions involving third parties, and 3) structural approaches to building trust.

Unilateral negotiator initiatives

Negotiators attempt to influence each other's perceptions and behaviors. This can include efforts to create a climate of mutual trust both by trying to elicit cooperative behavior from the other party, and by attempting to communicate their own trustworthiness and willingness to cooperate. Much of the literature on this trust-building process has been motivated by recognition of the circular relation between trust and cooperation (Deutsch, 1973): Trust tends to beget cooperation, and cooperation breeds further trust. Therefore, if a cycle of mutual cooperation can be initiated and sustained, trust will develop (Lindskold, 1978). This trust, in turn, will spur further cooperative acts.

Perhaps the simplest and most direct way to initiate such constructive change in the relationship between two wary negotiating groups is for one of the negotiators to make a gesture which interrupts the status quo. Such an effort is direct in that it immediately alters the pattern of interaction and simple in that it requires no third-party interventions or elaborate structural changes. Early studies pursuing this idea examined the use of unconditional pacifism to elicit cooperative responses. The experimental evidence regarding the efficacy of this strategy was discouraging. At least in the context of laboratory settings, unvarying or unconditional cooperation is puzzling to recipients and the tendency is to exploit it (Deutsch, 1986; Shure, Meeker, & Hansford, 1965; Solomon, 1960).

Although strategies of unconditional cooperation yield disappointing results, initiatives that involve contingent cooperation have proven more effective in eliciting and sustaining cooperative behavior. Early studies on this issue involved simple mixed-motives games in which a confederate made an initial cooperative move, inviting a reciprocal act of cooperation (Deutsch, 1973). Subsequent studies in this vein identify specific patterns of reciprocation that are efficacious in such situations. Osgood's (1962) strategy of graduated reciprocation in tension reduction (GRIT) was an early model of such patterns. Osgood's core insight was that a sequence of carefully calibrated and clear signals might initiate a sustainable process of mutual trust and cooperation. One of the appeals of this strategy, and perhaps one reason it attracted so much attention, was that it seemed to offer a mechanism for reducing distrust and suspicion between the nuclear superpowers. Thus, Etzioni (1967) used the GRIT framework to interpret the series of progressively conciliatory exchanges between President Kennedy and Premier Khruschev in the early 1960s.

Drawing on this theory, Lindskold and others undertook a sustained program of laboratory-based research on the dynamics of trust development (see Lindskold, 1978, 1986 for reviews). Several practical recommendations have emerged from this work. First, it is useful for negotiators to announce what they are doing ahead of time, and to carry out the initiatives as announced. In addition, it has been suggested that conciliatory initiatives should be irrevocable and noncontingent, so that they will be understood as efforts to resolve the conflict rather than to gain a quid pro quo. Also, they should be costly or risky to oneself, so that they cannot be construed as a cheap trick or trap. They should be continued for a period of time so as to put pressure on the other party to reciprocate and to give the other party time to rethink its policy. Two other pieces of advice are added by the current authors: Unilateral initiatives should be noticeable and unexpected so that they will provoke thought. Their users should try to demonstrate a good and lasting reason for wanting to change the relationship; otherwise such initiatives may be viewed as a flash in the pan.

The GRIT strategy proceeds from a logic of starting small in order to "jump start" a trust-building process. An alternative strategy, and one which reverses the logic a bit, involves an attempt by one party to "break the frame" of distrust and suspicion by making a large, dramatic conciliatory gesture. Because it entails such obvious and severe political costs to the negotiator making the initiative, its significance is hard to discount or ignore. An example is Egyptian President Anwar Sadat's trip to Jerusalem in 1978, which paved the way for peace between Egypt and Israel. Sadat stated the purpose of the trip was to improve Israeli trust in Egypt. Kelman (1985) has reported that most Israelis viewed this event as a genuine effort to improve relations. This strategy is not, however, unconditionally effective and may produce other than intended effects. Such initiatives risk alienating important constituents and may undermine a negotiator's credibility and effectiveness with constituents. And, as Sadat's experience demonstrated, sometimes this estrangement may even have fatal consequences.

Other studies indicate that cooperation leads to improved interpersonal and intergroup relations. In early studies on this topic, Sherif and his associates (Sherif et al., 1961) first produced animosity between two groups of boys in a summer camp by having them compete with and exploit each other. They were then able to dispel this animosity in a second phase by having them cooperate on "superordinate goals." Additional research suggests that even the anticipation of cooperation can also lead to improved interpersonal and intergroup relations (Ben-Yoav & Pruitt, 1984). There are many possible explanations for the positive trust-building effects of cooperation on relationships. Cooperation may lead to reward at the hands of the other party. It may provide favorable information about the other party that would not otherwise be available. It may enhance perceived similarity and break down the conceptual boundary between groups (Gaertner, Mann, Murrell, & Dovidio, 1989; see Brewer & Gaertner, this volume, chapter 22). Helping the other party may induce positive attitudes, another dissonance-resolving effect.

Such findings suggest that another route negotiators can employ to build trust through their own actions is via relationship-building activities. Most experienced, professional negotiators recognize that it is often useful to attempt to build a positive personal bond with another party, even if doing so entails some scrutiny by constituents (Friedman, 1994). This approach builds on recognition of the fact that trust is a central characteristic of mature and secure relationships, where people are likely to exhibit a combination of problem solving and concession making, which can lead to mutually beneficial, win–win agreements.

Carnevale and Pruitt (in press) have termed these sorts of relationships "working relationships." Working relationships are often found between people with emotional ties, such as friends, relatives, or married couples. Working relationships also are common between people with instrumental ties, such as colleagues whose jobs require them to cooperate, and negotiators in counterpart relationships. An example of the latter would be a salesperson and a regular client. Working relationships involve three related norms for dealing with mixed-motive settings: (a) A norm of *problem solving*, which specifies that if both parties feel strongly about an issue, they should try to find a way for both of them to succeed. (b) A norm of *mutual responsiveness*, which specifies that if only one party feels strongly about an issue or if problem solving fails, the party who feels less strongly should concede to the other's wishes. (c) A norm of *truth in signaling*, which specifies that the parties should be honest about the strength of their feelings. Truth in signaling is a necessary adjunct to the norm of mutual responsiveness, preventing people from exaggerating the strength of their needs. In the absence of this norm, neither party will trust the other's statements about issue importance, and the norm of mutual responsiveness will collapse. Weingart, Bennett, and Brett (1993) found evidence of the latter two norms in a study of multilateral four-party negotiation groups.

Third-party interventions and trust in intergroup negotiation

It has long been appreciated that third parties can play a significant role in the process of both creating and repairing damaged trust in intergroup negotiation (Carnevale & Arad, 1996; Kressel & Pruitt, 1989). Mediators inject cooperative norms, routines, and procedures into a negotiation. The effects of such interventions can be direct in terms of leading to better exchange of information and consideration of more integrative offers, but also modeling skills that the negotiators may then use themselves. Third parties often take even more active roles in trying to influence the negotiation processes between groups. In a study of labor mediators, Carnevale and Pegnetter (1985) found that trust in the mediator was one of the best predictors of whether or not agreement was achieved.

In a study investigating the efficacy of different third-party interventions, Keashly, Fisher, and Grant (1993) proposed that such interventions can be distinguished by their fundamental assumptions regarding the sources and dynamics of intergroup conflict. Specifically, they argued, third-party interventions involving *mediation* attempt to resolve conflict by focusing on creatively addressing the substantive issues in a conflict. Third-party *consultation*, in contrast, focuses on altering the relationship between the parties, including their attitudes and perceptions (misperceptions). Using an exercise called the intergroup conflict simulation, they demonstrated that both mediation and consultation produced comparable success with respect to resolution of the simulated dispute (a land settlement). However, consultation resulted in groups expressing more positive attitudes toward each other and also perceived the intergroup relationship itself as more collaborative. With respect to trust-building, therefore, it may be the case that consultation can enhance perceptions of the outgroup that contribute to higher perceptions of trustworthiness, including credibility, reliability, benevolence of motives, etc.

Structural approaches to creating and sustaining trust between groups

There is a large body of theory and research, mostly sociological, on institutional approaches to creating and sustaining trust (Zucker, 1986). The Standing Consultative

Commission (SCC) provides one illustration as to how institutional structures can be used to potentially improve and stabilize trust in complex, recurring, high-stakes negotiation, and especially when the parties are highly distrustful of each other (see Kahn, 1991 for history and overview).

The SCC was a product of the Strategic Arms Limitation Talks between the United States and Soviet Union begun in 1969. Thus, its creation was a direct result of a specific negotiation (the ABM treaty of 1972), but its aim was more general – the commission was to contribute to the continued viability and effectiveness of negotiated agreements by resolving questions of interpretation and concerns about compliance if and as they arose. It thus created an institutional mechanism for allowing the parties to reach an initial agreement, even though many details had not been worked out to the parties' respective satisfaction.

In discussing the utility of such a mechanism, Kahn (1991) noted that an important function of such an institution is that it enables the ongoing "interpretation and fleshing out of an agreement that is appropriately general rather than specific in many respects" (p. 161). In a related way, it builds flexibility into the "application of the agreement to new political and technological developments" (p. 161). In this respect, such structures enable the more open-ended, relational agreements exemplified by Japanese negotiations.

Another way of thinking about structural mechanisms for solving dilemmas of trust focuses on the efficacy of incentive systems at inducing trust and cooperation (Yamagishi, 1986). In these cases, an outside agency (e.g., a government) is implemented that either reinforces cooperation (by providing a bonus to those who are most cooperative), or punishes noncooperation (by imposing a penalty on those who are least cooperative). There is evidence that reward systems are more effective in inducing cooperation than penalty systems, which are more effective than no system (McCusker & Carnevale, 1995).

Reducing reliance on trust

Even when the necessary and sufficient conditions for trust do not exist, negotiators may be able to make some progress by simply reducing their dependence on trust. Noting that it is hard for people to cooperate in the absence of trust, Carnevale and Pruitt (in press) have argued that, when there is a desire or necessity to engage in negotiation, but trust between the parties is low, it may be possible to reduce reliance on trust by making decisions reversible. Hence an escape from any particular commitment is possible should the other party prove untrustworthy.

In support of this logic, Deutsch (1973) found higher levels of cooperation in a Prisoner's Dilemma when both parties were free to reverse their decisions again and again until mutually satisfactory outcomes were obtained. In the context of intergroup negotiation, such reversibility might be manifested as a rule, either explicitly stated or tacitly assumed, that no agreements are final until all points of contention have been mutually agreed upon by all parties. This rule makes it possible to concede on some issues without full assurance that the adversary will concede on all of the others that await resolution. Importantly, invocation of the rule by one party or the other will not be attributed to bad faith. In other words, backing out of a previous agreement or asking that an issue be revisited will not be viewed as defection, but a legitimate part of the process.

Another strategy for reducing dependence on trust is to *fractionate* a conflict by decomposing a complex multi-issue negotiation into many small issues, so that the risk associated with reaching agreement on any one issue is relatively low (Fisher, 1964). A negotiator can usually make a tiny cooperative move even if trust is low, and then wait to see if the other reciprocates before taking the next tiny move. Two negotiators can sometimes move toward settlement using this strategy by each making small concessions that are reciprocated by the other until they arrive at a common position. Much like GRIT, this strategy greatly reduces the perceived risk of misplaced trust. It has the additional benefit, like piecemeal reciprocity, that the parties learn that reaching agreement is possible (i.e., that it is possible to trust the other along at least some dimensions or with respect to some set of issues). Success on these early and comparatively easy issues may then build momentum and increase confidence on subsequent and more thorny issues, leading over time to greater trust between the negotiators.

Conclusions

A primary aim of our chapter was to review and assess recent theory and empirical research on the role of trust in intergroup negotiation. We suspect that the research optimist, encountering this growing literature for the first time, might easily see the glass as half full. Negotiation researchers and intergroup relations theorists interested in trust can draw on a much broader set of ideas regarding the origins and bases of trust than were available even a few years ago. And on the methodological front, recent experiments are employing more complex and realistic simulations of intergroup negotiation processes than early work in this area. Whereas past studies often used relatively simple binary-choice mixed-motive games as proxies for negotiation situations, more recent studies attempt to capture the flavor and complexity of real-world negotiation. Thus, substantial progress can be charted on both conceptual and methodological fronts. Taken together, this work points to the conclusion that trust is an important piece of the puzzle for understanding and improving intergroup relationships.

Although acknowledging these gains, the research pessimist is likely to perceive the glass only as half empty. Clearly, more can and needs to be done in terms of developing a comprehensive and integrative theory regarding the role of trust in intergroup negotiation. A concerted effort to develop a more interdisciplinary conception of trust in intergroup negotiation will push the boundaries of current social psychological theory and research in a fruitful direction. Such a conception would encompass not only the sort of psychological and social factors that social psychologists traditionally are enamored by, but also trace the impact of sociological and political considerations.

References

Adams, J. S. (1976). The structure and dynamics of behavior in organizational boundary roles. In M. D. Dunnette (Ed.), *Handbook of industrial and organizational psychology.* Chicago, IL: Rand McNally.

Allison, G. T. (1971). *The essence of decision: Explaining the Cuban Missile Crisis.* Boston, MA: Little, Brown.

Axelrod, R. (1984). *The evolution of cooperation.* New York: Basic Books.

Barber, B. (1983). *The logic and limits of trust.* New Brunswick, NJ: Rutgers University Press.

Barley, S. R. (1991). Contextualizing conflict: Notes on the anthropology of disputes and negotiations. In M. H. Bazerman, R. J. Lewicki, & B. H. Sheppard (Eds.), *Research on negotiation in organizations* (Vol. 3). Greenwich, CT: JAI Press.

Bendor, J., Kramer, R. M., & Stout, S. (1991). When in doubt: Cooperation in the noisy Prisoner's Dilemma. *Journal of Conflict Resolution, 35*, 691–719.

Ben-Yoav, O., & Pruitt, D. G. (1984). Resistance to yielding and the expectation of cooperative future interaction in negotiation. *Journal of Experimental Social Psychology, 34*, 323–335.

Blake, R. R., & Mouton, J. S. (1986). From theory to practice in interface problem solving. In S. Worchel & W. G. Austin (Eds.), *Psychology of intergroup relations* (pp. 67–82). Chicago, IL: Nelson-Hall.

Brewer, M. B. (1979). Ingroup bias in the minimal intergroup situatuion: A cognitive motivational analysis. *Psychological Bulletin, 86*, 307–324.

Brewer, M. B. (1981). Ethnocentrism and its role in interpersonal trust. In M. B. Brewer & B. Collins (Eds.), *Scientific inquiry in the social sciences* (pp. 345–359). San Francisco, CA: Jossey-Bass.

Brewer, M. B. (1996). Ingroup favoritism: The subtle side of intergroup discrimination. In D. M. Messick & A. Tenbrunsel (Eds.), *Codes of conduct* (pp. 160–171). New York: Russell Sage Foundation.

Brewer, M. B., & Brown, R. J. (1998). Intergroup relations. In D. Gilbert, S. Fiske, & G. Lindzey (Eds.), *Handbook of social psychology* (Vol. 2, pp. 554–594). Boston, MA: McGraw-Hill.

Brewer, M. B., & Silver, M. (1978). Ingroup bias as a function of task characteristics. *European Journal of Social Psychology, 8*, 393–400.

Burt, R., & Knez, M. (1995). Kinds of third-party effects on trust. *Journal of Rationality and Society, 7*, 255–292.

Butler, J. K. (1995). Behaviors, trust, and goal achievement in a win–win negotiating role play. *Group and Organization Management, 20*, 486–501.

Carnevale, P. J. (1985). Accountability of group representatives and intergroup relations. In E. J. Lawler (Ed.), *Advances in group processes: Theory and research* (Vol. 2). Greenwich, CT: JAI Press.

Carnevale, P. J., & Arad, S. (1996). Bias and impartiality in international mediation. In J. Bercovitch (Ed.), *Resolving international conflicts: The theory and practice of mediation* (pp. 39–53). Boulder, CO: Lynne Rienner.

Carnevale, P. J., & Pegnetter, R. (1985). The selection of mediation tactics in public-sector disputes: A contingency analysis. *Journal of Social Issues, 41*, 65–81.

Carnevale, P. J., & Probst, T. (1998). Social values and social conflict in creative problem solving and categorization. *Journal of Personality and Social Psychology, 74*, 1300–1309.

Carnevale, P. J., & Pruitt, D. G. (1992). Negotiation and mediation. *Annual Review of Psychology, 43*, 531–582.

Carnevale, P. J., & Pruitt, D. G. (in press). *Negotiation in social conflict* (2nd ed.). Buckingham, UK: Open University Press.

Carnevale, P. J., Pruitt, D. G., & Seilheimer, S. (1981). Looking and competing: Accountability and visual access in integrative bargaining. *Journal of Personality and Social Psychology, 40*, 111–120.

Davis, G. F., Kahn, R. L., & Zald, M. N. (1990). Contracts, treaties, and joint ventures. In R. L. Kahn & M. N. Zald (Eds.), *Organizations and nation-states: New perspectives on conflict and cooperation* (pp. 55–98). San Francisco, CA: Jossey-Bass.

Dawes, R. (1988). *Rational choice in an uncertain world.* New York: Harcourt Brace.

De Dreu, C. K. W., Giebels, E., & Van de Vliert, E. (1998). Social motives and trust in integrative negotiation: The disruptive effects of punitive capability. *Journal of Applied Psychology, 83,* 408–422.

Deutsch, M. (1973). *The resolution of conflict.* New Haven, CT: Yale University Press.

Deutsch, M. (1986). Strategies of inducing cooperation. In R. K. White (Ed.), *Psychology and the prevention of nuclear war.* New York: New York University Press.

Dodge, K. (1985). Attributional bias in aggressive children. In P. Kendall (Ed.), *Advances in cognitive-behavioral research and therapy* (Vol. 4, pp. 131–160). New York, Academic Press.

Etzioni, A. (1967). The Kennedy experiment: Unilateral initiatives. *Western Political Quarterly, 20,* 12–23.

Fisher, R. (1964). Fractionating conflict. In R. Fisher (Ed.), *International conflict and behavioral science: The Craigville Papers.* New York: Basic Books.

Friedman, R. A. (1994). *Frontstage, backstage: The dramatic structure of labor negotiations.* Cambridge, MA: MIT Press.

Fukuyama, F. (1995). *Trust: The social virtues and the creation of prosperity.* New York: Free Press.

Gaertner, S. L., Mann, J., Murrell, A., & Dovidio, J. F. (1989). Reducing intergroup bias: The benefits of recategorization. *Journal of Personality and Social Psychology, 57,* 239–249.

Gambetta, D. (1988). Can we trust trust? In D. Gambetta (Ed.), *Trust: making and breaking cooperative relationships.* Oxford, UK: Blackwell.

Ginzel, L., Kramer, R. M., & Sutton, R. (1991). Organizational impression management as a reciprocal influence process: The neglected role of the organizational audience. In B. M. Staw & L. L. Cummings (Eds.), *Research in organizational behavior* (Vol. 15, pp. 227–266). Greenwich, CT: JAI Press.

Goffman, E. (1969). *Strategic interaction.* Philadelphia, PA: University of Pennsylvania Press.

Granovetter, M. (1985). Economic action and social structure: The problem of embeddedness. *American Journal of Sociology, 91,* 481–510.

Greenhalgh, L., & Kramer, R. M. (1990). Strategic choice in conflicts: The importance of relationships. In R. L. Kahn & M. N. Zald (Eds.), *Organizations and nation states: New perspectives on conflict and cooperation* (pp. 181–220). San Francisco, CA: Jossey-Bass.

Hardin, R. (1992). The street-level epistemology of trust. *Annals der Kritikal, 14,* 152–176.

Insko, C. A., & Schopler, J. (1997). Differential distrust of groups and individuals. In C. Sedikides, J. Schopler, & C. Insko (Eds.), *Intergroup cognition and intergroup behavior* (pp. 75–108). Mahwah, NJ: Erlbaum.

Insko, C. A., Schopler, J., Hoyle, R., Dardis, G., & Graetz, K. (1990). Individual-group discontinuity as a function of fear and greed. *Journal of Personality and Social Psychology, 58,* 68–79.

Jervis, R. (1976). *Perception and misperception in international politics.* Princeton, NJ: Princeton University Press.

Kahn, R. L. (1991). Organizational theory. In PIN (Processes of International Negotiations) Project (Ed.), *International negotiation: Analysis, approaches, and issues* (pp. 148–163). San Francisco, CA: Jossey-Bass.

Kahn, R. L., & Zald, M. N. (1990). *Organizations and nation states: New perspectives on conflict and cooperation.* San Francisco, CA: Jossey-Bass.

Keashly, L., Fisher, R. J., & Grant, P. R. (1993). The comparative utility of third-party consultation and mediation within a complex simulation of intergroup conflict. *Human Relations, 46,* 371–393.

Kelley, H. H., & Stahelski, A. J. (1970). Social interaction basis of cooperators' and competitors' beliefs about others. *Journal of Personality and Social Psychology, 16,* 190–197.

Kelman, H. C. (1985). Overcoming the psychological barrier: An analysis of the Egyptian–Israeli peace process. *Negotiation Journal, 1*, 213–235.

Kennedy, R. F. (1969). *Thirteen days: A memoir of the Cuban Missile Crisis.* New York: Norton.

Kimmel, M., Pruitt, D. G., Magenau, J., Konar-Goldband, E., & Carnevale, P. G. (1980). The effects of trust, aspiration, and gender on negotiation tactics. *Journal of Personality and Social Psychology, 38*, 9–23.

Kramer, R. M. (1989). Windows of vulnerability or cognitive illusions? Cognitive processes and the nuclear arms race. *Journal of Experimental Social Psychology, 25*, 79–100.

Kramer, R. M. (1991). The more the merrier? Social psychological aspects of multi-party negotiations in organizations. In M. B. Bazerman, R. J. Lewicki, & B. H. Sheppard (Eds.), *Research on negotiation in organizations* (Vol. 3, pp. 307–332). Greenwich, CT: JAI Press.

Kramer, R. M. (1994). The sinister attribution error: Paranoid cognition and collective distrust in organizations. *Motivation and Emotion, 18*, 199–230.

Kramer, R. M. (1998). Paranoid cognition in social systems: Thinking and acting in the shadow of doubt. *Personality and Social Psychology Review, 2*, 251–275.

Kramer, R. M. (1999). Trust and distrust in organizations: Emerging perspectives, enduring questions. *Annual Review of Psychology, 50*, 569–598.

Kramer, R. M., Meyerson, D., & Davis, G. (1991). How much is enough? *Journal of Personality and Social Psychology, 58*, 984–993.

Kramer, R. M., Pommerenke, P., & Newton, E. (1993). The social context of negotiation: Effects of social identity and interpersonal accountability on negotiator decision making. *Journal of Conflict Resolution, 37*, 633–654.

Kressel, K. (1981). Kissinger in the Middle East: An exploratory analysis of role strain in international mediation. In J. Z. Rubin (Ed.), *Dynamics of third-party intervention: Kissinger in the Middle East.* New York: Praeger.

Kressel, K., & Pruitt, D. G. (Eds.) (1989). *Mediation research: The process and effectiveness of third-party intervention.* San Francisco, CA: Jossey-Bass.

Larson, D. W. (1997). *Anatomy of mistrust: U.S.–Soviet relations during the Cold War.* Ithaca, NY: Cornell University Press.

Lewicki, R., & Bunker, B. (1995). Trust in relationships: A model of trust development and decline. In B. B. Bunker & J. Z. Rubin (Eds.), *Conflict, cooperation, and justice* (pp. 131–145). San Francisco, CA: Jossey-Bass.

Lewis, J. D., & Weigert, A. (1985). Trust as a social reality. *Social Forces, 63*, 967–985.

Lindskold, S. (1978). Trust development, the GRIT proposal, and the effects of conciliatory acts on conflict and cooperation. *Psychological Bulletin, 85*, 772–793.

Lindskold, S. (1986). GRIT: Reducing distrust through carefully introduced conciliation. In S. Worchel & W. G. Austin (Eds.), *Psychology of intergroup relations* (pp. 305–322). Chicago, IL: Nelson-Hall.

Lindskold, S., & Han, G. (1988). GRIT as a foundation for integrative bargaining. *Personality and Social Psychology Bulletin, 14*, 335–345.

McCusker, C., & Carnevale, P. J. (1995). Framing in resource dilemmas: Loss aversion and the moderating effects of sanctions. *Organizational Behavior and Human Decision Processes, 61*, 190–201.

Messick, D. M., & Mackie, D. M. (1989). Intergroup relations. *Annual Review of Psychology, 40*, 45–81.

Neale, M. A., & Bazerman, M. H. (1991). *Cognition and rationality in negotiation.* New York: Free Press.

Osgood, C. E. (1962). *An alternative to war and surrender.* Champaign, IL: University of Illinois Press.

Polzer, J. T. (1996). Intergroup negotiations: The effects of negotiating teams. *Journal of Conflict Resolution, 40,* 678–698.

Probst, T., Carnevale, P. J., & Triandis, H. C. (1999). Cultural values in intergroup and single-group social dilemmas. *Organizational Behavior and Human Decision Processes, 77,* 171–191.

Pruitt, D. G. (1981). *Negotiation behavior.* New York: Academic Press.

Pruitt, D. G., & Kimmel, M. J. (1977). Twenty years of experimental gaming: Critique, synthesis, and suggestions for the future. *Annual Review of Psychology, 28,* 363–392.

Pruitt, D. G., & Rubin, J. Z. (1986). *Social conflict: Escalation, statement, and settlement.* New York: Random House.

Robert, C., & Carnevale, P. J. (1997). Group choice in ultimatum bargaining. *Organizational Behavior and Human Decision Processes, 72,* 256–279.

Ross, W., & Lacroix, J. (1996). Multiple meanings of trust in negotiation theory: A literature review and integrative model. *International Journal of Conflict Management, 7,* 314–360.

Rothbart, M., & Hallmark, W. (1988). Ingroup–outgroup differences in the perceived efficacy of coercion and conciliation in resolving social conflict. *Journal of Personality and Social Psychology, 55,* 248–257.

Rothbart, M., & John, O. P. (1985). Social categorization and behavioral episodes: A cognitive analysis of the effects of intergroup contact. *Journal of Social Issues, 4*(3), 81–104.

Rotter, J. B. (1971). Generalized expectancies for interpersonal trust. *American Psychologist, 26,* 443–452.

Sato, K. (1988). Trust and group size in a social dilemma. *Japanese Psychological Research, 30,* 88–93.

Sherif, M. (1966). *Group conflict and co-operation: Their social psychology.* London: Routledge & Kegan Paul.

Sherif, M., Harvey, L. J., White, B. J., Hood, W. R., & Sherif, C. W. (1961). *Intergroup cooperation and competition: The Robbers Cave experiment.* Norman, OK: University Book Exchange.

Shure, G. H., Meeker, R. J., & Hansford, E. A. (1965). The effectiveness of pacifist strategies in bargaining games. *Journal of Conflict Resolution, 9,* 106–117.

Slovic, P. (1993). Perceived risk, trust, and democracy. *Risk Analysis, 13,* 675–682.

Solomon, L. (1960). The influence of some types of power relationships and game strategies on the development of trust. *Journal of Abnormal and Social Psychology, 61,* 223–230.

Stephan, W. G., & Stephan, C. W. (1996). *Intergroup relations.* Boulder, CO: Westview Press.

Sumner, W. G. (1906). *Folkways.* New York: Ginn.

Tajfel, H. (1970). Experiments in intergroup discrimination. *Scientific American, 223*(2), 96–102.

Taylor, D. M., & Moghaddam, F. M. (1987). *Theories of intergroup relations: International social psychological perspectives.* New York: Praeger.

Thompson, L. (1998). *The mind and heart of the negotiator.* Upper Saddle River, NJ: Prentice-Hall.

Thompson, L., Valley, K. L., & Kramer, R. M. (1995). The bittersweet feeling of success: An examination of social perception in negotiation. *Journal of Experimental Social Psychology, 31,* 467–492.

Webb, W. M., & Worchel, P. (1986). Trust and distrust. In S. Worchel & W. G. Austin (Eds.), *Psychology of intergroup relations* (pp. 213–228). Chicago, IL: Nelson-Hall.

Weick, K. (1979). *The social psychology of organizing* (2nd ed.). New York: Addison-Wesley.

Weingart, L. R., Bennett, R. J., & Brett, J. M. (1993). The impact of consideration of issues and motivational orientation on group negotiation process and outcome. *Journal of Applied Psychology, 78,* 504–517.

Wrightsman, L. S. (1991). Interpersonal trust and attitudes toward human nature. In J. Robinson, P. Shaver, & L. Wrightsman (Eds.), *Measures of personality and psychological attitudes* (pp. 373–412). San Diego, CA: Academic Press.

Yamagishi, T. (1986). The provision of a sanctioning system as a public good. *Journal of Personality and Social Psychology, 51*, 110–116.

Yamagishi, T., & Yamagishi, M. (1994). Trust and commitment in the United States and Japan. *Motivation and Emotion, 18*, 129–166.

Zucker, L. G. (1986). Production of trust: Institutional sources of economic structure. In B. M. Staw & L. L. Cummings (Eds.), *Research in organizational behavior* (Vol. 8, pp. 53–111). Greenwich, CT: JAI Press.

CHAPTER TWENTY-TWO

Toward Reduction of Prejudice: Intergroup Contact and Social Categorization

Marilynn B. Brewer and Samuel L. Gaertner

The purpose of this chapter is to summarize the history and current status of social psychology's unique contributions to the reduction of prejudice and social discrimination. The type of prejudice and discrimination that we address in this chapter can exist as either differential positive evaluation and treatment favoring the ingroup or as differential negative evaluation and treatment intended to disadvantage the outgroup, or both (see Brewer, 1999; Gaertner et al., 1997; Mummendey & Wenzel, 1999). Our focus here is on reducing discriminatory behavior in intergroup settings, and as such this chapter is complementary to other chapters in this volume that deal with intrapersonal prejudice, stereotyping, and stereotype change.

Both theoretically and empirically, social psychology's contributions to prejudice reduction embody two major research traditions – contact hypothesis and social categorization/social identity theory. We begin by tracing the development of the contact hypothesis. Then we discuss the importance of the social categorization approach for understanding the etiology of prejudice and discrimination as well as the implications of this perspective for understanding the processes by which the contact hypothesis may operate. Three different models for category-based prejudice reduction – decategorization, recategorization, and mutual differentiation – are reviewed and compared. Finally, we present an integration of these approaches that suggests that these models may represent complementary, rather than competing, processes underlying prejudice reduction.

Preparation of this chapter was supported by NSF Grant No. SBR 95-14398 (to the first author) and NIMH Grant MH 48721 (to the second author).

The Contact Hypothesis

The "contact hypothesis" is a general set of ideas about reducing intergroup prejudice and discrimination that developed among social scientists in the 1940s in the context of inter-racial relations in the United States (Allport, 1954; Watson, 1947; Williams, 1947). The basic idea behind the hypothesis is that hostility between groups is fed by unfamiliarity and separation and that *under the right conditions*, contact among members of different groups will reduce hostility and promote more positive intergroup attitudes.

Classic studies

According to Allport (1954), the four most important of these qualifying conditions were (a) integration has the support of authority, fostering *social norms* that favor intergroup acceptance, (b) the situation has high "acquaintance potential," promoting *intimate contact* among members of both groups, (c) the contact situation promotes *equal status* interactions among members of the social groups, and (d) the situation creates conditions of *cooperative interdependence* among members of both groups. Each of these conditions was derived from results of early research on racial desegregation and intergroup contact in the United States, on which the hypothesis was initially based.

Social and institutional support. Unambiguous institutional support was assumed to create a climate for emergence of social norms of tolerance and acceptance. Two early studies of racially integrated housing projects in the United States (Deutsch & Collins, 1951; Wilner, Walkley, & Cook, 1955) documented the close relationship between institutional endorsement and changes in prevailing social norms. Compared to White residents of segregated housing projects, residents in the integrated projects expressed significantly more favorable attitudes toward interracial interaction, particularly when they believed that such interactions were expected and normative.

Acquaintance potential. Two basic reasons were expressed for why intimate, personalized contact should have more positive impact than brief, casual, or formal contact. One reason is that the development of close relationships is in itself rewarding – positive affect that would potentially generalize to the outgroup as a whole (Cook, 1962). Second is the potential to acquire new, more accurate information about outgroup members that would disconfirm negative stereotypes (Cook, 1978) and increase perceived intergroup similarity (Pettigrew, 1971; Stephan & Stephan, 1984).

The early housing project studies found that the relative proximity between Black and White families was an important correlate of positive attitude change. Greater proximity was associated with more frequent and more intimate contact between groups, and those with the most interactive contact with their Black neighbors developed the most favorable racial attitudes (Wilner et al., 1955).

Equal status. Segregated groups are often unequal in status, with associated negative stereotypes about the lower status group members' competence and abilities. The framers of the contact hypothesis were aware that contact situations that perpetuate status differentials would reinforce rather than disconfirm such negative expectations and hence emphasized the importance of equal-status participation within the contact situation. Residential integration most often provides opportunity for contact under equal-status conditions, but contact in work or school settings may not. When contact with members of a disadvantaged group places the outgroup member in a subordinate role, stereotypic expectations are strengthened rather than weakened (Cohen, 1984). Most field studies confirm the importance of equal-status contact as a necessary if not sufficient condition for positive attitude change (Amir, 1976).

Cooperative interaction. The condition of contact that has received the most attention and research since the 1950s is the stipulation regarding cooperative interdependence between members of the different social groups in the contact situation. This focus is due in large part to the influence of the now classic field experiment conducted by Muzafer Sherif and his colleagues in the summer of 1954 in a boys' camp in Robbers Cave, Oklahoma (Sherif, Harvey, White, Hood, & Sherif, 1961).

The researchers divided 22 eleven-year-old boys into two separate groups prior to their arrival at summer camp and initially kept these groups apart to develop their group identities. Then, in accord with Sherif et al.'s (1961) functional theory of intergroup relations, the introduction of group-oriented, competitive activities (e.g., tug-of-war, football, baseball) instigated intergroup hostility, including hostile verbal exchanges and actual fighting between members of the two groups. Subsequent intergroup contact under neutral, noncompetitive conditions, however, did not calm the ferocity of these exchanges. Only after the research team introduced a series of superordinate goals, ones that could not be achieved without the full cooperation of both groups, did the relations between the two groups become more harmonious. Supportive of Sherif's theoretical perspective, the descriptive record and systematic measures provide rich documentation of the effectiveness of cooperative interaction in reducing conflict and promoting cross-group friendships.

From Robbers Cave onward, many field studies of intergroup contact have confirmed that intergroup cooperation leads to more friendliness and less ingroup bias than situations that do not promote or require cooperative interaction. Probably the most extensive application of the contact hypothesis has been the implementation of cooperative learning programs in desegregated school classrooms. There is a sizable body of evidence that demonstrates the effectiveness of cooperative learning groups for increasing attraction and interaction between members of different social categories (Aronson, Blaney, Stephan, Sikes, & Sanpp, 1978; Johnson & Johnson, 1975; Slavin, 1983). Meta-analyses of studies in ethnically mixed classrooms confirm the superiority of cooperative learning methods over individualistic or competitive learning in promoting cross-ethnic friendships and reduced prejudice (Johnson, Johnson, & Maruyama, 1984).

Laboratory experiments: Defining the limits

The elements of the Robbers Cave experiment provided a prototype for subsequent laboratory experiments on the contact hypothesis and its moderating conditions.

The basic laboratory paradigm is essentially a scaled-down version of the summer camp model.

A brief review of these laboratory experiments identifies a number of factors that either inhibit or facilitate the effectiveness of contact to reduce ingroup–outgroup biases and promote positive attitudes toward outgroup members. Among the moderating variables confirmed by experimental studies are the frequency and duration of intergroup interaction (Worchel, Andreoli, & Folger, 1977; Wilder & Thompson, 1980), the presence of intergroup anxiety (Stephan & Stephan, 1985; Wilder & Shapiro, 1989), the structure of cooperative tasks (Bettencourt, Brewer, Croak, & Miller, 1992; Deschamps & Brown, 1983; Gaertner, Dovidio, Rust et al., 1999; Marcus-Newhall, Miller, Holtz, & Brewer, 1993), the outcome of cooperation (Worchel et al., 1977), and status equalization (Cohen, 1984). In general, results of laboratory experiments confirm the premises of the contact hypothesis but also indicate the complexity – and potential fragility – of effects of intergroup contact even under highly controlled conditions.

The issues of generalization

Despite the wealth of experimental evidence documenting the potential for prejudice reduction following cooperative intergroup contact, a number of issues regarding the validity of the contact hypothesis remain. One concern is whether findings obtained under the relatively benign conditions of intergroup relations between experimentally created groups in the laboratory can be generalized to real-world social groups with a history of conflict and hostility, inequalities of status and power, and political struggle. With established groups, resistance to contact and cooperative interdependence may be strong enough to make questions of the conditions of contact moot (Brewer, 2000a), and the history of outcomes of forced desegregation and contact is mixed at best (e.g., Cook, 1985; Gerard & Miller, 1975; Stephan, 1986).

Another issue is whether any positive effects of contact, when they do occur, are generalized from the immediate contact experience to attitudes toward the outgroup as a whole. A majority of laboratory experiments on contact effects are limited in that they assess only attitudes toward ingroup and outgroup participants within the contact setting. Presumably, however, the ultimate goal of contact interventions is reduction of prejudice toward whole social groups, not simply creation of positive attitudes toward specific group members. Evidence regarding the effectiveness of contact in this generalized sense is more sparse.

In what is probably the most comprehensive laboratory test of interracial contact effects, Cook (1971, 1984) conducted a series of experiments in which highly prejudiced White subjects worked with a Black confederate in an ideal contact situation (equal status, cooperative interdependence, with high acquaintance potential and equalitarian social norms) over an extended period of time. Perceptions of the Black co-worker were measured at the completion of the contact experience, and general racial attitudes were assessed before, immediately after, and up to three years following the experimental sessions. Across all variations of this experiment, White participants displayed predominantly positive behaviors toward their Black co-worker and expressed highly favorable evaluations in the post-experimental questionnaires. Whether liking for this individual member of the outgroup resulted in changed attitudes toward Blacks and race-related issues, however, varied across the experiments and for different attitude measures.

One major reason why generalization fails is that the newly positively valued outgroup member is regarded as an exception and not typical or representative of the outgroup in general (Allport, 1954; Rothbart & John, 1985; Wilder, 1984). In Cook's studies, significant differences in post-contact attitude change among those who participated in the contact experience compared to control subjects were obtained only in an initial experiment in which what Cook (1984) referred to as a "cognitive booster" was introduced during the course of the experiment. This added element was a guided conversation (led by a research confederate) in which the negative effects of discriminatory policies and practices were directly connected to the now-liked Black co-worker. This booster served to make salient the co-worker's category membership and to establish a link between feelings toward this individual and members of the group as a whole. In a later, conceptually related experiment, Van Oudenhoven, Groenewoud, & Hewstone (1996) found that Dutch students' evaluations of Turkish people in general were more positive after an episode of cooperative interaction with an individual Turkish person when his ethnicity was explicitly mentioned during the cooperative session than when ethnicity remained implicit only. Again, the explicit linkage appears to be a necessary mechanism for generalized contact effects.

Contact: The theoretical challenge

The basic idea behind the original contact hypothesis was elegantly simple: If separation and unfamiliarity breed stereotypes and intergroup prejudice (negative attitudes, hostility), then these effects should be reversible by promoting contact and increased familiarity between members of different groups or social categories. The underlying theoretical assumptions were that contact under cooperative interactive conditions provides opportunity for positive experiences with outgroup members that disconfirm or undermine previous negative attitudes and ultimately change attitudes toward and beliefs about the group as a whole.

Outside of the laboratory, research on the effects of contact during the 1960s and 70s took place almost entirely in these highly politicized field contexts (i.e., schools, public housing, the military) where a multitude of variables determined the social and psychological conditions of contact and the success or failure of the contact experiences (cf. Amir, 1969; Cook, 1985). Even laboratory experiments have unveiled a plethora of moderating variables that further qualify the basic assumptions regarding contact effects. As a consequence, the contact hypothesis itself accumulated a growing list of qualifiers and modifications (beyond the initial list of equal-status, intimate, cooperative contact) based primarily on experience rather than underlying theory. By the late 1970s (as one social psychologist put it), the elegant hypothesis had become more like a "bag lady, encumbered with excess baggage" (Stephan, 1987).

In his review of the current status of contact research, Pettigrew (1998) suggested that the challenge is to distinguish between factors that are *essential* to the processes underlying positive contact experiences and their generalization, and those that merely *facilitate* (or inhibit) the operation of these processes. To make this distinction, contact researchers needed a more elaborated theory of what the underlying processes are and how they mediate the effects of intergroup contact under different conditions. During the 1980s, research on the contact hypothesis was enriched by one such theoretical perspective that arose from European research on social categorization and social identity.

Social Categorization/Social Identity Theory

Social identity theory, as articulated by Tajfel (1978) and Turner (1975, 1985), represents the convergence of two traditions in the study of intergroup attitudes and behavior – social categorization, as represented in the work by Doise (1978), Tajfel (1969), and Wilder (1986), and social comparison, as exemplified by Lemaine (1974) and Vanneman and Pettigrew (1972). The theoretical perspective rests on two basic premises:

1. Individuals organize their understanding of the social world on the basis of categorical distinctions that transform continuous variables into discrete classes; categorization has the effect of minimizing perceived differences *within* categories and accentuating intercategory differences.
2. Since individual persons are themselves members of some social categories and not others, social categorization carries with it implicit *ingroup–outgroup* (we–they) distinctions; because of the self-relevance of social categories, the ingroup–outgroup classification is a superimposed category distinction with affective and emotional significance.

These two premises provide a framework for conceptualizing any social situation in which a particular ingroup–outgroup categorization is made salient. In effect, the theory posits a basic *intergroup schema* with the following characteristic features:

1. assimilation within category boundaries and contrast between categories such that all members of the ingroup are perceived to be more similar to the self than members of the outgroup (the *intergroup accentuation* principle);
2. positive affect (trust, liking) selectively generalized to fellow ingroup members but not outgroup members (the *ingroup favoritism* principle);
3. intergroup social comparison associated with perceived negative interdependence between ingroup and outgroup (the *social competition* principle).

The affective and behavioral consequences of this schema lead to intergroup situations characterized by preferential treatment of ingroup members, mutual distrust between ingroup and outgroup, and intergroup competition. According to this theoretical perspective, the starting point for intergroup discrimination and prejudice is a cognitive representation of the social situation in which a particular categorical distinction is highly salient. The role of category salience in intergroup bias has been well documented in experimental research using the minimal intergroup paradigm (Brewer, 1979; Diehl, 1990; Tajfel, Billig, Bundy, & Flament, 1971; Turner, 1981). Given a salient ingroup–outgroup distinction, preferential treatment of the ingroup is fueled by motivational factors including the need for self-esteem and positive distinctiveness (Turner, 1975), reduction of uncertainty (Hogg & Abrams, 1993), and the needs for belonging and differentiation (Brewer, 1991).

Because of the affective ties between self and ingroup, the primary process underlying intergroup discrimination is *ingroup favoritism,* or preferential attitudes and behavior toward the ingroup and its members relative to the outgroup. Whether ingroup bias also extends to derogation and negative treatment of the outgroup is more uncertain (Brewer, 1979, 1999; Mummendey & Wenzel, 1999), depending on whether the structural relations between groups and associated social norms foster and justify hostility or contempt. But ingroup differentiation and associated biases lay the groundwork for all forms of social discrimination and prejudice. In essence, social identity theory provides a perspective on intergroup relations as a complex interplay between cognitive and motivational processes within individuals and structural features of the social environment that make group distinctions salient and meaningful.

Combining Contact and Categorization Theories: Alternative Models for Reducing Ingroup Bias and Intergroup Discrimination

One advance toward a more integrative theory of intergroup relations was achieved when contact research was combined with concepts of social categorization and social identity theory to provide a theoretical framework for understanding the cognitive mechanisms by which cooperative contact is presumed to work (see Brewer & Miller, 1984; Gaertner, Mann, Murrell, & Dovidio, 1989; Hewstone, 1996; Hewstone & Brown, 1986; Wilder, 1986). From the social categorization perspective, the issue to be addressed is how intergroup contact and cooperation can be structured so as to alter cognitive representations in ways that would eliminate one or more of the basic features of the negative intergroup schema. Based on the premises of social identity theory, three alternative models for contact effects have been developed and tested in experimental and field settings, namely: Decategorization, recategorization, and mutual differentiation. Each of these models can be described in terms of (a) the structural representation of the contact situation that is recommended, (b) the psychological processes that promote attitude change within the contact setting, and (c) the mechanisms by which contact experiences are generalized to changed attitudes toward the outgroup as a whole.

Decategorization: The personalization model

The first model is essentially a formalization and elaboration of the assumptions implicit in the contact hypothesis itself (Brewer & Miller, 1984). A primary consequence of salient ingroup–outgroup categorization is the deindividuation of members of the outgroup.

Social behavior in category-based interactions is characterized by a tendency to treat individual members of the outgroup as undifferentiated representatives of a unified social category, ignoring individual differences within the group. The personalization perspective on the contact situation implies that intergroup interactions should be structured so as to reduce the salience of category distinctions and promote opportunities to get to know outgroup members as individual persons.

The conditional specifications of the contact hypothesis (equal status, intimate, cooperative interaction) can be interpreted as features of the situation that reduce category salience and promote more differentiated and personalized representations of the participants in the contact setting. Attending to personal characteristics of group members not only provides the opportunity to disconfirm category stereotypes, it also breaks down the monolithic perception of the outgroup as a homogeneous unit (Wilder, 1978). In this scheme, the contact situation encourages attention to information at the individual level that replaces category identity as the most useful basis for classifying participants.

Repeated personalized contacts with a variety of outgroup members should, over time, undermine the value and meaningfulness of the social category stereotype as a source of information about members of that group. This is the process by which contact experiences are expected to generalize – via reducing the salience and meaning of social categorization in the long run (Brewer & Miller, 1988).

A number of experimental studies provide evidence supporting this perspective on contact effects (Bettencourt et al., 1992; Marcus-Newhall et al., 1993). Miller, Brewer, and Edwards (1985), for instance, demonstrated that a cooperative task that required personalized interaction with members of the outgroup resulted not only in more positive attitudes toward outgroup members in the cooperative setting but also toward other outgroup members shown on a videotape, compared to cooperative contact that was task-focused rather than person-focused.

The personalization model is also supported by the early empirical evidence for the effects of extended, intimate contact on racial attitudes, reviewed above. More recently, extensive data on effects of intergroup friendships have been derived from surveys in Western Europe regarding attitudes toward minority immigrant groups (Hamberger & Hewstone, 1997; Pettigrew, 1997; Pettigrew & Meertens, 1995). Across samples in France, Great Britain, the Netherlands, and Germany, Europeans with outgroup friends scored significantly lower on measures of prejudice, particularly affective prejudice (Pettigrew, 1998). This positive relationship did not hold for other types of contact (work or residential) that did not involve formation of close personal relationships with members of the outgroup. Although there is clearly a bi-directional relationship between positive attitudes and extent of personal contact, path analyses indicate that the path from friendship to reduction in prejudice is stronger than the other way around (Pettigrew, 1998).

Other recent research also reveals two interesting extensions of the personalized contact effect. One is evidence (again from European survey data) that personal friendships with members of one outgroup may lead to tolerance toward outgroups in general and reduced nationalistic pride – a process that Pettigrew (1997) refers to as "deprovincialization." A second extension is represented by evidence that contact effects may operate indirectly or vicariously. Although interpersonal friendship across group lines leads to reduced prejudice, even knowledge that an ingroup member befriended an outgroup member has potential to reduce bias (Wright et al., 1997). Also, interpersonal processes involving the arousal of empathic feelings for an outgroup member, can increase positive attitudes toward members of that group more widely (Batson et al., 1997).

Recategorization: The common ingroup identity model

The second social categorization model of intergroup contact and prejudice reduction is also based on the premise that reducing the salience of ingroup–outgroup category distinctions is key to positive effects. In contrast to the decategorization approaches described above, recategorization is not designed to reduce or eliminate categorization but rather to structure a definition of group categorization at a higher level of category inclusiveness in ways that reduce intergroup bias and conflict (Allport, 1954, p. 43). Specifically, the common ingroup identity model (Gaertner & Dovidio, 2000; Gaertner, Dovidio, Anastasio, Bachman, & Rust, 1993; Gaertner, Dovidio, Nier, Ward, & Banker, 1999) proposes that intergroup bias and conflict can be reduced by factors that transform participants' representations of memberships from two groups to one, more inclusive group. With common ingroup identity, the cognitive and motivational processes that initially produced ingroup favoritism are redirected to benefit the former outgroup members. Among the antecedent factors proposed by the common ingroup identity model are the features of contact situations (Allport, 1954) that are necessary for intergroup contact to be successful (e.g., interdependence between groups, equal status, equalitarian norms). From this perspective, cooperative interaction, for example, enhances positive evaluations of outgroup members, at least in part, because cooperation transforms members' representations of the memberships from "Us" and "Them" to a more inclusive "We."

To test this hypothesis directly, Gaertner, Mann, Dovidio, Murrell, and Pomare (1990) conducted a laboratory experiment that brought two three-person laboratory groups together under conditions designed to vary independently the members' representations of the aggregate as one group or two groups (by varying factors such as seating arrangement) and the presence or absence of intergroup cooperative interaction. Supportive of the hypothesis concerning how cooperation reduces bias, among participants induced to feel like two groups, the introduction of cooperative interaction increased their perceptions of one group and also reduced their bias in evaluative ratings relative to those who did not cooperate during the contact period. Also supportive of the common ingroup identity model, reduced bias associated with introducing cooperation was due to enhanced favorable evaluations of outgroup members. In further support for the common ingroup identity model, this effect of cooperation was mediated by the extent to which members of both groups perceived themselves as one group.

Three survey studies conducted in natural settings across very different intergroup contexts offered converging support for the proposal that the features specified by the contact hypothesis can increase intergroup harmony in part by transforming members' representations of the memberships from separate groups to one more inclusive group. Participants in these studies included students attending a multi-ethnic high school (Gaertner, Rust, Dovidio, Bachman, & Anastasio, 1994), banking executives from a wide variety of institutions across the United States who had experienced a corporate merger (Bachman, 1993), and college students who were members of blended families whose households wre composed of two formerly separate families trying to unite into one (Banker & Gaertner, 1998).

To provide a conceptual replication of the laboratory studies of cooperation, the surveys included items (specifically designed for each context) to measure participants' perceptions of the conditions of contact, their representations of the aggregate (i.e., one group, two subgroups within one group, two separate groups and separate individuals), and a measure of intergroup harmony or bias. Across these three studies, conditions of contact reliably predicted the measures of intergroup harmony and bias. Also, as expected, the conditions of contact systematically influenced participants' representations of the aggregate. Supportive of the hypothesized mediating process, the relationships between the conditions of contact and bias in affective reactions among high school students, intergroup anxiety among corporate executives, and stepfamily harmony were reliably weaker after the mediating role of group representations was taken into account. The more the aggregate felt like one group, the lower the bias in affective reactions in the high school, the less the intergroup anxiety for the bankers, and the greater the amount of stepfamily harmony (Gaertner, Dovidio, & Bachman, 1996).

Challenges to the decategorization/recategorization models

Although the structural representations of the contact situation advocated by the decategorization (personalization) and recategorization (common ingroup identity) models are different, the two approaches share common assumptions about the need to reduce category differentiation and associated processes. Because both models rely on reducing or eliminating the salience of intergroup differentiation, they involve structuring contact in a way that will challenge or threaten existing social identities. Both cognitive and motivational factors conspire to create resistance to the dissolution of category boundaries or to re-establish category distinctions across time. Although the salience of a common superordinate identity or personalized representations may be enhanced in the short run, these may be difficult to maintain across time and social situations.

Brewer's (1991) optimal distinctiveness theory of the motives underlying group identification provides one explanation for why category distinctions are difficult to change. The theory postulates that social identity is driven by two opposing social motives – the need for inclusion and the need for differentiation. Human beings strive to belong to groups that transcend their own personal identity, but at the same time they need to feel special and distinct from others. In order to satisfy both of these motives simultaneously, individuals seek inclusion in distinctive social groups where the boundaries between those who are members of the ingroup category and those who are excluded can be clearly drawn. Highly inclusive superordinate categories do not satisfy distinctiveness needs, while high degrees of individuation fail to meet needs for belonging and for cognitive simplicity and uncertainty reduction (Hogg & Abrams, 1993). These motives are likely to make either personalization or common ingroup identity temporally unstable solutions to intergroup discrimination and prejudice.

Pre-existing social-structural relationships between groups may also create strong forces of resistance to changes in category boundaries. Cognitive restructuring may be close to impossible (at least as a first step) for groups already engaged in deadly hostilities. Even in the absence of overt conflict, asymmetries between social groups in size, power, or status create additional sources of resistance. When one group is substantially numerically smaller than the other in the contact situation, the minority category is especially salient and minority group members may be particularly reluctant to accept a superordinate category identity that is dominated by the other group. Another major challenge is created by pre-existing status differences between groups, where members of both high- and low-status groups may be threatened by contact and assimilation (Mottola, 1996).

The mutual differentiation model

These challenges to processes of decategorization/recategorization led Hewstone and Brown (1986) to recommend an alternative approach to intergroup contact wherein co-operative interactions between groups are introduced without degrading the original ingroup–outgroup categorization. More specifically, this model favors encouraging groups working together to perceive complementarity by recognizing and valuing mutual superiorities and inferiorities within the context of an interdependent cooperative task or common, superordinate goals. This strategy allows group members to maintain their social identities and positive distinctiveness while avoiding insidious intergroup comparisons. Thus, the mutual differentiation model does not seek to change the basic category structure of the intergroup contact situation, but to change the intergroup affect from negative to positive interdependence and evaluation.

In order to promote positive intergroup experience, Hewstone and Brown recommend that the contact situation be structured so that members of the respective groups have distinct but complementary roles to contribute toward common goals. In this way, both groups can maintain positive distinctiveness within a cooperative framework. Evidence in support of this approach comes from the results of an experiment by Brown and Wade (1987) in which work teams composed of students from two different faculties engaged in a cooperative effort to produce a two-page magazine article. When the representatives of the two groups were assigned separate roles in the team task (one group working on figures and layout, the other working on text), the contact experience had a more positive effect on intergroup attitudes than when the two groups were not provided with distinctive roles (see also Deschamps & Brown, 1983; Dovidio, Gaertner, & Validzic, 1998).

Hewstone and Brown (1986) argue that generalization of positive contact experiences is more likely when the contact situation is defined as an *intergroup* situation rather than an interpersonal interaction. Generalization in this case is direct rather than requiring additional cognitive links between positive affect toward individuals and representations of the group as a whole. This position is supported by evidence, reviewed above, that cooperative contact with a member of an outgroup leads to more favorable generalized attitudes toward the group as a whole when category membership is made salient during contact (e.g., Van Oudenhoven, Groenewoud, & Hewstone, 1996; Brown, Vivian, & Hewstone, 1999).

Although ingroup–outgroup category salience is usually associated with ingroup bias and the negative side of intergroup attitudes, cooperative interdependence is assumed to override the negative intergroup schema, particularly if the two groups have differentiated, complementary roles to play. Because it capitalizes on needs for distinctive social identities, the mutual differentiation model provides a solution that is highly stable in terms of the cognitive-structural aspects of the intergroup situation. The affective component of the model, however, is likely to be more unstable. Salient intergroup boundaries are associated with mutual distrust (Insko & Schopler, 1987) which undermines the potential for cooperative interdependence and mutual liking over any length of time. By reinforcing perceptions of group differences, the differentiation model risks reinforcing negative beliefs about the outgroup. In the long run, intergroup anxiety (Greenland & Brown, 1999; Islam & Hewstone, 1993), and the potential for fission and conflict along group lines remains high.

Hybrid Models: An Integration of Approaches

As reviewed above, each of the cognitive-structural models of intergroup contact and prejudice reduction has its weaknesses and limitations, particularly when one seeks to generalize beyond small group interactions in laboratory settings. These criticisms have led a number of writers to suggest that some combination of all three models may be necessary to create conditions for long-term attitude change (e.g., Brewer, 1996; Gaertner et al., 1996; Hewstone, 1996; Pettigrew, 1998). In this final section, we discuss some of these hybrid approaches and their implications for the reduction of prejudice and discrimination in pluralistic societies.

Multiple social identities

Individuals are members of multiple social groups which imply different social identities and ingroup loyalties. Yet social identities have been treated as if they were mutually exclusive, with only one social categorization (ingroup–outgroup differentiation) salient at any one time. New research has begun to challenge this assumption of exclusivity and to explore the implications of holding multiple group identities, or identities at different levels of inclusiveness, simultaneously.

Hierarchical dual identities. In recent work regarding the development of a common ingroup identity, it has been proposed that embracing a more inclusive superordinate identity does not necessarily require each group to forsake its original group identity completely (Gaertner et al., 1990, 1994). In many contexts this may be impossible or undesirable. In some intergroup contexts, however, when members simultaneously perceive themselves as members of different groups but also as part of the same team or superordinate entity, intergroup relations between these subgroups are more positive than if members only considered themselves as separate groups (Brewer & Schneider, 1990). For example, minority students in the multi-ethnic high school who identified themselves using both a minority subgroup and an American superordinate identity had lower intergroup bias than those students who identified themselves using only their minority group identity (Gaertner et al., 1994). Also, the greater the extent to which majority and minority students perceived the study body as ". . . different groups . . . all playing on the same team" (the dual identity item), the lower their degree of intergroup bias. By contrast, the more they conceived of the student body as "belonging to different groups" the higher the intergroup bias.

Moreover, a dual identity compared to a revised more inclusive purely one group identity may facilitate the generalization of the benefits of contact to members of the outgroup not specifically included within the recategorized representation. With a dual identity the associative link to others beyond the contact situation remains intact (see also Hewstone, 1996; Hewstone & Brown, 1986).

Other research also supports the value of a dual identity for reducing bias and improving intergroup relations. Two studies further suggest that the intergroup benefits of a strong superordinate identity remain relatively stable even when the strength of the subordinate identity becomes equivalently high (Huo, Smith, Tyler, & Lind, 1996; Smith & Tyler, 1996). This suggests that identification with a more inclusive social group does not require individuals to deny their ethnic identity. In addition, a dual identity can also lead to even more positive outgroup attitudes than those associated with a superordinate identity alone (Hornsey & Hogg, 2000). In terms of promoting more harmonious intergroup interactions, a dual identity capitalizes on the benefits of common ingroup membership as well as those accrued from mutual differentiation between the groups.

Crosscutting identities. Embedded categories at different levels of inclusiveness represent only one form of multiple ingroup identities. Individuals may also be members of social categories that overlap only partially, if at all. Many bases of social category differentiation – gender, age, religion, ethnicity, occupation – represent crosscutting cleavages. From the standpoint of a particular person, other individuals may be fellow ingroup members on one dimension of category differentiation but outgroup members on another. (For instance, for a woman business executive, a male colleague is an ingroup member with respect to occupation but an outgrouper with respect to her gender identification.) It is possible that such orthogonal social identities are kept isolated from each other so that only one ingroup–outgroup distinction is activated in a particular social context. But there are reasons to expect that simultaneous activation of multiple ingroup identities both is possible and has potential for reducing prejudice and discrimination based on any one category distinction.

Evidence from both anthropology (e.g., Gluckman, 1955) and political sociology (e.g., Coser, 1956) has long suggested that societies characterized by crosscutting loyalty structures are less prone to schism and internal intergroup conflict than societies characterized by a single hierarchical loyalty structure. More recently, social psychologists have also begun to consider the implications of such multiple crosscutting social identities for reduction of ingroup bias at the individual level (Brown & Turner, 1979; Deschamps & Doise, 1978; Marcus-Newhall et al., 1993; Vanbeselaere, 1991). A number of mechanisms have been proposed for why crosscutting group memberships would decrease ingroup bias and intergroup discrimination. For one thing, the increased complexity of a multiple social categorization reduces the salience or degree of differentiation associated with any one ingroup–outgroup distinction. Beyond the cognitive effects of category complexity, motivational factors also enter in to reduce the likelihood of intense ingroup–outgroup discrimination. First, the presence of multiple group loyalties potentially reduces the importance or significance of any one social identity for self-definition or belonging. Further, cross-category connections and consistency (balance) motives militate against negative attitudes toward outgroups that contain members who are fellow ingroupers on some other category dimension. Finally, crosscutting category memberships increase the degree of interpersonal interaction and contact across any particular category boundaries (Brewer, 2000b).

Experimental studies with both natural and artificial categories have demonstrated that adding a crosscutting category distinction reduces ingroup bias and increases positive attitudes toward crossed category members compared to simple ingroup–outgroup differentiation (Vanbeselaere, 1991) or compared to situations in which category distinctions are convergent or superimposed (Bettencourt & Dorr, 1998; Marcus-Newhall et al., 1993; Rust, 1996). In these studies, cooperative interaction in the context of crosscutting social identities and roles increases intracategory differentiation and reduces perceived intercategory differences, resulting in less category-based evaluations of individual group members. Further, the benefits of cross-categorization may be enhanced when both category distinctions are embedded in a common superordinate group identity (Gaertner, Dovidio, Nier et al., 1999; Rust, 1996). Thus, crossed categorization and recategorization may work together to produce enhanced inclusiveness and reduced intergroup discrimination.

Limitations of dual identification. The effectiveness of dual identities for increasing harmony between groups may vary across intergroup domains. For example, maintaining strong identification with the earlier subgroup identities following a corporate merger may threaten the primary goal of the merger. Similarly, in stepfamilies, the salience of the former family identities, even with the simultaneous recognition of a more inclusive family identity, may violate members' expectations about what their ideal family should be like. Whereas in the survey studies of executives who experienced a corporate merger (Bachman, 1993) and of stepfamily members (Banker & Gaertner, 1998) the perception of a one-group identity was positively related to favorable conditions of contact and to better outcomes (e.g., reduced bias and family harmony) the dual identity representations seemed to be diagnostic of serious problems. As these "dual identities" become stronger in the merger and stepfamily contexts the conditions of contact were more unfavorable and negative outcomes increased. In contrast, in the multi-ethnic high school study (Gaertner et al., 1994), the strength of the dual identity was related to positive conditions of contact and to reduced intergroup bias. Here, the salience of the subgroup identities, within the context of a superordinate entity that provides connection between the subgroups, may signal the prospects for good intergroup relations without undermining the goals of the school or those of the different ethnic or racial groups.

Crosscutting category memberships, also, do not always result in reduced category salience and greater intergroup acceptance (Vanbeselaere, 1991). If one category distinction is more socially meaningful or functionally important than others, intergroup discrimination based on that categorization may be unaffected by the existence of crosscutting memberships in other, less important groups. More important, multiple group identities may be combined into a single ingroup (e.g., categorization based on shared ethnicity *and* gender) which is more exclusive than either category membership considered separately (Brewer, 2000b). Whether multiple social identities can contribute to the reduction of prejudice and discrimination ultimately depends on whether individuals can be made aware of their multiple category memberships under conditions that promote inclusiveness rather than differentiation (Urban & Miller, 1998).

Reciprocal process models

The utility of each of the categorization-based strategies for reducing intergroup bias – that is, decategorization, recategorization, and mutual differentiation – has received empirical support. But the question remains as to how these alternatives that seem so different, even opposite, relate to one another? Should the three models be conceptualized as competitors, that is, as independent processes that reduce bias through different pathways? Or, are they different processes that are complementary and which can reciprocally facilitate each other?

Pettigrew (1998) has proposed that the essential conditions of intergroup contact reduce prejudice over time by initiating a sequence of strategies for reducing bias. He suggests that the sequence unfolds beginning with decategorization, followed in turn by mutual differentiation and recategorization. Pettigrew's reformulated contact theory (1998) proposes that this combination, over time, can maximally reduce prejudice toward outgroup members, and also generalize across situations, to different outgroup members, and even to different outgroups (see Pettigrew, 1997).

The order in which these category-based processes unfold, however, probably depends upon specific features of the contact situation, such as whether contact emphasizes group-on-group interaction (as at Robbers Cave) or interaction among individuals from different groups (as among neighbors). Nevertheless, the cogency of Pettigrew's general perspective receives converging support from a re-analysis of Sherif et al.'s detailed descriptions of Robbers Cave (Gaertner, Dovidio, Banker et al., 2000), and from recent laboratory studies that were designed to examine the possible interplay between decategorization, recategorization, and mutual differentiation (e.g., Dovidio et al. 1997).

Gaertner et al.'s (2000) analysis of the Robbers Cave study revealed that introducing superordinate goals instigated a sequence of social processes that alternated between recategorization, decategorization, mutual differentiation (when groups were respectful to one another), as well as categorization (when intergroup relations were conflictual). Indeed, Sherif and his colleagues (Sherif et al., 1961) emphasized that intergroup harmony was achieved gradually, only after the groups cooperated on a series of superordinate goals. A close analysis of their detailed description of events during the summer camp experiment reveals that an alternation pattern among the different categorization processes was evident throughout the gradual transition from conflicted to harmonious relations between the groups. In one instance, after the groups cooperated to move a stalled truck carrying their food, the boys immediately rejoiced, chanting repeatedly, "We won the tug-of-war against the truck." The inclusive pronoun "we" signals the momentary recategorization of these groups that was followed by the boys intermingling across group lines with friendlier, more interpersonal interactions. Over time, mutual differentiation began to replace the original categorized representation until finally, as camp concluded, recategorization and friendlier interpersonal relations across group lines characterized the boys' interactions.

The sequence which proceeded from recategorization to friendlier interpersonal relations observed at Robbers Cave was replicated in a laboratory experiment (Dovidio et al., 1997) in which the members of two groups were induced to conceive of themselves as one group or two groups and then given the opportunity to self-disclose or to offer assistance to an ingroup or outgroup member. As expected, the degrees of self-disclosure and prosocial behavior toward outgroup members were together *generally* greater among participants in the one-group relative to the two-group condition. Self-disclosure and prosocial behaviors are particularly interesting because they elicit reciprocity which can further accelerate the intensity of positive interpersonal interactions across group lines even when the initial recategorization process lasts only temporarily. In terms of a longitudinal analysis, these increasingly positive interpersonal relations can fuel the progression to a next stage in the sequence, for example, mutual differentiation or the formation of a more permanent recategorized bond between the memberships. This possibility is illustrated in a laboratory study in which personalized, self-disclosing interactions among the members of two groups meeting group-on-group transformed their perceptions of the aggregate from two groups to one group (Gaertner, Rust, & Dovidio, 1997).

Within an alternating sequence of categorization processes, mutual differentiation may emerge frequently to neutralize threats to original group identities posed by the recategorization and decategorization processes. As suggested by a recent laboratory experiment (Dovidio, Gaertner, & Validzic, 1998), however, mutual differentiation can facilitate recategorization among equal status groups which may otherwise experience threats to the distinctiveness of their group identities. Groups with equal status that earlier were instructed to approach their common problem from different perspectives more strongly perceived themselves as one group and had lower intergroup levels of bias compared to groups that earlier were assigned the same task perspective, or groups that were unequal in status regardless of whether they earlier shared the different task perspectives. Thus, recategorization, decategorization, and mutual differentiation processes seem to share the capacity to facilitate each other, supporting the view that when viewed over time, these processes are complementary and reciprocal.

Conclusions: Implications for Multicultural Societies

The contact hypothesis, with its conceptual and empirical elaborations, is a prescription for promoting positive intergroup relations within a context where groups must live together interdependently. The same basic principles apply whether we are considering two nuclear families joining into a common household, departments or companies combined within an organization, diverse ethnic or religious groups within a nation, or nation-states within an international community. In any of these contexts, the goals of contact and cooperation compete with natural tendencies toward ingroup–outgroup differentiation, separation, and exclusion. Personalization across category boundaries and formation of common superordinate identities – processes that reduce the social meaning of category boundaries – are in tension with pluralistic values that seek to maintain cultural variation and distinct social identities.

The tension between differentiation and integration must be recognized and acknowledged in any complex social system. Exclusive focus on either assimilation or separation as the solution to intergroup discrimination and conflict is neither desirable nor realistic. Proponents of multiculturalism assert that alternatives to these extremes are possible, that groups can maintain distinct identities at the same time as their members participate in a shared, superordinate group structure. Berry (1984), for instance, has argued that there are four different forms of interethnic relations possible in a pluralistic society, depending on how members of the diverse ethnic groups relate to their own ethnic identity and to their role in the society at large. In Berry's classification system, integration is the form of intercultural relations in which identification with ethnic subgroups and identification with the larger society are both engaged. We believe that the reciprocal relations among processes of personalization, recategorization, and mutual differentiation discussed above are compatible with this view of social integration and constitute the necessary underpinnings for an equalitarian multicultural society.

References

Allport, G. W. (1954). *The nature of prejudice.* Cambridge, MA: Addison-Wesley.

Amir, Y. (1969). Contact hypothesis in ethnic relations. *Psychological Bulletin, 71*, 319–342.

Amir, Y. (1976). The role of intergroup contact in change of prejudice and ethnic relations. In P. Katz (Ed.), *Towards the elimination of racism* (pp. 245–308). New York: Pergamon.

Aronson, E., Blaney, N., Stephan, C., Sikes, J., & Sanpp, M. (1978). *The jigsaw classroom.* London: Sage.

Bachman, B. A. (1993). *An intergroup model of organizational mergers.* Unpublished Ph.D. dissertation, University of Delaware, Newark, DE.

Banker, B. S., & Gaertner, S. L. (1998). Achieving stepfamily harmony: An intergroup relations approach. *Journal of Family Psycholgy, 12*, 310–325.

Batson, C. D., Polycarpou, M., Harmon-Jones, E., Imhoff, H., Mitchener, E., Bednar, L., Klein, T., & Highberger, L. (1997). Empathy and attitudes: Can feeling for a member of a stigmatized group improve feelings toward that group? *Journal of Personality and Social Psychology, 72*, 105–118.

Berry, J. W. (1984). Cultural relations in plural societies: Alternatives to segregation and their sociopsychological implications. In N. Miller & M. Brewer (Eds.), *Groups in contact: The psychology of desegregation* (pp. 11–27). New York: Academic Press.

Bettencourt, B. A., Brewer, M. B., Croak, M. R., & Miller, N. (1992). Cooperation and reduction of intergroup bias: The role of reward structure and social orientation. *Journal of Experimental Social Psychology, 28*, 301–319.

Bettencourt, B. A., & Dorr, N. (1998). Cooperative interaction and intergroup bias: Effects of numerical representation and crosscut role assignment. *Personality and Social Psychology Bulletin, 24*, 1276–1293.

Brewer, M. B. (1979). In-group bias in the minimal intergroup situation: A cognitive-motivational analysis. *Psychological Bulletin, 86,* 307–324.

Brewer, M. B. (1991). The social self: On being the same and different at the same time. *Personality and Social Psychology Bulletin, 17,* 475–482.

Brewer, M. B. (1999). The nature of prejudice: Ingroup love or outgroup hate? *Journal of Social Issues, 55,* 429–444.

Brewer, M. B. (2000a). Superordinate goals versus superordinate identity as bases of intergroup cooperation. In D. Capozza & R. Brown (Eds.), *Social identity processes* (pp. 117–132). New York: Sage.

Brewer, M. B. (2000b). Reducing prejudice through cross-categorization: Effects of multiple social identities. In S. Oskamp (Ed.), *Reducing prejudice and discrimination* (pp. 165–183). Mahwah, NJ: Erlbaum.

Brewer, M. B., & Miller, N. (1984). Beyond the contact hypothesis: Theoretical perspectives on desegregation. In N. Miller & M. Brewer (Eds.), *Groups in contact: The psychology of desegregation* (pp. 281–302). New York: Academic Press.

Brewer, M. B., & Miller, N. (1988). Contact and cooperation: When do they work? In P. Katz & D. Taylor (Eds.), *Eliminating racism: Means and controversies* (pp. 315–326). New York: Plenum.

Brewer, M. B., & Schneider, S. K. (1990). Social identity and social dilemmas: A double-edged sword. In D. Abrams & M. Hogg (Eds.), *Social identity theory: Constructive and critical advances* (pp. 169–184). London: Harvester Wheatsheaf.

Brown, R. J., & Turner, J. C. (1979). The criss-cross categorization effect in intergroup discrimination. *British Journal of Social and Clinical Psychology, 18,* 371–383.

Brown, R. J., Vivian, J., & Hewstone, M. (in press). Changing attitudes through intergroup contact: The effects of group membership salience. *European Journal of Social Psychology, 29.*

Brown, R. J., & Wade, G. (1987). Superordinate goals and intergroup behaviour: The effect of role ambiguity and status on intergroup attitudes and task performance. *European Journal of Social Psychology, 17,* 131–142.

Cohen, E. G. (1984). The desegregated school: Problems in status power and interethnic climate. In N. Miller & M. Brewer (Eds.), *Groups in contact: The psychology of desegregation* (pp. 77–96). New York: Academic Press.

Cook, S. W. (1962). The systematic analysis of socially significant events. *Journal of Social Issues, 18,* 66–84.

Cook, S. W. (1971). *The effect of unintended interracial contact upon racial interaction and attitude change.* (Final report, Project No. 5-1320). Washington, DC: U.S. Department of Health, Education, and Welfare, Office of Education.

Cook, S. W. (1978). Interpersonal and attitudinal outcomes in cooperating interracial groups. *Journal of Research and Development in Education, 12,* 97–113.

Cook, S. W. (1984). Cooperative interaction in multiethnic contexts. In N. Miller & M. Brewer (Eds.), *Groups in contact: The psychology of desegregation* (pp. 155–185). New York: Academic Press.

Cook, S. W. (1985). Experimenting on social issues: The case of school desegregation. *American Psychologist, 40,* 452–460.

Coser, L. A. (1956). *The functions of social conflict.* New York: Free Press.

Deschamps, J.-C., & Brown, R. J. (1983). Superordinate goals and intergoup conflict. *British Journal of Social Psychology, 22,* 189–195.

Deschamps, J.-C., & Doise, W. (1978). Crossed category memberships in intergroup relations. In H. Tajfel (Ed.), *Differentiation between social groups* (pp. 141–158). Cambridge, UK: Cambridge University Press.

Deutsch, M., & Collins, M. E. (1951). *Interracial housing: A psychological evaluation of a social experiment.* Minneapolis, MN: University of Minnesota Press.

Diehl, M. (1990). The minimal group paradigm: Theoretical explanations and empirical findings. In W. Stroebe & M. Hewstone (Eds.), *European review of social psychology* (Vol. 1, pp. 263–292). Chichester, UK: Wiley.

Doise, W. (1978). *Groups and individuals: Explanations in social psychology.* Cambridge, UK: Cambridge University Press.

Dovidio, J. F., Gaertner, S. L., & Validzic, A. (1998). Intergroup bias: Status differentiation and a common ingroup identity. *Journal of Personality and Social Psychology, 75,* 109–120.

Dovidio, J. F., Gaertner, S. L., Validzic, A., Matoka, K., Johnson, B., & Frazier, S. (1997). Extending the benefits of re-categorization: Evaluations, self-disclosure, and helping. *Journal of Experimental Social Psychology, 33,* 401–420.

Gaertner, S. L., & Dovidio, J. F. (2000). *Reducing intergroup bias: The common ingroup identity model.* Philadelphia: Psychology Press.

Gaertner, S. L., Dovidio, J. F., Anastasio, P. A., Bachman, B. A., & Rust, M. C. (1993). The common ingroup identity model: Recategorization and the reduction of intergroup bias. In W. Stroebe & M. Hewstone (Eds.), *European review of social psychology* (Vol. 4, pp. 1–26). London: Wiley.

Gaertner, S. L., Dovidio, J. F., & Bachman, B. A. (1996). Revisiting the contact hypothesis: The induction of a common ingroup identity. *International Journal of Intercultural Relations, 20,* 271–290.

Gaertner, S. L., Dovidio, J. F., Banker, B., Houlette, M. Johnson, K. M., & McGlynn, E. A. (2000). Reducing intergroup conflict: From superordinate goals to decategorization, recategorization, and mutual differentiation. *Group Dynamics, 4,* 98–114.

Gaertner, S. L., Dovidio, J. F., Banker, B., Rust, M. C., Nier, J., & Ward, C. M. (1997). Does pro-Whiteness necessarily mean anti-Blackness? In M. Fine, L. Powell, L. Weis, & M. Wong (Eds.), *Off White* (pp. 167–178). New York: Routledge.

Gaertner, S. L., Dovidio, J. F., Nier, J. A., Ward, C. M., & Banker, B. S. (1999). Across cultural divides: The value of a superordinate identity. In D. Prentice & D. Miller (Eds.), *Cultural divides: Understanding and overcoming group conflict* (pp. 173–212). New York: Russell Sage Foundation.

Gaertner, S. L., Dovidio, J. F., Rust, M. C., Nier, J. A., Banker, B., Ward, C. M., Mottola, G. R., & Houlette, M. (1999). Reducing intergroup bias: Elements of intergroup cooperation. *Journal of Personality and Social Psychology, 76,* 388–402.

Gaertner, S. L., Mann, J. A., Dovidio, J. F., Murrell, A. J., & Pomare, M. (1990). How does cooperation reduce intergroup bias? *Journal of Personality and Social Psychology, 59,* 692–704.

Gaertner, S. L., Mann, J. A., Murrell, A. J., & Dovidio, J. F. (1989). Reduction of intergroup bias: The benefits of recategorization. *Journal of Personality and Social Psychology, 57,* 239–249.

Gaertner, S. L., Rust, M. C., & Dovidio, J. F. (1997). *The value of a superordinate identity for reducing intergroup bias.* Unpublished manuscript, University of Delaware, Newark, DE.

Gaertner, S. L., Rust, M. C., Dovidio, J. F., Bachman, B. A., & Anastasio, A. (1994). The contact hypothesis: The role of a common ingroup identity on reducing intergroup bias. *Small Groups Research, 25,* 224–290.

Gerard, H. B., & Miller, N. (1975). *School desegregation: A long-term study.* New York: Plenum.

Greenland, K., & Brown, R. J. (1999). Categorization and intergroup anxiety in contact between British and Japanese nationals. *European Journal of Social Psychology, 29,* 503–521.

Gluckman, (1955). *Customs and conflict in Africa.* London: Blackwell.

Hamberger, J., & Hewstone, M. (1997). Inter-ethnic contact as a predictor of prejudice: Tests of a model in four West European nations. *British Journal of Social Psychology, 36,* 173–190.

Hewstone, M. (1996). Contact and categorization: Social psychology interventions to change intergroup relations. In C. N. Macrae, C. Stangor, & M. Hewstone (Eds.), *Stereotypes and stereotyping* (pp. 323–368). New York: Guilford Press.

Hewstone, M., & Brown, R. J. (1986). Contact is not enough: An intergroup perspective on the "contact hypothesis." In M. Hewstone & R. Brown (Eds.), *Contact and conflict in intergroup encounters* (pp. 1–44). Oxford, UK: Blackwell.

Hogg, M. A., & Abrams, D. (1993). Towards a single-process uncertainty-reduction model of social motivation in groups. In M. Hogg & D. Abrams (Eds.), *Group motivation: Social psychological perspectives* (pp. 173–190). London: Harvester Wheatsheaf.

Hornsey, M. J., & Hogg, M. A. (2000). Subgroup relations: A comparison of the mutual intergroup differentiation and common ingroup identity models of prejudice reduction. *Personality and Social Psychology Bulletin, 26*, 242–256.

Huo, Y., Smith, H., Tyler, T. R., & Lind, E. A. (1996). Superordinate identification, subgroup identification, and justice concerns: Is separatism the problem; is assimilation the answer? *Psychological Science, 7*, 40–45.

Insko, C. A., & Schopler, J. (1987). Categorization, competition, and collectivity. In C. Hendrick (Ed.), *Group processes. Review of personality and social psychology* (Vol. 8, pp. 213–251). Beverly Hills, CA: Sage.

Islam, M. R., & Hewstone, M. (1993). Dimensions of contact as predictors of intergroup anxiety, perceived outgroup variability, and outgroup attitude: An integrative account. *Personality and Social Psychology Bulletin, 19*, 700–710.

Johnson, D. W., & Johnson, R. T. (1975). *Learning together and alone.* Englewood Cliffs, NJ: Prentice-Hall.

Johnson, D. W., Johnson, R. T., & Maruyama, G. (1984). Goal interdependence and interpersonal attraction in heterogeneous classrooms: A meta-analysis. In N. Miller & M. Brewer (Eds.), *Groups in contact: The psychology of desegregation* (pp. 187–212). New York: Academic Press.

Lemaine, G. (1974). Social differentiation and social originality. *European Journal of Social Psychology, 4*, 17–52.

Marcus-Newhall, A., Miller, N., Holtz, R., & Brewer, M. B. (1993). Crosscutting category membership with role assignment: A means of reducing intergroup bias. *British Journal of Social Psychology, 32*, 125–146.

Miller, N., Brewer, M. B., & Edwards, K. (1985). Cooperative interaction in desegregated settings: A laboratory analogue. *Journal of Social Issues, 41*(3), 63–79.

Mottola, G. (1996). *The effects of relative group status on expectations of merger success.* Ph.D dissertation. University of Delaware. Newark, DE.

Mummendey, A., & Wenzel, M. (1999). Social discrimination and tolerance in intergroup relations: Reactions to intergroup differences. *Personality and Social Psychology Review, 3*, 158–175.

Pettigrew, T. F. (1971). *Racially separate or together?* New York: McGraw-Hill.

Pettigrew, T. F. (1997). Generalized intergroup contact effects on prejudice. *Personality and Social Psychology Bulletin, 23*, 173–185.

Pettigrew, T. F. (1998). Intergroup contact theory. *Annual Review of Psychology, 49*, 65–85.

Pettigrew, T. F., & Meertens, R. W. (1995). Subtle and blatant prejudice in Western Europe. *European Journal of Social Psychology, 25*, 57–75.

Rothbart, M., & John, O. P. (1985). Social categorization and behavioral episodes: A cognitive analysis of the effects of intergroup contact. *Journal of Social Issues, 41*(3), 81–104.

Rust, M. C. (1996). *Social identity and social categorization.* Unpublished doctoral dissertation. University of Delaware.

Sherif, M., Harvey, O. J., White, B. J., Hood, W. R., & Sherif, C. W. (1961). *Intergroup conflict and cooperation: The Robbers Cave experiment.* Norman, OK: University of Oklahoma Book Exchange.

Slavin, R. E. (1983). *Co-operative learning.* New York: Longman.

Smith, H. J., & Tyler, T. R. (1996). Justice and power: When will justice concerns encourage the advantaged to support policies which redistribute economic resources and the disadvantaged to willingly obey the law? *European Journal of Social Psychology, 26,* 171–200.

Stephan, W. G. (1986). The effects of school desegregation: An evaluation 30 years after *Brown.* In M. Saks & L. Saxe (Eds.), *Advances in applied social psychology* (Vol. 3, pp. 181–206). Hillside, NJ: Erlbaum.

Stephan, W. G. (1987). The contact hypothesis in intergroup relations. In C. Hendrick (Ed.), *Group processes and intergroup relations: Review of personality and social psychology* (Vol. 9, pp. 13–40). Beverly Hills, CA: Sage.

Stephan, W. G., & Stephan, C. W. (1984). The role of ignorance in intergroup relations. In N. Miller & M. Brewer (Eds.), *Groups in contact: The psychology of desegregation* (pp. 229–255). New York: Academic Press.

Stephan, W. G., & Stephan, C. W. (1985). Intergroup anxiety. *Journal of Social Issues, 41*(3), 157–175.

Tajfel, H. (1969). Cognitive aspects of prejudice. *Journal of Social Issues, 25,* 79–97.

Tajfel, H. (1978). Social categorization, social identity, and social comparison. In H. Tajfel (Ed.), *Differentiation between social groups* (pp. 61–76). London: Academic Press.

Tajfel, H., Billig, M., Bundy, R., & Flament, C. (1971). Social categorization and intergroup behaviour. *European Journal of Social Psychology, 1,* 149–178.

Turner, J. C. (1975). Social comparison and social identity: Some prospects for intergroup behaviour. *European Journal of Social Psychology, 5,* 5–34.

Turner, J. C. (1981). The experimental social psychology of intergroup behaviour. In J. Turner & H. Giles (Eds.), *Intergroup behaviour* (pp. 66–101). Oxford, UK: Blackwell.

Turner, J. C. (1985). Social categorization and the self-concept: A social cognitive theory of group behavior. In E. Lawler (Ed.), *Advances in group processes* (Vol. 2, pp. 77–122). Greenwich, CT: JAI Press.

Urban, L. M., & Miller, N. (1998). A theoretical analysis of crossed categorization effects: A meta-analysis. *Journal of Personality and Social Psychology, 74,* 894–908.

Vanbeselaere, N. (1991). The different effects of simple and crossed categorizations: A result of the category differentiation process or of differential category salience? In W. Stroebe & M. Hewstone (Eds.), *European review of social psychology* (Vol. 2, pp. 247–278). Chichester UK: Wiley.

Van Oudenhoven, J. P., Groenewoud, J. T., & Hewstone, M. (1996). Cooperation, ethnic salience, and generalization of interethnic attitudes. *European Journal of Social Psychology, 26,* 649–661.

Vanneman, R. D., & Pettigrew, T. F. (1972). Race and relative deprivation in the urban United States. *Race, 13,* 461–486.

Watson, G. (1947). *Action for unity.* New York: Harper.

Wilder, D. A. (1978). Reduction of intergroup discrimination through individuation of the out-group. *Journal of Personality and Social Psychology, 36,* 1361–1374.

Wilder, D. A. (1984). Intergroup contact: The typical member and the exception to the rule. *Journal of Experimental Social Psychology, 20,* 177–194.

Wilder, D. A. (1986). Social categorization: Implications for creation and reduction of intergoup bias. In L. Berkowitz (Ed.), *Advances in experimental social psychology* (Vol. 19, pp. 291–355). New York: Academic Press.

Wilder, D. A., & Shapiro, P. N. (1989). Role of competition-induced anxiety in limiting the beneficial impact of positive behavior by an out-group member. *Journal of Personality and Social Psychology, 56,* 60–69.

Wilder, D. A., & Thompson, J. E. (1980). Intergroup contact with independent manipulations of in-group and out-group interaction. *Journal of Personality and Social Psychology, 38,* 589–603.

Williams, R. M., Jr. (1947). *The reduction of intergroup tensions.* New York: Social Science Research Council.

Wilner, D. M., Walkley, R. P., & Cook, S. W. (1955). *Human relations in interracial housing.* Minneapolis, MN: University of Minnesota Press.

Worchel, S., Andreoli, V., & Folger, R. (1977). Intergroup cooperation and intergroup attraction: The effect of previous interaction and outcome of combined effort. *Journal of Experimental Social Psychology, 13,* 131–140.

Wright, S. C., Aron, A., McLaughlin-Volpe, T., & Ropp, S. A. (1997). The extended contact effect: Knowledge of cross-group friendships and prejudice. *Journal of Personality and Social Psychology, 73,* 73–90.

PART VIII

Applications

CHAPTER TWENTY-THREE

When and How School Desegregation Improves Intergroup Relations

Janet W. Schofield and Rebecca Eurich-Fulcer

For centuries humankind has struggled with conflicts among racial and ethnic groups. This conflict shows no sign of abating. Indeed, in recent years animosity between groups has sparked problems ranging from genocidal wars in Bosnia and Rwanda to individual hate crimes around the globe (Levin & McDevitt, 1993; Mays, Bullock, Rosenweig, & Wessells, 1998). Thus, the issue of how to improve intergroup relations is still of vital importance.

In the United States, school desegregation has been viewed as a possible route for improving intergroup relations, as indicated in the famous social science brief filed in the *Brown* v. *The Board of Education* case that laid the basis for school desegregation there. Thus, a substantial amount of research has focused on this outcome. A smaller amount of similar research has been conducted in other countries, most especially Israel. Although pertinent research from other countries is included in this chapter, the vast majority of the works cited here are from the United States because so much of the research on school desegregation has been produced there. In this chapter we explore the conditions under which school desegregation is likely to positively impact intergroup relations. However, before turning to that we first briefly examine some of the complexities arising in determining whether, generally speaking, school desegregation can be viewed as a social policy successful in improving intergroup relations.

Assessing the Success of Desegregation as a Social Policy for Improving Intergroup Relations

Research suggests that school desegregation often, but far from always, has positive effects on intergroup relations (Schofield, 1995b). Specifically, there is a modest-sized body of work suggesting that desegregation tends to have long-term positive effects on relations between individuals from different backgrounds (Stephan & Stephan, 1996). For example, students who attend desegregated schools are more likely to work and live in desegregated environments as adults than their peers from segregated schools (e.g., Astin, 1982; Braddock & McPartland, 1989; Braddock, McPartland, & Trent, 1984). Similarly, having attended a desegregated school is associated with more positive responses to White co-workers among adult African Americans (Braddock & McPartland, 1989).

However, research on the short-term effects of desegregation on intergroup relations suggests a more mixed picture (Schofield, 1991; St. John, 1975). Indeed, Stephan and Stephan (1996) conclude that desegregation more often reduces than increases prejudice among African American students but that the opposite is true for White students. Similarly, work in Israel suggests that contact between students can lead to either improved or worsened relations (Ben-Ari & Amir, 1986).

Other factors in addition to these somewhat inconsistent results contribute to the difficulty of coming to a definitive conclusion about whether, generally speaking, desegregation is a successful mechanism for improving intergroup relations. First, there are numerous ways to define success. Conceptualizing success as the creation of schools in which students from diverse backgrounds function without significant amounts of overt conflict might well lead to a different conclusion than conceptualizing it as creating schools which positively change the attitudes that students carry with them to other settings since these two changes do not necessarily go hand in hand. In fact, in one desegregated school the first author and her colleagues found generally neutral to positive peer-oriented classroom behavior (Schofield & Francis, 1982), improvements in intergroup behavior over time (Schofield & Sagar, 1977), and increased racial prejudice on the part of White students over time (Schofield, 1989). Patchen's (1982) large-scale study of 12 desegregated high schools in a Midwestern city in the United States similarly found varying results, with attitudes toward outgroup members as a group, the amount of friendly interaction with outgroup members, and the amount of unfriendly interaction with outgroup members being influenced by different aspects of the school situation.

A number of methodological problems also limit our ability to draw unambiguous conclusions about desegregation's impact on intergroup relations. Researchers working on this topic face serious measurement challenges. For example, some human subjects committees object to measures inquiring about negative relations between students from different racial and ethnic backgrounds, fearing that completing such instruments might spark conflict. Furthermore, there are often practical constraints on the length of measurement instruments related to concerns over lost class time. Finally, evaluation apprehension and social desirability are especially serious challenges here since evaluation of students by adults is the norm in schools and intergroup relations is such an emotion-laden topic.

Studies in this area have also been criticized for flaws related to the uncritical borrowing of instruments from earlier work that make it difficult to interpret their meaning. For example, the dependent measures in almost two-thirds of the studies considered for a meta-analysis on school desegregation (Schofield & Sagar, 1983) were structured so that improvement in minority/majority relations could occur only if students began to choose outgroup members *rather than* ingroup members, thus embodying the questionable assumption that intergroup relations can improve only at the expense of intragroup relations. In addition, many studies have used sociometric techniques that capture information on children's best friends (Asher, 1993; Schofield & Whitely, 1983). Although friendship is important in fostering improved intergroup attitudes (Pettigrew, 1997), using a stringent criterion such as best friendship as a measure of change in desegregated schools seems likely to lead to the conclusion that there has been little or no change in situations where change in less stringent outcomes, such as willingness to associate with outgroup members, may have occurred. Finally, measures developed using one population, often Whites, have been too readily used with other populations without adequate attention to whether the phenomena studied are parallel enough in the different populations to justify this (Schofield 1995b).

There are also several issues of study design that undercut the conclusiveness of findings in this area. First, desegregation studies are often plagued by self-selection problems at both the institutional and individual levels (Schofield, 1995b). Second, much of this research is correlational in nature, leaving open the question of the causal direction of any links found between school policies and student outcomes (Schofield, 1991, 1995a). Third, the majority of research dealing with the impact of desegregation is cross-sectional (i.e., comparing different groups of students with varying degrees of exposure to desegregation) rather than longitudinal (i.e., measuring the same students at various points in time, usually before and after desegregation) (Schofield, 1995b).

Unfortunately, even longitudinal studies in this area frequently have serious problems. Few span more than one year, often the first year of desegregation, which limits generalization from their findings since all involved are in the midst of adjusting to the desegregated situation during that year (Schofield, 1995b). Although occasional studies do span two to five or more years (e.g., Gerard & Miller, 1975; Savage, 1971; Schofield, 1979, 1989; Smith, 1971), they often have marked attrition problems. For example, Gerard and Miller lost approximately one-third of their sample during three years of data collection. Finally, many longitudinal studies employ no control group because of difficulties associated with locating appropriate ones (Schofield, 1995b). Given that there are both age trends (see Aboud & Amato, this volume, chapter 4) and historical trends in many of the variables studied as outcomes of desegregation, this is an especially serious problem.

Moreover, the production of research on desegregation slowed dramatically after the mid-1970s for a variety of reasons (Schofield, 1991). The mere fact that much of this research is 20 or more years old does not necessarily invalidate it (Schofield, 1998). It does, however, limit its usefulness for drawing conclusions about the present given that substantial changes in racial attitudes have taken place over that time period (Schuman, Steeh, Bobo, & Krysan, 1997). Furthermore, demographic changes mean that schools increasingly serve multiple groups of children from diverse backgrounds rather than virtually exclusively White and African American children which was often the case in the United States in the desegregated schools studied in earlier years (Orfield & Yun, 1999). This clearly changes the nature of many of the intergroup relations issues that arise (Peshkin, 1991).

Another factor that makes it difficult to reach a definitive conclusion about the success of desegregation is that researchers have often ignored the fact that desegregation can be

implemented in very different ways, and that these differences may well affect their outcomes (Cook, 1979). For example, school desegregation can occur as a result of a court
order or voluntarily. Either of these kinds of desegregation can be achieved through a
wide variety of mechanisms such as pairing previously segregated schools, closing segregated schools, or redistricting. Additionally, studies of schools with diverse student populations are often seen as part of this literature even though no formal desegregation plan
was involved because many of the intergroup relations issues that can be addressed in
such milieus are similar to those addressed in studies of schools under formal desegregation orders. Further, researchers sometimes do not provide clear descriptions of the situation and implementation process, making it difficult to decide if a study involves formal
desegregation or not, in addition to inhibiting comparisons across studies that might illuminate the factors accounting for their varied results.

Despite these important limitations, which make it difficult to assess the overall success
of desegregation as a social policy designed to improve intergroup relations, the literature
does offer substantial insight into when and how school desegregation may improve
intergroup relations among students. Thus we now turn to an exploration of this topic.

Conditions that Promote Positive Intergroup Contact within Desegregated Schools

The social psychological perspective that has most importantly influenced work on school
desegregation is known as the contact hypothesis. Allport's (1954) classic statement of
this approach emphasized that the nature of the contact between groups would influence
its effect and highlighted the importance of several specific factors including (a) the existence of opportunities to engage in close personalized contact with members of the other
group; (b) an emphasis on cooperative rather than competitive activities; (c) the existence
of equal status within the situation for members of all groups; and (d) the explicit support
of relevant authority figures for positive intergroup relations. Since then researchers from
around the world have suggested additional situational factors conducive to improving
intergroup relations (e.g., Ben-Ari & Amir, 1986). Although this approach has been
widely criticized as being little more than a "laundry list" whose increasing length has
limited its utility (Pettigrew, 1986, 1998), the contact hypothesis has generated and
helped organize a large body of research on school desegregation (Pettigrew, 1986). We
now turn to a discussion of findings from school desegregation research organized by the
set of conditions most commonly associated with the contact hypothesis.

Opportunities for close personalized contact with outgroup members: Contact as a necessary but not sufficient condition

From the perspective of the contact hypothesis, contact is a necessary but not sufficient
condition for improving intergroup relations, since the structure of the contact situation
is a moot point if there is no contact. Ironically, experience demonstrates that resegregation within desegregated schools is common (Eyler, Cook, & Ward, 1983; Schofield

1995b), suggesting that even mere contact may be much less frequent there than one would expect. Indeed, in one racially mixed school a student remarked, "All the segregation in this city was put in this school," reflecting the fact that although students from different backgrounds attended that school they had little contact with each other there (Collins & Noblit, 1978, p. 195).

A number of common educational practices foster resegregation within desegregated schools. The most obvious and widespread of these are tracking and ability grouping. Schools that categorize students on the basis of standardized tests, grades, or related criteria tend to have resegregated classrooms (Epstein, 1985). Furthermore, it is difficult to provide an education for children for whom English is not a first language without a certain amount of resegregation, although constructive approaches to this situation have been suggested (California State Department of Education, 1983; Carter & Chatfield, 1986; Cazabon, Lambert, & Hall, 1993; Fernandez & Guskin, 1978; Garcia, 1976; Gonzalez, 1979; Heleen, 1987; Lindholm, 1992; Morrison, 1990; Ovando, 1990a, 1990b; Roos, 1978; Wright & Tropp, 1998).

Although being in classes together is a start, sitting in the same classroom may well not be enough to bring about substantial change over time as both Klein and Eshel's (1980) study of desegregated schools in Israel and Gerard, Jackson, and Conolley's work (1975) in the United States suggest. Anxiety about dealing with outgroup members is often prevalent and can lead to avoidance of the very opportunities for contact that might help to improve intergroup relations (Stephan & Stephan, 1985). Indeed, students often voluntarily resegregate themselves due to anxiety and other causes (Cusick & Ayling, 1973; Friedlaender, Lazarin, Soukamneuth, & Yu, 1998; Gerard, Jackson, & Conolley, 1975; Pinderhughes, 1998; Rogers, Hennigan, Bowman, & Miller, 1984; Schofield, 1989). For example, one set of studies of seating patterns in the cafeteria of a school whose student body was roughly half African American and half White reported that only about 5% of the students sat next to someone of the other race on a typical day (Schofield, 1979; Schofield & Sagar, 1977) in spite of the fact that there was little overt racial friction there.

Unfortunately, this resegregation is often especially marked during free time and extracurricular activities in school – situations quite likely to allow the kind of sustained and close personalized contact that contact theorists suggest is crucial to improving relations between students from diverse backgrounds (Amir, 1969, 1976). Although certain kinds of partial resegregation can serve useful purposes, such as helping minority adolescents cope with the personal impact of racial stereotypes (Davidson, 1996; Tatum, 1995, 1997), it is undeniably true that extensive resegregation undermines opportunities for the kind of close personalized contact which Allport (1954) and his intellectual heirs such as Cook (1978) and Pettigrew (1998) propose as an important first step toward improved intergroup relations.

Cooperation in the pursuit of common goals

One way in which opportunities for personalized interaction among members of diverse groups occur is through cooperative interaction in the pursuit of common goals. Consistent with this, Allport (1954) argues that it is important that the contact situation foster cooperation rather than competition. The type of cooperation most likely to lead to improved intergroup relations is cooperation toward achieving a shared goal that cannot be accomplished without the contribution of members of both groups (Bossert, 1988/89; Johnson & Johnson, 1992). Cooperation that is based solely on the receipt of shared rewards (i.e., reward interdependence) does not appear to reduce intergroup hostility (Brewer & Miller, 1984).

Schools in numerous countries have historically stressed competition which research suggests can lead to stereotyping, unwarranted devaluation of the other group's accomplishments, and marked hostility, even when the groups initially have no history that might predispose them to negative reactions to each other (Worchel, 1979). Thus, schools are not typically milieus particularly conducive to promoting cooperation.

However, during the past 30 years seven distinct approaches to cooperative learning suitable for use in schools have been developed and tested over substantial periods in field settings (Slavin, 1995). This research has been carried out in the United States with groups of African American, Hispanic, Asian, and White students; in Canada with recent European immigrants, West Indian immigrants, and Anglos (Ziegler, 1981); and in Israel with various groups as well.

All of these approaches pay careful attention to the way cooperation is structured. For example, in the jigsaw method each student in a heterogeneous six-person group is given information on a subtopic related to the unit on which their group is working. After reading and discussing this segment of the unit in another group composed of individuals from other teams in the class who are also responsible for this particular information, students return to their original group to share this information with its members so they can achieve their common goal of learning the entire unit. Thus students on a team have a common goal, all students play an essential part in their groups, and the impact of possible pre-existing status differentials relating to academic achievement or other factors is mitigated by all students having the opportunity to become an "expert" on their particular topic (Aronson, Blaney, Stephan, Sikes, & Snapp, 1978). Another of these approaches, group investigation, which has been developed and tested extensively in Israel, emphasizes mechanisms that produce participation and joint decision making regarding joint products by small heterogeneous groups of students (Sharan & Sharan, 1992).

A host of researchers have found positive results in experiments on the impact of these cooperative team approaches with children from diverse backgrounds (Aronson et al., 1978; Aronson & Gonzales, 1988; Bossert, 1988/89; Cook, 1985; DeVries and Edwards, 1974; Hertz-Lazarowitz & Miller, 1992; Johnson & Johnson, 1982; Johnson, Johnson, & Maruyama, 1983, 1984; Sharan, 1980; Sharan & Sharan, 1992; Slavin, 1997). Such cooperative groups appear not only to foster improved intergroup relations but also to have positive academic consequences (Johnson, Maruyama, Johnson, Nelson, & Skon, 1981; Slavin, 1995).

Although research on cooperation in extracurricular activities is much more limited than research on cooperative learning teams, extracurricular activities, especially those that foster cooperation, can also play a constructive role in desegregated schools (Hawley et al., 1983). For example, Patchen (1982) found that participation in extracurricular activities had a stronger relation to interracial friendship than almost any of the numerous other variables in his study. Consistent with this, one of the few variables correlated with a variety of positive intergroup attitudes and behaviors in Slavin and Madden's (1979) study was participation in integrated athletics. Similarly, Clement and Harding (1978) found that participation in a group designed to help teachers maintain order in a desegregated school created a sense of cohesiveness among the sixth grade students that fostered positive relations among them. Unfortunately, given the preceding, extracurricular activities are often segregated, becoming the "turf" of one group or another in a school (Schofield & Sagar, 1983).

Although cooperation holds great potential for improving intergroup relations, it must be carefully structured (Hertz-Lazarowitz, Kirkus, & Miller, 1992; Miller & Harrington, 1992; Slavin, 1992). For example, inter-team competition has been found to reduce the benefits of cooperative interdependence among team members (Johnson, Johnson, & Maruyama, 1983; Sharan, 1980). Furthermore, it is important that the students involved contribute to group efforts in ways that do not reinforce traditional modes of interaction between majority and minority group members. For example, Cohen (1972) has found that when White and African American children interact with each other, the White children tend to be more active and influential even when the children have been matched on a wide variety of factors likely to influence their performance. Only after a carefully planned program that included having the Black children teach their White peers new skills did this tendency abate (Cohen & Lotan, 1997). Moreover, it has been suggested that in order for cooperation to positively impact intergroup relations students should be assigned to groups in a manner that makes their race or ethnicity low in salience (Miller & Harrington, 1992), although more recent studies found that positive change does not generalize well under such circumstances (Brown, Vivian, & Hewstone, 1999; Van Oudenhoven, Groenewoud, & Hewstone, 1996). Thus, although conditions conducive to improving intergroup relationships are found in many cooperative situations, they are neither inevitable aspects of all cooperative situations nor are they strictly limited to them.

Reducing the salience of racial/ethnic identities. One approach to reducing the salience of any one social category is to create what are called crosscutting categories (Schofield & McGivern, 1979; Vanbeselaere, 1991). It appears that creating additional, orthogonal bases of social categorization reduces the importance of any one categorization, such as race or ethnicity. Thus, for example, having African American and White students on each of two different cooperative learning teams means that racial background and team membership are crosscut. That is, students from different racial backgrounds now share something (i.e., team membership) with some members of the racial outgroup and simultaneously differ on that dimension from some members of their racial ingroup. If the social category that crosscuts racial or ethnic background is valued, meaningful, and salient, it may well undermine the tendency to discriminate based on the former (Brewer & Miller, 1984). Crosscutting role assignments with social categorizations during cooperative activities can also decrease intergroup bias (Bettencourt & Dorr, 1998) although it may not always be beneficial (Pepels, 1998).

Another constructive strategy is to create or emphasize shared social-category memberships for youths of different backgrounds, such as membership in a particular school or community (which rather than being crosscut with these memberships may be inclusive of them). Gaertner, Rust, Dovidio, Bachman, and Anastasio (1994) argue that the conditions espoused by contact theorists work because they induce individuals to alter their cognitive representations from that of separate ingroups and outgroups to a superordinate ingroup which encompasses previous outgroups. Based on this assumption, they conducted a study in a high school with a heterogeneous student body which measured students' perceptions of the extent to which the student body was one group or different groups. Students who held stronger perceptions that the student body was a unified group tended to show lower levels of bias than others. Thus, the creation of meaningful signs and symbols of shared identity (ranging from school T-shirts and traditions to special songs or the like) whether crosscutting racial identities or inclusive of them should be helpful in improving relations among diverse groups of students.

Creating affectively positive environments. Research on cooperation suggests that its impact on intergroup relations may be influenced by the outcome of the cooperative effort. Specifically, cooperation appears to be beneficial when individuals experience success on the task, whereas failure has been found to be detrimental to intergroup relations since it can lead to scapegoating of the outgroup (Worchel, Andreoli, & Folger, 1977). Such findings are consistent with research demonstrating that positive emotions caused by a wide variety of events (including presumably those stemming from success in cooperative efforts) increase self-disclosure and interaction with previously unknown others (e.g., Cunningham, 1988).

Serow and Solomon's (1979) findings that the teacher's warmth and acceptance of children, which presumably create a positive atmosphere, were correlated with positive interracial peer behavior suggest that positive emotions may also operate to improve intergroup relations in desegregated settings. However, the relationship between positive emotions and positive intergroup relations is not necessarily a simple one since there is also research demonstrating that positive affect can lead to greater stereotyping and increased perceptions of outgroup homogeneity (Wilder & Simon, this volume, chapter 8).

Equal status

According to Allport (1954) the contact situation must also be structured in a way that gives equal status to the groups involved. Although some have concluded that equal status is not absolutely essential for improving intergroup relations (e.g., Patchen, 1982), others emphasize its importance (e.g., Amir, 1976; Brown, 1995; Schofield, 1979). Researchers working in the area of school desegregation have tended to distinguish between equal status among groups *within* the contact situation and equal status among the groups *outside* the contact situation (i.e., on the basis of pre-existing factors such as socioeconomic status).

The relative status of racial or ethnic groups within a school may be influenced by the composition of the student body (Longshore & Prager, 1985). For example, if only a small number of students of a given background are present, they are unlikely to enjoy equal status since they form such a small group they will be unlikely to exert much influence in the institution. Consistent with the contact hypothesis, when minorities are a very small proportion of the total student body self-segregation seems to be heightened (Crain, Mahard, & Narot, 1982; Schofield & Sagar, 1983). For this and other reasons, experts suggest that minorities should represent at least 20% of the student body (Hawley et al., 1983) although some studies conducted in Israel have found no link between school composition and attitudinal change (Bizman & Amir, 1984).

The composition of the faculty and the administration is also important in the achievement of equal status within schools since, as in most organizations, the various occupational roles there are ordered in a status hierarchy. Unfortunately, there is a marked decline and shortage in the number of African American and other minority individuals who hold relatively high-status positions as teachers and administrators in schools in the United States (Boyer & Baptiste, 1996; Irvine & Irvine, 1983; King, 1993). Indeed, King (1993) notes that a large number of African Americans lost their jobs as teachers and administrators as a result of desegregation. Consequently, the way desegregation was implemented contributed to the under-representation of such individuals in high-status positions in the schools, which works against the improvement of intergroup relations.

Tracking and ability grouping, practices that clearly influence students' formal status within a school, are often instituted or emphasized in schools with heterogeneous student bodies. Unfortunately, given the substantial relationship between social class and academic achievement, unequal social status outside the school is likely to translate into unequal distribution of students from different backgrounds into the high- and low-status groups. Research suggests that tracking can undermine the achievement and motivation of students in lower tracks and has a negative effect on intergroup relations (Collins & Noblit, 1978; Epstein, 1985; National Opinion Research Center, 1973; Oakes, 1992). For example, Schofield (1979) reported that middle school students who had shown an increasing propensity to sit with other-race peers during lunchtime when they were seventh graders in heterogeneous classrooms moved toward more racially isolated seating patterns as eighth graders attending heavily tracked classes in the same school.

It is also important to realize that the extent to which the contact situation affords equal status to different groups may be a matter of interpretation (Robinson & Preston, 1976). Take something as apparently straightforward as the racial composition of the student body, which can be linked to status within the school as indicated earlier. Groups may misinterpret objective reality in a way that makes them feel disadvantaged. For example, Schofield (1989) reports that White students in a school that was roughly 50% African American were prone to overestimate the proportion of the student body that was Black, with one student even asserting it was "wall to wall Blacks" (p. 167). Furthermore, groups may have quite different views of whether a given procedure indicates that they have equal status in a situation. For example, in this same public school White parents generally believed admissions polices were fair. However, their Black counterparts pointed out that all White children applying there were accepted whereas hundreds of Black children were turned away out of concern for racially balancing the school, a situation which they argued suggested that Black students were treated as less desirable than White ones.

Even if schools avoid practices and policies that foster unequal status within their walls by reflecting status differences outside of the school, differences in group status outside the contact situation can influence the evolution of intergroup relations within it. For example, Bizman and Amir's (1984) work suggests that the intergroup attitudes of Israeli minority group members may change more positively when their group has higher status than their majority peers, whereas an equal status situation produces the most positive change for majority group members. Furthermore, as previously mentioned, research stimulated by status expectations theory suggests that external status differentials may replicate themselves in specific contact situations by influencing individuals' expectancies. Thus, characteristics such as age, sex, race, or ethnicity may generate expectations that shape interactions by influencing the power and prestige order that emerges (Cohen & Lotan, 1997).

Finding ways to prevent the unequal status of students in the larger society from creating unequal status within the school is a difficult problem that has not yet been satisfactorily solved. However, efforts to achieve equal status within the contact situation do seem to make some difference. For example, textbooks often ignore or demean the experiences and contributions of minority group members (Boateng, 1990; McAdoo & McAdoo, 1985; National Alliance of Black School Educators, 1984; Oakes, 1985) which is not conducive to creating equal status for all students within the schools. However, efforts to remedy this can have positive results. For example, Stephan and Stephan (1984) conclude that multiethnic curricula have a positive effect on intergroup relations when the program elements are of some reasonable complexity and duration. A more recent review by Banks (1995) comes to the same conclusion. In addition, status intervention treatments developed by Cohen (Cohen & Lotan, 1997) also show encouraging results. Finally, Epstein (1985) found a clear positive link between equal status programs (e.g., emphasis on the equality and importance of all students and avoidance of inflexible, academically based grouping) and African American students' attitudes toward desegregated schooling.

Support of authorities for positive relations

Finally, Allport (1954) contends that the support of authority, law, and custom for positive equal status relationships is vital to producing positive change through intergroup contact. Indeed, Pettigrew (1961) found that when authorities sanctioned desegregation the events surrounding it transpired less violently than otherwise. Moreover, research which examines individual cases of school desegregation within the United States suggests that both community and leadership support are key variables associated with the successful implementation of desegregation plans (Beck, 1980; Stave, 1995).

Support from authorities is likely to lead to beneficial effects partly because it fosters the formation of values supporting positive intergroup contact. Consistent with this, Brewer and Brown (1998) argue that decisions such as the 1954 Brown ruling and the British Race and Sex Discrimination Acts of 1965 and 1975 created a social climate in which it became unacceptable to openly degrade or discriminate against minorities.

However, such rulings are not likely to be translated directly into changes in students' intergroup attitudes and behavior although they are important symbolically.

For schoolchildren the most relevant authorities are probably their school's principal, their teachers, and their parents. In addition, as children move into adolescence peers become increasingly important arbiters of opinion and behavior. Although there is little research that empirically links principals' attitudes and behaviors to students' intergroup outcomes, those familiar with the functioning of desegregated schools generally agree that principals play an important role in shaping intergroup relations (Hawley et al., 1993). Principals can influence the course that desegregation takes through their actions toward teachers, students, and parents. First, they play an enabling function; that is, they make choices that facilitate or impede practices that promote positive intergroup relations, such as the adoption of cooperative learning teams. Second, they can model positive intergroup attitudes and behavior. Although there is no guarantee that others will follow the principal's example, it is likely to be helpful. Third, they can play a sensitizing function by putting the issue of intergroup relations on the school's agenda. Finally, the principal has the power to reward positive behavior and to discourage negative behavior through sanctions. Preventing negative intergroup behaviors is crucial because they can stimulate other negative behaviors in an escalating spiral. Indeed, one of the strongest predictors of unfriendly intergroup contact for both White and African American students is the students' general aggressiveness (Patchen, 1982). This highlights the importance of the principal's role in constructing an environment in which aggressive behavior is minimized.

Teachers are also important authority figures whose behavior affects relations between students. For example, Epstein (1985) found that teachers with positive attitudes toward desegregation use equal status instructional programs more than others and that students in such classrooms have more positive attitudes toward desegregation than peers in other classrooms. Patchen (1982) found a clear link between teachers' negative intergroup attitudes and White students' tendency to avoid their African American classmates. Gerard et al. (1975) found a relationship between teachers' prejudice and White children's acceptance of minority group students as friends that appeared to be mediated by the teachers' willingness to assign students to heterogeneous small groups for some of their classwork. Finally, Wellisch, Marcus, MacQueen, and Duck (1976) found more interracial mixing in informal settings among elementary school children whose teachers used classroom seating assignment policies that resulted in a lot of cross-race proximity than among children whose teachers tended to group children by race in their classrooms.

Awareness on the part of school authorities of the fact that individuals in a desegregated school may misunderstand each other's motives or intentions can be helpful. Also important is care in handling situations likely to result in intergroup conflict. For example, Greenfield's (1998) qualitative study of multiethnic sports teams in California high schools suggests that the coach's leadership style is crucial. The coach of the team that ended up having the fewest ethnic and racial tensions made it clear that intergroup hostility would not be accepted by meting out immediate public punishment to the team members when one member, a Euro-American boy, spoke in a disrespectful way to his African American teammate. In contrast, the coach of a team that ended up rife with such conflict typically avoided dealing with it or dealt with it as a private and individual manner, thus failing to set clear public norms against such behavior.

Although, as Aboud and Amato (this volume, chapter 4) point out, children's racial attitudes are not simply a mirror of their parents' attitudes, parents are also important authority figures whose attitudes and behaviors can make a difference (Flanagan, Gill, & Gallay, 1998). For example, the active and violent resistance of parents in Boston to school desegregation, which included stoning buses and keeping their children out of school, clearly exacerbated the problems that occurred in implementing the desegregation plan there as did the actions of parents in many cities in the southern United States as well (Lukas, 1985). Furthermore, Patchen's (1982) work demonstrates that students who perceived negative parental attitudes toward the racial outgroup were likely to avoid intergroup encounters and to have more unfriendly intergroup encounters than their peers who perceived more positive parental attitudes. It is possible that participants in this study misperceived their parents' attitudes, so that this connection is a function of their own attitudes rather than those of their parents. However, this and similar studies provide at least suggestive evidence of the importance of parental attitudes.

Thus, finding ways to encourage parents to support positive intergroup contact is likely to be important. Involving parents early in the planning process for desegregation, creating school and community-wide multiethnic committees involving parents, and providing information and opportunities for parental contact with the school all appear to be helpful (Hawley et al., 1983). Indeed, a study by Doherty, Cadwell, Russo, Mandel, and Longshore (1981) suggests that parent involvement in school activities can create more positive attitudes toward majority group members on the part of minority group students.

Peers may also be conceptualized as serving as authorities whose attitudes and behaviors regarding intergroup relations matter. Especially during adolescence, most students are members of peer groups and these tend to be important in influencing behavior, especially in times of anxiety or uncertainty when individuals tend to look to others for cues about their behavior (Fine, Weis, & Powell, 1997). Indeed, Blanchard, Lilly, and Vaughn's (1991) work shows that peers influence each other's expression of racist opinions. In addition, Patchen (1982) found that individuals' avoidance of outgroup members was clearly related to negative racial attitudes among their same race peers, which suggests that concerns about peer disapproval of intergroup contact can contribute to resegregation. Similarly, recent studies of multiracial schools by Carlson and Lein (1998), Friedlaender et al. (1998), and Pinderhughes (1998) suggest that peers play a strong role in influencing intergroup relations. Indeed, it seems likely that peer attitudes can inhibit or facilitate the development of intergroup friendships which is important in light of the accumulating evidence that such friendships positively influence intergroup attitudes (Pettigrew, 1997; Wright, Ropp, & Tropp, 1998).

Since pre-existing peer groups are likely to be racially homogeneous prior to desegregation, and contact may increase the salience of racial group membership, students are likely to look to their same-race peers for cues that influence them in important ways. Indeed, recently Wright, Aron, McLaughlin-Volpe, and Ropp (1997) concluded that there is considerable support for the idea that knowing that an ingroup peer has a close relationship with an outgroup member leads to more positive intergroup attitudes. This idea was tested in a recent quasi-experiment (Liebkind & McAlister, 1999). In this study, conducted with almost 1500 Finnish students aged 13–15 in schools with varying densities of foreign pupils, students in the experimental schools were presented with printed stories of ingroup members engaged in close friendships with members of the outgroup that were said to result in positive change in their attitudes toward the outgroup. They also participated in a discussion of these stories structured to elicit positive responses. Attitudes toward foreigners improved or remained stable in the experimental schools but declined or remained stable in the control schools in which students neither read the stories nor participated in the related discussion.

Although a well-structured contact situation is likely to be very important in influencing intergroup behavior, it must also be recognized that students often encounter each other outside of school in contexts that may be less well structured and that tensions from those encounters can spill over into the school day. Thus, peer tensions generated outside the contact situation may well affect what happens inside that situation. Furthermore, and more positively, work like that of Aboud and Doyle (1996), Tatum and Brown (1998), and Barroso, McAlister, Ama, Peters, and Kelder (1998) demonstrates that creative approaches can be developed to fostering peer processes to support positive intergroup relations.

Conclusions

In sum, there is no simple answer to the question of whether school desegregation has been successful in improving intergroup relations. A number of studies suggest that desegregation does have a positive long-term impact on intergroup realtions, but short-term outcomes appear to be more mixed. However, a substantial body of research has accumulated which provides useful guidance about the conditions that are likely to promote positive relations among students from diverse backgrounds, providing us with insights with the potential to enhance the known benefits of desegregation and to minimize possible negative outcomes.

Ironically, just as this body of research has accumulated, alongside a body of research that suggests that desegregation has modest positive effects on academic achievement and adult earnings for African Americans (Schofield, 1995b; Stephan & Stephan, 1996), commitment to desegregation as a social policy in the United States has virtually disappeared. A series of Supreme Court decisions in the 1990s changed the legal landscape significantly. Mandatory desegregation plans are being dissolved, voluntary ones are being challenged, and major districts in all regions of the country are phasing out their desegregation plans (Orfield & Yun, 1999). Furthermore, there appears to be a widespread public perception that desegregation has failed (Orfield, 1996), including an inaccurate perception that it has led to the massive exodus of Whites from the school districts involved. It is undeniable that desegregation has not eradicated the stubborn achievement gap between students of different backgrounds, that it has not automatically produced respectful positive relations between all students, and that some Whites leave desegregated districts (Rossell, 1990). Yet, in light of its documented accomplishments, the knowledge that has accumulated about how to enhance these outcomes, and the paucity of viable alternatives being considered to achieve the goals it serves, it seems shortsighted to abandon this policy because its benefits are less consistent and smaller in magnitude than many originally hoped they would be.

References

Aboud, F. E., & Doyle, A. B. (1996). Parental and peer influences on children's racial attitudes. *International Journal of Intercultural Relations, 20,* 371–383.

Allport, G. W. (1954). *The nature of prejudice.* Cambridge, MA: Addison-Wesley.

Amir, Y. (1969). Contact hypothesis in ethnic relations. *Psychological Bulletin, 71,* 319–342.

Amir, Y. (1976). The role of intergroup contact in change of prejudice and ethnic relations. In P. A. Katz (Ed.), *Towards the elimination of racism.* New York: Pergamon Press.

Aronson, E., Blaney, N., Stephan, C., Sikes, J., & Snapp, M. (1978). *The jigsaw classroom.* Beverly Hills, CA: Sage.

Aronson, E., & Gonzalez, A. (1988). Desegregation, jigsaw, and the Mexican-American experience. In P. A. Katz & D. A. Taylor (Eds.), *Eliminating racism: Profiles in controversy* (pp. 301–314). New York: Plenum Press.

Asher, S. R. (1993, May). *Assessing peer relationship processes and outcomes in interracial and interethnic contexts.* Paper presented at the Carnegie Corporation Consultation on Racial and Ethnic Relations in American Schools, New York.

Astin, A. (1982). *Minorities in American education.* San Francisco, CA: Jossey-Bass.

Banks, J. A. (1995). Multicultural education and the modification of students' racial attitudes. In W. D. Hawley & A. W. Jackson (Eds.), *Toward a common destiny* (pp. 315–339). San Francisco, CA: Jossey-Bass.

Barroso, C., McAlister, A., Ama, E., Peters, R. J., & Kelder, S. (1998, November). *Reducing prejudice and promoting tolerance among Hispanic high school students: Preliminary results from a quasi-experimental pilot study in Houston, Texas.* Paper presented at the Workshop on Research to Improve Intergroup Relations Among Youth, National Research Council, Washington, DC.

Beck, W. W. (1980). Identifying school desegregation leadership styles. *Journal of Negro Education, 49,* 115–133.

Ben-Ari, R., & Amir, Y. (1986). Contact between Arab and Jewish youth in Israel: Reality and potential. In M. Hewstone & R. Brown (Eds.), *Contact and conflict in intergroup encounters* (pp. 45–58). Oxford, UK: Blackwell.

Bettencourt, B. A., & Dorr, N. (1998). Cooperative interaction and intergroup bias: Effects of numerical representation and cross-cut role assignment. *Personality and Social Psychology Bulletin, 24,* 1276–1293.

Bizman, A., & Amir, Y. (1984) Integration and attitudes. In Y. Amir & S. Sharan (Eds.), *School desegregation: Cross-cultural perspectives.* Hillsdale, NJ: Erlbaum.

Blanchard, F. A., Lilly, T., & Vaughn, L. A. (1991). Reducing the expression of racial prejudice. *Psychological Science, 2,* 101–105.

Boateng, F. (1990). Combating deculturalization of the African-American child in the public school system: A multi-cultural approach. In K. Lomotey (Ed.), *Going to school: The African-American experience* (pp. 73–84). Albany, NY: State University of New York Press.

Bossert, S. T. (1988/89). Cooperative activities in the classroom. In E. Z. Rothkopf (Ed.), *Review of research in education* (Vol. 15, pp. 225–250). Washington, DC: American Educational Research Association.

Boyer, J. B., & Baptiste, H. P., Jr. (1996). The crisis in teacher education in America: Issues of recruitment and retention of culturally different (minority) teachers. In J. Sikula, T. J. Buttery,

& E. Guyton (Eds.), *Handbook of research on teacher education* (2nd ed., pp. 779–794). New York: Simon & Schuster Macmillan.

Braddock, J. H., & McPartland, J. M. (1989). Social-psychological processes that perpetuate racial segregation: The relationship between school and employment desegregation. *Journal of Black Studies, 19*, 267–289.

Braddock, J., McPartland, J., & Trent, W. (1984). *Desegregated schools and desegregated work environments*. Paper presented at the annual meeting of the American Educational Research Association, New Orleans, LA.

Brewer, M. B., & Brown, R. J. (1998). Intergroup relations. In D. T. Gilbert, S. T. Fiske, & G. Lindzey (Eds.), *Handbook of social psychology* (Vol.2, 4th ed., pp. 554–594). Boston, MA: McGraw Hill.

Brewer, M. B., & Miller, N. (1984). Beyond the contact hypothesis: Theoretical perspectives on desegregation. In N. Miller & M. B. Brewer (Eds.), *Groups in contact: The psychology of desegregation* (pp. 281–302). Orlando, FL: Academic Press.

Brown, R. (1995). *Prejudice. Its social psychology*. Oxford, UK: Blackwell.

California State Department of Education. (1983). *Desegregation and bilingual education – partners in quality education*. Sacramento, CA: California State Department of Education.

Brown, R. Vivian, J., & Hewstone, M. (1999). Changing attitudes through intergroup contact: The effects of group membership salience. *European Journal of Social Psychology, 29*, 741–764.

Carlson, C., & Lein, L. (1998). *Intergroup relations among middle school youth*. Paper presented at the Workshop on Research to Improve Intergroup Relations Among Youth, National Research Council, Washington, DC.

Carter, T., & Chatfield, M. L. (1986). Effective bilingual schools: Implications for policy and practice. *American Journal of Education, 95*, 200–232.

Cazabon, M., Lambert, W. E., & Hall, G. (1993). *Two-way bilingual education: A progress report on the Amigos Program*. Santa Cruz, CA: National Center for Research on Cultural Diversity.

Clement, D. C., & Harding, J. R. (1978). Social distinctions and emergent student groups in a desegregated school. *Anthropology and Education Quarterly, 8-9*, 272–282.

Cohen, E. (1972). Interracial interaction disability. *Human Relations, 25*, 9–24.

Cohen, E. G., & Lotan, R. A. (Eds.) (1997). *Working for equity in heterogeneous classrooms: Sociological theory in practice*. New York: Teachers College Press.

Collins, T. W., & Noblit, G. W. (1978). *Stratification and resegregation: The case of Crossover High School, Memphis, Tennessee* (Final report). Washington, DC: National Institute of Education.

Cook, S. W. (1978). Interpersonal and attitudinal outcomes in cooperating interracial groups. *Journal of Research and Development in Education, 12*, 97–113.

Cook, S. W. (1979). Social science and school desegregation: Did we mislead the Supreme Court? *Personality and Social Psychology Bulletin, 5*, 420–437.

Cook, S. W. (1985). Experimenting on social issues: The case of school desegregation. *American Psychologist, 40*, 452–460.

Crain, R. L., Mahard, R., & Narot, R. (1982). *Making desegregation work*. Cambridge, MA: Ballinger.

Cunningham, M. R. (1988). Does happiness mean friendliness? Induced mood and heterosexual self-disclosure. *Personality and Social Psychology Bulletin, 14*, 283–297.

Cusick, P., & Ayling, R. (1973, February). *Racial interaction in an urban secondary school*. Paper presented at the meeting of the American Educational Research Association, New Orleans, LA.

Davidson, A. (1996). *Making and molding of identity in schools: Students' narratives on race, gender, and academic engagement*. Albany, NY: State University of New York Press.

DeVries, D. L., & Edwards, K. (1974). Student teams and learning games: Their effects on cross-race and cross-sex interaction. *Journal of Educational Psychology, 66*, 741–749.

Doherty, W. J., Cadwell, J., Russo, N. A., Mandel, V., & Longshore, D. (1981). *Human relations study: Investigations of effective human relations strategies* (Vol. 2). Santa Monica, CA: System Development Corporation.

Epstein, J. L. (1985). After the bus arrives: Resegregation in desegregated schools. *Journal of Social Issues, 41*(3), 23–43.

Eyler, J., Cook, V., & Ward, L. (1983). Resegregation: Segregation within desegregated schools. In C. H. Rossell & W. D. Hawley (Eds.), *The consequences of school desegregation* (pp. 126–162). Philadelphia: Temple University Press.

Fernandez, R. R., & Guskin, J. T. (1978). Bilingual education and desegregation: A new dimension in legal and educational decision-making. In H. LaFontaine, B. Persky, & L. H. Glubshick (Eds.), *Bilingual education* (pp. 58–66). Wayne, NJ: Avery Publishing.

Fine, M., Weis, L., & Powell, L. C. (1997). Communities of difference: A critical look at desegregated spaces created for and by youth. *Harvard Educational Review, 67,* 247–284.

Flanagan, C., Gill, S., & Gallay, L. (1998, November). *Intergroup understanding, social justice, and the "social contract" in diverse communities of youth: Foundations for civic understanding.* Paper presented at the Workshop on Research to Improve Intergroup Relations Among Youth, National Research Council, Washington, DC.

Friedlaender, D., Lazarin, M., Soukamneuth, S., & Yu, H. C. (1998, November). *From intolerance to understanding: A study of intergroup relations among youth.* Paper presented at the Workshop on Research to Improve Intergroup Relations Among Youth, National Research Council, Washington, DC.

Garcia, G. F. (1976). The Latino and desegregation. *Integrated Education, 14,* 21–22.

Gaertner, S. L., Rust, M. C., Dovidio, J. F., Bachman, B. A., & Anastasio, P. A. (1994). The contact hypothesis: The role of a common ingroup identity on reducing intergroup bias. *Small Group Research, 25,* 224–249.

Gerard, H. B., Jackson, D., & Conolley, E. (1975). Social context in the desegregated classroom. In H. B. Gerard & N. Miller (Eds.), *School desegregation: A long-range study* (pp. 211–241). New York: Plenum Press.

Gerard, H. B., & Miller, N. (Eds.) (1975). *School desegregation: A long-range study.* New York: Plenum Press.

Gonzalez, J. M. (1979). *Bilingual education in the integrated school.* Arlington, VA: National Clearinghouse for Bilingual Education.

Greenfield, P. (1998). *How can sports teams promote racial tolerance and positive intergroup relations? Key lessons from recent research.* Paper presented at the Workshop on Research to Improve Intergroup Relations Among Youth. Washington, DC.

Hawley, W., Crain, R. L., Rossell, C. H., Smylie, M., Fernandez, R., Schofield, J., Tompkins, R., Trent, W. P., & Zlornik, M. (1983). *Strategies for effective desegregation: Lessons from research.* Boston, MA: Lexington Books, D. C. Heath.

Heleen, O. (Ed.). (1987). Two-way bilingual education: A strategy for equity [Special issue]. *Equity and Choice, 3*(3).

Hertz-Lazarowitz, R., Kirkus, V. B., & Miller, N. (1992). Implications of current research on cooperative interaction for classroom application. In R. Hertz-Lazarowitz & N. Miller (Eds.), *Interaction in cooperative groups* (pp. 253–280). New York: Cambridge University Press.

Hertz-Lazarowitz, R., & Miller, N. (Eds.) (1992). *Interaction in cooperative groups.* New York: Cambridge University Press.

Irvine, I. W., & Irvine, J. J. (1983). The impact of the desegregation process on the education of Black students: Key variables. *The Journal of Negro Education,* 410–422.

Johnson, D. W., & Johnson, R. T. (1982). The study of cooperative, competitive, and individualistic situations: State of the area and two recent contributions. *Contemporary Education, 1*(1), 7–13.

Johnson, D. W., & Johnson, R. T. (1992). Positive interdependence: Key to effective cooperation. In R. Hertz-Lazarowitz & N. Miller (Eds.), *Interaction in cooperative groups* (pp. 174–199). New York: Cambridge University Press.

Johnson, D. W., Johnson, R., & Maruyama, G. (1983). Interdependence and interpersonal attraction among heterogeneous and homogeneous individuals: A theoretical formulation and meta-analysis of the research. *Review of Educational Research, 53*(1), 5–54.

Johnson, D. W., Johnson, R. T., & Maruyama, G. (1984). Goal interdependence and interpersonal attraction in heterogeneous classrooms: A meta-analysis. In N. Miller & B. Brewer (Eds.), *Groups in contact: The psychology of desegregation* (pp. 187–212). Orlando, FL: Academic Press.

Johnson, D. W., Maruyama, G., Johnson, R., Nelson, D., & Skon, L. (1981). Effects of cooperative, competitive, and individualistic goal structures on achievement: A meta-analysis. *Psychological Bulletin, 89*, 47–62.

King, S. H. (1993). The limited presence of African-American teachers. *Review of Educational Research, 63*(2), 115–149.

Klein, Z., & Eshel, Y. (1980). *Integrating Jerusalem schools.* New York: Academic Press.

Levin, J., & McDevitt, J. (1993). *Hate crimes: The rising tide of bigotry and bloodshed.* New York: Plenum Press.

Liebkind, K., & McAlister, A. L. (1999). Extended contact through peer modelling to promote tolerance in Finland. *European Journal of Social Psychology, 29*, 765–780.

Lindholm, K. J. (1992). Two-way bilingual/immersion education: Theory, conceptual issues, and pedagogical implications. In R. V. Padilla & A. H. Benavides (Eds.), *Critical perspectives on bilingual education research* (pp. 195–220). Tempe, AZ: Bilingual Press/Editorial Bilingue.

Longshore, D., & Prager, J. (1985). The impact of school desegregation: A situational analysis. *Annual Review of Sociology, 11*, 75–91.

Lukas, J. A. (1985). *Common ground.* New York: Knopf.

Mays, V. M., Bullock, M., Rosenzweig, M. R., & Wessells, M. (1998). Ethnic conflict: Global challenges and psychological perspectives. *American Psychologist, 53*, 737–742.

McAdoo, H. P., & McAdoo, J. W. (Eds.) (1985). *Black children: Social educational and parental environments.* Beverly Hills, CA: Sage.

Miller, N., & Harrington, H. J. (1992). Social categorization and intergroup acceptance: Principles for the design and development of cooperative learning teams. In R. Hertz-Lazarowitz & N. Miller, (Eds.), *Interactions in cooperative groups* (pp. 203–222). New York: Cambridge University Press.

Morrison, S. H. (1990). A Spanish–English dual-language program in New York City. In C. B. Cazden & C. E. Snow (Eds.), *English plus issues in bilingual education* (pp. 160–169). Newbury Park, CA: Sage.

National Alliance of Black School Educators. (1984). *Saving the African-American child.* Washington, DC.

National Opinion Research Center (1973). *Southern schools: An evaluation of the effects of the Emergency School Assistance Program and of school desegregation* (Vols. 1 & 2). Chicago, IL.

Oakes, J. (1985). *Keeping track: How schools structure inequality.* New Haven, CT: Yale University Press.

Oakes, J. (1992). Can tracking research inform practice? Technical, normative, and political consideration. *Educational Researcher, 21*(4), 12–21.

Orfield, G. (1996). Plessy parallels: Back to traditional assumptions. In G. Orfield & S. E. Eaton, and the Harvard Project on School Desegregation (Eds.) *Dismantling desegregation: The quiet reversal of Brown v. Board of Education.* New York: New Press.

Orfield, G., & Yun, J. T. (1999). *Resegregation in American schools.* Cambridge, MA: The Civil Rights Project, Harvard University.

Ovando, C. J. (1990a). Intermediate and secondary school curricula: A multicultural and multilingual framework. *The Clearing House, 63*(7), 294–298.

Ovando, C. J. (1990b). Politics and pedagogy: The case of bilingual education. *Harvard Educational Review, 60*(3), 341–356.

Patchen, M. (1982). *Black-White contact in schools: Its social and academic effects.* West Lafayette, IN: Purdue University Press.

Pepels, J. (1998). *The myth of the positive crossed categorization effect.* The Netherlands: Thela Thesis.

Peshkin, A. (1991). *The color of strangers, the color of friends.* Chicago, IL: University of Chicago Press.

Pettigrew, T. F. (1961). Social psychology and desegregation research. *American Psychologist, 15,* 61–71.

Pettigrew, T. F. (1986). The intergroup contact hypothesis reconsidered. In M. Hewstone & R. Brown (Eds.), *Contact and conflict in intergroup encounters* (pp. 169–195). Oxford, UK: Blackwell.

Pettigrew, T. F. (1997). The affective component of prejudice: Empirical support for the new view. In S. A. Tuck & J. K. Martin (Eds.), *Racial attitudes in the 1990s: Continuity and change.* Westport, CT: Praeger.

Pettigrew, T. F. (1998). Intergroup contact theory. *Annual Review of Psychology, 49,* 65–85.

Pinderhughes, H. (1998, November). *Forging a multicultural school environment: An examination of intergroup relations at an innercity high school – The P.R.O.P.S. program.* Paper presented at the Workshop on Research to Improve Intergroup Relations Among Youth, National Research Council, Washington, DC.

Robinson, J. W., & Preston, J. D. (1976). Equal-status contact and modification of racial prejudice: A reexamination of the contact hypothesis. *Social Forces, 54,* 911–924.

Rogers, M., Hennigan, K., Bowman, C., & Miller, N. (1984). Intergroup acceptance in classrooms and playground settings. In N. Miller & M. B. Brewer (Eds.). *Groups in contact: The psychology of desegregation* (pp. 213–227). New York: Academic Press.

Roos, P. D. (1978). Bilingual education: The Hispanic response to unequal educational opportunity. *Law and Contemporary Problems, 42,* 111–140.

Rossell, C. H. (1990). *The carrot or the stick for school desegregation policy.* Philadelphia: Temple University Press.

St. John, N. H. (1975). *School desegregation: Outcomes for children.* New York: Wiley.

Savage, L. W. (1971). *Academic achievement of Black students transferring from a segregated junior high school to an integrated high school.* Unpublished master's thesis, Virginia State College, Petersberg, VA.

Schofield, J. W. (1979). The impact of positively structured contact on intergroup behaviors: Does it last under adverse conditions? *Social Psychology Quarterly, 42,* 280–284.

Schofield, J. W. (1989). *Black and White in school: Trust, tension or tolerance?* New York: Teachers College Press.

Schofield, J. W. (1991). School desegregation and intergroup relations: A review of the literature. In G. Grant (Ed.), *Review of research in education* (Vol. 17, pp. 335–409). Washington, DC: American Educational Research Association.

Schofield, J. W. (1995a). Improving intergroup relations among students. In J. A. Banks & C. A. McGee Banks (Eds.), *Handbook of research on multicultural education* (pp. 635–646). New York: Macmillan.

Schofield, J. W. (1995b). Review of research on school desegregation's impact on elementary and secondary school students. In J. A. Banks & C. A. McGee Banks (Eds.), *Handbook of research on multicultural education* (pp. 597–616). New York: Macmillan.

Schofield, J. W. (1998). *Research on intergroup relations: The state of the field.* Paper presented at the meeting of the Forum on Adolescence, National Research Council, National Academy of Sciences, Washington, DC.

Schofield, J. W., & Francis, W. D. (1982). An observational study of peer interaction in racially mixed "accelerated" classrooms. *The Journal of Educational Psychology, 74,* 722–732.

Schofield, J. W., & McGivern, E. P. (1979). Creating interracial bonds in a desegregated school. In R. G. Blumberg & W. J. Roye (Eds.), *Interracial bonds* (pp. 106–119). Bayside, NY: General Hall.

Schofield, J. W., & Sager, H. A. (1977). Peer interaction patterns in an integrated middle school. *Sociometry, 40,* 130–138.

Schofield, J. W., & Sagar, H. A. (1983). Desegregation, school practices, and student race relations. In C. H. Rossell & W. D. Hawley (Eds.), *The consequences of school desegregation* (pp. 58–102). Philadelphia: Temple University Press.

Schofield, J. W., & Whitley, B. E. (1983). Peer nominations vs. rating scale measurement of children's peer preference. *Social Psychology Quarterly, 46,* 242–251.

Schuman, H., Steeh, C., Bobo, L., & Kryson, M. (1997). *Racial attitudes in America: Trends and interpretation, revised edition.* Cambridge, MA: Harvard University Press.

Serow, R. C., & Solomon, D. (1979). Classroom climates and students' intergroup behavior. *Journal of Educational Psychology, 71,* 669–676.

Sharan, S. (1980). Cooperative learning in teams: Recent methods and effects on achievement, attitudes, and ethnic relations. *Review of Educational Research, 50,* 241–272.

Sharan, Y., & Sharan, S. (1992). *Expanding cooperative learning through group investigation.* New York: Teachers College Press.

Slavin, R. E. (1992). When and why does cooperative learning increase achievement? Theoretical and empirical perspectives. In R. Hertz-Lazarowitz & N. Miller (Eds.), *Interaction in cooperative groups* (pp. 145–173). New York: Cambridge University Press.

Slavin, R. E. (1995). Cooperative learning and intergroup relations. In J. A. Banks & C. A. McGee Banks (Eds.), *Handbook of research on multicultural education* (pp. 628–634), New York: Macmillan.

Slavin, R. E. (1997). Cooperative learning and student diversity. In Y. Amir, R. Ben-Ari, & Y. Rich (Eds.), *Enhancing education in heterogeneous schools: Theory and application* (pp. 215–247), Ramat-Gan: Bar-Ilan University Press.

Slavin, R. E., & Madden, N. A. (1979). School practices that improve race relations. *American Educational Research Journal, 16,* 169–180.

Smith, L. R. (1971). *A comparative study of the achievement of Negro students attending segregated junior high schools and Negro students attending desegregated junior high schools in the City of Tulsa.* Unpublished doctoral dissertation, University of Tulsa.

Stave, S. A. (1995). *Achieving racial balance: Case studies of contemporary school desegregation.* Westport, CN: Greenwood Press.

Stephan, W. G., & Stephan, C. W. (1984). The role of ignorance in intergroup relations. In N. Miller & M. B. Brewer (Eds.), *Groups in contact: The psychology of desegregation* (pp. 229–255), Orlando, FL: Academic Press.

Stephan, W. G., & Stephan, C. W. (1985). Intergroup anxiety. *Journal of Social Issues, 41(3),* 157–175.

Stephan, W. G., & Stephan, C. W. (1996). *Intergroup relations.* Boulder, CO: Westview Press.

Tatum, B. D. (1995). Talking about race, learning about racism: The application of racial identity development theory in the classroom. *Harvard Educational Review, 62,* 1–24.

Tatum, B. D. (1997). Identity development in adolescence: "Why are all the Black kids sitting together in the cafeteria?" In B. D. Tatum, *"Why are all the Black kids sitting together in the cafeteria?" And other conversations about race* (pp. 52–74). New York: Basic Books.

Tatum, B. D., & Brown, P. C. (1998, November). *Improving interethnic relations among youth: A school-based project involving teachers, parents, and children.* Paper presented at the Workshop on Research to Improve Intergroup Relations Among Youth, National Research Council, Washington, DC.

Van Oudenhoven, J. P., Groenewoud, J. T., & Hewstone, M. (1996). Cooperation, ethnic salience, and generalization of interethnic attitudes. *European Journal of Social Psychology, 26,* 649–661.

Vanbeselaere, N. (1991). The different effects of simple and crossed social categorizations: A result of the category differentiation process or of differential category salience? In W. Stroebe & M. Hewstone (Eds.), *European review of social psychology* (Vol. 2, pp. 247–278). Chichester, UK: Wiley.

Wellisch, J. B., Marcus, A., MacQueen, A., & Duck, G. (1976). *An in-depth study of Emergency School Aid Act (ESAA) schools: 1974–1975.* Report to the Department of Health, Education and Welfare, Office of Education. Washington, DC: System Development Corporation.

Worchel, S. (1979). Cooperation and the reduction of intergroup conflict: Some determining factors. In W. G. Austin & S. Worchel (Eds.), *The social psychology of intergroup relations* (pp. 262–273). Monterey, CA: Brooks/Cole.

Worchel, S., Andreoli, V., & Folger, R. (1977). Intergroup cooperation and intergroup attraction: The effect of previous interaction and outcome of combined efforts. *Journal of Experimental Social Psychology, 13,* 131–140.

Wright, S. C., Aron, A., McLaughlin-Volpe, T., & Ropp, S. A. (1997). The extended contact effect: Knowledge of cross-group friendships and prejudice. *Journal of Personality and Social Psychology, 73*(1), 73–90.

Wright, S. C., Ropp, S. A., & Tropp, L. R. (1998, August). *Intergroup contact and the reduction of prejudice: Findings in support of the friendship hypothesis.* Paper presented at the meeting of the American Psychological Association, San Francisco, CA.

Wright, S. C., & Tropp, L. R. (1998). Language of instruction and contact effects: Bilingual education and intergroup attitudes. Submitted to the *Journal of Educational Psychology.*

Ziegler, S. (1981). The effectiveness of cooperative learning teams for increasing cross-ethnic friendship: Additional evidence. *Human Organization, 40,* 264–268.

CHAPTER TWENTY-FOUR

Addressing and Redressing Discrimination: Affirmative Action in Social Psychological Perspective

Faye J. Crosby, Bernardo M. Ferdman, and Blanche R. Wingate

Social justice has been a recurring theme in social psychology. Theorists and researchers in our field have long been interested in understanding how interactions among groups and individuals relate to broader patterns of intergroup relations. Because typically such patterns include quite negative forms, including domination, discrimination, prejudice, and exclusion, much of social psychology's attention has focused on ways to ameliorate these problems. More recently, social psychologists have also attended to positive forms of intergroup relations, such as intergroup cooperation and organizational diversity initiatives. Nevertheless, the field's dominant tenor has been that intergroup relations are fundamentally problematic. It is in this context that social psychologists have considered the implications and effects of affirmative action (AA), or more generally, societal and organizational policies designed to proactively reduce or eliminate unfair group-based historical disadvantages.

AA policies have been the object of much contention. In this chapter, we delineate the social psychological issues involved in the controversies over AA in the United States and review both theory and empirical research regarding reactions to AA policies. First placing AA in the context of historical patterns of discrimination, we go on to describe what AA is and why it is needed. We then review evidence regarding reactions to AA by both direct beneficiaries and members of privileged groups. Finally, we provide perspectives for enhancing future theory and research on AA.

The authors are grateful to Carol Bronson, Alice Eagly, David Kravitz, and the editors of this volume for carefully and thoughtfully commenting on earlier versions of this chapter.

Intergroup Discrimination and Exclusion

AA policies and programs exist in the context of and in response to long societal histories of systematic and institutionalized exclusion and discrimination. For example, in the United States, women have long been denied entry to the full range of educational and professional opportunities. Before the 1964 Civil Rights Act, legal segregation and discrimination by race were widespread. Past prejudice and discrimination have had persistent effects. Currently in the United States, racism and sexism mean that despite civil rights and other legislation designed to create equality, the experience and opportunities available to individuals are shaped by the relationships of their group to other groups (Benokraitis, 1997; Dovidio & Gaertner, 1998; Jones, 1997; Operario & Fiske, 1998).

While affirmative action policy is designed to overcome a long-term legacy of invidious intergroup discrimination, AA is not a perfect policy. Nor is it always perfectly implemented. This makes AA a particularly rich and challenging subject for psychologists. It is also a topic on which psychologists must be self-reflective. Although many psychologists attempt to portray their approach as objective and racially unbiased, the legacy of the field has been otherwise (Morawski, 1997) and one cannot really remain neutral on the topic. Views of affirmative action – pro and con – link to views about the proper relations among various groups (e.g., women and men) and between individuals within groups.

How investigators approach their research reveals a great deal about their assumptions regarding the phenomena of interest. In the case of AA, some researchers (e.g., Heilman, 1996; Nacoste, 1994) have made pronouncements about AA's potentially deleterious effects on the basis of results from experiments in which participants reacted to either merit-based or category-based selections of people for tasks and rewards. The persistent juxtaposition of merit-based versus category-based selection is based on the assumption that one cannot simultaneously pay attention to both merit and group membership. Yet most identity-conscious AA programs do exactly that. Some experimental designs assume, in other words, that selecting individuals for positions in a group-conscious fashion necessarily means that merit cannot be considered. But as Konrad and Linnehan (1999) point out, research designs that ask participants to consider both qualifications and group membership would more closely parallel actual AA practices. If they are to avoid bias, researchers must not expect their participants to assume that anyone selected for a job will be qualified except for persons from under-represented groups, such as men and women of color, or White women. The term "qualified minority" or "qualified woman" carries many associations, including the implication that these associations are not commonly expected. In the United States, however, we do not usually see – in the context of selection for jobs – the term "qualified majority group member."

Affirmative Action: What is it and Why is it Needed?

Affirmative action is a term that often appears in the media but that rarely is defined. In the broadest sense, AA occurs whenever an organization expends energy to make sure that equal opportunity exists. AA policies exist in a number of countries, including Australia (Kramer, 1994), Belgium, France, the Netherlands (Chalude, De Jong, & Laufer, 1994; De Vries & Pettigrew, 1994), Canada (Leck & Saunders, 1992), Malaysia (Abdullah, 1997), and Pakistan (Waseem, 1997). It is in the United States that AA has the longest – and possibly the most complicated – history.

In employment, AA has been the law in the United States since 1965, when President Johnson signed Executive Order 11246. At that time "classical affirmative action" (American Psychological Association, 1996) began. Classical AA essentially involves two steps. First, using well-established guidelines, an organization monitors its own practices to make sure it employs qualified people in designated groups in proportion to their availability. Second, if imbalances between availability and utilization are discovered, corrective measures are taken. Clearly, the monitoring processes require an organization to be aware of people's group memberships to make sure that it utilizes qualified people from the targeted groups (e.g., White women; African American, Hispanic, Native American, and Asian American men and women) in proportion to their availability. Since 1965, practices such as "set-asides" (reserving a specific proportion of jobs or contracts for members of a given set of groups) and "quotas" (requiring the hiring of specific numbers in targeted groups) were instituted by some organizations. Such practices rarely withstand legal challenge. President Clinton's administration has sought to eradicate practices that do not conform to the classical definition of AA (Stephanopoulos & Edley, 1995).

In education, as in employment, the thrust of AA is to rid the system of hidden pockets of previously unacknowledged privilege and to open institutions to people from all backgrounds. Consider the University of California where the Regents have forbidden officials to notice ethnicity or gender in admissions. Administrators there support vigorous outreach programs to high schools and even to elementary schools. In addition, leaders like Chancellor Berdahl at Berkeley have urged reform of the admissions formula. Currently, extra points are awarded to Advanced Placement (AP) courses. Thus a B in an AP course receives four points – just the same number as an A in a "regular" course. Admissions to the university are determined in large part by a student's high school grade point average. Because wealthy school districts can afford to offer AP courses while poor ones cannot, the system unfairly advantaged wealthy people, who are disproportionately White. Now that vigilance has revealed the problem, thoughtful minds can work on solutions.

AA has had a critical role in reducing discrimination in the United States. A number of studies by economists have documented that both gender and ethnic disparities in pay are less pronounced among AA employers than among other employers (Tomasson, Crosby, & Herzberger, 1996). Recent scholarship has also shown that AA employers are more profitable than other employers (Reskin, 1998). AA has apparently fostered selection procedures that are more fair and valid than previous procedures (Konrad & Linnehan, 1999), perhaps especially by opening the doors to highly qualified applicants of all backgrounds.

What accounts for the superior economic effectiveness of affirmative action relative to passive equal opportunity? The superior effectiveness derives at least in part from the way that AA minimizes the consequences of a set of psychological processes that have been the object of intense study in the last decade. In 1982 Crosby first described what she has called "the denial of personal disadvantage." Over a dozen investigations have now replicated Crosby's essential finding that individuals from disadvantaged groups tend to imagine that they personally are exempt from the problems that they know affect their group. It seems that people only notice the personal relevance of societal discrimination when the injustices are flagrant. In addition, a set of laboratory studies has demonstrated how even very intelligent and highly educated decision makers have difficulty detecting small inequities unless the data are presented in aggregated form (Clayton & Crosby, 1992). Because AA does not rely on aggrieved individuals to come forward on their own behalf, it helps organizations avoid allowing small injustices accumulate to the boiling point. Because classical AA operates by aggregating information, furthermore, it allows administrators to head off problems before they erupt into explosive situations. Research by Konrad and Linnehan (1995a) showed that identity-conscious strategies adopted because of AA were more likely to have a positive impact on the employment status of White women and men and women of color, while identity-blind structures did not lead to improved outcomes for members of these groups.

Reactions to Affirmative Action Programs

AA policy and AA programs (AAPs) are highly controversial. Why does one person endorse AA and another resist or disfavor it? While some polemicists (e.g., Steele, 1991) explain people's reactions in simplistic terms, most scholars (e.g., Bergmann, 1996; Bobo & Kluegel, 1993; Kravitz et al., 1997; Reskin, 1998; Tomasson et al., 1996; Turner & Pratkanis, 1994) acknowledge that a number of factors contribute to the range of reactions among White men, White women, and men and women of color in the United States.

Conceptualizing the factors

Some researchers focus on self-interest (including interested reactions on behalf of one's group) as one influence on people's reactions both to the policy and the practice of AA (Esses & Seligman, 1996). With few exceptions (Murrell, Dietz-Uhler, Dovidio, Gaertner, & Drout, 1994) women favor AA more than men do (Dovidio, Mann, & Gaertner, 1989; Golden, Hinkle, & Crosby, 1998; Goldsmith, Cordova, Dwyer, Langlois, & Crosby, 1989; Kravitz & Platania, 1993; Little, Murray, & Wimbush, 1998; Ozawa, Crosby, & Crosby, 1996; Tickamyer, Scollay, Bokemeier, & Wood, 1989). Endorsement of AA is greater among people of color than among Whites (Bobo & Kluegel, 1993; Bobo & Smith, 1994; Fine, 1992a; Golden et al., 1998; Kinder & Sanders, 1990; Konrad & Linnehan, 1995b; Kravitz, Klineberg, Avery, Nguyen, Lund, & Fu, in press; Little et al., 1998; Sigelman & Welch, 1991; Tomasson et al., 1996). Sometimes (Klineberg & Kravitz, 1999; Kravitz & Platania, 1993) but not always (Vargas-Machuca & Kottke, 1999) the reactions of Latinos fall somewhere between those of Whites and Blacks.

Given the vehement opposition to AA on the part of some Black men (e.g., Carter, 1991; Sowell, 1994; Steele, 1991) and some White women (e.g., Heilman, 1996), it seems unlikely that narrow self-interest is the only determinant of people's reactions to AA. Similarly, the resolute endorsement of AA specifically and of diversity initiatives generally by many White men shows that opinions about affirmative action are not simply dictated by personal self-interest (see e.g., Bowen & Bok, 1998; Ferdman & Brody, 1995; Wu & Taylor, 1996), Other factors must be at play.

Another important factor is fairness. For many people, AA is equated with unjustified preferential treatment (Belkin, 1998; Crosby & Cordova, 1996; Fine, 1992a), which violates basic principles of procedural or distributive justice (Clayton & Tangri, 1989; Opotow, 1997; Tyler, this volume, chapter 17). Unlike "equal opportunity" policies, AA may appear to some to penalize White males (Crosby, 1994; Heilman, 1996). Members of both dominant and nondominant groups react most favorably to outreach and other "soft" AAPs and least favorably to programs which are construed as giving preferential treatment to specific target groups (Kravitz, 1995; Kravitz & Platania, 1993; Nacoste, 1985).

Yet considerations of fairness may not be as straightforward as they first appear. Whether one sees AA as a fair or unfair policy may itself be an indicator of one's commitment to the dominant ideology in the United States. According to Kluegel and Smith (1986), three cognitions combine in the dominant meritocratic ideology. These cognitions are: (1) that everyone has an opportunity to succeed economically; (2) that success and failure are caused by individual factors instead of structural factors; and (3) that unequal outcomes are appropriate because they reflect the inequality of contributions. Those who are skeptical about the dominant ideology or distrust how the meritocratic ideal works in reality may see AA as a means to achieve real fairness (Crosby & Cordova, 1996; Haney & Hurtado, 1994), while those who subscribe to the dominant ideology and trust the operation of the meritocratic ideal may dislike AA (Crosby, 1994). The group-based systemic approach of AA, furthermore, may be uncongenial to individualistically oriented Americans, even when those Americans perceive that a problem exists (Ozawa et al., 1996). Deep ideological rifts may thus explain how opponents of AA can genuinely bristle at what they see as the injustice of the policy while proponents can, with equal sincerity, be dismayed at the hidden injustices of so-called "equal opportunity" which they envision as being exposed and corrected by AA.

When opposition to AA derives from a reluctance to acknowledge (let alone dismantle) the privileges of those at the top of the social hierarchy, then opposition may also be linked to racism and sexism. The unthinking equation of diversity with a lowering of standards is certainly racist and sexist. Racial prejudice is the belief that racial differences are tantamount to inherent superiority of a particular race. In their theory of aversive racism, Gaertner and Dovidio (1986) propose that White people are able to adopt egalitarian values while still possessing negative perceptions of Black people. McConahay (1986) argues that although modern racists shun traditionally racist beliefs, they have not entirely discarded their negative attitudes toward Black people. Based on these theories, it seems likely that there will be a relationship between attitudes toward AA and prejudice. If racism were dead in the United States, how could we explain that White people endorse programs designated to help (White) women overcome discrimination more than they endorse programs designated to help Black people overcome discrimination (Tomasson et al., 1996)? The finding that White students who think they are judging journalists' essays evaluate anti-AA editorials more positively than pro-AA editorials, especially when a Black writer is supposed to have written the editorial against AA (Sheppard & Bodenhausen, 1992) supports the proposition that racism helps fuel anti-AA sentiment. Similarly, sexist attitudes have been shown to affect not only men's general evaluations of various AA plans but also how just they perceive the plans to be (Tougas, Crosby, Joly, & Pelchat, 1995).

Of course, people's reactions to AA must be analyzed in terms of their understanding of the term. Many people openly admit that they are unsure about what AA really is and how it operates (Winkelman & Crosby, 1994). Political rhetoric muddies the waters considerably (Crosby, 1998). At least one survey has shown that people's definitions of AA influence their attitudes toward AA, even after taking into account gender, ethnicity, social class, and political orientation (Golden et al., 1998). Those who understand AA to be a system whereby organizations monitor themselves to make sure that utilization matches availability endorse the policy, but those who conceive of AA as a quota system do not. Researchers have demonstrated that they can affect people's assessment of AA by how they frame the issues (Kinder & Sanders, 1990).

Empirical evidence: Attitudes of the direct beneficiaries

Predictors of endorsement for affirmative action among direct beneficiaries. What factors are associated with endorsement for or opposition to AA among those who are not part of society's dominant group and who are members of groups typically targeted by AA programs? The data are not copious, but several studies are available.

Fairness is one factor determining how men of color and women react to AA. Vargas-Machuca and Kottke (1999) surveyed 126 Latino and 105 White women college students and employees about gender-based AA plans. The most powerful predictor of attitudes was perceived fairness: Women who thought AA was fair endorsed it. Perceptions of discrimination and acculturation did not predict attitudes toward the AAP, and self-interest and ethnic identity did, but much less strongly than fairness. Similarly, in a telephone survey of Hispanic immigrants and native-born Whites, Blacks, and Hispanics, Klineberg and Kravitz (1999) found that, overall, the key predictors of opposition to the typical AAP were the beliefs that AA gives unfair advantages to women and minorities and that the typical AAP involves strong preferential treatment. The belief that AA involves strong preferential treatment was not a significant predictor in the Hispanic groups, however.

Ideology has also been shown to be important. In a secondary analysis of election studies, Fine (1992b) looked at how age, education, income, gender, partisan affiliation, and core values (e.g., belief in hard work) statistically influenced opinions about governmental programs such as AA. Only 13% of the respondents disliked AA, while 26% endorsed it moderately and 61% endorsed it strongly. Those who believed in hard work were more likely to favor AA.

Self-interest matters too. Kravitz (1994) reported the results of five studies, including a telephone survey of 60 adults (13 White, 23 Black, and 24 Hispanic) employed in the

Miami area. The survey assessed attitudes toward AAPs targeted at Blacks or Hispanics. Respondents' attitudes were more positive when the AAP was targeted toward their own ethnic group.

It is unclear whether knowledge (either first hand or theoretical) about AA is a strong predictor of attitudes among its direct beneficiaries. In an early case study by Goldsmith et al. (1989), a random sample of women and men employees and women students at Smith College spoke with an interviewer about AA and also rated the extent of their knowledge of AA. Trained coders also transcribed and coded the interviews for degree of knowledge about the law and its operation. Neither self-rated nor coder-rated knowledge predicted attitudes toward AA among the women employees or students. More recently, in a much larger-scale interview of randomly sampled Chicago area residents, Golden et al. (1998) found self-rated knowledge to predict endorsement of AA among women but not men and among ethnic minorities but not White people in the sample. Golden et al. also found that those with higher self-rated knowledge (and with more education) were more likely to characterize AA as a monitoring system whereas those with lower self-rated knowledge (and less education) were more likely to characterize AA as a quota system. Taylor-Carter, Doverspike, and Alexander (1995) presented a gender-based AA plan to respondents, accompanied by a strong argument in favor or against the fairness of the plan. They found a clear effect for the persuasive communication and no clear effect for raters' involvement or experience with AA.

Also unclear are the effects of first-hand experiences with racism and sexism. Vargas-Machuca and Kottke (1999) found that their participants' attitudes did not vary as a function of experiences with racism and sexism or of acculturation. On the other hand, in a series of studies, Matheson, Echenberg, Taylor, Rivers, and Chow (1994) found large differences between women in college and women working in the trades. The latter group, who had had more opportunities to experience sexism first-hand, supported AA much more strongly than the former.

Affirmative action and self-doubt. Shelby Steele (1991) and others (Carter, 1991; Heilman, 1996) have proposed that AA can stigmatize its intended beneficiaries. Steele has voiced the related idea that the Black people who endorse and rely on AA are those with damaged pride. Similar ideas are often repeated in the media (e.g., Connerly, 1995). Meanwhile, other scholars (e.g., Branscombe & Ellemers, 1998) have proposed that opposition to AA among members of disadvantaged groups may indicate that the target has internalized society's stigma so that he or she can only bolster self-esteem and personal status by alienation from the ingroup.

What does the empirical evidence show? Although not voluminous, it shows that most women and most men of color do not feel diminished by AA policies. A 1995 Gallup poll asked 708 White women and minority group members the question, "Have you ever felt that your colleagues at work or school privately questioned your abilities or qualifications because of affirmative action or have you never felt this way?" (Gallup Short Subjects, 1995). Results showed that only 8% of White women, 19% of African American women, and 29% of African American men answered yes.

While most disadvantaged people feel undermined when told that they received benefit through special privilege instead of merit (Arthur, Doverspike, & Fuentes, 1992; Heilman, 1994, 1996; Nacoste, 1994; for a review, see Kravitz et al., 1997), only a minority of society's disadvantaged confuse AA with special privilege. In an early study (Ayers, 1992), a small sample of women of color reported on their reactions to being selected through AA for honors, awards, or jobs. One young woman was angered to have been chosen as the "best Black" student, but the older women expressed gratitude for being given an opportunity to show their value. A very senior administrator articulated the opinion that White people's distrust of an AA candidate is simply White people's contemporary "acceptable" form of racism, a form that is less detrimental than previous forms. A recent in-depth study of 800 women of color in U.S. corporations conducted by Catalyst (1998) echoes the results of Ayers's study: Most women of color see AA as a set of practices which enhance, and do not displace, the true reward of merit.

The positive effect is not limited to women. Taylor (1994) studied the responses of 319 White women, 40 Black women, and 32 Black men who were employed by companies that either did or did not have an AAP in place. Taylor found no evidence of AA's supposed deleterious effects. Instead, she found strong positive effects for workplace AAPs. For example, Black men employed by firms that utilized AA reported more occupational ambition and less cynicism than those who worked for companies without AAPs. One might wonder how (tiny) self-doubt that may arise from participating in an affirmative action program compares to the (enormous) self-doubt that arises from unemployment.

Nor do students appear undermined in their self-esteem by AA policies. In one survey (Truax, Cordova, Wood, Wright, & Crosby, 1998), 351 undergraduate students were asked their reactions to AA and also whether they wondered if their peers and professors thought that they had been admitted to college because of their ethnicity and not their intellectual abilities. Few of the White and Asian American students but a great majority of the African American, Hispanic, and Native American students felt that others doubted their ability in this way. These students also felt that their academic abilities were judged on the basis of ethnic stereotypes. Yet they overwhelmingly endorsed AA. Support for affirmative action and worry about the perceptions of Whites were positively although marginally correlated.

Schmermund, Sellers, Mueller and Crosby (1998) extended Truax et al.'s work by administering surveys to 181 Black students at five institutions in Western Massachusetts. Although Truax et al. could infer from the pattern of their data that students of color had not internalized what Major, Feinstein, and Crocker (1994) call "suspicion of inferiority," they had no direct evidence of students' academic self-esteem. The students in Schmermund et al.'s study also strongly endorsed AA and often claimed that their fellow students and professors viewed them with suspicion. While approximately 60% of the students thought other students doubted their competence and 50% thought professors did, less than one-third of the sample admitted that they sometimes doubted their own academic merit. Interestingly, there was a marginally significant negative association between self-doubt and endorsement for AA: Students who disliked AA felt more academically insecure than those who liked the policy. This relationship is the opposite of what Shelby Steele (1991) or some others (e.g., Heilman, 1996) would predict.

Data exist for samples even younger than college students. Miller and Clark (1997) asked 161 U.S. high school students about their faith in the American dream. The students endorsed the dream, but Black students agreed less than Hispanic, Asian, or White students with the concept that the United States provides equal opportunities for all races and classes. For these students, concluded Miller and Clark, outreach programs and other forms of AA were essential for the preservation of hope.

Empirical evidence: Attitudes among members of privileged groups

The great majority of studies have been done in the last decade among White males and others whom the researchers do not envision as the direct beneficiaries of AA. Many, but not all, of the studies include college students as the participants. Most, but not all, assess a number of different attitudes to see which of the attitudes alone and in concert statistically predict opinions about AA. To date there is no standard scale measuring attitudes toward AA, so some of the variability across studies may be due to differences in question wording.

Taken as a whole the available studies do warrant some conclusions in spite of variations. First, resistance to AA is often associated with prejudice. Second, opposition to AA among privileged people cannot be understood wholly in terms of prejudice or other undesirable traits such as base self-interest. Third, the association between prejudice and negative attitudes toward AA has remained fairly stable throughout the 1990s. All three conclusions are visible in Table 24.1, which like the text, presents the studies in chronological order to underscore the third point.

In chronological order, the first study published in the 1990s was a quasi-experiment conducted by Kravitz and Platania (1993). They asked 349 undergraduates – diverse in gender and ethnicity – to define AA and then to evaluate 24 practices (e.g., hiring to meet quotas, giving special training) as to how likely they were to be part of an affirmative plan and as to how good they were. For one-third of the participants, AA was framed in terms of women; for another third, it was framed in terms of minorities; and for the last third it was framed in terms of the "handicapped." Participants supported AA measures involving quotas less than other measures, and they supported AA for those with disabilities more than for women or ethnic minorities. Although, as we have already noted, women and ethnic minorities supported AA more strongly than men and White participants, there were no interactions involving gender or ethnicity of participants and of target groups.

Another study that found participants more set against AA programs for ethnic minorities than for others was conducted by Murrell et al. (1994). These researchers asked White students to evaluate AAPs that differed in terms of the target group (elderly, physically handicapped, or Black) and that were or were not justified by an explanation of their necessity. Reactions toward policies presented with justification were more positive than to those presented without justification. Programs said to benefit Blacks were evaluated much less favorably than programs said to benefit the elderly or the handicapped, especially when the programs were not justified in terms of diversity goals or past injustices.

The influences both of prejudice and of fairness considerations were demonstrated again – in nonstudent samples – in two quasi-experiments by Tougas et al. (1995). A neo-sexism scale was used to divide samples of male managers and professionals into those high or low in sexism. Participants were randomly assigned to read about programs in which merit was or was not emphasized and were then asked to evaluate the worthiness and fairness of the programs. Neo-sexism predicted low support for the programs in both studies, and explanations stressing merit predicted high ratings of fairness.

To test the hypothesis that attitudes toward AA are derived from perceptions of fairness, Kravitz (1995) used a questionnaire to assess attitudes of White and Hispanic university students toward eight different AA plans directed at Blacks. He found that attitudes toward specific AAPs were completely mediated by perceptions of fairness and not by evaluations of personal or collective self-interest. Attitudes toward AA as a policy varied as functions of self-interest and racism.

Nosworthy, Lea, and Lindsay (1995) used a similar methodology. In a study of Canadian undergraduates, they found that support depended on the nature of the AA program described to respondents. They also found that racial prejudice and adherence to justice norms contributed – both separately and in conjunction – to the students' feelings about the "soft" programs such as outreach. While all students were opposed to the use of quotas or to "hard" AA programs, only those who were racist or had a strong belief in the just world took issue with mild forms of AA such as an advertising campaign.

Clayton (1996), in two studies designed to evaluate college students' opinions about categorizing people on the basis of group membership, manipulated both the type of social group involved and the purpose of the categorization. Participants objected most to categorizing people on the basis of race, religion, or sexual orientation.

Sidanius, Pratto, and Bobo (1996) analyzed three extensive data sets. In a large random sample of White students at the University of Texas, they found that opposition to AA increased as a function of racism and also of conservatism. They replicated these findings in a random sample of White residents of Los Angeles County, among whom they also found that anti-Black hostility had little predictive value and that opposition to AA was greatest among those who believed that society ought to be hierarchically ordered. This was especially true among college graduates. The third sample of White students came from UCLA. Again, attitudes toward AA were most positive among nonracist liberals who desired an egalitarian rather than a hierarchical society.

Dietz-Uhler and Murrell (1998) asked 79 university students to evaluate a woman applying for admission to either their own university (ingroup condition) or another university (outgroup condition) where the institution used standard or "affirmative action" (undefined) admissions programs. The standard admissions policy was seen as more just than the AA policy and highly qualified applicants received more favorable evaluations than applicants with weaker qualifications. Evaluations of the ingroup applicant were affected by the perceived fairness of the AA policy, but evaluations of the outgroup member were not.

Bobocel, Song Hing, Davey, Stanley, and Zanna (1998) conducted three studies to investigate whether people oppose AA because they perceive it to be unfair or because they are prejudiced. They found that, independent of prejudice level, opposition to AAPs was correlated with perceived violation of distributive and procedural justice norms. However, when participants were asked to evaluate AAPs that did not explicitly violate justice norms, opposition was positively associated with prejudice level. The authors concluded that prejudice and concern for justice are distinct sources of opposition to AA.

In a survey of Chicago area residents, Golden et al. (1998) found that people's definitions of AA significantly predicted their evaluations of the policy – even after controlling for ethnicity, gender, and political orientation. People who equated AA with a monitoring system endorsed the policy significantly more strongly than those who equated AA with quotas. Only 16% of the sample strongly opposed AA.

Little et al. (1998) surveyed university students (60% female, 21% non-White) about to enter the workforce regarding their opinions on equal opportunity employment and AA. Participants with lower levels of self-esteem were more likely to think that AAPs in the workplace would impair their future self-interests. A relationship between respondents' negative perceptions of AAPs and conviction that women and minorities were being given unfair advantages in society was also found.

Kravitz and Klineberg (1999) used data from an annual public opinion telephone survey of 424 U.S.-born Whites. Reactions to a tiebreak procedure (i.e., a statement explaining that a company would choose a Black candidate over a White candidate when they both had identical qualifications and Blacks were underrepresented in the company) were contrasted with reactions to a typical AAP. White respondents preferred the tiebreak procedure to other procedures, and the preference was strongest among the politically conservative.

Swim and Miller (1999) also reported multiple studies with college and noncollege populations. They examined the relationships among prejudice, White guilt, and attitudes toward a type of AA which some (e.g., Clayton & Tangri, 1989) would call "retributive affirmative action" in four different samples. Racial prejudice and White guilt were inversely related. Multiple regression analyses showed that prejudiced and guiltless Whites were more likely to dislike retributive AA.

Kravitz et al. (in press) conducted two studies designed to assess attitudes toward AA in the workplace. It was found that positive attitudes toward AA are related to the belief that the target group needs help and that AA will not impair organizational performance, but that White respondents whose AA schemata featured Black and Hispanic targets harbored negative attitudes toward AA.

In sum. Table 24.1 presents a summary. Nine of the surveys published in the 1990s assessing attitudes toward AA among the privileged members of society showed a link between prejudice and opposition to AA. Meanwhile, from seven of the studies one could infer that considerations of fairness were also influential.

Of course, we would be naive to assume that people's perceptions of fairness are unrelated to their preconceptions or prejudices. Consider in this regard the study by Kravitz and Klineberg (1999) where Whites endorsed a tiebreak procedure. It should be noted that other evidence, summarized by Dovidio and Gaertner (1998), suggests that it is highly unlikely that White judges would evaluate the same qualifications equally when held by Blacks and by Whites. Thus, a prejudiced person who values impartiality may see himself or herself as being impartial even when he or she is not (see also Brief et al., 1997).

Unlike the literature on attitudes among the direct beneficiaries reviewed above, only one survey of White people (Swim & Miller, 1999) linked attitudes toward AA with attitudes towards the ingroup. The lack of parallel is interesting. Why do so few researchers

Table 24.1. Studies of the Bases of Reactions to Affirmative Action among the Privileged

Date	Researcher(s)	Population	Basis of Reactions			
			Fairness	*Prejudice*	*Self-interest*	*Other*
1993	Kravitz & Platania	Undergraduate students	X			
1994	Murrell et al.	White students	X	X		
1995	Tougas et al.	Male managers	X	X		
		Students rating AA policy	X	X		
1995	Kravitz	Students rating AA plans	X		No	
1995	Nosworthy et al.	Canadian students			X	
1996	Clayton	Students				X
		White students in Texas		X		
1996	Sidanius et al.	White people in Los Angeles		X		X
		White students at UCLA		X		X
1998	Dietz-Uhler & Murrell	Students	X			
1998	Bobocel et al.	3 samples	X	X		
1998	Golden et al.	Chicago residents			X	X
1998	Little et al.	University students				X
1999	Kravitz & Klineberg	Telephoned sample of Whites				X
1999	Swim & Miller	Various samples		X		
In press	Kravitz et al.	Whites		X	X	

look at how attitudes toward affirmative action relate to identity issues among White people? Perhaps researchers are right to think that affirmative action poses no threat to the self-concept of Whites. Or maybe the researchers are just assuming that Whites are relatively invulnerable because American scholarship presumes that White people are the standard against which all other groups must be compared.

Expanding the Conversation

Even people who agree that equality is desirable and that discrimination should be both avoided and redressed disagree on how best to achieve the desired results. The debate often can be reduced to the issue of whether group-conscious or identity-blind approaches are preferable (Ferdman, 1997). Group-conscious approaches to making choices about individuals take into consideration their identities and the group contexts that have shaped them. Identity-blind approaches seek to apply general principles to all individuals, regardless of group memberships (or at least those group memberships assumed to be irrelevant to the decision at hand). Affirmative action is a group-conscious approach for addressing discrimination; it seeks to proactively identify, assist, and include members of targeted groups that have been hurt by current or historical patterns of exclusion.

Both in the workplace and in education, much of the controversy over AA has to do with whether one sees people as members of a group or as isolated individuals. Many people, especially in Western cultures, react negatively when asked to think about themselves and others in terms of their ethnic group memberships (Ferdman, 1995; Markus & Kitayama, 1994; Sampson, 1989) because they believe that doing so is unfair. From an *individualistic perspective*, the ideal of justice is based on the notion that group memberships should not determine what happens to individuals (Ferdman, 1997; Gottfredson, 1988; Kluegel & Smith, 1986). Those taking a *group perspective* see rampant individualism as a way to obscure the disparate treatment and differential power that have characterized the history of race and ethnic relations in the United States (see e.g., Alderfer & Thomas, 1988; Gaines & Reed, 1995; Glasser, 1988; Jones, 1997; McIntosh, 1988; Nemetz & Christensen, 1995; Palmer, 1994). Indeed, a number of scholars (e.g., Haney & Hurtado, 1994; Ibarra, 1995; Pettigrew & Martin, 1987; Schofield, 1986) have shown how meritocratic policies in the United States, under the guise of being race-blind, have actually served to maintain and even enhance privilege for Whites. For example, most people find their jobs through someone they know. Because social networks are quite divided by race (Sincharoen & Hu, 1999), predominantly White organizations are more likely to find White applicants for job openings, unless proactive steps are taken to advertise among people of color. Also, the criteria used to define "merit" in most organizations are based on majority-culture norms. Ignoring group memberships will simply serve to perpetuate those norms and therefore give preferences to members of the dominant culture (Ferdman, 1997). Similarly, not paying attention to gender can be a way of reinforcing organizational cultures that give preference to traditionally masculine styles and characteristics (Jacques, 1997; Maier, 1999).

Not all subordinate groups in the United States share the same relation to dominant groups. The current and historical patterns of power relations between the groups, and the specific nature of contact and/or conflict between the groups are all variables that can impact and interact with AA policies. Thus, implementation of an outreach program for women that ends up targeting primarily White women may be seen quite differently by the mostly White men in a law firm than a selection system targeted at African American men and women. The latter may be seen, for example, as more different, less likely to assimilate, and as greater threats to the intergroup hierarchy (Sidanius & Pratto, 1999). Programs geared at Latinos in general have often not resulted in increased representation of Chicanos and Puerto Ricans, relative to the increase in other Latino subgroups, even though these are the two Latino groups that have been most discriminated against historically. This could be, in part, because the patterns of intergroup relations between Anglo Whites on the one hand and South Americans and Cubans on the other are quite different and generally less conflictual than those between Anglo Whites and Chicanos or Puerto Ricans.

Affirmative action practices share two goals, but not always in equal measure. First, AA exists to enhance diversity in specified groups such as undergraduate students or corporate managers. Second, AA exists to achieve fairness for all. AA's road to fairness rests on two underlying assumptions. The first is that fairness requires an explicit effort, especially given the unfair discrimination and oppression of yesterday and, oftentimes, of today. The second assumption is that fairness to individuals within categories is aided by taking cognizance of those categories. Thus, for example, if we are to assure the fair treatment of women and men, we must first notice who is male and female and note the treatment of people in each category. In this view, justice involves treating the whole group equally, not only selected individuals (Ferdman, 1997).

The importance of noting categorical information is probably greatest when previously monolithic groups embark on the quest for diversity (Dass & Parker, 1999; Ferdman & Brody, 1996; R. Thomas, 1990). But as organizations, and indeed society as a whole, come to embrace diversity, number counts will need to give way to more sophisticated analyses. Assessment of group representation purely in terms of numbers often tends to be framed from an assimilationist perspective (see Ferdman, 1997; Jones, 1998; Miller & Katz, 1995). When psychologists come to value truly diverse ways of thinking and acting, and when even the privileged White people see diversity as being in their own self-interest (Potts, 1994; Wheeler, 1994, 1995), we can help assure that AA goes beyond addressing and redressing discrimination toward diversity and inclusion. If we are thoughtful about affirmative action, we may come to consider not only the problems but also the opportunities created by intergroup distinctions.

References

Abdullah, F. H. (1997). Affirmative action policy in Malaysia: To restructure society, to eradicate poverty. *Ethnic Studies Report, 15*, 189–221.

Alderfer, C. P., & Thomas, D. A. (1988). The significance of race and ethnicity for understanding organizational behavior. In C. L. Cooper & I. T. Robertson (Eds.), *International review of industrial and organizational psychology* (pp. 1–41). Chichester, UK: Wiley.

American Psychological Association. (1996). *Affirmative action: Who benefits?* Washington, DC.

Arthur, W., Jr., Doverspike, D., & Fuentes, R. (1992). Recipients' affective responses to affirmative action interventions: A cross-cultural perspective. *Behavioral Sciences and the Law, 10*, 229–243.

Ayers, L. R. (1992). Perceptions of affirmative action among its beneficiaries. *Social Justice Research, 5*, 223–238.

Belkin, L. (1998, November). She says she was rejected by a college for being White. Is she paranoid, racist, or right? *Glamour, 96*, 278.

Benokraitis, N. V. (Ed.) (1997) *Subtle sexism: Current practice and prospects for change.* Thousand Oaks, CA: Sage.

Bergmann, B. R. (1996). *In defense of affirmative action.* New York: Basic Books.

Bobo, L., & Kluegel, J. R. (1993). Opposition to race-targeting: Self-interest, stratification ideology, or racial attitudes? *American Sociological Review, 58,* 443–464.

Bobo, L., & Smith, R. A. (1994). Antipoverty policies, affirmative action, and racial attitudes. In S. H. Danziger, G. D. Sandefur, & D. H. Weinberg (Eds.), *Confronting poverty: Prescriptions for change* (pp. 365–395). Cambridge, MA: Harvard University Press.

Bobocel, D. R., Son Hing, L. S., Davey, L. M., Stanley, D. J., & Zanna, M. P. (1998). Justice-based opposition to social policies: Is it genuine? *Journal of Personality and Social Psychology, 75,* 653–669.

Bowen, W. G., & Bok, D. (1998). *The shape of the river: Long-term consequences of considering race in college and university admissions.* Princeton, NJ: Princeton University Press.

Branscombe, N. R., & Ellemers, N. (1998). Coping with group-based discrimination: Individualistic versus group-level strategies. In J. K. Swim & C. Stangor (Eds.), *Prejudice: The target's perspective* (pp. 37–60). San Diego, CA: Academic Press.

Brief, A. P., Buttram, R. T., Reizenstein, R. M., Pugh, S. D., Callahan, J. D., McCline, R. L., & Vaslow, J. B. (1997). Beyond good intentions: The next steps toward racial equality in the American workplace. *Academy of Management Executive, 11*(4), 59–72.

Carter, S. J. (1991). *Reflections of an affirmative action baby.* New York: Basic Books.

Catalyst (1998). *Women of color in corporate management: Dynamics of career advancement.* New York: Catalyst Inc.

Chalude, M., De Jong, A., & Laufer, J. (1994). Implementing equal opportunity and affirmative action programmes in Belgium, France, and The Netherlands. In M. J. Davidson & R. J. Burke (Eds.), *Women in management: Current research issues* (pp. 289–303). London: Paul Chapman.

Clayton, S. (1996). Reactions to social categorization: Evaluating one argument against affirmative action. *Journal of Applied Social Psychology, 26,* 1472–1493.

Clayton, S., & Crosby, F. J. (1992). *Justice, gender, and affirmative action.* Ann Arbor, MI: University of Michigan Press.

Clayton, S. D., & Tangri, S. S. (1989). The justice of affirmative action. In F. A. Blanchard & F. J. Crosby (Eds.), *Affirmative action in perspective* (pp. 177–192). New York: Springer-Verlag.

Connerly, W. (1995, May 3). UC must end affirmative action. *San Francisco Chronicle.*

Crosby, F. J. (1982). *Relative deprivation and working women.* New York: Oxford University Press.

Crosby, F. J. (1994). Understanding affirmative action. *Basic and Applied Social Psychology, 15,* 13–41.

Crosby, F. J. (1998). What is affirmative action? *Burkenroad Symposium.* A. B. Freeman School of Business. Tulane University.

Crosby, F. J., & Cordova, D. I. (1996). Words worth of wisdom: Toward an understanding of affirmative action. *Journal of Social Issues, 52,* 33–49.

Dass, P., & Parker, B. (1999). Strategies for managing human resource diversity: From resistance to learning. *Academy of Management Executive, 13*(2), 68–80.

Dietz-Uhler, B., & Murrell, A. J. (1998). Evaluations of affirmation action applicants: Perceived fairness, human capital, or social identity. *Sex Roles, 38,* 933–951.

Dovidio, J. F., & Gaertner, S. L. (1998). On the nature of contemporary prejudice. In J. L. Eberhardt & S. T. Fiske (Eds.), *Confronting racism: The problem and the response* (pp. 3–32). Thousand Oaks, CA: Sage.

Dovidio, J. F., Mann, J., & Gaertner, S. L. (1989). Resistance to affirmative action: The implications of aversive racism. In F. A. Blanchard & F. J. Crosby (Eds.), *Affirmative action in perspective* (pp. 83–102). New York: Springer-Verlag.

Esses, V. M., & Seligman, C. (1996). The individual-group distinction in assessment of strategies to reduce prejudice and discrimination: The case of affirmative action. In R. M. Sorrentino &

E. T. Higgins (Eds.), *Handbook of motivation and cognition: The interpersonal context* (Vol. 3, pp. 570–590). New York: Guilford Press.

Ferdman, B. M. (1995). Cultural identity and diversity in organizations: Bridging the gap between group differences and individual uniqueness. In M. Chemers, S. Oskamp, & M. A. Costanzo (Eds.), *Diversity in organizations: New perspectives for a changing workplace* (pp. 37–61). Thousand Oaks, CA: Sage.

Ferdman, B. M. (1997). Values about fairness in the ethnically diverse workplace. *Business and the Contemporary World, 9*, 191–208.

Ferdman, B. M., & Brody, S. E. (1996). Models of diversity training. In D. Landis & R. Bhagat (Eds.), *Handbook of intercultural training* (2nd ed., pp. 282–303). Thousand Oaks, CA: Sage.

Fine, T. S. (1992a). The impact of issue framing on public opinion toward affirmative action programs. *Social Science Journal, 29*, 323–334.

Fine, T. S. (1992b). Public opinion toward equal opportunity issues: The role of attitudinal and demographic forces among African Americans. *Sociological Perspectives, 35*, 705–720.

Gaertner, S. L., & Dovidio, J. F. (1986). The aversive form of racism. In J. F. Dovidio & S. L. Gaertner (Eds.), *Prejudice, discrimination, and racism* (pp. 61–89). Orlando, FL: Academic Press.

Gaines, S. O., & Reed, E. S. (1995). Prejudice: From Allport to Du Bois. *American Psychologist, 50*, 96–103.

Gallup Short Subjects (July, 1995). *Gallup Poll Monthly, 358*, 34–61.

Glasser, I. (1988). Affirmative action and the legacy of racial injustice. In P. A. Katz & D. Taylor (Eds.), *Toward the elimination of racism: Profiles in controversy* (pp. 341–357). New York: Plenum Press.

Golden, H., Hinkle, S., & Crosby, F. J. (1998). Reactions to affirmative action: Substance and semantics. *Institute for Research on Women and Gender Working Paper*. Ann Arbor, MI: University of Michigan, IRWAG.

Goldsmith, N., Cordova, D., Dwyer, K., Langlois, B., & Crosby, F. J. (1989). Reactions to affirmative action: A case study. In F. A. Blanchard & F. J. Crosby (Eds.), *Affirmative action in perspective* (pp. 139–146). New York: Springer-Verlag.

Gottfredson, L. S. (1988). Reconsidering fairness: A matter of social and ethical priorities. *Journal of Vocational Behavior, 33*, 293–319.

Haney, D., & Hurtado, A. (1994). The jurisprudence of race and meritocracy: Standardized testing and "race neutral" racism in the workplace. *Law and Human Behavior, 18*, 223–248.

Heilman, M. E. (1994). Affirmative action: Some unintended consequences for working women. *Research in Organizational Behavior, 16*, 125–169.

Heilman, M. E. (1996). Affirmative action's contradictory consequences. *Journal of Social Issues, 52*, 105–109.

Ibarra, H. (1995). Race, opportunity, and diversity of social circles in managerial networks. *Academy of Management Journal, 38*, 673–703.

Jacques, R. (1997). The unbearable whiteness of being: Reflections of a pale, stale male. In P. Prasad, A. J. Mills, M. Elmes, & A. Prasad (Eds.), *Managing the organizational melting pot: Dilemmas of workplace diversity* (pp. 80–106). Thousand Oaks, CA: Sage.

Jones, J. M. (1997). *Prejudice and racism* (2nd ed.). New York: McGraw-Hill.

Jones, J. M. (1998). Psychological knowledge and the new American dilemma of race. *Journal of Social Issues, 54*, 641–662.

Kinder, D. R., & Sanders, L. M. (1990). Mimicking political debate with survey questions: The case of White opinion on affirmative action for Blacks. *Social Cognition, 8*, 73–103.

Klineberg, S. L., & Kravitz, D. A. (1999, April). *Ethnic differences in support for a "typical" affirmative action plan*. Paper presented at the Society for Industrial and Organizational Psychology meetings, Atlanta.

Kluegel, J. R., & Smith, E. R. (1986). *Beliefs about inequality: Americans' views of what is and what ought to be.* New York: Aldine de Gruyter.

Konrad, A. M., & Linnehan, F. (1995a). Formalized HRM structures: Coordinating equal employment opportunity or concealing organizational practices? *Academy of Management Journal, 38,* 787–820.

Konrad, A. M., & Linnehan, F. (1995b). Race and sex differences in line managers' reactions to equal employment opportunity and affirmative action interventions. *Group and Organization Management, 20,* 409–439.

Konrad, A. M., & Linnehan, F. (1999). Affirmative action: History, effects, and attitudes. In G. N. Powell (Ed.), *Handbook of gender and work* (pp. 429–452). Thousand Oaks, CA: Sage.

Kramer, R. (1994). Affirmative action in Australian organizations. In M. J. Davidson & R. J. Burke (Eds.), *Women in management: Current research issues* (pp. 277–288). London: Paul Chapman.

Kravitz, D. A. (1994, April). Public perceptions of affirmative action. In D. A. Kravitz (Chair), *Affirmative action: Psychological research and practitioner reactions.* Symposium conducted at the Society for Industrial and Organizational Psychology meetings, Nashville.

Kravitz, D. A. (1995). Attitudes toward affirmative action plans directed at Blacks: Effects of plan and individual differences. *Journal of Applied Social Psychology, 25,* 2192–2220.

Kravitz, D. A., Harrison, D. A., Turner, M. E., Levine, E. L., Chaves, W., Brannick, M. T., Denning, D. L., Russell, C. J., & Conrad, M. A. (1997). *Affirmative action: A review of psychological and behavioral research.* Bowling Green, OH: Society for Industrial and Organizational Psychology.

Kravitz, D. A., & Klineberg, S. L. (1999, April). *Predicting Whites' attitudes toward two affirmative action plans (AAPs).* Paper presented at Society for Industrial and Organizational Psychology meetings, Atlanta.

Kravitz, D. A., Klineberg, S. L., Avery, D. R., Nguyen, C. L., Lund, C., & Fu, E. J. (in press). Attitudes toward affirmative action: Correlations with demographic variables and with beliefs about targets, actions, and economic effects. *Journal of Applied Social Psychology.*

Kravitz, D. A., & Platania, J. (1993). Attitudes and beliefs about affirmative action: Effects of target and of respondent sex and ethnicity. *Journal of Applied Psychology, 78,* 928–938.

Leck, J. D., & Saunders, D. M. (1992). Canada's Employment Equity Act: Effects on employee selection. *Population Research and Policy Review, 11,* 21–49.

Little, B. L., Murray, W. D., & Wimbush, J. C. (1998). Perceptions of workplace affirmative action plans. *Group & Organization Management, 23,* 27–47.

Maier, M. (1999). On the gendered substructure of organization: Dimensions and dilemmas of corporate masculinity. In G. N. Powell (Ed.), *Handbook of gender and work* (pp. 69–93). Thousand Oaks, CA: Sage.

Major, B., Feinstein, J., & Crocker, J. (1994). Attributional ambiguity of affirmative action. *Basic and Applied Social Psychology, 15,* 113–141.

Markus, H. R., & Kitayama, S. (1994). A collective fear of the collective: Implications for selves and theories of selves. *Personality and Social Psychology Bulletin, 20,* 568–579.

Matheson, K., Echenberg, A., Taylor, D. M., Rivers, D., & Chow, I. (1994). Women's attitudes toward affirmative action: Putting action in context. *Journal of Applied Social Psychology, 24,* 2075–2096.

McConahay, J. B. (1986). Modern racism, ambivalence, and the Modern Racism Scale. In J. F. Dovidio & S. L. Gaertner (Eds.), *Prejudice, discrimination, and racism* (pp. 91–125). Orlando, FL: Academic Press.

McIntosh, P. (1988). *White privilege and male privilege: A personal account of coming to see correspondences through work in women's studies.* Working Paper No. 189. Center for Research on Women, Wellesley College, Wellesley, MA.

Miller, F., & Clark, M. A. (1997). Looking toward the future: Young people's attitudes about affirmative action and the American dream. *American Behavioral Scientist, 41*, 262–271.

Miller, F. A., &. Katz, J. H. (1995). Cultural diversity as a developmental process: The path from monocultural club to inclusive organization. In J. W. Pfeiffer (Ed.), *The 1995 Annual: Volume 2, Consulting* (pp. 267–281). San Diego, CA: Pfeiffer.

Morawski, J. G. (1997). White experimenters, White blood, and other White conditions: Locating the psychologist's race. In M. Fine, L. Weis, L. C. Powell, & L. Mun Wong (Eds.), *Off White: Readings on race, power, and society* (pp. 13–28). New York: Routledge.

Murrell, A. J., Dietz-Uhler, B., Dovidio, J., Gaertner, S., & Drout, C. (1994). Aversive racism and resistance to affirmative action: Perceptions of justice are not necessarily color blind. *Basic and Applied Social Psychology, 15*, 71–86.

Nacoste, R. B. (1994). If empowerment is the goal . . . : Affirmative action and social interaction. *Basic and Applied Social Psychology, 15*, 87–112.

Nacoste, R. W. (1985). Selection procedure and responses to affirmative action: The case of favorable treatment. *Law and Human Behavior, 9*, 225–242.

Nemetz, P. L., & Christensen, S. L. (1995). The challenge of cultural diversity: Harnessing a diversity of views to understand multiculturalism. *Academy of Management Review, 21*, 434–462.

Nosworthy, G. J., Lea, J. A., & Lindsay, R. C. (1995). Opposition to affirmative action: Racial affect and traditional value predictors across four programs. *Journal of Applied Social Psychology, 25*, 314–337.

Operario, D., & Fiske, S. T. (1998). Racism equals power plus prejudice: A social psychological equation for racial oppression. In J. L. Eberhardt & S. T. Fiske (Eds.), *Confronting racism: The problem and the response* (pp. 33–53). Thousand Oaks, CA: Sage.

Opotow, S. (1997). What's fair? Justice issues in the affirmative action debate. *American Behavioral Scientist, 41*, 232–245.

Ozawa, K., Crosby, M., & Crosby, F. (1996). Individualism and resistance to affirmative action: A comparison of Japanese and American samples. *Journal of Applied Social Psychology, 26*, 1138–1152.

Palmer, J. (1994). Diversity: Three paradigms. In E. Y. Cross, J. H. Katz, F. A. Miller, & E. W. Seashore (Eds.), *The promise of diversity: Over 40 voices discuss strategies for eliminating discrimination in organizations* (pp. 252–258). Burr Ridge, IL: Irwin.

Pettigrew, T. F., & Martin, J. (1987). Shaping the organizational context for Black American inclusion. *Journal of Social Issues, 43*, 41–78.

Potts, J. (1994). White men can help – but it's hard. In E. Y. Cross, J. H. Katz, F. A., Miller, & E. W. Seashore (Eds.), *The promise of diversity: Over 40 voices discuss strategies for eliminating discrimination in organizations* (pp. 165–169). Burr Ridge, IL: Irwin.

Reskin, B. (1998). *The realities of affirmative action in employment.* Washington, DC: American Sociological Review.

Sampson, E. E. (1989). The challenge of social change for psychology: Globalization and psychology's theory of the person. *American Psychologist, 44*, 914–921.

Schmermund, A., Sellers, R., Mueller, B., & Crosby, F. (1998). *Attitudes toward affirmative action as a function of racial identity among Black college students.* Unpublished manuscript.

Schofield, J. W. (1986). Causes and consequences of the colorblind perspective. In J. F. Dovidio & S. L. Gaertner (Eds.), *Prejudice, discrimination, and racism* (pp. 231–253). Orlando, FL: Academic Press.

Sheppard, L. A., & Bodenhausen, G. (1992, August). *Prejudice and the persuasion process: Perceptions of affirmative action opponents and proponents.* Paper presented at the American Psychological Association Annual Convention, Washington, DC.

Sidanius, J., & Pratto, F. (1999). *Social dominance: An intergroup theory of social hierarchy and oppression.* Cambridge, UK: Cambridge University Press.

Sidanius, J., Pratto, F., & Bobo, L. (1996). Racism, conservatism, affirmative action, and intellectual sophistication: A matter of principled conservatism or group dominance? *Journal of Personality and Social Psychology, 70*, 476–490.

Sincharoen, S., & Hu, L-T. (July, 1999). *Background characteristics and ethnic identity among African Americans.* Paper presented at the International Society for Political Psychology, Amsterdam, The Netherlands.

Sigelman, L., & Welch, F. (1991). *Black Americans' views of racial inequality: The dream deferred.* Cambridge, UK: Cambridge University Press.

Sowell, T. (1994). *Race and culture: A world view.* New York: Basic Books.

Steele, S. (1991). *The content of our character: A new vision of race in America.* New York: Morrow.

Stephanopoulos, G., & Edley, C., Jr. (1995, July 19). Affirmative action review. *Report to the President.* Washington, DC: Government Printing Office.

Swim, J. K., & Miller, D. L. (1999). White guilt: Its antecedents and consequences for attitudes toward affirmative action. *Personality and Social Psychology Bulletin 4*, 500–514.

Taylor-Carter, M. A., Doverspike, D., & Alexander, R. (1995). Message effects on the perceptions of the fairness of gender-based affirmative action: A cognitive response theory-based analysis. *Social Justice Research, 8*, 285–303.

Taylor, M. C. (1994). Impact of affirmative action on beneficiary groups: Evidence from the 1990 General Social Survey. *Basic and Applied Social Psychology, 15*, 143–178.

Thomas, R. R. (1990). From affirmative action to affirming diversity. *Harvard Business Review, 68*(2), 107–117.

Tickamyer, A., Scollay, S., Bokemeier, J., & Wood, T. (1989). Administrators' perceptions of affirmative action in higher education. In F. A. Blanchard & F. J. Crosby (Eds.), *Affirmative action in perspective* (pp. 125–138). New York: Springer-Verlag.

Tomasson, R., Crosby, F. J., & Herzberger, S. (1996). *Affirmative action: The pros and cons of policy and practice.* Washington DC: American University Press.

Tougas, F., Crosby, F., Joly, S., & Pelchat, D. (1995). Men's attitudes toward affirmative action: Justice and intergroup relations at the crossroads. *Social Justice Research, 8*, 57–71.

Truax K., Cordova, D. I., Wood, A., Wright, E., & Crosby, F. (1998). Undermined? Affirmative action from the targets' point of view. In J. Swim & C. Stangor (Eds.), *Prejudice: The target's perspective* (pp. 171–187). New York: Academic Press.

Turner, M. E., & Pratkanis, A. R. (1994). Affirmative action as help: A review of recipient reactions to preferential selection and affirmative action. *Basic and Applied Social Psychology, 15*, 43–69.

Vargas-Machuca, I., & Kottke, J. L. (1999, April). *Latinos and affirmative action: Self-interest, fairness, past discrimination, and acculturation.* Poster presented at the Society for Industrial Organizational Psychology meetings, Atlanta.

De Vries, S., & Pettigrew, T. F. (1994). A comparative perspective on affirmative action: *Positieve aktie* in the Netherlands. *Basic and Applied Social Psychology, 15*, 179–199.

Waseem, M. (1997). Affirmative action policies in Pakistan. *Ethnic Studies Report, 15*, 223–244.

Wheeler, M. L. (1994). *Diversity training: A research report.* Report R-1083, The Conference Board, 845 Third Avenue, New York, NY 10022.

Wheeler, M. L. (1995). *Diversity: Business rationale and strategies: A research report.* Report 1130-95-RR, The Conference Board, 845 Third Avenue, New York, NY 10022.

Winkelman, C., & Crosby, F. J. (1994). Affirmative action: Setting the record straight. *Social Justice Research, 7*, 309–328.

Wu, C. M., & Taylor, W. L. (1996). *The resource: An affirmative action guide.* Washington DC: The Citizen's Commission on Civil Rights.

CHAPTER TWENTY-FIVE

Intergroup Relations and National and International Relations

Thomas F. Pettigrew

Social psychology has long aspired to contribute to humane and rational public policy. This aspiration has been especially strong among those who focus on intergroup relations. Kurt Lewin, for example, established two research centers late in his life – one for basic group research at the Massachusetts Institute of Technology, the other for applied group research 200 miles away in New York City. He hoped to achieve "full-cycle" social psychology with basic and applied work mutually enhancing each other (Cialdini, 1995).

The discipline's ambitious policy aspirations have been only partially fulfilled. Yet there are many instances from around the world where social psychology has played an important role in shaping intergroup policy. A few examples of this influence are broad, dramatic, and well known. Most examples, however, are more circumscribed, out of view, and often achieved in concert with other social sciences. This chapter samples both types to provide an overview of the discipline's impact on policy. These varied cases then suggest critical issues that arise when social psychology ventures into the "real world" of intergroup relations.

Six Examples of Major Policy Influence

The racial desegregation of American schools

The first significant involvement of social psychology in dramatic social change remains the best-known instance of the discipline's influence. Kenneth Clark, working with the legal staff of the National Association for the Advancement of Colored People, rallied his social psychological colleagues to the cause of ending the racial segregation of the public schools in the United States. The list of those who testified as expert witnesses in federal district courts about the harmful effects of such segregation on African American children reads like a who's who of American social psychology at the time: Jerome Bruner, Kenneth Clark, Isadore Chein, Stuart Cook, Otto Klineberg, David Kretch, and Brewster Smith (Kluger, 1987).

Once the school cases were consolidated and reached the U.S. Supreme Court, Clark, Chein, and Cook prepared a social science appendix to the plaintiff's brief. Thirty-two experts signed this review of the evidence, with social psychologists joined by anthropologists, psychiatrists, and sociologists. In an unusual action, the High Court cited social science evidence in its historic opinion in the famous footnote 11 (U.S. Supreme Court, 1954). Having stated flatly that the "segregation of white and colored children in public schools has a detrimental effect upon the colored children," the Supreme Court found this finding to be "amply supported by modern authority." This social science authority, as listed in the footnote, cited specific papers by Clark and Chein on how racial segregation harmed the personality development of African American children. The Court also cited sociological evidence of the structural damage wrought by segregation as developed by Franklin Frazier and Gunnar Myrdal.

Later social psychologists again served as expert witnesses in shaping the implementation orders of lower courts in specific school districts. Here the distinction between merely desegregated and genuinely integrated schools became important. The distinction relied on Allport's (1954) intergroup contact hypothesis and the relevant contact research (Pettigrew, 1975). For further details, see Schofield and Eurich-Fulcer's chapter on school integration in this volume.

Worker participation in group decisions

Group dynamics were introduced into Japan after World War II by American occupation authorities and encouraged directly by Kurt Lewin (Sugiman, 1998). Japanese social psychologists soon replicated the classic Lewinian finding of the superiority of group decisions in behavior change (Lewin, 1952).

Japanese industry applied this extensive research to such programs as quality control circles and self-managed group activities. These programs altered the nature of employer–employee relations by providing workers' input into the decisions that directly affected the work process. Widely credited as a key factor in Japan becoming a low-cost producer of high quality goods, these worker participation programs became famous as an integral part of the nation's industrial efficiency. The irony is that this Western idea got recycled back to its origins as part of the widespread industrial adoption of "Japanese" methods (Sugiman, 1998). Japanese firms embraced this social psychological contribution to industrial policy while Western manufacturing resisted it until it saw Japan's success.

Second-language learning

Changing public perceptions on a crucial issue is difficult. But, if achieved, this new perspective can have major policy consequences. Wallace Lambert (1992) and his McGill

University colleagues provide a striking example. In an extended project, McGill's social psychologists have addressed the intergroup language conflict in Canada's Quebec Province.

Their effort centered on developing bilingualism among children of English-speaking parents. Conventional wisdom and earlier research held bilingualism to be a serious handicap for school achievement, measured intelligence, and even adjustment. Lambert found this research literature extremely weak. No controls for social class, testing conducted only in the monolinguals' language, and other inadequacies characterized previous work. His research produced sharply different results. Bilingual children scored higher than monolingual children on a variety of tests of linguistic flexibility and on some cognitive tests as well. Nor were these results limited to Canada. Similar research showing advantages for bilinguals has been reported in Israel, Singapore, South Africa, Switzerland, and the United States with a variety of languages (Balken, 1970; Ben-Zeev, 1972; Ianco-Worrall, 1972; Torrence, Gowan, Wu, & Alioti, 1970).

Encouraged by such findings, Lambert set up "immersion education." English-speaking children spent their first three years of school almost exclusively surrounded by French with monolingual French teachers. The success of this effort has been widely recognized and emulated. In a reversal of traditional methods, second-language learning now employs immersion techniques in Canada and throughout the world. Despite some critical controversy, Lambert's research has substantially altered public perceptions about bilingualism and how it should be taught.

A bilingual compromise

While Lambert focused on the English-speaking side of Quebec's bilingual issue, Richard Bourhis brought social psychological insights to the French-speaking side. As a cultural and linguistic minority within Canada, Francophones view Quebec as the last enclave in North America of a distinctive French society. Until the 1960s, English was the language of work and prestige in Quebec even though Francophones comprised most of the population. But then the Quebec government enacted a series of language laws designed to enhance the status of the French language. Anglophones resisted these new acts, and tensions between the groups heightened (Bourhis, 1994a, 1994b).

The controversy came to a boil in 1977 when the provincial government passed Bill 101. It banned the use of all languages other than French on all commercial and many road signs. Following a ruling by the Canadian Supreme Court on freedom of expression, the Quebec government had to consider a compromise. Militant Quebec nationalists wanted to retain only French on public signs, while Anglophones wanted a return to freedom of language choice.

At this point, Bourhis was called in by the Quebec government. He conducted research for the *Conseil de la Langue Française* that had a major influence in shaping a compromise. He proposed that bilingual signs again be allowed with the provision that French had to be twice as prominent as other languages.

Why the two-to-one split in favor of the French language? Bourhis based the ratio on research with the minimal group paradigm (Sachdev & Bourhis, 1991). By manipulating power differentials between ad hoc ingroup and outgroup members, these studies showed that respondents preferred membership in a dominant group whose share of power was not absolute (100%) but twice as much as that of the outgroup (Bourhis, 1994c). Then he tested his laboratory finding in the field with a probability survey of the Quebec population. The survey's results showed that relative to freedom of choice or French only, the majority of Francophones and Anglophones gave their preference for the 67–33% split. In 1993, the Quebec government allowed bilingual commercial signs with the two-thirds French requirement. Three years later, the compromise was even defended by the separatist *Parti Quebecois* minister who had originally crafted Bill 101.

Sex stereotypes and discrimination

The first U.S. Supreme Court recognition of social psychology's understanding of stereo-typing came in 1989. Susan Fiske testified as an expert witness in *Hopkins* v. *Price Water-house*, a precedent-setting case involving sex discrimination.

Ann Hopkins, a competent professional at the accounting firm, was denied partner-ship in part because the firm evaluated her as "macho" and in need of becoming "more feminine" (Fiske, Bersoff, Borgida, Deaux, & Heilman, 1991, p. 1050). Fiske testified on her behalf. A major contributor to this literature, she focused on the discipline's research on stereotyping – the conditions that furthered it, indicators that reveal it, consequences of it, and remedies for it. On all counts, Fiske found that the firm had fashioned a situation where stereotypes can shape discriminatory treatment. Hopkins' solo situation encouraged stereotypes and did nothing to limit them.

In this and later cases, Fiske's testimony followed the outline she used in her writings on the subject (Fiske, 1998). Biases have automatic features; and in some ways such biases are socially pragmatic – people act on them or not according to the situation. Further-more, if they are motivated, people can control their biases. And organizations and other social structures have the demonstrated power to motivate people to hold their biases in check. Each of these four steps in Fiske's testimony is supported by the discipline's avail-able evidence (Fiske, 1998).

Increasing the importance of the case for psychology, the American Psychological Asso-ciation (1991) filed an *amicus curiae* brief. It challenged the defendant's argument that Fiske's testimony was "intuitively divined" by providing a review of the evidence. Hopkins eventually won her discrimination suit, with the social psychological evidence on stereo-typing playing a significant role throughout the seven-year litigation.

Peace in the Middle East

Many of the Palestinian and Israeli negotiators who engaged in the discussions that led to the Oslo Peace agreement in 1993 had worked together before. They shared a common vision that they could shape a win–win solution to achieve peace. Considering the long hostilities between the two opponents, how was this remarkable situation possible?

In part, it was achieved through the tireless efforts of Herbert Kelman. For more than two decades, Kelman (1997; Rouhana & Kelman, 1994) has applied his social psychological approach to Arabs and Israelis. His conflict resolution efforts use workshops that stress interactive problem solving. Numbering between 8 and 16 people, these small groups include social science facilitators. Politically influential people from both sides meet for unofficial and confidential interaction. Part of Kelman's skill is selecting the participants. They must be people who seriously entertain the notion of a peaceful solution to the conflict.

These workshops have a dual purpose (Kelman, 1997). One intention is to induce changes in the participants themselves as they develop a more differentiated view of their opponents. The workshops also increase the likelihood that the insights and proposals developed in the problem-solving interaction feed back into each community's political debate. The groups serve as a setting for direct interaction and have the potential of initiating coalitions of peace-minded participants across conflict lines. And the workshops present a model for a new relationship between the parties.

Amidst the varied influences operating in the Middle Eastern search for peace, one cannot isolate the full effects of Kelman's efforts. At the least his many workshops have developed cadres of Israelis and Palestinians who can conduct productive negotiations. And many have served in high-ranking positions in both communities.

Areas of Policy Influence

Beyond these dramatic cases, social psychology has influenced intergroup policy by applying its perspective to a host of specific issues. Intergroup issues often are directly raised when such factors as race and gender are involved. But intergroup concerns also are relevant in more subtle ways. "We" and "they" differentiations are readily triggered when ordinary citizens encounter specialized professionals in such central institutions as the law, education, medicine, and governmental bureaucracies.

Influence on the law

It is hardly coincidental that two of the cited examples involve the courts. There are numerous instances of social psychological influence on precedent-setting litigation. Two focal areas have received major attention: eyewitness identification and testimony; and jury selection, size, voting rules, and decision making. Some social psychologists, such as Elizabeth Loftus (1986), routinely serve as expert witnesses and consultants in major trials. Two cases under different legal systems provide a glimpse into these contributions.

South African courts now accept social psychological phenomena as extenuating factors in murder trials involving mob violence. Colman (1991) presented to the courts an array of such established processes as obedience to authority, deindividuation, bystander apathy, and the fundamental attribution error. And this testimony helped spare the lives of numerous African defendants.

In Canada, Neil Vidmar (1996) influenced Canada's Supreme Court to broaden "probable cause" for challenging potential jurors. The Court cited Vidmar in finding that racial prejudice may be detrimental to a minority defendant in many ways – especially if there is "a perceived link" between race and the alleged crime. Accordingly, the Court held that widespread community bias raised "a realistic potential of partiality" and overturned a robbery conviction of an Aboriginal (*Regina* v. *Williams*).

There also are glaring instances when the discipline's findings go unheeded. Eyewitness identification made in court testimony remains highly influential in determining criminal trial outcomes. Yet the predominant conclusion of relevant research is the untrustworthiness of such testimony under a wide array of conditions (Tollestrup, Turtle, & Yuille, 1994). Cross-racial identification is especially problematic (Brigham & Barkowitz, 1978).

Similarly, decades of research have established the biasing effects of selecting only jurors who can conscientiously vote for the death penalty. Such "death-qualified jurors" are more likely than others to return guilty verdicts. Yet the U.S. Supreme Court in 1986 ruled this evidence constitutionally irrelevant and that such juries did not violate a defendant's right to a fair trial (Bersoff, 1987). Ellsworth (1988) relates a similar story of how the same court has disregarded research evidence in upholding capital punishment. Indeed, capital punishment remains in American law even though its disproportionate use against African Americans is a matter of record.

Influence on education

The classroom is a prime example of a social psychological specialty – situational dynamics. Not surprisingly, then, the discipline has devoted considerable attention to education – particularly to cooperative learning involving diverse groups. For instance, Elliot Aronson's ingenious jigsaw classroom substitutes intragroup cooperation for individual competition (Aronson & Patnoe, 1997). Inspired by the earlier work by Morton Deutsch (1949) and Muzifer Sherif (Sherif, Harvey, White, Hood, & Sherif, 1961), this technique has led to positive results for a variety of children around the globe: Australians (Walker & Crogan, 1998), Germans (Eppler & Huber, 1990), Israelis (Hertz-Lazarowitz, Sharan, & Steinberg, 1980), Japanese (Araragi, 1983), and Mexican Americans (Aronson & Gonzalez, 1988). The jigsaw approach has proven especially useful for schools with both majority-group and minority-group students.

Other cooperative techniques also have been developed, tested, and widely adopted in schools. Robert Slavin's (1986) extensive work has been particularly influential in changing educational policy. From his Center for Research on Effective Schooling for Disadvantaged Students at Johns Hopkins University, Slavin has demonstrated advantages for cooperative learning for a range of groups at risk in American schools – racial, cultural, and handicapped. These advantages include enhanced achievement, intergroup friendships, and intergroup relations generally.

With education's growing interest in classrooms with diverse students, intergroup contact theory (Allport, 1954; Pettigrew, 1998a) has proven particularly influential. Social psychologists have used the theory largely for improving relations between racial and ethnic groups. But educational specialists have used it to shape research and policy for a variety of groups. Extensive research literatures now exist on the contact effects of having children with physical and learning disabilities attend classes with nondisabled children. Meta-analyses of contact research reveals that these studies show an average reduction in prejudice toward the handicapped that is nearly comparable to that of racial and ethnic contact (Pettigrew & Tropp, 2000). Such results have played a major role in advancing the "mainstreaming" of handicapped children in regular classrooms.

Influence on medicine

Public health has served as an institutional bridge for social psychology to apply its perspective to medicine. In coordination with other social science disciplines and medical specialties, the discipline has influenced a great variety of health programs (Taylor, 1995). Social psychological work has been especially influential in efforts to combat AIDS (Weiss, Nesselhof-Kendall, Feck-Kandath, & Baum, 1990; Fisher & Misovich, 1990) and reduce tobacco use (Evans & Raines, 1990). It also has played a role in large-scale community health promotion programs (Loken, Swim, & Mittelmark, 1990). These efforts have intergroup implications, because stigmatized groups generally are medically underserved while being at greater risk.

Often social psychology takes the perspective of the less powerful and suggests changes in the behavior of the powerful. This micro-level tactic has the potential for macro-level alterations, since it is the powerful who control institutional settings. This recurrent theme often occurs in attempts to influence medical practice. For example, medical doctors are urged to change the way they interact with their patients to increase the likelihood that treatment recommendations are followed (Greenfield, Kaplan, Wary, Yano, & Frank, 1988). These changes are especially needed when the patients are from lower-status groups. Yet resistance is likely when change in the procedures of the powerful are recommended. Doctors typically oppose changing their routine ways of behaving when they view their patients as the cause of treatment recommendations not being followed.

Influence on service organizations

This theme of recommending institutional changes based on clients' perspectives characterizes the discipline's influence in numerous service organizations beyond medicine. Valerie Braithwaite provides an illustration involving the Australian Tax Office. As a member of a government task force, she persuaded the taxation officials to alter how they treat taxpayers so as to increase both trust and compliance.

Braithwaite's compliance model drew on theories of procedural justice, social identity, and cognitive consistency. Initial encounters with the Tax Office regarding noncompliance are framed by showing respect for the individual as a valued member of the community and by discourse that emphasizes citizenship, fairness, and strong and effective government. Harmony and security values are emphasized to anchor tax payment within the context of shared values. Research had repeatedly shown these values to be stable and widely supported by Australians (Braithwaite, 1997, 1998). Using values as a consensual base, the identity as a citizen is strengthened, and noncompliance is approached in a co-operative rather than adversarial fashion.

Braithwaite's model does not exclude the rewards and punishments that are fundamental to legal and economic responses to noncompliance. These levers for eliciting tax compliance remain, but they are not triggered until cooperative problem solving has failed. As with many social psychological applications, this institutional effort to preserve clients' sense of worth and dignity is given a place alongside traditional legal and economic theories of compliance.

Nine Difficult Issues Inherent in Influencing Policy

The translation of social psychological theory and research into policy is neither easy nor simple (Archer, Aronson, & Pettigrew, 1993; Pallak, 1990). This complexity applies with special force to intergroup applications. Nine difficult issues arise. Some issues are internal to the discipline; others involve the political context within which the applications occur.

Intradisciplinary issues

1. Social psychology is largely an inductive, empirically driven science. As such, it is less ready to apply its perspective to specific public problems. By contrast, economics, as a more deductive, theory-driven field, more easily shapes its existing models to provide timely guidance to policy makers. Social psychology is, however, slowly developing bold theory. In intergroup relations, social identity theory offers a promising example, but it remains an exception. As broader models emerge in social psychology, however, this barrier to rapid, custom-designed applications to critical policy decisions should diminish.

2. Social psychology's inexperience with implementing applications and influencing policy makers. Compared with other social scientists, social psychologists until recently have had little opportunity to implement their findings and shape public policy. In many countries, social science rose to prominence in social policy during the 1950s and 1960s. But during these years social psychologists focused on basic laboratory research to gain acceptance within psychology departments dominated by skeptical experimentalists. So, unlike other social sciences, the discipline generally failed to develop networks with policy makers and an understanding of how to gain acceptance of its applications.

Being "out of the policy loop" restricts the discipline's influence in many ways. For instance, it makes it less likely that a decision-making agency will directly sponsor social psychological research. And this lack of sponsorship limits policy influence as well as financial support. Caplan, Morrison, and Stambaugh (1975) found that 86% of the cases in which American government decision makers used social science knowledge involved research funded by the users' own agencies.

But times are changing. Increasingly, social psychologists specialize in these policy realms. They are in law, business, medical, and public health schools, in the mass media or directly in government. They "know the ropes," and can help their academic colleagues in the policy process. And new institutional bridges have emerged. At the Australian National University, for instance, the policy-oriented Research School of Social Sciences includes social psychologists on its interdisciplinary staff of social scientists.

3. The laboratory versus the "real world" issue. A popular explanation for social psychology's failure to make more of a policy difference concerns the external validity of laboratory research. The weak form of this view has merit. Decision makers frequently question the relevance of laboratory findings. The strong form of this contention, however, can be challenged. In many areas, laboratory results *have* proven robust in the field. Critics make too much of mundane realism (Aronson, Brewer, & Carlsmith, 1985; Berkowitz and Donnerstein, 1982). The generalizability of laboratory results is an empirical question, and the use of multiple methods strengthens the case.

Tetlock (1998, p. 773) cites three examples in world politics. (1) Laboratory research has shown how simpler modes of cognitive processing arise when time pressure, information load, and threat surpass optimal levels. (2) It has also shown the relative effectiveness of a tit-for-tat strategy in bargaining, and (3) an array of judgment biases. Archival and qualitative studies document all these phenomena on the world stage. Other examples of reasonably good fits between the laboratory and the field have been noted in aggression and organizational research (Anderson & Bushman, 1997; Locke, 1986).

Of course, field methods will not necessarily support all laboratory findings. But social psychologists who wish to influence public policy should seek – and are likely to find – confirmation of their findings with a variety of methods. Bold theories supported by a variety of research methods are the basis of effective applications to specific "real-world" intergroup problems.

4. Can policy applications be consistent across cultures and societies? We noted how Lambert's work on second-language learning by immersion and Aronson's work on the jigsaw classroom have generalized widely across cultures and societies. Such generalization is not unusual for social psychological applications. Yet cultural and structural factors impinge strongly on social psychological processes (Moghaddam, Taylor, & Wright, 1993; Triandis, 1994). Is there a paradox here?

Sharp cultural and structural differences across societies that relate to social psychological processes are common. It does *not* follow, however, that basic social psychological principles will therefore operate inconsistently across societies. Consider overcrowding. The principal conclusions of the crowding research in North America are still valid given the cultural and structural conditions under which these studies were conducted. With differences in such macro-conditions, crowding may not have the same detrimental effects in such dense countries as India. Yet such mediators of crowding effects as perceived control operate in India as they do in North America (Ruback & Pandey, 1991). Further work on crowding in dense nations could expand our understanding of the phenomenon. This expansion would entail carefully specifying the mediating links between the macro-societal, meso-situational, and micro-individual levels of analysis. Such specification requires diverse sampling of structural contexts.

One such effort tested the basic social psychological processes underlying intergroup prejudice in France, Germany, Great Britain, and the Netherlands (Pettigrew et al., 1998). These nations have sharply different intergroup situations, histories, and levels of prejudice; and their outgroups range from Turks to West Indians. Yet the same correlates and processes operate in similar ways across them. To be sure, distinctive features characterize each nation and target group. But the thrust of these findings highlights the comparable operation of such processes as social identification and group relative deprivation acting as proximal causes of prejudice and mediators for social factors acting as distal causes.

These results suggest two interlocking hypotheses (Pettigrew et al., 1998). *The universality hypothesis* predicts that social psychological processes operate in similar ways across cultures and societies although the macro-contexts vary widely. *The mediation hypothesis* holds that key social psychological predictors serve as critical mediators of the effects of social factors on dependent variables at the level of individuals. Hence, given divergent distal social factors, the same social psychological processes can lead to distinctly different outcomes in diverse settings.

Figures 25.1A and 25.1B illustrate these hypotheses (taken from Pettigrew, 1998b). The diagrams fit the same nearly saturated path model to data from two contrasting national samples concerning different minority targets. The model employs four predictors of blatant prejudice. Education is a consistently negative distal predictor of prejudice, and three proximal variables mediate its effects.

Sharpening the test, the two samples differ on four of the model's variables. The Dutch are better educated ($p < .0001$) and more authoritarian ($p < .0005$), the British more conservative ($p < .0001$) and prejudiced ($p < .0001$). Yet the models fit both situations. As predicted by the universality and mediation hypotheses, the proximal predictors mediate education's effects in highly similar ways in the contrasting samples. For both the British and Dutch, the well educated express less prejudice partly because they are less authoritarian and conservative and especially because they have more intergroup friends.

These data cover only Western countries; comparable work in non-Western nations is badly needed. This is what makes the Brewer and Campbell (1976) volume on intergroup attitudes in East Africa so valuable. Indeed, applications of social psychology in non-Western countries are sparse in general. This lacuna represents the most serious weakness in establishing the international utility of social psychology.

5. Missed opportunities. Social psychologists have neglected some issues of critical societal importance. For example, Pruitt (1998) notes that, while two-party negotiation is well studied, the more policy-relevant forms of multiparty and intergroup negotiation have been slighted. And, while the discipline understands the propaganda side of persuasion, it has developed few policy guidelines for how to promote deliberative persuasion (Pratkanis & Aronson, 1992).

The discipline has neglected policy-relevant issues even in areas of special strength. Thus, social psychologists in both Europe and the United States have paid scant

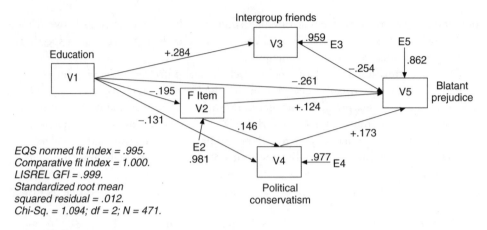

Figure 25.1A. British blatant prejudice against West Indians.

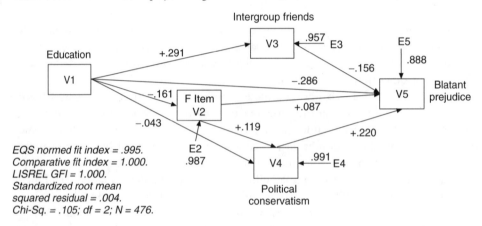

Figure 25.1B. Dutch blatant prejudice against Turks.

attention to the prejudice and discrimination directed against new immigrant minorities. For instance, the vast social identity literature has rarely examined minority relations in Europe. From 1986 to 1996, the 12 leading English-language journals of the discipline published only 18 such papers – 10 from the Netherlands alone (Ulrich Wagner's analysis in Pettigrew et al., 1998).

6. Connecting with the macro-level of analysis. We noted how such bridge institutions as public health have furthered social psychological contributions to social policy. Effective influence on the law has occurred within the courtroom where legal rules and the adversarial system operate. And most social psychological policy offerings have been advanced as part of a broader social science intervention where the macro-fields supplied a structural context. Useful social psychological policy contributions, then, have typically been structurally grounded.

Yet social psychology often broaches its findings and theory in a societal and institutional vacuum. Social policy, however, is embedded in societal and institutional contexts.

Hence, the discipline's socially ungrounded models appear irrelevant to policy makers – even though untested social psychological assumptions permeate their decisions. Objections to the field's ungrounded models are often raised in terms of the lack of integrated or "bold" theory (Cartwright, 1978, 1979; Kelley, 1983; Pettigrew, 1991) or that the discipline's theories are not "social" enough (Cartwright, 1978, 1979; Steiner, 1974).

Of course, social psychology can supply only parts of the puzzle of any major policy issue. All such issues, from peace to poverty, involve factors at all major levels of analysis. This makes it essential that the field shapes its contributions to link with the macro-levels of culture and social structure. Social psychological insights will not be useful to macro-level policy makers unless social psychologists themselves provide these cross-level links.

None the less, policy makers need social psychological contributions. Kelman (1997, p. 217) notes that even for international conflict ". . . there are . . . processes central to conflict resolution – such as empathy or taking the perspective of the other . . . and creative problem solving – that . . . take place at the level of individuals and interactions between individuals."

Add to this the unique contribution that social psychology can make by specifying the situational processes that mediate between the structural and individual levels of analysis. Other disciplines consider situations, but only social psychology focuses on situational mediation systematically. In doing so, the discipline provides both distinctive variables and explanations that usually involve subjective interpretations of the social environment. It is this situational and subjective perspective that is the discipline's unique contribution and forms the core of its applications to social policy (Ross & Nisbett, 1991). Moreover, situations frequently offer the optimal level at which to intervene. They require neither the "trickle down" effects of macro-changes nor time-consuming individual therapy.

Issues involving the political context

7. The question of values. Social psychologists rarely concern themselves with the problem of values in policy applications. This neglect reflects the fact that most members of the discipline, unlike other social sciences, are not particularly politically active and share a relatively narrow range of center-left to center political persuasions. This situation also is changing. Both the political left (Billig, 1977; Sampson, 1981) and right (Tetlock, 1994) have challenged the discipline's unspoken value consensus. Like it or not, policy applications invoke values, and the discipline has yet to address the problem. So, these writers perform a service by opening the discussion.

It is too simple, however, merely to call for a "socially committed social psychology" (Billig, 1977). Nor is it helpful to claim "objectivity" for one's position while castigating opponents for their political bias (Tetlock, 1994). Social psychologists are human beings with their own values who study human beings. So value assumptions in theory and research are unavoidable. And the role of values is enhanced further when there is an attempt to influence social policy.

Gunnar Myrdal (1944) held that values are inherent in social science. Be aware of your values, he maintained, struggle against their biasing effects, and alert your readers to them.

Objectivity becomes, then, a sought-for goal that is never fully attainable. This does *not* exclude social commitment. But such commitment must be made clear to others and combined with an equally strong commitment to competent research. Science and values need not conflict. Campbell (1959) argued that strong motivation can lead to a greater investment in tracing an accurate map of reality. Goal commitment, then, can lead to good science. The problem comes when the desired ends distort the means. This travesty results not only in poor science but in poor support of one's values as well. It is here that the Myrdalian struggle against value bias is relevant.

8. Protecting against the political misuse of social psychological theory and research. There is no ultimate defense against the political misuse of scientific contributions. Yet there are ways of limiting such misuse. Social psychologists can take care to avoid victim blaming and to disseminate their findings widely.

Consider the widespread tendency to blame the victims of social problems (Ryan, 1971). Since psychology centers on individuals, it constantly runs the danger of having its analyses appear as if the victims of social problems are fundamentally the cause of these problems (Caplan & Nelson, 1973). Thus, such valuable concepts as relative deprivation and learned helplessness can be easily twisted into victim blaming once they enter the political arena. This is not to deny that difficult human conditions can cause changes in their victims that in turn exacerbate social problems. But it is to assert that such victim characteristics are not the basic cause of social problems, nor are remedial attempts that ignore structural causes likely to prove helpful. Linking findings and recommendations to their macro-level bases helps to avoid victim blaming. Once we include culture and social structure in an analysis, holding individuals solely responsible becomes untenable.

Another issue concerns information for whom. Information is power, and it is a two-edged sword. So, for whom do we do research? Becker (1967) points out that information flows up the status hierarchy. It provides elites with a more complete view and greater capability. Therefore, those who would effectively and ethically apply social psychology must be careful to make their results known throughout the status hierarchy – not just to the elites who may have sponsored the research. Becker also notes that when social scientists give equal access to non-elites, critics often perceive them as politically biased to the left. This raises another issue.

9. It's hot in the kitchen. Social psychologists rarely are prepared for how scalding hot it is in the social policy kitchen. Intervention to influence policy arouses resistance. One soon learns that different perspectives apply outside of academia. Expert witnesses in American racial school desegregation cases were surprised by how defense lawyers questioned their research (Pettigrew, 1979). Had anyone conducted the research *in their particular city?* Just because massive studies had sampled schools throughout the country, why, lawyers asked, would anyone expect the results to hold true for their area?

Tense conflicts produce strong emotions. Kelman (1983) published a report on two lengthy interviews he held with Yasser Arafat, chair of the Palestine Liberation Organization. The article and its author were immediately attacked. Critics viewed it as cavorting with the enemy; they sternly rejected taking Arafat's word seriously. We now can see that this controversial paper was prophetic. It held that Arafat "has the capacity and will to negotiate an agreement with Israel, based on mutual recognition and peaceful coexistence, if afforded necessary incentives and reassurances" (Kelman, 1983, p. 203). The Oslo agreement a decade later proved Kelman correct.

Frequently the heat is generated within the discipline. Full consensus in any research area is rare in science. Suedfeld and Tetlock (1992), in *Psychology and Social Policy*, managed to find someone somewhere to attack the discipline's dominant consensus in many policy areas. Often the same critics are the challengers on many fronts. Elliott (1989, 1991, 1993), for example, not only opposes affirmative action for women in psychology but challenges the consensus views about death-qualified jurors and eyewitness testimony described earlier.

Besides pointed political differences, the critics and activists disagree about the standard required before scientific evidence should be used to influence social policy. Critics favor a standard higher than that required for scientific audiences. Activists counter that social psychologists should "tell what we know" rather than "wait for Godot" (Ellsworth, 1991). Science is open ended and dynamic; final conclusions are never reached; *all* the evidence is never in. Besides, they maintain, the standard that will prevail if no social science evidence is introduced is hardly exacting; it will consist only of the conventional wisdom of decision makers (Langenberg, 1991).

A Final Word

Compared with other social sciences – especially economics – social psychology has not had the impact on public policy that its adherents desire. Although social psychological assumptions saturate public policies, policy makers often ignore the discipline's relevant work (Pettigrew, 1988, 1998b). This harsh conclusion is true even for intergroup relations despite the urgency of intergroup conflict around the globe.

Those applications to broad social issues that have been effective have employed an extensive array of social psychological ideas. Thus, when Abrams, Hinkle, and Tomlins (1999) studied in 1992 the attitudes and intentions of Hong Kong residents in the midst of massive social transition, they drew upon five different theories of the discipline. The major contentions of social identity, reasoned action, relative deprivation, locus of control, and subjective norms all proved helpful. Abrams and his colleagues illuminated their subjects' critical decision concerning whether to stay or leave following the transfer of the colony to China. Moreover, their analysis allowed informed speculations about the future – such as the later Asian economic crisis.

Often ideas for policy-oriented work derive from both within and without the discipline. Kelman's efforts in the Middle East have employed a wide assortment of ideas. Thus, he culls insights from Floyd Allport's (1933) overlooked classic on institutional behavior and work by Lewin (1952) and others on participation. He finds useful Uri Bronfenbrenner's (1961) and Ralph White's (1965) mirror imaging of opponents' conceptions of each other. He draws widely on the attitude change literature and the work on mechanisms for neutralizing disconfirming information (Ross & Ward, 1995). Most directly, Kelman's approach relates to conflict negotiation principles (Pruitt, 1998) and the human need theory of the international relations specialist, John Burton (1979, 1984, 1988).

These successful cases illustrate the feedback that policy applications can provide for basic theory – the seldom recognized other side of the full-cycle process envisioned by Lewin. By drawing on a wide range of thought, policy studies provide important leads as to how the discipline's array of seemingly disparate ideas can be melded into the bolder, more inclusive theory so badly needed by social psychology.

References

Abrams, D., Hinkle, S., & Tomlins, M. (1999). Leaving Hong Kong? The roles of attitude, subjective norm, perceived control, social identity, and relative deprivation. *International Journal of Intercultural Relations, 23*, 319–338.

Allport, F. (1933). *Institutional behavior.* Chapel Hill, NC: University of North Carolina Press.

Allport, G. W. (1954). *The nature of prejudice.* Reading, MA: Addison-Wesley.

American Psychological Association. (1991). In the Supreme Court of the United States: *Price Waterhouse* v. *Ann B. Hopkins. American Psychologist, 46*, 1061–1070.

Anderson, C. A., & Bushman, B. J. (1997). External validity of "trivial" experiments: The case of laboratory aggression. *Review of General Psychology, 1*, 19–41.

Araragi, C. (1983). The effect of the jigsaw learning method on children's academic performance and learning attitude. *Japanese Journal of Educational Psychology, 31*, 102–112.

Archer, D., Aronson, E., & Pettigrew, T. F. (1993). Making research apply: High stakes public policy in a regulatory environment. *American Psychologist, 47*, 1233–1236.

Aronson, E., Brewer, M., & Carlsmith, J. M. (1985). Experimentation in social psychology. In G. Lindzey & E. Aronson (Eds.), *Handbook of social psychology* (Vol. I). New York: Random House.

Aronson, E., & Gonzalez, A. (1988). Desegregation, jigsaw, and the Mexican-American experience. In P. A. Katz & D. A. Taylor (Eds.), *Eliminating racism: Profiles in controversy.* New York: Plenum Press.

Aronson, E., & Patnoe, S. (1997). *The jigsaw classroom* (2nd ed.). New York: Longman.

Balkan, L. (1970). *Les effets du bilingualisme français-anglais sur les aptitudes intellectuelles* [The effects of French-English bilingualism on intellectual aptitudes]. Brussels: Aimav.

Becker, H. (1967). Whose side are we on? *Social Problems, 14*, 239–247.

Ben-Zeev, S. (1972). The influence of bilingualism on cognitive development and cognitive strategy. Unpublished doctoral dissertation, University of Chicago, IL.

Berkowitz, L., & Donnerstein, E. (1982). External validity is more than skin deep: Some answers to criticisms of laboratory experiments. *American Psychologist, 37*, 245–257.

Bersoff, D. N. (1987). Social science data and the Supreme Court: *Lockhart* as a case in point. *American Psychologist, 42*, 52–58.

Billig, M. (1977). The new social psychology and "fascism." *European Journal of Social Psychology, 7*, 393–432.

Bourhis, R. Y. (1994a). *Conflict and language planning in Quebec.* Clevedon, UK: Multilingual Matters.

Bourhis, R. Y. (1994b). Ethnic and language attitudes in Quebec. In J. W. Berry & J. Laponce (Eds.), *Ethnicity and culture in Canada: The research landscape.* Toronto: Toronto University Press.

Bourhis, R. Y. (1994c). Power, gender, and intergroup discrimination: Some minimal group experiments. In M. P. Zanna & J. M. Olson (Eds.), *The psychology of prejudice: The Ontario symposium* (Vol. 7). Hillsdale, NJ: Erlbaum.

Brewer, M. B., & Campbell, D. T. (1976). *Ethnocentrism and intergroup attitudes: East African evidence.* Beverly Hills, CA: Sage.

Braithwaite, V. (1997). Harmony and security value orientations in political evaluation. *Personality and Social Psychology Bulletin, 23,* 401–414.

Braithwaite, V. (1998). The value balance model of political evaluations. *British Journal of Psychology, 89,* 23–247.

Brigham, J. C., & Barkowitz, P. (1978). Do "They all look alike?" The effect of race, sex, experience, and attitudes on the ability to recognize faces. *Journal of Applied Social Psychology, 8,* 306–318.

Bronfenbrenner, U. (1961). The mirror image in Soviet–American relations: A social psychologist's report. *Journal of Social Issues, 17*(3), 45–56.

Burton, J. W. (1979). *Deviance, terrorism, and war.* New York: St. Martin's Press.

Burton, J. W. (1984). *Global conflict.* Brighton, UK: Wheatsheaf.

Burton, J. W. (1988). Conflict resolution as a function of human needs. In R. A. Coate & J. A. Rosati (Eds.), *The power of human needs in world society.* Boulder, CO and London: Lynne Rienner.

Campbell, D. T. (1959). *Systematic errors to be expected of the social scientist on the basis of a general psychology of cognitive bias.* Paper presented at the annual meeting of the American Psychological Association, Cincinnati, OH.

Caplan, N. A., Morrison, A., & Stambaugh, R. J. (1975). *The use of social science knowledge in policy decisions at the national level: A report to respondents.* Ann Arbor, MI: Institute for Social Research, University of Michigan.

Caplan, N. A., & Nelson, S. D. (1973). On being useful: The nature and consequences of psychological research on social problems. *American Psychologist, 28,* 199–211.

Cartwright, D. (1978). Theory and practice. *Journal of Social Issues, 34*(4), 168–180.

Cartwright, D. (1979). Contemporary social psychology in historical perspective. *Social Psychology Quarterly, 42,* 82–93.

Cialdini, R. B. (1995). A full-cycle approach to social psychology. In G. G. Brannigan & M. R. Merrens (Eds.), *The social psychologists: Research adventures.* New York: McGraw-Hill.

Colman, A. M. (1991). Social psychology in South African murder trials. *American Psychologist, 46,* 1071–1079.

Deutsch, M. (1949). A theory of cooperation and competition. *Human Relations, 2,* 129–152.

Elliott, R. (1989). Preferential hiring for women in psychology is unwarranted and unwise: Reply to Bronstein and Pfennig. *American Psychologist, 44,* 1549–1550.

Elliott, R. (1991). Social science data and the APA: The *Lockhart* brief as a case in point. *Law and Human Behavior, 15,* 59–76.

Elliott, R. (1993). Expert testimony about eyewitness identification: A critique. *Law and Human Behavior, 17,* 423–437.

Ellsworth, P. C. (1988). Unpleasant facts: The Supreme Court's response to empirical research on capital punishment. In K. Hass & J. Inciardi (Eds.), *Challenging capital punishment: Legal and social science approaches.* Beverly Hills, CA: Sage.

Ellsworth, P. C. (1991). To tell what we know or wait for Godot? *Law and Human Behavior, 15,* 77–90.

Eppler, R., & Huber, G. L. (1990). Wissenserwerb im Team: Empirische Untersuchung von Effekten des Gruppen-Puzzles. *Psychologie in Erziehung und Unterricht, 37,* 172–178.

Evans, R. I., & Raines, B. E. (1990). Applying a social psychological model across health promotion interventions: Cigarettes to smokeless tobacco. In E. Edwards, R. S. Tindale, L. Heath, & E. J. Posavac (Eds.), *Social influence processes and prevention*. New York: Plenum Press.

Fiske, S. T. (1998). Stereotyping, prejudice and discrimination. In D. T. Gilbert, S. T. Fiske, & G. Lindzey (Eds.), *The handbook of social psychology* (Vol. 2., 4th ed.). New York: McGraw-Hill.

Fiske, S. T., Bersoff, D. N., Borgida, E., Deaux, K., & Heilman, M. E. (1991). Social science research on trial: Use of sex stereotyping research in *Price Waterhouse* v. *Hopkins. American Psychologist, 46,* 1049–1060.

Fisher, J. D., & Misovich, S. J. (1990). Social influences and AIDS-preventive behavior. In E. Edwards, R. S. Tindale, L. Heath, & E. J. Posavac (Eds.), *Social influence processes and prevention*. New York: Plenum Press.

Greenfield, S., Kaplan, S. H., Wary, J. E., Yano, E. M., & Frank, H. J. L. (1988). Patients' participation in medical care: Effects on blood sugar control and quality of life in diabetes. *Journal of General Internal Medicine, 3,* 448–457.

Hertz-Lazarowitz, R., Sharan, S., & Steinberg, R. (1980). Classroom learning style and cooperative behavior of elementary school children. *Journal of Educational Psychology, 72,* 99–106.

Ianco-Worrall, A. D. (1972). Bilingualism and cognitive development. *Child Development, 43,* 1390–1400.

Kelley, H. H. (1983). The situational origins of human tendencies: A further reason for the formal analysis of structures. *Personality and Social Psychology Bulletin, 9,* 8–30.

Kelman, H. C. (1983). Conversations with Arafat: A social-psychological assessment of the prospects for Israeli–Palestinian peace. *American Psychologist, 38,* 203–216.

Kelman, H. C. (1997). Group processes in the resolution of international conflicts: Experiences from the Israeli–Palestinian case. *American Psychologist, 52,* 212–220.

Kluger, R. (1987). *Simple justice.* New York: Knopf.

Lambert, W. E. (1992). Challenging established views on social issues: The power and limitations of research. *American Psychologist, 47,* 533–542.

Langenberg, D. N. (1991). Science, slogans, and civic duty. *Science,* 361–364.

Lewin, K. (1952). Group decision and social change. In G. E. Swanson, T. M. Newcomb, & E. L. Hartley (Eds.), *Readings in social psychology*. New York: Holt.

Locke, E. A. (Ed.) (1986). *Generalizing from laboratory to field settings.* Lexington, MA: Lexington Books.

Loftus, E. M. (1986). Ten years in the life of an expert witness. *Law and Human Behavior, 10,* 241–263.

Loken, B., Swim, J., & Mittelmark, M. B. (1990). Heart health program: Applying social influence processes in a large-scale community health promotion program. In E. Edwards, R. S. Tindale, L. Heath, & E. J. Posavac (Eds.), *Social influence processes and prevention*. New York: Plenum Press.

Moghaddam, F. M., Taylor, D. M., & Wright, S. C. 1993. *Social psychology in cross-cultural perspective*. New York: Freeman.

Myrdal, G. (1944). *An American dilemma.* New York: Harper & Row.

Pallak, M. S. (1990). Public policy and applied social psychology. In E. Edwards, R. S. Tindale, L. Heath, & E. J. Posavac (Eds.), *Social influence processes and prevention*. New York: Plenum Press.

Pettigrew, T. F. (1975). The racial integration of the schools. In T. F. Pettigrew (Ed.), *Racial discrimination in the United States*. New York: Harper & Row.

Pettigrew, T. F. (1979). Tensions between the law and social science: An expert witness view. In *Schools and the courts: Desegregation* (Vol. I). Eugene, OR: ERIC Clearinghouse for Educational Management, University of Oregon.

Pettigrew, T. F. (1988). Influencing policy with social psychology. *Journal of Social Issues, 44*(2), 205–219.

Pettigrew, T. F. (1991). Toward unity and bold theory: Popperian suggestions for two persistent problems of social psychology. In C. Stephan, W. Stephan, & T. F. Pettigrew (Eds.), *The future of social psychology.* New York: Springer-Verlag.

Pettigrew, T. F. (1998a). Intergroup contact theory. *Annual Review of Psychology, 49,* 65–85.

Pettigrew, T. F. (1998b). Applying social psychology to international social issues. *Journal of Social Issues, 54*(4), 663–675.

Pettigrew, T. F., Jackson, J., Ben Brika, J., Lemaine, G., Meertens, R. W., Wagner, U., & Zick, A. (1998). Outgroup prejudice in Western Europe. *European review of social psychology, 8,* 241–273.

Pettigrew, T. F., & Tropp, L. (2000). Does intergroup contact reduce prejudice? Recent meta-analytic findings. In S. Oskamp (Ed.), *Reducing prejudice and discrimination: Social psychological perspectives.* Mahwah, NJ: Erlbaum.

Pratkanis, A. R., & Aronson, E. (1992). *Age of propaganda.* New York: Freeman.

Pruitt, D. G. (1998). Social conflict. In D. T. Gilbert, S. T. Fiske, & G. Lindzey (Eds.), *The handbook of social psychology* (Vol. II, 4th ed.). New York: McGraw-Hill.

Ross, L., & Nisbett, R. E. 1991. *The person and the situation: Perspectives of social psychology.* New York: McGraw-Hill.

Ross, L., & Ward, A. (1995). Psychological barriers to dispute resolution. In M. Zanna (Ed.), *Advances in experimental social psychology* (Vol. 27). New York: Academic Press.

Rouhana, N. N., & Kelman, H. C. (1994). Promoting joint thinking in international conflicts: An Israeli–Palestinian continuing workshop. *Journal of Social Issues, 50*(1), 157–178.

Ruback, R. B., & Pandey, J. (1991). Crowding, perceived control, and relative power: An analysis of households in India. *Journal of Applied Social Psychology, 21,* 315–344.

Ryan, W. (1971). *Blaming the victim.* New York: Pantheon Books.

Sachdev, I., & Bourhis, R. Y. (1991). Power and status differentials in minority and majority group relations. *European Journal of Social Psychology, 21,* 1–24.

Sampson, E. E. (1981). Cognitive psychology as ideology. *American Psychologist, 36,* 730–743.

Sherif, M., Harvey, O. J., White, D. J., Hood, W. R., & Sherif, C. F. (1961). *Intergroup conflict and cooperation: The Robbers Cave experiment.* Norman, OK: University of Oklahoma Book Exchange.

Slavin, R. E. (1986). Cooperative learning: Engineering social psychology in the classroom. In R. S. Feldman (Ed.), *The social psychology of education: Current research and theory.* New York: Cambridge University Press.

Steiner, I. D. (1974). Whatever happened to the group in social psychology? *Journal of Experimental Social Psychology, 10,* 94–108.

Suedfeld, P., & Tetlock, P. E. (Eds.), *Psychology and social policy.* New York: Hemisphere.

Sugiman, T. (1998). Group dynamics in Japan. *Asian Journal of Social Psychology, 1,* 51–74.

Taylor, S. E. (1995). *Health psychology* (3rd ed.). New York: McGraw-Hill.

Tetlock, P. E. (1994). Political or politicized psychology: Is the road to scientific hell paved with good moral intentions? *Political Psychology, 15,* 509–530.

Tetlock, P. E. (1998). Social psychology and world politics. In D. T. Gilbert, S. T. Fiske, & G. Lindzey (Eds.), *The handbook of social psychology* (Vol. II, 4th ed.). New York: McGraw-Hill.

Tollestrup, P. A., Turtle, J., & Yuille, J. (1994). Actual victims and witnesses to robbery and fraud: An archival analysis. In D. Ross, J. Reed, & M. Toglia (Eds.), *Adult eyewitness testimony: Current trends and developments.* New York: Cambridge University Press.

Torrence, E. P., Gowan, J. C., Wu, J. M., & Alioti, N. C. (1970). *Journal of Educational Psychology, 61,* 72–75.

Triandis, H. C. (1994). *Culture and social behavior.* New York: McGraw-Hill.

U.S. Supreme Court (1954). *Brown v. Board of Education – I.* 347 U.S. 483.

Vidmar, N. (1996). Pretrial prejudice in Canada: A comparative perspective on the criminal jury. *Judicature, 79,* 249–255.

Walker, I., & Crogan, M. (1998). Academic performance, prejudice, and the jigsaw classroom: New pieces to the puzzle. *Journal of Community and Applied Social Psychology, 8,* 381–393.

Weisse, C. S., Nesselhof-Kendall, S. E. A., Feck-Kandath, C., & Baum, A. (1990). Psychosocial aspects of AIDS prevention among heterosexuals. In E. Edwards, R. S. Tindale, L. Heath, & E. J. Posavac (Eds.), *Social influence processes and prevention.* New York: Plenum Press.

White, R. K. (1965). Images in the context of international conflict: Soviet perceptions of the US and USSR. In H. C. Kelman (Ed.), *International behavior: A social psychological analysis.* New York: Holt, Rinehart, & Winston.

Index

Bold page numbers refer to tables and italic page numbers refer to figures.